Before the Paper Chase

Before the Paper Chase

The Scholarship of Law School Preparation and Admissions

Edited by

Tim Alan Garrison
Professor, Portland State University

Frank Guliuzza
Professor and Dean of Academic Affairs,
Patrick Henry College

Carolina Academic Press
Durham, North Carolina

Library of Congress Cataloging-in-Publication Data

Garrison, Tim Alan, 1961-
Before the paper chase : the scholarship of law school preparation and admissions / Tim Alan Garrison and Frank Guliuzza.
p. cm.
Includes bibliographical references.
ISBN 978-1-59460-615-1 (alk. paper)
1. Law schools--United States--Admissions. I. Guliuzza, Frank. II. Title.

KF285.G37 2012
340.071'173--dc23

2011052379

Carolina Academic Press
700 Kent Street
Durham, North Carolina 27701
Telephone (919) 489-7486
Fax (919) 493-5668
www.cap-press.com

Printed in the United States of America

For Our Students

Contents

Acknowledgments

It is our distinct pleasure, as teachers, to advise pre-law students. Advising often allows us to work with students much more closely than we are able to do in a traditional classroom setting. And, because it is very focused teaching, we have the unique opportunity to change the lives of many of our students if only because we can share our expertise in ways that help guide them to where they might really want and need to go. Both of us can recount story after story of young people who we have had the opportunity to assist, and who, in turn, have become quite memorable to us and have gone on to successful careers in a variety of fields. Every outstanding pre-law advisor knows what we mean and feels the same way.

Of course, to enjoy the blessings of working closely with a wide range of wonderful pre-law students, one must, in fact, become an effective advisor and teacher. Both of us are extremely grateful for our experiences with the Western Association of Pre-law Advisors (WAPLA). It is fair to say that each of us had a lot to learn as advisors. From the first WAPLA conference that we attended, it was clear just how much we did not know: about the application process, about the kinds of information that law school admissions specialists are looking for when evaluating particular applicants, about how to help an individual student select the law school that might be best for him or her, about how to finance law school, or about issues related to securing employment once one graduates from law school. WAPLA's exceptional leaders, folks like Jim Riley, the late Phil Whitman, Chuck Fimian, Claudia Tomlin, Marilyn Hoffman, Verlaine Walker, Marty Sommerness, Marsha Yowell, Doug Costain, and especially Eileen Crane, who served as president of WAPLA when we were both introduced to the organization, provided us with their warm friendship and were forthcoming with their expertise. We have also benefitted from our conversations with a new generation of WAPLA board members, including extraordinary advisors such as Joseph Behrens, Catherine Bramble, Kris Tina Carlston, Rebecca Gill, Julie Givans, Ellen Grigsby, Lori Hausegger, Sara Lyness, Amy Urbanek, and Sandra Voller. Thanks to WAPLA, we are both substantially better advisors, and our students have reaped the rewards. Later, when each of us would serve as the president of WAPLA, we were very mindful to be faithful to the traditions established by our friends and predecessors.

WAPLA is but one of six pre-law organizations, all with similarly funny acronyms, that represent colleges and universities in various regions throughout the country: the Midwest Association of Pre-Law Advisors (MAPLA), the Northeast Association of Pre-Law Advisors (NAPLA), the Pacific Coast Association of Pre-Law Advisors (PCAPLA), the Southern Association of Pre-Law Advisors (SAPLA), and the Southwestern Association of Pre-Law Advisors (SWAPLA). Between us, we've had the privilege of speaking with folks from each organization, and we can attest to the time, effort, and resources the advisors in those organizations spend to educate the pre-law advisors in their own regions.

Several years ago, the regional "APLAs" gave birth to a national organization, the Pre-Law Advisors National Council (PLANC). PLANC serves to represent the APLAs to outside groups (e.g., the Law School Admissions Council and its member law schools, the Council on Legal Education Opportunity, the National Association of Law Placement, the American Bar Association, and the Access Group). PLANC also sponsors a quadrennial conference to teach rookie advisors how to ply their craft and veterans how to improve their skills. The six APLAs and PLANC have served to "professionalize" the occupation of pre-law advising. We are very grateful to the service that PLANC has provided on behalf of pre-law advisors and pre-law students. Both of us have found the PLANC conferences to be an invaluable educational experience for advisors. We want to recognize Charles Neal, Eileen Crane, Nim Batchelor, James Calvi, Mel Hailey, and Heather Struck for their formal leadership while serving as chair of PLANC during our time as pre-law advisors. We also are deeply grateful to the gentlemen who were among the founders (or long-standing sages) of PLANC: Jerry Polinard, Frank Homer, and, of course, the incomparable Gerald Wilson. They provide the institutional memory, good humor, and wisdom that are indispensable to the group. We also want to pay a special tribute to Anne Brandt, the LSAC's extraordinary liaison to PLANC and pre-law advisors in general. Anne has always been a knowledgeable, energetic, and kind friend of the pre-law advisor.

We also want to express our appreciation to all of those law school deans, directors of admissions, and other law school officials who have been our friends and acquaintances over the years. While the law schools come in for some criticism in this book, we do want to say that we have always had enjoyable and fruitful relationships with our law school friends (who are too many in number to name here without fear of forgetting some of them). We have found them all to be generous, thoughtful, and supportive of our objectives and endeavors. Like the pre-law advisors, they also are motivated by a fundamental desire to help students fulfill their dreams and ambitions.

Several years ago WAPLA started to encourage the "scholarship of pre-law advising" at our conferences. Advisors have lots of opinions on the admissions process, the value of the LSAT, how law school "rankings" affect pre-law students, the value of undergraduate "law" classes, and the like. We found that while advisors often held strong opinions about such subjects, there was very little empirical evidence to support their views. Hence, WAPLA started to invite scholars who were doing original research on topics related to the enterprise of advising pre-law students to present their work at its annual conference. It was this emphasis upon the scholarship of advising that served as the inspiration for this project.

We are very thankful to the scholars who have allowed us to showcase their work. We've included pieces on a wide variety of the subjects mentioned above. If we have chosen to emphasize some topics over others, or have included scholarship that some might believe has become "vintage," it's because we were impressed by the quality of the work. We are certainly hoping that some of the many fine pieces that are included in this book might serve as inspiration to future scholars who will pick up the mantle and take on these questions applying the best tools available to social scientists, historians, and legal scholars.

We especially want to acknowledge and thank those who helped us pull this book together. First, the editors and staff of Carolina Academic Press have been unfailingly kind, supportive, and patient with us. In particular, we want to express our appreciation to Keith Sipe, our publisher and the man who sanctioned this strange idea, and Emily Utt, Zoë Oakes, Linda Lacy, Suzanne Morgen, Tim Colton, Charlesy Rutan, and Katie Herzog. Karen Clayton deserves special thanks for her formatting expertise. We also want to thank Laura Dewey, who created our index. We also could not have completed the manuscript without the help of Katie Roberts, Katie Donnelly, and Gayle Reinhardt.

Of course, we have to thank our colleagues and students at Portland State University, Weber State University, and Patrick Henry College. They have all helped to enrich our personal and professional lives in ways that we cannot fully express.

Lastly, we offer our very special appreciation to our families. They have always supported our work and appreciated our desire to help our students. We thank Kathy and Cindy, and our children, for giving us the time to complete this project.

Publication Acknowledgments

"Asking the Lost Question: What is the Purpose of Law School?," by Bethany Rubin Henderson, first appeared in the *Journal of Legal Education*, Volume 53, Number 1, pages 48–79, in March, 2003. Reprinted with the permission of the author and the *Journal of Legal Education.*

"The Reach of Our Pedagogy: Political Science Undergraduate Classes and Pre-Law Academic Preparation," by Ellen Grigsby and Amelia A. R. Murphey, is an original article produced for this anthology.

"'But the Emperor Has Nothing On': Testing the Myths about Undergraduate Law Classes," by Frank Guliuzza, is an original article produced for this anthology.

"Performance in Law School: What Matters in the End?," by Richard A. Ippolito, first appeared in the *Journal of Legal Education*, Volume 54, Number 3, pages 459–464, in September, 2004. Reprinted with the permission of the author and the *Journal of Legal Education.*

"Merit and Diversity: The Origins of the Law School Admissions Test," by William P. LaPiana, first appeared in the *Saint Louis University Law Journal*, Volume 48, pages 955–990, in Spring, 2004. Reprinted with the permission of the author and the *Saint Louis University Law Journal*, © 2004, St. Louis University School of Law, St. Louis, Missouri

"The LSAT Myth," by Jeffrey S. Kinsler, first appeared in the *Saint Louis University Public Law Review*, Volume 20, pages 393–416, in 2001. Reprinted with permission of the author and the *Saint Louis University Public Law Review* © 2001 St. Louis University School of Law, St. Louis, Missouri.

"Predicting Law School Academic Performance from LSAT Scores and Undergraduate Grade Point Averages: A Comprehensive Study," by David A. Thomas, first appeared in the *Arizona State Law Journal*, Volume 35, pages 1007–1028, in Fall, 2003. Reprinted with the permission of the author and the *Arizona State Law Journal.*

"Predicting LSAT Scores from SAT Scores," by David S. Mann, is an original article produced for this anthology.

"In Praise of Law School Rankings: Solutions to Coordination and Collective Action Problems," by Russell Korobkin, first appeared in the *Texas Law Review*, Volume 77, pages 403–428, in December, 1998. The author and the *Texas Law Review* have provided permission to use only the English language version of this article.

"Do Rankings Matter? The Effects of *U.S. News and World Report* Rankings on the Admissions Process of Law Schools," by Michael Sauder and Ryon Lancaster, first appeared in *Law & Society Review*, Volume 40, Issue 1, pages 105–134, in March, 2006. Reprinted with the permission of the authors, *Law and Society Review*, and John Wiley and Sons. © 2006, John Wiley and Sons.

"Student Quality as Measured by LSAT Scores: Migration Patterns in the *U.S. News* Rankings Era," by William D. Henderson and Andrew P. Morriss, first appeared in *Indiana Law Journal*, volume 81, pages 163–203, in 2006. Reprinted with the permission of the authors and the *Indiana Law Journal.* ©2006 by the Trustees of Indiana University.

"Rankings and Reactivity: How Public Measures Recreate Social Worlds," by Wendy Nelson Espeland and Michael Sauder, first appeared in *American Journal of Sociology*, volume 113 (1) pages 1–40, in July, 2007. Reprinted with the permission of the authors, the *American Journal of Sociology*, and the University of Chicago Press. © 2007 University of Chicago.

"The Interplay between Law School Rankings, Reputation, and Resource Allocation: Ways Rankings Mislead," by Jeffrey Evans Stake, first appeared in the *Indiana Law Journal*, Volume 81, pages 230–270, in 2006. Reprinted with the permission of the author and the *Indiana Law Journal.* ©2006 by the Trustees of Indiana University.

"Why Not Rank Law Schools by Student Credentials?: Replacing the 'Junk Science' of *U.S. News* Rankings," by David A. Thomas, is an original piece produced for this anthology.

A portion of " 'A Great Devourer of Good Men' and Women: A Review of the Employment and Student Debt Status of Current Law School Graduates," by Deborah D. Thornton, first appeared in the December, 2010 edition of *Policy Studies.* This article is reprinted with the permission of the author and *Policy Studies.*

"Socratic Method and the Irreducible Core of Legal Education," by Donald G. Marshall, first appeared in *Minnesota Law Review*, Volume 90, pages 1–17, in November, 2005. Reprinted with the permission of the author's estate and the *Minnesota Law Review.*

"The Relationship Between Law School and the Bar Exam: A Look at Assessment and Student Success" by Lorenzo A. Trujillo, first appeared in the *University of Colorado Law Review,* Volume 78, pages 69–114, in 2007. Reprinted with the permission of the author and the *University of Colorado Law Review.*

"Institutional Denial about the Dark Side of Law School, and Fresh Empirical Guidance for Constructively Breaking the Silence," by Lawrence S. Krieger, first appeared in the *Journal of Legal Education*, Volume 52, pages 112–129, in September, 2002. Reprinted with the permission of the author and the *Journal of Legal Education.*

"Opportunity Lost: How Law School Disappoints Law Students, the Public, and the Legal Profession," by Jason M. Dolin, first appeared in the *California Western Law Review,* Volume 44, pages 219–255, in 2007–2008. Reprinted with the permission of the author and the *California Western Law Review.*

"On Being a Happy, Healthy, and Ethical Member of an Unhappy, Unhealthy, and Unethical Profession," by Patrick J. Schiltz, first appeared in *Vanderbilt Law Review*, volume 52, pages 872–951, in May, 1999. Reprinted with the permission of the author and the *Vanderbilt Law Review.*

Introduction

The "Business" of Preparing Pre-Law Students

In the United States we seem to have a love-hate relationship with lawyers. Most people have a favorite lawyer joke, and we often refer to those in the profession as "shysters" suggesting that they are people of dubious character who will do almost anything for a buck. At the same time, attorneys rank highly in occupational prestige ratings, and people certainly respect their training and expertise.

One thing is for certain; love them or hate them, there are a lot of lawyers. There are about 1.2 million attorneys in the United States and about 150,000 students currently enrolled in J.D. programs. Hence, not only do attorneys help keep the train that is big business rolling down the tracks, the law is a big business itself. Further, educating attorneys, and preparing future attorneys for admission to law school, is likewise a substantial business.

One might suggest, however, that preparing students for admission to law school is a rather *strange* business. First, it is a multi-faceted enterprise. Students require preparation to take the Law School Admission Test (LSAT). They need to know how to present themselves to the various law schools so that they might earn admission—and, oftentimes, the 200-plus law schools have slightly different priorities when evaluating candidates. And, should they be fortunate enough to earn admission, applicants will often require help paying for law school—or even knowing how to walk in the world of those who can help them finance a legal education.

Second, some components of the business are well established and lucrative. There are scores of test preparation companies ready to teach you how to get ready for the LSAT. There are also lots of financial outfits who are willing to educate pre-law students as to how they should pay for their legal education—and, subsequently, to lend them the money necessary to attend law school (should they, of course, prove to be credit worthy—one score that might be more important than the LSAT). Moreover, there are a host of specialized businesses directly or indirectly related to preparing students for admission to law school. For instance, there are groups that work with students from historically underrepresented populations, and others that will provide simulated first-year classes to prepare admitted students for the time they stand "on their feet" before their own version of Professor Kingsfield at X, Y, or Z College of Law.

Third, one might argue that the process of directly advising pre-law students is a rather strange one indeed. Although companies consistently emerge that purport to advise students successfully with regard to the admissions process, the advising enterprise is still largely virgin territory. Perhaps that is because, until relatively recently, students were either thought to not need a whole lot of advising ("Gosh, can't they just talk to a lawyer?"), or, alternatively, it assumed that this component of preparing students for admission to law school was ceded over to the colleges and universities. After all, isn't advising an important part of the educational function of higher education? In fact, many colleges and universities do not provide support for prelaw advising at their institutions.

Even if they do, preparing students for the admissions process is no small task. Even if an advisor learns nothing about the specific parts of the LSAT, or how a student might finance his or her legal education, the advisor should know about the admissions process itself. The advisor will want to learn about how to prepare the application, how a student might showcase her accomplishments on a resume, the complexities of preparing a personal statement, and whom the student might look for when requesting letters of recommendation. Sadly, this very large and hugely important aspect of the business is utterly hit-and-miss. When we were on the Pre-Law Advisors National Council (PLANC), we participated in discussions in which it was suggested credibly that *perhaps 60–70 percent of pre-law students have advisors that are thoroughly inadequate.*

If a student wants to know what kind of pre-law advising they might receive at a given academic institution, there are things to look for. At many schools, the "pre-law advisor" (PLA) is a faculty member who has been drafted to do the job. Actually, that is how we entered into the pre-law "profession." Tim has a law degree and teaches constitutional history. Frank taught constitutional law in a Political Science department. Since we were seen as the "law guys" at our respective institutions, we were asked to work with pre-law students.

The problem with having the "law guys" serve as advisors is that generally professors receive very little reward for this assignment. In a profession where one is evaluated primarily by the quality of one's teaching, or, increasingly, for the quantity of one's scholarly output, working with pre-law students is often a rather thankless task. Unless one makes it an important professional priority, pre-law advising is likely to be placed on the back burner—the very back burner. The professor often comes into the advising session armed with two pieces of information—the student's LSAT score and a copy of the *U.S News & World Report* edition which ranks the various law schools. In such a setting, the advisor will look at the score, and, based upon the data in the magazine, she might recommend a set of schools to the student.

Some schools turn the process of advising pre-law students over to their advising office/centers/programs. At any given institution, this is the outfit that does the advising for the entire college or university. Hence, the advising office is responsible for helping to make sure that hundreds or, more typically, thousands of students are in a position to complete their degrees in a fairly timely manner—so that Mom and Dad are not shelling out tuition for eight or nine years. If the school asks one of the general advisors to work with pre-law students, there is no reason to expect this advisor to be any better prepared than his or her academic counterpart. Even for experienced "advisors," pre-law advising often comes as an additional task or duty, and, absent some very specialized training, one is still as likely to work a limited set of data, e.g., the LSAT score and the aforementioned popular magazine.

We certainly recognize that there are many extraordinary PLAs that were and are drafted from academic departments—the "law guys." And, of course, some of the best PLAs in the country come out of advising centers/offices/programs. We have had the opportunity to work with some of the best PLAs in the United States. They take their responsibility seriously, and are often fluent in how to prepare for the LSAT, financing law school, the application process, or post-graduation placement opportunities. We dare say that most of the experienced and accomplished advisors will admit, however, that there is a tremendous dearth of quality pre-law advising at the vast majority of colleges and universities in the United States.

As a result, students are forced to get much of their information from a variety of sources: the PLA on campus (whom we have already discussed); companies who recognize that there is money to be made advising pre-law students; what they can learn "on the streets"—talking with other students in the same boat; and what they might learn from traditional and online publications.

Pre-law students can find a variety of sources of information, and most of these sources are not shy in sharing opinions. They will share their thoughts regarding the "5 myths about the LSAT," the "12 myths about the legal profession," or, perhaps, the "10 myths about applying to law school," or the "8 mistakes" students make when preparing the personal statement, or "the real law school rankings." One thing is almost as certain as death and taxes: the aforementioned sources like to share information. The problem is that, often, the information they share is not consistent. Further, it almost certainly is not based on any sort of consistent, longitudinal, empirical research. The advice might not be bad. It is just generally anecdotal.

In fact, even the best pre-law advisors, when they get together and swap advising stories and strategies, much the way a group of excellent guitarists might sit together and jam, will often present their respective points of view about the racial biases in the LSAT, or the value of the test, or the way to prepare personal statements, the law school rankings, and the like, almost exclusively from personal experience. And, when they differ, each PLA is certain that he or she is correct.

That begs the question (with respect to some of these questions that are of great importance to PLAs and pre-law students): Has anyone done any empirical work? Are there studies that address some of the questions that often frustrate pre-law students and require answers from PLAs?

The Purpose of This Book

That is our goal in this project: to present the work done by scholars to answer the questions that PLAs and law school admissions personnel most often raise in their conversations about the process:

"The LSAT is an awful instrument to predict success in law school." "*Not true, the LSAT serves its purpose well and provides important information to the law schools.*"

What does the literature say?

"One should never take undergraduate law classes. We'll teach you all the law that you need to know when you get to law school." "*Are you kidding? Undergraduate law classes are the best diagnostic tool available to students to find out if they will like or be good at law school.*"

Have experts taken up this question?

"Law school rankings are an important tool for those who are considering law school. They are valuable to the 'customers.'" "*No way. Rankings distort the process; the law schools cater their 'product' to how it will affect their respective scorecards.*"

Is there any significant scholarship that addresses the issue?

In our book, we present what we hope is some of the best scholarship written to address some of the questions that we have discussed above. Most of the articles in this volume have been published previously. A few are examples of new scholarship in the field; all of the articles are of fairly recent vintage, for we know that the admissions and evaluation process does change over time.

Our hope is to introduce some of this scholarship to those who have a stake in the process of preparing students to navigate through the admissions process. We want PLAs, and others involved in this process of working with students, to be able to discuss important questions the way others might in academic discourse. They should be able to present evidence—and cite to such evidence. We certainly do not want to minimize the importance of the anecdotal evidence. Rather, we want to expand the kind of information available to professionals in the field of pre-law advising, and to enable them to have this information available when necessary. Quite obviously one of our objectives is to encourage additional scholarship. When we listen to advisors raise issues about the LSAT, the law school rankings, the success of certain kinds of personal statements, and the like, we believe that these are testable questions. They are the kinds of things that scholars can and should test and, in so doing, the product of this work will only serve to improve the product.

What's in the Book?

We divide the book into five parts. In **Part One**, we present a number of articles that address how a student might prepare for the law school decision. In her essay, Bethany Rubin Henderson tackles a fundamental question that cuts to the core of legal education. She identifies at length the criticism about legal education, and argues that these complaints are valid. Further, she argues that they cannot be solved with cosmetic solutions (e.g., more courses, better buildings, more professors). Rather, she claims that law schools need to ask the basic questions: "Why are we here? What is the purpose of legal education?" Moreover, even when one articulates the purposes of legal education that are common to all institutions, each law school still needs to define its own particular purpose.

Every PLA is asked repeatedly about the particular courses or majors that a given student should take. Ellen Grigsby and Amelia A. R. Murphy take a preliminary stab at answering the former. They study the kinds of courses that students might take within a Political Science curriculum to see if certain kinds of courses better prepare students to be successful in the admissions process. They conclude that "skills-related learning/choices" are more significant than the particular courses that students might select from within the discipline. Frank Guliuzza addresses a related question: do courses on law offered by undergraduate departments in history, political science, communications, or criminal justice aid or hinder the first-year law student? Many law school personnel actually encourage students to avoid such courses; Guliuzza begs to differ with some preliminary quantitative evidence. In the final article in this portion of the book, Richard Ippolito argues that, even when "holding constant standard measures of ability like the LSAT," there are hidden indexes of success and failure of law students when measuring their first-year performance. Some of these are related to the behavior of particular students, e.g., where they sit in the classroom and the likelihood that they skip class. He shares with law schools how they might successfully identify these "nontraditional signals of superior performance."

Part Two looks at the Law School Admissions Test—the dreaded LSAT. What does the test measure? How effective is the exam at predicting the future success of law school students? And has the exam been too great an emphasis in the admissions process?

William Lapiana's essay returns back to the origins of the LSAT. He challenges the notion that the test was ever intended to be sole criterion for making admissions decisions. Nor was the average test score of admitted students ever intended to be the seminal means of evaluating the quality, or at least the ranking, of particular schools. Moreover, he contends that the purpose of an objective test was to increase access to legal education—and to increase diversity within the legal profession.

Those who work with pre-law students understand that the LSAT is the most important single component of one's application package—whether it was ever intended to serve that purpose or not. Jeffrey Kinsler insists that is because law school admissions personnel believe that the LSAT score is the most important variable when predicting the likelihood of success in law school. Is that hypothesis valid? Kinsler studied graduating students at Marquette University Law School and found that other variables such as undergraduate grade point average, the reputation of a student's undergraduate institution, and a combination of grade point average and institutional reputation actually were better at predicting law school performance than the LSAT. Similarly, David Thomas challenges the preeminence of the LSAT as the most important predictor of success in law school. He notes that while the Law School Admission Council (LSAC), which administers the LSAT, properly discourages law schools from an overreliance on the exam as an admissions tool, LSAC does tout the predictive power of the test. In his study, however, he challenges the ability of the test to predict "overall law school academic performance." He compares the LSAT's predictive value of overall performance with "first-year academic performance." He also compares the value of undergraduate grade point average as a predictor of overall performance and first-year performance. David S. Mann, in "Predicting LSAT Scores from SAT Scores," offers data that suggests that an undergraduate student's SAT score might provide an early indication of how one will perform on the law placement exam. Mann's findings are preliminary and narrowly focused, and we hope our publication of his research will entice other scholars to study the correlations between the two exams in greater detail.

In **Part Three**, we turn our attention to the value of law school rankings. As one might expect, there is a wide variety of data and opinion on this hot-button topic. We start with an essay by Russell Korobkin who argues that, despite the ease with which critics take pot shots at them, law school rankings serve an important purpose. He argues that the primary purpose of the rankings is to "coordinate the placement of law students with legal employers." Accordingly, they serve a purpose, and it is a purpose that is not directly related to the admissions process—one that is quite apart from the accuracy of such rankings. Further, he provides a normative argument. The rankings create public goods that might otherwise fail to be produced by the law school marketplace without this rudimentary attempt to assess outcome.

Michael Sauder and Ryon Lancester link the rankings directly back to the admissions process. They claim that, although the rankings purport to measure law school quality, they can become a self-fulfilling prophecy which affects future rankings. Hence, the rankings can help create differences rather than simply reflect these differences among law schools, thereby distorting the very thing that they claim to measure—the quality of the various law schools.

William D. Henderson and Andrew P. Morriss argue that the introduction of the rankings into the admissions world has had an enormous impact on how law schools admit students and allocate resources. Specifically, law schools have implemented a variety of strategies to help raise their median LSAT scores. Why? Because data suggests that ninety percent of the differences in rankings are attributable to the median LSAT score of the entering classes. Accordingly, the authors study the change in entering-class median LSAT score. Drawing upon their findings, they suggest that the current "LSAT arms race" produced by the current rankings competition actually threatens the viability of the existing model of legal education. In response, they offer several recommendations to law school deans and the editors of *U.S. News & World Report.*

Wendy Nelson Espeland and Michael Sauder use the impact of law school rankings to measure the impact of reactivity as an inevitable result of human reflexivity. They discuss how the need for transparency and accountability, the "audit explosion," has produced a proliferation of testing, evaluations, and rankings. This, of course, has an effect on those who produce services, e.g., how decisions made by those in legal education will affect the particular law school's "scorecard." They use the *U.S. News* rankings of law schools as a case study. They conclude that the *U.S. News* rankings produce self-fulfilling prophecy and commensuration, and "three important effects of reactivity: the redistribution of resources, the redefinition of work, and a proliferation of gaming strategies by the law schools."

Jeffrey Evans Stake's article on law school rankings is far less theoretical—although he might largely agree with Espeland and Sauder with regard to the tangible impact these rankings have had on legal education. He asserts that the *U.S. News* rankings have changed legal education in the United States. He claims that, unfortunately, that these rankings are unquestionably misleading. They mislead schools into thinking they are offering a quality of schooling that is not true—in fact they often pursue a "path of operation that reduces the quality." They mislead the student into thinking that school A will offer a better education and, subsequently, a better quality of life, than other schools which might be a better fit for this particular student. Too, they mislead the public, which depends upon law schools in the United States to produce effective attorneys.

Perhaps the problem is not the effort to rank law schools, but rather, with the exaggerated acquiescence to those doing the ranking. In this article, David A. Thomas targets the *U.S. News* rankings specifically, claiming them to be the product of "junk science." Thomas recognizes that his criticisms of the *U.S News* rankings are not unique, and argues that the demand for a ranking system is not going to go away. There certainly is a demand for law school rankings from a variety of constituencies. Accordingly, he advocates for a better way to rank law schools. Using many of the same variables that *U.S. News* employs in its methodology, Thomas provides an alternative set of rankings that demonstrates his claim that several schools are either significantly overrated or underrated by *U.S. News.*

Deborah Thornton's article in **Part Four** points out that the recent recession has negatively impacted the job market for new attorneys. Thornton argues that the present economy, combined with the fact that law students graduate with an average of $100,000 in student debt, makes the future very grim for students interested in pursuing a career in the law. She calls on students to look carefully at tuition rates before they make their enrollment decision, to consider the possibility of attending law school on a part-time basis, and to live frugally as they work their way through the curriculum. We looked long and hard for articles on the subjects of tuition and student debt; unfortunately, Thornton's article was the only recent one on point. As editors, we were disappointed that scholars have not devoted more attention to the issues of rising tuition, increasing student debt loads, and the impact of those factors on long-term law student satisfaction and success; and we hereby call for more research on these very important topics.

In **Part Five,** we discuss scholarship on the experience of attending law school. Naturally, many of these articles, especially those critical of the way legal education is delivered in the United States, offer alternative methods of instructional delivery and, occasionally, even more substantial reforms.

We begin with Donald G. Marshall's defense of the Socratic Method. Marshall says that "genuine dialogue" is the irreducible core of legal education. He is critical of alternative approaches to instructional delivery including lectures or what he calls "disguised lectures." Marshall, therefore, calls for a revival of the Socratic Method and uses the article to "teach" how to teach the Socratic Method.

Lorenzo Trujillo argues that law schools have a moral and ethical obligation to society to prepare successful professionals. The national data on bar passage rates calls into question how well law schools are meeting this need. Based upon his own study of law students at the University of Colorado, Trujillo recommends a serious of reforms to legal education, and to the way students prepare for the bar exam; and he suggests some alternatives to the bar exam itself.

While Trujillo examines how effectively law schools train future lawyers, Lawrence Krieger looks at law students themselves. Krieger asserts that law students are unhappy. He examines data that suggests heightened depression, alcoholism, suicide, and the like among law students. Further, he notes that unhappy law students are likely to become unhappy lawyers. He notes, unfortunately, that there is a systematic denial by law professors of this "collective distress and unhappiness of our students and lawyers they become." Building upon his own previous work, he suggests different approaches to the failing paradigms at the heart of legal education that will enable law school faculty to become more effective in addressing this significant problem.

Jason Dolin claims that law students are graduating without adequate preparation to practice law. While his argument may not be original, he does reassert the oft-heard complaint that many law school graduates cannot do even the most basic practical "stuff" required by attorneys in their practice. He places the lion's share of the blame on the law schools which keep churning out a glut of graduates (because they have a financial incentive to do so), and which essentially use the same pedagogy that was introduced by C.C. Langdell (because "we all had to do it, and it worked for us"). He suggests some remedies to the predicament, and urges "the bench and the bar" to push for the reforms necessary to make law schools more effective.

Finally, we offer the lengthy article by Patrick Schiltz. Schiltz notes that, for many prospective attorneys, admission to an upper-echelon ("tier one"?) law school is the grand prize in the admissions process because it best provides for the opportunity to secure employment at an upper-echelon/national-international ("tier one"?) law firm. Why? Because pre-law students are told that for one to earn an offer from an A-list law firm in a major city is indeed the ticket to the good life. Such firms are successful in selling this image to students who are excited about the prospect of a top-flight salary and substantial occupational prestige. Unfortunately, Schiltz warns, life in these big firms is often fraught with disaster: young lawyers are typically unhappy, and are often inadvertently seduced into unethical behavior. Sadly, Schiltz warns, faculty at the elite law schools typically are ill-equipped to head off problems for their students. He notes that many measure success in the profession as employment in a top-tier law firm, and he touts other options available to outstanding law students—and outlines how one might have a happy, healthy, and ethical life in the law.

Two notes on our format and structure: First, because these articles are authored by a wide, interdisciplinary group of scholars, it would have been unfair to impose one particular citation format on any one of them. For that reason, we retained the format included in the original article or the one provided by the author. Second, some readers, particularly those who maintain an extremely positive view of the current system, may bridle at the overall perception of legal education presented herein. We found that the scholarship has been extremely critical of legal education for the last two decades, and many of these articles call for dramatic reforms in the admissions, ranking, and teaching processes. We agreed at the outset that we would follow the scholarship wherever it led us, and we believe that these selections fairly represent the general tenor of the current scholarly conversation. Still, at the end of this process, we feared that we might be presenting a picture that was overtly negative; and we went back again to search for work that presented legal education in a positive light. Unfortunately, while there are plenty of graduation orations and bar newsletter articles praising the law school, we found little concomitant praise in the quantitative or qualitative *scholarship*. We do believe that law schools are especially good at preparing students to become engaged in the intellectual and theoretical understanding of the law, that they offer an education that prepares students for a variety of occupations beyond just the legal profession, and that they are adept at training people to think in an analytical fashion. In closing, we call upon the legal profession to provide the quantitative date to support our belief.

Part One

Preparing for the Law School Decision

Asking the Lost Question: What Is the Purpose of Law School?

*Bethany Rubin Henderson**

Introduction

Law students frequently are critical of both what they learn in law school and how they are being taught. One set of common complaints focuses on the lack of diversity in courses offered. For example, students object that the curriculum overemphasizes corporate and private-practice courses to the detriment of courses focusing on crucial social problems. Many students who do not understand why various required courses are mandatory resent being forced into them. Another set of concerns focuses on what occurs in the classroom. Students despair at the lack of faculty guidance on what and how they should be learning. They contend that the classroom environment discourages them from making meaningful intellectual contributions and engaging in vital intellectual and political discourse. They yearn for regular, meaningful feedback from faculty who are as committed to teaching as they are to research. They also object to the standard grading system, in which a course grade is based solely on a final exam, as arbitrary and at best minimally reflective of students' intellectual and lawyering capacities. Yet another frequent critique is that the issues addressed and the skills taught in law school are far removed from the everyday problems lawyers encounter.

What should be most disturbing to legal educators and the legal profession, however, is the increasingly widespread complaint about the effect of legal education on students' perceptions of the law and its role in society. Students arrive at law school full of excitement about the law's capacity to further social justice. Yet many leave law school disillusioned, perceiving the law as a value-neutral instrument and lawyers as persons who wield that instrument without regard for its impact on society. Students further contend that law schools' institutional and administrative practices, coupled with high tuition, contribute to this perception. For example, a common protest is that law schools herd students into private law firm practice but at best do not effectively assist and at worst impede students' efforts to enter the legal profession in other capacities.

Students are not the only ones expressing concerns about legal education. Faculty, law school administrators, and professional organizations also offer frequent criticisms. The recognition of how wide and deep student concerns run has spurred some faculty and administrators to turn a critical eye on their own practices. Their assessments of where legal education is failing students derive from a belief that student concerns are generally valid and merit a response. Apprehension about the efficacy of the predominant law school pedagogies—the Socratic and case methods—has prompted numerous other critiques. Professional organizations such as the American Bar Association also periodically query how well law schools prepare students for practice.

Why do these criticisms of legal education matter? Given that law schools continue to graduate large numbers of new lawyers each year, most of whom engage in relatively successful legal careers, should we be at all concerned when we hear complaints about legal education? The answer is an emphatic yes. There are two reasons. First, what happens in law schools directly contributes to the much-discussed "crisis" in the legal profession. Yale Law School dean Anthony T. Kronman aptly describes this crisis as,

> in essence, a crisis of morale. It is the product of growing doubts about the capacity of a lawyer's life to offer fulfillment to the person who takes it up. Disguised by the material well-being of lawyers, it is a spiritual crisis that strikes at the heart of their professional pride.[1]

The criticisms of legal education demonstrate that today's law students doubt their ability to lead fulfilling lives as lawyers, despite the financial rewards of private practice. Students' complaints reveal that not only is attending law school generally unfulfilling, but also that legal education alienates students from their values and ideals. As law school is students' first systematic introduction to the ideals of professional excellence, its deleterious impact on students' perceptions of professional norms should greatly concern the legal profession.

Furthermore, law school is the appropriate forum to inculcate professional norms and a vision of law as a noble public profession. A fundamental role of any education is to socialize students into the culture and norms of the community. The values and norms both implicit and explicit in students' law school experience greatly affect their perception of the legal profession. As Kronman says, "It is in the law school classroom that lawyers are introduced to the culture of the profession and here that their professional self-conception first takes shape."[2] As law teachers encounter prospective lawyers before their impressions of the legal profession are fully formed, they "have a unique opportunity to influence the attitude of the nascent lawyer committed to their classrooms at the embryonic stage of his legal career."[3] Law schools have long recognized their socialization capacity; they have served as the "primary cultural and ideological device[s] in the making and shaping of the American legal profession" since the late nineteenth century.[4] Therefore, law schools are not simply an appropriate avenue through which to instill the norms and culture of the legal profession in its members. They represent the primary opportunity for the legal profession to pull itself out of its present crisis.

Finding the Source of the Concerns about Legal Education

Typically analysts explain away students' dissatisfaction with law school by blaming the actors. One theory blames the students. Rather than consider how law school practices mesh with student goals, experiences, and abilities, some claim the real problem is law students' sense of entitlement, lack of work ethic, and generally whiny attitude. If students were not so spoiled, were better prepared, and were willing to work hard, they argue, there would be no problems in law schools.

Blaming students for legal education's problems has several flaws. Most critically, it does not recognize the real differences between today's law students and those of the

1870s, for whom traditional legal education was designed. Students in the 1870s were relatively homogeneous-middle- and upper-middle-class white Protestant males of approximately the same age, educated in philosophy, classical studies, and political science, and planning to be personal lawyers, appellate lawyers, judges, and statesmen. But today's law students are decidedly heterogeneous. They are men and women of all ages, races, ethnicities, religions, socioeconomic classes, and educational backgrounds. They aspire to (and enter) a wide range of careers and professions; in fact, many attend law school because they believe it is a good general degree, not because they have a strong desire to spend their entire professional lives as lawyers. Nevertheless, the blame-the-student argument assumes that what was taught to law students in the 1870s is still appropriate today. It disregards not only that law students have changed considerably, but also that lawyers play different—and many more—roles in the twenty-first century than they did in the nineteenth. Finally, this argument often degenerates into the critic's perception of his own success in law school: "I learned the old hard way. It worked for me, and it should work for everyone."

A second theory blames law teachers, for a variety of reasons. For example, some claim that the "scholarly culture" in law schools undermines the message that law is a noble profession. They believe the focus on philosophies of law—like legal realism, law and economics, and critical legal theory—distracts faculty from their mission of teaching people how to become practicing lawyers. In fact, they contend, law teachers' total absorption in academic aspects of law causes them to teach law solely as an academic subject, to be considered from a contemplative distance rather than from a practitioner's up-close-and-personal viewpoint.

Others claim that law teachers nearly uniformly ascribe to an ideology that excludes emotion from the classroom on the grounds that this is the way to develop logical and rational thinking. This suppression of emotion drains intellectual discussions of meaning, alienating students and limiting their ability to locate their arguments in a broader moral or philosophical framework.[5] A third—and similar—claim is that faculty present all materials, including contextual ones, only from "a traditional legal perspective, i.e., the legal structures or principles they involve."[6] By so limiting students' ability to conceptualize the interrelationship of the law and other disciplines, teachers impress upon students a narrow, value-neutral, and alienating vision of the law. A fourth claim argues simply that law teachers lack the grounding in educational and learning theory to instruct their students effectively. The students' struggle to overcome poor teaching results in disenchantment with law school and a distancing from the law itself.

Blaming the faculty for legal education's flaws is every bit as inadequate as blaming students. First, law teachers' academic research and writing are vital to our legal system. Few practicing lawyers and judges have the time or the opportunity to reflect on the larger societal impact of their actions. Instead they turn to the writing of academics for information and commentary. Second, despite the compliance of many faculty in perpetuating the widely deplored aspects of legal education, faculty themselves are not the ultimate source of the problem. Not every law teacher demands the exclusion of emotions from the classroom or projects a value-neutral conception of the law. Many, in fact, try hard to provide students a broader, more contextualized perspective. However, in several ways law teachers are limited in their ability to have systemic impact on either students or the legal profession. Law school classes are so large that most faculty rarely develop meaningful relationships with their students. Additionally, the massive writing requirements of the tenure process tether the most junior faculty, the ones most willing to explore alternative pedagogies, to predominantly academic endeavors.

Variations on the blame theme include blaming administrators rather than teachers, blaming ABA and state bar requirements, and blaming the historical elitism of the legal profession. These explanations also fall short. Since faculty typically control many decisions, administrators are often more limited than teachers in their ability to effect change at law schools. ABA requirements may indeed place some constraints on law schools, but they certainly do not prevent the schools from providing students a fulfilling education. Lastly, the residue of history is no excuse for the shortcomings of today.

Most importantly, all of the blame-theme explanations for the problems in legal education suffer the same fatal flaw. All fail to offer any considered justification for the existence of law school.[7]

Asking the Lost Question: What Is the Purpose of Law School?

Discussion about the shortcomings of legal education is futile unless we can agree why law schools exist.[8] Without an understanding of the purpose of law school, assessments of schools' practices are hollow. As one writer on legal education recognized, "Only when the purpose [of legal education] is identified can determinations be made as to subject-matter and educational methods."[9]

Therefore, any discussion of legal education must begin not with what (is happening in law schools) or who (is doing these things), but why (are we doing anything at all). Why does law school exist? What purpose does it serve? Ascertaining its purpose provides a framework within which to have a meaningful discussion of what law schools should and should not be doing. Law school's purpose is the measuring stick against which to evaluate not just the abundant complaints and criticisms that legal education attracts but also the efficacy and relevance of law schools' practices.

In this paper I propose that the source of legal education's problems is that law schools' practices, which are based on the way law schools have been operating for more than 100 years, do not correspond to the purpose of law school today.[10] I first explore the fundamental question: what is the current purpose of law school? I conclude that the purpose of law school is to teach a heterogeneous group of people, who come from widely different backgrounds and with widely differing goals, to think like lawyers. I next explore exactly what teaching these people to think like lawyers means. After undertaking a functional analysis of the roles lawyers play in our society, to understand what it is that lawyers actually do, I conclude that "teaching people to think like lawyers" is not simply a matter of cultivating nascent skills in logical reasoning, as is commonly assumed, but instead entails helping students develop a broad range of skills and knowledge.

I then describe today's law schools' practices (which are remarkably consistent across the country) and compare them against law school's current purpose. My comparison reveals gaps between the current purpose and the present practices—gaps that coincide with oft-expressed concerns about legal education. This suggests that bridging the purpose/practice divide can alleviate much of the dissatisfaction with law school and potentially ameliorate the crisis in the legal profession. I conclude by offering some preliminary suggestions of ways to align law schools' practices with law school's purpose.

The Current Purpose of Law School

How Do We Determine What the Purpose of Law School Is?

There are two primary ways to determine an institution's purpose. The first is to look at what the institution claims to be its purpose. The second is to consider an institution's current practices in light of its history—why it developed in the way it did and what historical purposes it served.

Although mission statements are the standard institutional proclamations of purpose, law school mission statements do not reveal much. Neither the AALS nor the ABA offers a mission statement for the institution of law school.[11] Many individual schools, however, do have mission statements. Consistency among them might provide insight into the current purpose of the institution of law school. But unfortunately law schools appear to treat mission statements as a formality. A recent survey of law school deans revealed that the schools' mission statements do not accurately reflect what deans believe to be their school's internal strengths, public image, or core values—primary elements that schools use in making strategic decisions.[12] Thus, seeking an underlying consistency in mission statements is not a reliable way to determine the current purpose of law school.

Examining law school's historical development, while somewhat more fruitful, also does not fully elucidate its present purpose. Law schools as we know them—schools teaching only law that are part of larger universities—did not emerge until the 1820s.[13] Blackstone gave the first known lecture on the common law at Oxford in 1753.[14] It was not until 1779, however, that American universities began appointing professors of law. Such a professor, at that time, was like a professor of philosophy or government; he had no separate department, and his purpose was simply to lecture to the university community about interesting legal issues.[15] In 1784 the first school to focus solely on training lawyers opened its doors. Litchfield, a private, stand-alone establishment, was fundamentally a vocational school. It claimed to be superior to the standard law office apprenticeship because it "taught the law as a science, and not merely nor principally as a mechanical business, nor as a collection of loose independent fragments."[16] In practice, however, Litchfield and its peers were merely the "natural outgrowth of an office overcrowded with students who sought to "read law" under a particular lawyer's tutelage.[17]

Throughout the 1800s universities absorbed private law schools like Litchfield for their profit-making capacities.[18] Yet university law schools of the mid-nineteenth century bore little resemblance to those of today. Many liberal arts programs included occasional lectures on legal issues,[19] because the study of law was considered useful not just for prospective lawyers but also "for men not intending to practice, but who wished to fit themselves for public office."[20] Law departments, however, "were marginal to the main purpose" of their host universities and often competed for students with the liberal arts curriculum.[21] Most law departments had only a couple of faculty, whose job was to lecture about the law to large groups of students.[22] Like their private predecessors, university-based law schools in the mid- to late-nineteenth century "were primarily trade schools."[23]

The introduction of the case method by Harvard Law School dean C. C. Langdell in 1870 revolutionized law school. Perceiving law as a science "provided a justification for the existence of law schools.... If law really was a science, then it deserved serious academic study."[24] By the 1890s the ABA had embraced both the case method and Langdell's model of an academic and professional law school as the appropriate mechanisms to raise professional standards and "control the number and, perhaps, the ethnic and religious derivation of new entrants to the bar."[25] As Robert Stevens has said, "the concept of providing part of legal training through an institution known as the law school had become associated with the parallel aspect of institutionalization—the urge to raise standards and so make the bar more competent and more exclusive."[26] University law schools' purpose shifted from training gentlemen, lawyers, and statesmen to establishing and controlling the culture and ideology of the professional bar. University law schools evolved past the vocational training of their private competitors as they "sought to ritualize language, elite traditions, legal consciousness, social characteristics, and political thought." For the elite lawyers of the late nineteenth and early twentieth century, then, "law schools were to function as the appropriate transmitter of established legal culture."[27]

Nevertheless, until the end of the nineteenth century "the vast majority of the legal profession ... still experienced only on-the-job legal education."[28] Apprenticeships remained more common than law school attendance, and law school requirements were minimal.[29] In fact, many people who attended law school did so in addition to, not instead of, serving an apprenticeship.[30] Furthermore, men who attended law school had no edge on passing the bar over those who took the apprenticeship route.[31]

During the twentieth century, however, law schools pushed out apprenticeships as the standard legal education. The transition came largely as a result of the pressure on the professional bar to raise standards and the growing desire to curb the exponential increase in the number of lawyers.[32] In the 1920s the ABA and the AALS recommended that all prospective law students complete two years of college work, and by the end of the 1930s most states had adopted this requirement.[33] By the 1960s four years of college and three years of full-time law school had become the norm.[34] The concept of a unitary bar (in which all lawyers require the same skills and knowledge), first introduced in 1878 at the original organizational meeting of the ABA,[35] had become an "irrebuttable presumption"; its natural counterpart was uniform standards, which resulted in homogeneity among law schools.[36]

Clearly the purpose of law school has evolved and changed alongside the needs and interests of the public and of the legal profession. Although law school's history does not define its present purpose, it does help us determine that present purpose. It tells us that, as a result of their historical evolution, present-day law schools are the primary gatekeepers for the legal profession.[37] The vast majority of state bar associations require that prospective lawyers earn a law school degree in order to be eligible for state bar admission. By far the most common path to becoming a lawyer is to attend law school. Less than one-tenth of one percent of people who passed the bar exam during the 1990s did not attend law school.[38] Law schools' admissions processes are thus the first hurdle to becoming a lawyer. Through the admissions process, law schools select who will ultimately be eligible to sit for the bar examination.

Furthermore, as a result of the institutionalization of university-based law schools, present-day law schools are fundamentally academic institutions. They confer postbaccalaureate degrees, not licenses to practice law. They are closely tied to universities that influence their operations, decisions, and budgets. And while ABA and state bar requirements certainly inform law schools' decisions and practices, they do not control them.

Defining the Purpose—What It Means to "Think Like a Lawyer"

The most important thing this historical look has shown us is that the purpose of law school has evolved in accordance with the needs and interests of the legal profession and of the public. The purpose of law school in the 1780s was not the same as the purpose of law school in the 1870s, and neither defines the purpose of law school today. The current purpose emerges from the unique role law schools now play in lawyers' development. Law schools encounter prospective lawyers at their most formative stage and offer them their first formalized introduction to the legal profession. As primarily academic institutions, law schools are most capable of teaching novices the cognitive skills lawyering requires. In short, then, given law schools' capacities and novice lawyers' needs, the purpose of law school can be summed up in the recognizable phrase: to teach people to think like lawyers.[39]

The inquiry into the purpose of law school cannot end with that simple assertion, however. When we consider whether an institution is meeting its purpose, our terminology must be precisely delineated.[40] Imprecision in defining an institution's purpose allows into the dialog hidden assumptions that undermine the assessment of institutional practices against that purpose. So the critical first step to understanding the purpose of law school is to define what it means to "think like a lawyer." Although this is an oft-stated justification for law school, no consensus exists about what "thinking like a lawyer" means. Furthermore, the concept of thinking like a lawyer is loaded with notions, accumulated over time, about what a lawyer does. We need to reexamine and clearly define what it means to "think like a lawyer" before we can begin to assess lawyers' practices.

At the most generic level, teaching people to think like a lawyer means teaching them how to approach situations as a lawyer would. Thinking like a lawyer involves two elements, one functional and one normative.

The Functional Component

The functional element defines how lawyers think in terms of what lawyers do.[41] What skills and knowledge lawyers rely on depends upon what functions they perform. If we figure out what lawyers actually do, we can then trace back from that understanding to determine what skills and knowledge are critical to lawyering.

One standard way of defining what lawyers do is in terms of the clients they serve and the size of the offices in which they practice. Lawyers do either public or private work. They practice solo or work in a large, medium, or small private firm, for the government, or for a nonprofit legal services center. They work as in-house counsel for corporations or other typically nonprofit organizations. Another common way to categorize lawyers is by the legal issues they work on. Lawyers' work is either a litigation (trial or appellate) practice or a transactional practice; it focuses on specific subjects, such as employment law or admiralty law.

Although such categorizations are interesting, they obscure several realities about being a lawyer.[42] Lawyers in fact perform similar functions regardless of who their client or employer is and how much money either has. Furthermore, lawyers perform multiple functions regardless of who their employer is, who their client is, or what specific area of the law they focus on.

A better way to understand what lawyers do is to look at the functions lawyers actually perform. If we can define a set of lawyering functions, we can examine them to see what types of skills and knowledge they require. Those clusters of skills and knowledge constitute the functional elements of thinking like a lawyer.

Lawyering functions. Lawyers perform a wide range of functions that are common across the legal profession and can be grouped into four broad categories.

Lawyers are *advocates and advisers.*[43] Lawyers work to secure the best possible outcomes for the clients they represent or the social causes for which they advocate. To do this, they provide clients with all necessary information to make an informed decision about what actions to take and then assist clients in pursuing their chosen course of action. They help clients assess legal, personal, and financial problems, and assist clients on moral issues.[44] They conduct legal and factual research, and synthesize arguments about possible interpretations of laws and the application of laws to particular sets of facts, to present clients with solutions to problems or risk analysis.

One common means by which lawyers advocate for causes or clients is litigation. Lawyers prosecute criminals, bring civil suits against people or entities that violate the law or breach private agreements, and defend the government against challenges to its actions and decisions. They also bring and defend lawsuits on behalf of private clients or for the purpose of furthering a particular social policy. In pursuit of such lawsuits, lawyers make written and oral arguments in court about the correct interpretations of laws, negotiate with opposing counsel, testify in front of government entities, draft contracts, participate in alternative dispute resolution processes, and lobby government officials. They investigate potential claims both for and against their clients or cause. They investigate and depose potential witnesses and seek out evidence. They prepare clients for depositions and trial. They advocate for interpretations of statutes that support their client's claims. They advocate for the application of common law in a manner that supports their client's or cause's interests.

Other common ways in which lawyers advocate for clients or causes include acting as public spokespersons on their behalf, organizing groups of like-minded persons for community and legal action, testifying in front of government and regulatory bodies on behalf of clients or causes, and negotiating contracts and lobbying for legislation favorable to their clients or causes.

Lawyers are makers and implementers of policies and rules. Lawyers draft, design, and interpret rules and policies for government and for private and nonprofit entities; they make sure those rules and policies are implemented in the way intended and according to the law. For example, lawyers draft legislation and corporate policies, consult with interested parties, and negotiate preliminary and final versions of these documents. They write rules to govern the legal profession, such as the Federal Rules of Evidence, the Federal Rules of Civil Procedure, and the Model Rules of Professional Conduct. They craft the platforms of political parties and represent the interests of the United States and its citizens and corporations in dealing with foreign governments, citizens, and corporations. Lawyers also hold senior management and executive positions in private, public, and nonprofit organizations, in law firms, and in government agencies.[45] They act as directors on corporate and nonprofit boards and frequently serve as elected officials.

Lawyers also employ their specialized knowledge about the law to comply with the legal rules and processes their clients' or causes' needs demand. For example, they ensure that contracts and corporate documents comply with governing laws. They conduct due diligence for mergers and acquisitions to ensure that all corporate papers are in order. They prosecute patents in accordance with the rules of the U.S. Patent and Trademark Office. They meet all procedural rules of litigation in timely fashion and comply with discovery requests.

Lawyers are *adjudicators, negotiators, and mediators*. They adjudicate disputes between parties, write judicial opinions, and preside over juries charged with passing judgment on a particular matter. Lawyers also help parties resolve disputes without litigation[46]—for example, by helping them negotiate settlements.[47] They also serve as both court-appointed and "volunteer" neutral mediators and arbitrators to assist competing third parties in resolving disputes.

Lawyers are *educators*. As educators, lawyers instruct others about the legal system, legal institutions, lawyers' services, the legal profession, and the interpretation of statutory and common law. Lawyers teach other lawyers about specialized legal issues through continuing legal education programs. Senior lawyers teach junior lawyers the skills and knowledge necessary to succeed in law practice. Lawyers teach law students the norms and culture of the legal profession as well as the skills and knowledge necessary to be a lawyer.[48] Lawyers instruct the public about legal issues by speaking at public forums, making public comments via the media and the Internet, visiting with classes of schoolchildren and community groups, writing articles for both academic and more general audiences, and discussing law-related issues with neighbors, friends, and colleagues.

Lawyering capacities. What sorts of skills and knowledge must lawyers have to perform the lawyering functions described above? Although it is common to define what lawyers need to know as knowledge or skills, either alone is insufficient; it is the ability to synthesize knowledge and skills that lawyers require. There are three definable clusters of knowledge and skills both common and critical to the lawyering functions I've described: judgment capacity, legal reasoning capacity, and communication capacity.

Judgment capacity entails the ability to exercise sound and reasoned judgment in light of an "integrated understanding" of the complex factual patterns, conflicting interests, potentially applicable legal theories, and pragmatic considerations involved in any given legal issue.[49] It includes knowing how to discern existing or potential problems based on (usually incomplete) knowledge of facts and familiarity with the relevant legal doctrine; how to investigate the factual, legal, ethical, and practical aspects of problems, including undertaking legal research; how to identify stakeholders and investigate their interests and needs; and how to locate and call upon potential legal and nonlegal collaborators.[50] A key component of sound judgment capacity is being able to use all of this information to craft solutions that recognize and account for the many—often conflicting—factors and interests. To exercise sound judgment, lawyers must know how to organize knowledge, both legal and nonlegal, and recognize in new situations patterns that correspond to knowledge they already possess.[51]

Legal reasoning capacity means being able to identify legal concerns, assess legal risks, and propose legal solutions based on a comprehensive understanding of relevant legal doctrine. This requires knowledge of legal doctrines and the ability to evaluate the applicability of various legal theories in light of factual and pragmatic factors.[52] It demands familiarity with the substance and procedures of both traditional legal pathways like litigation and alternative dispute resolution options like negotiation. It requires the ability to locate, read, parse, and understand the interpretations and precedential value of relevant cases as well as the interpretations and applicability of relevant statutes. Effectively interpreting cases and statutes further requires knowledge of the historical, political, and judicial contexts in which cases were decided and statutes were passed. Legal reasoning capacity also entails the ability to draft, understand, and evaluate legal documents, including contracts, personal documents such as wills, and corporate documents.

Communication capacity involves the ability to communicate effectively with a wide variety of audiences for a wide variety of purposes.[53] One element of communication capacity is the ability to both speak and write persuasive legal, political, and ideological arguments. This involves knowledge of the structure of legal arguments, comprehension of the rationale for particular legal regimes, and skill at packaging and presenting arguments to different audiences. For lawyers desiring to make their communication official—to file a brief with the court, for example, or to establish a corporation in a particular jurisdiction—it also requires knowledge of the appropriate forms of legal documentation.[54]

A second—equally important—element of communication capacity is basic people skills, including listening, empathy, and sensitivity to the concerns, interests, needs, and biases of the audience. Good people skills benefit lawyers instrumentally, by helping them to better understand others' goals and motivations, as well as affectively, by helping them learn to empathize with others, and thus better understand how others interpret interactions, construct values, and perceive society at large.[55]

The Normative Component

In addition to the functional element, there is a normative component to thinking like a lawyer. It defines how lawyers think and act in terms of professional norms. Like other professions, the legal profession has its own values, culture, and ideology that inform its members' thought processes and actions. In the legal profession these norms enjoy particularly high status. They are enshrined in codes of professional responsibility. Every prospective lawyer must pass a character examination, typically in the form of a professional responsibility exam, to ensure that he is familiar with professional norms and able to comply with them. Violating a professional norm subjects a lawyer to discipline; blatant violations can result in eviction from the profession. Consequently, lawyers always approach situations against the backdrop of the legal profession's culture and norms.

Another aspect of the normative component is recognizing the unique social responsibility being a lawyer entails. As David Barnhizer has said, law is "inextricably tied to social action and the application of power."[56] Lawyers' responsibilities do not end with their duty to a particular client. Lawyers have a duty to society at large to uphold the rule of law and ensure its just application. This duty stems from their unique position of power over the implementation and application of laws. Law is an inherently political profession; every application of the law involves an interpretation of what the rules and norms of our society should be.

The normative component of thinking like a lawyer entails first and foremost a comprehensive understanding of the role of lawyers, and thus of law, in our society. It demands knowledge of and facility with the rules of professional responsibility, including comprehension of why they exist and what purposes they serve. It includes being able to identify, recognize, avoid, and resolve potential breaches of professional norms and values.[57] It also involves the ability to work effectively within the confines of professional responsibility to address problems and resolve legal issues.

In conclusion, there are four elements to thinking like a lawyer: judgment capacity, legal reasoning capacity, communication capacity, and comprehension of professional norms and responsibilities. Each of these components has both knowledge and skills aspects. Now the purpose of law school can be more clearly stated: to teach prospective lawyers the knowledge and skills necessary to exercise sound judgment, develop sound legal reasoning capacity, communicate effectively, and function at all times in accordance with professional norms and responsibilities.

Law Schools' Current Practices

How does what is actually happening in law schools today compare with what the purpose of law school suggests we should expect to see occurring? The two aspects of law schools' practices with direct impact on the teaching of students to think like lawyers are pedagogy—what occurs in faculty-student interactions both in and outside of the classroom—and curriculum—course content, diversity of course selection, and required courses.[58] In this section I examine law schools' current pedagogical and curricular practices. I first present the expectations raised by the purpose of law school, as I have defined it. Then I review law schools' current practices, pointing out where the schools are meeting expectations and where they are failing to do so.

Before I begin, it is important to note that few empirical studies have been done on law school practices. Much of the evidence for what law schools actually do is anecdotal, but the anecdotal observations are remarkably consistent. Although individual law schools will vary to some degree, my composite picture of a law school should be recognizable to nearly every law student and indicative of most students' experiences.

Pedagogy

Expectation

The four components of thinking like a lawyer—judgment, legal reasoning, communication, and comprehension of professional norms—demand a highly interactive pedagogy. Because those elements are abstract and complex, students cannot learn how to think like lawyers simply by reading a casebook or listening to a lecture about what lawyers do. They need to actively grapple with identifying and evaluating complex legal problems, practice communicating to a wide variety of audiences, and receive extensive feedback on their efforts. So we should expect to see assignments and classroom exercises challenging students to develop their judgment, legal reasoning, and communications skills. We should expect to find reading assignments that provide students the necessary background in the role of law and lawyers in our society, and in legal doctrine and how it developed. We should also expect to witness classroom activities and assignments that challenge students to ground their identification and resolution of complex legal problems in both historical and pragmatic contexts.

Since using these pedagogies requires a significant faculty commitment, we should expect to find law teachers expending a significant portion of their time on preparing lessons, interacting with students, and offering feedback on both students' abilities and their grasp of historical, contextual, and doctrinal materials.

Since the mechanisms used to assess students' performance also should reflect the components of thinking like a lawyer, we should expect to observe students being tested on their ability to exercise and defend their judgments, on their capacity to understand and work with legal doctrines and different sources of law, on their facility at communicating both orally and in writing with a number of audiences, and on their capability to recognize and effectively handle situations that raise issues of professional responsibility.

Reality

Faculty-student interaction and classroom activities. Do law schools meet such expectations of faculty-student interaction and classroom activities? Yes and no. Although some practices contribute to the engaged, interactive classroom environment that thinking like a lawyer demands, most law schools' current practices detract from their ability to provide such an environment. Furthermore, although classroom instruction effectively prepares students to analyze and distinguish cases, often this is accomplished at the expense of instruction in other necessary lawyering capacities.

The standard law school class is large, limiting in-class opportunities for meaningful faculty-student interaction. First-year classes almost uniformly are taught in large sections. Upper-level seminars, while becoming more common, are still not the norm. Large classes, ranging in size from 50 to more than 200, frequently keep students and faculty from getting to know each other well. Nevertheless, students' success in securing such elite positions as clerkships and fellowships is heavily dependent on faculty recommendations. The predictable result is that the louder, more confident students jockey for the teacher's attention; the less loquacious or less self-assured students end up participating less, meaning they have fewer institutionalized opportunities to interact with their teachers and classmates.[59] Large classes also protect unprepared students: the larger the class, the less likely any one student will be called on. Furthermore, since teachers are unable to monitor student activity in large classes, students can—and often do—cut class, come to class unprepared, or disengage from the classroom discussion for an extended time, without concern for immediate repercussions. Consequently, few law students actually experience the active in-class engagement that the purpose of law school demands.

The Langdellian case method remains the predominant pedagogy at American law schools, particularly in first-year classes: students read judicial decisions, usually appellate ones, and the teacher questions them about the facts, principles, and theories behind those decisions. The goal is to teach students how to analyze a case in order to ascertain the doctrinal and theoretical justifications for its holding, and thus to comprehend the case's precedential value and its applicability to different fact patterns. The case method is quite successful at doing that, but it does not offer students the historical and contextual grounding lawyers require, nor does it engage students in practicing skills other than analyzing and reasoning from cases.

Law teachers regularly use some version of the Socratic method in conjunction with the case method. They pose questions to students that challenge students' assumptions and interpretations, often leading them down the wrong path intentionally to demonstrate the fallacy of a line of reasoning. The goal of the Socratic method is to hone students' reasoning skills through active engagement with the teacher—or observation of another student's active engagement. Traditionally teachers called on students with no warning. Nowadays, more commonly, they inform certain students in advance that they will be called on, or they mix cold-calling with requests for volunteers. Also common is allowing a student to pass if the student is called on without warning and is unprepared. A 1996 survey of law faculty revealed that over 90 percent use the Socratic method in first-year and upper-level large classes for an average of 53 percent of class time. Sixty-seven percent use the Socratic method in seminars, and 54 percent use it in "skills courses," although it is not the primary way faculty and students interact in small-class settings."[60]

Lecture is also a dominant law school pedagogy: 94 percent of faculty lecture in upper-level courses, 82 percent in seminars, and 86 percent in skills courses, for anywhere from one-fifth to one-third of class time.[61]

Pedagogies other than lecture or Socratic dialog are far less common. In large first-year and upper-level courses, less than one-third of faculty use alternative pedagogies, and they do so for less than 10 percent of class time.[62]

In sum, there is little open conversation in class among faculty and students, and thus little feedback to students, except for those few who are called upon or who volunteer to participate. Combined with large class sizes, which ensure that a student will be called on at most a few times during a semester, the result is an abundance of passive learning. Students generally receive information from books, lectures, or observation of another student in Socratic dialog rather than construct knowledge and develop skills through active engagement.

Faculty emphasis on teaching. Law schools generally fail to meet expectations about teaching. They neither offer incentives for good teaching nor even define it. The only consistent feedback on their teaching that law teachers receive comes from end-of-term student evaluations.[63] Furthermore, law schools offer little, if any, teaching support to their faculty. Instead they encourage faculty to focus primarily on scholarship—researching, writing, and publishing—and they create, through the tenure process, a very real disincentive for faculty to expend more than minimal energy on teaching. In decisions on hiring, promotion, tenure, and salary, scholarship is the weightiest factor; significant publications more than make up for barely passable teaching.[64]

Little pedagogical direction is available even for interested faculty, despite the fact that law teachers typically have had little exposure to learning theory. Few schools provide teaching workshops, much less require that their faculty attend. Although there are some postgraduate programs designed to help law faculty develop their teaching abilities, only a few people attend them. For example, only a very small minority of law professors attend the annual three-day AALS Workshop for New Law Teachers or the periodic Conference on New Ideas for Experienced Teachers.[65] Consequently, faculty tend to model their teaching styles on their own professors and mentors, replicating in today's classes the teaching methods of earlier generations.[66]

Assignments. Law schools demonstrate mixed success in meeting the expectation of reading assignments that provide students with a foundation in the role of law and lawyers in our society, and in legal doctrine and how it developed.

Law schools still rely primarily on casebooks—introduced by Langdell in the late nineteenth century—for reading assignments. Like their predecessors, modern casebooks consist almost entirely of appellate opinions even though most legal disputes never appear in court and many courts of limited jurisdiction do not rigidly follow precedent. The focus on appellate opinions obscures the fact that lawyers' role in shaping cases is just as important as precedent, if not more so, to a judge's decision. Unlike the earlier casebooks, which contained nothing but judicial decisions, modern ones do include selections from law review articles, directive questions, limited commentary, and occasional historical and political background materials.[67] Such material does help to put judicial decisions in context, but in most casebooks it is heavily edited and relatively sparse. Furthermore, the most substantive commentary offers theoretical perspectives on cases' doctrinal value and theoretical justifications for or criticisms of judges' decisions. Rarely does any commentary give students a broad contextual background for judicial decisions or any insight into lawyers' actions.[68] Furthermore, students frequently read only the cases and skip the other materials, confident that class discussion will almost certainly revolve around the facts and principles of cases, not the casebook's selected theoretical commentary.

In many courses, to be sure, casebooks are not the sole source of reading material. It is becoming increasingly common for teachers to put together reading packets containing law review articles, newspaper articles, and other commentary on cases and legal doctrines. Such packets are a good step toward giving students the kind of contextualized understanding that thinking like a lawyer demands and that casebooks lack. But the very fact that these materials are supplemental to a casebook lends them an implicit air of inferiority; students may think that if the materials were truly important, the casebook editors would have seen fit to include them. A teacher can, of course, ameliorate this message of inferiority by giving the packet materials at least equal airtime in class or by not assigning a casebook at all. However, given the prominence of casebooks in law classrooms and the emphasis placed on them, particularly during the first year, students may feel shortchanged when teachers focus on reading packets instead.

Assessments. Law schools generally fail to meet expectations regarding assessments. Because of the low level of student-faculty interaction, feedback and assessments typically come through grades—usually based on one examination at the end of the semester. Modern law school exams still resemble the exams Langdell gave in the 1870s. The two most common types of questions call for rule application and issue spotting.[69] Occasionally a teacher requires or allows a paper instead of an exam, but it is rare that speaking in class counts toward students' grades or that there is more than one graded assignment. Students typically do not get their exams or papers back, or receive any written or oral comments about their work. Although students usually can ask to see their exam or paper after receiving their grade, they typically will find few, if any, marks on the pages. Large classes contribute to this situation; teachers have to grade so many exams or papers that they can spend only limited time on each one. For the most part, assessment of law students neither tests them on the many-faceted capacities they will require as lawyers nor gives them significant feedback on their performance.

Curriculum

Expectation

The four components of thinking like a lawyer necessitate that the curriculum include a broad range of content. To be able to identify, investigate, and resolve legal problems, students must have a basic understanding of common law and statutory legal doctrine, including both the elements of particular doctrines and the historical, political, ideological, and pragmatic influences on doctrinal development. To effectively act in accordance with professional norms, students must have basic knowledge of the role of law and lawyers in our society, the rules of professional conduct, and the reasons for those rules. They must also have opportunities to practice judgment, legal reasoning, and communications skills.

In a course catalog we should expect to see, at a minimum, courses on legal doctrine, doctrinal evolution, and legal history and philosophy; courses on professional responsibility and lawyers' roles in society; and courses emphasizing skills development.[70] Furthermore, we should expect to find that the required courses provide students the background historical, contextual, and doctrinal knowledge, and the understanding of the professional legal culture, that they need to exercise sound judgment, legal reasoning, and communications skills when approaching legal problems.

Reality

Course selection. Law schools do a reasonably good job of providing doctrinal knowledge and exposure. The curriculum consists mainly of doctrinal or "substantive" courses. According to a 1997 survey of new courses that law schools added between 1994 and 1997, over two-thirds of the new courses addressed substantive areas of the law. Less than one-third focused on lawyering skills, legal institutions in context, or the role(s) lawyers play in society.[71] Although doctrinal courses are typically heavily corporate-focused, courses addressing issues of social justice are becoming more common. The 1997 survey revealed that a majority of new doctrinal courses introduced in the mid-1990s addressed topics related to social justice, such as family law, human rights law, environmental law, healthcare law, constitutional law, criminal law, discrimination law, and labor and employment law.[72]

Law schools do much less well, however, at instruction in the other skills and knowledge lawyering requires. In fact, the ABA's most recent assessment of legal education, the MacCrate Report, concludes that "relatively few law students have exposure to the full range of professional skills offerings."[73]

For example, although all law schools require students to take a course on professional responsibility, typically worth two credits, there is little systematic effort to inculcate a sense of professional responsibility among students. The course usually employs the case method to instruct students on the rules tested on the ethics portion of the bar exam, instead of challenging students to actively explore the complex ethical issues lawyers regularly confront in practice.[74] It typically focuses not on "the social responsibilities of the lawyer or the profession, but rather the legal responsibility of the individual practitioner vis-à-vis his clients and the ethical considerations he 'ought' to take into account in properly exercising his private role as an attorney."[75] Tenured faculty generally decline to teach the professional responsibility courses, leaving instruction on lawyers' public roles to outside lecturers and junior faculty.[76] Furthermore, the rule orientation of the case method ensures that legal ethics and professional norms are rarely discussed systematically in doctrinal courses.[77] The resulting message is that comprehending lawyers' public responsibilities is not a complex and real concern that merits much of students' attention.

Skills are also shortchanged in the law school curriculum. The two ways in which standard curricula do directly address skills—legal writing programs and clinical programs—demonstrate law schools' general disregard for skills training.

Legal writing courses emerged in the middle of the twentieth century in response to calls for more egalitarian legal education focused on professional skills.[78] However, as writing programs matured, competing purposes, competing conceptions of how to implement programs, limited resources and the unwillingness of most full-time faculty to supervise student writing have limited their efficacy and value.[79] Today most law schools address legal writing through one required first-year writing course[80] and perhaps an upper-level required seminar paper or research paper. Writing typically is taught separately from doctrinal subjects, signaling "that legal writing is a 'skill' separate and independent from legal analysis" and that "the only relevance of 'legal writing' is as a finished product."[81] Writing supervisors tend not to be full-time faculty.[82] Instead, upper-class students, recent graduates, and adjunct or visiting faculty commonly instruct a tutorial group of ten to twenty students in the use of the library and legal research and supervise limited writing assignments on artificial problems. The additional fact that writing courses typically carry less academic credit than doctrinal courses signals that writing skills are less important than understanding doctrine.[83]

Clinical legal education became common in law schools beginning in the 1960s. The general purpose of clinical education is to introduce students to the factual, procedural, ethical, and human complexities of practice, including dealing with clients, working with other attorneys, navigating social institutions, and discerning legal problems from complicated and incomplete facts.[84] Students work in legal aid clinics and represent actual clients, typically indigent persons, under the guidance of a clinical instructor who is a practicing lawyer.

Although clinical education can introduce students to complexities the case method only hints at, law schools resist clinical education and have affirmatively limited its growth and its impact.[85] First, schools typically keep clinical education "separate, even invisible, from the rest of legal education as a matter of curriculum, space, and time, thereby preventing contamination of the university law school's basic concepts and structures."[86] Clinical courses are reserved for upper-level students and sometimes restricted to third-years. Many clinics operate off campus, or on the periphery, often in dingy, utilitarian quarters.

Second, law schools tacitly and subtly suggest that clinical education has a second-class status in the academy. For example, while most doctrinal classes focus on corporate and institutional legal problems, most clinics serve indigent clients who are experiencing legal problems in their personal lives. The disconnect between classroom lessons and clinical work, coupled with the predominance of classroom studies, signals to students that the lessons learned in the clinic are less important than those learned in the classroom. Clinical work typically earns fewer academic credits than traditional courses, even when students spend more hours on clinical work than on classroom work. Lastly, most law schools reserve the benefits of tenure for classroom faculty, again indicating that clinical teachers do not merit equal status.[87]

Required courses. The required curriculum in most law schools does not provide students the background knowledge of history, sociopolitical context, doctrine, and the professional culture that they need in order to exercise sound judgment, legal reasoning, and communications skills when approaching legal problems. It usually consists solely of a smattering of first-year doctrinal courses—typically torts, property, criminal law, civil procedure, constitutional law, and contracts—plus token courses in professional responsibility and legal research and writing. Many schools also recommend that students take additional doctrinal courses such as corporations, tax, and accounting.

In short, many of law schools' current practices are holdovers from the nineteenth century that fail to achieve the twenty-first-century purpose of law school—to teach a heterogeneous group of students how to think like lawyers.

Bridging the Purpose-Practice Divide

It is plain that many of law schools' current practices not only fail to support but in fact actually undermine law school's current purpose. To be truly useful for the twenty-first century, then, law schools must free themselves of the shackles of the outmoded nineteenth-century practices that have become so entrenched as to be nearly invisible. This is easier said than done; there are reasons why law schools operate as they do, and any attempt to change law schools' practices must take account of them. Therefore, before conceiving of changes to law schools' practices, we must first understand the obstacles in our path—the reasons law schools are the way they are today.

Obstacles to Change

Law schools' practices are based on tradition, not on a regular assessment and reassessment of the needs of the public, students, and the legal profession. That these practices persist is largely due to a combination of institutional inertia and financial disincentives for change.

The entrenchment of the case method is a prime example. Even in the face of challenges from the legal profession itself, like the AALS Curriculum Committee's 1944 effort to "isolate legal skills and so to articulate the rationales underlying legal education," the case method has not fallen out of favor. The few law schools that undertook broad experiments with alternative pedagogies during the twentieth century inevitably returned to it.[88] Today the case method remains omnipresent; it is the primary pedagogy at virtually every American law school, including all of the elite schools.[89]

The case method reigns supreme in spite of suffering nearly constant criticism since its inception and in spite of "the fact that Langdell's justification for developing and using [it]—his belief that law is a science that can be reduced to fundamental rules through scientific analysis—has long since been repudiated."[90] What explains the case method's persistence despite its recognized severance from its theoretical moorings?

There are several reasons for the method's continued supremacy. First, the case method's central role in justifying law schools and professionalizing the bar has entrenched its position. Law schools have made significant efforts over the last century to distinguish themselves from trade schools.[91] The depiction of law as a science, a justifiable branch of academic study, was central to law schools' ability to make that distinction. The case method transformed law training into an academic pursuit and law into a profession. Law schools today still blindly cling to the misperception that it is the case method that gives them intellectual and professional credibility. This is a classic example of institutional inertia.

Second, the case method makes financial sense. It allows for a "low-cost, high-return law school."[92] It made it possible for law schools to be financially feasible at a time when they were trying to differentiate themselves from both the impersonal, passive learning of lectures and the personal but nondoctrinal instruction of apprenticeships.[93] Today the case method still enables semipersonalized instruction of large numbers of law students at a relatively low cost, and at a relatively high student-faculty ratio.[94]

Institutional inertia and financial disincentives also explain the persistence of other practices that no longer support law school's current purpose. For example, law schools themselves face significant financial and structural disincentives to change their practices. Instruction requiring greater faculty-student interaction would compel faculty to spend much more time on teaching than they do now. A much higher faculty-student ratio is necessary to preserve the faculty's ability to spend time on research—an activity that brings great acclaim to the host law school—and at the same time to encourage and facilitate more time-intensive pedagogies. Hiring more teachers is costly, as is the less desirable alternative of shrinking the student body.[95] Furthermore, unless all law schools act in concert, a school that places greater emphasis on teaching ability in tenure decisions may not be able to attract many of the productive scholars whose star power brings acclaim, alumni donations, and students. This may explain why elite law schools stress scholarship "as the most important element in almost everything they do," relegating teaching to secondary status.[96] Even law schools' physical infrastructures pose a constraint on changing practices. Classrooms designed for large, Socratic, case-method classes are not easily adaptable to smaller, more intimate groups or to experiential learning. Remodeling would be costly.

In addition to institutional inertia and financial disincentives, structural disincentives—influences built into the fabric of law schools' behavior—also constrain law schools' willingness and ability to change their practices. Two in particular are worth mentioning here because of their broad-ranging impact. First, the ABA tacitly approves the standard practices in today's law schools via its accreditation requirements. Although the ABA requirements do not address pedagogy or curriculum directly, they indirectly influence these decisions. For example, the ABA now requires accredited law schools to have a student/faculty ratio no greater than twenty to one.[97] Despite the prevalence of adjunct and part-time faculty, the ABA does not include them in calculating that ratio. Most full-time faculty spend only ten to twelve hours per week in the classroom. This combination of a low faculty-student ratio and the few hours law professors actually spend teaching contributes to large class size and minimal attention to pedagogy. Second, law schools are part of universities, and standard university tenure processes frequently emphasize scholarship over teaching ability.

Suggestions

Despite these obstacles, change is indeed both possible and critical. Unless law schools do adapt, they may soon find they have outlived their usefulness. But attempts to bridge the gulf between law school's purpose and law schools' practices must recognize the influences of institutional inertia and both financial and structural disincentives. Change will incur significant costs, both financial and personal, as law schools reconstruct themselves to better achieve their current purpose. Given these constraints, change must be incremental and evolutionary.

Following are several suggestions of ways to begin bridging the purpose-practice divide. These are not meant to be a complete list of the changes law schools should undertake, nor are they meant to limit the scope of options readers might imagine. Instead they offer a starting point, an example of the way creative thinking within the purpose-practice framework can help resolve the problems of legal education and, perhaps, ameliorate the crisis in the legal profession as well.

Make sure law students have sufficient foundation in legal institutions, the role of law, and the role of lawyers. As the discussion of lawyering functions and capacities made apparent, a solid grounding in the history, operation, and impact of legal institutions, in the role of law, and in the role of lawyers is necessary for all lawyers. Students must acquire this foundation either before or during law school. It is critical not only to understanding legal doctrine and the legal profession, but also to choosing a career path in the law. Following are a few ways law schools can make sure their students are properly versed in these foundational topics.

Require a prelaw curriculum. Medical schools in the United States require a premed curriculum; all applicants must take a certain set of courses before they are eligible to apply for and attend medical school.[98] There is no comparable requirement for law students. Requiring a prelaw curriculum would relieve law schools of some of the financial burden of ensuring that students have adequate foundation in areas such as the role of law in our society, legal philosophy and legal history, and communication and analytical skills. Like the premed curriculum, a prelaw curriculum would need to be tailored to the types of instruction general colleges and universities can, and already do, provide. It should not, however, be so extensive as to prohibit students from majoring in any subject, whether directly law-related or not, that interests them.

A prelaw curriculum might also serve as an extra screening mechanism for law school applicants; taking a set of courses requires a commitment far greater than filling out an application. Thus, it might help curb the increasing number of law students who are biding their time while getting what they consider to be a good general degree. If all law students shared an equally deliberate focus and interest in the law, students' motivation and learning might improve significantly.

Redesign the first-year curriculum. The review of law schools' practices demonstrated that the required first-year curriculum barely broaches the foundational material for thinking like a lawyer, such as professional norms and ethics, the role of law in society, and the role of lawyers in society. It also demonstrated that professional responsibility courses generally fail to give students meaningful exposure to, comprehension of, and experience with the norms of the legal profession. Given law schools' unique ability to affect students' perceptions of the legal profession, it is important to socialize students into the norms of the legal community from the moment they first arrive at law school. A required first-year curriculum should fulfill this responsibility in a meaningful way.

For example, instead of focusing on standard legal doctrine, case analysis, and research and writing skills, the first-year curriculum ought to emphasize legal history, the role of law and lawyers in society, and the norms of the legal profession. Students ought to learn such foundational materials before they begin studying legal doctrine or lawyering skills. Additionally, legal doctrine and skills need not be learned in isolation from professional responsibility issues. If all three topics appear simultaneously as a cohesive unit within the confines of one course taught by a full-time tenure-track teacher, students can actively experience and grapple with the interconnections between knowledge, skills, and norms that, as practicing lawyers, they will encounter on a daily basis.

Improve teaching in law schools. Improved teaching can and should lead to more meaningful assessment mechanisms, greater student-faculty interaction, greater engagement of students in the classroom and with reading materials, and more meaningful and productive in-class, out-of-class, and research assignments. Particularly in the isolationist and individualistic university environment, pedagogical changes will not be effective if they are imposed on faculty. Instead, law schools ought to facilitate the faculty's exposure to and understanding of the benefits of alternative pedagogies and assessment mechanisms, and then enable the faculty to pursue those pedagogies. Following are some concrete suggestions of ways law schools might accomplish this.

Give faculty incentives to focus on teaching. The institutional emphasis on scholarship over teaching is one of the biggest obstacles to pedagogical change, yet it is also one over which law schools have considerable control. There are numerous relatively low-cost and high-return ways for law schools to shift this incentive structure. First and foremost, law schools must define standards for teaching against which professors' and applicants' teaching may be measured. Meaningful standards that are enforced (through hiring or promotion decisions) will force law faculty to attend to their teaching abilities while simultaneously giving them a tangible goal to strive for in their teaching. Additionally, law schools could condition summer research stipends on attendance at teaching workshops and creation of new lesson plans. Law schools could recalibrate the hiring and tenure processes to increase the importance of good teaching. Law schools could also provide, and require attendance at, periodic teaching workshops or faculty roundtables focused on teaching and learning theory.[99]

Establish minimum practice requirements for tenure-track faculty. The fact that the average practical experience of tenure-track faculty is quite low has significant implications for law schools. Academic lawyers (i.e., law professors) tend to fashion academic lawyers, even though very few law graduates remain in academia. Furthermore, many law teachers have spent little time practicing the skills and knowledge about which they instruct students.[100] Consequently, they have minimal experience with the complex problems their students will face every day as practicing lawyers. Requiring time spent away from the academy before or during a teaching career would help to correct this imbalance. Law teachers who have had practice experience would be better able to incorporate the complexities of practice into their classes, instead of teaching solely from observations about the law made from a comfortable distance.[101]

A practice requirement should not be construed narrowly. Law schools and law students will benefit most when faculty have practice experience across a broad range of practice settings, legal activities, substantive areas of the law, and clients, including people, entities, and causes. To maximize the value of a faculty practice requirement, law schools should encourage faculty to spend practice time in a context that corresponds with their research and teaching interests.

Restructure the curriculum and pedagogy to focus on developing students' lawyering capacities. The current law school curriculum provides extensive instruction in doctrinal and substantive areas of the law but minimal instruction in lawyering capacities other than specific aspects of legal reasoning. Neglect of judgment capacity, communication capacity, and aspects of legal reasoning beyond case analysis and application results in new lawyers who are by and large unprepared for practice. Since effective use of these capacities depends heavily on knowledge of substantive law and relevant facts, it is important that students develop these capacities in conjunction with, not separately from, learning legal doctrine and theory. The current norm is to teach skills in separate courses from doctrine. Law schools must restructure their curriculum, and encourage the requisite faculty professional development, to enable both the skills and the knowledge elements of lawyering capacities to be taught within the confines of a single course.

For example, a course in contracts could include students' drafting a contract for an actual (or simulated) client. Students could learn corporations by advising an actual (or simulated) corporation. All such curricular and pedagogical revisions entail two things. First, they involve an overhaul of the standard pedagogy, the case method, which is ill-equipped to develop lawyering capacities other than case analysis and the ability to apply common law precedent to discrete bodies of fact. Second, they require not only that faculty receive extensive training in how to conduct such courses, but also that the law school support faculty—both financially and with other resources such as teaching assistants or credit toward the tenure scholarship requirement—in their endeavors to implement this new curriculum and pedagogy.

Improve students' facility with and comprehension of professional norms. Lawyers need a solid grounding in professional norms. Yet law schools provide minimal instruction in this area. The failure is not due to the schools' lack of capacity, but rather to a lack of either desire or effort, or both. Since lawyers must make all of their decisions against the backdrop of professional responsibilities and norms, it is imperative that law schools, where prospective lawyers first encounter the legal profession, communicate the importance of professional norms to students. Following are two suggestions of ways law schools might accomplish this.

Require instruction in professional responsibility in all courses. Part of the problem with current instruction is that professional responsibility is presented in isolation from other legal topics. It is taught as a separate body of rules, rather than as an integral part of the daily decisions and activities of lawyers. Requiring all faculty to address issues of professional responsibility in the context of their courses could help counter the implicit message students now receive about the relevance of professional responsibility and professional norms. For example, in the context of a case analysis a teacher could lead a discussion of the involved lawyers' responsibilities to their clients or of the judge's responsibilities for dealing with the case. Furthermore, integrating instruction in professional responsibility into all courses might help engage students who find doctrinal instruction alienating because it seems detached from the personalities and characteristics of the people involved, the practical issues of case management, and any historical or political context.

Require pro bono service. Law schools could require all students to complete a certain number of pro bono hours as a graduation requirement.[102] That could improve students' comprehension of professional norms in at least two ways. First, a pro bono requirement in law school would parallel the existing ABA recommendation that all lawyers spend at least fifty hours per year on pro bono work.[103] Inculcating this norm of service in lawyers from the moment they enter the profession, i.e., when they start law school, should result in a larger percentage of lawyers actually complying with that recommendation. Second, a satisfying experience serving underprivileged clients might encourage students to continue pro bono work after they enter the workforce.

* * *

The complaints about legal education are loud, and the problems with legal education are real. They cannot be remedied by merely adding a few more courses, hiring a few more teachers, or building a few more classrooms. These purported solutions implicitly and wrongly assume that what law schools need is simply more of the same. Despite the alarming implications of the persistence of outdated nineteenth-century practices, however, law schools can change. They just have not gone about change the right way.

The key to change in law schools is to start at the beginning and ask the fundamental question: why are we here? Not why were we originally established, or why were we around fifty years ago, but why are we here now? What is the current purpose of the institution of law school, and what is the current purpose of my law school in particular? Although the purpose of the institution—to teach students to think like lawyers—is common to all, individual law schools serve communities with different needs and students with different needs, skills, and aspirations. Thus, determining the purpose of a particular law school is just as important as defining the purpose of the institution of law school. It is only by answering the purpose questions that we can begin to have a meaningful discussion about what law schools should be doing and why. It is only through regular revisiting of these questions that we can ensure law school's continued relevance and survival.

Law schools not only can change, they must change. Widespread, loud, and relentless student concerns are the law schools' miner's canary;[104] they signal that something is so direly wrong in legal education that the very existence of law schools is threatened.[105] Their persistence reveals that the Band-Aids and stop-gap measures that have been tried do not resolve the critical underlying problem—that law schools' practices do not adequately reflect law school's purpose.

Law schools' failure to adapt, to correlate their practices with their purpose, threatens not only the schools themselves, but the legal profession in general. Lawyers no longer join the legal profession *sua sponte*, as they did in the eighteenth and nineteenth centuries. Instead, lawyers today are fully the products of their law schools. To quote Justice Frankfurter: "In the last analysis, the law is what the lawyers are. And the law and the lawyers are what the law schools make them."[106]

Notes

* I very much appreciate the guidance and encouragement I received from Lani Guinier and Daniel Coquillette. My heartfelt thanks also to my father, a consummate lawyer and law professor, Michael Rubin, for his support and input.

1. The Lost Lawyer: Failing Ideals of the Legal Profession 2 (Cambridge, Mass., 1993).

2. *Id.* at 269.

3. John R. Peden, Goals for Legal Education, 24 J. Legal Educ. 379, 382 (1972).

4. Robert Granfield, Making Elite Lawyers: Visions of Law at Harvard and Beyond 27–29 (New York, 1992).

5. Angela P. Harris & Marjorie M. Shultz, "A(nother) Critique of Pure Reason": Toward Civic Virtue in Legal Education, 45 Stan. L. Rev. 1773, 1775–85 (1993). Proponents see this ideology as derived from the concept of law as a science and reinforced by the legal profession's ideals of lack of bias, fairness to all, and dispassionate approach to the law. *Id.* at 1775–79.

6. Steven H. LeLeiko, Legal Education—Some Crucial Frontiers, 23 J. Legal Educ. 502, 507 (1971).

7. The ABA assessments of legal education, which attempt to focus not on blame but instead on practices they believe law schools should adopt, share this weakness. For example, although the MacCrate Report recognizes the need to determine what skills and values lawyers require, it takes law schools' existence and relevance for granted. Section of Legal Education and Admissions to the Bar, American Bar Association, Report of the Task Force on Law Schools and the Profession: Narrowing the Gap, Legal Education and Professional Development—An Educational Continuum (Chicago, 1992) [hereinafter MacCrate Report].

8. Taking the purpose of education as the foundation for all other discussions about education is a concept frequently used in discussions of K–12 education. See, e.g., Patricia Albjerg Graham, Schools: Cacophony About Practice, Silence About Purpose, Daedalus, Fall 1984, at 29.

9. Peden, *supra* note 3, at 387.

10. My understanding of the source of problems with legal education is not unique. For example, in 1995 Gary L. Blasi argued that "[o]ur legal education system is predicated on unstated and generally unexamined assumptions about what lawyers do." What Lawyers Know: Lawyering Expertise, Cognitive Science, and the Functions of Theory, 45 J. Legal Educ. 313, 324 (1995). The MacCrate Report also recognizes the importance of basing what occurs in law school on a comprehensive understanding of what lawyers actually do today. MacCrate Report, *supra* note 7, at 7.

11. The MacCrate Report. supra note 7, does set forth the ABA's vision of the legal profession, the skills and values new lawyers should seek to acquire, and what legal education resources should provide what training. But the report is primarily descriptive and does not offer a succinct purposive mission statement for law school.

12. See Gordon T. Butler, The Law School Mission Statement: A Survival Guide for the Twenty-first Century, 50 J. Legal Educ. 240, 248–53 (2000).

13. For a history of American law schools, see Robert B. Stevens, Law School: Legal Education in America from the 1850s to the 1980s 3–34 (Chapel Hill, 1983).

A few stand-alone law schools still exist today. But even the ABA recognizes that "[i]n terms of their structure, curriculum, and academic emphasis, [these] schools are virtually indistinguishable from their university-based counterparts." MacCrate Report, *supra* note 7, at 3 n. 1.

14. Arthur E. Sutherland, The Law at Harvard 2 (Cambridge, Mass., 1967).

15. Stevens, supra note 13, at 4–5.

16. Id. at 4.

17. Marian C. McKenna, Tapping Reeve and the Litchfield Law School 59–60 (New York, 1986) (noting that Reeve, the school's founder, "never made any distinction between his office and his school").

18. Stevens, supra note 13, at 35–36.

19. Id. at 35.

20. Sutherland, supra note 14, at 25.

21. Stevens, supra note 13, at 35.

22. Russell L. Weaver, Langdell's Legacy: Living with the Case Method, 36 Vill. L. Rev. 517, 523–25 (1991). Students' preparatory work for these lectures consisted primarily of reading legal treatises. Id. at 525.

23. Stevens, supra note 13, at 35.

24. Weaver, supra note 22, at 529.

25. John J. Costonis, The MacCrate Report: Of Loaves, Fishes, and the Future of American Legal Education, 43 J. Legal Educ. 157, 162 (1993). See Granfield, *supra* note 4, at 26–33 (detailing how the elite bar developed an interest in creating and maintaining standards within the legal profession). Although the implementation of high standards directly contributed to creating the profession of law, this movement, and the entrenchment of university law schools in response to it, had a darker side. Under the guise of maintaining high standards by requiring law school attendance, many minorities who previously could have read apprenticeships to pass the bar were effectively blocked entirely from the practice of law.

26. Stevens, *supra* note 13, at 24.

27. Granfield, *supra* note 4, at 27. During Langdell's 25-year deanship, 1870–1895, institutionalized legal training was established as *de rigueur* for leaders of the profession." Stevens, *supra* note 13, at 36.

28. Stevens, *supra* note 13, at 24.

29. Law schools often accepted students who did not gain admission to their host university's liberal arts curriculum. Stevens, *supra* note 13, at 37–38. Graduation from high school, much less college, was not a standard prerequisite for admission to law school. *Id.* Law was an undergraduate degree, and students attended classes for eighteen months to two years. *Id.* at 36–37. A mandatory three years of law school was not imposed until 1899, and law did not become a graduate course of study until after World War I. *Id.*

30. *Id.* at 25. It was not until the 1890s that a requirement of formal study or apprenticeship was instituted in the majority of states. *Id.*

31. Only the few law schools with a diploma privilege, which allowed students to be admitted to practice upon examination by three of their law school teachers, could offer their students an immediate practical advantage over an apprenticeship. See *id.* at 26. During the last decades of the nineteenth century, oral bar examinations began to give way to written ones. *Id.* at 25.

32. See *id.* at 173–216. For an alternative perspective on the impetus for change in the legal profession, see Bernard J. Hibbitts, Representing the American Lawyer as Reformer: A Prospectus (2001) (unpublished manuscript) (discussing the impact of lawyers' perceptions of themselves as law and social reformers).

33. Stevens, *supra* note 13, at 172–79. In their attempts to standardize legal education, the ABA and the AALS made several other recommendations, including lowering maximum student-faculty ratios and increasing the number of books held by law school libraries. Id. Many states adopted extra requirements in addition to those urged on them by the ABA and the AALS. *Id.* at 179–80. The professional bar's move to increase control over legal education was quite successful; during this era, partly in response to the demands of increasing standards and partly in response to the economic climate, the number of unaccredited law schools declined dramatically. *Id.* at 172–80.

34. *Id.* at 209.

35. MacCrate Report, *supra* note 7, at 105–06.

36. Stevens, *supra* note 13, at 205–08.

37. The MacCrate Report defines the judiciary as the gatekeeper of the legal profession. MacCrate Report, *supra* note 7, at 114–19. Through its regulatory role the judiciary does indeed perform a gatekeeping function. But even before prospective lawyers become subject to judicial regulation, they must be accepted into law school. While the judiciary, in conjunction with the organized bar, monitors the passage between law school and law practice, law schools control who gets in the front door of the legal profession.

38. I arrived at this figure by dividing the total number of persons who passed all state bars in a particular year by the number of those passers who had not gone to law school and then averaging the numbers across years. I used the statistics provided by the National Conference of Bar Examiners, at <http://www.ncbex.org/stats/content.htm> (last visited Mar. 27, 2002). Although this is admittedly a very rough calculation, over the years for which the NCBEX makes statistics readily available, the percentage of non-law-school attendees who passed a bar examination and thus became eligible in some states to practice law averaged well below .1 percent of all persons eligible to practice law.

39. Several writers have suggested that a second purpose of law school is to produce legal scholarship. See, e.g., Butler, *supra* note 12, at 241L; Derek Bok, A Flawed System of Law Practice and Training, 33 J. Legal Educ. 570, 581 (1983). Law schools clearly do perform this function. Although evaluating this claim in full is beyond the scope of this paper, I will briefly address it here. I submit that producing

legal scholarship is a *secondary* purpose of law school, one that should complement, but not supersede, law school's primary purpose of teaching people to think like lawyers. For this claim I offer two brief justifications. First, law schools do not hold a monopoly on legal scholarship as they do on training prospective lawyers. Think tanks, law-related nonprofits, and individual practicing lawyers, for example, contribute greatly, and regularly, to legal discourse. Second, the time demands of legal scholarship are intensive. Today's law teachers, who are under immense pressure from tenure requirements and their peers to produce scholarly publications, find it tempting to, and often do, subordinate their teaching responsibilities to their research. As a result, the teaching of students, clearly a primary purpose of law school, suffers. Thus, while faculty's legal scholarship is indeed valuable, it should be done in a manner that supports students' education, and should not be used as an excuse for inadequate teaching.

40. See Deborah Meier, The Power of Their Ideas: Lessons for America from a Small School in Harlem 161 (Boston, 1995) (discussing the importance of terminological precision in defining the purpose of education).

41. See Nancy Schultz, How Do Lawyers Really Think? 42 J. Legal Educ. 57, 57 (1992) (asserting that "we cannot really teach students how lawyers think without teaching them at the same time what lawyers do").

42. Furthermore, particularly on law school campuses, the public/private distinction is politically charged. Underlying consideration of what legal job to accept is the often unspoken apprehension that public equals good and private equals selling out. Such value judgments contribute to the manner in which client-centric characterizations of lawyers obscure the functions lawyers actually perform. For further discussion of this, see Robert Granfield, Constructing Professional Boundaries in Law School: Reactions of Students and Implications for Teachers, 4 S. Cal. Rev. L. & Women's Stud. 52, 69–74 (1994).

43. Lawyers performing advocacy and advising functions draw on five of the elements the MacCrate Report lists as fundamental lawyering skills: problem solving, legal analysis and reasoning, legal research, factual investigation, and counseling. See MacCrate Report, *supra* note 7, at 138–39, 141–72, 176–84.

44. The ABA Model Rule of Professional Conduct 2.1 explicitly states that "a lawyer may refer not only to law but to other considerations such as moral, economic, social, and political factors, that may be relevant to the client's situation."

45. The MacCrate Report lists effective "organization and management of legal work" as one of the ten fundamental lawyering skills. MacCrate Report. supra note 7, at 199–202. Although lawyers often have need of business skills beyond simply managing legal work or a legal office, many of the broad skills that the report lists in this category are readily transferable to other business environments.

46. The MacCrate Report lists "Litigation and Alternative Dispute Resolution Procedures" as a fundamental lawyering skill. *Id.* at 191–98.

47. The MacCrate Report defines negotiation as one of the ten fundamental lawyering skills. *Id.* at 139, 185–90.

48. This happens both in formal law school environments and through summer associate programs, clinical programs, and students' part-time legal work.

49. Blasi, *supra* note 10, at 326. Systematic surveys of the skills used by practicing lawyers repeatedly reveal "the importance of a lawyer's ability to integrate factual and legal knowledge and to exercise good judgment in light of that integrated understanding." *Id.*

50. The ABA's most recent comprehensive review of legal education, the MacCrate Report, lists problem-solving skills first among fundamental lawyering skills. MacCrate Report, *supra* note 7, at 141–51.

51. Blasi, *supra* note 10, at 318–19.

52. This aspect of judgment capacity incorporates three of the MacCrate Report's fundamental lawyering skills—legal reasoning and analysis, legal research, and factual investigation. MacCrate Report, *supra* note 7, at 138–39, 151–72.

53. See id. at 172–76.

54. See id. at 174–75.

55. Carrie Menkel-Meadow, Narrowing the Gap by Narrowing the Field: What's Missing from the MacCrate Report—Of Skills, Legal Science and Being a Human Being, 69 Wash. L. Rev. 593, 619–20 (1994).

56. Freedom to Do What? Institutional Neutrality, Academic Freedom, and Academic Responsibility, 43 J. Legal Educ. 346, 350 (1993).

57. See MacCrate Report, *supra* note 7, at 140, 203–07 (listing "recognizing and resolving ethical dilemmas" as one of the ten fundamental lawyering functions).

58. A third practice at many law schools is extracurricular activities. Law schools often expect students to develop judgment capacity and communication capacity through participating in extracurricular activities such as journals, moot court teams, and law societies. However, the availability of extracurricular activities, as well as their intensity, depth, and preparatory value, varies greatly. Students have limited access to extracurricular activities; only a relatively small percentage of students, for example, have the opportunity to serve on a law journal or law review. Thus, extracurriculars are an insufficient mechanism for law schools to rely on to achieve their purpose. Furthermore, the very term extracurricular implies that law schools view such activities as additional to, rather than a fundamental part of, students' law school experiences.

59. Studies showing that women, on average, participate less frequently in class and perform less well academically in law school than men raise the concern that this classroom dynamic has a disproportionately negative impact on women. See Sarah Berger et al., "Hey! There's Ladies Here!!" 73 N.Y.U. L. Rev. 1022 (1998) (summarizing and analyzing five studies of gender-differentiated performance, participation, and interest in law school).

60. Steven I. Friedland, How We Teach: A Survey of Teaching Techniques in American Law Schools, 20 Seattle U. L. Rev. 1, 27 (1996). Law teachers who used the Socratic method did so for only 26 percent of the time in seminars and only 12 percent of the time in skills courses.

61. *Id.*

62. *Id.* (noting that 62 percent of faculty use small groups in upper-level classes, but only for 3 percent of the time).

63. The validity of course evaluations as a barometer of teaching ability is questionable. Typically students fill out the evaluations during the last few minutes of one of the last classes of the semester, before they take finals or receive grades. Consequently, when students fill out course evaluations, they are not in the best position to assess the teacher's effectiveness.

64. See John D. Copeland & John W. Murry, Jr., Getting Tossed from the Ivory Tower: The Legal Implications of Evaluating Faculty Performance, 61 Mo. L. Rev. 233, 241 (1996).

65. Weaver, *supra* note 22, at 544.

66. Although 90 percent of law school faculty say they choose their teaching techniques because they believe they are most effective, 59 percent also admit that being comfortable with a technique is important to their pedagogical choice, and 32 percent explicitly believe that learning a technique in law school affects this choice. Friedland, *supra* note 60, at 31.

67. Weaver, *supra* note 22, at 566–72.

68. Even when such materials are available, many law teachers only examine them in class from a traditional legal perspective, i.e. the legal structures or principles they involve. LeLeiko, *supra* note 6, at 507. This narrow approach limits students' ability to gain a contextualized understanding of a body of doctrine and how it relates to other legal doctrines, to other disciplines, and to societal concerns. Weaver, *supra* note 22, at 570–71.

69. Weaver, *supra* note 22, at 577. Policy questions are becoming more common as well. *Id.*

70. Many of these content areas can, and should, be covered in one well-designed course. Thus, even schools with limited faculty resources can offer students the necessary curriculum.

71. Deborah Jones Merritt & Jennifer Cihon, New Course Offerings in the Upper-Level Curriculum: Report of an AALS Survey, 47 J. Legal Educ. 524, 537 (1997). The survey asked schools to identify courses with writing or skills elements. Responding administrators designated just over 40 percent of courses as having some sort of writing or skills element, but it is unclear from both the survey questions and the results what these elements are or how comprehensive they are. *Id.* at 534–35.

72. *Id.* at 537. The survey found, however, that only 8.2 percent of all new courses were attributed primarily to student requests. *Id.* at 533. It also found that nearly two-thirds of courses added in response to student demand are taught by adjuncts and non-tenure-track faculty, while slightly less

than two-thirds of other new courses were taught by tenure-track faculty. *Id.* at 534. These figures indicate that law schools place low value on meeting student interests.

73. MacCrate Report, *supra* note 7, at 240. The report further found that "clinical programs are generally available to only 30 percent of law students at schools where live client clinics are offered" and that "professional skills training occupies only nine (9%) percent of the total instructional time available to law schools." *Id.*

74. Philip C. Kissam, Lurching Towards the Millenium: The Law School, the Research University, and the Professional Reforms of Legal Education. 60 Ohio St. L. J. 1965, 2004–05 (1999). Out of 31 new professional responsibility courses added at law schools between 1994 and 1997, only one-third explored ethical issues encountered in particular types of practice and less than 50 percent included a writing or skills component despite the fact that "professional responsibility requires close examination of law practice." Merritt & Cihon, *supra* note 71, at 559.

75. James P. Rowles, Toward Balancing the Goals of Legal Education, 31 J. Legal Educ. 375, 386 (1981).

76. MacCrate Report, *supra* note 7, at 246. The fact that full-time tenure-track faculty regularly shun professional responsibility courses helps create the impression that such courses are less important than doctrinal ones. *Id.* The MacCrate Report recognizes this problem and recommends that "law schools should assign primary responsibility for instruction in professional skills and values to permanent, full-time faculty." Id. at 245.

77. Kissam, *supra* note 74, at 2003–05.

78. *Id.* at 1986. Advocates of legal writing saw an opportunity for students to use writing "as an experience-based learning process to acquire legal knowledge and a variety of skills." *Id.* at 1987. Initially, in response to these demands, writing programs were "designed to provide writing opportunities that would be different from the writing of examinations, would involve much individualized feedback from more experienced writers and would entail much rewriting, especially of memorandums that attempt to resolve client problems." *Id.* at 1986.

79. *Id.* at 1986–87. For example, Harvard Law School requires that all students complete a term paper (commonly called the third-year paper) by the end of their third year. The course catalog encourages students to start this paper during their second year, work on it over the course of at least a year, and spend one-quarter of their time working on it in the semester in which they receive credit for it. Yet the average third-year paper earns students only one or two credits out of the 52 second- and third-year credits required to graduate, far less than one-quarter of the total required credit hours. This disjunction between the amount of time suggested and the minimal credits received often discourages extensive, advance work on papers, particularly as students are faced with a course load of 10 to 15 credit hours per term.

80. Often the course combines writing with legal research, further limiting the time focused on writing skills.

81. Kissam, *supra* note 74, at 1989 (noting that first-year students, at whom most legal writing courses are aimed, are least capable of independently perceiving how to use legal writing "to acquire and generate substantive and procedural legal knowledge"). Other skills courses suffer this same fate. "What is perhaps most problematic about legal methods courses is that the novice student often concludes that these methodological skills are somehow discrete because they are taught in a doctrinal vacuum." Linda Levine & Kurt M. Saunders, Learning to Think Like a Lawyer, 29 U.S.F. L. Rev. 121, 132 (1994).

82. The Merritt and Cihon survey found that tenure-track faculty teach 56.1 percent of new writing or skills courses and are "as likely to teach new writing or skills courses as other new courses." Merritt & Cihon, *supra* note 70, at 535. But the definition of writing or skills courses is unclear. The survey appears to count any and all courses which the responding administrator indicated had some unspecified amount of writing or skills elements as a writing or skills course. See *id.* at 534–35.

83. Kissam, *supra* note 74, at 1990. Law schools' persistence in grading student writing according to a traditional academic grading scale creates tension in the relationship between the student and the writing mentor and greatly increases the amount of work for the instructor. *Id.* at 1991. This tension diminishes the incentive for collaborative work, constructive and sympathetic rather than negative feedback, and repeated revisions of the same document. *Id.* at 1991–92.

84. Kissam, *supra* note 74, at 1993–97.

85. *Id.* at 1997.

86. *Id.* See also Levine & Saunders, *supra* note 80, at 130 ("Although clinics have been a major innovation to the standard law school curriculum, they remain ancillary to the case method and doctrinal course work.").

87. *Id.* at 1997–98.

88. Stevens, *supra* note 13, at 214–15.

89. Weaver, *supra* note 22, at 543.

90. *Id.* at 545–46. Even emerging pedagogical techniques, such as the problem method, tend to be "consistent with Langdell's basic assumptions about how law should he taught." *Id.* at 543. In other words, like the case method, emerging pedagogies approach law as a science best studied through books and best understood by reference to precedent.

91. *Id.* at 529. Advocates of apprenticeship viewed law as a craft that could best be learned by doing, rather than by listening to lectures about it. *Id.*

92. Costonis, *supra* note 25, at 161.

93. *Id.* The case method was such a cost-effective way to educate large numbers of students that in the late nineteenth and early twentieth centuries law schools were actually profitable. Stevens, *supra* note 13, at 63.

94. Certainly many law faculty do believe that the case method is "the proper way to teach law" and adequately serves law schools' fundamental educational goals of teaching students how to analyze cases critically and think like lawyers. Weaver, supra note 22, at 544. The issue, however, is not whether the case method has, or at any time had, intrinsic pedagogical value—I would argue that it does—but whether it should continue as the primary method of teaching today's heterogeneous students the cognitive skills that today's lawyers require. We cannot begin to consider whether or not the case method should remain until we understand the purposes law schools need it to serve today. Since there has been no such systematic exploration, we can best understand teachers' admiration of the case method as located in its historical role and purpose, rather than its present role and purpose.

95. Frank R. Strong, The Pedagogic Training of a Law Faculty, J. Legal Educ. 226, 232–33 (1973). These financial disincentives are often magnified for public universities, in which the size of the student body typically determines and justifies the size of the budget.

96. Butler, *supra* note 12, at 266.

97. Section of Legal Education and Admissions to the Bar, American Bar Association. Standards for Approval of Law Schools, Interpretation 402-2 (providing that the ABA may accredit, under certain circumstances, law schools with a student/faculty ratio tip to 30-to-1).

98. See Ronald H. Fishbein, Origins of Premedical Education, 76 Acad. Med. 425. 426 (2001).

99. Remedying the dearth of organizational and institutional forums in which to discuss pedagogy and teaching could also greatly contribute to increased faculty attentiveness to these topics. At present only one American journal, the Journal of Legal Education, is dedicated to these topics. Other American law journals publish articles about teaching only sporadically, at best.

100. This is particularly problematic in the realm of professional responsibility, where the complexities of law practice frequently challenge adherence to professional norms. Teachers with minimal practice experience will have neither the exposure to, nor the facility in dealing with, the sorts of ethical dilemmas practicing lawyers regularly encounter.

101. This practice requirement could be instituted in any number of ways. For example, law schools could require that applicants have a minimum of a certain number of years of law practice before being eligible for full-time faculty positions. Alternatively, schools could require their faculty to work on a set number of actual law practice projects (like lawsuits, negotiations, or transactions) each year, for private clients, the government, legal services clients, nonprofits, or social causes. Although the potential for conflicts of interest arises when faculty represent clients, the many faculty who regularly do so effectively, without compromising their teaching responsibilities, demonstrate that it is indeed possible. A third option is for law schools to require their faculty to take periodic sabbaticals during which they must represent clients or causes in legal matters, rather than teach, travel, or conduct scholarly research.

102. Whether or not to require law students to perform *pro bono* work has been a subject of much debate. Several American law schools, including Harvard Law School, have already implemented a

pro bono requirement. For further discussion on a student *pro bono* requirement, see American Association of Law Schools, Learning to Serve, at http://www.aals.org/probono/report.html (last visited Mar. 26, 2002); Dolores M. Coulter, The Pro Bono Priority: By Formally Promoting Pro Bono Service, Michigan's Law Schools Can Help Students Live Up to the Profession's Ethical Ideals, Mich. B. J., Sept. 2001, at 68; Sabrina A. Hall & Tammy R. Wavle, A Vision for the Future: Mandatory Pro Bono Programs in Texas Law Schools, Hous. Law., Jan./Feb. 2001, at 18; Deborah L. Rhode, Essay: The Pro Bono Responsibilities of Lawyers and Law Students, 27 William Mitchell L. Rev. 1201 (2000).

An alternative to a *pro bono* requirement is a requirement mandating that all students take a certain number of clinical courses or credits for graduation. Although it is not the main goal of clinical courses to instill the *pro bono* ethos, introducing students to the values of providing legal services to the poor is a likely side effect.

103. Model Rules of Professional Conduct 6.1 (2000).

104. I borrow this analogy from Lani Guinier & Gerald Torres, The Miner's Canary: Enlisting Race, Resisting Power, Transforming Democracy (Cambridge, Mass., 2002).

105. I am not the first to express concern that law schools are becoming increasingly irrelevant. David Rosenberg has argued that so long as law schools fail to reform themselves in accordance with "Holmes's ideas about educating lawyers so that they can make useful contributions to solving pressing questions of public policy, ... law schools and courts are traveling a path of increasing social irrelevance and irresponsibility." The Path Not Taken, 110 Harv. L. Rev. 1044, 1044 (1997).

106. Letter from Felix Frankfurter, Professor, Harvard Law School, to Mr. Rosenwald 3 (May 13, 1927) (Felix Frankfurter papers, Harvard Law School library), *quoted* in Rand Jack & Dana Crowley Jack, Moral Vision and Professional Decisions: The Changing Values of Women and Men Lawyers 156 (Cambridge, Mass., 1989).

The Reach of Our Pedagogy: Political Science Undergraduate Classes and Pre-Law Academic Preparation

*Ellen Grigsby & Amelia A. R. Murphy**

I. Introduction

Four questions prompted us to undertake the investigation described in this chapter: (1) Which of our political science courses are most frequently selected by our pre-law students? (2) What kind of learning contributes to the success of these pre-law students? (3) What, if any, academic choices separate successful from unsuccessful pre-law students? (4) How can we begin to collect empirical data to answer these questions? The first three questions are subsumed under the general description of what we term the "reach" of our pedagogy; that is, we are inquiring about a) which of our political science classes reach the greatest number of our pre-law students and b) which of the many lessons we attempt to teach in our classes are reaching students and are reflected in the academic choices they make. The final question concerns methodological challenges associated with our study.

Our paper finds that skills-related learning/choices are more significant than political science course selections in distinguishing successful v. unsuccessful pre-law students. We define pre-law students as students who register with the Law School Admission Council (LSAC). We define successful pre-law students as those who gain admission to at least one ABA-accredited law school and unsuccessful ones as those who fail to gain such admission. Our work concludes with a discussion of the limits of our study (small n, non-random sample generated by student self-selection in releasing identifying data) as well as the need for ongoing efforts—despite serious limitations posed by the Law School Admission Council's confidentiality policies—to do the empirical research we are seeking to undertake. Indeed, without empirical data addressing the questions we explore, we are severely impaired in assessing the reach of our pedagogy and the content of our academic advisement to the pre-law students in our departments. If we can find a way to more fully answer the question "do successful pre-law students make unique—relative to unsuccessful pre-law students—choices during their undergraduate careers," then we can enhance the empirical foundation of pre-law academic resources and can also, perhaps, more critically explore the implications of our pedagogy for the pre-law students who seek out our courses.

II. The Scholarship of Teaching and Learning and Scholarship on Preparation for Legal Education

A number of recent works in political science have documented an interest in translating pedagogical questions into topics of scholarly inquiry (Kehl 2002, 229; "Transcript" 2002). Not only do we locate our efforts within this disciplinary literature, but we also view our study as part of a larger body of work generally referred to as the scholarship of teaching and learning (STL). STL scholars call for rethinking a presumed teaching v. research opposition/divide in favor of scholarly practices that would preclude defining any element associated with a discipline's scope—including, for example, for political scientists, the communication of politically relevant concepts inside an undergraduate classroom—as extraneous to disciplinary research agendas (Huber 1999; Hutchings and Schulman 1999; Schulman 2000; Kreber 2002). One might view STL as a multidisciplinary reiteration of former APSA President Lawrence Lowell's 1910 admonition to political scientists to become more reflective teachers (Lowell 1910, 6) or of Elinor Ostrom's more recent urging that members of the profession ask themselves to consider the relevance of their scholarly practice for "high school and undergraduate students" (Ostrom 1998, 18).

Indeed, our experiences suggest that many of the high school and undergraduate students who express initial interest in a political science curriculum do so from a perspective that accommodates a possible inclination toward pre-law preparation; meeting Ostrom's challenge entails finding a way to better answer their questions about whether our classes can help them become more competitively positioned with respect to law school admissions.

Our present study also addresses questions assuming central significance in a number of recent works in legal education. Law faculty and law school admission officers continue to debate the utility of various measurements of pre-law student performance and achievement. The legal education scholarship's interest in these measurements shares our concern with improving our understanding of pre-law student academic decision-making and its relationship to later success or failure. Among the most debated topics is the reliance on UGPA and LSAT scores in evaluating pre-law student preparation for law school and entry into the legal profession. Lempert et al. report "little correlation between the numerical entry credentials ... [such as] undergraduate grade point average (UGPA) and Law School Admission Test (LSAT) scores—on the one hand and any of our measures of achievement after law school on the other" (2000). More recently, Sander's controversial article in *Stanford Law Review* has suggested: "A student who gains special admission to a more elite school on partly nonacademic grounds is likely to struggle more ..."(2004).

Henderson's work has raised the possibility that it is law school pedagogy—not student achievement—that drives continued heavy reliance on the LSAT in evaluating pre-law students. In Henderson's research, the "LSAT was a relatively robust predictor of in-class exams and a relatively weak predictor of take-home exams and papers" while UGPA "was a relatively stable predictor of all three testing methods" (2004). Moreover, Garfield and Levi have found that "under-prepared" pre-law students who gain admission to law school and who subsequently use academic support programs while in law school "are able to compete on an even playing field" (2004). That is, if Garfield and Levi are correct, the consequences of sub-optimal choices made by pre-law students may be surmountable if law schools choose to provide academic support resources.

As significant as the above studies are in scrutinizing measurements of the preparation levels of pre-law students, they stop short of raising questions about the broader patterns of academic and curricular choices of successful v. unsuccessful pre-law students. Our work expands the range of questions—e.g., beyond LSAT and UGPAs—regarding what separates successful and unsuccessful pre-law students.

III. Data and Method

The Law School Admission Council (LSAC) provides to registered pre-law advisors both (a) general aggregate-level information on registered pre-law students at the home institution and (b) individual-level data on pre-law students who give LSAC permission for the release of individual-level data to a registered pre-law advisor at the home institution. Aggregate datasets provide no means of identifying individual students and thus no opportunity for matching institutional student records with LSAC data. However, individual-level LSAC records include individual-specific information (e.g., student name, whether admitted to an ABA-approved law school, LSAT scores) that makes possible the matching of LSAC and institutional records. LSAC data are essential for identifying which of our pre-law students are actually successful in gaining law school admission. If a student releases her individual-level information through LSAC, it is possible to divide individual students into categories of "admitted" v. "not admitted" to an ABA-approved law school and then search for patterns in course selections and general academic choices within the admitted/not admitted categories.

Only 408 students (49%) out of a total of 824 registrants between 1999 and 2004 gave LSAC permission to release individual-level data; consequently, our study is limited to those students and LSAC confidentiality procedures preclude our access beyond the sample of self-selected individuals. Table A illustrates the gender, race, major, and mean LSAT score composition of our sample in relation to the entire population of UNM pre-law students for the period.

While not random, our sample is very similar to the entire UNM pre-law student population for the period under examination in terms of distribution of gender and ethnicity, and in terms of majors and mean LSAT score. Indeed, with respect to LSAT scores, for only one year (1999-2000) is the difference in mean scores as great as 1.1. With respect to ethnicity, white students are under-represented in our sample each year, and as much as 5% in 2003-2004 and 7.2% in 2002-2003. Men are slightly under-represented in our sample for four of the reported years, but, in only one year (2000-2001), by as much as 4%. None of these variations are statistically significant. The only statistically significant differences between the sample and full population are found in the percentage of political science majors for 00-01 (more in our sample than the population; $p = .02$) and 02-03 (fewer in the sample than in the population; $p = .056$).

Using the LSAC-generated list of 408 students, we examined students' complete academic transcripts to record a) all political science courses taken, b) semester GPAs for semesters 1-10, and c) number of incompletes, withdrawals, internships, grades below C, and presence/absence of transfer credits for *all* classes (i.e., not simply for political science classes). We then tested differences in choices made by successful and unsuccessful students for statistical significance.

Table A. Comparison of Study Population versus Sample on LSAC Available Measures

LSAC Year	03-04		02-03		01-02		00-01		99-00	
Gender	Population	Sample	Population	Sample	Population	Sample	Population	Sample	Population	Sample
Female	55.5%	55.9%	59.2%	61.8%	52.5%	52.8%	54.4%	58.2%	53.9%	52.1%
Male	44.5%	44.1%	40.8%	38.2%	47.5%	47.2%	45.6%	41.8%	46.1%	47.9%
	100.0%	100.0%	100.0%	100.0%	100.0%	100.0%	100.0%	100.0%	100.0%	100.0%
Race										
Hispanic	30.2%	36.1%	35.8%	38.9%	38.6%	40.5%	38.7%	38.5%	33.6%	36.8%
Other Minority	12.2%	11.3%	13.9%	18.1%	9.4%	9.5%	8.5%	9.2%	10.2%	8.8%
White	57.6%	52.6%	50.3%	43.1%	52.0%	50.0%	52.8%	52.3%	56.3%	54.4%
	100.0%	100.0%	100.0%	100.0%	100.0%	100.0%	100.0%	100.0%	100.0%	100.0%
Mean LSAT Score	150.9	150.6	149.4	149.3	150.7	151.1	149.4	150.8	150.1	151.2
% Pol Sci Majors	17.0%	18.6%	23.4%	15.8%	14.5%	12.4%	13.3%	19.4%	18.4%	16.4%
Number	**182**	**102**	**175**	**76**	**179**	**89**	**147**	**67**	**141**	**73**
% of Population	56.0%		43.3%		49.7%		45.6%		51.8%	

IV. Political Science Course Choices of Pre-Law Students

Table B illustrates how the 408 UNM pre-law students for whom we have identifying data made choices among the many political science course offerings during 1999-2004. Table B reports the number of pre-law students choosing particular classes, the percentage of pre-law students selecting particular classes, and levels of statistical significance across successful and unsuccessful pre-law student subgroups.

Table B. Political Science Course Choices of Pre-Law Students

	% Taking Course (n)	*Admitted*	**Not Admitted**
Introductory and General Courses			
The Political World (Intro)	11.0% (47)	12.2%	10.8%
Introductory Political Topics	0.3 (1)	.0	.7
Special Topics			
Political Topics*	23.4 (92)	25.8	19.3
Advanced Political Topics	10.2 (40)	9.7	11.0
Department Honors			
Undergraduate Seminar*	3.6 (14)	4.8	1.4
Senior Thesis**	2.5 (10)	4.0	0.0
Internships and Independent Studies			
Internships**	11.4 (46)	13.8	7.4
Independent Study**	5.1 (20)	7.3	1.4
Core Courses			
US Government*	47.5 (190)	50.8	41.9
Comparative Politics	24.3 (97)	26.1	21.1
International Relations	22.9 (92)	24.4	20.3
Political Theory*	20.6 (83)	22.8	16.9
Public Policy	11.8 (47)	12.7	10.1
Intro. To Political Analysis**	12.7 (51)	15.0	8.8
American Politics			
NM Politics	9.5 (38)	9.8	8.8
Comparative State Politics	1.5 (6)	1.2	2.1
Law and Society	18.4 (74)	18.5	18.2
Group Politics	2.0 (8)	2.0	2.1
Public Opinion and Electoral Behavior*	2.8 (11)	1.6	4.8
Political Parties	4.1 (16)	4.4	3.4
Politics of Ethnic Groups	3.8 (15)	4.4	2.8
Hispanics in US Politics	8.6 (34)	9.3	7.5
Black Politics	3.1 (12)	3.6	2.1
Legislative Process*	24.4 (98)	26.9	20.3
Con Law: Rights, Powers or Liberties	16.2 (65)	16.5	15.5
Women and the Law	1.5 (6)	2.0	.7
Women's Contemporary Legal Issues	0.7 (3)	1.2	.0
The American Presidency	10.2 (40)	10.5	9.6
Women in American Politics	2.3 (9)	3.2	.7

Table B. Political Science Course Choices of Pre-Law Students, *continued*

	% Taking Course (n)	*Admitted*	Not Admitted
Comparative Politics			
Topics in Comparative Politics**	4.8 (19)	6.5	2.1
Comparative Politics: Developing Countries	3.3 (13)	4.0	2.1
Human Rights and Political Violence	0.8 (3)	.8	.7
Western European Politics	1.8 (7)	2.8	.0
Central American Politics	1.8 (7)	2.0	1.4
Political Development in Latin America	5.1 (20)	5.7	4.1
Russian and Eurasian Government & Politics	2.3 (9)	1.6	3.4
Political Economy of Latin America	0.5 (2)	.8	0.0
International Politics			
Topics in International Relations	3.3 (13)	3.6	2.7
American Foreign Policy	5.9 (23)	6.1	5.5
Inter-American Relations	2.8 (11)	3.2	2.1
Intl Conflict, Arms Control and Disarmament	1.0 (4)	.8	1.4
Intl Peacekeeping and Conflict Resolution	0.3 (1)	.0	.7
Seminar in International Studies	0.3 (1)	.0	.7
Political Theory			
Ancient and Medieval Political Theory	2.3 (9)	2.4	2.1
Modern Political Theory	2.8 (11)	3.2	2.1
Public Policy			
Public Finance	2.3 (9)	2.0	2.7
Public Management and Administration	1.3 (5)	2.0	0.0
Population Policy and Politics	0.8 (3)	.4	1.4
Environmental Politics	0.8 (3)	.8	.7

Fisher's Exact Test (1-sided): * Statistically significant at .1 ** Statistically significant at .05

Only five political science courses were selected by 90 or more pre-law students in our sample. One might expect law-related courses to be among the most popular classes. However, not a single law-related courses appeared in the list of top five classes. Rather, the following classes were most popular among pre-law students: 1) Introduction to U.S. Government, 2) Political Topics, 3) Introduction to Comparative Politics, 4) Introduction to International Relations, and 5) Legislative Process. The most frequently taken political science course for the pre-law students—both majors and non-majors—in our sample was Introduction to U.S. Government, taken by 50.8% of successful pre-law students and 41.9% of unsuccessful students. However, this relationship is only statistically significant at the p = .1 level (one-tailed test). The only remaining statistically significant patterns among successful v. unsuccessful pre-law students among these most frequently chosen courses were also weak and involved 1)Political Topics and 2) Legislative Process (p = .1, one-tailed test for both courses).

The only course chosen by at least 50 pre-law students and exhibiting a statistically significant pattern among successful v. unsuccessful students at a level of .05 was Introduction to Political Analysis, which covers basic research design and statistics. Fifty-one pre-law students selected this course—only 12.7% of the sample. However, 15% of successful pre-law students chose the course while only 8.8% of unsuccessful students selected it.

Perhaps the most striking finding is the limited reach of Constitutional Law courses in the academic choices of the pre-law students in our sample. Only 16.2% (65 students) took at least one of the three Constitutional Law courses offered by our department. Constitutional Law course selection patterns separating successful v. unsuccessful pre-law students were statistically insignificant. This finding may be of particular interest to scholars who share Graber's recent misgivings about what he terms the problem of "unimaginative teaching" in Constitutional Law courses that fail to include scholarly treatment of behavioral and critical approaches to public law (2005).

V. General Academic Choices of Pre-Law Students

Statistically significant differences in decision-making patterns between successful v. unsuccessful pre-law students were more pronounced when we examined not specific political science course selections but, rather, general academic choices. Table C provides an overview of the academic choices we measured.

Table C. General Academic Choices of Pre-Law Students

	Admit	Not Admit
No Internships**	86%	92%
No Incompletes**	83	77
No Withdraws*	46	30
No Below C***	58	32
No Transfer*	42	34

Fisher's Exact Test (1-sided):* Statistically significant at .1 ** Statistically significant at .05 ** Statistically significant at .001

We found that successful pre-law students were more likely to have completed their undergraduate careers without incompletes (p = .05) and without any grades below a C (p = .001). When one compares the number of incompletes for successful v. unsuccessful pre-law students, the means are .24 and .46, respectively; the means for grades below a C for the two groups are 1.36 and 3.18, respectively.

Successful pre-law students were more likely than unsuccessful ones to have taken a political science internship (.p = .05); however, the majority of students in both categories took no such internships. The number of political science internship credits for successful pre-law students was a mean of 0.40 and for unsuccessful pre-law students was 0.16. Although the level of statistical significance is weak, successful pre-law students were more likely to complete their undergraduate careers without a recorded withdrawal (withdrawal after six weeks) from a class (p = .10). When comparing the number of course withdrawals for successful v. unsuccessful pre-law students, the means are 1.53 and 2.52, respectively. Finally, we have weak indicators that successful pre-law students were less likely to have transfer work (p = .10) than were unsuccessful pre-law students.

Moreover, we found statistically significant differences (.p = .001 for all semesters) in the semester UGPAs for all semesters measured (semesters 1-10) separating successful and unsuccessful pre-law students. Semester UGPAs are illustrated in Table D.

Table D. Semester UGPA* for Pre-Law Students

	Admitted	Not Admitted
Semester 1 UGPA	3.26	2.94
Semester 2 UGPA	3.31	2.96
Semester 3 UGPA	3.38	3.01
Semester 4 UGPA	3.44	2.97
Semester 5 UGPA	3.48	3.07
Semester 6 UGPA	3.44	3.14
Semester 7 UGPA	3.50	3.07
Semester 8 UGPA	3.48	3.09
Semester 9 UGPA	3.45	3.13
Semester 10 UGPA	3.50	3.12

* Semesters are individual to each student; therefore, UGPA for Semester 6 is not indicative of 'junior year' performance for all individuals, merely the 6th semester of coursework undertaken at UNM.

How might we interpret the above results? We believe the data suggest, perhaps, that the most significant lessons for pre-law students to learn are lessons about skills in self-assessment and academic seriousness and resourcefulness as regards judicious approaches to incompletes in classes, internships, grades below C, withdrawals from courses, and semester-by-semester undergraduate grade point averages (UGPA). In addition to teaching disciplinary content and critical analysis thereof, our findings suggest that, if we can concomitantly teach our students to assess their own academic progress, to make strategic decisions regarding their individual UGPAs, and to be sophisticated and cautious in making choices about such matters as withdrawals, incompletes, and grades below C, we are helping them learn what is associated with admission to law school. In short, learning the skills related to sound academic decision making appears to matter in a way that taking most political science courses appears not to have mattered to our students whose objective is admission to an ABA-accredited law school.

Conclusions

When we return to the four questions that have framed our study, we find that our results have prompted a conceptual shift in how we think about the "reach" of our pedagogy for the pre-law students we examined. Analyzing—and improving—the reach of our pedagogy might be thought of as having less to do with comparing pre-law student enrollments across political science classes than with opening up the possibility for pedagogy in all our classes to include explicit concentration on assisting students in developing self-assessment skills as regards their general academic choices. In our sample, the students who learned the skills to assess the meanings that institutions of higher education attach to completing classes selected, finishing classes on time, earning a C or above in all classes, and, when needed, having the foresight and sound academic planning skills to withdraw from a class prior to the period when withdrawal becomes part of a permanent record were more likely to gain admission to an ABA-accredited law school, irrespective of classes selected. Our results are consistent with the recommendations of the Pre-Law Committee of the American Bar Association Section of Legal Education and Admissions to the Bar, in that the Committee advises that skills matter and particular courses/disciplines do not, as regards success in law school and in the legal profession.

Our sample is necessarily non-random, given LSAC's commitment to the confidentiality of student records. While the limited nature of non-random sampling is evident, so is the need for building an empirical database on pre-law academic choices in order to ensure that we as academics are as thoughtful about the reach of our pedagogy as are many of our pre-law students. Our work could also be combined with focus group research in which we ask pre-law students about their reasons for selecting some courses rather than others and about the factors they weigh in overall academic planning. Additional studies at other institutions are needed to determine whether our findings are unique. Moreover, while our study makes no distinctions between ABA-accredited law schools to which our students seek admission, our method could accommodate such distinctions. Specifically, our definition of "successful" pre-law students could be refined to take into account admission to higher- v. lower-tiered law schools. In addition, with collaboration from law schools themselves, a study such as ours could be expanded to examine not simply successful admission to law school but also successful completion of law school.

Bibliography

American Bar Association, Pre-Law Committee of the ABA Section of Legal Education and Admissions to the Bar. "Preparation for Legal Education." http://www.abanet.org/legaled/prelaw/prep.html.

Garfiled, Leslie Yalof and Kelly Koenig Levi. 2004. "Finding Success in the 'Cauldron of Competition:' The Effectiveness of Academic Support Programs." *Brigham Young University Educational And Law Journal* 1: 1-50.

Henderson, William. 2004. "The LSAT, Law School Exams, and Meritocracy: The Surprising And Undertheorized Role of Test Taking Speed." *Texas Law Review* 82 (March) 975-1051.

Huber, Mary Taylor. 1999. "Disciplinary Styles in the Scholarship of Teaching: Reflections on the Carnegie Academy for the Scholarship of Teaching." Paper presented at the 7th International Improving Student Learning Symposium, 6-8 September 1999, University of York, UK, http://www.carnegiefoundation.org/eLibrary/docs/disciplinarystyles.

Hutchings, Pat and Lee S. Shulman. 1999. "The Scholarship of Teaching: New Elaborations, New Developments." *Change* 31 (September/October): 11-15.

Kehl, Jenny. 2002. "Indicators of the Increase of Political Science Scholarship on Teaching and Learning in Political Science." *PS: Political Science and Politics* 35 (2): 229-232.

Kreber, Carolin. 2002. "Controversy and Consensus on the Scholarship of Teaching." *Studies in Higher Education* 27 (2): 151-167.

Lempert, Richard O. et al. 2000. "Michigan's Minority Graduates in Practice: The River Runs Through Law School." *Law and Social Inquiry* 25 (Spring): 395-506.

Lowell, A. Lawrence. 1910. "The Physiology of Politics: Presidential Address, Sixth Annual Meeting of the American Political Science Association." *American Political Science Review* 4: 1-15.

Ostrom, Elinor. 1998. "A Behavioral Approach to the Rational Choice Theory of Collective Action: Presidential Address, American Political Science Association, 1997." *American Political Science Review* 92: 1-22.

Sander, Richard H. 2004. "A Systemic Analysis of Affirmative Action in American Law Schools." *Stanford Law Review* 57 (November): 367-483.

Shulman, Lee S. 2000. "From Minsk To Pinsk: Why A Scholarship of Teaching and Learning?" *The Journal of Teaching and Learning* 1 (1): 48-53.

"Transcript: Roundtable on the Scholarship of Teaching and Learning in Political Science." 2002. PS: Political Science and Politics 35: 223-228.

Note

* An earlier version of this paper was presented at the Annual Meeting of the Western Political Science Association, Albuquerque, NM March 16, 2006. We wish to thank Christopher Butler, William Hudson, and Kimi King for their helpful comments and suggestions.

"But the Emperor Has Nothing On": Testing the Myths about Undergraduate Law Classes

Frank Guliuzza

Introduction

While very few colleges and universities offer "pre-law" *majors* or *minors,* most are mindful of their pre-law *students.* As a result, those responsible for advising pre-law students often suggest a number of courses that their law school aspirants should take to be prepared for the LSAT or for the first year of law school. It seems that increasingly, and perhaps unfortunately, undergraduate *law* courses (e.g., Constitutional Law, Rights & Liberties, Criminal Law, Business Law) are excluded by pre-law advisers from these weighty lists of essential preparatory courses. Clearly, pre-law advisers did not come up with this advice without guidance. They are reacting to law school admissions personnel who discourage undergraduate students from taking "law" classes. The purpose of this project is to test empirically the wisdom of this advice. Through the usage of survey data, I hope to see whether a preference against undergraduate law classes exists among law school admissions officers and, increasingly, among pre-law advisers. Furthermore, by surveying practicing attorneys, I hope to evaluate the importance of undergraduate law classes as among those courses that provide excellent if not essential preparation for pre-law students.

Why Undergraduate Law Classes?

Bob Dylan noted that "the times, they are a changing.'" That inference appears particularly apt when one discusses the attitudes of pre-law advisers and law school admissions officers toward undergraduate "law" courses. At one time undergraduate law classes must have been highly regarded by the law schools and by college and university pre-law advisers. In fact, they were thought to be an integral component of a pre-law student's undergraduate training. Political science departments made their constitutional law course(s) a staple within their curricula. "Con law" was a bread-and-butter course for pre-law students.[1]

Although Constitutional Law is still taught in most political science departments, and law-related courses now appear across the curriculum in most universities, they are now often discouraged by pre-law advisers. University of California professor Martin Shapiro maintains that, "At best, the law schools are indifferent to undergrad con law and, at worst, hate it."[2] Pre-law advisers seem to be heeding Professor Shapiro's warning. In the *Pre-Law Handbook* published at Florida State University, students are told, "The law school curriculum is designed upon the assumption that the student has little or no specific knowledge of the law. Law schools prefer that you reserve your legal study for law school."[3] The pre-law advisory committee at The College of New Jersey boldly states that "the *best* candidates for law school come from majors unrelated to law."[4] Judge Richard Poland, of Flagler College, raised the question about whether law should be studied at the undergraduate level. "Traditionally," Poland notes, "the answer to this much debated question has been no."[5]

There are several reasons for the lukewarm to hostile reception that law schools and, subsequently, pre-law advisers, reserve for undergraduate law classes. First, they claim that undergraduate instructors are often not effective at teaching law the way it should be taught in law school. Thus, law school professors have to correct bad habits developed by students in undergraduate law courses. Shapiro observes, "The former mechanic always messed up the car as far as the later mechanic is concerned."[6] The authors of Florida State's pre-law handbook argue, "[W]hile pre-law courses introducing you to broad legal principles can aid you in deciding whether to pursue a legal education, they rarely are taught with the same depth and rigor as actual law school courses."[7] Furthermore, law school admissions officers suggest that since these students will learn the law anyway, their time is better spent obtaining the broadest liberal arts education possible. Thus, law schools prefer that prospective students hold off their legal studies until law school and, instead, fill their "undergraduate curriculum with broad, diverse, and challenging courses."[8]

Perhaps this trend toward marginalizing undergraduate law courses by pre-law advisers is troublesome. One might argue that, despite the biases held by the law schools, undergraduate law courses have always provided some substantial benefits to potential law students. For instance, first, *such courses can serve a diagnostic function.* They enable the student to see if he or she has either the aptitude for or interest in law. Even those pre-law advisers who discourage their students from taking law-related classes concede this point. The authors of the *Pre-Law Handbook* at Florida State acknowledge that the traditional pre-law courses introduce students "to broad legal principles and can aid you in deciding whether to pursue a legal education."[9] The pre-law advisers at Tufts admit that law-related courses "offer students an opportunity to test their academic interest in law."[10]

At Weber State, I have worked with a number of students—determined to go to law school—who discovered in undergraduate law classes that they are unable to read and analyze court cases. Their grades are solid, and they possess the skills necessary to score well on the LSAT. Yet they realize that they cannot make sense of court decisions—even when the others in the class are able to do so.[11] Occasionally, we have encountered students who do not find case analysis to be particularly daunting. They realize, however, that they simply do not like it. When confronted with the reality that this is the kind of work that they will have to do throughout their respective law school careers, and the kind of work that they will perform as practicing attorneys, they decide to do something else. Graduate school in philosophy or business suddenly sounds appealing. Certainly these are conclusions best reached before these students commit to law school. They are not, however, the kind of discoveries that students generally can ferret out from taking other kinds of classes or from preparing for the LSAT.

Second, *these courses serve a vital educational function.* Undergraduate law classes are a different entity than their law school counterparts. The law school folks are right. Constitutional law, criminal law, business law, and school law are indeed taught differently in law school than they might/should be in the Political Science, History, Criminal Justice, Management, or Teacher Education departments at a given university. The objective for those professors teaching such classes in law school is to prepare students to become attorneys. Their counterparts who teach undergraduate law classes understand them to be a component of their student's liberal arts education or vocational/professional training (e.g., criminal law for those in law enforcement or school law for teachers).

While there are several scholars who are critical of contemporary legal education,[12] one oft-repeated observation is that foundational law school classes are too vocational in their nature. They fail to provide an adequate political and social context from which aspiring lawyers might view judicial decisions.[13] Such is not the case with undergraduate law classes. If one looks at the kind of research that, for example, political scientists in the public law subfield are doing, then one might get a sense of the varieties of topics and literature introduced in their undergraduate law courses. In addition to the interpretive scholarship on the Supreme Court's case law and work that blends history and moral philosophy with legal argument,[14] other recent interpretive inquiries discuss issues of social and political power.[15]

Furthermore, even those who do teach their undergraduate law classes much the way they might be taught in law school recognize that quite a number of their students do not intend to go on to law school. Hence, their undergraduate course in constitutional law is intended to augment the student's understanding of American politics—not prepare one to practice law. Therefore, these professors are cognizant of their need to introduce the political and social dimension into the study of case law. Leslie Goldstein notes:

> I do think there is value in teaching the old undergrad case law courses that basically take a more-or-less law school approach and march students through the elements of legal arguments, trying to help them pick up a feel for legal reasoning, as part of what the Supreme Court has been wallowing in for the last 200 years. The reason I say a 'more-or-less' law school approach is that I am confident that all of us political science Ph.D.'s let students in on the open secret that the Supreme Court operates within a political context and that the Court often takes highly politically charged cases with serious political consequences. The typical first con law case taught, *Marbury v. Madison*, can hardly be taught without attentiveness to this reality. It may be that law school professors by this time let their students in on this important piece of the picture, but there is no guarantee that they will nor that all con law students will go on to law school. As political scientists we are better able to impart to students a clear sense of the degree to which, and the sense in which, the courts and especially the U.S. Supreme Court, function as a MIX of legal and a political institution. That is an important lesson for undergraduates to learn about American politics, and one that I offer no apologies for attempting to impart.[16]

Poland agrees. He believes that, "Law should be taught in a limited manner, to enhance the liberal arts tradition."[17] To bolster his claim, Poland quotes Justice Louis Brandeis who argued: "The study of law should be introduced as part of a liberal education, to train and enrich the mind.... I am convinced that, like history, economics, and metaphysics—and perhaps even to a greater degree than these—the law could be advantageously studied with a view to the general development of the mind.[18]

Third, *such courses serve a sustaining function.* Arguably, undergraduate law courses help prepare students for law school in that they contribute to an excellent undergraduate education principally because they provide students with particular knowledge (and in unique contexts) that law students should have attained prior to matriculating. Moreover, undergraduate law classes provide a sustaining function in that they enhance a student's "comfort zone" when they attend law school.

In the pre-law advising program at Weber State we have worked with students who have been accepted to a wide range of law schools. When they report back, these students confirm the stereotypes about the first year experience. Without fail they are intimidated by the atmosphere in law school, and find the work load to be more than a bit daunting. We have discovered, however, that those with some exposure to the law and the United States legal system as undergraduates, regardless of their major, find law school to be far less terrifying. They do not enter law school cocky about what they already know. Nor can they escape the pressures associated with the Socratic method or the heavy workload. They simply feel more comfortable when a professor refers to a case in a certain jurisdiction or asks them to explain a court's holding.

Quite apart from the education they receive *in toto,* prospective law students are encouraged to take classes that will help them to get into law school and/or courses that will help them to succeed once they matriculate. If undergraduate law classes can provide essential background to students, provide a context for the vast body of law they will learn in the foundational courses, and help facilitate students' success, then they must certainly fall within the category of classes that should be encouraged for pre-law students. It certainly makes sense to suggest that such students take at least one undergraduate law class rather than to sway students to avoid them altogether.

Methodology

The hypothesis undergirding this project is that undergraduate law classes are of benefit to pre-law students—enough benefit to warrant the inclusion of at least one such course in the written/oft unwritten list of courses suggested to pre-law students by pre-law advisers. First, they serve as an important diagnostic tool helping to measure one's aptitude for or interest in the law. Second, these courses can provide essential knowledge and skills that serve to offer a measure of security to those who take them that is simply not available to those students who do not.

I tested this hypothesis by collecting survey and interview data, and a limited content analysis, from three groups: Law school admissions personnel, pre-law advisers, and practicing attorneys. To collect information from law school admissions personnel, I asked pre-law students to call the admissions offices of several accredited law schools. Among the questions they asked were: "Would you recommend that I take a "law" class while an undergraduate?"; and "Are such classes good/helpful classes or not?" To collect information from pre-law advisors, I went to the pre-law advising pages at several colleges and universities. I looked to see if the advisors recommended undergraduate law classes as among those that their students should take; or, alternatively, did the advisors either recommend against undergraduate law classes—or were they agnostic about the subject. Finally, to collect information from attorneys I sent out the list of questions that are included as an appendix to the text.

Consistent with the hypothesis, I expected to find that:

- Law school officers are not supportive of undergraduate law classes. At best they are cavalier; when they are most vitriolic they are fully opposed to such courses.

- Pre-law advisers are more difficult to predict. I would expect a large percentage of advisers to echo the line articulated by the law schools. Some, however, especially those advisers who teach law-related courses, should be more far more favorable toward these courses.
- The answers from attorneys should be the most complex. Some attorneys should indicate their support of the classes for the reasons identified in the hypothesis. Others will argue that the courses were of little value. "We surpassed everything I learned in my undergraduate business (con law, criminal law) class in two weeks in my law school class," is a standard line advanced in my preliminary interviews.

Findings

As one can see from Table I, law school admissions personnel did not recommend undergraduate law classes. Instead, they preferred a wide variety of classes (e.g., Upper-level English, Logic, Communication, Econ, Philosophy, Writing, Political Science, "Traditional Humanities").

Further, they gave a number of reasons for advising prospective applicants to shy away from undergraduate law classes. Some were rather flippant ("You're better off to take history; go and visit museums and gain an appreciation of art; go see a symphony"). Others argued that undergraduate classes simply cannot adequately prepare students for law school ("It might help prepare you but law school requires learning in a different way"; "Some professors think that their programs are similar but law school classes are much more difficult. Undergrad classes are not the same thing"; "The law professors don't think that law classes should be taken seriously"). Alternatively, one admissions director felt that the classes may be counterproductive precisely because they are too hard ("Don't drop your GPA for those courses"). Finally, most of those who opposed law classes suggested that they would take away from the breadth and depth of one's undergraduate education just to teach students something that they will learn later ("Law school will teach you anything you need to know"; "You will get all the education that you need in law school").

Table I. Law School Admissions Personnel and Undergraduate Law Classes

Do you recommend undergraduate law classes?		Are undergraduate law classes good/helpful?	
Yes	7%	Yes	67%
No	87%	No	33%
Maybe	6%		

While law school admissions personnel do not recommend undergraduate law classes, they find such classes to be of value. By a two-to-one margin, the same people said that law classes are good or helpful. Most indicated that they would provide "a good introduction," or help "establish familiarity," or even might "instill confidence."

Pre-law advisors are a bit more complicated. As I indicated above, some advisors are academics—often political scientists or professors from other disciplines who have been asked to advise students as part of their service requirement to the institution. Other pre-law advisors are, in fact, professional advisors. Clearly, some of the pre-law advising pages were constructed by the latter. These tend to quote from the American Bar Association, or some other authoritative outfit, with regard to the importance of undergraduate law classes. Consequently, most of these are "agnostic" with regard to their value. Other advising pages were created by professors or, more particularly, are a part of an academic department's home page (most often a political science department home page). Perhaps not surprisingly, these advisors recommend law classes—most often courses that introduce the law, or some variation of Constitutional Law—as important/essential for pre-law students. This information is reflected in Table II.

Table II. Pre-Law Advisors and Undergraduate Law Classes

Recommend	35.3%
No Opinion or "Agnostic"	47.1%
Don't Recommend	17.6%

Finally, I assumed that many attorneys would look fondly at their undergraduate law classes while others would be protective of the law school experience. The latter cluster would, accordingly, suggest that they covered everything they learned in an undergraduate course in just a few weeks in a related law school class.

Table III indicates that undergraduate law classes did enrich the undergraduate education of those surveyed. Evidence shows that the courses also enriched the undergraduate major. The courses were often case intensive, and many employed the Socratic Method. Those surveyed were less enthusiastic, however, when they evaluated these courses in terms of their importance in shaping the decision to attend law school; whether they provided a "comfort zone" at law school; whether they helped to develop skills necessary to succeed in law school; and, finally, whether they actually imparted specific knowledge that they would eventually reencounter in law school. The responses to questions #14–17 all clustered at 2.0 or below.

After looking at the results from all undergraduate law classes and all majors, I decided to see if there was a difference in the many types of undergraduate law classes. I did a comparison of those whose undergraduate experience was limited to Business and/or Criminal Law and those who took Constitutional Law and/or some type of Judicial Process course. Table IV indicates the results.

There does appear to be a substantial difference between those in the Business/Criminal law cluster and those who took Constitutional Law/Judicial Process. Those surveyed seemed to find the courses to be more valuable; they were more likely to be case intensive, use the Socratic Method, and require students to brief cases; and they were a bit better in preparing students to succeed in law school although, the data still suggests, with regard to questions #14–17, that the help they provide is limited.

Finally, I decided to see how one's major affected the way one viewed their undergraduate law classes. I looked at those who majored in Business, English, Arts & Sciences, and Political Science/History. Again, the data in Table V suggests that there is a difference. Those in Business seemed to have a more valuable experience in their undergraduate law classes than those in English or Arts & Sciences. Those in Political Science/History appeared to have an even better experience. But, with regard to the key questions #14-17, only those in Political Science scored better than a "2" on the four-point scale.

Table III. Totals: All Majors, All Classes

Never, Not Really, No/Little Impact	1
Some, A Few	2
Quite a Bit, Several, Were Very Helpful	3
Most Significant, Law School Almost Duplicative	4
#9 (Enrich Undergraduate Education):	2.48
#10 (Enrich Undergraduate Major):	2.35
#11 (Case Intensive):	2.59
#12 (Brief Cases):	1.98
#13 (Socratic Method):	2.23
#14 (Affect Your Decision to Attend Law School):	1.80
#15 (Comfort Level at Law School):	1.75
#16 (Skill Development):	1.58
#17 (Specific Knowledge in Particular Courses):	2.03

Table IV. Totals By Type of Undergraduate Law Course(s)

Question #:	9	10	11	12	13	14	15	16	17
Business Law/ Criminal Law	2.22	1.94	2.17	2.08	1.79	1.79	1.32	1.32	1.58
Con Law/ Judicial Process	3.0	2.64	3.0	2.29	2.18	2.14	2.0	1.82	2.05

Table V. Totals by Major

Question #:	9	10	11	12	13	14	15	16	17
Business (Accounting/ Economics)	2.34	2.08	1.86	1.43	2.0	1.52	1.54	1.36	1.85
English	2.0	1.75	1.75	1.5	1.25	1.25	1.0	1.0	1.25
Other (Fine Arts, Communication, Psychology, Sociology)	2.33	2.17	2.5	2.0	2.0	1.5	1.4	1.33	1.5
Political Science/ History	3.0	3.06	3.22	2.71	2.71	2.22	2.11	1.77	2.39

Conclusion

As indicated above, the times do seem to be changing. Once thought to be a staple of a pre-law curriculum/program, undergraduate law classes are now far less popular with law school representatives and, often, among pre-law advisers.

In this study I learned that law school representatives are almost schizophrenic about undergraduate law classes. By an overwhelming margin, they do not recommend that pre-law students take these classes. By a two-to-one margin, however, they believe that these classes are rigorous, good, and helpful.

The survey administered to attorneys was also revealing. It indicates that the attorneys do not believe that undergraduate law classes provide much of a diagnostic or sustaining function. The data does suggest that all classes are not created equally. Those students who majored in Political Science and History found their "law" classes to be far more beneficial than those from other majors. In addition, students who took Constitutional Law enjoyed the experience substantially more than those who concentrated in Business Law or Criminal Law. They certainly provide support for the argument that such classes provide an important educational experience. Nonetheless, even though those in Political Science, and those who took a course in Constitutional Law, are far more positive about their undergraduate law classes, they are much more lukewarm with respect to their diagnostic or sustaining effects.

Appendix A: Questionnaire

QUESTIONNAIRE:

UNDERGRADUATE "LAW" CLASSES

1.) Undergraduate major? ______________________

2.) Undergraduate institution?

a.) National University?

b.) Regional University?

c.) National Liberal Arts College?

d.) Regional Liberal Arts College?

______

3.) Gender?

a.) Male?

b.) Female?

______

4.) Age?

a.) Under 25?

b.) 25-30?

c.) 31-40?
d.) Over 41?

5.) Undergraduate G.P.A.?
a.) 3.75 or above?
b.) 3.5-3.74?
c.) 3.0-3.49?
d.) 2.5-2.99?
e.) Under 2.5?

6.) LSAT score? (Current scoring system/percentile)
a.) 165-180? (upper 10%)
b.) 159-164? (upper 20%)
c.) 154-158? (upper 35%)
d.) 150-153? (upper 50%)
e.) 147-149? (upper 60%)
f.) Below 147? (lower 40%)

7.) Did you take any "law" classes (e.g. Constitutional Law, Business Law, Criminal Law) while you were an undergraduate student? [*If you select a.), skip to question #18*].
a.) I never took an undergraduate law class
b.) I took one undergraduate law class.
c.) I took two undergraduate law classes.
d.) I took more than two undergraduate law classes.

8.) Of the undergraduate law classes, what did you take? Check all that apply:
a.) Constitutional LawlRights & Liberties.
b.) Business Law or Criminal Law?
c.) Judicial ProcesslElements ofLaw/History of Law/Jurisprudence
d.) Other(s).

9.) Did these courses help to enrich your undergraduate education?

a.) Not really.

b.) Some. They certainly added to my undergraduate education, but did not stand out as particularly special.

c.) Quite a bit. They were an important part of my undergraduate education.

d.) They were among the most significant and meaningful courses I took while an undergraduate.

e.) Don't recall.

____

10.) Did these courses help to enrich your major course of study?

a.) Not really.

b.) Some. They certainly added to my major, but did not stand out as particularly special.

c.) Quite a bit. They were an important part of what I gleaned from my major.

d.) They were among the most significant and meaningful courses I took within my major course of study.

e.) Not applicable--law-related courses were not a component of my major.

f.) Don't recall.

____

11.) Was the class/were the classes "case intensive"?

a.) We were never asked to read court cases.

b.) We read a few court cases.

c.) We read several court cases throughout the term.

d.) We were required to read court cases for nearly each class session.

e.) Don't recall.

____

12.) Were you required to "brief" court cases?

a.) We never briefed court cases.

b.) We briefed a few seminal cases throughout the term.

c.) We briefed several court cases throughout the term.

d.) We were required to brief a number of court cases for nearly each class session.

e.) Don't recall.

____

13.) Did the instructor use the "Socratic method" in his or her course?

a) No. The instructor presented the law-related material by lecturing.
b.) Some. The instructor generally lectured but would occasionally direct questions to the class.
c.) Yes. The instructor did use the Socratic method, but directed questions toward the class generally rather than to single out a particular individual.
d.) Yes. The instructor would usually "call on"/direct questions to one person in the class.
e.) Don't recall.

______

14.) How did these courses affect your decision to attend law school?

a.) They had no/very little impact upon my decision to attend law school.
b.) They were of some help to me in making my decision to attend law school.
c.) They were very helpful in my decision to attend law school.
d.) After taking these classes I was determined to attend law school.
e.) Don't remember.

______

15.) How did these courses affect your "comfort" level once you arrived at law school?

a.) They had little-to-no effect. I was terrified.
b.) They were of some help to me. I felt a bit more secure because of the undergraduate law courses, but was generally confused.
c.) They were very helpful to me. While I was still nervous, they provided me with a level of security I could see that my classmates with no undergraduate law experience did not have.
d.) I felt like I was on extremely sure footing. The first few weeks were not nearly as scary as I had been led to believe.
e.) Don't remember.

______

16.) How effective were these courses at teaching you some of the skills you would need to succeed in law school?

a.) They did not teach me the skills I would need in law school.
b.) They were of some help. I did learn skills, but I would have learned them very quickly in law school.
c.) They were quite helpful. Many of the skills I would need to do well in law school were emphasized in my undergraduate "law" courses.
d.) Apart from legal writing and/or oral argument, I came to law school with nearly all the skills necessary to succeed in my classes.
e.) Don't recall.

______

17.) With regard to course content, how much knowledge did you bring to law school from particular courses?

a.) Almost none. Nearly everything I learned about a particular subject (e.g., Con Law, Crim Law, Business Law) I learned in law school.

b.) Some knowledge--they did give me some familiarity.

c.) They provided me with a solid foundation for my law school courses. In fact, they helped me to understand the law school material more completely.

d.) At best the law school courses were almost duplicative. I actually learned more from one/some of the undergraduate classes.

e.) Don't recall.

____

18.) Class rank in law school?

a.) Upper 10% of my class.

b.) Upper 25% of my class.

c.) Upper 50% of my class.

d.) Lower 50% of my class.

____

19.) Type of law you practice?

____

Notes

1. Leslie Goldstein, in "Roundtable: Author Meets Critics. Martin Shapiro and the Study of Public Law and Judicial Politics," Address presented at the Annual Meeting of the American Political Science Association, Chicago, IL (Aug. 31–Sept. 3, 1995), notes "(T)he numbers in terms of professional membership were always there, because departmental hiring policies were shaped by the perception that student demand would always be there for a constitutional law course ..." In fact, some law professors accuse *LSAC* of harboring this positive bias toward constitutional law. Michael DeBow & Roger Clegg, in "Pre-Law Prerequisites: A Guide to the Post-Socialist World," 67 POL'Y REV. 74, at 75 (1994), write:

> The (LSAC) reading list's emphasis mirrors the tendency of entering law students to overestimate the importance of 'con law' to their understanding of other areas of the law; indeed, many seem to think that constitutional law is the foundation for all other areas of law—thus confusing public and private law, as well as the public and private sectors.

2. Martin Shapiro, "Judicial Politics or Public Law: The Search," presented at the Annual Meeting of the Western Political Science Association, Tucson, AZ (March 14, 1997).

3. *Florida State University College of Law Pre-Law Handbook* (August 24, 1998), www.law.fsu.edu/admissions/prelaw_handbook/prelaw curriculum.

4. William Ball, "Pre-Law at The College of New Jersey," www.tcnj.edu/-ball/prelaw. Emphasis added.

5. Richard Poland, "Should Law be Studied at an Undergraduate Level," *Pre-Law*, Flagler College, www.flagler.edu/academics/prelaw/article.

6. Shapiro, *supra* note 2, at 9.

7. FSU Handbook, *supra* note 2, at 9.

8. Id. Some pre-law advisers do not recommend that students abandon law-related courses. They do suggest, however, that law schools would prefer that they be limited. For example, the Pre-Law Advising Program Handbook at Tufts University warns that "(L)aw schools urge undergraduates not to take these (law-related) courses in such numbers that they prevent them from taking a broad range of course in the liberal arts and engineering." See *Pre-law Advising Program HANDBOOK,* Tufts University, www.tufts.edu/as/undergra_edu/law/lawhk. Other advisers note that since the ABA's Pre-Law Committee does not mention law-related knowledge as essential for prospective law students, then it is better to steer such students away from the law courses and toward a more general liberal arts education. See "Preparation for Legal Education," prepared by the Pre-Law Committee of the ABA Section of Legal Education and Admissions to the Bar, www.abanet.org/legaled/prep.

9. FSU Handbook, *supra* note 3.

10. Tufts Handbook, *supra* note 7.

11. We worked with one student who scored a 167 on the LSAT. He took the test early in his college career (after his freshman or sophomore year). Later he took Constitutional Law. He found that as hard as he worked, and as much as he tried, he was unable pull arguments and reasoning from cases. If the exam questions called for him to talk about the significance of a case, or if he were asked to put the case into a historical or analytical context, he would do fine. Alternatively, if he were asked to read a new case and to mesh it in with the relevant body of law in a particular area, he was lost. He was very concerned about his chances for success in law school, but with an LSAT score in the 96th percentile he was heavily recruited and it was just too inviting to pass up.

12. See S.J. Becker, "Advice for the New Law Professor," 42 J. LEGAL ED. 241 (1992); M. Moskovtz, "Beyond the Case Method: It's Time to Teach Problems," 41 J. LEGAL ED. 289 (1991); A. D'Amato, "Rethinking Legal Education," 74 MARQ. L. REV. 1 (1990); Timothy Terrell, "What Does & Does Not Happen in Law School to Prepare Students to Practice Law? A View From Both Sides of the Academia/Pratice Dichotomy," 83 L. LIB. J. 493 (1991); Cecilia Bryant, "The Fork in the Road: The Bifurcated Purposes of Legal Education," 71 FLA. B. J. 48; Larry Edwards, "Another 'Postcript' to "The Growing Disjunction Between Legal Education and the Legal Profession," 69 WASH. L. REV. 561 (1994); Robert MacCrate, "'The Lost Lawyer' Regained: The Abiding Values of the Legal Profession," 100 DICKINSON L. REV. 587 (1996); MacCrate, "A Fresh Look at Lawyers' Education," 27 U. RICH. L. REV. 21 (1992); William Trail & William Underwood, "Essay: The Decline of Professional Legal Training and a Proposal for Its Revitalization in Professional Law Schools," 48 BAYLOR L. REV. 201 (1996); SCOTT TUROW, ONE L (1988); JOHN BONSIGNORE, et al., BEFORE THE LAW (1994).

13. C.E. Klafter, "The Influence of Vocational Schools on the Origins of American Legal Thought," 37 AM. J. LEGAL HIST. 307 (1993); J.M. Balkin & Sanford Levinson, "The Canons of Constitutional Law," 111 HARV. L. REV. 963. For a different perspective, see MARY ANN GLENDON, A NATION UNDER LAWYERS (1994) at 104. Professor Glendon argues that law schools should be more vocational if by vocational one means that students should learn the nuts and bolts of the law (in lieu of the alternatives discussed above).

14. See, for example, JOHN BRIGHAM, THE CULT OF THE COURT (1987); RONALD KAHN, THE SUPREME COURT & CONSTITUTIONAL THEORY (1994); LIEF CARTER, AN INTRODUCTION TO CONSTITUTIONAL INTERPRETATION (1991); STEPHEN MACEDO, LIBERAL VIRTUES: CITIZENSHIP, VIRTUE & COMMUNITY IN LIBERAL COMMUNITARIANISM (1990); SOTERIOS BARBER, THE CONSTITUTION OF JUDICIAL POWER (1993); GRAHAM WALKER, MORAL FOUNDATIONS OF CONSTITUTIONAL THOUGHT (1990); CHRISTOPHER WOLFE, JUDICIAL ACTIVISM (1991); MATTHEW FRANCK, AGAINST THE IMPERIAL JUDICIARY (1996).

15. See HOWARD GILLMAN, THE CONSTITUTION BESIEGED (1993); MICHAEL McCANN, RIGHTS AT WORK (1994); KEVIN McGUIRE, THE SUPREME COURT BAR (1993); SUSAN BURGESS, CONTEST FOR CONSTITUTIONAL AUTHORITY (1992); GERALD ROSENBERG, THE HOLLOW HOPE (1991); LEE EPSTEIN & JOSEPH KOBYLKA, THE SUPREME COURT & LEGAL CHANGE (1992); SUSAN LAWRENCE, THE POOR IN COURT (1990). For an excellent summary of theoretical work in public law, see Michael McCann's essay, "It's Only Law & Courts, But I Like It," presented at the Annual Meeting of the American Political Science Association, Chicago, IL (August 31–Sept. 3, 1995). Of course this does not include the myriad works produced by political scientists who the study judiciary as a political institution (and whose scholarship is far more quantitative in its nature) or who do doctrinal or comparative analyses including Lawrence Baum, Paul Brace, Gregory

Calderia, Bradley Cannon, Sue Davis, Donald Downs, James Gibson, Mark Graber, Joel Grossman, Frank Guliuzza, Melinda Hall, Donald Kommers, Herbert Jacob, Lynn Mather, Walter Murphy, David Neubauer, David O'Brien, David Rhode, Austin Sarat, Jeffrey Segal, Elliot Slotnick, Christopher Smith, Harold Spaeth, John Stookey, G. Alan Tarr, Sidney Ulmer, and Stephen Wasby.

16. Goldstein, *supra* note 1.

17. Poland, *supra* note 5, at 2.

18. Id.

Performance in Law School: What Matters in the End?

Richard Ippolito

In a previous article, I evaluated the performance of students entering George Mason University School of Law in the fall of 1999.[1] I emphasized student performance in a mandatory economics class during their first year (Concepts in Economic and Legal Analysis, hereafter simply Economics), and I looked at grades in a few traditional law courses. The article reported two findings. First, students who excelled in Economics had higher aptitude in mathematics as measured by their SAT math score and by a variable indicating that they had taken calculus or a similarly advanced math course in college. Second, overall performance at the start of law school seemed to depend on attributes that typically are unmeasured during the application and evaluation process. These attributes could be inferred from several measures of behavior in law school: choice of row in a ten-row lecture hall and number of lectures missed, both measured from my spring Economics class; an indicator (GRADY) that incoming students chose to take Torts from Dean Mark Grady, a nationally known torts expert who teaches from his own textbook, instead of with Assistant Professor John Hasnas; and the HASNAS SIGNAL, which denoted students who turned down his invitation to get a one-third grade point bonus in exchange for signing in "ready and prepared" in 25 out of 28 lectures.[2]

By now these students have completed law school. This note reports which variables mattered in the end and, in particular, whether some of the nontraditional measures of personal attributes still mattered in GPA. In short, they did. Performance after the first year is arguably the best index of success because it follows attrition of the poorer students. All the hidden attributes matter in these results. Two of the hidden attributes predict final performance, even though the population was truncated to include only those who made it to graduation. Specifically, students who choose to sit in the back of the classroom and occasionally skip class have a lower final grade point average. These two variables are as important in the final grade as 10 points in the LSAT score. The results also suggest that age plays some role in success in law school, and that SAT math and verbal scores add significant predictive power to the LSAT for final performance.

A Few Changes in Sample Size and Data Measures

When I did the original empirical work, I included a total of 224 students who took Economics during the fall semester of 1999. Of these, 20 were either transfer students or master's students. To track the performance of the J.D. students to graduation, I limited the universe this time to the 204 J.D. students who completed their first semester of law school. It turned out that the empirical results for the J.D.-student-only population were almost identical to those I published for the slightly larger universe, and so I do not repeat them here. I also replaced the self-reported LSAT scores with official LSAT scores, but this change had no important implications for the results.[3]

Performance in All First-Year Courses

Column 1 in Table 1 shows the results as of the end of the first year of law school. The dependent variable is the GPA earned by students after completing one year of law school. The LSAT score matters, but not overwhelmingly. All else equal, students with 10 additional LSAT points accumulate on average .27 incremental points in their first-year GPA. College SAT scores also matter. Holding constant the LSAT score, a student who scored an extra 100 points in both verbal and math parts of the SAT would gain about .15 grade points in law school GPA. The verbal score variable does not reach significance at the 90 percent level, but nevertheless is on the same order of magnitude as the math score. SAT scores appear to add valuable information to law school success, even after accounting for LSAT scores.

Perhaps the most interesting result is that all four measures of hidden student attributes matter importantly in first-year performance. Students who selected into Grady's Torts class enjoyed an increase in first-year GPA performance equal in magnitude to 10 points in LSAT score. One expects Hasnas's decliners to score .33 lower on their Torts exam, by construct of the bonus. What is fascinating is that the Hasnas decliners earned a .33 lower GPA, on average, in all of their first-year classes. Clearly, the GRADY and HASNAS variables convey information about student attributes that are correlated with success in law school; and yet these attributes are not fully captured by standard measures of performance such as LSAT and SAT scores. Together, the coefficients on the two Torts variables are twice as important as a 10-point advantage in LSAT score.

Moreover, even holding constant the Torts signals, absenteeism and row choice still enter into first-year grades in a significant way. All else equal, students who chose to miss three out of fourteen lectures in Economics II (spring semester, first year) earned .09 lower first-year GPAs in law school. Those who chose to sit in the rear of the Economics II class had another .11 reduction in first-year GPA. I presume that students' absenteeism and seat choice patterns in Economics reflect their behavior in other courses. [Table 1.]

Hidden attributes, which are unmeasured at the admissions stage, seem to matter more than LSAT scores in determining first-year performance. The kind of student who is willing to choose the dean for Torts, who accepts the possibility of being called upon during class, and who takes a seat in the front of the class and attends all the lectures

Table 1. Determinants of First-Year and Final Grade Point Averages

	All Students Completing First Year	All Students Completing Law School (On Time)	
Independent Variables	**First-Year GPA (1)**	**First-Year GPA (2)**	**Final Law School GPA (3)**
Intercept	2.91 (22.75)	2.85 (22.62)	2.93 (22.33)
Evening student	0.05 (0.56)	–0.05 (0.57)	–0.01 (0.01)
Female	0.07 (1.23)	0.07 (1.27)	0.07 (1.20)
Age 26–30	0.11 (1.39)	0.06 (0.82)	.16* (1.85)
Age over 30	0.1 (1.00)	0.04 (0.43)	0.1 (1.06)
Work full time now	–0.06 (0.53)	0.12 (1.00)	0.06 (0.51)
Worked 3 or fewer years full time but not now	0.11 1.27)	0.13 (1.51)	0.05 (0.55)
Worked more than 3 years full time but not now	–0.09 (0.74)	–0.1 (0.1)	0.01 (0.10)
Some economics in college (none omitted)	–0.06 (1.07)	–0.06 (1.09)	–0.1 (–1.6)
B.S. in economics or better	0.2 (1.53)	.23* (1.86)	0.19 (1.43)
Official LSAT (minus mean)	.027** (2.9)	.017** (2.6)	.024** (3.41)
SAT math (minus mean)	.0007* (1.82)	.0008** (2.24)	0.0005 (1.38)
SAT verbal (minus mean)	0.0006 (1.45)	.0009** (2.31)	.0009** (2.18)
College math (took calculus or higher in college)	0.05 (0.75)	0.01 (0.28)	–0.01 (0.19)
HASNAS SIGNAL	–.33** (4.22)	–.22** (2.66)	–0.04 (0.51)
GRADY	.25** (2.38)	.17* (1.70)	0.12 1.13)
Absences in Economics II (out of 14 lectures)	–.03* (1.84)	–.03** (1.97)	–.06** (3.49)
Sat in back in Economics II	–.11* (1.75)	–0.09 (1.46)	–.12* (1.89)
Number of observations	200	173	173
R^2	0.41	0.43	0.34

Numbers in parentheses are t-values. *(**) denote that the coefficient is statistically different from zero at the 90 (95) percent level of significance (two-tail test).

earns .78 additional grade points on average (compared to one who does none of these things).[4] A law school that could somehow measure these kinds of attributes in its applicant pool could presumably increase the success rate of its graduates dramatically without necessarily altering the LSAT composition of the class.

Attrition of Students Who Finish the First Year

I next look at overall performance in law school at the time of graduation. Of course, not all law students who complete the first year end up graduating. Of 200 students who completed their first year, 27 did not make it to graduation on time. For the most part, those who left or did not complete the program in three years were relatively poor performers.[5] The natural question arises: do the variables that matter in first-year performance still matter for the truncated sample consisting entirely of successful students?

Column 2 of Table 1 shows the first-year GPA results for the 173 survivors. For the most part, the results overall are not much different from those for all 200 students who completed their first year. Some of the coefficients are lower. For example, the GRADY and HASNAS variables in column 2 have coefficients that are about two-thirds of their magnitudes reported in column 1. Similarly, the coefficient on LSAT scores falls from .027 to .017. The reduction in the magnitude of these coefficients for the final 173 suggests that hidden attributes help predict who will not successfully complete the program. Among survivors to graduation, these measures still help predict relative success, but not as importantly as before the truncation occurs.

It is worth noting that both math and verbal SAT scores remain important in explaining first-year GPA in the truncated sample. Holding constant LSAT score, the coefficients on both SAT variables are positive and significantly different from zero at the 95 percent level of significance. A student who gets 100 extra points on her verbal and math SAT expects to have a .17 higher GPA after one year in law school.[6] This effect is equal in magnitude to a 10-point difference in LSAT score. These results suggest that law schools ought to be interested in factoring both LSAT and SAT scores into their admissions process.

GPA at Graduation

First-year GPA performance may be a better measure of the overall importance of the attributes than the final GPA, because all first-year students take the same courses and they take most of them in large classes where a grading curve is strictly observed. Beyond the first year, course selection is a factor in determining the final GPA.

Some students seek out smaller classes (where it is harder to enforce a curve) and gravitate toward more lenient graders, while better students may tend to take the hard courses. At the same time, some students mature and learn how to perform better in a system that might have been foreign to them during their first year. So GPA scores at graduation reflect a mixture of ability, hard work, learning, maturing, and gaming.

Column 3 in Table 1 gives the final GPA results for the 173 J.D. students who graduated on time from the entering class of fall 1999.

The coefficient on LSAT is .024 and is statistically different from zero at the 99 percent level of confidence. A 10-point swing in LSAT score is worth about one-quarter of a grade point in the final average. To put this number in perspective, consider that the average GPA upon graduation for this class is 3.07 with a standard deviation of .4. Thus, a 10-point swing in LSAT on average is worth 60 percent of a standard deviation in final outcome. SAT scores continue to make a contribution to final grade (though the math score drops below conventional levels of significance). An extra 100 points in both math and verbal SAT scores results in about .14 higher GPA or about 60 percent as much as 10 points in LSAT score.[7]

Interestingly, the coefficients on the GRADY and HASNAS SIGNAL variables are much smaller in the final tally. Students who shied away from the dean during their first semester, or who were reluctant to be called upon by Hasnas, either learned how to become better students or were better at gaming their grade point average in their second- and third-year classes. In contrast, the variable that captures the number of absences in Economics II is even more important than it was in determining first-year performance. Presumably, students prone to skip Economics also either skipped other classes or exhibited the same lack of enthusiasm for learning in other classes as they did in Economics. Students willing to skip four of fourteen Economics lectures during their first year had on average a .24 lower final GPA, precisely the contribution that 10 points in LSAT makes.

Additionally, holding constant absenteeism, LSAT scores, and all other things, students who sat in the back of their Economics II class during their first year, and who survived the first-year cut, were prone to graduate with a lower GPA. On average they had .12 lower GPAs than their counterparts who sat closer to the front of the class in Economics.

The overall thrust of the results reported in this article and its predecessor is that while numbers matter, they may not matter that much in relation to personal attributes that determine success. The LSAT score consistently matters, but not in an overwhelmingly important way.[8] At George Mason 10 points in LSAT score translates to about a quarter of a grade point among those who make it to graduation (about an 85 percent completion rate). This is in comparison to a standard deviation of final GPA of .40. If law schools pay attention to numbers, my results suggest that they would do well to add SAT scores to their list of criteria for admission to law school. Holding constant LSAT score, math and verbal SAT scores consistently help predict law school success, and on balance are about as important as the LSAT itself.

Perhaps more interestingly, the results show that personal attributes can swamp the importance of LSAT in predicting success in law school. Presumably, this is the reason why many undergraduate programs and law schools look for some evidence of hard work and motivation in their application procedure. Students who choose to sit in the back of the lecture hall and are prone to skip class may signal these attributes by their behaviors during college. Are these the students who when in college failed to participate in extracurricular activities? Are they the ones who failed to work in summer jobs or the ones who worked? Are they the ones who held positions in their fraternities and sororities or are they the ones who did not join any group?

Holding constant standard measures of ability like the LSAT, the results suggest that law schools that could successfully identify nontraditional signals of superior performance might gain a dramatic advantage over the competition in terms of the success of their graduates. The key to identifying these traits is the collection of data upon entry, together with a careful tracking of performance in law school and beyond as a function of these variables. Few law schools, I suspect, are sufficiently disciplined to pursue this exercise diligently, but those that do may reap an impressively high return on their investment.

Notes

1. Richard A. Ippolito, The Sorting Function: Evidence from Law School, 51 J. Legal Educ. 533 (2001).

2. The GRADY and HASNAS SIGNAL variables are described in *id.*

3. There was a small upward bias in students' self-reported scores. The coefficients on the official LSAT scores were higher and attained higher levels of significance but did not materially affect any of the other results. I also acquired official undergraduate GPA records, but I found that, like the self-reported undergraduate GPAs, they had no predictive power on performance in law school.

4. For this calculation, I assume that those who do not attend class every day miss three times out of 14.

5. Six students transferred to other law schools after their first year; these normally were good performers. Eight withdrew of their own volition, and eight were asked to leave. Nine were still enrolled at the time of their scheduled graduation. Some of the latter students failed their first year and simply started anew; others may have had to repeat some classes or take a leave of absence. Of the 204 J.D. students who completed their first year, 173 graduated on time—an 85 percent completion rate.

6. These coefficients are as large as those on math and verbal SAT scores when entered as determinants of undergraduate GPA. For example, see Julian Betts & Darlene Morell, The Determinants of Undergraduate Grade Point Average: The Relative Importance of Family Background, High School Resources, and Peer Group Effects, 34 J. Human Resources 268 (1999).

7. It is worth noting that while the LSAT scores are official, the SAT scores are self-reported. Since I also had self-reported LSAT scores, I could make some judgment about the importance of getting official scores. I found that when I used official scores, the coefficient and its level of significance increased quite significantly. Self-reported LSAT scores are a bit biased high, but also are noisier than the official numbers. These statistical manipulations suggest that official SAT scores might perform better in my regressions than is suggested by results based on self-reported SAT scores.

8. I could not find any influence of undergraduate GPA on performance at George Mason. It could well be that the GPA screen employed by the admissions department works to limit entry to those who otherwise exhibit some promise. But after admission undergraduate GPA does not affect law school performance, despite a great variance in the distribution of GPAs among admitted students.

Part Two

The Law School Admissions Test

Merit and Diversity: The Origins of the Law School Admissions Test

William P. Lapiana

I. Introduction

This Article discusses the creation of the Law School Admissions Test (LSAT) and is based on surviving archival materials.[1] This story is particularly important today, fifty-five years after the first administration of the LSAT, because the use of an individual's LSAT score in law school admission is in some ways at the heart of the controversy regarding affirmative action in law school admissions, a role upon which the United States Supreme Court has recently ruled. In *Grutter v. Bollinger*, a divided Court found that the University of Michigan's admission policies, which were carefully tailored to take race into account as an element of diversity, did not violate the Equal Protection Clause.[2] In short, the so-called objective measures—grade point average and the LSAT score—need not be the only criteria by which applicants are judged. In the Court's view, the LSAT plays an important, though limited, role. It remains a useful law school admissions tool.

One thesis of this article is that the LSAT was created to be a tool and that it was not intended to be the sole criterion for making admission decisions, an assertion strongly supported by the historical record. A second thesis is inferred from the record by placing it in context. Given the circumstances facing American law schools after the second World War, the creation of an "objective" test as an aspect of law school admissions increased access to legal education. Finally, this article argues that it is reasonable to conclude that this expansion of access was the aim of at least some of the legal academics involved in the creation of the test.

A thorough investigation of how the test, and indeed other "objective" measures, came to be regarded as the sole measure of whether an applicant is worthy of admission is beyond the scope of this Article, but the conclusions presented lead to some suggestions for investigation of that question.

II. History of Admissions Testing

The first step in understanding the hopes and plans of the creators of the LSAT is understanding the history of admissions testing before the second World War. Two tests were well-known and used. In the mid-1920s, George D. Stoddard, a psychologist at the University of Iowa, and Merton L. Ferson, dean at North Carolina and then at Cincinnati, collaborated on a test published by West.[3] Starting in 1930, Yale Law School used a test developed by the university's Department of Personnel Study.[4] Both of these tests were consciously and explicitly designed to supplement other criteria, and especially to provide some control on the wide variation in the meaning of college records. As one of the principal participants in the Yale effort put it, the purpose was "to provide some check upon the validity of undergraduate records and to furnish a common denominator of educative promise."[5] Fifteen years earlier, Dean Ferson made the same points, and also emphasized the possibility of using such a test as a tool for counseling prospective students.[6]

All those who discussed these tests in print, however, acknowledged that they were not, and neither could nor should be, the sole criteria by which admissions decisions were made. As Henry Witham of the University of Tennessee stated in reporting his school's experience with the Stoddard-Ferson test: "The tests discover inherent mental ability (as applied to law), but do not show the will to work nor the capacity for work."[7] According to Witham, the test's usefulness came in its ability to predict lack of success—students who did poorly on the aptitude test usually did poorly in law school.[8] The predictive value of the test, he added, was enhanced when it was combined with a judgment about the applicant's desire and ability to work.[9] He explained those criteria:

> Desire to work is self-explanatory. Under ability to work are included health and prior education, work outside of law school such as newspaper work, college annual, college sports, etc., social activities, and any number of outside distractions which might claim the student's time and thought. A student has ability to work in direct proportion to perfect health and prior education and in inverse proportion to his interest in outside distractions.[10]

At Yale, according to the dean, the school's own aptitude test formed part of the second stage of a two-step admissions process.[11] Applicants who survived screening based on a written application, "which required the applicant to disclose most of his life history, good or bad," college grades, and two letters of recommendation were invited to take the test and have an interview with a member of the admissions committee.[12] While exact processes varied, it seems that schools that did use aptitude tests adamantly maintained that the resulting scores were but a part of the admissions decision. To an important degree, judgments were made on a subjective judgment of capacity and willingness to work.

Whatever role subjective judgments played in admission decisions, discussions of testing also revealed a strong underlying belief in the existence of "aptitude" and the ability to measure it. The Stoddard-Ferson and Yale tests resembled each other. Both made use of various tests of verbal skills, as represented by questions dealing with synonyms and antonyms, verbal analogies, reading comprehension and recall, and some sort of test designed to be specifically "legal."[13] The Stoddard-Ferson effort even included a test of reading comprehension based on an excerpt from Langdell's Summary of Contracts (which Dean Ferson, at least at one time, thought might be too difficult).[14] At the University of Wisconsin, a study of various predictive measures found that the Yale test had no advantage over a standard intelligence test,[15] which, according to one of the Wisconsin researchers, it resembled.[16] The point, of course, is that the "legal" tests were based on the sort of intelligence tests developed in preceding decades and widely used for the first time to test Army recruits during the first World War.

The very use of the tests indicates a willingness to sort young men on the basis of probability rather than on an individualized judgment of the character, intelligence, and prospects of each individual. In 1930, John Henry Wigmore wrote in the *Illinois Law*

Review a short editorial about what he called the science of "juristic psychopoyemetrology," or "the science of measuring capacity for mental achievement."[17] Wigmore believed that the cultivation of his newly-named science was a good thing. "Vocationally," he wrote, "who can undervalue the immense saving of misguided effort that would be gained if, at the outset of preparation for a career, dependable advice could positively disparage one's choice?"[18] Wigmore decided to put the Stoddard-Ferson test to the test, and had it administered to the class that entered Northwestern in October 1925.[19] Because the course of study was three years for those with a college degree and four years for those with three years of college study, the results were not tabulated until July 1929.[20] Wigmore found a novel, and probably unique, way to analyze the results. Rather than using statistics and especially correlation coefficients, he created charts, showing graphically where those who placed in the four quartiles of the aptitude scores placed in their law school work, measured both by the number of A's and the number of A's and B's they received.[21] Wigmore believed that his charts showed the test to be gravely deficient.[22] Individuals from all four quartiles of the aptitude scores found themselves in the top quarter of the class.[23] The professor concluded, therefore, that the Stoddard-Ferson test was of little use in predicting any one individual's capacity for success in legal study, at least at Northwestern.[24]

Not surprisingly, Wigmore's article drew responses from advocates of testing. Both Albert Crawford of the Yale Department of Personnel Study (which created the Yale test) and George D. Stoddard, co-author of the test Wigmore used, emphasized the need to make admission decisions based on probabilities. As Stoddard stated: "There is only one way in which Professor Wigmore's fervent hopes for adequate prognostication *for the individual* can be realized. That is by fixing to the individual student of known accomplishment, say on a test, a figure representing the *probability* of success for that category of students in which he is reliably placed."[25] The advocates of testing, of course, promoted the tests as merely one factor in the admissions decision. Nevertheless, the small controversy occasioned by Wigmore's criticism indicates the growing power of the idea of large-scale sorting based on standardized testing. The experience with similar tests during the first World War surely contributed to the acceptance of the probabilistic or statistical idea. As John Carson has written, the aptitude tests used by the Army marked "a significant break with civilian intelligence-measuring instruments."[26] Besides the modifications necessary for mass administration and grading, more unusual "was the orientation of the test toward the production of qualified results completely objectively determined."[27] In Carson's view, the creation of the Army tests "completed a process—already begun, to be sure, within civilian psychology—of remaking mental testing into a new sort of endeavor, one in which professional judgment was subordinated to objective determination and statistical manipulation."[28]

There are many ways to look at the transformation Carson describes when trying to place it in the context of admission to law school, setting aside for the time being any question of what the tests "really" measured or of their formal statistical validity. On the one hand, Wigmore's objections speak to a world in which such decisions are made by measuring each applicant individually. The use of tests does not necessarily mean the complete abandonment of such measures. As Dean Gulliver reported, applicants to Yale first submitted to a preliminary screen based on a written application, the college record, and recommendations, and only then were invited to take the aptitude test and submit to an interview.[29] The relative weight given the "objective" measure of the test and the subjective impression of the interview is difficult to recapture, but there must have been wide latitude for interviewers to indulge their preconceptions, prejudices, intuitions, and guesses. The use of such factors, of course, not only allow one to identify those who do not test well or whose college efforts were handicapped by the need to work, but also allow the indulgence of invidious discrimination. Dean Henry Witham of Tennessee, in fact, used the results of the Stoddard-Ferson test in conjunction with his judgment of the student's willingness to apply himself to law school work.[30] One can only imagine what factors, beyond those he openly discussed, went into that determination. On the other hand, if one believes in the relative validity of the test results, then their widespread use in the admissions decision can be seen as a net gain for fairness. To the extent that the role of individual prejudice is reduced, possibilities are assumed to be opened to more and more people. In this story, these possibilities even eventually would be extended to women.

In the pre-war period, however, aptitude testing of applicants for law school was seen as a device for weeding out those who would not be able to successfully complete the course of study. The goal was not identifying the best and the brightest to whom the bountiful opportunities of a legal career would be opened, but rather to be able to tell the least talented that attendance at law school would be a waste of time and money. Testing was not so much a means of selecting future lawyers as it was a means of discouraging the manifestly incapable from applying to law school and of increasing the "efficiency" of legal education. While it might be difficult to rigorously document, one of the stories told most often about law school admissions before the LSAT (and perhaps for sometime after its creation) is the admonishment given to first year students on their first day of class to look to their right and left and realize that one of the three will not make it past the first year.[31] How widespread the policy of admitting a large number of students and dismissing a significant proportion after the first year of study cannot be known with precision, but it could not be efficient and would certainly encourage a culture of competition and extreme individualism in first-year classes. Testing before admission was an alternative.

III. Law School Admissions

A. Pre-War Admissions

Given the often-stated uses of testing, it seems that the gate to the legal profession was guarded not by admissions testing but by more subtle social pressures and attitudes that told young men—and certainly all but a very few young women—that certain goals were simply beyond their reach. Any attempt to understand the existence of invidious discrimination in law school admissions before the creation of the LSAT must begin with the fact that American law schools were not as homogenous in the first half of the twentieth century as they became at its end, and that a college degree was not a prerequisite to a legal education and admission to the bar until after the Second World War.[32] Although some members of the profession, both practitioners and academics, did everything they could to eliminate part-time legal education (usually in night schools) and make a college degree a necessary credential for every lawyer, they did not succeed.[33] Throughout the 1920s and 1930s, the professionalizing and standard-raising ideology of some lawyers was met and to a great degree countered by the idea that becoming a lawyer was a peculiarly American way to advance in the world and become successful. Ritual invocations of the privations endured by Abraham Lincoln in his quest for education outside of formal institutions actually seemed to express a powerful belief that simply would not be denied.

Equally important to understanding the pre-LSAT world of admission to law school is an attempt to recapture the contours of discrimination and social stratification in the pre-war period. Specifically, the extent and virulence of discrimination against Catholics and Jews, whether or not they or their parents were actually immigrants, played an important role in shaping American life in the period before the second World War.[34] Prohibition, of course, has long been recognized as an attack on the culture of European immigrants and their descendants who were not of Anglo-Saxon stock.[35] The collapse of much of the power of these exclusionary sentiments—at least in the major urban areas of the United States—in the wake of the New Deal and the war, is only beginning to receive attention.[36] In short, admissions testing before the war was not needed to exclude cultural minorities. Discrimination against them was acceptable and quite frankly practiced.[37]

With the end of the second World War, American society found itself on the threshold of a new world. Returning veterans were promised educational benefits, which would mean that young men who had never imagined gaining a college education now had the financial ability to do so.[38] They also might have found the imagining somewhat easier. As the war continued and the need for trained enlisted men and officers increased, many young working-class white men not only received training in technical specialties, but also had the opportunity to become officers. Having had the experience of being leaders, they might have found it easier to believe that higher education was not beyond their abilities. For whatever reason, white male veterans returned from the war with new possibilities for making their place in American society. A significant transformation of American society was beginning. The story of the beginnings of the LSAT is an important part of the story of the birth of a new age.

B. The Development of an Admissions Test

As the second World War came to an end, higher education in the United States faced the challenge of accommodating the returning veterans whose ability to attend college and university had been greatly enhanced by the G.I. Bill's educational provisions.[39] It is not clear whether the potential influx of students made law schools more conscious of their admission procedures, but given the attention to testing in the pre-war period, it is not surprising to find a letter dated May 17, 1945 from Frank H. Bowles, admissions director at Columbia Law School, to the then-president of the College Entrance Examination Board (CEEB or College Board), John Stalnaker. Bowles suggested that the two men discuss the creation of "a law capacity test" to use in admissions decisions.[40] The current test used by Columbia, in Bowles's judgment, was unsatisfactory.[41] He set out seven criteria for the new instrument: (1) "[h]igh predictive value," defined as a correlation coefficient of .70 or higher; (2) "discrete measure of capacity for law study insofar as that capacity can be isolated;" (3) "[h]igh reliability;" (4) no more than one and one-half hours in length; (5) "[s]ensible and observable relation to the study of law;" (6) "[r]esults easy to interpret," and (7) low cost.[42] The reply came from the new head of the CEEB, Henry Chauncey. The project was of interest to the CEEB, but Chauncey cautioned Bowles that some of his aims might have to be sacrificed to achieve others.[43] Bowles's aims were not different from those of the pre-war advocates of testing. All except Wigmore wanted something easy to administer, tried to tie the substance of the test to the actual study of law, and talked in terms of correlation in the realm of .50–.70 as acceptable and more than .70 as very reassuring.[44]

For whatever reason, matters appear to have gone nowhere until the summer of 1947, when representatives from Columbia met with representatives of the testing organization.[45] Present at that meeting, along with Bowles, was Professor Willis Reese of Columbia, who would play the leading role in the development of the LSAT.[46] William Turnbull's memorandum of the meeting, headed "Meeting with Columbia Representatives re Law Aptitude Examination," was dated July 30, 1947.[47] In his view, the primary purpose of the meeting was to familiarize Reese with the CEEB.[48] Bowles, whom Turnbull described as "apparently the person who has pushed to have the Board take over the problem" of improving Columbia's procedures, wished to invite Harvard and Yale to join the project to design a test, the results of which would correlate with first-year grades, "on the assumption that first-year performance is highly correlated with later success in law school and in legal practice."[49] Correlation with success in taking the bar examination was rejected because candidates take them several times and "virtually everybody passes them sooner or later."[50] In addition, there was preliminary discussion of the contents of the test, and "paragraph reading, analogies, syllogistic reasoning, 'inconsistencies,' and practical judgment" were all mentioned.[51] Finally, Bowles suggested that the project be financed by contributions of three or four thousand dollars per year from each of the three schools.[52]

All the important themes in the story of the creation of the LSAT are evident in this report of the first substantive meeting between the testing professionals and the legal educators. First, and perhaps most importantly, the validity of the LSAT was linked to its correlation with grades in the first year of law study. A similar correlation was used to measure the usefulness of the pre-war tests, and the dismissal of the criterion of success on the bar examination was even more telling. As the modern American law school solidified its position in the profession and extended, and to some degree realized, its claim to being the best possible preparation for the practice of law, its relationship to the bar examination became more and more problematic. Except for those few schools that retained the "diploma privilege," which allowed their graduates to automatically become members of the bar, law schools and the bar examination authorities were forced into an often uncomfortable relationship.[53] The student with a law degree, the product of a legal education, had to pass yet another hurdle, one over which the school had no control. Langdell himself had tried to separate graduation from admission, emphasizing the differences between an examination in a course, set by a teacher who had taught a specific approach to a subject, and a bar examination, the content of which is determined by other criteria.[54] At the very beginning, then, the LSAT was linked to success in law school, not success at the bar. Of course, the use of first-year grades as the measure of validity was a practical decision. Access to those grades was completely within the schools' control, and the use of first-year grades would allow the first validity studies to be made quickly.

The content of the test was also set at that first meeting. The items described in Turnbull's memorandum were familiar: "paragraph reading, analogies, syllogistic reasoning, 'inconsistencies,'and practical judgment."[55] It was not surprising, of course, that the test would look like other aptitude tests, especially if it was to be administered for the first time in a matter of months. Chauncey wrote to an assistant dean at New York University later that fall: "The first test which will be tried out will contain materials from our files that seem a priori to be appropriate. Later we will prepare, with the help of representatives from the law schools, materials that are tailor-made for this purpose."[56] In fact, the composition of the test was the least of the problems to be faced and solved in the short time before the first administration. Spreading the word of the new project and finding law schools willing to participate were more important. Increased participation would provide greater numbers for testing validity and spread more widely the costs.

On August 15, 1947, representatives of Columbia, Yale, and Harvard law schools met with Chauncey and other representatives of the College Board to discuss the new test.[57]

On August 18, 1947, Reese reported to his dean on the meeting. Columbia and Yale were reported to be very willing to go along with the plan, while the Harvard representative cautioned that he was less sure his faculty would be willing to participate, given their seeming satisfaction "with their present procedure and results."[58] Chauncey then outlined the College Board's plan, which included a policy committee of law school representatives (Policy Committee) to advise the College Board on the construction of the test, the administration of an experimental test in the fall of 1947 preparatory to a March 1948 administration for use in admissions to the fall 1948 class, the testing of all candidates rather than just those "whose college grades placed [them] in the "doubtful category," and an estimate of costs between $10,000 and $15,000 per year.[59]

It seems that the only real objection raised with respect to Chauncey's plan concerned the cost of development of the test. Chauncey had suggested that each school contribute $4,000 per year for three years with a like amount contributed by the College Board.[60] He further proposed that other "co-operating" law schools interested in taking part in the development of the test share in the cost.[61] The decision was made to write to all the members of the College Board that had law schools, as well as to the University of Michigan, and invite them to join with Harvard, Yale, and Columbia in planning and financing the test.[62] Reese's narrative is carefully couched in the passive voice, making it impossible to know who first suggested seeking more participants.[63] It was a most important decision, however, because it helped ensure that the creation of the test would also create a new organization of law schools.

The next few months were spent seeking support for the project. In August, a form letter went to the deans of the law schools whose universities were members of the College Board, along with the dean of the University of Michigan's law school.[64] The letter invited the school to serve on the Policy Committee for the test, contribute to the cost of the test, and give one-quarter of a faculty member's time to work on test development.[65] An accompanying memorandum dated August 18, 1947, outlined what had been decided at the August 15, 1947, meeting, including the creation of the Policy Committee, testing of validity by comparison with law school grades, and financing arrangements.[66] The participating schools would provide $12,000, while the College Board pledged $4,000 and promised to repay the schools when the test became self-supporting.[67] After that, excess receipts would go into a reserve fund to cover future losses and perhaps pay for special research projects.[68] The CEEB would charge the test account all direct costs, a portion of overhead, and a seven and one-half percent override "to be used for basic research in the field of testing."[69] Chauncey also held out the promise that the test might help to study the relationship between success in law school and in later life.[70]

The replies were favorable, though no dean was willing to donate a portion of a faculty member's time to the project.[71] Even if a particular school did not use a test (though many did) or, like New York University's school, was "as yet unconvinced about the usefulness of an aptitude test as a method of selecting law students," they had "an open mind" and were quite willing to participate in what most described as an experiment.[72] Monetary support would be forthcoming, too, although several schools first had to seek approval of the central university administration.[73]

On October 20, 1947, Chauncey had what was probably the most crucial meeting in the quest to create support for a law school admissions test. He traveled to Cambridge for an audience with Erwin Griswold, dean of the Harvard Law School.[74] Griswold told Chauncey that Harvard certainly could use such a test to make decisions on "those borderline on college record and those from unknown colleges."[75] Harvard, as Tepler described many years later, had "a very complex system for the evaluation of college grades, and ... had built up a lot of tables predicting what a certain average at a particular college meant."[76] The dean told Chauncey that those tables were based on the classes of 1928–1934 and were hopelessly "out of date," and that no new data could be expected until approximately 1954.[77] Tepler described the problem as "the return of the veterans and the flood of candidates from many places and many colleges" for which no data existed; "there wasn't any reasonable way to work the old system anymore."[78] The test would be of real benefit to the school and Griswold promised cooperation.[79]

Before meeting with Griswold, Chauncey had sent a letter to the dean of the law schools at Rutgers, Northwestern, Syracuse, Stanford, Cornell, the University of Southern California, New York University, the University of Pennsylvania, Yale, and Harvard that invited them to a meeting in Princeton to discuss the proposed test.[80] If the LSAT has a birthday, it is the date of that meeting, November 10, 1947.[81] In attendance were Chauncey, Director of the College Board,[82] his assistant director, Richard H. Sullivan, William Turnbull of the College Board, Dean Elwood H. Hettrick of Boston University, Willis Reese from Columbia, Livingston Hall from Harvard, Albert Newmann from Michigan, Francis Putnam from New York University, George Braden from Yale, Willard Pedrick from Northwestern, Dean George Harris from Rutgers, the Dean of Syracuse's law school, Paul Andrews, and two College Board research associates, Harold Guilksne and John French.[83] From this meeting came several decisions about the test that would shape it for the next fifty years.

C. The LSAT

First was the name. Although the exact title "Law School Admission Test" was decided on administratively after the meeting, it was Willard Pedrick who suggested that the schools should avoid using the term "aptitude test."[84] Decades later he recalled:

> My thought at the time was that we didn't want the people to think we were grading their aptitude, that we were grading their suitability for law school study, and apparently I felt then, I guess I would still feel today, that it's better to tell somebody that his/her qualities, however great they may be, are not well-tailored to law school.[85]

Pedrick's suggestion was not unproblematic. The test would henceforth be advertised as an "admissions" test—a test designed to predict the likelihood of success in law studies. On the other hand, the test would have some qualities of an aptitude test as well. The discussion at the November meeting brought out the ambiguity.

The law professors were presented with some sample questions that Braden, Reese, and Lon Fuller had helped to select after the August meeting in New York.[86] From the contemporary record of the meeting, it appears that the questions presented to the group involved memory and comprehension, word meanings, and sentence completion. The emphasis in the first group of questions was on memory; Chauncey indicated that the assumption was that memory was important in legal work, an assumption Dean Harris of Rutgers confirmed.[87] Dean Andrews then described the next group of questions as a vocabulary test.[88] Dr. Turnbull attempted to explain the rationale behind these particular questions: "The idea is to pick out the meaning and then select a word from a number which have been given different meanings.... It is a logical process rather than a vocabulary process."[89] Andrews was also concerned that one question required knowledge of Greek philosophy.[90] Again, Turnbull demurred, pointing out that the question required the candidate to complete a sentence based on information given by the question.[91]

More interesting, and revealing perhaps, is the discussion of what did not appear among the proposed question types. Dean Andrews weighed in with the suggestion that the test include some sort of examination of knowledge of "general culture."[92] In his view, "[t]he general cultural note strikes me as very important to determine whether [the candidate] will be a good lawyer or a licensed legal mechanic."[93] Professors Braden and Reese disagreed. Braden went so far as to assert that a candidate is "eligible from a cultural point of view if you have a college degree and a good college record plus a legal aptitude test."[94] He emphasized that, while Yale does take "men in the social sciences," the admissions process takes into account both the college record and Yale's aptitude test, but that an applicant from an "unknown" college needs a better score.[95] Andrews then remarked that he had denied admission to a candidate with an A average from "a college of applied science which is recognized as a good engineering education" because the applicant had taken only one English and one elementary history course and did "a fair job" on the verbal section of the test Syracuse used.[96] Livingston Hall of Harvard then added, "I don't think I have ever seen a record that went that far," presumably in its omission of "cultural study."[97] Reese noted that, when faced with a candidate offering a record like the one Andrews described, Columbia had denied admission.[98]

This colloquy on "general culture" would not end the discussion by any means. During the next several years, the LSAT would experiment with questions designed to test general knowledge before abandoning the whole enterprise. At this formative moment, however, it might have been significant that the advocate of testing for "general culture" was the dean of a local school in upstate New York and opposition to the idea was expressed at once by the representatives of Yale and Columbia. Although all seemed to agree that they had turned down applicants lacking a background in literature and history, the representatives of the national schools saw no need to include questions testing that knowledge as part of the new admissions test. These different views of what the test should include might have reflected the applicant pools of the schools. Perhaps Dean Andrews found himself attempting to judge among applicants whose cultural *bona fides* were less obvious than those of the applicants to the Ivy League schools. For him, the test would be more useful if it helped to discriminate on a "cultural" basis. The national schools, with applicant pools representing the best graduates of a number of colleges from throughout the nation, had no need for a cultural filter. Even more importantly, the discussion was about excluding those whose education was too technical and too rooted in the sciences. If we accept that the legal academics discussing the question meant what they said, they were not talking about excluding cultural minorities through the use of a test of general, cultural knowledge. William (Ben) Schrader, an Educational Testing Service (ETS) specialist in testing and statistics, remembered the view of the "law school group": "As long as you went through college, you would be on an equal footing with anybody else."[99] Because the G.I. Bill certainly made college more accessible to white male veterans, the decision to limit the test to aptitude and avoid testing specific knowledge might actually diminish cultural bias, at least toward some white males who might otherwise be stigmatized as working-class ethnics. The issue would be revisited, however, within the first decade of the LSAT's existence.

The next topic to lead to extensive discussion is perhaps the most surprising to those who have grown up in a world in which the LSAT is taken for granted. The original proposal from the testing professionals did not include reporting of the test scores to the candidates.[100] Richard H. Sullivan's memorandum of November 7, 1947 entitled "Legal Aptitude Test: Plan of Administration" suggested that candidates be told "that the scores are considered confidential and will be sent only to the law schools as requested by the candidate. No score reports will be issued to candidates themselves, to their families, or friends."[101] The temptation to indulge in counterfactual history raised by this proposal is irresistible. Were scores reported only to schools, the admissions process would have been much more mysterious than it has turned out to be. Unable to factor their scores into strategic decisions about an application strategy, students with good college records might have applied more adventurously and aimed higher. Schools might have found it easier to keep from the public the weight given to factors other than scores and grades, and the entire notion of and debate about affirmative action would have been different. If the scores were withheld from the candidates, the schools might have found it possible to withhold information about the scores of candidates they did accept, and the entire modern ranking system might never have developed. The question of taking the test more than once would never have arisen. On the other hand, the less information candidates have, the less accountable are the decision-makers.

For the moment, the important datum is that the law professors gathered in Princeton in November 1947 unanimously voted to report scores to the candidates.[102] The discussion leading to that decision was marked by two important factors. First, several participants disagreed about how anxious candidates were to see their scores, and, second, there was an undercurrent of indifference to the ultimate solution of the question. Henry Chauncey was clearly in favor of disclosure as a means to keep the admissions officers honest.[103] In his view, college admissions officers "wanted to be able to hide behind scores, they want to be able to discriminate and use the scores as an excuse and they do not want to show their hands."[104] The law professors acknowledged that, in Reese's words, the score was a "weapon" in the hands of a rejected candidate, yet he believed that "people are not very inquisitive as to what they get on their tests."[105] Braden disagreed. Applicants to Yale want to know their score on the Yale test—"they want to know if they have legal aptitude."[106] He believed that candidates should receive their scores, or at least enough information to allow them to make a decision about applying to another law school. The discussion ended with agreement on giving the scores to the candidates, but a slightly different question opened up a different line of discussion.[107]

The schools represented at the November meeting were literally paying for the creation and administration of the new test. Should other schools be allowed to use the scores in making admission decisions? The decision on that question—any school can ask for the scores and use them, but only those who contribute to the expenses of the testing program may have a hand in setting policy—was less important than the accompanying discussion about the rankings of colleges used by some of the law schools to interpret undergraduate grades. Chauncey proposed the "pay to participate" solution and then suggested that part of the testing program involve the ranking of colleges.[108] Livingston Hall was adamant. He stated, "We [Harvard Law School] do not feel that we should make generally available to colleges the relative standing of other colleges as shown by our own records."[109] Braden and Reese admitted that only their admissions personnel understand the Yale and Columbia ranking systems anyway.[110] The discussion ended with agreement that the testing professionals would consider correlating scores and college grades but there would be no publicity for the law schools' ranking systems.[111] The last subject of extended discussion was the calendar for administration of the test. The discussion was dominated by attempts to accommodate each school's particular admission policies. Eventually, dates at the end of February and early May were selected.[112]

Work continued after that November meeting. Willard Pedrick continued to put forward his view that the test should not be advertised as an aptitude test. In September 1947, he had written Sullivan suggesting that the announcement of the test be modified by striking the word "mental" from the phrase "to measure the mental abilities that are important" for law study.[113] Sullivan and the testing professionals eventually agreed. He wrote to Pedrick, "[S]everal of us worried around with the wording descriptive of what the test is designed to measure and finally had to settle upon the phrase in your draft copy as the most appropriate."[114]

The content of the test was further discussed at a meeting at Princeton on January 30, 1948. Many of the participants in the November meeting attended, along with a large complement of ETS personnel.[115] Once again, the point was made that the test was to measure the qualities important for success in law school rather than whatever was needed to be a successful practicing lawyer, and that it was to be a test of aptitude (though that word would not be used in public).[116] According to the memorandum of the meeting in the ETS files, the participants agreed that the qualities for which the candidates should be tested fell into four categories. First were those satisfactorily measured by the existing batteries of questions: precision in analysis and logical thinking, feeling for relevance, clarity, perception of analogy, vocabulary and verbal comprehension, command of language, clarity and precision in writing, ability to organize argument, ability to get the essence from reading matter, persistence and industry, concentration, executive ability, and capacity to work under pressure.[117] Further experimentation was required to develop questions to test memory, rapidity of reaction, practical judgment, meticulousness, ingenuity, and imagination.[118]

Questions might be developed to test the ability to apply principles to specific cases, to see the uses and possibilities of an argument, to move from abstract to concrete and vice versa, to recognize the adequacy of data, and something described as "semantic insight."[119] Finally, questions should be developed to test for analytical versus emotional thinking, suspicion of generalities, willingness to question premises, creativity and the ability to synthesize, ability to recreate a situation, drive to get behind premises, intellectual curiosity, patterns of interest, intellectual achievement, emotional balance, character and dependability, qualities of leadership, force, and drive.[120]

Behind the lengthy list recorded in the memorandum is an important part of the story. When asked to recall the events of 1947 and 1948 decades later, some of the law professors remembered that they did not have much of a role in deciding the content of the test. Willard Pedrick recalled:

> [I]n those early days [the professors who attended the November 1947 meeting] believed that somebody who is pretty good at almost any kind of intellectual endeavor would be a good prospect for law school. So we started, I think, with the notion that a test that had some relationship to an IQ test would be appropriate.[121]

Constructing that test was another matter, however. Pedrick believed that Reese had some input on the content of the test, but noted, "I think the rest of us were willing to look at ETS as the technicians and let them have a go at it and then come back later and see how it was working."[122] Reese himself, when asked whether the professors showed any interest in the technical side of writing the test, answered: "There was not any."[123] The same conclusion was drawn on the ETS side. French noted in late 1948 that "there seemed to be little inclination on the part of the law professors to do any work on test construction."[124] For their part, the testing professionals often found the law professors to be less than ideal students. John Winterbottom of ETS, who began a long association with the test in the mid-1950s, felt that few of the legal academics "really understood what was going on, and I'm not sure that many of them really understood validity studies and all that sort of thing we sent out to them."[125] Ben Schrader, also from ETS, disagreed with Winterbottom.[126] On the other hand, Louis Toepfer found Schrader "totally and utterly incomprehensible," and Emerson Spies agreed that Schrader "failed to understand how little we understood."[127]

The law professors might not have believed themselves competent to write the test they wanted, but they certainly knew what that test was supposed to do. From the first stirrings of interest in a "legal capacity" test, the goal was to create a predictive tool tied to success in law school, as defined by first-year grades. That was also the goal of the pre-war admission tests, although none of those tests were consulted by the ETS personnel writing the first LSAT.[128] The law professors did not want to get involved in some sort of testing of personality, no matter how enthusiastically some ETS members lobbied for it. Chauncey, in particular, believed in the ability of testing to sort American society both efficiently and accurately, not only for intellectual ability, but for personality traits as well.[129] The law professors, however, would have no part of it, at least in the early days of the LSAT. They were concerned only with one narrow measure of "success"—performance in the first year of legal study. As Ben Schrader remarked decades later, by the time he came to work on the LSAT in 1950, the idea that the test was designed only to predict first-year grades was "carved in stone."[130] In 1955, Winterbottom wrote a memorandum summarizing the policies behind the test and declared that, before the first administration of the LSAT in February 1948, it had been decided "that the main purpose of the test would be to predict scholastic achievement in law school."[131] And the law professors decided to accomplish that end, as Schrader noted, by having an aptitude test.

Of course, the word "aptitude" did not appear in the name of the test, thanks at least in part to Willard Pedrick's consistent advocacy. Yet there is little doubt that the test was intended to be a test of capacity rather than knowledge. In his 1955 memorandum, Winterbottom summarized the decisions made in 1948:

> [S]ince it seemed desirable not to do anything which would tend to limit law school entrants to those students having a particular kind of subject-matter background, it was further decided that the test should be as free as possible of questions based on specific information available only to those who had taken certain courses or who had some familiarity with the law.[132]

Looking back on the contemporary record and later recollections, then, it is clear that the law professors involved in the creation of the LSAT in the winter of 1947–1948 knew what they wanted. The professors wanted a test that could predict success as measured in terms of first-year grades by measuring capacity or aptitude rather than knowledge, but were reluctant to describe the test in those terms and had very little idea of how to construct a test to measure those qualities.[133] The testing professionals at ETS did have that knowledge, and they put together the first LSAT from questions in the item files, according to Chauncey.[134] Those items were of the following types: contrary and irrelevant statements, debate, figure classification, paragraphs, reading comprehension, reasoning, sentence completion, verbal analogies, and word classification.[135] And to everyone's great pleasure, the test worked. The experimental tests given to law school students in the fall of 1947 correlated well with their grades.[136]

After the first administrations on February 28 and May 8, 1948, it was also clear that the program was a financial success. More than fifty-six hundred applicants took the test on those dates, generating so much revenue that ETS found itself holding a surplus of $23,200 attributable to the new testing program.[137] It was clear that the contributions from the schools would be repaid by the end of 1948.[138] More importantly, the validity studies that had been carried out indicated that the test was a useful predictor of success in law school, at least within the limits of what could be considered statistically significant and practically useful.[139] Financially and practically successful then, the LSAT began its life under the best of auspices. During the next ten years or so, two important lines of development played themselves out. First, the debate about the content of the test called into question the meaning of the aptitude test. Second, the question of the governance of the LSAT became more and more important as revenues increased.

IV. The Meaning and Governance of the LSAT

The LSAT was designed to be an aptitude test, but at the very beginning, suggestions were made that there be an effort to gauge the general culture or general background of the candidates. The discussion and controversy that culminated in the decision in 1957 to introduce a test of general background took place in a world in which "cultural bias" did not mean what it would mean ten, let alone forty, years after the decision was made. Both the content of the discussion and the way the decision was made provide an important perspective on the later and continuing controversy.

Before considering the parameters of the debate, however, it is important to state as strongly as possible what the LSAT was not designed to do. The creators of the LSAT did not intend the test to be the sole criterion for admission to law school. The entire rationale for the test was the need to supplement the information supplied by the undergraduate record. The original understanding, Winterbottom wrote in 1955, was that "[s]cores on the test were to be used *along with pre-law grades*, recommendations and other information as an aid in admissions."[140] In addition, while some schools might have been in the position to be highly selective in admissions, Schrader remembered that in the "early days," the mean score of those admitted to law school was not much higher than the mean score of all applicants.[141] Years later, Emerson Spies put it simply: "There was not a great growth in those initial years. That's because there wasn't a great need for the test in those early years, let's face it."[142] A single vignette, however, says it all. In March 1950, a law school representative wrote A. Pemberton Johnson, Winterbottom's predecessor as project manager for the LSAT, explaining, at his admission committee's request, why they admitted a candidate whose LSAT was fifty points lower than that of the next lowest admitted candidate. The candidate was a college and medical graduate and "had just returned after a long period of war service in the Army Medical Corps" and, therefore, was "out of touch with the ordinary collegiate academic materials and procedures."[143] He did a respectable job in his first-year studies.[144] Johnson replied, "We firmly believe that the general findings of the validity of the LSAT combined with pre-law college grades are no substitute in certain individual cases like this for the exercise of sound judgment based on experience."[145] From the beginning, the LSAT was meant to be a tool, and from the beginning, the magic of the "objective" numerical score exercised its power over the legal mind.

Questioning the LSAT's emphasis on the measurement of aptitude did not take long to start. In 1954, ETS was asked to work on questions to test understanding of human institutions and values, an undertaking suggested by the Association of American Law School's committee on pre-legal education.[146] The 1954 meeting of the Policy Committee voted against cooperation in a study of ways to measure understanding of values. First, the testing of values requires a judgment about the "excellence of values reflected in the test materials."[147] Second, because the LSAT was an aptitude test, "[i]t was not evident that the proposed kind of test would be useful in this respect."[148]

There the matter sat until Louis Toepfer of Harvard was elected to lead the Policy Committee in 1956. Years later, Toepfer candidly admitted, "I had that problem of everybody having high scores."[149] This led him to try to find ways to discriminate among those high scores.[150] With Toepfer as the chair, the Policy Committee discussed the use of the Graduate Record Examination Area Tests (the Area Tests) to find the applicants with "narrow" backgrounds "who have majored in rather technical fields like business and who, in many cases, have expended their electives on trivialities."[151] The 1957 meeting of the Policy Committee referred the question to a subcommittee that asked ETS to report the scores on the Area Tests of students now in law school.[152] Unfortunately, ETS identified only three students now in law school who had attended colleges where they were required to take the Area Tests and could find scores for only one of them.[153] Thought next turned to a new one- or two-hour test of "general culture." Toepfer continued to believe that the importance of a broad and liberal education to a lawyer made measuring what candidates have learned in college worthwhile.[154] His colleague on the subcommittee, John Bainbridge from Columbia, told Toepfer that the proposed addition to the LSAT would give "something of substantial value to those of us concerned with our culture and the traditional concepts of our profession."[155]

Those attending the June 1958 meeting of the Policy Committee gave the matter a thorough discussion. The minutes summarized the arguments of those in favor as making two points. The new cultural material might increase the validity of the test and its very inclusion "would help to show that law schools are seriously interested in encouraging their applicants to acquire a broad background during their undergraduate training."[156] The opposition pointed out the difficulty of finding material, "particularly in the area of philosophy, on which there would be general agreement regarding its suitability;" that the material might be "coachable;" and that the addition of the material would diminish "the unique contribution of the LSAT" as a measure of aptitude.[157] The information on general background is available in the undergraduate record in any event.[158] A motion to cease experimentation with testing of general culture was defeated and the committee voted to proceed with an experimental test to be administered in the fall of 1958 and validated against first-year grades.[159]

The new test was not universally popular with those responsible for guiding the LSAT. At a December 1959 meeting of the committee charged with furthering the development of the test, opinion on the usefulness of the test of general background was deeply divided. A majority of the committee recommended adopting the test as part of the LSAT in November 1961, even though the studies carried out after the experimental administrations showed that the test was useless as a predictor of law school grades.[160] The majority position was that the new test "might be a more efficient measure of achievement and reveal abilities not apparent from the college record."[161] It also identified those who had acquired "the liberal education so strongly recommended by all law schools, recommended not because men so educated would necessarily enjoy any greater academic success but because they would probably become more effective members of the profession."[162] The minority raised two points. The first was the impropriety of designing a test to do anything other than measure legal aptitude, "the only appropriate activity of the Law School Admission Test Board."[163] The second was the possible effect on an undergraduate's choice of courses.[164]

The new test, along with questions designed to test writing ability, became part of an afternoon testing session in 1961.[165] The first discussion of the new test took place at a meeting of the test development committee in February 1963.[166] Several legal educators wrote to Toepfer beforehand, presumably to give information they would not be present to recount in person. At least three of these letters belittled the test of general background. One correspondent assured Toepfer that he could learn all he needed to know about the breadth of education from the candidate's transcript. "Who cares," William Shane wrote, "if he doesn't recognize a picture of Michelangelo's Moses?"[167] Norman Penney told Toepfer that his school did not use the afternoon scores in the admissions process, except to the extent that "possibly a few students get some help ... when they are on the borderline. I doubt that any school really uses them more than this."[168] Yet another writer was more sympathetic to the general background test because they might identify those who do not do well on the rest of the LSAT, but who "nevertheless may do successful law school work."[169] But unless the test of general background can identify those persons, it is not worth it.[170]

The last comment was the most telling. What impressed Winterbottom the most at the meeting on February 22, 1963 "was the way in which considerations of statistical validity dominated the discussion."[171] In his view, the general background test was not designed to rise or fall on its ability to predict grades.[172] He thought it had been adopted originally for its "backwash effect [in influencing undergraduate study] and in order to provide information which may help law schools to select students for qualities which have no very close relationship with grades."[173] Toepfer agreed with Winterbottom's assessment of the tone of the meeting, but was far from happy with it. In his view, the fascination with statistical validity illustrates the "fundamental weakness" of the committee members.[174] He complained that "[n]one of them know beans about admissions and apparently have closed their minds to learning."[175] For Toepfer, "[t]he only good way to assess a test is to examine it and then ask yourself whether you would rather have a man who stood high on this measure than one who stood low."[176]

This controversy about the test of general background is clearly important for understanding the development and role of the LSAT in law school admissions, but how we should interpret it more than forty years after the event is far from self-evident. At first blush, the subject of the test is clearly "cultural," an ideal means of creating and perpetuating cultural bias, and would be conclusive evidence for some that the LSAT's very roots are sunk deep into the earth of racism and invidious discrimination.[177] But the historical record reveals a far more complex situation. There certainly is no evidence that anyone intended the general background test to exclude any particular group. Louis Toepfer, perhaps its strongest advocate, saw it as a way to answer his own peculiar problem as the person responsible for admissions to Harvard Law School. All his applicants had "high scores," and he believed that the general background test would give him some basis on which to sort his own applicant pool.[178] In fact, recalling the controversy about the general background test, Toepfer asserted that "the only thing" that sorted people the way the rest of the test did not "was really the knowledge of current events."[179]

People do have differing opportunities to acquaint themselves with current events and differing views about what events are sufficiently important to warrant attention. Asserting that the goal of the general background test was to sort out candidates who were interested in the world around them does not absolve the test of bias in construction or result. On the other hand, the opposition to and eventual abandonment of the general background test reveal one of the most important consequences of the use of standardized testing in law school admissions. As Winterbottom noted and Toepfer lamented, by the early 1960s, discussion of the value of testing was firmly rooted in the belief that the testing was appropriate only to the degree that it could predict law school performance. The most damning thing that could be said about the general information test was that it did not predict.

The emphasis on prediction was not new, of course. The pre-war admission tests had also been subject to validation studies based on correlations between test scores and performance in law school. The LSAT, however, was more widely used and subjected to ongoing supervision. Year in and year out, the legal educators who sat on the Policy Committee and its various subcommittees, especially those devoted to development of and research on testing, heard ETS personnel subject every suggestion for modification of the test to one criterion: how well did a new question-type predict performance? Those outside the LSAT organization read literature that told them that the test was designed to predict success in law school—specifically, first-year grades. Beginning in 1960, conferences for admission personnel of law schools spread the gospel of prediction even more widely.

V. The Role of Prediction

One meaning of the story of the general background test is that prediction became the rationale for objective testing. Tests that did not aid prediction—general background and the contemporary tests of writing ability—were discarded. The emphasis on prediction had another, and perhaps unexpected, effect. What the LSAT could not do became as important as what the test could do. The test did say something about ability to do law school work as measured by first-year grades, but its very limitation helped to focus attention on other factors in admission decisions.

One of the factors investigated was "personality," a term meaning all the aspects of a person that lead him or her to work hard at a task.[180] By investigating personality, the legal educators and ETS personnel thought they might find a way to identify the under- and over-achiever, or, in cruder terms, to identify both the lazy and those who would have to struggle to keep up. Even though members of both groups might do well on the LSAT, they might not be the best risks for admission. In the fall of 1956, experimental personality tests were administered at ten different law schools to about thirteen hundred students.[181] Three different types of tests were given. Two were designed to measure "flexibility" and "aspiration," and the third was an "omnibus" test intended to measure a broad range of personality traits.[182] The tests were to be evaluated against grades, and one hope was to identify those who might drop out, especially for reasons other than poor academic performance.[183] The goal was to find an objective test of the qualities Henry Witham identified in 1930 as necessary components of success in law school. A memorandum prepared in preparation for the testing gives further indication of the sort of thinking behind the new project. One test would involve sentence completion because "[t]here is good evidence to support the idea that *variability* in response to the same sentence completion stems, over several occasions, is a good measure of an important quality that might be called "Tolerance of Ambiguity," "Tolerance of Complexity," or, in a particular sense, "Flexibility."[184] The results of such a test would be useful because of the "reputed fact" that some students fail because they cannot cope with the discovery that law is not certain and rigorously logical.[185]

In retrospect, the assumptions behind this psychological testing might seem a bit naive, but the effort was a serious one. The Policy Committee spent a considerable sum, more than $25,000, in the effort.[186] The actual implementation of the study was handed over to John R. Hills, director of the office of testing and guidance of the Regents of the University System of Georgia. In April of 1959, he reported to Winterbottom that the entire project had turned up little useful information. "Most of the leads we followed," he wrote, "have petered out, as far as prediction of grades in law school goes."[187] Winterbottom replied that no one was expecting the study to have "immediate application" to admissions decisions, and it was sufficient to have increased knowledge about personality.[188] Winterbottom added, "I think that we should look on this study as the close of a chapter so far as the LSAT Policy Committee is concerned."[189]

The failure of the mid-1950s study did not, however, mark the end of concern with the personality of applicants. In 1960, the LSAT Research Committee (Research Committee) was talking about investigating motivation and attitudes.[190] In 1961, the entire Policy Committee heard the Research Committee's report that discussed "at length" the possibility of using "such sensitive information as religious affiliation, family income, parent's education, and the like."[191] The committee believed that gathering such information was not necessary because "[t]he applicant's social and cultural background, it is believed, is determinative only to the extent that it produces certain attitudes, drives, and characteristics."[192] There should be no objection to using some device to measure these attitudes directly, "without regard to the background that produced them."[193] At that same meeting, the Policy Committee voted to appropriate $3,000 to hire experts to assist in the design of research on the role of "non-intellectual factors" in law school success.[194] Louis Toepfer summed up the goal of this research when he answered a British legal academic's questions about the use of the LSAT at Harvard. The test, he wrote, provided a useful common basis for comparing students of diverse backgrounds, and it "assists greatly in arriving at a decision about admission" of candidates "whose other attainments leave us doubtful or often openminded."[195] Just as important, however, is what the test does not do:

> You will see when you examine this test that it measures largely qualities in the general area of verbal reasoning. It does not include measures of likes and dislikes, ambition, motivation and other personal qualities which are closely related to successful performance. For this reason, it is not very useful by itself but taken with undergraduate records and other appraisals it becomes a very helpful tool.[196]

As Toepfer acknowledged, however, the test could not be the only tool. Indeed, the need for additional tools would almost certainly become acute. The legal academics and ETS personnel knew the demographic facts. The "population boom" was approaching law-school age, and the number of applicants was likely to increase.[197] One view was that the increase would put even greater demands on the LSAT to predict not only success, but also superior performance as the number of competent applicants increased and the competition for scholarships increased.[198] At the same time, as H.B. Reese told the Research Committee, "many of us in admissions administration are using standards of selection other than success in law school."[199] The additional criteria might include trying to predict what sort of practitioners graduates would be. "Another possible criterion might emerge," he believed, "from judgments about the kind of student body we want, apart from their capacities."[200]

As the 1960s began and the baby boom came into the sights of law school admissions officers, the LSAT had contributed to the creation of a culture in which prediction of success in law school was an important part of the admission decision, but was clearly understood by those most familiar with the test and its development to be not the only part. The quest continued for better ways to determine which candidates would have a more difficult time because of their "personality," especially as expressed in motivation for study. At the same time, the ability to predict that the LSAT provided made it clear that other factors entered into the admission decision.

VI. The Role of the LSAT Today

Somehow, in spite of the consistent message that the LSAT was merely one factor in law school admissions, the test score has assumed an overwhelming importance. The position of the plaintiff in *Grutter v. Bollinger*[201] can be understood at the most general level as expressing the idea that a candidate with a higher score should always be admitted in preference to a candidate with a lower score, although perhaps it is more accurate to say that the argument is that a preference based on race cannot offset a lower score.[202] The current "ratings" of law schools, which mirror the median LSAT of their students, are often blamed for the overemphasis on test scores and certainly could contribute to the idea of test score as entitlement. When a candidate can see that he or she has an LSAT score above a school's median, rejection begins to look suspicious.

Not so long ago, however, it was the test score itself that was suspicious. The "truth-in-testing" movement of the 1970s was predicated on the belief that the tests were unfair and had too great an influence in the lives of those who had no option but to surrender their futures to a standardized test. ETS, the creator of most of these tests (though not the LSAT, which was produced after the creation of the independent Law School Admissions Council), was seen as "powerful, unaccountable, and secretive."[203] The result of the movement for greater accountability on the part of ETS was the enactment of a "truth-in-testing" law in New York State in 1979.[204] The result for ETS was a decision to treat the New York statute as if it had nationwide effect and to release copies of all tests when they were given.[205] The same provisions, of course, applied to the LSAC and the LSAT.

The result for the test-preparation business was increased opportunity and respectability. The release of the tests gave the review companies raw material with which to work and a much greater ability to claim success by measuring their students' improvement by comparing "before-and-after" results on examinations that were the real thing. To put it crudely, aptitude could be bought.[206] As Nicholas Lemann notes in his study of the standardized test in America, the market was large and vigorous, powered by the understandable desire of baby-boom-generation parents to ensure their children's future and prevent the disaster of downward mobility.[207]

If the rewards of a high test score become an entitlement, then any interference with that entitlement will be resisted, and there seems little doubt that affirmative action based on race is widely seen as just such interference. The secretive and elitist testing agency has been replaced as an object both of fear and scorn by an interfering government and by secretive and elitist educational institutions.[208] The situation is complicated, of course, by electoral politics and votes presumably to be gained by opposing racially based affirmative action.

The world of legal education itself has also contributed to the transformation of the role of the LSAT. In the first place, the American Bar Association's (ABA) accreditation standards require that a law school require applicants to take a "valid and reliable admission test to assist the school in assessing the applicant's capability of satisfactorily completing the school's educational program," and the presumption is that the LSAT is the test to take.[209] As part of maintaining accreditation, the ABA requires law schools to submit an annual questionnaire, which, among much other required information, requires the schools to report the LSAT scores of matriculating students. The scores are then reported in the ABA Law School Guide.[210] While such information is certainly valuable to an applicant who is trying to decide on an application strategy, there is no way to limit its use. The LSAT scores of a school's students have become important in commercial rankings, especially those by *U.S. News and World Report.* A statistical analysis of those rankings commissioned by Association of American Law Schools (AALS) found that "virtually all of the differences in the overall ranks among schools could be explained by the combination of two of the *U.S. News* factors. These factors are student selectivity (which is driven by the school's median LSAT score) and academic reputation."[211]

The need to stand out in these rankings, of course, becomes a powerful impetus to report the most impressive scores possible. The LSAC itself has recognized that the LSAT is subject to what it does not call, but surely can be described as, abuse. In 1999, as part of a comprehensive series of recommendations on the proper use of test scores in admissions, the anonymous authors of the study noted:

> It is generally acknowledged that too few resources are dedicated to the increasingly complex law school admission process. There was a time when the number of faculty and staff allocated to this function was adequate to the demand, but that was before recruiting, marketing, counseling, customer service, computer expertise, research, e-mail, data management, continuing education, and many other functions became a part of the admission operation. Law schools with staff that are too small, with too little power to effect change, may have contributed to expedient uses of standard predictors and the resultingly thin records of other criteria used to make decisions.[212]

To some degree the law schools themselves have contributed to the overwhelming importance of the LSAT score, although it must be noted that the deans of law schools have severely criticized the commercial rankings that have contributed to the outsized importance of the LSAT.[213]

The prominence of the LSAT score in these despised, but clearly influential rankings, has helped to transform a test that was designed to provide guidance to applicants and, as this article argues, to increase the diversity of the profession by helping to show that many people had the ability to do law school work. In addition, the test was never meant to have anything to do with any sort of prediction of whether a candidate would be a successful lawyer, whatever that term means. Today, however, the LSAT—that is, the mean and median test scores of the student body—has become the most important factor distinguishing one law school from another.

VII. Conclusion

The homogenization of American legal education in the period after the second World War eliminated the variety noted in Alfred Reed's reports authored for the Carnegie Foundation.[214] The three-year course of study for full-time students became the norm, the college degree the universal prerequisite, and the casebook, rather than the treatise, the basis of classroom instruction. Many different factors helped to bring about change, including the ambitions of law school faculties, the ability of the ABA to convince state authorities that only graduates of ABA-approved schools would be allowed to sit for the bar examination, and the resulting power of the ABA accreditation requirements and, to a lesser degree, the requirements for AALS membership.[215]

Reed's studies, however, were more than descriptive. His great insight was that the wide variety of legal practice in the United States meant that not all lawyers needed to be trained in the same way and that all law schools need not look alike. He was particularly concerned that men (at least) from all classes be able to aspire to the bar:

> Humanitarian and political considerations unite in leading us to approve of efforts to widen the circle of those who are able to study law. The organization of educational machinery especially designed to abolish economic handicaps—intended to place the poor boy, so far as possible, on an equal footing with the rich—constitutes one of America's fundamental ideals. It is particularly important that the opportunity to exercise an essentially governmental function should be open to the mass of our citizens.[216]

Reed was not concerned with race or with gender, but his concern for a representative legal profession led him to envision a system of legal education that maximized diversity in the American legal profession. The LSAT was created to further that aim. Whether it can continue to do so is the challenge of law school admissions in the twenty-first century.

Notes

1. These materials form the records of both the Law School Admissions Council (LSAC) and of the Educational Testing Service (ETS). The author was given access to them by the LSAC, which has in its possession the relevant ETS records on microfiche. The interpretations and conclusions in this Article are those of the author alone and are not in any sense the official view of the LSAC or of ETS.

2. Grutter v. Bollinger, 123 S. Ct. 2325, 2347 (2003).

3. See Merton L. Ferson, *Law Aptitude Examinations*, 5 AM. L. SCH. REV. 563, 564 (1925).

4. See Albert B. Crawford & Tom Jay Gorham, *The Yale Legal Aptitude Test*, 49 YALE L.J. 1237, 1238 (1940). For a complete discussion of the Yale test, see *id.* at 1237–49.

5. *Id.* at 1238.

6. Ferson, *supra* note 3, at 563–65.

7. Henry B. Witham, Correspondence, *Legal Aptitude Tests*, 25 ILL. L. REV. 448, 449 (1931).

8. *Id.* at 450.

9. *Id.*

10. *Id.*

11. A. G. Gulliver, *The Use of a Legal Aptitude Test in the Selection of Law School Students*, 9 AM. L. SCH. REV. 560, 560 (1940).

12. *Id.*

13. See Ferson, *supra* note 3, at 564.

14. *Id.*

15. Richard Wellington Husband, *Prediction of Law School Success*, 1939 WIS. L. REV. 285, 291 (1939).

16. *Id.* at 286 n.3.

17. John H. Wigmore, *Juristic Psychopoyemetrology—Or, How to Find Out Whether a Boy Has the Makings of a Lawyer*, 24 ILL. L. REV. 454, 455 (1929).

18. *Id.*

19. *Id.* at 456.

20. *Id.* at 456–57.

21. *Id.* at 457.

22. Wigmore, *supra* note 17, at 463.

23. *Id.* at 461.

24. *Id.* at 463.

25. George D. Stoddard, Correspondence, *Legal Aptitude Tests*, 25 ILL. L. REV. 446, 447 (1931).

26. John Carson, *Army Alpha, Army Brass, and the Search for Army Intelligence*, 84 ISIS 278, 286–87 (1993). The unreliable and biased nature and the misuse of the results of the Army tests are fully examined in STEPHEN JAY GOULD, THE MISMEASURE OF MAN 192–233 (1981).

27. Carson, *supra* note 26, at 287.

28. *Id.*

29. Gulliver, *supra* note 11, at 560.

30. Witham, *supra* note 7, at 450.

31. In 1925, Merton Ferson, author of one pre-LSAT admissions test, wrote: "The student mortality continues high in law school, and it is not the indolent alone who fail." Ferson, *supra* note 3, at 563.

32. Any study of the heterogeneity of American legal education in the pre-LSAT period must begin with two reports of the Carnegie Foundation, both authored by Alfred Z. Reed: *Training for the Public Profession of the Law*, published in 1921, and *Present-Day Law Schools in the United States and Canada*, published in 1928. A college degree followed by three years of full-time study, the accepted standard today, was the sole method of obtaining a degree at only three schools during the 1927–1928 academic year, and curricula varied widely. See ALFRED ZANTZINGER REED, PRESENT-DAY LAW SCHOOLS IN THE UNITED STATES AND CANADA 169, 222–36 (1928). In the earlier study, Reed identified "four broadly distinguished types of law schools" based on the length of the course of study, entrance requirements, and whether students were considered part-time or full-time. ALFRED ZANTZINGER REED, TRAINING FOR THE PUBLIC PROFESSION OF THE LAW 414–16 (1921).

33. WILLIAM P. LAPIANA, LOGIC AND EXPERIENCE: THE ORIGIN OF MODERN AMERICAN LEGAL EDUCATION 162–64 (1994).

34. For a useful summary of some of the literature and of the various schools of interpretation of the immigrant experience of "Americanization," see Gary Gerstle, *Liberty, Coercion, and the Making of Americans*, 84 J. AM. HIST. 524 (1997).

35. WILLIAM E. NELSON, THE LEGALIST REFORMATION: LAW, POLITICS, and IDEOLOGY IN NEW YORK, 1920–1980, at 41, 384–85 nn. 51–52 (2001).

36. See, e.g., *William E. Nelson, The Changing Meaning of Equality in Twentieth-Century Constitutional Law*, 52 WASH. & LEE L. REV. 3 (1995).

37. Educational institutions were not exempt from these attitudes. In discussing *Goldstein v. Mills*, 57 N.Y.S.2d 810 (N.Y. Sup. Ct. 1945) (suit challenging the tax exemption of Columbia University on the grounds that the New York City Tax Commission had not found that Columbia did not discriminate in admissions as mandated by statute, and ultimately dismissed on procedural grounds), William E. Nelson writes: "Everyone knew, of course, that Columbia, like most other colleges and universities, did discriminate, especially against Jews and occasional other groups such as Italian Catholics." Nelson, *supra* note 35, at 152.

38. ALAN BRINKLEY, THE END OF REFORM: NEW DEAL LIBERALISM IN RECESSION AND WAR 257–59 (1995).

39. Servicemen's Readjustment Act of 1944, Pub. L. No. 78-346, 58 Stat. 287.

40. Letter from Frank H. Bowles, Admissions Director, Columbia Law School, to John Stalnaker, President, College Entrance Examination Board (May 17, 1945), *microformed on* Educational Testing Service Archives Microfiche (on file with the LSAC) [hereinafter ETS Archives] at Series 1, Box 1, Folder 1.

41. *Id.*

42. *Id.*

43. Letter from Henry Chauncey, President, College Entrance Examination Board, to Frank H. Bowles, Admissions Director, Columbia Law School (May 22, 1945), *microformed on* ETS Archives, supra note 40, at Series 1, Box 1, Folder 1.

44. See Crawford & Gorham, *supra* note 4, at 1241–42, 1241 n.6; Husband, *supra* note 15, at 290.

45. See Memorandum from William W. Turnbull, College Entrance Examination Board, *Meeting with Columbia Representatives Re Law Aptitude Examination* (July 30, 1947), *microformed on* ETS Archives, *supra* note 40, at Series 3, Box 8, Folder 1 [hereinafter Memorandum from William W. Turnbull].

46. See *id.* At the time Reese interested himself in the creation of a law school admissions test, Columbia University was still led by Nicholas Murray Butler who had imposed ceilings on the number of Jewish students at Columbia and whose administration had tried to impose ceilings on the dental school by merging it with the medical school, which did have admissions ceilings. NELSON, *supra* note 35, at 152. There is no evidence that this author has been able to find, but it is possible, and certainly pleasing to contemplate, that Reese was trying to find a way to stymie Butler and his supporters by creating an objective test of ability, which, at the very least, would make it embarrassing to turn away clearly qualified applicants because they were members of groups to which unpleasant characteristics were ascribed.

47. Memorandum from William W. Turnbull, *supra* note 45.

48. *Id.*

49. *Id.*

50. *Id.*

51. *Id.*

52. Memorandum from William W. Turnbull, *supra* note 45.

53. For a thorough discussion of the diploma privilege and its extent in the late 1920s, see REED, PRESENT-DAY LAW SCHOOLS IN THE UNITED STATES AND CANADA, *supra* note 32, at 53–72.

54. LAPIANA, *supra* note 33, at 56–57.

55. Memorandum from William W. Turnbull, *supra* note 45.

56. Letter from Henry Chauncey, President, College Entrance Examination Board, to Russell D. Niles, New York University Law School (Oct. 10, 1947), *microformed on* ETS Archives, *supra* note 40, at Series 1, Box 1, Folder 1 [hereinafter Letter from Henry Chauncey].

57. *See* Letter from William W. Turnbull, College Entrance Examination Board, to Edward S. Noyes, Board of Admissions, Yale Law School (Aug. 18, 1947), *microformed on* ETS Archives, supra note 40, at Series 1, Box 1, Folder 1 [hereinafter Letter from William W. Turnbull].

58. *Id.*

59. *See* Memorandum from Henry Chauncey, President, College Entrance Examination Board, *Proposal for Development of Legal Aptitude Test* (Aug. 18, 1947), *microformed on* ETS Archives, *supra* note 40, at Series 1, Box 1, Folder 1 [hereinafter Memorandum from Henry Chauncey]; Memorandum from Henry Chauncey, President, College Entrance Examination Board, *Conference with Dean Griswold and Professor Dodd on the Legal Aptitude Test October 20, 1947* (Oct. 21, 1947), *microformed on* ETS Archives, *supra* note 40, at Series 1, Box 1, Folder 1.

60. *See* Memorandum from Henry Chauncey, *supra* note 59.

61. *Id.*

62. *See* Letter from William W. Turnbull, *supra* note 57.

63. Emerson Spies believed "that that was sort of a private decision made by Willis Reese," and Lawrence Tepler remembered that "in the beginning it didn't seem to me that there was anything political." Oral History Transcript of Emerson Spies, in EDUCATIONAL TESTING SERVICE ORAL HISTORY PROJECT (on file with the LSAC) [hereinafter ORAL HISTORY PROJECT]. William Turnbull of the College Board described the decision to use the College Board's membership as a mailing list as "a logical compromise between the hundred or so accredited law schools in the country and the three prime movers." Letter from William W. Turnbull, *supra* note 57.

64. Letter from William W. Turnbull, *supra* note 57.

65. *Id.*

66. Memorandum from Henry Chauncey, *supra* note 59.

67. *Id.*

68. *Id.*

69. *Id.*

70. *Id.*

71. See Letter from Russell D. Niles, New York University Law School, to Henry Chauncey, President, College Entrance Examination Board (Oct. 6, 1947), *microformed on* ETS Archives, *supra* note 40, at Series 1, Box 1, Folder 1.

72. *Id.*

73. *See id.*

74. *Conference with Dean Griswold and Professor Dodd on the Legal Aptitude Test October 20, 1947*, *supra* note 59.

75. *Id.*

76. Oral History Transcript of Lawrence Tepler, in ORAL HISTORY PROJECT, *supra* note 63.

77. Memorandum from Henry Chauncey, *supra* note 59.

78. Oral History Transcript of Lawrence Tepler, *supra* note 76.

79. For details of Chauncey's meeting with Griswold, see *Conference with Dean Griswold and Professor Dodd on the Legal Aptitude Test October 20, 1947*, *supra* note 59, and Oral History Transcripts of Emerson Spies, Lawrence Tepler, and John A. Winterbottom, in ORAL HISTORY PROJECT, *supra* note 63. Willis Reese had similar memories of the situation at the end of the war. He told Millard Ruud, who interviewed him for the LSAC oral history project, that "there was increased demand from the veterans returning from World War II. So there were applications from a lot of individuals that we found it more difficult to evaluate." Oral History Transcript of Willis Reese, in ORAL HISTORY PROJECT, *supra* note 63. At the time Ruud interviewed Reese, Reese was terminally ill. Even the transcript gives the impression that talking was an effort and the brevity and general nature of most of the conversation was no doubt because of Reese's physical condition.

80. Transcript of Conference of Law Schools on Legal Aptitude Test 1 (Nov. 10, 1947), *microformed on* ETS Archives, *supra* note 40, at Series 3, Box 8, Folder 1 [hereinafter Transcript of Conference].

81. *See id.*

82. Chauncey would soon become the head of the ETS to be formed on January 1, 1948 by the merger of the College Board with the testing functions of the Carnegie Foundation and the American Council Testing Organization. *See* Transcript of Conference, *supra* note 80, at 1.

83. *See* Brief of the Conference on Legal Aptitude Tests 1 (Nov. 10, 1947), microformed on ETS Archives, supra note 40, at Series 3, Box 8, Folder 1.

84. *Id.* at 5.

85. Oral History Transcript of Willard Pedrick, in ORAL HISTORY PROJECT, *supra* note 63.

86. Transcript of Conference, *supra* note 80, at 7.

87. *Id.* at 9.

88. *Id.* at 10.

89. *Id.*

90. *Id.*

91. Transcript of Conference, *supra* note 80, at 10.

92. *Id.* at 12.

93. *Id.*

94. *Id.*

95. *Id.*

96. Transcript of Conference, *supra* note 80, at 13.

97. *Id.*

98. *Id.*

99. Oral History Transcript of William B. Schrader, in ORAL HISTORY PROJECT, *supra* note 63.

100. *See* Memorandum from Richard H. Sullivan, Legal Aptitude Test Plan of Administration (Nov. 7, 1947), *microformed on* ETS Archives, *supra* note 40, at Series 3, Box 8, Folder 1.

101. *Id.*

102. Transcript of Conference, *supra* note 80, at 19.

103. *Id.* at 17.

104. *Id.*

105. *Id.* at 19.

106. *Id.*

107. Transcript of Conference, *supra* note 80, at 19.

108. *Id.* at 20.

109. *Id.*

110. *Id.* at 21.

111. *Id.*

112. Transcript of Conference, *supra* note 80, at 26.

113. Letter from Willard Pedrick, Northwestern University Law School, to Richard H. Sullivan, College Entrance Examination Board (Dec. 5, 1947), *microformed on* ETS Archives, *supra* note 40, at Series 1, Box 1, Folder 1.

114. Letter from Richard H. Sullivan, College Entrance Examination Board, to Willard Pedrick, Northwestern University Law School (Dec. 8, 1947), *microformed on* ETS Archives, *supra* note 40, at Series 1, Box 1, Folder 1.

115. Those representing the law schools included Paul Andrews from Syracuse, George Braden from Yale, Paul Bruton from Pennsylvania, Lon Fuller from Harvard, Willard Pedrick from Northwestern, Willis Reese from Columbia, and Louis Tyree from Rutgers. Those representing ETS included Henry Chauncey, Richard H. Sullivan, William W. Turnbull, John French, Miss Mann, Mr. Schultz, and Miss Huddleston. The schools all had been represented at the November meeting, and Lon Fuller and Louis Tyree replaced Livingston Hall and Dean George Harris for the January meeting. *See* Memorandum, *Meeting to Plan Law School Admission Test* (Jan. 30, 1948), *microformed on* ETS Archives, *supra* note 40, at Series 3, Box 8, Folder 2.

116. *Id.*

117. *Id.*

118. *Id.*

119. *Id.*

120. Memorandum, *Meeting to Plan Law School Admission Test*, *supra* note 115.

121. Oral History Transcript of Willard Pedrick, *supra* note 85.

122. *Id.*

123. Oral History Transcript of Willis Reese, *supra* note 79.

124. Handwritten Note by John N. French on Memorandum from Richard H. Sullivan, to William W. Turnbull & John French (Oct. 26, 1948) (on file with LSAC Archives at Record Group 1, Series Group 1).

125. Oral History Transcript of John A. Winterbottom, in ORAL HISTORY PROJECT, *supra* note 63.

126. *Id.*

127. Oral History Transcript of Emerson Spies, *supra* note 63.

128. John Winterbottom stated:

> I have never seen any evidence in the ETS records that any of them [admissions tests already in use] was [sic] used in any sense as a model for the LSAT, or even consulted to see what

> was in them. They seem to have been out there, and we knew about them, but as far as I can tell, there was no effort to mine them or to go to the authors of them or find out what experience there had been with these things.

Oral History Transcript of John A. Winterbottom, *supra* note 125.

129. See Nicholas Lemann, *The Great Sorting*, ATLANTIC MONTHLY, Sept. 1995, at 88.

130. Oral History Transcript of William B. Schrader, *supra* note 99.

131. Memorandum from John A. Winterbottom, *The Policy Committee of the Law School Admission Test—Its Origin and Activities* (Jan. 14, 1955), *microformed on* ETS Archives, *supra* note 40, at Series 3, Box 8, Folder 11 [hereinafter Memorandum from John A. Winterbottom].

132. *Id.*

133. According to Pedrick, the professors were sure of one thing—they did not want questions involving geometric figures and arithmetic. Their first reaction was that they themselves could not cope with such questions, but the argument that impressed ETS was the assurance that candidates would rebel because such questions did not seem to have anything to do with law. Oral History Transcript of Willard Pedrick, *supra* note 85.

134. See Letter from Henry Chauncey, *supra* note 56.

135. LYNDA M. REESE & RUTH ANNE COTTER, A COMPENDIUM OF LSAT AND LSAC-SPONSORED ITEM TYPES, 1948–1994, at 3–5, Table 1 (1994).

136. *See* W.B. Schrader & Marjorie Olsen, *The Law School Admission Test as a Predictor of Law School Grades* (1950) (LSAC-50-1), in REPORTS OF LSAC SPONSORED RESEARCH: VOLUME I, 1949–1969, *microformed on* ETS Archives, *supra* note 40.

137. Memorandum, *Meeting with Law School Representatives*, (May 25, 1948), *microformed on* ETS Archives, *supra* note 40, at Series 3, Box 8, Folder 2.

138. *See id.*

139. Memorandum from A. Pemberton Johnson, LSAT Project Manager, ETS, to Members of the Law School Admission Test Policy Committee (Feb. 13, 1951), *microformed on* ETS Archives, *supra* note 40, at Series 1, Box 1, Folder 3.

140. Memorandum from John A. Winterbottom, *supra* note 131.

141. Oral History Transcript of William B. Schrader, *supra* note 99. On the other hand, the Dean at Stanford, Carl B. Spaeth, reported to Richard H. Sullivan that Stanford received approximately one thousand applications for the 1947–1948 academic year and admitted two hundred and twenty five students. Letter from Carl B. Spaeth, Dean, Stanford School of Law, to Richard H. Sullivan, College Entrance Examination Board (Dec. 22, 1947), *microformed on* ETS Archives, *supra* note 40, at Series 1, Box 1, Folder 1. In 1953, Dean Henry Brandis, Jr., of the University of North Carolina told A. Pemberton Johnson that applicants with the required three years of college and an average of "middle C" were admitted "regardless of test score," but applicants with averages barely above the minimum and low test scores were advised that they "probably will have scholastic trouble in Law School." Letter from Henry Brandis, Jr., Dean, University of North Carolina School of Law, to A. Pemberton Johnson, LSAT Project Manager, ETS (May 5, 1953), *microformed on* ETS Archives, *supra* note 40, at Series 3, Box 8, Folder 1. In 1955, Johnson reported to Dean John T. Fey of George Washington University that several schools on the West Coast had set 400 as the minimum score for admission because so many with scores below that failed in the first year. A school in the Mid-Atlantic states set a "practical minimum" score of 475. He suggested that George Washington University set a minimum of score of 450 and adjust it based on experience. Letter from A. Pemberton Johnson, LSAT Project Manager, ETS, to John T. Fey, Dean, George Washington University Law School (June 9, 1955), *microformed on* ETS Archives, *supra* note 40, at Series 1, Box 1, Folder 4.

142. Oral History Transcript of Emerson Spies, *supra* note 63.

143. Letter from George J. Thompson, Law School Representative, to A. Pemberton Johnson, LSAT Project Manager, ETS (Mar. 1, 1950), *microformed on* ETS Archives, *supra* note 40, at Series 1, Box 1, Folder 2.

144. *Id.*

145. Letter from A. Pemberton Johnson, LSAT Project Manager, ETS, to George J. Thompson, Law School Representative (Mar. 9, 1950), *microformed on* ETS Archives, *supra* note 40, at Series 1, Box 1, Folder 2.

146. Memorandum from A. Pemberton Johnson, to LSAT Policy Committee (July 30, 1954), *microformed on* ETS Archives, *supra* note 40, at Series 3, Box 8, Folder 10.

147. *Id.*

148. *Id.*

149. Oral History Transcript of Louis A. Toepfer, in ORAL HISTORY PROJECT, *supra* note 63.

150. *Id.*

151. Memorandum from John A. Winterbottom, *Comments on Agenda* (n.d.), *microformed on* ETS Archives, *supra* note 40, at Series 3, Box 8, Folder 14 [hereinafter *Comments on Agenda*].

152. *See* Minutes of the Policy Committee (June 7, 1957), *microformed on* ETS Archives, *supra* note 40, at Series 3, Box 8, Folder 14; Memorandum from John A. Winterbottom, *Meeting of Sub-Committee of Area Tests and Writing Samples* (Nov. 22, 1957), *microformed on* ETS Archives, *supra* note 40, at Series 3, Box 8, Folder 15.

153. Letter from Robert S. Pasley, to Louis A. Toepfer, Chairman, LSAT Policy Committee (Feb. 13, 1958), *microformed on* ETS Archives, *supra* note 40, at Series 3, Box 8, Folder 15.

154. Memorandum from Louis A. Toepfer, to LSAT Policy Committee (May 22, 1958), *microformed on* ETS Archives, *supra* note 40, at Series 3, Box 8, Folder 16.

155. Letter from John Bainbridge, LSAT Policy Committee, to Louis A. Toepfer, Chairman, LSAT Policy Committee (Mar. 21, 1958), *microformed on* ETS Archives, *supra* note 40, at Series 3, Box 8, Folder 15.

156. Minutes of the LSAT Policy Committee 4 (June 5, 1958), *microformed on* ETS Archives, *supra* note 40, at Series 3, Box 8, Folder 16.

157. *Id.*

158. *Id.*

159. *Id.*

160. Report of the Test Development Committee (Dec. 1959), *microformed on* ETS Archives, *supra* note 40, at Series 3, Box 9, Folder 20.

161. *Id.*

162. *Id.*

163. *Id.*

164. *Id.*

165. Minutes of the Policy Committee Meeting (June 3, 1960), *microformed on* ETS Archives, *supra* note 40, at Series 3, Box 9, Folder 20.

166. Memorandum from Paul Miller, to Members of the LSAT Test Development & Research Committee (Mar. 12, 1963), *microformed on* ETS Archives, *supra* note 40, at Series 3, Box 9, Folder 39.

167. Letter from William R. Shane, Assistant Dean, University of Pennsylvania Law School, to Louis A. Toepfer, Chairman, LSAT Policy Committee (Feb. 14, 1963), *microformed on* ETS Archives, *supra* note 40, at Series 3, Box 9, Folder 39.

168. Letter from Norman Penney, Associate Dean, Cornell Law School, to Louis A. Toepfer, Chairman, LSAT Policy Committee (Feb. 11, 1963), *microformed on* ETS Archives, *supra* note 40, at Series 3, Box 9, Folder 39.

169. Letter from A. Kenneth Pye, Associate Dean, Georgetown University Law Center, to Louis A. Toepfer, Chairman, LSAT Policy Committee (Feb. 20, 1963), *microformed on* ETS Archives, *supra* note 40, at Series 3, Box 9, Folder 39.

170. *Id.*

171. Letter from John A. Winterbottom, Program Director, ETS, to Louis A. Toepfer, Chairman, LSAT Policy Committee (Mar. 12, 1963), *microformed on* ETS Archives, *supra* note 40, at Series 3, Box 9, Folder 39.

172. *Id.*

173. *Id.*

174. Letter from Louis A. Toepfer, Chairman, LSAT Policy Committee, to John A. Winterbottom, Program Director, ETS (Mar. 19, 1963), *microformed on* ETS Archives, *supra* note 40, at Series 3, Box 9, Folder 39.

175. *Id.*

176. *Id.*

177. A recent example of this school of thought can be found in Daria Roithmayr, *Deconstructing the Distinction Between Bias and Merit*, 85 Cal. L. Rev. 1449, 1475–94 (1997).

178. *See supra* notes 149–150 and accompanying text.

179. Oral History Transcript of Louis A. Toepfer, *supra* note 149.

180. See Report of the Research Committee (Dec. 19, 1960), *microformed on* ETS Archives, *supra* note 40, at Series 3, Box 9, Folder 21.

181. *Comments on Agenda*, *supra* note 151.

182. *Id.*

183. *Id.* The schools were Columbia, Harvard, Michigan, Northwestern, Pennsylvania, Rutgers, Southern California, Stanford, the University of Washington and Washington University in St. Louis. *Id.*

184. Memorandum from D.R. Saunders, *Proposal for Use of Law School Groups for the Study of Experimental Personality Tests* (May 17, 1956), *microformed on* ETS Archives, *supra* note 40, at Series 2, Box 4, Folder 28.

185. *Id.*

186. Twenty-five thousand dollars was appropriated for research in personality, motivation, and interests during the period from mid-1954 to mid-1957. Minutes of the Policy Committee Meeting (June 9, 1954), *microformed on* ETS Archives, *supra* note 40, at Series 3, Box 8, Folder 10. Another $30,000 was appropriated in 1957 for research during the remainder of 1957 and for 1958. Minutes of the Policy Committee Meeting (June 7, 1957), *microformed on* ETS Archives, *supra* note 40, at Series 3, Box 8, Folder 14.

187. Letter from John R. Hills, Director of the Office of Testing and Guidance, The Regents of the University System of Georgia, to John A. Winterbottom, Program Director, ETS (Apr. 12, 1959), *microformed on* ETS Archives, *supra* note 40, at Series 3, Box 8, Folder 18.

188. Letter from John A. Winterbottom, Program Director, ETS, to John R. Hills, Director of the Office of Testing and Guidance, The Regents of the University System of Georgia (Apr. 17, 1959), *microformed on* ETS Archives, *supra* note 40, at Series 3, Box 8, Folder 18.

189. *Id.*

190. See Report of the Research Committee, *supra* note 180.

191. Minutes of the LSAT Policy Committee Meeting E-3 (June 2–3, 1961), *microformed on* ETS Archives, *supra* note 40, at Series 3, Box 9, Folder 27.

192. *Id.*

193. *Id.*

194. *Id.* at E-2.

195. Letter from Louis A. Toepfer, Chairman, LSAT Policy Committee, to A.W.B. Simpson, Lincoln College (Jan. 24, 1962), *microformed on* ETS Archives, *supra* note 40, at Series 3, Box 10, Folder 40.

196. *Id.*

197. *See* Minutes of the Test Development and Research Committee Meeting (Oct. 27, 1961), *microformed on* ETS Archives, *supra* note 40, at Series 3, Box 9, Folder 32; Memorandum from H.B. Reese, to the Research Committee (n.d.), *microformed on* ETS Archives, *supra* note 40, at Series 3, Box 9, Folder 22 [hereinafter Memorandum from H.B. Reese].

198. Minutes of the Test Development and Research Committee Meeting, *supra* note 197.

199. Memorandum from H.B. Reese, *supra* note 197.

200. *Id.*

201. 123 S. Ct. 2325 (2003).

202. *Id.* at 2332–33.

203. NICHOLAS LEMANN, THE BIG TEST: THE SECRET HISTORY OF THE AMERICAN MERITOCRACY 220 (1999).

204. *Id.* at 224–27.

205. *Id.* at 227.

206. The effects of "truth-in-testing" on the review business are described in LEMANN, *supra* note 203.

207. *Id.* at 228–29. For a review of the Lemann book, see William P. LaPiana, *Testing, Class, and Material Success, or How We Got to Be Professors*, H-Net Reviews in the Humanities and Social Sciences (2000), at http://www.h-net.msu.edu.proxy.lib.pdx.edu/reviews/showrev.cgi?path=1664796 6265537 (2000) (reviewing LEMANN, *supra* note 203).

208. Lemann describes in detail an important facet of the controversy, the enactment in California of Proposition 209 banning affirmative action based on race. LEMANN, *supra* note 203, at 225–336.

209. The relevant standard and its interpretations are as follows:

Standard 503. ADMISSION TEST.

> A law school shall require each applicant to take a valid and reliable admission test to assist the school in assessing the applicant's capability of satisfactorily completing the school's educational program.

Interpretation 503-1:

> A law school that uses an admission test other than the Law School Admission Test sponsored by the Law School Admission Council shall establish that such other test is a valid and reliable test to assist the school in assessing an applicant's capability to satisfactorily complete the school's educational program.

Interpretation 503-2:

> This Standard does not prescribe the particular weight that a law school should give to an applicant's admission test score in deciding whether to admit or deny admission to the applicant. Other relevant factors that may be taken into account include undergraduate course of study and grade point average, extracurricular activities, work experience, performance in other graduate or professional programs, relevant demonstrated skills, and obstacles overcome.

Interpretation 503-3:

> A pre-admission program of coursework taught by members of the law school's full-time faculty and culminating in an examination or examinations, offered to some or all applicants prior to a decision to admit to the J.D. program, also may be useful in assessing the capability of an applicant to satisfactorily complete the school's educational program, to be admitted to the bar, and to become a competent professional.

American Bar Association, *Standards for Legal Education*, *at* http:www.abanet.org/legaled/standards/chapter5.html (2003).

210. American Bar Association, *2003 Annual Questionnaire Part 2*, *at* http://www.abanet.org.proxy.lib.pdx.edu/legaled/questionnaire/questionnairefiles/enrollment.doc (2003).

211. STEPHEN P. KLEIN & LAURA HAMILTON, THE VALIDITY OF THE U.S. NEWS AND WORLD REPORT RANKING OF ABA LAW SCHOOLS, *at* http://www.aals.org.proxy.lib.pdx.edu/validity.html (1998).

212. LAW SCHOOL ADMISSION COUNCIL, NEW MODELS TO ASSURE DIVERSITY, FAIRNESS, AND APPROPRIATE TEST USE IN LAW SCHOOL ADMISSIONS 7 (1999).

213. Law School Admission Council, *Deans Speak Out*, at http://www.lsac.org/ LSAC.asp?url=lsac/deans-speak-out-rankings.asp (2003).

214. REED, PRESENT-DAY LAW SCHOOLS IN THE UNITED STATES AND CANADA, *supra* note 32, at 169.

215. The story of the transformation of one law school and the important role of the ABA and AALS is told in DAVID J. LANGUM & HOWARD P. WALTHALL, FROM MAVERICK TO MAINSTREAM: CUMBERLAND SCHOOL OF LAW, 1847–1997, at 118–42, 168–226 (1997).

216. Reed, *supra* note 32, at 398.

The LSAT Myth

Jeffrey S. Kinsler

Predicting which students will perform well in law school may seem like an impossible task, but law schools endeavor to do so every day, and the primary tool they use to make such predictions is the Law School Admission Test (LSAT), a standardized, 101-question multiple-choice examination. Over the past couple of decades, the LSAT has become "the single most important factor in the entire law school application process."[1] It is more important than the undergraduate grade point average (UGPA), the reputation of the undergraduate institution, or the rigor of the undergraduate major.[2] This article explores whether the LSAT warrants such prominence.

Using statistical and anecdotal evidence, this article analyzes recent graduates of Marquette University Law School (MULS) to ascertain whether: (1) the LSAT is a valid predictor of three-year performance in law school; (2) the LSAT is a better predictor of law school performance than the UGPA or the reputation of the applicant's undergraduate institution; (3) an applicant's undergraduate major is useful in predicting law school performance; and (4) an applicant's age at the time of entry into law school is a valid predictor of law school performance.[3]

I. Executive Summary

The statistical and anecdotal analyses of MULS's 1998 and 1999 graduating classes produced some noteworthy results. First, the LSAT was a very weak predictor of three-year law school performance at MULS; it was a valid predictor for less than 20% of students. Second, the UGPA was better at predicting law school performance than the LSAT. Third, the reputation of a student's undergraduate institution was also better at predicting law school performance than the LSAT. Fourth, a combination of the UGPA and reputation of undergraduate institution was a better predictor of law school performance than either a combination of the LSAT and UGPA or a combination of the LSAT and reputation of undergraduate institution. Fifth, there was no significant correlation between undergraduate majors and law school performance. Finally, there was no significant correlation between age and law school performance.

These findings support two hypotheses. First, law schools, like MULS, that rely heavily on LSAT scores in the admissions process are not admitting the best available students because there is little correlation between LSAT scores and law school performance. Second, if more reliance were placed on an applicant's UGPA and/or the quality of his or her undergraduate institution, law schools would attract better and brighter students.

The findings in this article should not surprise legal educators, as such findings are consistent with the evidence in the well-known case of *Grutter v. Bollinger*,[4] in which the court stated:

> One such solution would be to relax, or even eliminate, reliance on the LSAT. The evidence presented at trial indicated that the LSAT predicts law school grades rather poorly (with a correlation of only 10–20%) and that it does not predict success in the legal profession at all. If, as its admissions policy states, [the University of Michigan Law School] seeks students who "have substantial promise for success in law school" and "a strong likelihood of succeeding in the practice of law," one wonders why the law school concerns itself at all with an applicant's LSAT score.[5]

II. The LSAT's Preeminence

The LSAT's ascendency in law school admissions is attributable to at least three factors. First, the Law School Admission Council (LSAC), the entity that administers the LSAT test, proclaims that not only do "LSAT scores help to predict which students will do well in law school,"[6] but they are better at predicting law school performance than any other single factor.[7] And no one questions the LSAC. That is, until now.

Second, excessive reliance on the LSAT is "indicative of the colossal laziness" of law schools.[8] It is simply much easier to admit or reject an applicant on the basis of a three-digit number than on an extensive evaluation of an assortment of seemingly incomparable and indecipherable criteria, such as the quality of undergraduate institutions, the rigor of certain majors, or the comparability of undergraduate grade point averages at different colleges and universities.[9] Not surprisingly, therefore, the LSAT has become the primary, and, in some cases, sole factor in the admissions process of many law schools.[10]

Third, the *U.S. News & World Report* (*U.S. News*) annually ranks law schools based on various objective and subjective criteria. One such criteria is the median LSAT score, which comprises 12.5% of each school's ranking.[11] While 12.5% may seem inconsequential, it is one of the few criteria that law schools have the ability to influence or, arguably, manipulate. As a result, there is nothing law schools won't do to maintain the highest possible median LSAT scores, including, at times, automatically rejecting students with sub-par LSAT scores.[12]

III. Sample

This article analyzes the performance of the graduating classes of 1998 and 1999 of Marquette University Law School.[13] During these years, the student body of MULS was comprised of about 500 students.[14] MULS awards one degree, the Juris Doctor (JD). MULS awarded JDs to 140 students in 1998 and 143 students in 1999.[15] MULS is accredited by the American Bar Association and is a member of the Association of American Law Schools.[16] MULS is ranked in the Third Tier of the *U.S. News and World Report's* survey of U.S. law schools.[17] Considering its size and reputation, MULS is representative of many American law schools.

IV. Variables

This article analyzes the predictive validity of five factors used by law schools in the admissions process. The correlation between these variables and law school grade point averages (LGPA) is examined below using statistical and/or anecdotal evidence.

LSAT Score. The first factor analyzed in this article is the applicant's LSAT score.[18] All of the students in this study were tested under the post-1991 version of the LSAT, which has a minimum score of 120 and a maximum score of 180. The LSAT scores were reported to MULS by the Law School Data Assembly Service (LSDAS), an affiliate of the LSAC. The LSAT scores of MULS's 1998 graduating class ranged from 144 to 165. The top 25th percentile scored from 158 to 165; the bottom 25th percentile scored from 144 to 152. The LSAT scores of MULS's 1999 graduating class ranged from 145 to 167. The top 25th percentile scored from 157 to 167; the bottom 25th percentile scored from 145 to 153.

Undergraduate Grade Point Average. The UGPAs used in this study are those compiled by and reported to MULS by the LSDAS. The UGPAs of MULS's 1998 graduating class ranged from 1.88 to 3.95 on a 4.0 scale. The UGPAs of the top 25th percentile ranged from 3.46 to 3.95; the UGPAs of the bottom 25th percentile ranged from 1.88 to 2.86. The UGPAs of MULS's 1999 graduating class ranged from 2.15 to 4.0 on a 4.0 scale. The UGPAs of the top 25th percentile ranged from 3.47 to 4.0; the UGPAs of the bottom 25th percentile ranged from 2.15 to 2.90.

Reputation of Undergraduate Institution. The third factor analyzed in this article is the reputation of an applicant's undergraduate institution as measured by the *U.S. News and World Report's* most recent college and university rankings.[19] For purposes of this article, institutions grouped in the *U.S. News'* "Top 50 National Universities" and "Top 50 National Liberal Arts Colleges" are considered "Superior Undergraduate Institutions."

Undergraduate Major. The fourth factor analyzed in this article is the applicant's undergraduate major. For purposes of this article, undergraduate majors are divided into six categories: social sciences (e.g., sociology, political science, economics, history, geography, anthropology, psychology, international and foreign studies, government, pre-law); humanities (e.g., English, classical studies, foreign languages, art history, philosophy); natural sciences and math (e.g., biology, chemistry, zoology, mathematics, engineering); business (e.g., accounting, finance, management, marketing, business administration); communication (e.g., communication, journalism, speech communication); and others (e.g., physical education, nursing).

Age. The final factor analyzed in this article is the age of an applicant at the time of entry into law school. For purposes of this article, an applicant is considered "mature age" if he of she was 30 years of age or older at the time of entry into law school.

V. Predictive Validity

The ability of each of the five variables mentioned above to predict law school performance is analyzed below using statistical and/or anecdotal evidence.

A. Statistical Evidence

The LSAC regularly analyzes the correlation between first-year law school grades and LSAT scores. The LSAC uses a statistical model in which:

> correlation is stated as a coefficient for which 1.00 indicates an exact correspondence between candidates' test scores and subsequent law school performance. A coefficient of zero would indicate nothing more than a coincidental relationship between test scores and subsequent performance. The closer to 1.00 the correlation coefficient is, the greater the test's predictive validity. In other words, the closer to 1.00 the correlation coefficient is, the less chance there will be of candidates with high LSAT scores failing in their studies or candidates with low test scores performing at the top of their law school class.[20]

The LSAC's most recent study found that "[c]orrelations between LSAT scores and first-year law school grades ranged from .10 to .66," with a median of .39.[21] But is the LSAT a valid predictor of three-year performance in law school? In theory, the predictive validity of the LSAT should decline after the first year, as three-year law school performance is dependent more on work ethic and dedication (traits consistent with a high UGPA) than natural intelligence (a trait consistent with a high LSAT score). The results of this article support such a theory.

1. LSAT/LGPA Correlation

Using the same statistical model as the LSAC (i.e., where 1.0 indicates exact correlation and 0 indicates coincidence), the correlation coefficient for LSAT scores and law school grade point average ("LGPA") for MULS's 1998 graduating class was .192, a very weak correlation by any standard. Indeed, performance on the LSAT accounted for less than 4% of the variance witnessed in law school performance (i.e., an R Square of .037).

The correlation between LSAT scores and LGPA for the 1998 MULS graduating class is described more fully in the following tables:

MODEL SUMMARY

Model	R	R Square	Adjusted R Square	Std. Error of the Estimate
1	.192[a]	.037	.030	.31838

a. Predictors (Constant), LSAT

ANOVA[b]

Model	Sum of Squares	df	Mean Square	F	Sig.
1 Regression	.544	1	.544	5.364	.022[a]
Residual	14.191	140	.101		
Total	14.734	141			

a. Predictors (Constant), LSAT
b. Dependent Variable: LGPA

COEFFICIENTS[a]

Model	Understandardized Coefficients B Std. Error	Standardized Coefficients Beta	t	Sig.
1 (Constant)	.777 1.015		.766	.445
LSAT	1.516E-02 .007	.192	2.316	.022

a. Dependent Variable.: LGPA

The correlation coefficient for LSAT scores and LGPA for MULS's 1999 graduating class was *even lower* than it was for the 1998 class, namely, .179. Again, performance on the LSAT accounted for less than 4% of the variance witnessed in law school performance (*i.e.*, an R Square of .032), as described more fully in the following tables:

MODEL SUMMARY

Model	R	R Square	Adjusted R Square	Std. Error of the Estimate
1	.179[a]	.032	.025	.37587

a. Predictors (Constant), LSAT

ANOVA[b]

Model	Sum of Squares	df	Mean Square	F	Sig.
1 Regression	.663	1	.633	4.690	.032[a]
Residual	20.062	142	.141		
Total	20.724	143			

a. Predictors (Constant), LSAT
b. Dependent Variable: LGPA

COEFFICIENTS[a]

Model	Understandardized Coefficients B Std. Error	Standardized Coefficients Beta	t	Sig.
1 (Constant)	.264 1.332		.199	.843
LSAT	1.860E-02 .009	.179	2.166	.032

a. Dependent Variable.: LGPA

There are numerous studies indicating that males generally outperform females on multiple-choice examinations.[22] Thus, in theory the predictive ability of the LSAT—a multiple-choice test—may be worse for females than it is for males. No such disparity was detected, however, for MULS's recent graduates.

In 1998, the LSAT was a better predictor for females than it was for males; the correlation coefficients for LSAT scores and LGPA was .274 for females and .041 for males, with the latter figure being statistically insignificant (i.e., the figure cannot be confidentially distinguished from zero).

MODEL SUMMARY (FEMALE 1998)

Model	R	R Square	Adjusted R Square	Std. Error of the Estimate
1	.274[a]	.075	.058	.39952

a. Predictors (Constant), LSAT

ANOVA[b]

Model	Sum of Squares	df	Mean Square	F	Sig.
1 Regression	.486	1	.486	4.474	.039[a]
Residual	5.972	55	.109		
Total	6.458	56			

a. Predictors (Constant), LSAT
b. Dependent Variable: LGPA

COEFFICIENTS[a]

Model	Understandardized Coefficients B Std. Error	Standardized Coefficients Beta	t	Sig.
1 (Constant)	−.305 1.616		−.189	.851
LSAT	2.220E-02 .010	.274	2.115	.039

a. Dependent Variable.: LGPA

MODEL SUMMARY (MALE 1998)

Model	R	R Square	Adjusted R Square	Std. Error of the Estimate
1	.041[a]	.002	−.011	.30345

a. Predictors (Constant), LSAT

ANOVA[b]

Model	Sum of Squares	df	Mean Square	F	Sig.
1 Regression	1.229E-02	1	1.229E-02	.134	.716[3]
Residual	7.459	81	9.208E-02		
Total	7.471	82			

a. Predictors (Constant), LSAT
b. Dependent Variable: LGPA

COEFFICIENTS[a]

Model	Understandardized Coefficients B Std. Error	Standardized Coefficients Beta	t	Sig.
1 (Constant)	2.606 1.433		1.189	.073
LSAT	3.359E-03 .009	.041	.365	.716

a. Dependent Variable.: LGPA

By contrast, the LSAT was a better predictor for males than it was for females in 1999; the correlation coefficients for LSAT scores and LGPA was .105 for females and .227 for males.

MODEL SUMMARY (FEMALE 1999)

Model	R	R Square	Adjusted R Square	Std. Error of the Estimate
1	.205[a]	.011	–.006	.21828

a. Predictors (Constant), LSAT

ANOVA[b]

Model	Sum of Squares	df	Mean Square	F	Sig.
1 Regression	3.065E-02	1	.3.065E-02	.643	.426[a]
Residual	2.763	58	.109		
Total	2.794	59			

a. Predictors (Constant), LSAT
b. Dependent Variable: LGPA

COEFFICIENTS[a]

Model	Understandardized Coefficients B Std. Error	Standardized Coefficients Beta	t	Sig.
1 (Constant)	2.185 1.253		1.744	.087
LSAT	6.486E-03 .008	.105	.082	.426

a. Dependent Variable.: LGPA

MODEL SUMMARY (MALE 1999)

Model	R	R Square	Adjusted R Square	Std. Error of the Estimate
1	.227[a]	.051	.040	.33221

a. Predictors (Constant), LSAT

ANOVA[b]

Model	Sum of Squares	df	Mean Square	F	Sig.
1 Regression	.485	1	.485	4.395	.039[a]
Residual	8.940	81	.110		
Total	9.425	82			

a. Predictors (Constant), LSAT
b. Dependent Variable: LGPA

COEFFICIENTS[a]

Model	Understandardized Coefficients B Std. Error	Standardized Coefficients Beta	t	Sig.
1 (Constant)	-8.579E-03 1.509		-.006	.995
LSAT	2.038E-02 .010	.227	2.096	.039

a. Dependent Variable.: LGPA

2. UGPA/LGPA Correlation

The correlation between UGPA and LGPA was higher for MULS graduates than the correlation between LSAT and LGPA. In 1998, the UGPA was a much better predictor of law school performance than the LSAT; the UGPA explained three times more variance in law school performance than did the LSAT. The correlation coefficient (.349) for LSAT scores and LGPA for the 1998 MULS graduating class is described more fully in the following tables:

MODEL SUMMARY

Model	R	R Square	Adjusted R Square	Std. Error of the Estimate
1	.349[a]	.122	.116	.29615

a. Predictors (Constant), UGPA

ANOVA[b]

Model	Sum of Squares	df	Mean Square	F	Sig.
1 Regression	1.658	1	1.658	18.905	.000[a]
Residual	11.928	136	8.771E-02		
Total	13.586	137			

a. Predictors (Constant), UGPA
b. Dependent Variable: LGPA

COEFFICIENTS[a]

Model	Understandardized Coefficients B Std. Error	Standardized Coefficients Beta	t	Sig.
1 (Constant)	2.251 .201		11.182	.000
LSAT	.275 .063	.349	4.348	.000

a. Dependent Variable.: LGPA

The UGPA outperformed the LSAT as a predictor of law school performance again with respect to MULS's 1999 graduating class, as described more fully in the following tables:

MODEL SUMMARY

Model	R	R Square	Adjusted R Square	Std. Error of the Estimate
1	.267[a]	.071	.065	.36683

a. Predictors (Constant), UGPA

ANOVA[b]

Model	Sum of Squares	df	Mean Square	F	Sig.
1 Regression	1.453	1	1.453	10.799	.001[a]
Residual	18.973	141	.135		
Total	20.426	142			

a. Predictors (Constant), UGPA
b. Dependent Variable: LGPA

COEFFICIENTS[a]

Model	Understandardized Coefficients B Std. Error	Standardized Coefficients Beta	t	Sig.
1 (Constant)	2.281 .267		8.552	.000
UGPA	.276 .084	.267	3.286	.001

a. Dependent Variable.: LGPA

There was no significant variance in the correlation between UGPA and LGPA when males and females were considered separately. In 1998, the correlation coefficients for UGPA and LGPA was .436 for females and .274 for males. Conversely, the correlation coefficients for UGPA and LGPA was .299 for females and .449 for males in 1999.

3. LSAT, UGPA and LGPA Correlation

The correlation coefficient for LSAT scores and UGPA, combined, and LGPA is higher than that for LSAT scores or UGPA alone. This coefficient, however, is mostly attributable to the predictive validity of the UGPA, and not the LSAT. For example, the correlation coefficient for LSAT scores and UGPA, combined, and LGPA was approximately .40 for MULS's 1998 graduating class; however, UGPA alone had a correlation coefficient of nearly .35. The correlation between LSAT scores and UGPA, combined, and LGPA for the MULS's 1998 graduating class is described more fully in the following tables:

MODEL SUMMARY

Model	R	R Square	Adjusted R Square	Std. Error of the Estimate
1	.405[a]	.164	.151	.29008

a. Predictors (Constant), LSAT, UGPA

ANOVA[b]

Model	Sum of Squares	df	Mean Square	F	Sig.
1 Regression	2.227	2	1.113	13.230	.000[a]
Residual	11.360	135	8.415E-02		
Total	13.586	137			

a. Predictors (Constant), LSAT, UGPA
b. Dependent Variable: LGPA

COEFFICIENTS[a]

Model	Understandardized Coefficients B Std. Error	Standardized Coefficients Beta	t	Sig.
1 (Constant) UGPA LSAT	–.310 1.005 .289 .062 1.622E-02 .006	 .368 .205	–.309 4.657 2.599	.758 .000 .010

a. Dependent Variable.: LGPA

These findings held true for MULS's 1999 graduating class, as described more fully in the following tables:

MODEL SUMMARY

Model	R	R Square	Adjusted R Square	Std. Error of the Estimate
1	.326[a]	.106	.094	.36107

a. Predictors (Constant), LSAT, UGPA

ANOVA[b]

Model	Sum of Squares	df	Mean Square	F	Sig.
1 Regression	2.174	2	1.087	8.339	.000[a]
Residual	18.252	140	.130		
Total	20.426	142			

a. Predictors (Constant), LSAT, UGPA
b. Dependent Variable: LGPA

COEFFICIENTS[a]

Model	Understandardized Coefficients B Std. Error	Standardized Coefficients Beta	t	Sig.
1 (Constant)	-.789		-.593	.554
UGPA	1.332	.279	3.489	.001
LSAT	.289	.188	2.352	.020
	.083			
	1.953E-02			
	.008			

a. Dependent Variable.: LGPA

4. Summary of Statistical Findings

The statistical analyses of MULS's 1998 and 1999 graduating classes produced two notable findings. First, the LSAT was a very weak predictor of three-year law school performance; the LSAT accounted for less than 4% of the variance witnessed in law school performance. Second, the UGPA was a better predictor of three-year law school performance than the LSAT. These statistical findings are reinforced by anecdotal evidence in the next section.

B. Anecdotal Evidence[23]

Statistical analyses are fine and probably provide as much accuracy as possible under the circumstances. But the average applicant wants to know—in "English"—how he or she can expect to do in law school. The reason for such inquiry is obvious.

A legal education is an investment, and, like any investment, should be based, at least in part, on sound economic projections.[24] Before commencing a legal education, applicants should perform a cost-benefit analysis to determine whether law school is a wise investment. This analysis is particularly important for the ever-increasing number of mature age applicants, many of whom have established careers prior to entering law school.

Two factors comprise the cost-benefit analysis of a legal education. The first is the cost of a legal education, a factor easy to calculate once an applicant chooses a particular law school. Most law schools accurately estimate law school expenses in their application materials. The cost of a three-year legal education, including tuition, housing, food, books and supplies, may exceed $125,000.[25] For many students, a large portion of this amount will be financed at rates ranging from 8.25% to 9.5% for periods of up to twenty years.[26] As a consequence, some students leave law school with long-term debt exceeding $200,000.[27]

The second factor is the salary an applicant may expect upon graduation. Unlike the cost of law school, this factor is less predictable. While the starting salaries at major law firms exceed $130,000, the median starting salary for the graduating class of 1998 was $45,000.[28] If an applicant had reasonable assurance that he or she could secure a position in a major law firm upon graduation, law school may be a sound investment. Positions in major law firms, however, are generally reserved for those students who graduate at or near the top of their law school classes.

Applicants currently have access to the 25th and 75th LSAT and UGPA percentiles for each law school.[29] In order to make a sound cost-benefit analysis, however, applicants need to be able to predict—by comparing their LSAT scores and UGPAs with the LSAT and UGPA percentiles of various law schools—their chances of graduating in the top 25% of their law school class. Only then can a realistic cost-benefit analysis be conducted. This article endeavors to take some of the guess-work out of the application process by providing applicants with statistical and anecdotal evidence for use in projecting law school success.

For the following anecdotal analyses, the term "strong performance" is used to connote academic success in law school. Strong performance is defined as the top 25% of each graduating class. In 1998, thirty-five students graduated in the top 25% of their law school class; students in this group graduated from MULS with grade point averages exceeding 3.382 on a 4.0 system. In 1999, thirty-six students graduated in the top 25% of their law school class; students in this group graduated from MULS with grade point averages exceeding 3.338.

The top 25% was chosen because of the numerous benefits and advantages conferred upon this group (or at least parts thereof). The top 25% is often the cut-off used by major law firms to screen applicants. It is also used by many law schools to determine academic scholarships, law review membership, and clinical, extern and moot court opportunities. Many judges also use this figure to screen judicial clerkship applicants. Strong performance in law school can open many doors and lead to a successful, lucrative career.

By contrast, the term "weak performance" is used to connote a lack of academic success in law school. Weak performance is defined as the bottom 25% of each graduating class. In 1998, thirty-five students graduated in the bottom 25% of their law school class; students in this group graduated from MULS with grade point averages below 2.891. In 1999, thirty-five students graduated in the bottom 25% of their law school class; students in this group graduated from MULS with grade point averages below 2.965.

[Predictive Ability Chart 1] summarizes the predictive ability of the LSAT, UGPA and reputation of undergraduate institutions based on anecdotal evidence derived from MULS's 1998 and 1999 graduating classes. On this chart, 100% represents a perfect predictor and 25% represents random chance. The following charts are explained in more detail in Sections 1–3, *infra*.

[Predictive Ability Chart 2] summarizes the predictive validity of various combinations of the LSAT, UGPA, and reputation of undergraduate institution based on anecdotal evidence derived from MULS's 1998 and 1999 graduating classes.

1. Law School Admission Test

The LSAT scores of MULS's 1998 graduating class ranged from 144 to 165. The top 25th percentile scored from 158 to 165. Thirty-eight students in the 1998 graduating class scored in the top 25th percentile (158 and above) on the LSAT.[30] If the LSAT were a perfect

PREDICTIVE ABILITY CHART 1

	Prediction Rate of Strong Performance 1998	Prediction Rate of Weak Performance 1998	Prediction Rate of Strong Performance 1999	Prediction Rate of Weak Performance 1999	Average Rate of Prediction
LSAT SCORE	28.9%	35.3%	32.5%	21.6%	29.6%
UGPA	34.2%	48.6%	41.7%	37.1%	40.4%
SUPERIOR UNDERGRAD. INSTITUTION	44.7%	n/a	30.8%	n/a	37.8%

PREDICTIVE ABILITY CHART 2

	Prediction Rate of Strong Performance 1998	Prediction Rate of Weak Performance 1998	Prediction Rate of Strong Performance 1999	Prediction Rate of Weak Performance 1999	Average Rate of Prediction
LSAT AND UGPA	28.6%	77.8%	42.9%	42.9%	44.7%
LSAT AND SUPERIOR UNDERGRAD.	42.9%	n/a	41.7%	n/a	42.3%
UGPA AND SUPERIOR UNDERGRAD.	80%	n/a	50%	n/a	65%

predictor of strong performance, the thirty-five students who graduated in the top 25% of the 1998 class could all be expected to come from these thirty-eight. If the LSAT were no better at predicting performance than random chance, 9.5 (or 25%) of these students could be expected to graduate in the top 25% of the 1998 class. As it turns out, only eleven of the thirty-eight students from the top 25th LSAT percentile graduated in the top 25% of the 1998 class. This is a prediction rate of 28.9%, just slightly better than random chance. Even more disturbing is the fact that eight students in the top 25th LSAT percentile graduated in the bottom 25% of the 1998 class. This means 21.1%—nearly a quarter—of the top 25th LSAT percentile graduated in the bottom 25% of the 1998 class.

The bottom 25th percentile of the 1998 graduating class scored from 144 to 152 on the LSAT. There were thirty-four students in this group. If the LSAT were a perfect predictor of weak performance, all thirty-four students in this group could have been expected to graduate in the bottom 25% of the 1998 class. If the LSAT were no better at predicting performance than random chance, 8.5 (or 25%) of these students could have been expected to graduate in the bottom 25% of the 1998 class. As it turns out, twelve of the thirty-four students from the bottom 25th LSAT percentile graduated in the bottom 25% of the 1998 class. This is a prediction rate of 35.2%. By contrast, eight students in the bottom 25th LSAT percentile graduated in the top 25% of the 1998 class. This means that 23.5%—nearly a quarter—of the bottom 25th LSAT percentile graduated in the top 25% of the 1998 class.

The LSAT scores of MULS's 1999 graduating class ranged from 145 to 167. The top 25th percentile scored from 157 to 167. Forty students in the 1999 graduating class scored in the top 25th percentile (157 and above) on the LSAT. If the LSAT were a perfect predictor of strong performance, the thirty-six students who graduated in the top 25% of the 1999 class could all be expected to come from these forty. If the LSAT were no better at predicting performance than random chance, ten (or 25%) of these students could have been expected to graduate in the top 25% of the 1999 class. As it turns out, only thirteen of the forty students from the top 25th LSAT percentile graduated in the top 25% of the 1999 class. This is a prediction rate of 32.5%. By contrast, seven students in the top 25th LSAT percentile graduated in the bottom 25% of the 1999 class. This means that 17.5% of the top 25th LSAT percentile graduated in the bottom 25% of the 1999 class.

The bottom 25th percentile of the 1999 graduating class scored from 145 to 153. There were fifty-one students in this group. If the LSAT were a perfect predictor of weak performance, all thirty-five students who graduated in the bottom 25% of the 1999 class could have been expected to come from this group. If the LSAT were no better at predicting performance than random chance, 12.75 (or 25%) of these students could have been expected to graduate in the bottom 25% of the 1999 class. As it turns out, only eleven of the thirty-one students from the bottom 25th LSAT percentile graduated in the bottom 25% of the 1999 class. This is a prediction rate of 21.6%, a percentage below random chance. By contrast, eleven students in the bottom 25th LSAT percentile graduated in the top 25% of the 1999 class. This means that 23.5% of the bottom 25th LSAT percentile—nearly a quarter of the total and more than the number who graduated in the bottom 25% of the 1999 class—graduated in the top 25% of the 1999 class.

In sum, the LSAT prediction rates ranged from a high of 35.3% to a low of 21.6% on a scale in which 100% represents perfect prediction and 25% represents random chance. The average prediction rate of the LSAT for the graduating classes of 1998 and 1999 was 29.6%, a figure just slightly above random chance. And, contrary to a common misconception in the industry, the LSAT was a slightly better predictor of strong performance (30.7%) than weak performance (28.5%).[31] These results are consistent with the statistical analyses in the preceding section of this article.

2. Undergraduate Grade Point Average

The UGPAs of MULS's 1998 graduating class ranged from 1.88 to 3.95 on a 4.00 scale. The UGPAs of the top 25th percentile ranged from 3.46 to 3.95. Thirty-five students in the 1998 graduating class had UGPAs in the top 25th percentile (3.46 and above). If the UGPA were a perfect predictor of strong performance, all of the students who graduated in the top 25% of the 1998 class could all be expected to come from these thirty-five. If the UGPA were no better at predicting performance than random chance, 8.75 (or 25%) of these students could be expected to graduate in the top 25% of the 1998 class. As it turns out, twelve of the thirty-six students from the top 25th UGPA percentile graduated in the top 25% of the 1998 class. This is a prediction rate of 34.2%. By contrast, only five (14.3%) students in the top 25th UGPA percentile graduated in the bottom 25% of the 1998 class.

The UGPAs of the bottom 25th percentile of the 1998 class ranged from 1.88 to 2.86. There were thirty-five students in this group. If the UGPA were a perfect predictor of weak performance, all thirty-five students in this group could have been expected to graduate in the bottom 25% of the 1998 class. If the UGPA were no better at predicting performance than random chance, 8.5 (or 25%) of these students could have been expected to graduate in the bottom 25% of the 1998 class. As it turns out, seventeen of the thirty-five students from the bottom 25th UGPA percentile graduated in the bottom 25% of the 1998 class. This is a prediction rate of 48.6%. By contrast, only four students (11.4%) in the bottom 25th UGPA percentile graduated in the top 25% of the 1998 class.

The UGPAs of MULS's 1999 graduating class ranged from 2.15 to 4.00 on a 4.00 scale. The UGPAs of the top 25th percentile ranged from 3.47 to 4.00. Thirty-six students in the 1999 graduating class had UGPAs in the top 25th percentile (3.47 and above). If the UGPA were a perfect predictor of strong performance, all of the students who graduated in the top 25% of the 1999 class could be expected to come from these thirty-six. If the UGPA were no better at predicting performance than random chance, nine (or 25%) of these students could be expected to graduate in the top 25% of the 1999 class. As it turns out, fifteen of the thirty-six students from the top 25th UGPA percentile graduated in the top 25% of the 1999 class. This is a prediction rate of 41.7%. By contrast, only four (11.1%) students in the top 25th UGPA percentile graduated in the bottom 25% of the 1999 class.

The UGPAs of the bottom 25th percentile of the 1999 graduating class ranged from 2.15 to 2.90. There were thirty-five students in this group. If the UGPA were a perfect predictor of weak performance, all thirty-five students in this group could have been expected to graduate in the bottom 25% of the 1999 class. If the UGPA were no better at predicting performance than random chance, 8.75 (or 25%) of these students could have been expected to graduate in the bottom 25% of the 1999 class. As it turns out, thirteen of the thirty-five students from the bottom 25th UGPA percentile graduated in the bottom 25% of the 1999 class. This is a prediction rate of 37.1%. By contrast, only seven students (20%) in the bottom 25th UGPA percentile graduated in the top 25% of the 1999 class.

In sum, the UGPA prediction rates ranged from a high of 48.6% to a low of 34.2% on a scale in which 100% represents perfect prediction and 25% represents random chance. The average prediction rate of the UGPA for the graduating classes of 1998 and 1999 was 40.4%, a figure significantly higher than the LSAT prediction rate.

3. Quality of Undergraduate Institution

Thirty-six students from MULS's 1998 graduating class graduated from "Superior Undergraduate Institutions," which, for the purposes of this article, is defined as institutions listed in the *U.S. News'* "Top 50 National Universities" and "Top 50 National Liberal Arts Colleges." If attending a Superior Undergraduate Institution were a perfect predictor of strong performance, all of the students who graduated in the top 25% of the 1998 class could have been expected to come from these thirty-six. If attending a Superior Undergraduate Institution were no better at predicting performance than random chance, nine (or 25%) of these students could have been expected to graduate in the top 25% of the 1998 class. As it turns out, sixteen of the thirty-six students who graduated from Superior Undergraduate Institutions graduated in the top 25% of MULS's 1998 class. This is a prediction rate of 44.4%. By contrast, only six (16.7%) students who graduated from Superior Undergraduate Institutions graduated in the bottom 25% of MULS's 1998 class.

Thirty-nine students from MULS's 1999 graduating class graduated from Superior Undergraduate Institutions. If attending a Superior Undergraduate Institution were a perfect predictor of strong performance, all of the students who graduated in the top 25% of the 1999 class could have been expected to come from these thirty-nine. If attending a Superior Undergraduate Institution were no better at predicting performance than random chance, 9.75 (or 25%) of these students could have been expected to graduate in the top 25% of the 1999 class. As it turns out, twelve of the thirty-nine students who graduated from Superior Undergraduate Institutions graduated in the top 25% of MULS's 1999 class. This is a prediction rate of 30.8%. By contrast, only five (12.8%) students who graduated from Superior Undergraduate Institutions graduated in the bottom 25% of MULS's 1999 class.

In sum, the prediction rates for students who graduated from Superior Undergraduate Institutions ranged from a high of 44.4% to a low of 30.8% on a scale in which 100% represents perfect prediction and 25% represents random chance. The average prediction rate of the UGPA for the graduating classes of 1998 and 1999 was 37.8%, a figure significantly higher than the LSAT prediction rate.

4. Law School Admission Test and Undergraduate Grade Point Average

Seven students from 1998 graduating class scored in MULS's top 25th LSAT percentile and had UGPAs in MULS's top 25th percentile. Of these seven, only two graduated in the top 25% of MULS's 1998 graduation class. This is a rate of 28.6%, which is far lower than the prediction rate of UGPAs alone. Of the seven students who scored in MULS's top 25th LSAT percentile and had UGPAs in MULS's top 25th percentile, one (14.3%) graduated in the bottom 25% of MULS's 1998 graduation class.

Nine students from 1998 graduating class scored in MULS's bottom 25th LSAT percentile and had UGPAs in MULS's bottom 25th percentile. Of these nine, seven (77.8%) graduated in the bottom 25% of MULS's 1998 graduation class and none graduated in the top 25% of MULS's 1998 graduating class.

Seven students from 1999 graduating class scored in MULS's top 25th LSAT percentile and had UGPAs in MULS's top 25th percentile. Of these seven, only three graduated in the top 25% of MULS's 1999 graduation class. This is a rate of 42.9%, which is nearly identical to the prediction rate of UGPAs alone. Of the seven students who scored in MULS's top 25th LSAT percentile and had UGPAs in MULS's top 25th percentile, one (14.3%) graduated in the bottom 25% of MULS's 1999 graduation class.

Seven students from 1999 graduating class scored in MULS's bottom 25th LSAT percentile and had UGPAs in MULS's bottom 25th percentile. Of these seven, three (42.9%) graduated in the bottom 25% of MULS's 1999 graduation class and none graduated in the top 25% of MULS's 1998 graduating class.

In sum, the prediction rates of the LSAT and UGPA, combined, ranged from a high of 77.8% to a low of 28.6% on a scale in which 100% represents perfect prediction and 25% represents random chance. The prediction rates of these combined factors for strong performance was quite similar to the prediction rate of the UGPA alone. The prediction rates of these factors for weak performance, however, was higher than that of either the LSAT or UGPA alone.

5. Law School Admission Test and Quality of Undergraduate Institution

Seven students from 1998 graduating class scored in MULS's top 25th LSAT percentile and graduated from Superior Undergraduate Institutions. Of these seven, three graduated in the top 25% of MULS's 1998 graduation class. This is a rate of 42.9%, which is lower than the prediction rate of Superior Undergraduate Institutions alone. Of the seven students who scored in MULS's top 25th LSAT percentile and graduated from Superior Undergraduate Institutions, one (14.3%) graduated in the bottom 25% of MULS's 1998 graduation class.

Twelve students from 1999 graduating class scored in MULS's top 25th LSAT percentile and graduated from Superior Undergraduate Institutions. Of these twelve, five graduated in the top 25% of MULS's 1999 graduation class. This is a rate of 41.7%. Of the twelve students who scored in MULS's top 25th LSAT percentile and graduated from Superior Undergraduate Institutions, one (8.3%) graduated in the bottom 25% of MULS's 1999 graduation class.

In sum, the prediction rates of the LSAT and Superior Undergraduate Institutions ranged from a high of 42.9% to a low of 41.7% on a scale in which 100% represents perfect prediction and 25% represents random chance. The average prediction rate of these factors was 42.3%, which is significantly higher than the LSAT prediction rate and similar to the UGPA and Superior Undergraduate Institution rates.

6. Undergraduate Grade Point Average and Quality of Undergraduate Institution

Five students from 1998 graduating class scored in MULS's top 25th UGPA percentile and graduated from Superior Undergraduate Institutions. Of these five, four graduated in the top 25% of MULS's 1998 graduation class. This is a rate of 80%. Of the five students who scored in MULS's top 25th UGPA percentile and graduated from Superior Undergraduate Institutions, none graduated in the bottom 25% of MULS's 1998 graduation class.

Four students from 1999 graduating class scored in MULS's top 25th UGPA percentile and graduated from Superior Undergraduate Institutions. Of these four, two graduated in the top 25% of MULS's 1999 graduation class. This is a rate of 50%. Of the four students who scored in MULS's top 25th UGPA percentile and graduated from Superior Undergraduate Institutions, none graduated in the bottom 25% of MULS's 1999 graduation class.

In sum, the prediction rates of the UGPA and Superior Undergraduate Institutions ranged from a high of 80% to a low of 50% on a scale in which 100% represents perfect prediction and 25% represents random chance. The average prediction rate of these factors was 65%, which is significantly higher than the prediction rate of either (a) the LSAT and UGPA combined or (b) the LSAT and Superior Undergraduate Institutions combined.[32]

7. Undergraduate Major

There is a belief among some admissions officials that students from the so-called rigorous undergraduate disciplines, such as natural sciences, math and engineering, are generally smarter and, therefore, make better law students.[33] But is this true?

For purposes of this article, undergraduate majors are divided into six categories: social sciences (e.g., sociology, political science, economics, history, geography, anthropology, psychology, international and foreign studies, government, pre-law); humanities (e.g., English, classical studies, foreign languages, art history, philosophy); natural sciences and math (e.g., biology, chemistry, zoology, mathematics, engineering); business (e.g., accounting, finance, management, marketing, business administration); communication (e.g., communication, journalism, speech communication); and others (e.g., physical education, nursing).

The prediction rates of undergraduate majors for the graduating class of 1998 are set forth in the following chart:

1998 GRADUATING CLASS

Major	Representation in Graduating Class	Representation in Top 25% of Graduating Class	Representation in Bottom 25% of Graduating Class
Social Sciences	62.1%	62.9%	54.3%
Humanities	11.4%	14.3%	14.3%
Business	12.9%	17.1%	8.6%
Natural Sciences and Math	6.4%	5.7%	8.6%
Communications	5.7%	0%	11.4%
Others	1.4%	0%	2.9%

The prediction rates of undergraduate majors for the graduating class of 1999 are set forth in the following chart:

1999 GRADUATING CLASS

Major	Representation in Graduating Class	Representation in Top 25% of Graduating Class	Representation in Bottom 25% of Graduating Class
Social Sciences	52.4%	47.2%	65.7%
Humanities	9.8%	11.1%	11.4%
Business	19.6%	19.4%	14.2%
Natural Sciences and Math	11.2%	16.7%	2.9%
Communications	4.9%	5.6%	2.9%
Others	2.1%	0%	2.9%

These results seem to indicate that there was no significant correlation between majors and either strong or weak performance in law school. The only notable variance was the underperformance in 1998 by students with social science majors. This discrepancy, however, was not repeated in 1999.

8. Age of Student

There is a presumption among admissions officials that older students perform better in law school. This belief is based on the fact that older students are generally more mature and have significantly more life experience than the typical 23-year-old college graduate.

For purposes of this article, an applicant is considered "mature age" if he or she was 30 years of age or older at the time of entry into law school. The prediction rates of mature age students for the 1998 graduating classes are set forth in the following chart:

1998 GRADUATING CLASS—MATURE-AGE STUDENTS

Total Mature-Age Students	Mature Age Students in Top 25% of Graduating Class	Mature Age Students in Bottom 25% of Graduating Class
15.7%	11.4%	17.1%

The prediction rates of mature age students for the 1999 graduating classes are set forth in the following chart:

1999 GRADUATING CLASS—MATURE-AGE STUDENTS

Total Mature-Age Students	Mature Age Students in Top 25% of Graduating Class	Mature Age Students in Bottom 25% of Graduating Class
16.1%	16.7%	14.3%

The results of this analysis seem to indicate that there is little or no correlation between age and performance in law school.

VI. Conclusion

Using statistical and anecdotal evidence, this article analyzed recent graduates of MULS to ascertain whether: (1) the LSAT is a valid predictor of three-year performance in law school; (2) the LSAT is a better predictor of law school performance than the UGPA or the reputation of the applicant's undergraduate institution; (3) an applicant's undergraduate major is useful in predicting law school performance; and (4) an applicant's age at the time of entry into law school is a valid predictor of law school performance.

The statistical and anecdotal analyses of MULS's 1998 and 1999 graduating classes produced the following results. First, the LSAT was a very weak predictor of three-year law school performance; it was a valid predictor in fewer than two out of ten cases. Second, the UGPA was better at predicting law school performance than the LSAT. Third, the reputation of a student's undergraduate institution was also better at predicting law school performance than the LSAT. Fourth, a combination of the UGPA and reputation of undergraduate institution is a better predictor of law school performance than either a combination of the LSAT and UGPA or a combination of the LSAT and reputation of undergraduate institution. Fifth, there was no significant correlation between undergraduate majors and law school performance. Finally, there was no significant correlation between age and law school performance.

Notes

1. IAN VAN TUYL ET AL., THE BEST LAW SCHOOLS 31 (2000 ed.).

2. *Id.*

3. THE OFFICIAL GUIDE TO U.S. LAW SCHOOL 7 (2001 ed.). Other qualitative factors considered by law schools are the applicant's improvement in grades and graduate work. These factors are not considered in this article.

4. No. 97-CV-75928-DT, 2001 WL 293196 (E.D. Mich. March 27, 2001), at *1.

5. *Id.* at 43.

6. LSAT & LSDAS REGISTRATION & INFORMATION BOOK 121 (2000–2001 ed.).

7. Edward G. Haggerty (Media Relations Specialist for the LSAC), *LSAT: Uses and Misuses*, 70 N.Y. ST. BAR. J. 45 (Jun. 1998).

8. VAN TUYL, *supra* note 1, at 31.

9. Recently, the LSAC has acknowledged the "historic overreliance on the LSAT." Jess Bravin, *Law School Admission Council Aims to Quash Overreliance on LSAT*, THE WALL STREET J., Mar. 29, 2001, at B1.

10. At Marquette University Law School, the LSAT constitutes 65% of an applicant's Index Score. The applicant's undergraduate grade point average comprises the remaining 35%. The Index Score is often the sole factor in determining whether an applicant is admitted into law school.

11. *News You Can Use: Best Graduate Schools*, U.S. NEWS & WORLD REPORT, Apr. 10, 2000, at 74.

12. MULS exemplifies this point. Like most law schools, MULS has a rolling admissions process. At some point in the late spring or summer, MULS establishes a median LSAT goal. For students who apply after that point, the LSAT often serves as a 100% threshold. Those at or above the median LSAT goal are considered for admission; those below are not.

13. May, August and December graduates are included in the pool.

14. MULS commenced a part-time program in 1997. The analyses in this article do not include any students from this program, as none graduated before 2000.

15. Because the pool is comprised exclusively of graduates, it does not include MULS students who (a) transferred to other law schools, (b) withdrew voluntarily, or (c) were dismissed for academic reasons. These three groups would not consist of many students, considering that MULS's annual attrition rate is typically about 3%. And a significant portion of this 3% occurs before the end of the first year.

16. *See ABA Approved Law Schools, at* http://www.abanet.org/legaled/approvedlawschools/alpha.html (last visited May 25, 2001).

17. *News You Can Use: Best Graduate Schools*, U.S. NEWS & WORLD REP., Apr. 10, 2000, at 77.

18. MULS generally considers the applicant's highest LSAT score in the admissions process. VAN TUYL, *supra* note 1, at 22 (listing the law schools that use the highest LSAT score).

19. *News You Can Use: America's Best Colleges*, U.S. NEWS & WORLD REP., Sep. 11, 2000, at 104–30. These rankings are by no means fool-proof, but they are nonetheless heavily relied upon in the admissions process.

20. LSAT & LSDAS REGISTRATION & INFORMATION BOOK 121 (2000–2001 ed.).

21. *Id.* The LSAC recently commissioned a study of three-year performance in which it concluded that the correlation between LSAT scores and three-year law school performance was similar to the correlation between LSAT scores and first-year performance. LINDA F. WIGHTMAN, BEYOND FYA: ANALYSIS OF THE UTILITY OF LSAT SCORES AND UGPA FOR PREDICTING ACADEMIC SUCCESS IN LAW SCHOOL 16 (LSAC Research Council Aug. 2000). This study, however, did not analyze individual law schools.

22. See, e.g., Beth Dawson, et al., *Performance on the National Board of Medical Examiners Part 1 Examination by Men & Women of Different Race and Ethnicity*, J. AM. MED. ASS'N 674 (Sep. 7, 1994).

23. The prediction rates contained in this section are not based on generally accepted statistical models and, therefore, may not be as accurate as the statistical evidence in the preceding section.

24. There are, of course, non-economic reasons for attending (or not attending) law school. The importance of these factors varies widely among candidates and, in any event, are beyond the scope of this article.

25. LAW SCHOOL ADMISSION COUNCIL, *supra* note 3, at 31. This figure excludes opportunity costs.

26. The rates and terms quoted are those in effect for students entering law school in the Fall Semester, 2000.

27. This figure includes principal and interest for the maximum terms of the loans.

28. LAW SCHOOL ADMISSION COUNCIL, *supra* note 3, at 35.

29. *News You Can Use: Best Graduate Schools*, U.S. NEWS & WORLD REP., Apr. 10, 2000, at 73–77.

30. In some instances, the number of students in the LSAT percentiles is greater or less than the number of students in the corresponding law school graduation percentiles. This is due to ties in LSAT scores.

31. These percentages, of course, do not include students who failed to complete law school at MULS.

32. It was not possible to test the predictive validity of all three factors combined because there were no students in either the 1998 or 1999 graduating class who (a) scored in MULS's top 25th LSAT percentile, (b) had a UGPA in MULS's top 25th percentile, and (c) attended a Superior Undergraduate Institution.

33. Conversely, some applicants with degrees in natural sciences and math "think that they cannot or should not apply to law school because they lack a liberal arts degree." PETERSON'S LAW SCHOOLS 4 (2000 ed.).

Predicting Law School Academic Performance from LSAT Scores and Undergraduate Grade Point Averages: A Comprehensive Study

*David A. Thomas**

I. Introduction

According to the Law School Admission Council (LSAC), the entity that administers the Law School Admission Test (LSAT), the LSAT helps "predict which students will do well in law school."[1] LSAC rests this assertion on a series of validity studies "that examine the relationship between students' LSAT scores and their first-year grades in law school."[2] The "vast majority" of law schools participate in these studies.[3] Despite the unverified assumption that first-year law school grades are representative of "law school performance,"[4] and continuing criticism of the LSAT on other grounds,[5] the LSAT, according to one writer, "has become the primary, and, in some cases, sole factor in the admissions process of many law schools."[6] All of the more than 175 law schools participating in the latest *U.S. News & World Report* survey of law schools report the LSAT data they used in their admissions processes.[7] That magazine accords LSAT scores a weight of 12.5% in calculating each law school's ranking,[8] which may lead some law schools to exaggerate its importance in admission criteria.[9]

The LSAC cautions law schools against using LSAT scores as the primary admissions criterion: "[A] combination of students' scores and undergraduate grade-point averages (GPAs) gives a better prediction than either the LSAT or the GPA alone [apparently in reference to first-year law school performance]."[10] Nevertheless, the LSAC maintains "[t]he LSAT is a strong predictor of first year law school grades and compares very favorably with admission tests used in other graduate and professional fields of study."[11] The LSAC has also sponsored limited studies of how effectively LSAT and GPA can predict overall law school academic performance, concluding that predictive values change little from first-year to cumulative law school academic performance.[12]

"The LSAT is designed to measure skills that are considered essential for success in law school,"[13] and by general imputation, for success in the legal profession. These skills are "the reading and comprehension of complex texts with accuracy and insight; the organization and management of information and the ability to draw reasonable inferences from it; the ability to think critically; and the analysis and evaluation of the reasoning and arguments of others."[14] If LSAC has competently designed the LSAT, then how well the test predicts law school performance necessarily depends in part on how well each law school's faculty (1) teaches and measures learning of these skills in its own program, and (2) accurately expresses the success of its efforts in its grading system. That law schools vary greatly in achievement of these tasks is self-evident.

Statistically, the LSAC expresses the correlation between LSAT scores and first-year law school grades as a "coefficient for which 1.00 indicates an exact positive correspondence."[15] For the year 2001, the most recent available data, the median LSAT correlation coefficient at the 181 participating law schools was .41 (with individual law schools' coefficients ranging from .09 to .58).[16] The coefficient for LSAT and GPA combined was .49 (ranging from .28 to .66).[17] LSAC measures but does not report the coefficient for GPA alone.[18] This is unfortunate, because such a report could better reveal whether GPA or LSAT is better able to predict academic success in law school.

This official LSAC explanatory background for the LSAT's predictive power relative to law school academic performance raises several questions:

1. How important is it to predict first-year law school performance rather than overall law school performance (that is, first-year academic standing rather than academic standing upon graduation from law school)?
2. Is first-year law school academic performance a reasonably reliable predictor of overall law school academic performance?
3. Does the predictive power of (1) the LSAT or (2) GPA or (3) LSAT and GPA combined vary significantly from students' first-year law school academic performance compared with their overall law school academic performance?
4. Is the predictive power of either LSAT or GPA unacceptably low relative to the importance assigned to these factors in the admission processes at U.S. law schools?
5. If predictive values for the LSAT are low compared with predictive values of other measurements, can explanations be identified and improvements be incorporated into the LSAT design? In other words, if the LSAT predictive power is relatively low, is it possible that the skills for which the LSAT was designed are no longer so prevalently or effectively taught in U.S. law schools?

The study reported in this article is partially intended to identify the LSAT predictive value for overall law school academic performance compared with first-year law school academic performance. The study will also identify and compare GPA predictive value in both settings. Finally, the study will identify and compare, in both settings, the predictive value of the GPA/LSAT combination used at the author's own law school, a combination usually referred to by the LSAC as the "index," and which is customized to each law school's admission patterns.

Based on an analysis of twenty-seven years of admissions and academic records from Brigham Young University's J. Reuben Clark Law School, all of it fortunately available in digital form, the author will document the following conclusions:

1. The predictive power of the LSAT score, undergraduate GPA and a combination of those two measures in an "index" is about the same, both for first-year and for overall academic performance.
2. Although the differences may be small or statistically insignificant, the LSAT score is a better predictor than GPA of first-year law school performance, and GPA is a better predictor of overall law school performance. An index with a combination of LSAT score and GPA is substantially better than either LSAT score or GPA alone in predicting both first-year and overall law school performance.

3. The predictive power of any of these measures is not strong, and only the most general patterns may be discerned. Entering law students should not feel that their future academic success is either unduly limited or assured by the quality of their academic credentials.

Section II of this article describes the informational resources available for carrying out this study. Section III describes the methodology used, and Section IV displays the data generated by that methodology. In Section V the author analyzes the data for what they reveal about the power of LSAT and GPA credentials to predict law school academic performance, and Section VI contains a conclusion and summary.

II. Resources

Brigham Young University's J. Reuben Clark Law School (BYU) is relatively young, having commenced classes in August 1973.[19] Fortunately, the beginnings of office automation were available at that time, and all BYU law student admissions and academic records data have been stored electronically since that time. The student population has remained level at about 150 members of each entering class.[20] In its admission practices BYU has consistently sought students with both strong LSAT and strong GPA credentials.[21]

For this study, each student in each entering class was identified by an identification number, LSAT score, undergraduate GPA, and—for LSAT, GPA and index (combination of LSAT and GPA)—was assigned a ranking relative to other members of that class. As an example, suppose Student No. 1234 entered with an LSAT of 162, which ranked 75th of the 150 members in that class. Perhaps that same student also had a 3.85 undergraduate GPA, which ranked 25th in the class of 150. That student's index of 235[22] perhaps ranked 23rd in the class of 150. Next, for that same class, using the same student identification numbers, the students were ranked according to their academic class standing after the first year of law school and at graduation. As explained more fully in the next section on methodology, it was then possible to compare the three numerical rankings upon entry with each of the two academic rankings. This produced a set of six rankings for each student in each of the twenty-seven classes of BYU law students that have graduated since the founding of the law school. Again, as explained more fully in the next section, a way was devised to express the disparity, if any, between the numerical rankings upon entry into law school, and the academic performance rankings at the end of the first and third years of law school. These disparities then enable analysis and comparative evaluations of the absolute and relative power of the various credentials upon entry to predict academic performance in law school.

This information is summarized here in this resources section, because, with all pertinent BYU data in electronic form, the computer—when properly programmed—can conduct all of these calculations for all twenty-seven classes of law students, thus making the database and computer power an important resource indeed.

III. Methodology

The retrieval, sorting and arranging of data described in the preceding section is one part of the methodology, but not the most important part for this study. As described above, for each class of law students, six lists were created in which students are ranked according to LSAT, GPA and index, and compared with their respective class standings at the end of their first and third years of law school. So each list shows not only the students' ranking according to the indicated category (LSAT, GPA or index), but also compares that ranking to academic performance. The six lists are:

1. LSAT ranking[23] compared with first year class ranking
2. Undergraduate GPA ranking compared with first year class ranking
3. Index ranking compared with first year class ranking
4. LSAT ranking compared with class ranking upon graduation
5. Undergraduate GPA ranking compared with class ranking upon graduation
6. Index ranking compared with class ranking upon graduation.

The critical element of methodology in compiling these lists was to find a way of calculating and expressing how closely correlated the rankings upon entry are to the rankings upon graduation. In a limited way, the LSAC has been doing this for years. Each year the participating law schools submit to the LSAC class standing data for students admitted at the beginning of that academic year.[24] The LSAC then compares students' LSAT and GPA with their respective class standing at the end of the first year of law school and statistically produces a "correlation coefficient" to express how closely correlated entry credentials are to actual academic performance in the first year of law school.[25] The LSAC correlation coefficient is expressed as a decimal number, with 1.00 being a perfect correlation and anything under 1.00 being a less strong correlation.[26] As mentioned in the Introduction, the LSAC explains that these correlations vary from law school to law school.[27] The median correlation between LSAT score and first-year academic performance (described by the LSAC as first year law school grades) is .41, with a range of .09 to .58.[28] The median correlation between LSAT scores combined with GPA (the so-called "index") and first-year academic performance is .49, with a range of .28 to .66.[29]

The LSAC comparisons, while interesting and useful, suffer from two major limitations. First, for whatever reason, LSAC makes no comparisons with grades for the entire three-year law school experience. Thus LSAC makes no representations about the power of LSAT to predict overall law school academic performance, but confines its claims to LSAT power to predict only first-year law school performance. That deficiency is of little importance if only small differences arise overall between students' academic performances during the first year and during all three years of law school.

Second, the LSAC method is essentially unintelligible to persons without statistical training. This statement is not intended to challenge or discredit the data or conclusions drawn through the LSAC method, but only to suggest that it is awkward for law school administrators to apply this method in validating or extending findings for their own schools. In essence, each law school attempting to generate these types of studies on its own and affirm, challenge, reinforce or extend the LSAC data must reinvent or rediscover the wheel LSAC has invented. That is not an impossible task, but it does require some initiative and makes it more difficult to confirm the LSAC's representation that the "LSAT is a strong predictor of first-year law school grades."[30]

Because of these limitations in the LSAC methodology used to compute and express comparisons, this study employs a different methodology that should be more understandable to and usable by persons without statistical training. In this methodology, an entering student's LSAT, GPA or index ranking upon entry is compared with the same student's academic ranking at the end of the first and third years of law school. The disparity in those rankings is expressed as a percentage or the equivalent three-digit decimal number. For example:

1. Student 1234 has an LSAT of 160, which ranks 95th in the entering class of 150.
2. At the end of the first year of law school Student 1234 ranks 75th in the class of 150.
3. If the LSAT were a perfect predictor of class ranking, Student 1234 should have finished 95th in the class, so finishing 75th is a disparity of 20 places in ranking.[31] Twenty places out of 150 may be expressed as 20/150, or 13.3% or .133. That is how far short this result fell from achieving a perfect correlation, or 100% or 1.000. Thus the degree of correlation may be expressed as 100% – 13.3%, or 86.7% or .867. The closer the academic ranking is to the ranking upon entry in a particular category, the closer the correlation number is to 1.000. This correlation number is hereafter referred to as the "correlation score."

IV. Data

The available BYU law school data enables one to determine six different correlation scores for each student in each of the twenty-seven graduated classes. These correlation scores show how closely each student's academic ranking—at the end of the first or third years of law school—came to matching with the ranking of that student's credentials upon entry. That information, however, has relatively little institutional value. The law school is more interested in learning how high these correlations generally are, and whether correlations may be stronger for one type of credential than another—for instance, whether LSAT scores correlate better than undergraduate GPAs with law school academic performance. So for each category and for each class, one can display not only the individual student correlations, but also easily compute mean and median correlations for the entire class and readily identify trends and tendencies. These findings can then be reinforced by computing and comparing the correlations for all twenty-seven years of BYU law school data.

An important caution to remember is that these correlations between individual credentials upon entry into law school and ranking of law school academic performance are not intended to suggest that one can attribute academic performance to any one credential. Law school academic performance is achieved through combinations of each student's credentials, background, character, work habits and an infinite variety of external circumstances. Thus, the correlations between any one credential and the eventual academic performance will always be less than perfect, unless an occasional perfect match occurs by coincidence.[32]

It may also be important to learn whether students with strong combinations, referred to here as the "index"—high LSAT scores and high GPAs—are likely to achieve strongly correlated academic performances. For this purpose, it is helpful to calculate correlations for the index used by each law school. The index varies from law school to law school, according to the relative emphasis a law school places on LSAT and GPA in its admission practices. Nevertheless, it may be important for a law school to learn whether or not its particular emphasis in admissions translates into predictable academic success later on. If, for instance, a law school seeks to admit students with high LSAT scores, but is less concerned about undergraduate GPAs, and students with such credentials achieve relatively lower academic rankings, the law school may wish to reexamine its admissions criteria or priorities.[33] In this study using BYU Law School data, correlations for the law school's index are also calculated.

The charts in Appendices A and B show the data described above for the class that graduated from BYU Law School in 1997. In Appendix A the sample data show student rankings in individual categories; in Appendix B the correlation means are shown in a format enabling easier comparisons. The charts are produced by way of example; a similar set of charts with full data for all the students could be produced for each of the graduating classes considered in this study. In each chart the types of data are the same, but the correlation scores are different, depending on whether the correlation is with LSAT score, undergraduate GPA, or the combination of those two factors in the "index" used by the law school in its admission practices. The higher the correlation score—the closer it approaches 1.000—the smaller the disparity (either higher or lower) in ranking places between rank upon entry, according to the featured criterion of that chart, and academic rank in class. The correlation means for each class, when compared with correlation means from other classes, are weighted according to the number of students in each class.

For BYU Law School's graduating class of 1997, used here only by way of typical example, the correlation scores for credentials upon entry with academic performance may be summarized as shown below. The higher score indicates a stronger correlation. A .751 or 75.1% correlation score means that in class of 150, the student's academic ranking came within 37.5 positions, either higher or lower, of achieving a perfect correlation.

When these summaries are computed for all twenty-seven years of BYU Law School's graduated classes, the results may be depicted as follows:

27 Years of BYU Law School Graduated Classes

Grad Year	Grad Count	GPA: 1st Year Ranking Corr. Mean	GPA: Grad Ranking Corr. Mean	LSAT: 1st Year Ranking Corr. Mean	LSAT: Grad Ranking Corr. Mean	Index: 1st Year Ranking Corr. Mean	Index: Grad Ranking Corr. Mean
1976	147	0.742	0.654	0.758	0.688		
1977	154	0.710	0.656	0.700	0.692		
1978	140	0.756	0.676	0.753	0.678		
1979	148	0.719	0.633	0.747	0.661		
1980	136	0.693	0.661	0.694	0.667		
1981	149	0.727	0.657	0.697	0.580	0.752	0.679
1982	147	0.773	0.678	0.766	0.649	0.719	0.631
1983	143	0.702	0.689	0.729	0.661	0.729	0.664
1984	155	0.710	0.670	0.740	0.671	0.740	0.668
1985	144	0.692	0.656	0.714	0.632	0.692	0.613
1986	129	0.758	0.766	0.740	0.747	0.701	0.717
1987	144	0.725	0.735	0.748	0.762	0.742	0.764

27 Years of BYU Law School Graduated Classes *continued*

Grad Year	Grad Count	GPA: 1st Year Ranking Corr. Mean	GPA: Grad Ranking Corr. Mean	LSAT: 1st Year Ranking Corr. Mean	LSAT: Grad Ranking Corr. Mean	Index: 1st Year Ranking Corr. Mean	Index: Grad Ranking Corr. Mean
1988	143	0.716	0.752	0.739	0.787	0.703	0.756
1989	156	0.726	0.721	0.761	0.758	0.764	0.759
1990	159	0.727	0.750	0.752	0.772	0.733	0.746
1991	154	0.763	0.775	0.745	0.753	0.775	0.790
1992	150	0.791	0.792	0.770	0.763	0.820	0.816
1993	151	0.777	0.775	0.770	0.773	0.800	0.794
1994	146	0.774	0.770	0.791	0.793	0.801	0.801
1995	150	0.736	0.741	0.733	0.745	0.741	0.767
1996	153	0.762	0.770	0.717	0.716	0.770	0.760
1997	153	0.734	0.750	0.747	0.749	0.758	0.776
1998	139	0.731	0.727	0.742	0.717	0.769	0.746
1999	148	0.709	0.718	0.766	0.751	0.766	0.772
2000	136	0.757	0.759	0.780	0.782	0.793	0.791
2001	151	0.730	0.742	0.757	0.750	0.755	0.762
2002	143	0.746	0.745	0.761	0.765	0.768	0.777
Overall		0.740	0.733	0.744	0.730	0.759	0.744

Notes: Indexes were not regularly used in BYU Law School admissions processes until the class of 1981 entered law school in 1978. Also, the LSAT scoring system changed twice during the 27 years. These changes are not factors in the study because all comparisons are based on rankings, regardless of the scoring system in effect at any particular time.

Finally, the aggregate correlation scores for all students in all twenty-seven graduated classes may be summarized as follows:

1. LSAT and first-year ranking: .744
2. GPA and first-year ranking: .740
3. Index and first-year ranking: .759
4. LSAT and third-year ranking: .730
5. GPA and third-year ranking: .733
6. Index and third-year ranking: .744

V. Analysis

A. General Conclusions from the Correlation Scores

From the twenty-seven-year summary of correlation scores shown in the preceding paragraph, the following general observations may be stated:

1. The correlation scores for all categories in all years are relatively consistent, with the mean numbers ranging between .730 and .759.
2. The correlation scores are higher for first-year academic performance than they are for three-year academic performance. The mean correlation scores for first-year and three-year academic performance are shown below:

	First-Year	**Third-Year**
LSAT	.744	.730
GPA	.740	.733
Index:	.759	.744

3. As shown above, the LSAT score is a better predictor for first-year academic performance than is undergraduate GPA (.744 to .740), but GPA is a better predictor than LSAT score for third-year academic performance (.733 to .730). However, these minuscule differences are not statistically significant.
4. As shown above, the index is a better predictor for first-year and third-year performance (.759/.744) than either the LSAT score (.744/.730) or the undergraduate GPA (.740/.733). The index predicts first-year performance slightly more accurately than it predicts three-year performance (.759 to .744).

As far as admission practices are concerned, attributing extra weight to the LSAT score as a meaningful indicator or predictor of academic performance in law school is without validity, except where a form of customized weighting is included in each law school's index.

B. How Significant or Useful Are Entry Credentials in Predicting Academic Performance?

The differences in the mean correlation scores for the twenty-seven-year data seem rather small, but they may actually be significant because of the massive documentation that underlies the numbers. A more meaningful question is whether the correlation score itself, or any comparable attempt to identify correlation coefficients, enables one to draw any sensible conclusions. This question is explored in the following paragraphs.

Correlation scores at BYU Law School are based on a relatively stable student population. BYU Law School attempts to admit classes of about 150 students, and generally it graduates classes of about 150 students. If, according to the methodology used in this study, the long-term correlation between entry credentials and law school academic performance is about 75% (another way of expressing a correlation score of .750), a student would meet or exceed that correlation prediction by ranking within 37.5 places above *or below* a perfectly correlated rank. That is a spread that extends over one-half of the ranking positions in the class and is therefore not especially precise. Moreover, only one-half of the students would even achieve that much of a correlation, or better; the other half would experience a weaker correlation. If the long-term correlation were at 50%, so that the average student achieved a class ranking that was within 75 positions, either higher or lower, of a perfect correlation in a class of 150, then that covers the entire spectrum of the class and is no better than a random or coincidental correlation, with no predictive value at all.

Therefore, if 50% correlation has no predictive value, then 75% correlation is half-way between the no predictive value of 50% correlation and the perfect predictive value of 100% correlation. It's better than nothing, but only half as good as it could be.

Expressed in different terms, and by way of example, if a student enters law school with an LSAT score exactly in the middle of the group of entering students, that student's first-year grades have a 50% chance of falling in the second or third quartile of class rankings. That student's grades also have a 50% chance of falling somewhere in the top and bottom quartiles of the class. A student who enters law school with an LSAT score between the first and second quartiles of entering students' LSAT scores has a 50% chance of having first-year grades fall somewhere within the first and second quartiles of the class rankings at the end of the first year; but that same student also has a 50% chance of achieving a ranking in the third and fourth quartiles of first-year rankings.

So, with respect to any one student, one may predict only the most general probability that higher credentials will eventually yield higher academic performance. Students need not feel any sense of deterministic fatalism that lower credentials will consign them to the lower ranks of the class or exclude them from prestigious law review membership. This is abundantly borne out by the data for individual students shown in the charts for the BYU Law School class of 1997, set out in Appendix B. Similarly, no student is justified in feeling secure or smug that high credentials on entry will, by themselves, inevitably lead to comparable academic success in law school.

Undermining the predictive reliability of both LSAT score and GPA are (1) the possibilities for improving LSAT performance by preparation and (2) the vast variety of standards for grading throughout U.S. higher education, a variety that exists both within and among educational institutions.

As to the first factor, the LSAT is intended to measure mental abilities and should therefore be "preparation-proof." While that may be generally true, substantial anecdotal evidence suggests that intense, well-directed preparation can make a difference. From the author's experience of reading thousands of admission applicants' files and noting many files with multiple LSAT scores, it can be stated that only rarely does a re-take of the LSAT yield a lower score. Also, certain preparation courses seem to be conspicuously successful.

Regarding the second factor, the variety of grading standards and practices will always exist, and it seems that one way to even out those differences is to gather data from long-range and comprehensive studies. Thus, the twenty-seven-year data stream of this study would seem to produce more reliable general conclusions.

VI. Summary and Conclusions

This study has compiled and analyzed admission and academic performance data from twenty-seven graduating classes at Brigham Young University's J. Reuben Clark Law School. From this information, each student's Law School Admission Test (LSAT) score and undergraduate grade point average (GPA), ranked relative to the other entering students, has been compared with the student's academic class ranking at the end of the first year of law school and upon law school graduation. An index number, consisting of the LSAT score and GPA weighted and combined according the law school's admission practices, has also been computed and compared. How close these entry rankings compare to the academic rankings has been computed and expressed in a number referred to in this study as a correlation score. The correlation scores range from a perfect match of 1.000 to almost 0.000, and the means and medians for large groups of these scores generally range from .700 to .750. This article has explained the methodology for computing the correlation score. The article has also shown detailed data from one class, the class of 1997, and summary data for the entire group of twenty-seven BYU law school graduating classes.

From the data of all twenty-seven BYU Law School graduating classes, the following general conclusions have been drawn, relative to using entry credentials as predictors of academic performance in law school:

1. The correlation scores for all categories in all years are relatively consistent, with the mean numbers ranging between .719 and .771.
2. The correlation scores from all entry credentials are higher for first-year academic performance than they are for three-year academic performance.
3. The LSAT score is a better predictor for first-year academic performance than is undergraduate GPA, but undergraduate GPA is a better predictor than the LSAT score for third-year academic performance.
4. The index is a better predictor for first-year and three-year performance than either the LSAT score or the undergraduate GPA. The index predicts first-year performance slightly more accurately than it predicts three-year performance.

The common practice in law school admissions of attributing special weight to the LSAT score as a predictor of law school academic performance is without merit or validity.

This article also questions how significant or substantial the predictive value of entry credentials is for any individual student. From the charts displayed for the BYU Law School class of 1997, it appears that no entering law student need feel deterministically destined for either success or failure in law school because of the rank of one's entry credentials.

Appendix A

Sample Correlations of LSAT scores, GPA, and Index Scores to Class Rank after the First Year of Law School and upon Graduation from Law School

Note: In the following charts, Correlation refers to how close the academic rank came to the student's rank on entry in the particular category shown in the chart. For example, a student who entered law school ranked 10/151 in LSAT score and who then completed the first year of law school ranked 25th in the class would have a correlation of .901, having come within 15 places of perfect correlation in a class of 151: 136/151 = .901.

A. Sample Correlation of Pre-Law School LSAT and Ranking after First Year of Law School for Class of 1997 (151 Students)

Student No.	LSAT	LSAT Rank	GPA	Index	Rank after First Year	Correlation
xxx1	173	1	3.42	241	7	.953
xxx2	173	1	3.67	246	106	.298
xxx3	173	1	3.57	244	35	.768
xxx4	173	1	3.93	252	2	.967
xxx5	171	5	2.43	220	70	.570
xxx6	170	6	3.71	244	132	.166
xxx7	170	6	2.61	220	17	.927
xxx8	170	6	3.60	242	9	.980
xxx9	170	6	3.49	240	14	.947
xxx10	170	6	3.10	232	121	.238
xxx11	170	6	3.54	241	128	.192
xxx12	167	12	2.88	225	62	.669

B. Sample Correlation of Pre-Law School GPA and Ranking after First Year of Law School for Class of 1997 (151 Students)

Student No.	GPA	LSAT Rank	LSAT	Index	Rank after First Year	Correlation
xxx1	4.00	1	159	241	109	.285
xxx2	4.00	1	164	244	1	1.000
xxx3	4.00	1	160	240	52	.662
xxx4	3.94	4	162	241	61	.623
xxx5	3.93	5	173	252	6	.993
xxx6	3.91	6	164	242	7	.993
xxx7	3.91	6	163	241	4	.987
xxx8	3.91	6	158	236	26	.868
xxx9	3.91	6	162	240	42	.762
xxx10	3.90	10	NA	NA	3	.954
xxx11	3.90	10	164	242	34	.841
xxx12	3.88	12	167	245	99	.423

C. Sample Correlation of Pre-Law School Index and Ranking after First Year of Law School for Class of 1997 (151 Students)

Student No.	LSAT	LSAT Rank	Index	GPA	Rank after First Year	Correlation
xxx1	252	1	173	3.93	2	.993
xxx2	246	2	173	3.67	106	.311
xxx3	245	3	167	3.88	73	.536
xxx4	244	4	164	4.00	1	.980
xxx5	244	4	170	3.71	132	.152
xxx6	244	4	173	3.57	35	.795
xxx7	243	7	165	3.88	21	.907
xxx8	242	8	164	3.91	6	.987
xxx9	242	8	170	3.60	9	.993
xxx10	242	8	165	3.87	5	.980
xxx11	242	8	164	3.90	29	.861
xxx12	242	12	159	4.00	109	.358

D. Sample Correlation of Pre-Law School LSAT and Ranking upon Graduation from Law School for Class of 1997 (151 Students)

Student No.	LSAT	LSAT Rank	GPA	Index	Rank after First Year	Correlation
xxx1	173	1	3.42	241	2	.993
xxx2	173	1	3.67	246	72	.530
xxx3	173	1	3.57	244	37	.762
xxx4	173	1	3.93	252	6	.967
xxx5	171	5	2.43	220	100	.371
xxx6	170	6	3.71	244	129	.185
xxx7	170	6	2.61	222	23	.887
xxx8	170	6	3.60	242	22	.901
xxx9	170	6	3.49	240	38	.788
xxx10	170	6	3.10	232	117	.265
xxx12	170	6	3.54	241	121	.238
xxxl2	167	12	2.88	225	83	.530

E. Sample Correlation of Pre-Law School GPA and Ranking upon Graduation from Law School for Class of 1997 (151 Students)

Student No.	GPA	LSAT Rank	LSAT	Index	Rank after First Year	Correlation
xxx1	4.00	1	159	241	109	.285
xxx2	4.00	1	164	244	1	1.000
xxx3	4.00	1	160	240	52	.662
xxx4	3.94	4	162	241	61	.623
xxx5	3.93	5	173	252	6	.993
xxx6	3.91	6	164	242	7	.993
xxx7	3.91	6	163	242	4	.987
xxx8	3.91	6	158	236	26	.868
xxx9	3.91	6	162	240	42	.762
xxx10	3.90	10	NA	NA	3	.954
xxx11	3.90	10	164	242	34	.907
xxx12	3.88	12	167	245	99	.424

F. Sample Correlation of Pre-Law School Index and Ranking upon Graduation from Law School for Class of 1997 (151 Students)

Student No.	LSAT	LSAT Rank	Index	GPA	Rank after First Year	Correlation
xxx1	252	1	173	3.93	6	.967
xxx2	246	2	173	3.67	72	.536
xxx3	245	3	167	3.88	99	.364
xxx4	244	4	164	4.00	1	.980
xxx5	244	4	170	3.71	129	.172
xxx6	244	4	173	3.57	37	.781
xxx7	243	7	165	3.88	32	.834
xxx8	242	8	164	3.91	7	.993
xxx9	242	8	170	3.60	22	.907
xxx10	242	8	165	3.87	15	.954
xxx11	242	8	164	3.90	34	.828
xxx12	241	12	159	4.00	109	.358

Appendix B

Correlation of LSAT Scores, GPA and Index Scores with Law Students' First-Year and Three-Year Academic Performance: Examples from the Class of 1997

This appendix presents three groups of fifteen students each from a class of approximately 150 students. One group is from the upper range of that class, one group from the middle of the class, and one group from the lower range of that class. For this chart, students are arranged according to LSAT score. The purpose of this appendix is merely to illustrate the wide variety of and absence of pattern in individual correlation scores.

A. Upper Range of Class

Student No.	LSAT	GPA	Index	LSAT: 1/3-Yr. Corr.	GPA: 1/3-Yr. Corr.	Index: 1/3-Yr. Corr.
1	173	3.42	241	.961/.993	.377/.388	.947/.914
2	173	3.67	246	.316/.553	.656/.887	.311/.550
3	173	3.57	244	.789/.789	.735/.735	.808/.808
4	173	3.93	252	.987/.993	.980/.993	.993/.974
5	171	3.43	220	.572/.388	.470/.649	.570/.755
6	170	3.71	244	.171/.204	.404/.437	.159/.192
7	170	2.61	222	.934/.908	.126/.152	.272/.298
8	170	3.60	242	.993/.921	.623/.695	1.000/.927
9	170	3.49	240	.967/.822	.490/.636	.960/.894
10	170	3.10	232	.270/.309	.894/.854	.649/.689
11	170	3.54	241	.230/.289	.695/.755	.258/.318
12	167	2.88	225	.671/.546	.437/.563	.642/.768
13	167	3.08	229	.724/.730	.437/.430	.768/.762
14	167	3.44	236	.243/.171	.788/.715	.364/.291
15	167	3.56	238	.987/.961	.583/.868	.921/.894
Correlation means from upper range:				.654/.638	.580/.647	.641/.669

B. Middle Range of Class

Student No.	LSAT	GPA	Index	LSAT: 1/3-Yr. Corr.	GPA: 1/3-Yr. Corr.	Index: 1/3-Yr. Corr.
66	161	3.62	233	.829/.987	.795/.974	.748/.934
67	161	3.85	238	.743/.730	.947/.960	.987/1.000
68	161	3.39	229	.836/.704	.927/.940	.987/.881
69	161	3.58	233	.711/.789	.735/.815	.636/.715
70	161	3.09	223	.961/.809	.576/.728	.669/.821
71	161	3.82	237	.757/.612	.464/.318	.483/.338
72	160	3.60	232	.671/.954	.623/.901	.596/.881
73	160	3.57	231	.836/.684	.834/.689	.848/.669
74	160	3.67	233	.572/.638	.430/.497	.397/.464
75	160	4.00	240	.849/.836	.669/.682	.781/.795
76	160	3.61	232	.829/.796	.914/.881	.894/.861
77	160	3.54	231	.743/.974	.722/.954	.722/.954
78	160	3.44	229	.559/.697	.695/.828	.662/.795
79	159	4.00	241	.803/.816	.285/.298	.358/.371
80	159	3.81	235	.730/.625	.921/.974	.980/.914
Correlation means from middle range:				.762/.777	.702/.763	.716/.720

C. Lower Range of Class

Student No.	LSAT	GPA	Index	LSAT: 1/3-Yr. Corr.	GPA: 1/3-Yr. Corr.	Index: 1/3-Yr. Corr.
136	153	3.85	230	.382/.441	.848/.788	.715/.775
137	153	3.87	230	.822/.724	.371/.470	.841/.940
138	152	3.27	217	.724/.954	.828/.940	.709/.940
139	152	3.71	226	.954/.789	.417/.583	.874/.960
140	151	3.05	212	.625/.809	.603/.788	.609/.795
141	151	3.81	227	.842/.895	.417/.364	.907/.854
142	151	3.82	227	.434/.507	.788/.715	.662/.735
143	150	3.70	224	.645/.664	.715/.695	.775/.795
144	150	3.13	213	.987/.980	.629/.934	1.000/1.000
145	150	2.75	205	.533/.816	.510/.795	.510/.795
146	148	3.05	209	.974/.974	.947/.947	.967/.967
147	148	2.93	207	.993/.993	.993/.993	.987/.987
148	144	3.04	205	.980/.993	.967/.980	.980/.993
149	144	3.44	212	.987/.980	.709/.715	.980/.987
150	143	2.05	204	.954/.875	1.000/.927	.954/.881
Correlation means from lower range:				.789/.826	.716/.776	.831/.897

D. Comparison of Correlation Means from Upper, Middle and Lower Range Samples of the Class

	LSAT 1/3	GPA 1/3	Index 1/3
Correlation Means from Upper Range:	.654/.638	.580/.647	.641/.669
Correlation Means from Middle Range:	.762/.777	.702/.763	.716/.720
Correlation Means from Lower Range:	.789/.826	.716/.776	.831/.897

Notes

* The author is grateful to Vance Everett, BYU Law School Computer Systems Manager, for his significant contribution to retrieving the information used in this article. The author also acknowledges with gratitude the significant assistance of Dennis L. Eggett, BYU Professor of Statistics and Director of the Center for Statistical Consultation and Collaborative Research, and Jonathan L. Gatlin, graduate statistics student, in reviewing the technical statistics aspects of this study.

1. LAW SCHOOL ADMISSIONS COUNCIL, INC., LSAT & LSDAS REGISTRATION AND INFORMATION BOOK 121 (2003–2004 ed.) [hereinafter LSAC, REGISTRATION AND INFORMATION].

2. *Id.*

3. *Id.*

4. *Id.* The data in this study would enable a testing of the assumption that third-year law school grades do not differ significantly from first-year law school grades, but that study is not necessary for this article.

5. See, e.g., Dorothy A. Brown, *The LSAT Sweepstakes*, 2 J. GENDER RACE & JUST. 59 (1998); Richard Delgado, Official Elitism or Institutional Self Interest? 10 Reasons Why UC-Davis Should Abandon the LSAT (And Why Other Good Law Schools Should Follow Suit), 34 U.C. DAVIS L. REV. 593 (2001); Leslie G. Espinoza, *The LSAT: Narratives and Bias*, 1 AM. U. J. GENDER & L. 121 (1993); Edward G. Haggerty, *LSAT: Uses and Misuses*, 70 N.Y. ST. B.J., May–June 1998, at 45; William C. Kidder, *Does the LSAT Mirror or Magnify Racial and Ethnic Differences in Educational Attainment?: A Study of Equally Achieving "Elite" College Students*, 89 CAL. L. REV. 1055 (2001); William C. Kidder, *The Rise of the Testocracy: An Essay on the LSAT, Conventional Wisdom, and the Dismantling of Diversity*, 9 TEX. J. WOMEN & L. 167 (2000); William C. Kidder, *Portia Denied: Unmasking Gender Bias on the LSAT and Its Relationship to Racial Diversity in Legal Education*, 12 YALE J. L. & FEMINISM 1

(2000); Jeffrey S. Kinsler, *The LSAT Myth*, 20 St. LOUIS U. PUB. L. REV. 393 (2001); Naseem Stecker, *What's the Score: The LSAT and the Blind*, MICH. B.J., Jan. 2001, at 46; Dan Subotnik, *Goodbye to the SAT, LSAT? Hello to Equity by Lottery? Evaluating Lani Guinier's Plan for Ending Race Consciousness*, 43 HOW. L.J. 141 (2000); David M. White, *The Requirement of Race-Conscious Evaluation of LSAT Score for Equitable Law School Admissions*, 12 LA RAZA L.J. 399 (2001).

6. Kinsler, *supra* note 5, at 395.

7. *America's Best Graduate Schools*, U.S. NEWS & WORLD REP., 2004, at 28.

8. *Id.* at 29. Under the criterion of "Selectivity," the magazine assigns 25% of its ranking values; median LSAT score, which is not shown in its published data charts, is assigned 50% of the selectivity value, which means that the median LSAT score of a law school's admittees accounts for 12.5% of that school's ranking calculation. *Id.*

9. As reported in a local legal news daily, an Emory University Law School professor and dean candidate pitched his candidacy by proclaiming his school's need to rise in the rankings: "Emory ... needs to vault itself into the top 15, and then into the top 10. One of the school's top priorities, he said: "To get out of this not even 25 land that we've slipped into.'" Janet L. Conley, *Emory Dean Hopeful: We Must Beat UGA*, FULTON COUNTY DAILY REP., Feb. 26, 2002, at 1. Kinsler concluded, with respect to two recent graduating classes of his own law school, that "the LSAT was a very weak predictor of three-year law school performance." Kinsler, *supra* note 5, at 416. LSAC publicly measures LSAT scores only in relation to first-year law school performance, but still declares more generally "that LSAT scores help to predict which students will do well in law school." LSAC, Registration and Information, *supra* note 1, at 121.

10. LSAC, REGISTRATION AND INFORMATION, *supra* note 1, at 121; *see also* David A. Thomas, *The Law School Rankings Are Harmful Deceptions: A Response to Those Who Praise the Rankings and Suggestions for a Better Approach to Evaluating Law Schools*, 40 HOUS. L. REV. 419, 429–31 (2003).

11. LSAC, REGISTRATION AND INFORMATION, *supra* note 1, at 121.

12. E.g., LINDA F. WIGHTMAN, BEYOND FYA: ANALYSIS OF THE UTILITY OF LSAT SCORES AND UGPA FOR PREDICTING ACADEMIC SUCCESS IN LAW SCHOOL (2002). This study uses data from the LSAC National Longitudinal Bar Passage Study (Law School Admission Council, 1998), which uses data collected from 142 law schools over a five to six year period beginning in 1991. *Id.* at 1. The purpose of that study was to determine if bar passage rates for law student graduates of color were too low to justify affirmative action in admissions. *Id.* This same data collection was also used in the principal study cited in this note to determine if the predictive values of LSAT scores and undergraduate grade point averages for law school academic performance of law students of color differed significantly from the predictive values for white students. *Id.* at 2. This principal study also cites other limited studies of these predictive values, for both one-year and three-year law school academic performance, which studies yield mixed conclusions. *Id.*

13. LSAC, REGISTRATION AND INFORMATION, *supra* note 1, at 1.

14. *Id.*

15. *Id.* at 121.

16. Id.

17. *Id.*

18. *Id.* LSAC reports that the correlation between GPA and first-year grades varies from law school to law school, id., which must mean that LSAC is in fact measuring that correlation.

19. *See General Information about the Law School, at* http://www.law2.byu.edu/Services/about_law_school.htm (last modified May 9, 2000).

20. See BYU J. Reuben Clark Law School Bulletin 2004–2005, at 4.

21. According to information released in April, 2003, by *U.S. News & World Report*, relating to students entering law schools in 2002, only five law schools reported both a 75th–25th percentile LSAT range and a 75th–25th percentile GPA range higher than BYU's 75–25th percentile ranges for LSAT and GPA—Yale, Stanford, Harvard, Columbia, and the University of California, Boalt Hall School of Law. *America's Best Graduate Schools*, U.S. NEWS & WORLD REP., 2004, at 28.

22. The index is specific to each law school and consists of a weighted combination of LSAT score and undergraduate GPA. Currently at BYU the index consists of the LSAT score plus the undergraduate GPA

times nineteen, or LSAT + (19 x GPA) = Index. Law schools may adjust their index each year, and often do so in response to advice from the LSAC, which monitors the LSAT and GPA credentials of students actually admitted to that school. A law school placing more emphasis on LSAT than on GPA as an admission credential would adopt, for its index calculation, a smaller multiplier for GPA than that used by BYU. LAW SCHOOL ADMISSIONS COUNCIL, LAW SCHOOL ADMISSION REFERENCE MANUAL 2003–2004 43 (2003) [hereinafter LSAC, REFERENCE MANUAL]; LAW SCHOOL ADMISSIONS COUNCIL, REPORT ON FIRST-YEAR PERFORMANCE 26 (2003) [hereinafter LSAC, FIRST-YEAR].

23. To reiterate, the ranking here is based on the rank relative to other law students in that entering class.

24. LSAC, REFERENCE MANUAL, *supra* note 22, at 43; LSAC, FIRST-YEAR, *supra* note 22, at 26.

25. LSAC, REGISTRATION AND INFORMATION, *supra* note 1, at 121.

26. *Id.*

27. *Id.*

28. *Id.*

29. *Id.*; Kinsler, *supra* note 5, at 397–405.

30. LSAC, REGISTRATION AND INFORMATION, *supra* note 1, at 121.

31. If the student had finished with a class ranking of 115, rather than 75, the same disparity of 20 places would exist, with the same resulting correlation score.

32. Statistical methods for determining correlations, such as the method employed by the LSAC, may attempt to isolate each variable factor as much as possible. It is probably also true that the two most prominent factors in identifying a student's characteristics that will lead to eventual academic performance are the LSAT and GPA, and isolating these from each other may lead to revealing data.

33. A law school concerned about its own *U.S. News* ranking, for instance, will undoubtedly note that median LSAT scores of its entering students count for 12.5% of its *U.S. News* ranking, while median undergraduate GPA counts for only 10%. *See America's Best Graduate Schools*, *supra* note 21, at 29.

Predicting LSAT Scores from SAT Scores

David S. Mann

Introduction

The College of Charleston is a four-year, liberal arts, public institution in South Carolina. In a typical year, Law Services' Annual Action Reports indicate over 100 students to be enrolled in LSDAS. *See* Table 1 below for those and other data. This is a rather pedestrian campus, where about 2/3 of the students commute (approximately 2500 dorm beds) and many hold part-time jobs while they are in the "Holy City" of Charleston. The College of Charleston is a major "feeder school" to the University of South Carolina School of Law.

Hypothesis

Of primary interest is the notion that SAT can predict LSAT, all other things being equal (or, in statistical parlance, holding everything else constant). Although student populations differ from year to year, and applicant pools from different years cannot be compared in too much detail, there are trends. If there was a strong statistical relationship, some potentially powerful implications and ethical issues might follow. For instance, we *could* provide the regression equation to entering freshmen and show *them* how to predict their LSAT based on their SAT scores. We also could caution students, as an ETS report in 1963 stated (the gender pronouns are reproduced from the original):

> To the student with an outstanding record, strong motivation, and clearly defined aspirations, a high prediction will help to confirm the generally favorable prospects. Another student may have a similar record *except for low test scores.* If he is doing well in a college with high academic standards, it is possible that his earlier test scores are not a good indicator of … ability. Perhaps, however, he is making a good record, as some students do, *in spite of a relatively low ability level.* If so, he should realize that any slackening of effort will be extremely serious. (ETS, 1963, p. 6, emphasis added).

ETS would never admit that students may in fact be "good test takers," or poor ones. A strong correlation between the two scores, with or without looking at grade point average, might indicate such a trend.

By way of comparison, a separate hypothesis predicts LSAT scores from grade point averages, again holding everything else constant. There was no hypothesis about particular majors, races, genders, or states of residence.

The Databases

The data cover two segments of time—1991–3 (see Mann, Gibson, and Bolchoz, 1993) and 1994–5 through 1998–9—and are based on two sources. One is the Law Services Annual Action Report. The other is the Student Information System (SIS) transcript report from the College. The 1994–1999 database includes 238 students, their LSAT scores as reported by Law Services, gender, race, state of residence, undergraduate major, grade point average, and SAT scores when available. The 1991–3 database includes 161 students, their LSAT scores as reported by Law Services, grade point average and SAT scores when available. [Note: not anticipated were: (a) the large number of students for whom there was no SAT score available because the SIS does not record SAT scores for transfer students, and (b) the large number of students who do not wish their data to be provided in the Action Reports.]

In both studies, if a student took the SAT more than once, the highest verbal and math SAT scores were used. This decision corresponds with the College of Charleston Admissions policy criterion. The LSAT score recorded was the score reported in the Annual Action Report, which notes an asterisk if the student took the test more than once—and is an average score. The database does not record asterisks.

Table 1 shows some comparisons between the 1993 report and the current study, from a wide lens. Though the College undergraduate enrollment has increased from around 7800 to around 9500 in the eight year period, the number of students registered in LSDAS doesn't change much from year to year. Students covered in each Annual Action Report do not have LSAT scores or grade point averages different to a statistically significant degree from the larger number of students who were in the LSDAS but whose individual data were not released. In fact, note that a much larger percentage of students covered in the Action Reports are admitted to law school than students who did not wish their individual data to be released. It is cautious but appropriate to assume, therefore, that the students for whom we have data in the Action Reports *probably* are not meaningfully different from the larger number of students (other than the odds of their admission to law school) and *may* be considered "typical" of law school applicants from the College of Charleston. The highest individual LSAT score by any student in the database was 173.

Table 1 also shows that the grade point averages and LSAT scores are by no means stellar. The grade point averages reported are those from Law Services, not student transcripts. It is well known that Law Services re-computes grade point averages as a mechanism of standardization. Readers may wish to note that the College of Charleston grade scheme is 4.0 based, with 3.5 = B+ and 2.5 = C+. There are no A-, B-, or C- grades calculated. Law Services includes in its grade point calculations the scores from other schools students may have attended, but those scores are not broken down in the Annual Action Reports. Given all these considerations, the students who apply to law school from the College of Charleston *may* be "average" law school applicants. The highest individual grade point average for any student in the database was 4.0.

For the earlier study, Bolchoz ran the computer program using a then-current version of SAS. For the more recent study, Mann used Statview 4.5, published by Abacus.

Table 1. Descriptive Data

Y	N	%In	LSDAS	A	LSAT	GPA	ARLSAT	ARGPA	ACC	ACCR
1992–3	7821	79.0	121	56	150.7	2.90	152.9	3.06	40	30
1993–4	8051	77.3	113	63	151.9	2.93	152.9	3.06	37	29
1994–5	8227	74.8	125	65	151.0	2.92	151.6	2.89	57	41
1995–6	8582	72.5	112	41	150.6	2.94	152.0	3.00	46	27
1996–7	9006	69.8	103	42	151.9	2.96	151.5	2.95	48	28
1997–8	9252	66.9	121	52	151.7	3.07	152.7	3.18	68	41
1998–9	9484	66.5	98	31	151.6	2.96	152.2	3.07	49	23

AR = Students in Action Reports and discussed in this study. Undergraduate enrollment data are from College of Charleston Fact Book (http://eofc.edulinstitutionalreasearch/fastfacts/), accessed 9-14-01.
Y: Year undergraduate entered
N: Undergraduates entered
%IN: instate

LSDAS: # applied to LSDAS
A: Action Reports
LSAT: Average LSAT
GPA: Average GPA
ARLSAT: Action Report LSAT
ARGPA: Action Report GPA
ACC: #Accepted
ACCR: #Accepted on Action Reports

The Data

It seemed like a good idea at the time to organize some of the findings according to major. That rationale was from the perspective of a pre-law advisor, who too often is asked what the best major is to get into law school. See Table 2. A full thirty percent of the LSAT test takers were Political Science majors. Three departments lurk behind with about eleven percent each: English, History, and Business Administration. Only about eight majors offered at the College of Charleston are not listed here; but it is not difficult to guess why Political Science dominates. To the 18-year-old student in college, it might be intuitive, but some scholars, such as political scientist Murray Edelman, saw the linkage nearly a generation ago and suggested the overlap between interest in politics and interest in law:

> The form of legal language ... conveys a reassuring message regardless of its content. Because the language of statutes, constitutions, and treaties consists of definitions and of specific commands to judges, administrative officials, and the general public to behave in ways specified by elected representatives of the people, its very form offers reassurance of popular sovereignty and the rule of law. Lawyers take the ambiguity of legal language for granted in their practice, constantly disputing the meaning of terms; but to the general public legal language symbolizes precision and clarity in specifying the will of legislatures and constitutional conventions. (Edelman, 1977, pp. 17–8)

Perhaps it would have been wise (let alone politically correct on my campus) to avoid discussing majors, grade points, LSAT scores, and so forth altogether. Hence, grade point averages are deliberately omitted from Table 2. In terms of the LSAT, however, it does appear that the six percent of the test takers (16/238) who were Philosophy majors scored the best as a group. This should be taken with extreme caution because of the numeric disparity between the numbers of test takers for each major. For the dataset as a whole, the range of LSAT scores was from 173 to 135. The standard deviations do not provide much additional information. (Privacy concerns obliged me to omit the scores of single and double test takers for any specific major.) [Table 2.]

Table 2.

Major	LSAT Test N of Students	Takers by Major Ave. LSAT	1994–1999 LSAT s.d.
Art History	1		
Classics	1		
Communication*	6	151	4.26
Theatre	1		
English*	28	153	7.04
Fine Arts	1		
French	1		
Philosophy	16	157	4.47
Religious Studies	1		
Spanish	4	151	2.98
Accounting	3	150	0
Business Administration	24	152	5.74
Economics	2		
Biology	5	146	9.01
Marine Biology	2		
Geology	1		
Physics	1		
Anthropology	3	160	4.50
Education	7	150	3.30
History	26	152	7.13
Political Science	73	152	6.18
Psychology	14	153	6.20
Sociology	8	152	9.03
Urban Studies	1		
Totals; Averages	238	152	6.65

* Until Fall 1999, Communication had been subsumed in the English department. Some students reported the former anyway, as there was a "concentration" option.

Table 3 shows the SAT scores grouped by major. Single and double test takers in a major are again omitted, except to note when a student had no SAT score to report, which is noted separately (nr). For some majors, the single test taker had no SAT score, and the major is omitted from Table 3 entirely. There is a serious drop-off from 238 LSAT test takers to 134 SAT scores. At least when organized by major, the standard deviations for some scores is quite high but is most likely spurious, that is, unrelated to major *per se.*

Table 3. SAT Test Takers by Major

Major	# Students Ave.	SATTT	SATM	SATV	SAT s.d.
Classics	1	nr			
Communication	3	1110	553	556	40.41
English	17	1134	530	605	63.74
Philosophy	7	1257	647	610	72.57
Business Administration	10	1125	564	561	96.66
Biology	4	1107	522	585	114.41
Geology	1	nr			
Anthropology	3	nr			
Education	3	1130	550	580	34.64
History	17	1111	518	593	118.07
Political Science	45	1136	559	580	112.50
Psychology	11	1093	532	560	90.58
Sociology	5	1134	566	568	184.33
Totals/Averages	139	1138	555	584	122.27

Findings

The findings here are in two parts. The first is a summary of the 1991–93 study and is displayed as Figure 1 and Table 4. In 1993 we reported that all the correlations are strong, in the anticipated direction, and are statistically significant at levels that would be publishable in any respectable political science journal, which is the author's sole criterion. Figure 1 is the regression scatterplot for the 1991–93 dataset. The regression equation appears at the bottom of the figure. Table 4 displays the regression equation, which is statistically significant, and the $R^2 = .5038$, which to some may be a meaningful number. The correlation coefficient is .71. The quality of Figure 1 is a function of the fact that it is a copy of a copy of a printout.

The more recent data are similarly displayed in Table 5 and Figure 2. All the correlations remain strong, in the anticipated direction, and are statistically significant using the same criterion. These data show some decline in the size of the correlation compared with the 1991–3 data. Here the $R^2 = .443$, which remains a very good number. The correlation coefficient is .66. The regression equation is statistically significant and is reproduced at the bottom of Figure 2.

Figure 1. SAT and LSAT Analysis, Combination of 92 and 93 Correlations between LSAT and SAT

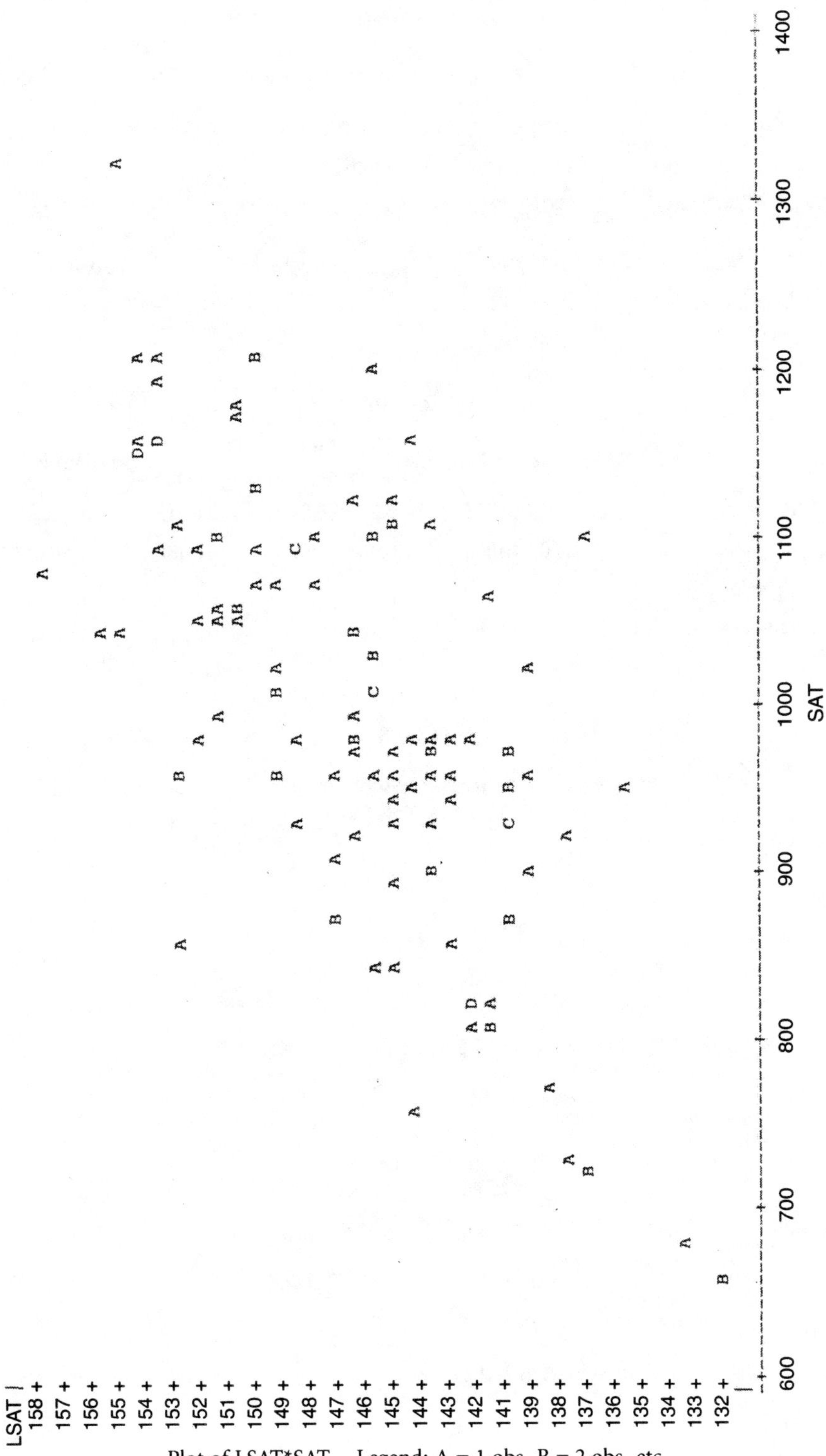

Plot of LSAT*SAT. Legend: A = 1 obs, B = 2 obs, etc.

Table 4. SAT and LSAT Analysis, Combination of 92 and 93 Correlations between LSAT and SAT

Analysis of Variance

Source	DF	Sum of Squares	Mean Square	F Value	Prob>F
Model	1	3478.47183	3478.47183	131.971	0.0001
Error	130	3426.52059	26.35785		
C Total	131	6904.99242			

Root MSE	5.13399	R-square	0.5038
Dep Mean	150.99242	Adj R-sq	0.4999
C.V.	3.40016		

Parameter Estimates

Variable	DF	Parameter Estimate	Standard Error	T for HO: Parameter=O	Prob > | T |
INTERCEP	1	111.083916	3.50259309	31.715	0.0001
SAT	1	0.040065	0.00348758	11.488	0.0001

Model: MODEL1
Dependent Variable: LSAT

Table 5.

Regression Summary LSAT vs. Total SAT

Count	135
Num. Missing	111
R	.666
R Squared	.443
Adjusted R Squared	.439
RMS Residual	4.959

ANOVA Table LSAT vs. Total SAT

	DF	Sum of Squares	Mean Square	F-Value	P-Value
Regression	1	2605.747	2605.747	105.957	<.0001
Residual	133	3270.802	24.592		
Total	134	5876.548			

Regression Coefficients
LSAT vs. Total SAT

	Coefficient	Std. Error	Std. Coeff.	t-Value	P-Value
Intercept	112.015	4.014	112.015	27.903	<.0001
Total SAT	.036	.004	.666	10.294	<.0001

Figure 2.

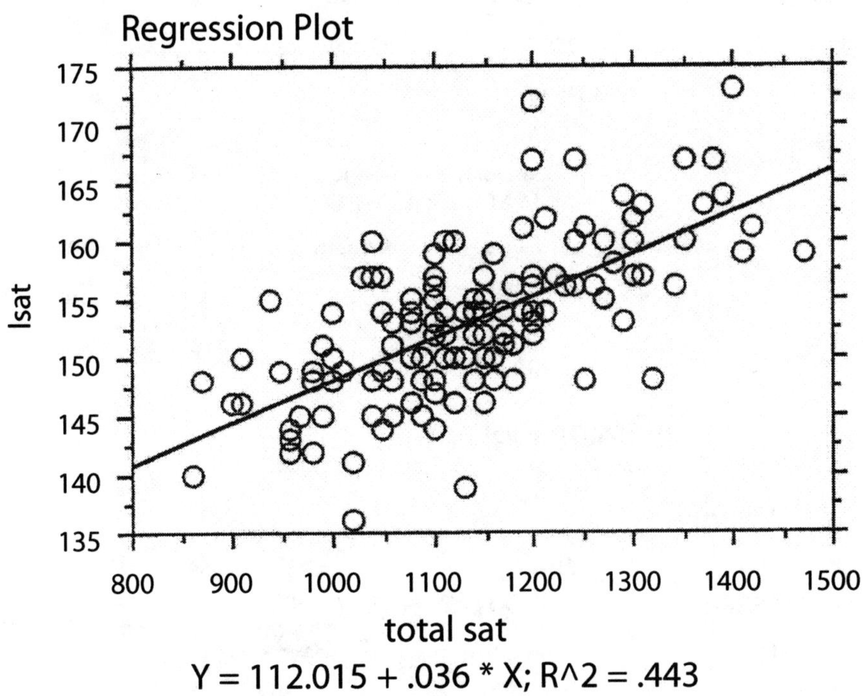

Table 6.

Regression Summary
LSAT vs. Total GPR

Count	237
Num. Missing	9
R	.298
R Squared	.089
Adjusted R Squared	.085
RMS Residual	6.277

ANOVA Table
LSAT vs. Total GPR

	DF	Sum of Squares	Mean Square	F-Value	P-Value
Regression	1	900.488	900.488	22.856	<.0001
Residual	235	9258.685	33.399		
Total	236	10159.173			

Regression Coefficients
LSAT vs. Total GPR

	Coefficient	Std. Error	Std. Coeff.	t-Value	P-Value
Intercept	140.889	2.578	140.889	54.648	<.0001
Total SAT	3.981	.833	.298	4.781	<.0001

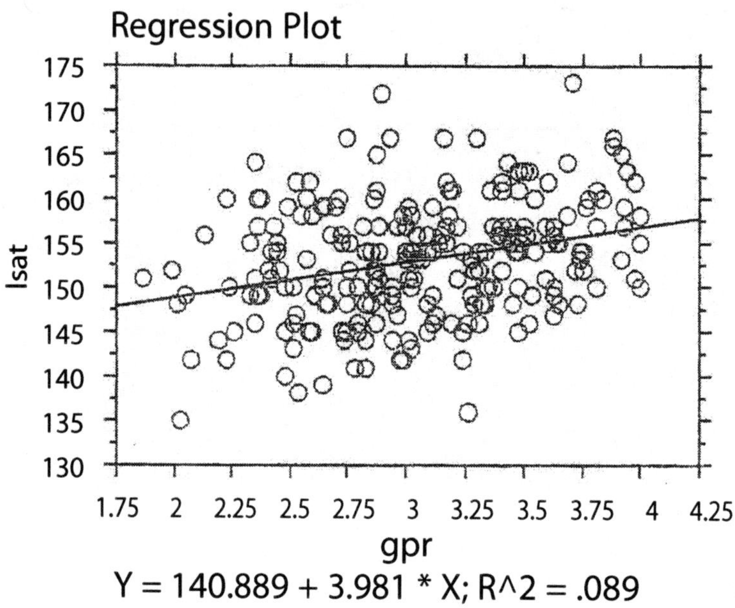

There is no straightforward explanation for the decline in the meaningful statistics between the earlier study and the more recent one. However, the data remain quite clear; there is a relationship, and it is strong and in the anticipated direction.

On a lark, since the data were in the matrix, it was a curiosity to see how good a predictor of LSAT was of a student's grade point average. A summary Table 6 shows the outcome for these students. Inspection of the scatterplot is most helpful, but for the numbers freaks, the $R^2 = .089$, and the correlation coefficient is .298. So while the regression equation is statistically significant, the regression line is visibly more flat compared with Figure 1 and Figure 2. Another curiosity was to see whether the SAT predicted the student's grade point average. While not displayed here, the $R^2 = .083$, or, almost identical to the grade point average-LSAT statistics.

During that number-crunching frenzy, MSAT and VSAT were regressed with LSAT. The data show that MSAT predicts LSAT ($R = .349$) better than VSAT ($R^2 = .309$). Both of the regression equations were statistically significant and in the anticipated direction. These statistics are not displayed.

The differences between men and women were negligible, as was the difference between in-state students and out-of-state students. There were the expected differences between whites and nonwhites both for SAT and LSAT scores, which are not reproduced here, in part because there were only 14 non-white students for whom there were SAT scores. To compare 125 white students' SAT scores with 14 non-white students' scores did not seem statistically appropriate.

Finally, at the last minute another set of numbers was generated. Table 7 and Table 8, an afterthought, displays basic regression data controlling for applicant pool year. It is dangerous to use regression data for small numbers of students. As with most basic statistics, assumptions are made based on the law of large numbers and normal curves.

Table 7. SAT to LSAT Regression Data by Year

Year	N of Students	R^2	F-Value	P-Value
1994	31	.391	18.633	.0002
1995	17	.595	22.032	.0003
1996	27	.485	23.565	.0001
1997	26	.445	19.238	.0002
1998	12	.405	6.809	.026
1999	22	.361	11.285	.003

Table 8. SAT to LSAT Regression Data by Year

Year	N of Students	R^2	F-Value	P-Value
1994	47	.038	1.756	.1918
1995	33	.214	8.450	.0067
1996	39	.338	18.877	.0001
1997	48	.027	1.275	.2646
1998	30	.111	3.502	.0718
1999	40	.015	.564	.4572

Such statistical rules warn that small numbers of students or scores may not reflect or predict accurately. With that giant red flag in mind, there is a trend downward in the ability of the SAT to predict LSAT scores. Note that since 1995, the R^2 is dropping, as is the probability function's confidence, though it dips and curves slightly. Obviously, if there were more students in the database, faith in this table would be enhanced. Nonetheless, it is a curious trend that is supported, in some sense, by the 1991–3 database, the R^2 figure for which was higher than the grouped data from 1994–9. One more thing: any of these results still predict LSAT better than grade point average. For support for that statement, see Table 8. With the exception of 1996 and possibly 1995, the R^2 are quite low and the regression equations are not statistically significant. Unlike Table 7, there is no upward or downward trend either in R^2 or statistical significance. A tentative conclusion when looking at these two tables could be: though the impact of SAT on LSAT *may* be declining, the effect is not explained by grade point average as a separate independent variable.

Discussion

The hypothesized model was that SAT scores predict LSAT scores. We found evidence to support that hypothesis in 1993, and the evidence remains in 2001. We hold constant: graduation date, age, race, gender, major, grade point average, high school attended, state of residence, and no doubt many other factors. In short, we hold constant the effects of at least three and a half years of college education and college life. But the relationship is clear and unmistakable. The higher the one score, the higher the other.

SAT predicts LSAT, and SAT predicts LSAT much better than grade point average predicts LSAT. Vanderkooi and Sterling reported in 1981 that grade point average is at least as good a predictor of law school performance as LSAT scores in most cases. Though their finding uses a different dependent variable (law school performance), their premise may be in conflict with results shown here.

Law school deans insist that LSAT predicts law school performance. Could we extrapolate: if SAT predicts LSAT, and if LSAT predicts success in law school, then should not SAT predict success in law school?

With the exception of reading comprehension (generally, see Katz, 1990), SAT and LSAT are very different tests. How can pre-law advisors explain the statistical relationship between SAT and LSAT? Better yet, how can Law Services explain the relationship? Is there a student self-selection process at work? Is there some truth to the notion that some students are simply better at taking standardized tests than other students? Should we, as advisors, use the prediction equation to weed out those who might otherwise be interested in going to law school but will not score well on the LSAT? What, in fact, do such standardized tests measure?

Sources

Edleman M. (1977). *Political Language: Words That Succeed and Policies That Fail.* New York: Academic Press.

ETS. (1963). "Using Scholastic Aptitude Test Scores in Counseling Prospective Graduate and Law Students." Statistical Report SR-63-62, October, 1963. Princeton: Educational Testing Service.

Katz, S. (1990). "Answering Reading Comprehension Items Without Passages on the SAT." Psychological Science 1: 122.

Mann, D., T.S. Gibson, and C. Bolchoz. (1993). "Predicting LSAT Scores from SAT Scores: A Preliminary Report." Presented at the Southern Association of Pre-Law Advisors' Annual Meeting, October 1–3, 1993, Louisville, Kentucky.

Vanderkooi, L.K., and J.S. Sterling. (1981). "Predictors of Achievement in Law School." Presented at the Annual Meeting of the Law and Society Association, June 12, 1981, Amherst, Massachusetts.

Part Three

The Value of Law School Rankings

In Praise of Law School Rankings: Solutions to Coordination and Collective Action Problems

*Russell Korobkin**

It has become a popular sport among law professors and administrators to criticize published rankings of law schools, especially, but not exclusively, the infamous annual rankings published by that erstwhile example of journalistic excellence, *U.S. News & World Report*. The criticism generally heard around the faculty coffee machine is that the rankings fail to measure accurately "quality" among law schools. Instead, they serve only to provide students with a false sense of security that they are receiving a top-rate education if they attend a top-ranked school, and a false sense of inferiority if they attend a lower-ranked school.

The complaints have been building over the nine-year history of the *U.S. News* survey and have now reached a crescendo of sorts.[1] Last year 150 law school deans signed a letter criticizing the U.S. News survey.[2] This year, in a more brazen frontal assault, the Association of American Law Schools (AALS) commissioned a study to investigate the validity of the *U.S. News* rankings.[3] The Law School Admission Council then mailed the study to more than 70,000 law school applicants,[4] along with a letter—this time signed by 164 law school deans—urging applicants not to pay attention to rankings when making matriculation decisions.[5] The extent of the criticisms—both formal and informal—of rankings is all the more remarkable considering that the fervor of all but those deans and professors at the very "top" schools must be somewhat chilled by the fear that carping might be perceived as sour grapes[6] or, at least, as a transparent and somewhat pathetic attempt to justify one's toil at a less than "elite" school.

This essay looks at law school rankings from an unconventional perspective and, in the process, defends their use. Part I presents a positive theory of law school rankings with normative undertones. It argues that the passionate critics of rankings misunderstand the primary purpose that rankings serve. Essentially, the critics despise rankings because rankings fail to serve the purpose the critics attribute to them. The critics attack ranking methodology because they believe the methodology fails to represent fairly the quality of education provided by the ranked institutions. The critics are no doubt correct, but in an empty sort of way. The primary purpose of rankings is to coordinate the placement of law students with legal employers, and how the rankings are determined is utterly irrelevant to this purpose. Hence, the first point developed in this essay: the *existence* of rankings fulfills the *purpose* of rankings, without reference to what the rankings claim to measure or how well they measure it.

Part II of this essay provides a normative theory of rankings as it attempts to demonstrate that the conclusions reached in Part I are neither inherently nihilistic nor even unduly cynical. Although methodology is irrelevant to the ability of rankings to serve a coordinating function, methodology can be relevant to how well rankings serve valuable secondary purposes. Well used, rankings can encourage the creation of public goods that otherwise would be inefficiently underproduced by the law school marketplace, thus solving what might otherwise be a stubborn collective action problem. The argument here is that scholarship is just such a public good that, without reinforcement of a rankings system, is quite likely to be underproduced relative to its social optimum. Consequently, rankings can serve a valuable social purpose by promoting the production of legal scholarship. To the extent that they do so, rankings should be commended; to the extent that they fail to do so, rankings should be criticized.

I. The Coordination Function of Rankings

A. Focusing on the Inadequacies of Existing Rankings Misses the Point

Critics of *U.S. News & World Report* and other attempts to rank law schools usually base their attacks on two criticisms of the Byzantine algorithms that the rankings employ.[7] The first criticism is that the rankings as a whole fail to measure accurately the quality of legal education provided by law schools. How can the number of books in the law school library plus the school's annual financial aid expenditure divided by the starting salary of those employed within six months and twelve days of the fortnight before graduation reveal anything about the quality of education provided to students at that law school?[8] The American Bar Association, the AALS, and other interested organizations, for example, have criticized the *U.S. News* rankings for failing "to inform the public about the relative merit of law schools."[9] In a similar vein, the recently commissioned AALS study criticizes the *U.S. News* rankings on the grounds that factors not considered by the survey are "just as important" as the ones that are considered.[10]

The second criticism is that factors used as inputs into the rankings are unreliable because they are not measured accurately. That is, regardless of the relevance of the number of books in the law school library, the surveys fail even to count the books correctly. The AALS study points out that although *U.S. News* provides a ranking of schools by judges and lawyers, the validity of those rankings is questionable given that there is no indication that the magazine samples lawyers and judges in anything approaching a random manner, and that the abysmally low response rate on the survey (approximately 33%) might create a skewed data set even of those included in the original sample.[11] An even more basic methodological error, as the AALS study points out, is that while *U.S. News* claims to give various factors precise weights in its final analysis, the magazine fails to control for differences in the standard deviations of scores between categories prior to creating the final analysis.[12] The consequence of this is that factors with large standard deviations in the scores (i.e., a lot of variance in the scores between schools) are actually given more weight in the final analysis than *U.S. News* claims, and that factors with small standard deviations (i.e., not much variance in scores from school to school) carry less weight than the magazine claims.[13]

The latter criticism is no doubt correct; *U.S. News*'s measurement techniques are unquestionably sloppy. But this charge is not very interesting or relevant given the critics' more basic charges. After all, if one does not think the number of library books is a relevant statistic in the first place, what difference does it make if the person who reports such worthless figures cannot count?

The former criticism—that the rankings fail to measure quality of education—is, of course, what really matters to the critics. And every critic, it seems, has a different opinion about which factors capture the concept of "quality" in legal education and are ignored or underweighted by the *U.S. News* rankings, and which factors relied upon by *U.S. News* do not reflect quality.[14] Not long ago, for example, Thomas Brennan, Dean of the Thomas Cooley Law School, issued his own set of "quality" rankings[15] that ignored students' scores on the Law School Admissions Test (LSAT) and the reputation of schools' faculty—both important components of the *U.S. News* methodology—on the grounds that the former "is not very significant" and the latter is "too subjective."[16] The problem is that while the critics might be correct in arguing that the rankings fail to measure educational quality, they can win only a Pyrrhic victory. Measuring educational quality is not the primary purpose that rankings serve, so *U.S. News*'s failure on this score is hardly damning.

At this point in the discussion, agitated critics are likely to argue that the failure of the rankings to measure educational quality accurately does matter if for no other reason than that prospective students believe that the rankings do serve this goal. Consequently, rankings are dangerous to the uninformed students who select their law school based upon its relatively high ranking, in the belief that they will receive a better quality education there than at a lower-ranked school, when such a conclusion is as likely to be wrong as to be right. This common sentiment is troubling for two reasons: it grossly and unfairly underestimates the intelligence of the would-be law students who read rankings, and it overestimates the importance of the critics' own institutions. These two issues are now considered in turn.

B. Students Are Not Dumb

There is not much doubt that many students do pay attention to law school rankings.[17] But while the AALS and other critics believe that rankings mislead students,[18] it is quite plausible that students are not so naive as to believe they will receive an intrinsically higher-quality legal education at the "#10 school" than at the "#15 school," or at a "second-tier" school than at a "third-tier" school.[19] Students understand that rankings serve a coordination function,[20] matching "high quality"[21] students first with each other[22] and then with the most sought-after employers.[23]

The most prestigious legal employers wish to hire the highest quality law students, and these students tend to wish to work for the most prestigious legal employers, or at least to keep open the option of doing so.[24] The problem is that other law students desire positions with the same employers, and employers have difficulty picking the most desirable students out of the passel. Employers know that comparing the grades of students who earned them at different law schools is not necessarily revealing, and that attempting to determine which students will make the best lawyers on the basis of a thirty-minute interview carries a dangerously high risk of error. Another way of stating the point is to say that "new lawyers," as a commodity "purchased" on the market by law firms, are "experience goods," meaning that it is quite difficult for the purchaser to evaluate the quality of the goods before purchasing them.[25]

"High quality" students, therefore, need a way to signal their quality to employers that cannot be imitated by "lower quality" students.[26] They do this by responding to rankings. By choosing a school with a high ranking, the student sends an important signal to future employers: he is brainy or clever enough to be accepted by a more selective school.[27] The higher-ranked school can be more selective because it is higher ranked, which increases the number of "high quality" students who apply.[28] The most selective legal employers respond to the signaling of students by interviewing and selecting students from the top-ranked law schools or at least the most highly ranked schools in their areas.[29] Like the students, the employers are not motivated by any belief that the highly-ranked schools offer an objectively superior legal education. Rankings exist to create a prestige hierarchy. Because they do this, the system is self-perpetuating and fully rational,[30] regardless of whether the rankings are based on unimpeachable data or cotton candy.

The available data on law school enrollment and employer recruiting is remarkably consistent with the theory that rankings serve a coordinating function, efficiently channeling students into post-law school employment. The LSAT scores of a school's students—a reasonable proxy for selectivity—tend to be higher the higher the school is ranked by *U.S. News*. The average LSAT score for students at the 75th percentile of their entering class was over 165 for schools in the "first tier" of U.S. News's 1997 rankings, while it was under 160 for schools in the "second tier" and under 153 for schools in the "fourth tier."[31] Part of this difference is no doubt due to the fact that LSAT scores are one input into the *U.S. News* rankings, but this almost certainly does not account for the entire difference.

Figure 1. Average LSAT Scores of Law Schools' Students

Tier, as Ranked in *U.S. News*	Number of Schools in Tier	Average LSAT Score of 75th Percentile Student
1	50	165.2
2	38	159.6
3	43	156.8
4	43	152.8

Just as "high quality" students, at least as measured by LSAT scores, appear to respond to rankings, it appears that the most prestigious legal employers do so as well. Stories of complaints levied by employers about the lack of practical knowledge imparted to students at the most prestigious law schools abound in the folklore of the legal profession. But what is most interesting about these anecdotes is that they never seem to result in the complaining employer ending its practice of hiring from these "impractical" institutions.[32] The available data bears out this observation. There is a strong correlation between a law school's *U.S. News & World Report* ranking and the number of legal employers per student that are members of the National Association of Law Placement (NALP) and recruit regularly at the school. The average "first-tier" school, as determined by *U.S. News*'s 1997 survey, has more than four times as many NALP employers regularly recruiting on campus per student than does the average second-tier school. Third-tier schools, on average, have even fewer NALP recruiters per student. And fourth-tier schools have only one third as many regular recruiters per student, on average, as do third-tier schools.[33] While the University of Chicago boasts more than two recruiters annually for each student in its graduating class (with Yale and Stanford close behind) no second-tier school has more than one recruiter visit for each two students in the graduating class, and no third or fourth tier school (with the sole exception of Howard Law School) has more than one NALP recruiter for each five students in the graduating class.[34]

Figure 2. NALP Recruiters per Graduating Student

Tier, as Ranked in *U.S. News*	Number of Schools in Tier	Average NALP Recruiters per Student
1	50	.69
2	37	.16
3	43	.12
4	39	.04

Even within the 50 schools in *U.S. News*'s first tier, the number of recruiters visiting a school is strongly correlated with the school's ranking.[35] In a regression containing only a school's ranking and the number of NALP recruiters it boasts, the ranking explains more than 70% of the variance in the number of NALP employers recruiting at each of the "top 50" law schools[36]—an extraordinary result for a single factor.

Figure 3. NALP Employers per Graduating Student: "Top 50" Schools

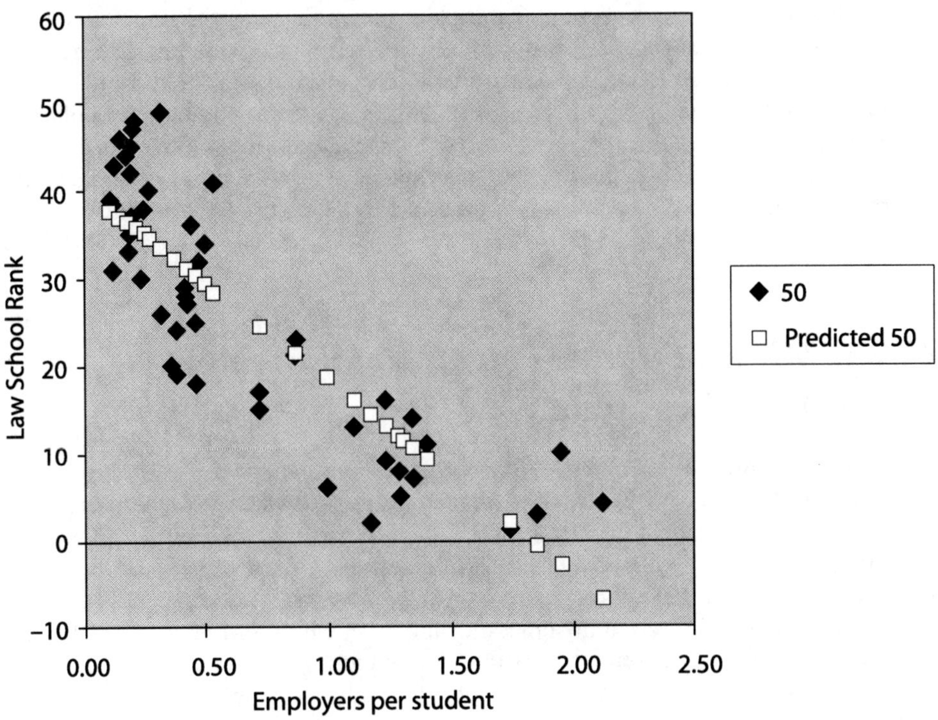

In a recent study, John Wehrli considered the channeling issue from a different perspective. He examined the educational background of each lawyer currently practicing with one of the nation's largest one-hundred law firms (as reported by the *American Lawyer* magazine),[37] a group of firms that serves as a proxy, albeit an imprecise one, for the category of "most prestigious legal employers." He then identified and ranked the top thirty law schools in the country on the basis of their per capita representation in the top one-hundred firms.[38] The top nine law schools in Wehrli's study were all among the top ten law schools in the 1998 *U.S. News* ranking.[39] Of the top twenty schools in Wehrli's ranking, nineteen appeared in the top twenty in *U.S. News*'s 1998 rankings.[40]

This data, taken together, indicates that high-quality students attend highly ranked schools, and that prestigious legal employers recruit at these same schools. Impressive as it is, the data cannot and does not prove that rankings play a causal role in the channeling of high-quality students to prestigious employers; it is possible that factors other than rankings attract top students and desired employers to the same law schools. But the most plausible inference to draw is that students and employers use rankings as an employment sorting mechanism: rankings channel the most desirable students into the most desirable jobs, the next most desirable students into the next most desirable jobs, and so on. The conclusion seems inescapable that, as one reporter recently observed, "educational pedigree still is paramount in the law and a middling student at a prestigious law school will typically have an edge over a top performer at a lower-ranked school," and that students know and respond to this reality.[41] Hence, if the primary concern of potential law students is to choose an institution that will maximize their chances of securing prestigious employment opportunities, paying close attention to law school rankings — regardless of how they are compiled — is a quite rational selection strategy. The importance of rankings for their own sake to law school applicants is clear.

Inexplicably, the primary purpose that rankings serve for potential students is more often than not completely ignored or misunderstood by critics of rankings. In the recent letter addressed to all law school applicants that accompanied the AALS study of the *U.S. News* rankings, the signatory deans "strongly urge[d]" students "to minimize the influence of rankings on [their judgment]" and instead to focus their inquiry on "the things [they] care about in a potential law school."[42] The letter thus failed even to consider the possibility that the factor many potential students care most about is the relative prestige of institutions, which is provided by the rankings!

C. The Minimal Upside Potential of Ranking "Quality" Education

Would the coordination function of rankings be better served if the schools that provided the objectively highest quality legal education received the highest rankings? Not necessarily. Legal employers that are able to hire the smartest students would benefit, of course, if their hires received the best legal education. On the other hand, however, other legal employers that are unable to attract the smartest students would benefit if their future employees received the highest quality legal education. From a social-value perspective, it is not at all clear whether the "best" education — whatever that means — is most efficiently provided to the most talented, least talented, or most average students. It seems at least as plausible to believe that the dullest students would benefit more from truly enlightening law school training than the smartest students (who will find it easier to learn good lawyering skills on the job and are likely to work for employers that have more resources to train them) as to believe the opposite.

That said, there certainly would be some social benefit if rankings were to reflect more accurately the quality of legal education. The existence of rankings creates an arms race among law schools, each seeking to climb its way to the top of the heap—or at least past its rivals.[43] If that competition were focused on true, objective quality of legal education, absolute quality would improve everywhere, even though the amount of relative quality cannot be increased. A rising tide raises all boats.

There are two problems, however, with focusing the inevitable arms race that rankings fuel on the goal of educational quality—one very pedestrian, the other somewhat profound. The pedestrian problem, which this essay will not belabor, is that no one has the foggiest idea how to judge objectively the quality of legal education across law schools. Consequently, any effort to "improve" ranking systems by focusing on measures of quality almost certainly is not worth the candle. The more profound problem is that even if we could identify objective quality in legal education, unleashing the competition for rankings based on the indicators identified is likely to create only a marginal social benefit. A more detailed discussion of this point is in order.

Every law professor who is not hopelessly delusional knows that the relative quality of a student's legal education is likely to have only a very marginal effect on her success in the practice of law. As much as professors would all like to believe that our brilliant lectures on the Rule Against Perpetuities can transform a blithering idiot into Clarence Darrow, it just is not true. A brilliant student will make an excellent lawyer even if he is forced to learn Trusts and Estates from the dimmest faculty member east or west of the Mississippi River. A quick mind and a little on-the-job training can make up for quite a few mediocre courses. Conversely, we law professors hope to help our most inept students become competent lawyers so that they serve their clients effectively and do not embarrass their institutions, but few of us suffer any illusions that our tutelage is likely to propel students to the Supreme Court someday.[44] In short, law professors provide their students with some basic knowledge and a few intellectual tools that will help prepare them to learn on the job. Of course, these things are not unimportant, but the magnitude of what professors can accomplish in the classroom is relatively limited, and, more importantly, the marginal value of a great education—whatever that is—compared to a merely competent one is probably small.[45]

Consider the likely benefit, then, of finding the "silver bullet" of education quality. Assume, for example, that a flawlessly designed scientific study conclusively demonstrated that the number of books in the law school library is the most important objective determinant of the quality of the legal education the school provides. What would be gained by reorienting all the rankings to reward the schools with the most books? In the drive for status, virtually all law schools would redouble their efforts to expand their libraries' collections. When the dust settled, there would still be twenty schools in the top twenty, and the best students would tend to gravitate toward them. There would undoubtedly be distributional effects, as the schools most adept at procuring books would advance in the rankings while others declined. But if the marginal value of a high-quality legal education relative to an average-quality one is small, as hypothesized in this essay, the net social benefit of the competition would be minimal.

Would a competition among law schools to provide higher-quality education result in society being "better represented" or ultimately "more just"? Perhaps, but probably not much. That the likely benefit of a competition to improve educational quality is small, of course, does not mean that it would not be worth pursuing in a world of unlimited resources. But the critical inquiry is whether the status competition that rankings fuel could be more socially productive if focused elsewhere. In Part II, this essay argues that it can.

II. Using the Rankings to Create Public Goods

To summarize: Rankings serve a valuable coordination function that well serves the best students and the most sought-after legal employers, and this purpose is equally well served if the rankings are based on the quality of education schools offer or the number of pushups their deans can do. This does not mean, however, that one should be indifferent to how rankings are determined. Rankings create status; status creates competition for status; and competition creates activity that can be put to productive use. Although ranking law schools based on the height of law buildings would effectively serve the coordination function, such an approach would be suboptimal because it would cause resources to be allocated to, and presumably largely wasted on, bricks and mortar. Rankings can be used optimally, from a social standpoint, by directing the energy that will inevitably go into competition for high rankings toward the creation of a socially desirable benefit that would otherwise go underproduced. Scholarship fits this description and, as such, this essay proposes, should be promoted explicitly by rankings systems.

A. Scholarship as a Public Good

In *The Logic of Collective Action*, Mancur Olson explained that when a group has a large membership, the contribution of each member to the whole is negligible so each has an incentive to free ride on the efforts of the others.[46] Unless the group has a large proportion of altruists, there will be little collective action unless the group can develop an incentive system to reward individual production.[47] Olson's logic can be applied to the production of scholarship. There are many law schools, and the scholarly contribution of any individual school is of small value to the legal profession or the academy as a whole. Scholarship will only be produced, therefore, if many law schools are altruists or if the collective creates an incentive for individual institutions to produce scholarship.

To fully understand this logic, one must take a step back and ask a question those in the academy rarely ask: Why should a law school or university administrator with the power of the purse reward scholarly output among members of the faculty?[48] The question does not suggest that legal scholarship is unimportant.[49] The problem is that scholarship is a public good, meaning that consumption of it by one person does not leave less for others and that the cost of excluding free riders from consuming it is prohibitive.[50] The creation of a scholarly work is usually funded by a single law school, while the benefit is shared by scholars (or sometimes lawyers, judges, students, or legislators) everywhere. Why would an institution with any sense of fiscal responsibility pay professors substantial salaries so that they can spend a good part of their time creating knowledge upon which the rest of the world can free ride? The answer is that the institution would not. Instead, it would pay professors only to spend their time doing work that creates a benefit the school could capture for itself.

So how can institutions of higher education sustain their tradition of scholarly output that inures to the public good? Returning to Olson's logic, such institutions have only two options: find a way to capture at least some of the benefits created by scholarly productivity or hire administrators who hold no concern for the bottom line. In the past, both methods ensured a high level of scholarly production. As to the first, prior to the rise of the *U.S. News* rankings, informal "rankings" of law schools were based primarily on the scholarly reputation of a school's faculty, which made it in the self-interest of law schools to support scholarship. This system, which still persists, although arguably to a lesser degree than it once did, can be understood as a "reputational tax-and-transfer system." The reputations of law schools that produce less than their pro rata share of scholarship are taxed and the reputational benefits are transferred to those schools that produce more than their pro rata share.

As to the second method, the financial viability of a law school in the free market was, in days past, a concern of very few institutions. Like most institutions of higher learning, law schools were funded by state treasuries or private philanthropists who did not ask for an annual profit and loss statement. If law professors and law school administrators wanted to spend a great deal of their time creating a public good, they met with little opposition.

Today, altruism among institutions of higher education appears to be on the decline. Budget cutting and belt tightening are, unfortunately, becoming ubiquitous at institutions of higher education coast to coast.[51] In the very near future, at all but the very wealthiest schools, scholarship will have to demonstrate that it can pay the bills; otherwise, faculty undoubtedly will be asked to devote more of their time to activities that will. The *death* of scholarship is not likely. There will always be some altruistic philanthropists who will endow chairs at prestigious institutions for the purpose of furthering scholarship, and governments of various levels will likely find it in their interest to support some level of basic research. But the *decline* of scholarship might be on the horizon unless the academy as a collective body continues to provide individual institutions with incentives to continue scholarly production. Rankings based in large measure on scholarship have historically provided such an incentive and can continue to do so in the future.

In a recent essay, Laurel Terry criticized the *U.S. News* rankings for evaluating law schools on the basis of a unitary set of standards.[52] Terry argues that an emphasis on scholarship in the rankings (still present, although diluted by the host of other factors also considered relative to the days of informal rankings) devalues the education of students and thus creates an incentive for "teaching" institutions to aspire to the priorities of "research" institutions—schools she defines as being relatively more concerned with developing theory than individual lawyers.[53] Rather than arguing that all law schools should place more emphasis on teaching and less on scholarship, Terry proposes the development of a second, parallel set of law school rankings that excludes consideration of scholarly productivity and instead emphasizes measurable characteristics of teaching value such as: student-faculty ratios, the amount of time faculty members are available to students outside of the classroom, the number of writing exercises in which faculty provide feedback to students, and the amount of faculty involvement in student co-curricular activities.[54] Such a ranking system would, presumably, offer institutions at which research is not a main priority the same opportunity for the type of status historically afforded to research institutions. In effect, this would deprive the latter institutions of the benefits of the reputational tax-and-transfer system that they have historically enjoyed.

Terry is quick to emphasize that, despite her proposal, she "strongly believe[s] that we need to have research institutions whose priority is theory development rather than personal development of [] students."[55] But without a reward paid in status for developing theory, which institutions would be altruistic enough to devote significant resources to the creation of a public good while their competitors devote all, or nearly all, of their resources to developing the skills of individual tuition payers, free riding on the scholarship of others? Terry views the issue of whether to emphasize research from the point of view of the individual faculty member who must allocate a finite amount of time between serving students and creating theory,[56] but this perspective obscures the fact that the production of scholarship is ultimately a matter of institutional, not individual, resource allocation. A research institution could pay its faculty to spend fifty percent of its time conducting research and still provide the same quantity of "teaching"—as Terry defines it—as does an institution that produces no scholarship merely by hiring twice as many professors.[57] If "research" law schools enjoyed no reputational advantage over "teaching" law schools, students would presumably opt for the type of institution that provided the most resources for their personal development per dollar of tuition paid.

Because creating scholarship costs money but does not directly benefit any individual tuition-paying student, producing scholarship without the reputational subsidy would be bad business unless students intrinsically value, and would be willing to pay for, the opportunity to bask in the glow of noted scholars. A recent survey of law students suggests that very few do. The *National Jurist* magazine ranks law schools on the basis of factors that students identified as important to them.[58] In that survey, students ranked teaching quality and various measures of job placement success as the most important measures of a law school; in contrast, they believed that having a "distinguished" faculty is relatively unimportant.[59]

Such student preferences suggest that to stay competitive in the market for students, "research" schools either would have to spend more money than their "teaching" school competitors or cut back on resources devoted to research. Over the long term, the likely result is a type of "race to the bottom," tempered only by haphazard philanthropic contributions to support the research enterprise.[60] Terry values the public good of scholarship, so long as institutions that create the public good are not compensated for doing so. Her desire for institutional altruism is understandable but, unfortunately, not very realistic.

For a glimpse of what the future could hold if scholarship is not rewarded by rankings systems, one need not look any further than Dean Brennan's 1996 rankings.[61] Stanford Law School,[62] perennially ranked in the top five in *U.S. News & World Report*'s survey, ranked a lowly thirtieth on Brennan's "quality" list. The reason for the disparity in Stanford's standing between the two surveys is no mystery. As Brennan himself explained, Stanford professors are among "the most visible legal scholars in the country," a fact for which the school is rewarded in the *U.S. News* rankings but not by his methodology.[63]

In the short run, of course, Stanford's reputation can well withstand a snubbing in a single, lightly read set of rankings. In fact, Stanford's poor showing in Brennan's rankings undoubtedly damaged the credibility of that set of rankings more than the reputation of the law school.[64] But what would happen if rankings that potential students and employers regularly read completely stopped taking into account scholarly production and, year after year, Stanford ranked outside of anyone's "top twenty"? A reasonable prediction is that, eventually, top students would begin to filter away to other schools—although, admittedly, this would probably take a long period of time. Employers would no doubt follow the students, feeding a downward spiral. If this were to happen, one would think that, sooner or later, the pressure would be great for Stanford to divert resources devoted to scholarship to other uses that would improve its ranking and stop student flight. In such a world of academe, where would the scholarly work—that professors like Terry "value" but don't wish to subsidize reputationally—come from?

B. Distinguishing the Public Goods Argument from Other Defenses of Scholarship

It is important to distinguish the "public goods" argument advanced in this essay from a very different argument commonly made in favor of rewarding academic institutions reputationally for their scholarly production. The usual argument underlies a set of rankings entitled *The Legal Gourmet Report: A Ranking of U.S. Law Schools by Educational Quality*, published annually by Brian Leiter as an alternative to the *U.S. News* survey. Leiter's rankings are notable for relying far more heavily on indicia of the quantity and quality of faculty scholarship than the *U.S. News* rankings.[65] While Leiter's emphasis on scholarship is appropriate, his motivation for this emphasis is misplaced.

In past years, Leiter has defended his methodology's emphasis on scholarship on the ground that "a faculty of distinguished scholars really is likely to provide a better education: one that is more intellectually demanding and current, based, as it will be, on a cutting-edge understanding of the field and its problems."[66] So justified, Leiter's survey turns out to be an alternative opinion about how to measure the "quality" of a legal education, and thus it ultimately differs from the *U.S. News* approach in the details but not in the overall view of the purposes rankings can and should serve. More importantly, his specific argument, variants of which legal scholars are all familiar with—that good scholarship informs or goes hand-in-hand with good teaching—is probably not true. Good teaching no doubt requires keeping abreast of scholarship in one's field, but there is little reason to suppose that good teaching requires producing the scholarship one's self.

In a recent study, James Lindgren and Allison Nagelberg show that—at least at three law schools—student evaluations indicate that the most frequently cited scholars are significantly better teachers than the least frequently cited scholars.[67] Such a correlation between strong teaching and strong scholarship is hardly surprising. Many of the qualities necessary to be a top scholar are important inputs to teaching excellence as well: outstanding analytical ability, creativity, a passion for the study of law, personal energy, and a strong work ethic, to name just a few.

If these qualities were equally distributed among all law professors, however, good scholarship and good law teaching probably would be inversely related for the simple reason that producing a piece of scholarship is infinitely more time consuming than reading the scholarship of others. This is to say that top-flight scholars might be excellent teachers, on average, but they probably could improve their teaching by spending the time they currently devote to writing their own books and articles studying and incorporating the scholarship of others into their lessons.[68] This conclusion follows from the simple observation that while some of the time spent producing a piece of scholarly writing has synergies with teaching, much of the time spent in the scholarly endeavor creates no such synergies. There is certainly overlap between law teaching and law scholarship, but creating scholarship is almost certainly not the most time-efficient method for members of any given faculty to transfer the wisdom of the legal academy to its students.

While this logic applies to all academic disciplines to some extent, it is probably more valid in the context of law schools than in most other academic departments.[69] Professors in disciplines that train doctoral candidates arguably must produce cutting-edge scholarship in order both to teach their graduate students advanced material and to serve as role models for the next generation of scholars in their fields. Law professors, in contrast, are primarily in the business of training lawyers, not academicians, and nearly all law school courses—even "upper level" courses—teach introductory material in a given field. Specialized "seminar" courses are the exceptions that prove the rule. As a result, law teaching offers only minimal opportunities for professors to share with their students the in-depth but highly specialized knowledge that they must develop in order to produce scholarly books and articles. In this respect, law teaching has much in common with undergraduate teaching.[70] A number of small liberal arts colleges that stress faculty attention to teaching rather than research productivity are renowned for the "high quality" of the education they provide. Similarly, it seems highly plausible that a law school with a dedicated teaching faculty conducting no original research could provide a higher quality education than a research-oriented faculty, assuming identical student bodies and financial resources.

Rankings should reward scholarship, then, not because an individual professor's scholarly work directly benefits the quality of education an individual student receives but because reputational rewards can serve as a private incentive to create the public good of scholarship.[71] If good scholarship leads to high rankings, it will also lead to financial reward for the institutions that best promote it. If it does not, in the emerging bottom-line oriented world of higher education, pressures will quickly mount for faculty to spend less time conducting research and more time teaching the Statute of Frauds and the collateral source rule. Such pressures would be individually rational for each individual institution, but, ironically, would leave the legal academy and profession as a whole worse off.[72]

C. Should Other Goods Be Considered in Rankings?

Assuming that emphasizing scholarship in law school rankings is justified not because of the spillover effects that the production of scholarship has on law teaching but because such an emphasis will encourage the production of a public good, the question naturally arises whether law school rankings ought to promote the production of other public goods instead. Surely there must be public goods more deserving—or at least equally deserving—of production as scholarship. What special claim does scholarship have to the resources that will inevitably be devoted to the arms race for status that rankings fuel?

Legal scholarship deserves special consideration as a basis for rankings because it is both: (1) a true public good, and (2) a good that law school infrastructure and personnel are uniquely able to produce. Law professors are particularly well suited to advance society's store of knowledge in the areas in which they teach, and the research university infrastructure, in which most American law schools reside, provides a useful resource base for this endeavor.

Few "other candidates" for rankings criteria measure up in both areas. No doubt, there are public goods that are more important than legal scholarship. Society might wish to encourage cleansing of the environment or the construction of interstate highways, for example, more than the production of legal scholarship. But law schools have no special competence in providing such goods. Readers who disagree with the quite unsupported assertion made above that the marginal value of a "great" law school education relative to a merely "good" one is small[73] might contend that rankings should be used to promote an arms race in educational quality. While it is true that quality law teaching is a good that law schools are uniquely situated to provide and that it has some public good aspects, quality legal education is predominantly a private good. At the margin, "outstanding" attorneys might create more social justice than merely "good" attorneys, and this increased justice can be viewed as a public good, because it creates a benefit that does not inure entirely to lawyers' clients. But most of the value of creating outstanding attorneys is privately appropriated. The products of an outstanding legal education can charge their clients more than they would be able to if they were products of a mediocre legal education. Thus, law students have a private incentive to pay for a high-quality education, and law schools, consequently, will always have an incentive to provide a high-quality education. To the extent that a "high-quality" education can be defined, students will have an incentive to pay for it regardless of whether or not it is rewarded with prestige.

This is not to say that scholarship is necessarily the only proper criterion for law school rankings. Rather, I mean to argue that scholarship is the most obvious proper criterion for rankings, and that other criteria should be added to rankings methodology only if they meet the standards of being primarily public goods that are within the particular competence of law schools to provide. Consider one possible example: The practice of public interest law is arguably a public good, and it is arguably within the special competence of law schools to either provide this good directly or to encourage its production by law school graduates. Consequently, either the number of public interest clients served by a law school's clinic, or its faculty, or the percentage of a school's graduates who pursue careers in public interest law might be appropriate for consideration in law school rankings.

III. Conclusion: Implementation Challenges

This essay has defended the publication and use of law school rankings by arguing that their utilitarian purpose is not to measure "quality" of legal education in the abstract, as most critics of rankings assume, but rather to coordinate the channeling of the most capable students to the most desirable legal employers. Despite the questionable methodological approaches employed by, among other publications, *U.S. News*, rankings succeed at fulfilling their primary goal, and thus serve a valuable social purpose. This essay also has argued that because the content of rankings is irrelevant to the fulfillment of their primary purpose, rankings can be most useful as a tool to encourage the production of public goods that would otherwise be underproduced relative to the social optimum. Because legal scholarship is such a public good, and one that law schools are uniquely competent to provide, this essay has proposed that rankings should be based primarily on the scholarly productivity of law school faculties, while leaving open the possibility that other public goods within the competence of law schools to provide might also be considered.

Even if readers are convinced on these two points, details relating to implementation remain to be considered. Assuming that all were to agree that it is socially optimal for law school rankings to be based largely, if not exclusively, on measures of faculty scholarly output, determining what measures should be used to judge the quality of that output is a problematic task that can never produce a first-best outcome. Rewarding a school's reputation in the scholarly community could encourage networking and politicking as much as scholarship. Awarding points for articles and pages published, *a la* the *Chicago-Kent Law Review*'s occasional rankings,[74] could encourage quantity of scholarship at the expense of quality. Judging quality by counting the number of times a scholar is cited[75] rewards scholars in popular fields and those with unique ideas, neither of which necessarily implies quality.[76] Combining these or similar approaches into a weighted average only begs the question of which are most relevant or least flawed.

The debate about how to measure the quality of scholarship will never be resolved perfectly or in a way that pleases everyone. Although this is unfortunate, it is far less troubling than the fact that the current debate concerning how to measure the "quality" of a legal education is focused on the wrong target altogether. Regardless of the precise measure or measures chosen, if rankings reward scholarship, law schools will have the necessary incentive to devote considerable resources to scholarly activity. In the long run, competition between law schools to produce scholarship, while not of immediate or obvious value to any single law student, is likely to create more social value than competition geared toward marginally increasing the direct quality of legal education, which most critics of the *U.S. News & World Report* rankings implicitly or explicitly advocate.

Notes

* This essay benefitted from the comments of Ian Ayres, Chris Guthrie, Cheryl Hanna, David Hyman, Andy Leipold, Brian Leiter, David Meyer, Daria Roithmayr, Laurel Terry, Tom Ulen, and Mark Weber, although none of these otherwise kind souls could be persuaded to take responsibility for any of the heresies contained herein. John Booher provided valuable research assistance.

1. A recent article in the *ABA Journal* referred to the legal education community's opposition to rankings as having "taken on the force of a jihad." Terry Carter, *Rankled by the Rankings*, A.B.A. J., Mar. 1998, at 46, 46.

2. *See* David E. Rovella, *A Survey of Surveys Ranks the Top U.S. Law Schools*, NAT'L L. J., June 2, 1997, at A1. The Association of American Law Schools, the American Bar Association, and the Law School Admission Council, in addition to the 150 individual deans, all oppose law school rankings. *See* M.A. Stapleton, *Push Is on for Unranked Guides to Schools*, CHI. DAILY L. BULL., Jan. 10, 1997, at 3. One student has noted the apparent hypocrisy of deans who insist on ranking their students despite differences in professors, tests, and courseloads, yet complain that it is misleading and unfair to rank law schools. *See* Alan R. Dayton, Letter to the Editor, *Rankings Are as Fair to Schools as to Students*, NAT'L L.J., June 23, 1997, at A14.

3. *See* Stephen P. Klein & Laura Hamilton, *The Validity of the* U.S. News & World Report *Rankings of ABA Law Schools* (visited Nov. 19, 1998) <http://www.aals.org.proxy.lib.pdx.edu/validity.htm>.

4. *See* Carter, *supra* note 1, at 46. *The New York Times* puts the number at 93,000. *See* Jan Hoffman, *Judge Not, Law Schools Demand of a Magazine That Ranks Them*, N.Y. TIMES, Feb. 19, 1998, at A1.

5. According to news reports, the mailing cost the Law School Admission Council $ 50,000. *See* Hoffman, *supra* note 4, at 46.

6. *The National Law Journal* refers to "the annual rite of whining that follows the *U.S. News & World Report* law school rankings, in which schools attack the survey while obsessing over their ranks." Rovella, *supra* note 2. Presumably, complaints emanating from all schools except Yale, the perennial number one, could be classified as whining. Even Harvard, the usual number two, could be accused of whining, since it presumably would love to beat out Yale for the top spot.

7. *See*, e.g., Editorial, *Breaking Ranks*, NAT'L L.J., June 2, 1997, at A14 (criticizing *U.S. News* for providing "consumers with an unexplained ranking number derived from a combination of dissimilar factors"); Brian Leiter, Letter to the Editor, *U.S. News Rankings: Unfair to State Schools?*, NAT'L L.J., Oct. 7, 1996, at A18 (insisting that the *U.S. News* rankings are "influenced by a bizarre host of factors that systematically penalize state schools").

JD/MBA student John Wehrli has published a set of law school composite quality rankings on the Internet that should win the gold medal for complicated methodology. Wehrli ranks the top 30 law schools by assigning a 70% weight to the average ranking of schools from 4 other sources, of which 2 are *U.S. News* reputational rankings and the third is the *U.S. News* overall rankings. The scores for each of these 4 sources are, in turn, determined by combining their current rankings with an average of their historical rankings. A 20% weight is assigned to "caliber of student" rankings, which are in turn derived by giving a 40% weight to a composite score of a school's students' undergraduate grade point averages and a 60% weight to a composite score of a school's students' LSAT scores. The composite GPA and LSAT scores are themselves determined by taking the median scores of the top 50% of a school's students. The remaining 10% weight is given to a "selectivity" score, which is calculated—mercifully—merely by dividing a school's total number of admits by its total number of applicants. *See* John E. Wehrli, *Methodology Used for Composite Rankings* (visited May 26, 1998) <http://wehrli.ilrg.com/method.html>. Wehrli warns his readers—and apparently not in jest—that all surveys and rankings suffer from what he terms "[a]rbitrary [f]ormula [b]ias." John E. Wehrli,

Methodology & Weaknesses of the Published Rankings (visited May 26, 1998) <http://wehrli.ilrg.com/weakness.html>.

8. This represents my best understanding of how *U.S. News & World Report* currently tabulates its rankings, but I offer no warranty concerning the accuracy of this representation.

9. Carl Monk, *The AALS Role in Opposing Rankings of Law Schools*, AALS NEWSL. (Association of Am. Law Schs., Washington, D.C.), Apr. 1997, at 4 (quoting a 1990 joint statement of the AALS, the ABA Section of Legal Education and Admissions to the Bar, the Law School Admission Council, and the National Association for Law Placement); *see also Annual Report of the Consultant on Legal Education to the American Bar Association* 44 (1993–94). Failing to perceive an important role for rankings independent of the inputs used to generate them, the *Report* responded:

> Although we have not had the opportunity to review the *U.S. News and World Report* article, we believe that any ranking or rating of law schools, based upon data the magazine has asked deans to provide, must be meaningless or grossly misleading. The survey does not and could not, measure many important factors involved in evaluating the quality of law schools.

Id.

10. Klein & Hamilton, *supra* note 3.

11. *See id.* A recent article in *The American Lawyer* criticized *U.S. News* for measuring schools' reputations by surveying people who cannot possibly have even heard of all the schools they are asked to rank, much less know anything about all of the schools. *See* Roger Parloff, *Who's Number One? And Who's Number 52, 91, and 137?*, AM. LAW., Apr. 1, 1998, at 5, 5.

12. See Klein & Hamilton, *supra* note 3, at 8, ¶ 28-29, 10 ¶ 36, and 12 ¶ 45.

13. *See id.* (analyzing the *U.S. News*'s "overall selectivity," "overall resources," and "overall placement" ranking methodologies).

14. *See, e.g.*, Franklyn D. Kimball, *The Ones to Rank Law Schools Are Employers*, NAT'L L.J., June 30, 1997, at A16 (criticizing *U.S. News*'s rankings for relying on student grades, LSAT scores, starting salaries, placement rates, faculty credentials, and student opinions, and for undervaluing the opinions of employers).

15. *See* THOMAS E. BRENNAN, JUDGING THE LAW SCHOOLS 15–19 (1996). Brennan provides "no less than 50 different primary rankings," including the overall "quality" ranking. *Id.* at 8.

16. Saundra Torry, *For Law School Deans, Rankings Can Rankle*, WASH. POST, Feb. 12, 1996, at F7. *U.S. News* responded to Brennan's rankings by claiming its criteria are "far more relevant to the quality of schools." *Id.* (quoting *U.S. News* Executive Editor Mel Elfin).

17. A recent study reported that 30% of college students considered rankings at least "somewhat important" to their matriculation decisions and 11% considered them very important. Kim Strosnider, *Study Measures Influence of College Rankings*, CHRON. HIGHER EDUC., Apr. 4, 1997, at A34. Last year's issue of *U.S. News* containing the magazine's college rankings was its second best-selling issue. Parloff, *supra* note 11, at 7. It would seem logical that the choices of professional schools would be even more affected by rankings, and anecdotal reports of law school administrators and pre-law counselors suggests this is the case. *See, e.g.*, Carter, *supra* note 1, at 48 (quoting University of Miami Law School Vice Dean Laurence M. Rose as saying "I wish I had a nickel for every student who's come up to me and asked where we rank in *U.S. News*.... I could stop teaching and retire"); Hoffman, *supra* note 4 (quoting Duke Law School Dean Pamela Gann as noting that the rankings "clearly matter" and "are extremely widely read and extremely widely relied upon"); Rovella, *supra* note 2 (quoting a UCLA pre-professional advisor as stating that "students are using [*U.S. News* law school rankings] as their sole counseling tool"); M.A. Stapleton, *School Ranking Doesn't Make Deans' List*, CHI. DAILY L. BULL., Mar. 8, 1996, at 3 (quoting Dean Thomas M. Mengler of the University of Illinois College of Law as calling rankings "significant factors in employment and admissions," and Dean Richard Matasar of Chicago-Kent Law School as saying "It's really a shame that some people rely on information that's so deeply flawed"). Stetson University College of Law reports an increase in the number of applicants due to the popularity of its trial advocacy program, recently ranked first in the specialized trial advocacy ranking by *U.S. News*. *See* Chris Klein, *Lower Tier-Dwellers Boost Their Notability by Carving out Niches*, NAT'L L.J., Mar. 31, 1997, at A12. Applications to Chicago-Kent Law School reportedly increased 30% in 1991 after it was named by *U.S. News* as among 5 up-and-coming law schools. *See* Carter, *supra* note 1, at 48. The suspicion that applicants do pay attention to rankings is reinforced

by revelations that some law schools have been caught reporting different—and more favorable—statistical information to *U.S. News* than to the ABA. See Frank T. Read, *Legal Education's Holy War over Regulation of Consumer Information: The Federal Trump Card*, 30 WAKE FOREST L. REV. 307, 318–19 (1995) (recounting that "42 of the 176 ABA-approved law schools reported different admissions data to [*U.S. News*] than those same schools reported to the ABA"); Carter, *supra* note 1, at 50 (reporting that "12–15 schools had played games between the ABA and *U.S. News* with differing data").

18. *See "Law School Rankings May Be Hazardous To Your Health!": A Message to Applicants from Law School Deans* (visited May 26, 1998) <http://www.lsac.org/dnbroch.htm> [hereinafter *Message to Applicants*] ("[W]e [law school deans] strongly urge you [law school applicant] to minimize the influence of rankings on your own judgment.").

19. Of course, a few students might believe this. God help their clients.

20. For an excellent description of tacit coordination strategies between people with common interests, see THOMAS C. SCHELLING, THE STRATEGY OF CONFLICT 54, 54–58 (1979) ("One does not simply predict where the other will go, since the other will go where he predicts the first to go, which is wherever the first predicts the second to predict the first to go, and so ad infinitum.").

21. The term "high quality" is used here as shorthand for "the kind of students most desirable to legal employers." It should go without saying that what legal employers value in their new hires has nothing to do with a student's inherent worth, and that what employers value might or might not bear a strong relationship to raw intellectual power or legal acumen.

22. Although this argument focuses on how rankings coordinate students with employers, rankings also serve an important coordination function by matching the best students with each other. *Cf.* Seymour Martin Lipset, *In Defense of the Research University*, *in* THE RESEARCH UNIVERSITY IN A TIME OF DISCONTENT 219, 223 (Jonathan R. Cole et al. eds., 1994) ("The best thing about an education at Harvard and Stanford, two schools I know well, is the quality of the undergraduates.... What makes these and other schools great educational institutions is that they attract brilliant students, who then find it easy to locate one another."). This coordination aspect of rankings is consistent with the thesis forwarded in this essay that rankings serve a valuable purpose regardless of how the rankings are determined.

23. *Cf.* Roger Parloff, *supra* note 11, at 7, 7 (noting that readers "devour[]" ratings because they want to know which school will "open the most doors").

24. These employers of choice are, generally speaking, the largest law firms. Whether the relentless pursuit of these employment opportunities is in the best long-term interests of law students individually or society collectively is, of course, another question entirely. *See generally* ANTHONY T. KRONMAN, THE LOST LAWYER: FAILING IDEALS OF THE LEGAL PROFESSION 271–314 (1993) (describing the trends among large firms that have produced low job satisfaction among large-firm lawyers).

25. For a discussion of "experience goods" and their counterpart, "search goods," *see* Phillip Nelson, *Information and Consumer Behavior*, 78 J. POL. ECON. 311, 311–12 (1970).

26. *Cf.* Michael Spence, *Job Market Signaling*, 87 Q.J. ECON. 355, 358 (1973) (explaining that the education levels of job applicants can serve as signals of productivity to employers assuming that signalling costs are negatively correlated with productivity).

27. Students' undergraduate matriculation decisions are probably also largely based on signalling concerns, as leading research universities continue to attract the top high school students. *See, e.g.*, Harvey Brooks, *Current Criticisms of Research Universities*, *in* THE RESEARCH UNIVERSITY IN A TIME OF DISCONTENT, *supra* note 22, at 231, 235. Hence, despite the widespread belief that many small colleges offer superior undergraduate education, Brooks notes:

> [T]here is little evidence from the market that [the focus on research] is turning undergraduates away from research universities.... The explanation given for this by critics is that undergraduates select universities on the basis of their research reputation or that of their professors because this reputation is the best assurance of a good job or admission to a preferred graduate or professional school after graduation.

Id.; *see also* Stephen M. Stigler, *Competition and the Research Universities*, *in* THE RESEARCH UNIVERSITY IN A TIME OF DISCONTENT, *supra* note 22, at 131, 148. Stigler, too, finds the signalling function of a degree from a research university to be compelling:

> There are thousands of undergraduate institutions in the country where virtually no research is carried out, and a fine education is available, usually at a significantly lower cost than at

> a research university. And yet, the major research universities remain in demand. Consumers ... are evidently willing to pay at current rates for what they are receiving, whether it be an education or simply reflected prestige.

Id.

28. If you think a top 10 school is not more selective than a number 20 school, just wait until the top 10 school stays in the top 10 for a few years and the number 20 school stays at number 20. Unless the number 20 school is close to a top surfing beach and the top 10 school is on the north slope of Alaska, the top 10 school will become more selective.

29. *Cf.* Alex M. Johnson, Jr., *Think Like a Lawyer, Work Like a Machine: The Dissonance Between Law School and Practice*, 64 S. CAL. L. REV. 1231, 1246 (1991) (arguing that through the admissions process law schools serve as gatekeepers to the profession).

Legal employers that have had enough experience with hiring students from different law schools can and sometimes do form their own internal rankings of the graduates from certain schools that they then follow when making hiring decisions. Developing an internal ranking system, though, is both costly and subject to the bias of attributing statistical significance to experiences gleaned from a small sample of students from different schools that may not be representative of those schools' student bodies generally. As a result, most employers probably hew fairly closely to external rankings of schools when they make interviewing or hiring decisions, although they might make slight adjustments to those rankings based on their experiences.

30. *Cf.* Carter, *supra* note 1, at 52 (quoting University of Texas law professor Brian Leiter as observing that "it's reasonable for [students] to be concerned with prestige and reputation, and rankings speak to that").

31. *See infra* Figure 1. ABA APPROVED LAW SCHOOLS: STATISTICAL INFORMATION ON AMERICAN BAR ASSOCIATION APPROVED LAW SCHOOLS 77–86 (Rick L. Morgan & Kurt Snyder eds., 1997).

32. One colleague relays a story of a prominent federal judge who, in recommending a former law clerk for an academic position, wrote that the candidate was an excellent clerk *in spite of* his Yale Law School education. Notice, however, that despite the sarcastic reference to the education offered by the nation's most highly-ranked law school, concerns about the quality of a Yale education did not stop the judge from hiring the young man as his law clerk in the first place!

33. *See infra* Figure 2. The figures were calculated by: (1) executing a search during August 1997, on Westlaw's NALP computer database for each ABA-accredited law school and tallying the number of employers who reported that they regularly recruit at each school; (2) dividing by 3 the total number of students enrolled in each law school, according to the 1996 *U.S. News & World Report* special edition on "The Best Graduate Schools"; (3) dividing the former number by the latter; and (4) averaging the results for schools in each of the four "tiers," as evaluated by *U.S. News*. Schools that were either not included in the 1997 *U.S. News* rankings or whose enrollment data was not included in the *U.S. News* 1996 Best Graduate Schools issue were not included in the calculation, which explains why the total number of schools is less than the total number of schools that make up the data in Figure 1, *supra*.

34. Complete calculations for each school are on file with the *Texas Law Review*. These calculations were derived from public data described *supra* note 33.

35. *See infra* Figure 3.

36. $R^2 = .71$. A more complex model might prove a causal relationship, but the exercise here is meant only to demonstrate the strong correlation between rankings and recruiter visits.

37. *See* John E. Wehrli, *Top 30 Law Schools at the Top 100 Law Firms, Adjusted for School Size* (visited May 26, 1998) <http://wehrli.ilrg.com/amlawnormt30.html> [hereinafter *Top 30 Law Schools*]; see also supra note 7 (describing the complicated methodology Wehrli used to calculate his law school rankings).

38. *See* Wehrli, *supra* note 37.

39. The schools are Harvard, Yale, Chicago, Columbia, Stanford, Michigan, Virginia, N.Y.U., and U.C. Berkeley (Boalt). Duke and the University of Pennsylvania were also in U.S. News's 1998 "top 10." Schools of Law, U.S. NEWS & WORLD REP., Mar. 2, 1998, at 78, 78.

40. The one school in the top 20 in terms of "top-firm penetration" that was not ranked in the 1998 *U.S. News* top 20 was Boston University, at #29. One of the 2 schools in the *U.S. News* top 20

that failed to make the top 20 in "top-firm penetration," Vanderbilt, ranked #21 in the latter category—compared to #16 in the *U.S. News* survey.

41. David Segal, *A Fall Harvest for Law Firms*, WASH. POST, Nov. 25, 1996, at F1.

42. *Message to Applicants*, *supra* note 18.

43. *Cf.* Carter, *supra* note 1, at 48 (reporting that enormous pressure is placed on law school admissions and career services officers to "get the numbers up, whatever it takes—or else."); *id.* at 50, 52 (reporting that Hastings Law School responded to its recent slide out of *U.S. News*'s top 50 by implementing an intensive job placement program).

44. The 99% of law professors who think they are smarter than all nine Supreme Court justices might think that the Supreme Court is a poor choice of an example chosen to represent "places where only smart lawyers get jobs," but I trust that they get the point anyway.

45. *See* William O. Barrett, Letter, *The Impact of Quality*, AM. LAW., June 1998, at 37, 37 (citing a study demonstrating that when the abilities of incoming students are controlled, the college a student chooses to attend has virtually no impact on his future earnings); *cf.* Ronald J. Gilson & Robert H. Mnookin, *Foreword: Business Lawyers and Value Creation for Clients*, 74 OR. L. REV. 1, 6 (1995) ("[O]nly a fraction of the students possesses judgment ... and we are skeptical whether the law school experience accounts for even this fraction. Indeed, we suspect that some students come to law school with practical wisdom already in hand and may well have had it when they were twelve years old.").

46. MANCUR OLSON, JR., THE LOGIC OF COLLECTIVE ACTION 15–16 (1971).

47. *See id.* at 44.

48. I have asked my classes this question in the past, suggesting that they might want to demand that the dean require me to teach four classes each semester and stop "wasting" my time on scholarship. This would cut the number of professors our school would need in half and, presumably, save the students a fair amount of tuition dollars. While some students seem tempted to bolt out of class and into the dean's office, others understand right away that scholarship helps build the school's reputation, and this reputation is part of what they pay for each semester.

49. In our darkest moments, of course, we all wonder if the scholarly articles that we spend thousands of hours sweating over provide any social benefit whatsoever, and occasionally some professor safely over the tenure hurdle writes a scathing article shamelessly playing on these secret moments of existential despair. *See, e.g.*, Kenneth Lasson, *Scholarship Amok: Excesses in the Pursuit of Truth and Tenure*, 103 HARV. L. REV. 926, 928 (1990) ("Scholarship could be valuable; most of it isn't. Whatever rich stew there might have been thins quickly into gruel through the sheer multitude of journals seeking fodder for their troughs. Slops fill the law reviews."); Elyce H. Zenoff, *I Have Seen the Enemy and They Are Us*, 36 J. LEGAL EDUC. 21, 21 (1986) ("Published articles lack originality, are boring, too long, too numerous, and have too many footnotes, which also are boring and too long." (footnotes omitted)). These attacks contain a good deal of truth, but they are almost certainly too pessimistic, as the value of legal scholarship should be judged by its best work, not its worst. *See* Richard A. Posner, *Legal Scholarship Today*, 45 Stan. L. Rev. 1647, 1655 (1993). I assume in this essay merely that legal scholarship is a "good"; I make no attempt to quantify its positive value. I leave a more complete response to those who might argue that legal scholarship has *no social value whatsoever* for another time and place.

50. *See, e.g.*, ROBERT COOTER & THOMAS ULEN, LAW AND ECONOMICS 40 (2d ed. 1997).

51. *See, e.g.*, Rick Karlin, *SUNY Towns Fight Cuts in Funds*, TIMES UNION (Albany), June 24, 1997, at A1; Richard Locker, *'97 Assembly Lacked Bombshells, but Little Laws Go a Long Way*, COM. APPEAL (Memphis), June 9, 1997, at A1 (noting that cuts to the higher education budget for Tennessee public universities "all but guarantee[] an increase estimated at 6 percent in tuition and registration fees"); Rosemary Shinohara, *UA to Raise Costs, Cut Classes, Staff*, ANCHORAGE DAILY NEWS, June 30, 1997, at B1 (discussing the impact of sizeable budget cuts on the University of Alaska system); Jane Stancill, *UNC-CH Gets New Arts and Sciences Dean*, NEWS & OBSERVER (Raleigh), July 12, 1997, at B1 (detailing the hiring of an administrator previously known for successfully handling deep budget cuts); Valerie Strauss, *UDC Chief Is Upbeat About Deal to Sell Radio Station*, WASH. POST, July 10, 1997, at D.C. 1 (demonstrating how the sale of a public university's assets was used to resolve a budget deficit); *WSU Faculty to Get 3 Percent Pay Increase*, SPOKESMAN REV. (Spokane), May 1, 1997, at B3 (describing a university faculty salary increase contingent upon cuts made elsewhere); Susan Young, *Mood Swings: Challenges Ahead Despite Boost in Support, Morale*, BANGOR DAILY NEWS, May 24–25, 1997, at A1 (recounting the effects of a pledge of private funds). Law schools are not immune to this trend. *See, e.g.*, Doug Caruso, *Law Schools Urged to Find Ways to Cut Costs*,

COLUMBUS DISPATCH, June 1, 1996, at 5D (reporting proposed budget cuts at Ohio's five public law schools); Phil McDade, *Money Woes Hurt UW Law Rating, Official Says*, WIS. ST. J., Mar. 17, 1996, at 3C (suggesting that budget cuts have caused the University of Wisconsin law school's drop in the *U.S. News* rankings).

52. *See* Laurel Terry, *Taking Kronman and Glendon One Step Further: In Celebration of "Professional Schools,"* 100 DICK. L. REV. 647, 667–75 (1996).

53. *See id.* at 670–71.

54. *See id.* at 672–73.

55. *Id.* at 674.

56. *See id.* at 673.

57. In fact, this bears a strong resemblance to the current state of affairs in the legal academy, as most research-oriented schools support scholarship by providing their faculty with lighter teaching loads than most teaching-oriented schools.

58. *See* Brett S. Martin, *How to Really Rank the Best Law Schools*, NAT'L JURIST, May/June 1997, at 32 (ranking law schools on factors identified as important by law students).

59. *Id.* at 29. According to the survey, quality of teaching is the #1 criterion among students, employment rate after 6 months is #2, placement office assistance is #3, and reputation among attorneys is #5. Having "distinguished" faculty members was only the #22 criterion—out of 39—in terms of importance to students, while the school's "reputation among law faculty," which would presumably be based on scholarly productivity, ranked #25. *Id.*

60. One prediction is that only professors with privately endowed "research" chairs would be provided the luxury of conducting research, while all others would be expected to devote all of their time to teaching. Of course, in such a world there likely would be fewer endowed chairs than there are today, because only philanthropists dedicated to the intrinsic worth of scholarship would endow them. Philanthropists who donate their money because they desire to enhance the prestige of an institution—usually their alma mater—would earmark that money for other uses.

61. *See* BRENNAN, *supra* note 15, at 10–14 (evaluating law schools on "five basic Indexes," none of which consider scholarship).

62. In the interest of full disclosure it should be noted that this is the author's alma mater.

63. Torry, *supra* note 16.

64. *See id.* (quoting George Washington University Law School Dean Jack Friedenthal as remarking that "any person who knows anything about legal education ... would howl" at Stanford's ranking).

65. Brian Leiter, *The Legal Gourmet Report, 1997–98: A Ranking of U.S. Law Schools by Educational Quality* (visited Oct. 9, 1998) <http://www.dla.utexas.edu/depts/philosophy/faculty/leiter/LGOURMET.HTM>. *The Legal Gourmet Report* views the scholarly activity of faculty through the lenses of publications per capita, faculty membership in the American Academy of Arts & Sciences, and the number of citations garnered by the top 10 faculty members.

66. *Id.*

67. *See* James Lindgren & Allison Nagelberg, *Are Scholars Better Teachers?*, 73 CHI.-KENT L. REV. 823, 827–29 (1998).

68. This point is supported indirectly by a recent statistical analysis, conducted by Deborah Merritt, that finds no relationship between scholarly productivity and success in garnering teaching awards among law professors with 7–11 years of professional experience. See Deborah Jones Merritt, *Research and Teaching on Law Faculties: An Empirical Exploration*, 73 CHI.-KENT L. REV. 765, 807 (1998). If it is correct that excellence in scholarship demands many of the same skills required for excellence in teaching, then top scholars should earn more than their fair share of teaching awards, all other things being equal. That they fail to do so suggests all other things are not equal, and what is unequal is probably time spent directly on teaching-related activities. The Lindgren and Nagelberg study shows top scholars are better-than-average teachers. *See* Lindgren & Nagelberg, *supra* note 67, at 832–33. The Merritt study suggests that they might fail to achieve recognition as the top teachers as often as they otherwise could. *See* Merritt, *supra* at 807.

This interpretation is also consistent with an interesting, although less rigorous, recent study by Fred Shapiro that finds that law review tributes to retiring or deceased authors of extremely influential legal scholarship mention the teaching prowess of the subject of the tribute far less often than do tributes to a control group of other law professors. *See* Fred R. Shapiro, *They Published, Not Perished, but Were They Good Teachers?*, 73 CHI.-KENT L. REV. 835, 839 (1998). Contrary to the suggestion of the article's title, this finding in no way suggests that "star" authors were not good teachers: only one tribute in the sample suggests at all that the scholar was a bad teacher. *See id.* at 840. It does suggest, however, that—whatever their classroom talents—this group tended to emphasize scholarship relative to teaching.

69. *Cf.* Francis X. Sutton, *The Distinction and Durability of American Research Universities, in* THE RESEARCH UNIVERSITY IN A TIME OF DISCONTENT, *supra* note 22, at 309, 315 ("For some of the graduate schools of research universities, strong research programs are clearly needed to maintain their attractiveness as graduate schools. But it is not clear that this is so for law or business schools.").

70. *Cf.* Brooks, *supra* note 27, at 235 (noting that the "perception that research and teaching are competitive, and largely mutually exclusive, activities ... is clearly more true at the beginning undergraduate level than it is at later stages in university education").

71. From a positive perspective, the reputational value of scholarly productivity is the reason often given for the emphasis that research universities place on scholarship relative to teaching in the hiring and promotion processes. *See, e.g.*, Lipset, *supra* note 22, at 222 ("[H]igher education in the United States gives infinitely more recognition to research and publication than to teaching.... The reason is obvious. Teaching reputations do not carry off campus; research ones do.").

72. In this sense, a law school's decision whether or not to devote resources to producing scholarship can be viewed as a multi-party "prisoner's dilemma," in which all schools are better off if all produce scholarship than if all do not, but each would prefer not to produce scholarship while the others continue to do so. The term "prisoner's dilemma" stems from the standard hypothetical in which two prisoners, held in different cells, are given the option by the police to finger the other for a crime. If one prisoner keeps quiet while the other squeals, the former serves a long sentence while the latter is released. If both keep quiet, both serve a short sentence for a lesser crime, and if both squeal, both serve a moderate sentence. Under this set of incentives, both prisoners have an incentive to squeal, although they would be better off if they both were to keep quiet. *See, e.g.*, DAVID M. KREPS, GAME THEORY AND ECONOMIC MODELLING 37–39 (1990); AVINASH K. DIXIT & BARRY J. NALEBUFF, THINKING STRATEGICALLY: THE COMPETITIVE EDGE IN BUSINESS, POLITICS AND EVERYDAY LIFE 11–14 (1991).

73. *See supra* text accompanying notes 43–45.

74. *See, e.g.*, Colleen M. Cullen & S. Randall Kalberg, *Chicago-Kent Law Review Faculty Scholarship Survey*, 70 CHI.-KENT L. REV. 1445 (1995); Janet M. Gumm, *Chicago-Kent Law Review Faculty Scholarship Survey*, 66 CHI.-KENT L. REV. 509 (1990).

75. *See, e.g.*, Ira Mark Ellman, *A Comparison of Law Faculty Production in Leading Law Reviews*, 33 J. LEGAL EDUC. 681 (1983); Fred R. Shapiro, *The Most-Cited Law Review Articles Revisited*, 71 CHI.-KENT L. REV. 751 (1996); Fred R. Shapiro, *The Most-Cited Articles From the Yale Law Journal*, 100 YALE L.J. 1449 (1991); Fred R. Shapiro, *The Most-Cited Law Review Articles*, 73 CAL. L. REV. 1540 (1985).

76. Citation counts can also benefit scholars with the most power—with whom others want to curry favor—and those with the most friends. *See generally* Frederick C. Thorne, *The Citation Index: Another Case of Spurious Validity*, 33 J. CLINICAL PSYCHOL. 1157, 1157 (1977) ("The ways in which the system can be manipulated and converted to ulterior purposes [are not] widely understood and deserve critical elaboration."). For a compelling argument that many citations in legal scholarship are motivated by factors other than the intellectual importance of the cited work, *see* Arthur Austin, *The Reliability of Citation Counts in Judgments on Promotion, Tenure, and Status*, 35 ARIZ. L. REV. 829, 832, 831–34 (1993) ("Ideology, academic politics, fun, sycophancy—any motivation is possible." (footnote omitted)); *see also* Joseph Goldstein, *Commentary*, 100 YALE L.J. 1485, 1485 (1991) (insisting that rankings based on citation counts bear "no relationship to scholarly merit"). *But see* J. Margolis, *Citation Indexing and Evaluation of Scientific Papers*, 155 SCIENCE 1213, 1214 (1967) (arguing that "the value of a scientific paper can be measured by the influence it has on others," which may be reflected in citation counts). For a tongue-in-cheek but insightful guide to how to increase your citation count, *see* J.M. Balkin & Sanford Levinson, *How to Win Cites and Influence People*, 71 CHI.-KENT L. REV. 843, 849, 855–56 (1996) (advising would-be citation "all-stars" to attend or teach at the most prestigious law schools, to write about subjects that are popular with other professors or law students, and to cite themselves).

Do Rankings Matter? The Effects of *U.S. News & World Report* Rankings on the Admissions Process of Law Schools

Michael Sauder & Ryon Lancaster

In recent years there has been a tremendous proliferation of quantitative evaluative social measures in the field of law as well as society generally. One of these measures, the *U.S. News & World Report* rankings of law schools, has become an almost obsessive concern of the law school community, generating a great deal of speculation about the effects of these rankings on legal education. However, there has been no attempt to systematically ascertain what, if any, effects these rankings have on the decisionmaking of students and schools in the admission process. This article documents some of these effects by conceptualizing rankings as a signal of law school quality, investigating (1) whether students and schools use this signal to make decisions about where to apply and whom to admit, and (2) whether the creation of this signal distorts the phenomenon—law school quality—that it purports to measure. Using data for U.S. law schools from 1996 to 2003 we find that schools' rankings have significant effects both on the decisions of prospective students as well as on decisions schools make in the admissions process. In addition, we present evidence that the rankings can become a self-fulfilling prophecy for some schools, as the effects of rank described above alter the profile of their student bodies, affecting their future rank. Cumulatively, these findings suggest that the rankings help *create* rather than simply reflect differences among law schools through the magnification of the small, and statistically random, distinctions produced by the measurement apparatus.

Introduction

Over the last fifteen years, there has been a great increase in the number of rankings of educational institutions published by widely circulating magazines and newspapers both in the United States and internationally.[1] Part of a general trend toward increased accountability and transparency through the development of social measures,[2] this proliferation of rankings has generated much concern about their validity, how students use them, and how the behaviors of schools are changed in reaction to them. Nowhere is this concern more palpable than in the field of legal education. Perhaps because there is a single publication that dominates the field of law school rankings—*U.S. News & World Report* (hereafter, *USN*)—or because every accredited law school (as opposed to just the top 25 or top 50 schools in most other fields) is ranked on a single dimension, law schools and their governing organizations[3] have made very public efforts to caution their constituencies about and discredit the rankings. But while this concern about the rankings has created a substantial amount of speculation and debate about the methodology, validity, and appropriateness of the rankings of education institutions (e.g., Klein and Hamilton 1998; Berger 2001; Schmalbeck 2001), there have been few studies—and none that have focused on the field of legal education[4]—that have attempted to determine whether or not these rankings actually affect the decision-making of the prospective students who are the primary audience of these publications or the behavior of the schools that the rankings evaluate.

The question of the effect of these rankings, however, is an important one, and the implications of the answer stretch beyond the boundaries of education. Rankings, in the language of economists, act as signals—observable indicators, such as price (Milgrom and Roberts 1986), advertising (Ippolito 1990) or warranties (Boulding and Kirmani 1993), of the underlying quality and properties of that which is being represented (Nelson 1970; Spence 1974). Signals, according to this view, are especially valuable in markets like legal education where quality is hard to measure and information is difficult for outsiders to gather themselves. Thus, rankings are especially useful to prospective law students because they provide clear (although, as we will discuss below, not necessarily accurate) indications of the underlying quality of law schools, a function that both proponents of rankings (e.g., Korobkin 1998) and the rankers themselves cite as sufficient justification for the rankings.

But the relationship between the signal and the quality it is signaling is not always pure. For example, recent work by economic sociologists (e.g., Podolny 1993; Benjamin and Podolny 1999) has pointed out that signals often become decoupled from what they are supposed to represent and can affect the behavior of actors independent of the underlying quality that the signals are designed to indicate. This argument resonates with criticisms made by opponents of the rankings who, although they do not formulate their positions in the language of economics, contend that the rankings are inaccurate and methodologically flawed: that is, the distribution of signals produced by the rankings does not correspond well to the actual distribution of quality among law schools but continues to influence the behavior of students and administrators.

Moreover, a close look at rankings draws attention to a separate potential problem concerning the use of these types of signals as proxies of actual quality. Namely, setting aside questions of accuracy, does the *process* of communicating these signals itself have independent effects on the objects it is supposed to be measuring? Signaling theory assumes that this communicative process is a neutral one; in the case at hand, this theory would posit that the signals produced by rankers simply reflect law school quality as they, the rankers, define it. But given the extremely precise distinctions made by the rankers, and in light of recent research documenting the powerful symbolic effects of quantification and commensuration (Porter 1995; Espeland 1998; Espeland and Stevens 1998), whether or not the communication of these signals has an independent effect on the institutions it is measuring—by, for example, amplifying small differences between schools—becomes a question of growing relevance as rankings of all sorts proliferate within and beyond the legal world.[5]

In this article, we conduct a statistical analysis of law school rankings to address both the practical and theoretical issues outlined above. First, using school-by-school applicant data and ranking data from *U.S. News & World Report*, we analyze whether the rankings have affected the admissions process at law schools. Here, we focus on two questions: (1) Is the behavior of prospective students affected by a school's *USN* rank? And, (2) Is the behavior of law schools altered in response to their rank? Next, we use the same data to examine whether the signals produced by the rankings affect the quality of a school's applicant pool independent of other factors. We do this by testing whether changes in a school's rank one year has reverberating effects on subsequent applicant pools; a "spiraling" scenario such as this would exemplify how these signals at least partially determine (and therefore distort) the law school quality which they purport to simply reflect or measure.

The Debate about Rankings

Rankings as Valuable Signals

While educational quality is a crucial factor in the decision-making process of prospective students, it is also a very difficult and costly factor for these students to gather direct information about on their own. Faced with this situation of high uncertainty, many prospective students will search for signals of educational quality. In the past, these signals most commonly included informal networks, pre-law advisors, and a few guidebooks that provided accounts—primarily qualitative in nature—of law schools.

Since 1990, however, the annual rankings of law schools published by *USN* have provided a new type of signal for legal education quality, a signal that is not only easily accessible (due to the wide circulation and relative inexpensiveness of the magazine) but is also presented in a format (precise relative valuations) that is compelling to outside audiences. Providing this new type of comparative information is, according to *USN*, the motivation behind the rankings. As the magazine asserted in an early rankings issue, "The sad truth is that it is easier to learn about the relative merits of compact-disk players than it is to compare and contrast America's professional schools. And some educators prefer to keep it that way" (March 19, 1990: 50).

This argument—that the rankings provide a valuable and previously unavailable signal of educational quality to prospective students and other constituents—is also put forward by analysts who believe that rankings are beneficial to legal education. For example, Berger (2001) reasons that rankings provide useful, convenient, and plausibly accurate signals to law school applicants, signals that also force law schools to be accountable for the legal education that they provide in a way that they were not prior to the rankings. Korobkin (1998) advocates for the signaling function of rankings even more explicitly in his defense of the value of rankings. He argues that the accuracy of the rankings is relatively unimportant; instead, the true worth of the rankings is to provide market signals that serve to match the best students with the best employers, a process that Korobkin believes is of great benefit to legal education.

Although many law school administrators and faculty agree that there have been some positive consequences of the rankings—most often citing the information provided to students and the institutional transparency or accountability that these rankings create—those who believe that these benefits outweigh the negative effects are in the minority. As one of the few deans who supported the rankings explained,

> Before the rankings, there wasn't a number that was running around; in the past a dean could pontificate about how great his program was but now it's harder to

> pull the wool over people's eyes. With these numbers, you can't just talk. The basic things that law schools do are still all there: we want to get the best students, the best faculty, and we want our students to be successful. Our job and our career goals haven't changed, but now we have metrics. I think it's just like Consumer Reports for cars. You can quarrel with individual things, you can quibble with the formula, but we have a wonderful product and it's good for people to know. Most deans think all of this is horrible—I'm a real outlier on this.[6]

Rankings as Distorting Signals

As the end of the previous statement implies, most in the law school community are not as sanguine about the effects of the rankings as *USN* and its proponents. While few question that the *USN* rankings provide a new signal of law school quality, opponents of the rankings believe that this signal also creates negative effects that overshadow any informational benefits. For example, the rankings, according to many law school administrators, change both how resources are distributed and how work is done within law schools because administrators feel pressure to make decisions based on what is best for the school's rank rather than what is best for the quality of the education provided by the school. Specifically, interviewed deans have noted a dramatic increase in money spent on marketing and advertising, a much greater emphasis on LSAT scores in the admissions process, a transition from need-based to merit-based scholarships, and the transformation of the focus of career services from providing career counseling to ensuring that employment numbers are as high as possible (Espeland and Sauder 2004). This emphasis on "the numbers" rather than educational quality is perhaps most striking in the strategies that schools have adopted to game the rankings. Writing as the acting president of the AALS, Dale Whitman (2002) lists six such strategies: encouraging under-qualified applicants to apply in order to raise selectivity ratios, "skimming" top students from other schools to keep entering first-year cohorts small (again raising the selectivity ratio), admitting students with higher LSAT scores over students who are otherwise better qualified and a better fit, and temporarily hiring unemployed graduates to boost employment statistics.

These effects of rankings would be far less problematic to opponents of the rankings if an improvement in rank always corresponded to an improvement in educational quality—that is, if the signal produced by the rankings was tightly coupled to the phenomenon it was measuring. But these critics argue that there is a disconnect between rankings and quality, a disconnect that stems from at least two sources. First, opponents of the rankings argue that they are methodologically inaccurate signals of the phenomenon they purport to measure; that is, the *USN* rankings do not effectively measure law school quality. Second, independent of measurement concerns, critics contend that the *process* of measurement itself provides a distorted representation of law school quality by amplifying insignificant differences between schools and creating differences where none existed before. In other words, rather than simply reflecting the distribution of quality among law schools, the signal produced by the rankings distorts this distribution and in doing so reshapes the reputational terrain of law schools.

Methodological Inaccuracy

USN creates precise relative comparisons among law schools by employing a formula that combines four primary measurements of law school quality—peer and professional assessment (40 percent of total), selectivity (25 percent), placement success (20 percent) and faculty resources (15 percent)—to generate an overall reputational rank for every law school accredited by the ABA (see Appendix 1 for a complete description of these factors). Although the way in which *USN* has made distinctions between schools has fluctuated somewhat over time, from 1993 until 2003 the basic structure of these rankings consisted of an ordinal ranking of the top 50 law schools and a division of the remaining (approximately 130) schools into tiers (second tier, third tier, fourth tier) in which they were listed alphabetically. Using this formula, *USN* creates a point total for each school which is then standardized to give the top school a final score of 100 and the remaining schools a score based on the percentage of their total points compared to the total points of the top school. So, for example, if Yale receives 22 total points and the University of Alabama receives 10.4, then Yale's score is standardized to100 and the University of Alabama's score is standardized to 47.3 (100 X 10.4/22). Schools are then sorted by their standardized scores and given a numerical rank if they rank in the top 50, or they are equally divided into one of three tiers if they do not.

One criticism of this methodology—that is, the accuracy of the signal produced by *USN*—is that it fails to take into account many of the attributes that constitute a quality law school. A prominent example of this opinion is a letter of protest written by the LSAC and signed by the vast majority of law school deans. Since 1997, this letter has been sent each year to all students who register to take the Law School Admissions Test (LSAT). The LSAC letter questions the quality of information provided by *USN*, alleging that the rankings cannot take each student's "special needs and circumstances into account," and fail to measure many factors that students claim are most important in their choice of law school, including measures for the quality and accessibility of teachers, faculty scholarship, and racial and gender diversity within the faculty and student body.[7]

Leaving aside what *USN* does not measure, other analysts have found that the measures that are used by *USN* to estimate law school quality are bad proxies for the actual quality of these schools. Klein and Hamilton (1998), for example, conclude that 90 percent of the overall differences in ranks among schools can be explained solely by the median LSAT score of their entering classes; this finding suggests that despite their stated weights, the numerous other factors that comprise the rankings have little effect on a school's overall rank. In a similar vein, Lempert (2001) characterizes the *USN* rankings as "pseudoscience" and, examining each component carefully, characterizes every factor used by *USN* as deeply flawed.

Finally, critics argue that the signal of law school quality provided by the rankings is largely a product of the weights given to each factor included in the formula used by *USN*. There is no inherent justification, for example, for making reputation 40 percent of law school quality, faculty resources 15 percent, or volumes in the library .75 percent; these weights were invented by the rankers. Although Klein and Hamilton (1998) minimize the importance of these weights, their influence is convincingly demonstrated in a web site developed by Jeffrey Stake that allows students to determine the weight of each factor according to their own preferences.[8] As Stake's "Ranking Game" shows, even small changes in the relative weights of these variables can make substantial differences in the rank ordering of schools. This suggests that methodological decisions play a crucial role in determining the signal created by *USN*.

Signal Distortion

Putting aside the accuracy with which *USN* measures law school quality, another line of criticism of the rankings contends that the process of creating this signal is itself a source of distortion. Recent sociological and historical work on commensuration (Espeland 1998; Espeland and Stevens 1998) and quantitative authority (Porter 1995), for example, convincingly argues that quantification is a unique type of signal, one that often alters the phenomena that it is representing. Opponents of rankings make similar claims about the signals produced by *USN*, arguing that by quantifying law school quality very precisely and creating hard lines of distinctions (the cut points between tiers, for instance) the rankings both amplify small differences between schools and create differences among schools that did not exist previously. That is, independent of *what* information is signaled by *USN*, *how* this information is signaled is a second important source of distortion.

Documenting this claim involves looking closely at how *USN* signals law school quality to its audiences, examining how the actual distribution of law school quality compares to the representation of this distribution put forth by *USN*. As we show below, *even when USN's own definition of law school quality is used as a proxy for actual law school quality*, there are significant differences between the actual distribution of law school quality and how this distribution is signaled by *USN*.

Using the information provided by *USN* in the 2000 through 2003 rankings, we were able to produce accurate estimates ($R^2 > .98$) of the distribution of law school quality—again, as defined by *USN*—for all ranked law schools during this period.[9]

Figure 1. Distribution of USN Quality Scores 2000–2003

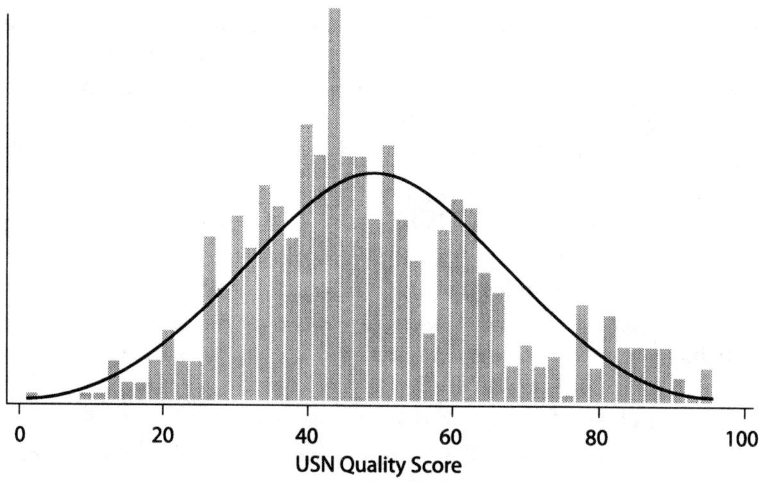

Figure 1 displays the density plot of the standardized score for the years 2000 through 2003, demonstrating that the underlying distribution of quality closely approximates a normal distribution.

However, if we look at how this approximately normal distribution is *represented* by the *USN* rankings, we see a different picture. Figure 2 shows how *USN* creates a very different distribution of schools than the distribution based on their own algorithm. Whereas Figure 1 shows that the standardized scores of law schools are very similar to one another near the center of the distribution, we can see in Figure 2 that this is where *USN* makes the decisive breaks between schools in the top tier, the second tier, and the third tier. In other words, very small differences at the center of the distribution can lead schools to change their rank or tier, since there is very little that separates them from the other schools. In addition, *USN*'s representation of the distribution portrays schools *within* the second, third and fourth tier schools as being of equal quality, and makes it appear as though there are large gaps between tiers even though the underlying distribution is continuous. Furthermore, the numerically ranked schools extend the high end of the distribution, creating large distinctions between schools. While this might be appropriate at the extreme of the distribution where schools are separated by relatively large values on the underlying quality dimension, it is far less accurate toward the center of the distribution where schools become very similar to one another—but this is precisely where *USN* creates its most precise distinctions.

Figure 2. Comparison of Distributions

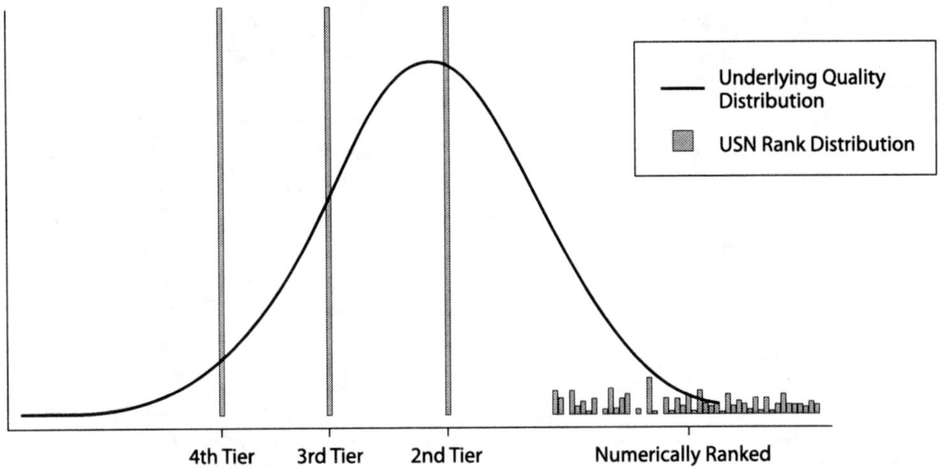

One of the consequences of this shift in the distribution is that there is a lot of fluctuation in the ranks of schools due to very small and statistically insignificant changes in their scores or the scores of the schools near them in the rankings. This applies to all schools ranked in the top 50 because the distinctions made by *USN* between these schools are so fine. As shown in Table 1, the top 50 ranked schools are more likely to experience a change in the rankings from the previous year than they are to remain the same.

Overall, in each year roughly 68 percent of schools experience a change in the rank from the previous year. This is largely because *USN* makes very fine distinctions among the top 50 schools even though the quality measures of these schools form a continuous normal distribution where schools towards the center of the distribution have very similar scores; in other words, the scores of these schools—especially those close to the center of the distribution—are very similar, so very small changes in their scores can have disproportionate effects on their rank. [See Table 1.]

Similarly small differences can become even more magnified at the margins of tiers. Again, despite that law school quality as measured by *USN* takes the shape of a normal distribution, the presentation of this distribution by *USN* implies that there is a meaningful and qualitative difference between "second tier" and "third tier" law schools. While these tier changes are less common—each year a little over 80 percent of the schools remain in the same tier as they were in the previous year—during our ten-year analysis period only 29 of the 130 schools who were not ranked in the top 50 throughout this period did not experience a change in tier (18 of these 29 schools remained in the fourth tier during this time).

Signal distortion of this type is very important to law schools because they believe that small differences in rank are meaningful to their outside constituencies: it matters whether a school is 9 or 12, 23 or 28, second tier or third tier because, they believe, these statistically insignificant differences have a significant influence on how outside constituencies perceive

Table 1. Number of Schools That Have Changed Tier or Rank, 1994–2003

	Tier				Rank			
	No Change	*Up*	*Down*	Total	*No Change*	*Up*	*Down*	Total
1994	127	23	21	171	15	5	4	24
	74.3%	*13.5%*	*12.3%*		*62.5%*	*20.8%*	*16.7%*	
1995	133	17	23	173	7	10	8	25
	76.9%	*9.8%*	*13.3%*		*28.0%*	*40.0%*	*32.0%*	
1996	135	18	20	173	13	16	17	46
	78.0%	*10.4%*	*11.6%*		*28.3%*	*34.8%*	*37.0%*	
1997	142	15	17	174	14	18	16	48
	81.6%	*8.6%*	*9.8%*		*29.2%*	*37.5%*	*33.3%*	
1998	155	12	7	174	16	16	16	48
	89.1%	*6.9%*	*4.0%*		*33.3%*	*33.3%*	*33.3%*	
1999	148	8	18	174	14	22	12	48
	85.1%	*4.6%*	*10.3%*		*29.2%*	*45.8%*	*25.0%*	
2000	143	16	14	173	9	18	22	49
	82.7%	*9.2%*	*8.1%*		*18.4%*	*36.7%*	*44.9%*	
2001	146	10	18	174	16	16	18	50
	83.9%	*5.7%*	*10.3%*		*32.0%*	*32.0%*	*36.0%*	
2002	142	21	11	174	16	14	18	48
	81.6%	*12.1%*	*6.3%*		*33.3%*	*29.2%*	*37.5%*	
2003	155	9	10	174	19	18	13	50
	89.1%	*5.2%*	*5.7%*		*38.0%*	*36.0%*	*26.0%*	
Total	1,426	149	159	1,734	139	153	144	436
	82.2%	*8.6%*	*9.2%*		*31.9%*	*35.1%*	*33.0%*	

and behave toward law schools (Espeland and Sauder 2004; Sauder and Espeland 2005). Therefore, law schools are pressured to continually optimize their ranking, by, for example, basing admissions decisions on LSAT scores, spending more money on merit-based scholarships in order to "buy" students whose LSAT scores will raise the school's median, or producing expensive glossy brochures to be sent to those who fill out the *USN* survey.

The belief that small differences matter to outside constituencies explains why law schools pay such close attention to the rankings even if they believe they are inaccurate. Interviews with law school administrators indicate that schools employ the aforementioned strategies to improve their rank because they perceive that even changes in rank caused by normal statistical fluctuations can have considerable effects on the actual quality of the school because these changes are viewed by external audiences as real changes in quality. As one dean explained,

> You have people who focus on whether or not the rankings are in fact valid, whether they really show anything, whether the methodology is good, and so on. And those debates can seem endless at times as everybody kind of decries the rankings. On the flip side you have the pragmatic reality of the rankings.... Whatever the validity of the methodology, it's difficult to pretend that the rankings don't matter. I mean prospective students use them; employers use them; university administrators use them. So whether we in legal academics think they're valid or not, whether they're reflective or not, the truth is that I don't think you can just ignore them.

The "pragmatic reality" of the rankings—the belief that outside constituencies make decisions based on where schools rank—is the primary driving force behind the influence of the rankings on legal education. In other words, law school rankings are consequential, regardless of their validity, because prospective students decide which schools to attend, employers decide whom to hire, and alumni decide how much to give to their alma maters based on where a school stands in the most current *USN* ranking.

But the pragmatic reality of the rankings is not limited to the one-time fluctuations a school might experience. Many administrators believe that the distorting effects caused by the precise evaluations made by the rankings can have long-term consequences as the next cohort of prospective students responds to the new rankings of the school. For example, the fear exists that a fall in the rankings will have a spiraling negative effect in which this drop in rank will lead to a negative response from these outside audiences (for example, a lower quality applicant pool) which will in turn lead to an even worse rank.[10] As one administrator told us,

> Ever since [a fall from the second to third tier] we've been scrambling to try to lift our rankings because it's a vicious cycle. Students say, "Well, why should I come to you? You're in the third tier." Employers say, "Why should I hire your people? You're in the third tier." So we get less-good students. So it just circulates.

The existence of such a spiral, negative or positive, would indicate an important way in which small changes in rank can become magnified to have extensive and long-lasting consequences for law schools. In addition, because these consequences of rankings could often be the result of the vagaries of the methodology employed by *USN* rather than any real change in educational quality, the existence of a spiral would also exemplify how the signal produced by the rankings can *create* new forms of inequality rather than simply reflect pre-existing inequalities among schools. In this situation the dangers of a loose coupling between a signal and what it is representing (Podolny 1993) become clear: the signal not only might misrepresent the phenomenon it is measuring, but it could also reify this misrepresentation as future actors base their actions or decisions on this signal.

Evidence of the Effects of Rankings

As proponents of the rankings have noted (see Berger 2001), it is striking that despite the debate and concern surrounding the rankings, there has been little attempt to systematically test these wide-ranging claims about their effects. Schmalbeck's (2001) study of measures of reputational standing over time is the only empirically grounded study of the effects of law school rankings to date, and this study provides little support for those who claim that the rankings have significant consequences. Schmalbeck finds that the reputations of law schools are relatively durable and that rankings have done little to change perceptions of school quality among those who fill out the *USN* survey: a drop in rank during one year, for instance, does not have a negative effect on a school's reputation score in the following year's survey.

Schmalbeck's study, however, does not address the effects of rankings on external constituencies, the audiences about which law school administrators are most concerned. And while no empirical research on this question has examined this issue in the field of legal education, analyses of the effects of rankings on other types of educational institutions lend justification to administrators' concerns. In their investigation of how prospective undergraduates use rankings, for example, McDonough et al. (1997) find that rankings intensify the "reputation game" played by colleges by focusing the attention of prospective students on the purported prestige of schools rather than on the fit between the school and the particular student's interests and needs. Likewise, Monks and Ehrenberg's (1999) study of elite colleges shows that movement in rank affects the number of applicants these colleges received, their selectivity in admissions, their yield rate, and how they deployed scholarship money. Finally, Elsbach and Kramer (1996) find that even small changes in business school rankings evoke identity crises within these organizations.

These studies highlight the fact that the crucial question in the debate about law school rankings has yet to be addressed empirically: Do the rankings affect the behavior of external audiences? Or, in the language of signaling theory: Do the signals produced by *USN* influence the behavior of external audiences?

To answer this question, the present study examines the effects that a school's rank has on what many consider the most important of these constituencies: prospective students. If students perceive the rankings to be a useful signal of law school quality, then they should respond to a school's rank independently of other schools' characteristics. Students will be more likely both to apply to higher ranked schools and to matriculate at these schools because these schools possess signals of higher quality. Similarly, after controlling for other school characteristics, students with better LSAT scores will be more likely to apply to schools towards the top of the rankings, while students with lower LSAT scores will be more likely to apply to schools with a lower ranking.

Hypothesis 1: *Controlling for school characteristics, the USN ranks will have an independent effect on students' decisions in the admissions process.*

In light of the pragmatic reality of the rankings, we next examine whether schools alter their admissions activity in anticipation of the effects that they believe correspond to rankings. If students do use the rankings as a signal for law school quality and make their decisions about which schools to apply to and where they accept offers from, then we expect that schools will also be influenced by the rankings in their own admissions decisions. That is, schools will accept a greater number of students as they decrease in the rankings because they expect fewer of their accepted applicants to actually matriculate. In addition, they might modify their tuition in response to the rankings—lowering tuition to make their school more appealing if they have a low rank or raising tuition to increase revenue if they are ranked high.

Hypothesis 2: *Controlling for school characteristics, the USN ranks will have an independent effect on schools' decisions in the admissions process.*

If the rankings do act as a signal and affect the decisions of students and schools in the admissions process, then there is also the possibility that changes in rank might actually affect the quality of schools. The factors that *USN* uses to create their rankings are precisely those factors that are affected by rank. Therefore, we would expect that the effects of the *USN* rankings on decisions will in turn affect future *USN* rankings.

Hypothesis 3: *Student and school decisions in response to the USN ranks will have a significant effect on future USN ranks, net of previous ranks.*

Data and Methods

To test the effects of the *USN* rankings on prospective students and law schools, we have collected data from two primary sources. Data on rankings were collected from the 1993 to 2003 editions of the *U.S. News and World Report Guide to Graduate Schools.* During this period, *USN* ranked the top 50 schools numerically and then grouped the remaining schools into three tiers within which their placement was determined alphabetically. In order to measure school characteristics that were not used in the construction of the *USN* scores, we collected data from the 1996 to 2003 editions of *The Official Guide to U.S. Law Schools,* now jointly published by the LSAC and the American Bar Association (ABA). *The Official Guide to U.S. Law Schools* is designed to provide prospective students with both a qualitative description of all accredited law schools in the U.S. as well as a wide variety of quantitative characteristics (e.g., school size, minority composition, volumes in the library, and a chart of the previous year's applicants chances of admission based on their LSAT scores and GPAs) of these same schools.[11] Prior to the 1996 edition, these data were published in different forms, preventing us from extending the analysis further into the past.

Dependent Variables

We test the effects that rankings have on a number of outcomes that are consequential for law schools. We begin by examining the effects of rank on three variables which reflect student decisions: how many students apply, the percentage of all students with top scores who apply, and the percentage of admitted applicants who matriculate (attend the school after they have been accepted). We operationalize these variables as follows. First, *number of applications* is taken directly from the school-by-school data reported in *The Official Guide to U.S. Law Schools.* Second, we measure the *percentage of top students* by calculating the portion of the applicant pool with LSAT scores that fall within particular ranges: 160 and above, 150 to 159, and 120 to 149. Because the current edition of the rankings used by students who are applying to law school in any given year is published two years before the corresponding school-by-school data is published in *The Official Guide to U.S. Law Schools,* we apply a two-year lag to both of these variables.

Finally, we calculated *percent matriculated* by dividing the total number of students who were accepted by each school by the number of students who chose to attend. Because rankings have a more immediate impact on matriculation—the *USN* rankings are published in March and most students make decisions about which school to attend in April—a one-year lag was implemented for this variable.

To determine if schools alter their behavior in response to changes in their rank, we next analyze two variables that speak to this issue. We measure *percentage of applicants accepted* by dividing the total applicant pool by the number of applicants accepted by the school, while *tuition* is measured by the annual tuition costs of each school.

USN *Ranks*

We calculate the effects of rankings in two ways. *USN* groups law schools into four broad categories, or tiers, based on the scores determined by a formula that combines measures of reputation, selectivity, employment success, and institutional resources.

Schools that score in the top 50 of all law schools[12] are placed in the first tier, and given a numerical rank based on their position within the tier. For example, Yale University Law School had the highest raw score in each of the years we consider here. This places Yale in the top tier, or tier 1, and within that tier Yale is ranked number 1. The second, third, and fourth tiers were determined by their raw score where, once the top 50 schools are removed, the top 33.3 percent of the remaining schools are placed in the second tier, the middle 33.3 percent in the third tier, and the bottom 33.3 percent in the fourth tier.

We first measure the effects of tier placement. Because schools in tiers 2, 3, and 4 are not assigned numerical ranks, this is the only level of differentiation for most schools. To test for tier effects, we constructed dummy variables for each tier, using tier 4 (low) as the reference category. That is, we created dichotomous (0/1) variables for tier 1, tier 2, and tier 3. The coefficients and levels of significance are measured relative to tier 4, so that the coefficients for the effects of tier are to be interpreted as the net effect relative to tier 4.

Second, we assess the effects of the specific numerical ranks assigned to schools in the first tier. We measure *rank* by using the *USN* ranks. Since only those schools in the first tier have numerical ranks, schools in the other tiers were not included in our analyses of numerical rank. We reverse coded the numerical rank of schools in order to simplify interpretation. That is, Yale Law School, which has always been ranked the top school in the country, is given a rank of 50, while the bottom school in the first tier is given a rank of 1. Thus higher ranked schools have a higher number than lower ranked schools.

Controls

We also include a number of control variables. Most importantly, we employ a fixed-effects panel regression, which allows us to include a separate dummy variable for each school. This provides us with the ability to control for all of the unique time-invariant school characteristics (such as reputation, whether the school is public or private, if the school is independent or attached to a university, etc.) that are not accounted for by our other variables. For example, if a school has a specialty program (for instance, tax law) that attracts a disproportionate number of applications from top students, our fixed-effect model allows us to control for this school-specific factor if it does not change during our analysis period. In other words, this model specification permits us to control for a broad range of factors that we are not able to measure directly.

In addition to using a separate dummy variable for each school, we included several other controls. We incorporate dummy variables for *year* from 1996 to 2003 with 1996 as the reference category. We also control for the *size* of each school, measured by the number of law students at the school and employ a log transformation to normalize this distribution. We ran the models with each of these variables, and they did not affect our coefficients for our measure of *USN* rank. Finally, we tested for the effects of *age* of the school and whether the school is *public or private*, but—because these two variables were highly collinear with size—they are not included in the final analyses.

Model

In order to test hypotheses one and two, we ran a pooled-cross section fixed effects Prais-Winsten regression. This model has four distinct strengths. First, as we explain above, the fixed-effect allows us to control for time-invariant school characteristics. Second, pooling multiple years allows us to examine schools over time. Third, because we have multiple observations of each school, our cases are not independent of one another; the fixed effects model, however, allows us control for unmeasured school characteristics as well as the non-independence of observations. Finally, the Prais-Winsten autoregressive function allows us to control for serial correlation within schools over time (Greene 2000).

In order to test hypothesis 3, we employ two different models. First, to determine what predicts which tier a school falls in, we use an ordered probit model because it uses an ordinal variable—such as tier—as its dependent variable. Although this model does not allow us to use a fixed effects term, we do control for previous tier which captures much of the same variation. As shown in Figure 1, the underlying distribution of quality is a normal distribution; this allows us to use an ordered probit, which assumes an ordinal division of a normal distribution. In order to predict the rank of a school, we used a random effects pooled-cross sectional regression with a Prais-Winsten correction for serial correlation. This is largely the same model as we used to test hypotheses 1 and 2 without the fixed effects term. The fixed effects term was removed because it is closely correlated with previous rank, which is of theoretical interest for this hypothesis.

Results

Number of Applications

The first two columns of Table 2 show the results of our tests on the effects that rank has on the total number of applications that schools receive. The first column presents our results for the effects of tier differences. Although our results show that there are not significant differences in the number of applications received by schools in the second, third, and fourth tiers, we find that schools in the first tier receive a much higher number of applications—on average these schools receive 177 more applications than schools in the fourth tier and 125 more than schools in the second tier. In addition, our dummy variables for year, which are all significant at $p < 0.01$, yield no surprises: we find that there was a dramatic drop in the total number of applications from 1996 to 2000 which was followed by an overall increase in applications from 2000 to 2003 (though still below 1996 levels), and that larger schools receive a greater number of applications.

The second column of Table 2 presents our results for the top 50 schools with numerical ranks. Here, we find that schools with higher ranks have a statistically significant higher number of applications. Controlling for year, size, and our fixed effect term for each school, we find that each rank a school increases leads to an increase of nearly 19 applications. Although our results show a similar pattern in the overall number of applications, we do not find a significant effect for the size of school.

Applications by LSAT Score

Columns three through eight in Table 2 demonstrate our results for the percentage of a school's applicant pool who have LSAT scores in the following ranges: 160 and above, 150 to 159, and 120 to 149. Our data show that there has been a slight decrease over time in the percentage of applicants with LSAT scores above 160 and between 150 and 159,

Table 2. Pooled Cross-Section Fixed-Effects Prais-Winsten Regression of the Effects of USN Ranks on Student Decisions

	Total Applications		Percentage of Applicants with LSAT 160+		Percentage of Applicants with LSAT 150+		Percentage of Applicants with LSAT 120+		Percent Matriculate	
	Tiers	Top 50	Tiers	Top 50	Tiers	Top 50	Tiers	Top 50	Tiers	Top 50
USN Rank									2.67	
Top Tier[a]	176.79		2.63		1.77		−3.03		(1.41)	
	(50.62)**		(0.69)**		(0.98)		(0.99)**		1.98	
Second Tier[a]	51.68		1.27		1.75		−2.00		(0.98)*	
	(30.31)		(0.42)**		(0.80)*		(0.86)*		2.15	
Third Tier[a]	11.07		0.26		0.93		0.21		(0.76)**	
	(18.30)		(0.28)		(0.59)		(0.59)			
Numerical Rank		18.55		0.13		−0.06		−0.06		0.18
		(3.82)**		(0.04)**		(0.04)		(0.03)		(0.04)**
Size	655.37	844.95	−1.68	11.67	13.93	5.34	−9.63	−16.31	5.93	19.50
	(114.06)**	(465.61)	(1.56)	(6.87)	(2.40)**	(5.40)	(2.92)**	(7.92)*	(2.22)**	(3.58)**
Year Controls[b]										
1997	−178.95		−2.87	−1.91	0.35	−0.11	2.59	1.81	−2.23	−1.15
	(20.84)**		(0.29)**	(0.82)*	(0.42)	(0.75)	(0.44)**	(0.97)	(0.50)**	(0.61)
1998	−445.21	−357.03	−1.68	0.34	−0.01	−0.38	2.14	0.55	−3.30	−2.48
	(24.28)**	(51.37)**	(0.32)**	(0.86)	(0.47)	(0.78)	(0.51)**	(0.99)	(0.52)**	(0.62)**
1999	−624.50	−664.19	−2.78	−0.35	−0.57	0.84	3.72	0.05	−2.71	−0.64
	(25.17)**	(57.90)**	(0.32)**	(0.92)	(0.48)	(0.82)	(0.55)**	(1.05)	(0.50)**	(0.62)
2000	−632.27	−608.65	−3.25	−0.16	−1.49	1.85	4.90	−1.33	−2.10	−1.74
	(26.23)**	(60.90)**	(0.32)**	(0.94)	(0.45)**	(0.84)*	(0.50)**	(1.07)	(0.50)**	(0.64)**
2001	−551.39	−449.87	−2.78	0.21	−1.90	1.67	5.25	−1.58	−2.77	−2.15
	(26.64)**	(59.82)**	(0.32)**	(0.91)	(0.46)**	(0.82)*	(0.50)**	(1.04)	(0.51)**	(0.68)**
2002	−481.14	−269.54	−3.05	−0.38	−1.55	1.98	4.91	−2.01	−2.22	−1.17
	(26.73)**	(58.63)**	(0.32)**	(0.89)	(0.46)**	(0.81)*	(0.49)**	(1.00)*	(0.51)**	(0.60)*
2003	−369.14	−91.32	−3.59	−0.82	−1.15	3.38	4.92	−1.92	−2.03	−1.35
	(26.21)**	(58.76)	(0.32)*	(0.91)	(0.46)*	(0.83)**	(0.50)**	(1.03)	(0.51)**	(0.65)*
Constant	−2,504.08	−2,339.54	18.54	−15.68	−50.94	−19.08	116.35	139.40	0.41	0.00
	(731.32)**	(3,145.20)	(10.02)	(48.16)	(15.42)**	(37.81)	(18.69)**	(55.46)*	(14.27)	(0.00)
N	1,298	365	943	258	943	259	943	259	1,218	372
N Schools	174	60	147	50	146	50	146	50	174	60

$^{*}p < 0.05$, $^{**}p < 0.01$. *Note:* All models include dummy variables for each school. These were omitted for the sake of brevity. Standard errors are in parentheses. [a]The fourth tier was used as the reference category. [b]1996 was the reference category for all models except for the effects of numerical ranks for total applications, where 1997 was the reference category.

while there has been a concurrent rise in the percentage of applicants with LSATs between 120 and 150; this suggests that more students with lower LSAT scores have been applying to law school between 1996 and 2003. The effects of *USN* ranks on these different types of applicants are relatively straightforward. Schools in the top 2 tiers have a higher percentage of their applicant pool with LSAT scores above 160 compared to schools in the third and fourth tier. Similarly, schools in the top 2 tiers have a significantly lower percentage of their applicant pool with LSATs between 120 and 150. The results for percentage of applicants with LSAT scores between 150 and 160 are mixed, with schools in the second tier having a significantly higher percentage of their students with these LSAT scores.

Not surprisingly, our results indicate that students with very high LSAT scores tend to apply to top schools. Students with LSAT scores above 150 are more likely to apply to second tier schools than schools in other tiers, which indicates that they realize that these are the schools into which they have the best chance of being accepted. Similarly, students with LSAT scores below 150 are much less likely to apply to schools in the top two tiers, where they have little chance of being accepted.

Our results for numerical rank are rather mixed. We find that for schools in the first tier, there is a significant ($p < 0.01$) effect for rank on applicants with LSAT scores of 160 and above; an increase in one rank leads to a small increase in the number of top applicants on the order of .13 percent. These results suggest that top applicants do pay attention to minor differences in rank. However, we do not find that rank has significant effects for the percentage of students with LSATs between 150 and 159 or between 120 and 149. This suggests that students with LSATs below 160 apply to top ranked schools at a relatively constant rate and do not strongly differentiate between schools in the top tier where they have significantly lower chances of being accepted.

Matriculation

The final two columns in Table 2 present our results for the percentage of accepted students who matriculate. We find that a higher percentage of students matriculate at larger schools; we hypothesize that this is because larger schools are more likely to be public schools with lower tuition costs. With respect to the *USN* rank, we find that schools in the top 3 tiers have on average a 2 percent increase in the percentage of their students who matriculate, controlling for other factors. However, the effects are not significant for the top tier even though it has the largest coefficient. This indicates that there is a significant amount of variation in the percentage of accepted students who matriculate in the top tier. As we can see in the final column of Table 2, this is largely because the effect of numerical rank is strong and statistically significant ($p < 0.01$); that is, each numerical rank increase leads to a .18 percent increase in the percentage of students who matriculate.

Table 3 presents our results for the responses of schools to the *USN* ranks. The first two columns show the results of our regressions of *USN* rank on the percentage of applicants accepted by schools. We find that there has been a general increase in the percentage of applicants accepted over time, closely following the decrease in applications shown in Table 2. Additionally, we find that larger schools are more likely to accept applicants than are smaller schools. The effects of *USN* ranks are not significant when schools are ranked by tier, which indicates that the different tiers have relatively stable acceptance rates. However, column 2 in Table 3 indicates that within the first tier schools with higher ranks accept a smaller percentage of their applicants. An increase of one rank leads to a .2 percent reduction in the percentage of students accepted ($p < 0.01$).

Our results for tuition are presented in columns 3 to 6 in Table 3. Overall, we find a general increase in both in-state and out-of-state tuition over this period. However, we find that size itself has no effect, indicating that size is not a driver of costs. The effects of the *USN* ranks on tuition are weak, with the only significant effect being that third tier schools have significantly lower tuition ($p < 0.05$ for both in-state and out-of-state) than do fourth tier schools. While the effect is not large, in that schools in the third tier charge $200 less than fourth tier schools, it is surprising.

Feedback Effects

Table 4 presents the results of our tests of hypothesis 3. The first two columns present our ordered probit regressions of school characteristics and previous tier on the current tier of schools. Column 1 presents the results with only controls for size and previous tier. Not surprisingly, we find that previous tier is a very strong predictor of current tier; this confirms what we found in Table 1, that schools do not change tier frequently. Our coefficients for tier are all significant at $p < 0.01$, and—because each coefficient sits squarely in the middle of each tier's range—they are robust predictors of current tier. Column 2 of Table 4 presents our results when we include the effects of student decisions from the previous year. Here we find that tier is still significant at $p < 0.01$. The effects of decisions are rather minimal, with the only significant effect being the percentage of students with LSATs above 160.

Columns 3 and 4 of Table 4 present the results of our regression of previous rank, school decisions, and student decisions on current rank for the top 50 ranked schools. Column 3 presents our model without student decisions, and we find that rank is a very strong predictor ($p < 0.01$), and the coefficient is nearly 1. This suggests that previous rank is a very strong predictor of current rank. When we include the effects of student and school decisions in our model (presented in column 4), we find that the effect of rank remains significant, though the coefficient is smaller than in the model in column 3. As in the models for tier, we find that the only consequential effect of decisions is the percentage of the applicants with LSATs above 160. Here we find each one point increase in the percentage of applicants with LSATs above 160 increase a school's rank by a half.

Discussion

Consistent with our hypotheses, we find that the *USN* ranks act as a signal to law school applicants. Independent of school characteristics, we find that these ranks affect how many students apply to a school, how many of those applicants have exceptionally high LSAT scores, the percentage of applicants who are accepted, and the percentage of accepted students who matriculate. In short, the *USN* rankings have a significant impact on the admissions process in law schools. Furthermore, these effects tend to be stronger for the top schools that are ranked numerically than for the majority of schools that are ranked by tier.

Table 3. Pooled Cross-Sectional Random-Effects Prais-Winsten Regressions of the Effects of *USN* Rank on School Decisions

	Percentage of Applicants Accepted		In-State Tuition (in thousands of dollars)	
	Tiers	Top 50	Tiers	Top 50
USN Rank				
Top Tier[a]	–1.83		–0.22	
	(1.39)		(0.40)	
Second Tier[a]	–0.77		–0.16	
	(1.13)		(0.15)	
Third Tier[a]	–1.13		–0.19	
	(0.84)		(0.08)**	
Numerical Rank		–0.20		–0.00
		(0.04)**		(0.02)
Size	6.80	12.18	–0.51	0.11
	(3.16)*	(4.44)**	(0.50)	(2.17)
Year Controls[b]				
1997	2.95	3.36	0.90	1.30
	(0.54)**	(0.52)**	(0.09)**	(0.20)**
1998	10.63	7.28	1.63	1.99
	(0.60)**	(0.62)**	(0.12)**	(0.26)**
1999	13.73	9.56	2.32	2.95
	(0.62)**	(0.61)**	(0.13)**	(0.28)**
2000	14.69	9.84	3.06	3.49
	(0.63)**	(0.61)**	(0.14)**	(0.30)**
2001	13.64	8.49	3.81	4.28
	(0.64)**	(0.60)**	(0.15)**	(0.30)**
2002	12.91	6.61	4.72	5.05
	(0.63)**	(0.59)**	(0.16)**	(0.31)**
2003	10.35	4.39	5.70	6.37
	(0.63)**	(0.58)**	(0.15)**	(0.31)**
Constant	–7.20	–62.31	8.05	1.04
	(20.34)	(32.17)	(3.25)*	(14.33)
N	1.255	374	1.313	400
N Schools	174	60	175	60

$^*p < 0.05$, $^{**}p < 0.01$. *Note:* All models include dummy variables for each school. These were omitted for the sake of brevity. Standard errors are in parentheses.

[a]The fourth tier was used as the reference category. [b]1996 was the reference category for all models except for the effects of numerical ranks for total applications, where 1997 was the reference category.

The grouping of schools into tiers tends to segment the market for law school admissions. The only tier effects for the total number of applications is that the numerically ranked schools (the top 50) tend to receive, on average, about 180 more applications than other schools. The status that accompanies a top tier ranking is a boon for applications. However, when we examine the effects of numerical ranks within the top tier, we find that each rank increases the applicant pool by nearly 19 applications. While not by itself very much, this indicates that a difference of ten ranks within the first tier yields roughly the same

Table 4. Ordered Logit and Random-Effects Regression of the Effects of Student and School Decisions on *USN* Rank

	Tier		Rank	
	(1)	(2)	(3)	(4)
Tier1[a]	12.93	9.62		
	(0.60)**	(0.78)**		
Tier2[a]	7.43	6.26		
	(0.39)*	(0.56)**		
Tier3[a]	3.90	3.47		
	(0.34)**	(0.45)**		
Rank		0.94	0.70	
		(0.02)**	(0.05)**	
Size	−0.02	0.65	0.44	0.58
	(0.12)	(0.34)	(0.83)	(1.60)
# of Applications		−0.00		0.00
		(0.00)		(0.00)
LSAT 160+		0.16		0.47
		(0.03)**		(0.15)**
LSAT 150–159		−0.00		0.25
		(0.03)		(0.17)
LSAT 120–149		−0.00		0.31
		(0.02)		(0.18)
Percentage of Acceptances		−0.02		0.01
		(0.01)		(0.06)
Percentage Matriculate		0.02		0.01
		(0.01)		(0.04)
Constant			−1.66	−36.10
			(5.33)	(18.08)*
Cut 3	9.90	15.55		
Cut 2	5.59	10.50		
Cut 1	1.73	5.90		
N	795	795	234	234
N Schools			48	48

$^*p < 0.05$, $^{**}p < 0.01$. *Note:* For the regressions on tier, we used an ordered probit model, while for the regressions on rank, we used a Prais-Winsten random-effects regression.
[a]Tier 4 is the reference category.

number of additional applications as does the difference between schools in the fourth tier and those in the first tier.

We see a similar pattern in the percentage of applicants with LSAT scores above 160. Compared to schools in the third and fourth tiers, schools in the second tier attract about 1.3 percent more of these applicants, while schools in the top tier attract 2.6 percent more. Within the top tier, each rank increases the percentage by .13 percent, where a difference of ten ranking positions equals the difference between second and fourth tier schools, while a 20 rank difference equals the difference between first and fourth tier schools. The percentage of students with LSAT scores in the 150 to 159 range is highest in second tier schools, and there are actually negative effects for being in the top two tiers for the percentage of applicants with LSAT scores between in the 120 to 149 range. We interpret this finding to mean that applicants use the *USN* tiers to match themselves to schools based on the students' own LSAT scores. That is, students with high LSAT scores are more likely to apply to the top ranked schools, while students with lower scores avoid the top ranked schools in favor of applying to the lower ranked schools. This strongly suggests that the *USN* ranks helps define how this market is segmented.

USN ranks also affect the percentage of accepted students who matriculate in the law school. Approximately 2 percent more accepted students choose to attend schools in the second and third tiers each year than do accepted students in the bottom tier. While the effect for first tier schools is of similar magnitude, it fails to attain significance. However, within the first tier, each rank change increases the matriculation rate by .2 percent, so that a difference of 10 ranks changes the percentage roughly the same amount as the difference between the bottom tier and the other tiers. Finally, the *USN* ranks have minor effects on the ability of schools to be more selective. While there were no significant effects for the tiers, schools within the first tier were able to be more selective the higher their rank.

Overall, the *USN* ranks have a consistent and independent impact on which schools students apply to, where they can hope to be accepted, and where they eventually matriculate. But, as shown above, this is not the full extent of the effects of the rankings. The responses of students to the signals produced by the *USN* rankings can affect the future rank of schools in a way that compounds the initial effects of rank. The strongest effect of *USN* rank in our model is its influence on the schools to which top students apply, a variable that we also found to be a strong predictor of future rank. In other words, the fluctuations in the ranks of schools—which are commonplace due to the precise distinctions made in the rankings and rarely anything more than random statistical variation—have a clear influence on where students with high LSAT scores apply, which in turn affects a school's future ranking. Moreover, this process affects the underlying quality of schools, as schools that drop in the rankings are unable to recruit as talented of students as before. This spiraling effect highlights the importance of LSAT scores in determining the rank of schools and provides support for Klein and Hamilton's (1998) emphasis on the importance of LSAT scores to the determination of *USN* rank.

Two examples of the effects of rankings on actual schools provide concrete demonstrations of the somewhat abstract implications of our predictive models. The University of Akron School of Law moved from the fourth tier in 1999 to the third tier in 2000. In the following year, Akron received 88 additional applications (1,150, up from 1,062). In addition, it was able to decrease the percentage of acceptance offers from 48 percent to 43 percent, while maintaining the same number of students who matriculate (199 in 2000 to 201 in 2001), resulting in an increase in its matriculation rate from 40 percent to 44 percent.

Within the top tier, the University of Wisconsin suffered a drop from 23 in the 1996 rankings to 43 in 1997, and the subsequent year's applicant pool decreased by more than 20 percent (from 1,915 to 1,536). In addition, this drop in the rankings also affected its ability to recruit top applicants. After dropping to 43, the percentage of applicants with LSATs above 160 went from 39 percent to 37 percent; in real numbers this translated to the loss of nearly 170 applicants.

Conclusion

In this article, we have demonstrated that the *USN* rankings provide a signal of law school quality that influences the behavior of both outside audiences and law schools. While the effects of these rankings on admissions have been the subject of much speculation in the law school community, this is the first study to empirically examine these effects in detail. We find that these effects are both statistically significant and substantively meaningful to the affected schools. Even if their magnitude is not immense—20 applicants here, a few matriculation points there—these are actual changes to student body quality that are recognized as important by law school administrators, and thus, as we discuss below, prompt many secondary effects of rankings—such as increases in marketing activity, attention to LSAT scores, and career services statistics—that magnify their influence.

When considering the impact that these signals have had on law schools it is also important to keep in mind that admissions is just one of the many aspects of legal education that are affected by the *USN* rankings. Administrators note that the rankings also affect how other outside constituencies—most importantly, employers, alumni, and university trustees—perceive and behave toward the school. As one dean explained:

> The law school faculties and the smart administrators all say, "This [the rankings] is a bunch of hooey, we don't care about this," until they drop and the board of trustees says, "Hey, you're dropping; why should we give you more money?" And the board of visitors from the law school say, "Man, your school's really going to pot and you haven't changed a thing.... Big changes need to be made here." And your monetary support—the alumni—say, "Well I'm not sure I want to support a school that's going in the wrong direction." And your money starts to dry up, and you go "We have got to have the money; we can't afford to lose funding or else it *will* spiral downhill and we will be a worse law school."

In addition, many administrators note that internal constituencies such as current students, faculty, and even members of the administration itself are affected by changes in rank; among the manifestations of these effects are morale changes, transfers in or out, changes in the ability to attract new faculty, and an increase or decrease in job security for administrators. While these effects fall outside the scope of our current study, they suggest that the admissions process is just one of many nodes within the institution that are affected by the rankings, and a valuable line of future research would be to examine if and how the behavior of these constituencies is influenced by the *USN* rankings.

In this article we have also demonstrated how the process of creating market signals can have unintended effects on the phenomenon that they are designed to simply measure or represent. While economic theories of signaling focus almost exclusively on what signals do (e.g., provide consumer information), sociologists have tended to point out the limitations of these signals, such as the disjuncture between what is signaled and the reality of what is being represented (Podolny 1993) and the influence of the signal independent of the phenomenon it is measuring (Benjamin and Podolny 1999; Uzzi and Lancaster 2004). Drawing on the insights of research on the effects of quantification (Porter 1995; Espeland 1998; Espeland and Stevens 1998), the present findings extend the sociological line of critique by demonstrating how the process of signaling itself—that is, how the signals are presented—can distort in consequential ways that which is being signaled, regardless of its methodological accuracy. We suggest two ways in which the signal created by *USN* has distorted law school quality.

First, by precisely quantifying the quality of each law school and then creating rigid and fine-grained distinctions between schools, *USN* misrepresents the actual distribution of law school quality *even if its own measure of quality is accepted as accurate*. This means that many of the exacting distinctions made by *USN*, especially those that are made toward the center of the distribution of law schools, do not indicate actual differences in law school quality. As our results demonstrate, however, this false precision has significant consequences for law schools because small differences in law school rank appear significant to influential outside audiences.

The effect of these small differences supports the views of those administrators who claim that small changes, changes that are often caused by random fluctuations in the statistical measurements used by *USN*, can have important consequences for the school by influencing the quality of the student body. In this light, the redistribution of resources in which many schools engage to maintain or raise their ranking is a rational, if unfortunate, strategy. Because a decrease in ranking can do real damage to a school, administrators often feel obliged to prevent such a fall; one dean expressed this well:

> It would be stupid in a competitive environment not to do the things that are better for the *USN*, if it could ultimately lead you to getting worse students overall. So the cost-benefits of making decisions cannot be done without considering what the external effect may be. I mean, I care about rankings because they hurt us if we don't get good rankings. I want to have a better ranking because it means that we'll have better students and they'll have more opportunity.

Second, the distortion created by these presentational choices can then be compounded as future decisions are made according to these signals. Our analysis shows how the effects of the rankings on the admissions process have the potential to create a feedback loop that appreciably increases the magnitude of these consequences for institutions that experience changes in rank. This spiraling effect would unfold as follows: a school at the cusp between tiers experiences a statistically insignificant change in its numerical rank that moves them from one tier to another; then, the benefits or detriments that the school experiences because of this change will push that school closer to the mean for that tier; finally, this movement toward the mean will solidify the school's position in the new tier. In this way, the consequences of a change in rank extend beyond the following year, and these compounding effects can have long-term effects on the quality of students the school can attract and, thus, the quality of the school. This is a case where the rankings, by transforming insignificant variations into significant consequences, play a clear role in creating—rather than simply reflecting—law school quality. While it is true that the rankings, as their advocates contend, provide useful and accessible information to prospective students and other audiences, our findings suggest a more careful consideration of the unintended, and sometimes unnoticed, consequences that these evaluations produce.

Appendix: Methodology of *USN* Law School Rankings (2003)

Reputation = 40% of the Overall Ranking		
(1) Reputation Score by Academics:	25%	(of the overall ranking)
(2) Reputation Score by Practitioners:	15%	
Selectivity = 25% of the Overall Ranking		
(1) Median LSAT:	50%	(of selectivity score)
(2) Median GPA:	40%	
(3) Acceptance Rate:	10%	
Placement Success = 20% of the Overall Ranking		
(1) Employed at Graduation:	30%	(of placement score)

(2) Employed 9 Months Later:	60%	
(3) Bar Passage Rate:	10%	
Faculty Resources = 15% of the Overall Ranking		
(1) Expenditure Per Student:	65%	(of faculty resource score)
(2) Student/Faculty Ratio:	20%	
(3) Per-Student Spending (other):	10%	
(4) Volumes in Library:	5%	

Notes

1. Rankers of note in the United States include *Atlantic Monthly, Business Week, Financial Times, U.S. News & World Report,* and *Wall Street Journal.* Internationally, prominent rankings of universities are published by magazines in, for example, Australia (*Australian Good University Guide*), Canada (*Macleans*), Germany (*Der Spiegel, Stern, Focus*), the United Kingdom, (*Times Higher Education Supplement*), and Asia (*Asiaweek*); there are also several rankings of institutions worldwide (e.g., in *Asiaweek* and *Times Higher Education Supplement*). This list does not include the multitude of rankings published by academics or institutes across disciplines and throughout the world.

2. Caron and Gely (2004) write, for example, "A tsunami of accountability and transparency is sweeping across American law and society. One manifestation is the insatiable public demand for ever more and increasingly sophisticated rankings in all aspects of American life" (2004:1553).

3. The rankings have prompted official responses, for example, the Law School Admissions Council (LSAC), the American Association of Law Schools (AALS), and the National Association of Law Placement (NALP).

4. See McDonough, et al. (1997) and Monks and Ehrenberg (1999) for evidence that the rankings of undergraduate institutions affect the perceptions and decisions of prospective students.

5. Over the past two decades, for example, there has been an enormous increase in the role of rankings in legal practice. In the United States, law firms are ranked by subjective ratings of other lawyers (*The Best Lawyers in America*), size (*The National Law Journal 250* and the *Of Counsel 500*), revenues (*The AmLaw 100*), the amount of pro bono work performed by their attorneys (*The American Lawyer*), and their commercial activity (*The American Lawyer Corporate Scorecard*). And this is not just an American phenomenon. Legal newspapers in Europe, such as *Chambers & Partners* and *The Lawyer 100* in the United Kingdom and *Décideurs Juridiques et Financiers* in France, also rank law firms, and *The Lawyer* ranks international firms in terms of the amount of business they do in the EU in *The Lawyer Euro100*.

6. All quotations and statements about the opinions of law school administrators and faculty are taken from a related study for which 135 in-depth interviews were conducted (Espeland and Sauder 2004). Among those interviewed were deans, associate deans, deans of admissions, directors of career services, and faculty from over 50 law schools across the United States.

7. In 2003, 178 of 186 of the deans of ABA accredited law schools signed this letter. The letter, entitled, "Deans Speak Out," is published along with a list of signers on the LSAC's website at www.lsac.org/deans-speak-out-rankings.

8. http://monoborg.law.indiana.edu/LawRank/rankgame.

9. While the data that we have do not allow us to compute the *USN* score exactly (insufficient data are provided by the magazine), we were able to gain a good estimate of each school's standardized score by employing a model based on the information about each school that *USN* does provide. Specifically, we ran a linear regression of the factors that constituted the point total on the standardized score that *USN* provided for the top 50 schools. For each year this provided an R^2 between 0.983 to 0.986, meaning that the model explained over 98 percent of the variation in the scores for these top 50 schools. Because *USN* does not provide standardized scores for schools in the second through fourth tier schools, we used the coefficients of this model to predict the standardized scores for these schools. We then combined the actual scores for the top 50 schools in each year with the predicted scores for the other 130 schools.

10. The opposite effect—a compounding rise in ranking and quality of students—is also sometimes mentioned, but with much less frequency. See Stabile (2000) for a report on how the University of Toledo College of Law attempted to take advantage of just such an effect.

11. Prior to the 2001 edition, qualitative descriptions were published by the ABA in a separate volume. Many view the merger of the ABA and LSAC volumes as an attempt to provide a better source of alternative information for prospective students in order to counter the influence of the *USN* rankings.

12. Due to ties, the number of schools in the top 50 is sometime more than 50. The top 50 schools are determined by the top 50 scores, so schools that have identical scores have the same rank.

References

Benjamin, Beth A. and Joel M. Podolny (1999) "Status, Quality, and Social Order in the California Wine Industry," 44 *Administrative Science Q.* 563–589.

Berger, Mitchell (2001) "Why the *U.S. News and World Report* Law School Rankings Are Both Useful and Important," 51 *J. of Legal Education* 487–502.

Boulding, William and Amna Kirmani (1993) "A Consumer-Side Experimental Examination of Signaling Theory: Do Consumers Perceive Warranties as Signals of Quality?," 20 *J. of Consumer Research* 111–450.

Caron, Paul L. and Rafael Gely (2004) "What Law Schools Can Learn from Billy Beane and the Oakland Athletics," 82 *Texas Law Rev.* 1483–1554.

Elsbach, Kimberly D. and Roderick M. Kramer (1996) "Members' Responses to Organizational Identity Threats: Encountering and Countering the Business Week Rankings," 41 *Administrative Science Q.*, 442–476.

Espeland, Wendy Nelson (1998) *The Struggle for Water: Politics, Identity and Rationality in the American Southwest.* Chicago: Univ. of Chicago Press.

Espeland, Wendy Nelson and Michael Sauder (2004) "*Quantitative Authority and the Reflexivity of Rankings.*" Paper presented at the Annual Meeting of the Law and Society Association. Chicago, IL (3–7 June).

Espeland, Wendy Nelson and Mitchell Stevens (1998) "Commensuration as a Social Process," 24 *Annual Rev. of Sociology*, 312–43.

Greene, William H. (2000) *Econometric Analysis*, 4th ed. Upper Saddle River, N.J.: Prentice Hall.

Ippolito, Pauline M. (1990) "Bonding and Nonbonding Signals of Product Quality," 63 *Journal of Business* 41–60.

Klein, Stephen and Laura Hamilton (1998) "The Validity of the *U.S. News and World Report* Rankings of the ABA Law Schools," Study commissioned by the American Association of Law Schools, available at http://www.aals.org/validity.html (accessed 4 November 2005).

Korobkin, Russell (1998) "In Praise of Law School Rankings: Solutions to Coordination and Collective Action Problems," 77 *Texas Law Rev.* 403–428.

Law School Admissions Council (with the American Bar Association, Association of American Law Schools) (1996–2003) *The Official Guide to ABA-Approved U.S. Law Schools*, 1999–2003. Eds. W. Margolis, et al.

Lempert, Richard (2002) "Pseudo Science as News: Ranking the Nation's Law Schools," Paper presented at American Association of Law Schools. New Orleans, LA (3–5 Jan.).

McDonough, Patricia, et al. (1997) "College Rankings: Who Uses Them and With What Impact," Paper presented at the Annual Meeting of the American Educational Research Association, Chicago, IL, March.

Milgrom, Paul and John Roberts (1986) "Price and Advertising Signals of New Product Quality," *J. of Political Economy* 796–821.

Monks, James and Ronald G. Ehrenberg (1999) "The Impact of *U.S. News and World Report* College Rankings on Admissions Outcomes and Pricing Policies at Selective Private Institutions," National Bureau of Economic Research Working Paper #7227.

Nelson, Phillip (1970) "Information and Consumer Behavior," 78 *J. of Political Economy* 311–329.

Podolny, Joel M. (1993) "A Status-based Model of Market Competition," 98 *American J. of Sociology* 829–872.

Porter, Theodore M. (1995) *Trust in Numbers.* Princeton: Princeton University Press.

Sauder, Michael and Wendy Nelson Espeland (2005) "Strength in Numbers? The Advantages of Multiple Rankings," Paper presented at the Next Generation of Law School Rankings Symposium. Indiana University School of Law (15 April).

Schmalbeck, Richard (2001) "The Durability of Law School Reputation," 48 *J. of Legal Education*, 568–590.

Spence, Michael (1974) *Market Signaling: Informational Transfer in Hiring and Related Processes.* Cambridge: Harvard University Press.

Stabile, Tom (2000) "How to Beat *U.S. News.*" 10 *National Jurist* 19.

Uzzi, Brian and Ryon Lancaster (2004) "Embeddedness and Price Formation in Corporate Law Markets," 69 *American Sociological Rev.* 319–44.

Whitman, Dale (2002). "Doing the Right Thing," *The Newsletter of the Association of American Law Schools* 1–4 (April).

Student Quality as Measured by LSAT Scores: Migration Patterns in the *U.S. News* Rankings Era

*William D. Henderson & Andrew P. Morriss**

This study examines the change in entering-class median LSAT score, a key input into the U.S. News & World Report ("U.S. News") *rankings, between 1993 and 2004. Using multivariate regression analysis, the authors model several factors that can influence the direction and magnitude of this change. The study presents six specific findings: (1) the market for high Law School Admission Test (LSAT) scores is divided into two segments that operate under different rules; (2) initial starting position is a strong predictor of the future gain or loss in LSAT scores; (3) the allure of the high-end corporate law firms appears to cause a significant portion of students to discount the importance of rankings in favor of locational advantages related to the regional job market; (4) students will pay a tuition premium to attend elite law schools but, when deciding among non-elite schools, are willing to forgo a higher-ranked school for lower tuition; (5) there is little or no association between change in lawyer/judge and academic reputation and median LSAT scores; and (6) two well-known gaming strategies for driving up median LSAT scores appear to work.*

Drawing upon these results, the authors suggest that the current rankings competition among law schools has all the hallmarks of a "positional arms race" that undermines social welfare. The authors outline the emerging equilibrium in which non-elite schools engage in costly strategies to boost their reputations while elite law schools are able to further leverage their positional advantage. Because this dynamic spawns rapidly escalating costs in the form of higher tuition, continuation of the ranking tournament threatens the long-term viability of the current model of legal education. The authors conclude with four specific recommendations to law school deans and the editors of U.S. News.

Introduction

The annual ranking of law schools by *U.S. News & World Report* ("*U.S. News*") is a topic that regularly generates considerable controversy. While some commentators have praised the signaling and market-clearing functions the *U.S. News* rankings provide law students and legal employers,[1] others lament how the rankings have obscured the emphasis on "true" educational quality.[2] Yet, whether one defends or attacks the *U.S. News* ranking or its methodology, virtually everyone within the legal academy agrees that the advent of rankings has dramatically affected how law schools admit students and allocate resources.

Although *U.S. News* relies upon a methodology that encompasses a variety of substantive factors, including faculty reputation, library resources, faculty-student ratios, and bar passage, student Law School Admission Test (LSAT) scores have assumed (albeit inadvertently) an importance far greater than their current, direct 12.5% weighting.[3] According to a 1998 study commissioned by the Association of American Law Schools (AALS), "90% of the overall differences in ranks among schools can be explained solely by the median LSAT score of their entering classes."[4] Not surprisingly, during the last several years, law schools have attempted a wide variety of strategies in the hope of raising their median LSAT score.[5] As noted by one commentator, *U.S. News* has produced an LSAT "arms race" among law schools.[6] Although effective law school administration undoubtedly has an effect on the direction and magnitude of changes in LSAT median scores, this study suggests that the competition among law schools occurs on a playing field that strongly favors some participants and strongly disadvantages others regardless of an individual school's strategies. In other words, in terms of attracting students with higher LSAT scores, there is only so much a skillful dean or admissions office can accomplish.

The purpose of this Article is to develop a model of the market for high-LSAT students. Using multivariate regression analysis, we explore how gains and losses in median LSAT scores during the *U.S. News* rankings era have been influenced by a variety of factors, such as initial starting position, a law school's geographic proximity to large legal markets, gaming strategies, and average student debt. The main thrust of this Article is empirical rather than normative. Part I frames the research question and provides a brief literature review. Part II summarizes our data set and project methodology. Part III presents the project results. Finally, Part IV discusses the implications of this study, including recommendations based on our results for law school administrators and faculties.

I. Research Question

A. Law School Competition and the Median LSAT

The first *U.S. News* story on law school rankings appeared in 1987.[7] The methodology was simplistic: *U.S. News* asked 183 law school deans to name the ten best law schools. The article then ranked the top twenty law schools based on their level of inclusion. Harvard and Yale, which appeared on 91.7% of all responses, were tied for number one. Wisconsin, which was mentioned on 5.2% of all responses, was ranked number twenty. In 1990 and 1991, *U.S. News* published more comprehensive rankings of the nation's twenty-five "best law schools," which included numerical rankings on a variety of criteria, including academic reputation, lawyer/judge reputation, admissions selectivity, placement success, graduation rate, instructional resources, average starting salary, and average LSAT scores.[8] The first *U.S. News* ranking of all ABA-accredited law schools (then 175 schools) appeared in 1992. The top twenty-five were ranked in order, with the remaining 150 schools listed alphabetically within four quartiles—a precursor to the present day "tier" format, which began in 1994.

Unfortunately, there are at least two obstacles that preclude a direct comparison of change in *U.S. News* rankings over time. First, *U.S. News* has altered its rankings methodology several times, including, excluding, and changing the weighting formula for various "input" variables.[9] Second, the ordinal ranking of law schools has gradually expanded from twenty-five (1990–1993) to fifty (1994–2002) to one hundred (2003–2005), with the remainder of law schools listed alphabetically in tier or quartile format. Because *U.S. News* only publishes a subset of the data it uses to produce its annual rankings, and some of the data it uses (e.g., median LSAT and median GPA) are not available in published sources elsewhere, it is essentially impossible to calculate accurate ranking scores for all individual law schools for either current or past years.[10]

Notwithstanding these limitations, the *U.S. News* rankings provide some uniform data that permit a comprehensive comparison of quantitative measures of law schools over time. Since 1992, *U.S. News* has consistently published four input variables for all ABA-approved law schools: (1) reputation among academics, (2) reputation among lawyers and judges, (3) acceptance rate, and (4) student LSAT scores (median or 25th and 75th percentiles).[11]

This Article focuses on the changes over time of one *U.S. News* input variable—median LSAT scores. Our decision to focus only on LSAT scores requires some context. As a preliminary matter, we want to make clear that this study is the first part of a larger project on law school rankings and the nature of law school competition. We believe it is obvious to everyone within the legal academy that law school rankings have become "the 800-pound gorilla of legal education."[12] With important issues of resource allocation and educational policy hanging in the balance, a careful empirical analysis of the *U.S. News* rankings, including their ongoing influence on law schools, prospective employers, legal employers, and alumni donors, is long overdue. As a first step toward a comprehensive analysis of the impact of the *U.S. News* rankings on legal education, we begin with a look at the changes in median LSAT scores.

We decided to begin the larger project with an initial focus on median LSAT scores for two reasons. First, changes in median LSAT scores over time reflect, at least in part, the market preferences of prospective law students. Thus, changes in median LSAT scores provide a window into the relative importance of a variety of factors related to a student's enrollment decision, including law school prestige, the price elasticity of tuition, loan indebtedness, geographic location, and employment prospects upon graduation. Second, we believe that LSAT scores have achieved a rather peculiar and hallowed status among law school administrators and faculty. Unlike reputation among academics or practitioners, or even student selectivity, median LSAT score is a discrete annual benchmark that offers the hope (or fear) that it will produce a change in the *U.S. News* rankings. Each year, miniscule changes in median LSAT scores are causes for celebration or gnashing of teeth at dozens of reputable law schools populated by otherwise sensible faculty and administrators.[13] Yet it is hard to believe that a one-or two-point change in median LSAT has any appreciable impact on either student body quality[14] or overall program quality. In other words, we are beginning our ranking project with the LSAT because we believe it is the most provocative input variable and that studying it will garner support for additional empirical work on law school rankings. Our specific research objective is to (a) identify the relative winners and losers over time in the competition for the finite number of high-LSAT students, and (b) examine, through multivariate regression analysis, factors that can explain, at least in part, the underlying pattern in the movements of LSAT scores at law schools.

B. Literature on Rankings

Although the *U.S. News* rankings have attracted the attention of several legal commentators,[15] there is a paucity of empirical research on how rankings actually affect law schools (the subject of the rankings) vis-a-vis prospective law school students (the target audience and ultimate rankings consumers).[16] However, in 1998 the Law School Admission Council (LSAC) published two research monographs by the late Charles Longley, a renowned pre-law advisor at Bucknell University, that provided some preliminary evidence on factors that influence the market for law school applicants. Specifically, Longley's studies focused on how the broad systemic fluctuations in law school applications from the mid-1980s to the mid-1990s affected the numerical credentials of law school entering classes[17] and what characteristics of individual law schools explained proportionately large (or small) changes in application volume.[18]

Longley's first study documented the fairly intuitive proposition that the ebb and flow of law school applicants produces corresponding changes in acceptance rates, median undergraduate GPA (UGPA), and median LSAT scores. Longley observed that during the ten-year span between 1985 and 1995, applications to ABA-approved law schools started at a low of 231,952 in 1985, steadily rose to a peak application volume of 426,173 in 1992, and then tapered off to 361,726 by 1995.[19] Longley found that during both the "cycle of increase" and the "cycle of decrease" changes in application volume were strongly correlated with changes in acceptance rates for both public and private law schools.[20] Longley found a corresponding relationship between changes in application volume and the increase or decrease in the median UGPA and LSAT scores of entering students, although the statistical relationship was much weaker for UGPA than for the LSAT scores.[21] Further, Longley noted that while application volume had a virtually identical effect on public versus private law schools in terms of acceptance rate and median LSAT scores, the relationship between application volume and median UGPA was statistically significant only for private law schools,[22] thus causing Longley to conclude that "private law schools may be more subject to the ebb and flow of the application market."[23]

One of the most interesting questions lurking within the data of Longley's first study is why some law schools failed to benefit from the overall growth in the law school applicant pool. For example, for the 1985 to 1992 time period, when the total number of law school applicants increased by over 83%, over one-fifth of all law schools experienced a decline in their median UGPA.[24] Longley's study also documented similarly large disparities in how application volume affected median LSAT scores. Specifically, even though virtually all law schools experienced an increase in their median LSAT scores between 1985 and 1992, this increase was one point or less at twenty-six law schools (16%) while forty-eight law schools (30%) gained five or more points.[25] Similarly, when total application volume to all ABA-approved law schools fell by over 15% from 1992 to 1995, the median LSAT scores actually increased at twenty-six law schools (15%). In other words, some law schools appeared to be struggling in a highly favorable admissions environment while other law schools thrived even when the total applicant volume dropped off significantly. It is these dynamics (i.e., the relative winners and losers in the competition for high-LSAT students, regardless of systemic market factors) that are the primary focus of our study.

Longley's second study used multivariate regression analysis to examine the relationship between a law school's application volume and three independent variables: institutional reputation, starting salary of graduates, and annual tuition.[26] Since higher applicant volume is closely associated with higher entering credentials, Longley's second study provides indirect evidence of what types of law schools are likely to fare better in terms of increasing median LSAT scores. During the 1993 to 1996 admission cycles, Longley found that approximately 70% of application variation between law schools could be explained by these three factors, but that "salary and reputation, respectively, are persistently the most important factors."[27]

With respect to tuition, Longley observed divergent patterns for public and private law schools. Although Longley found no statistically significant relationship (or, for one year, a slight negative relationship) between application volume and tuition at public law schools, his data showed a fairly robust positive coefficient for tuition at private law schools—in other words, the higher the tuition, the greater the volume of applicants—even when controlling for reputation and starting salary.[28] Longley, who worked for over two decades as a pre-law advisor, attributed this seemingly anomalous finding to the "Chivas Effect" in which students believe that "if it costs more, it must be worth it."[29]

Another possibility, which Longley apparently overlooked, is that most elite law schools, which generally have higher published tuition rates,[30] are also the most generous in terms of providing financial aid to highly qualified applicants. High-LSAT students, after all, have become a coveted good. Their education can be subsidized by students with lower entering credentials who are willing and able (at least, with the help of loans) to pay the full published tuition.[31] In contrast, public law schools may lack the resources and flexibility to effectively utilize this strategy.[32] Longley also did not control for local market conditions, something we found to be an important part of explaining the quality of applicants and, therefore, something that we believe would also be an important part of explaining the quantity of applications.

Finally, it is worth noting the various ways in which Longley constructed his reputation variable. Longley initially used a simple average of academic and lawyer/judge reputation scores for each law school as reported in the prior year's *U.S. News* rankings.[33] He marginally improved the predictive validity of his model by using the mathematical log of this reputation variable, which accounts for the possibility that highly ranked law schools may be "hyper-attractive[ ]" to prospective law students.[34] Reacting to criticisms that the *U.S. News* reputation variables are too subjective or based on unrepresentative samples, Longley constructed a reputation variable based on various published objective inputs such as a law school's median LSAT, median GPA, student-faculty ratios, and volume of library holdings. Regardless of whether Longley utilized the *U.S. News* reputation variable, his objective index of reputation, or some combination of both, all of his models had virtually identical predictive power.[35]

For the purposes of our study, the most important aspect of Longley's findings on reputation and application volume is that some hierarchy of reputation or ranking has a positive effect on application volume and so, by extension, on median LSAT scores. Delineating the precise contours of this reputation construct is a difficult undertaking. It is unclear whether the annual *U.S. News* rankings merely reflect true estimations of reputation, or whether the ranking itself has become its primary determinant for future years.[36] That said, Longley's findings are strong support for concluding that a law school's starting position has a significant effect on its ability to effectively compete for highly qualified students.

II. Sample, Variables, and Methodology

A. Law Schools in Sample

For the purposes of this study, we assembled a data set of all published information included in the *U.S. News* rankings since the appearance in 1992 of the first comprehensive list of all ABA-accredited law schools. The overwhelming majority of U.S. law schools are comparable in the dimensions examined here. However, for a variety of reasons, we eliminated some law schools from the data set and excluded a handful of other law schools from some or all of our statistical tests.

First, we excluded the three law schools in Puerto Rico (Pontifical Catholic University, University of Puerto Rico, Inter American University) from our data set despite their ABA-accredited status because we do not consider them to be competing in the same market as other U.S. law schools.[37]

Second, there are a number of schools accredited only in a single state (nineteen in California alone), unaccredited (fifteen in California alone), or with some sort of provisional accreditation.[38] The graduates of these schools are generally allowed, if they fulfill certain other requirements, to take the bar exam in the state where the school is located, but are unable to sit for the bar in other states.[39] These schools are not ranked by *U.S. News* and therefore could not be included in our analysis.

Third, several law schools began operation during the period covered by our data set (1992 to 2004), including Appalachian School of Law, Ave Maria University School of Law, Barry University School of Law, Florida A&M, Florida Coastal, Florida International University, University of Nevada School of Law, and University of St. Thomas School of Law. Obviously, we could not include these schools for analyses that required data for years before they were in existence and so each is excluded from some or all of the statistical analyses, depending on the availability of data.

Finally, Widener University operates two campuses (Harrisburg, Pennsylvania and Wilmington, Delaware) but reports consolidated data. We considered the two Widener campuses as separate law schools since they are located in two different Metropolitan Statistical Areas (MSAs) and some important independent variables in our model are dependent on location. For variables derived from sources using Widener's consolidated data, however, we were forced to use the same values for both campuses.

B. Dependent Variable

Our dependent variable is change in a law school's median LSAT score between the 1992 entering class (the first year the LSAT was scored on a 180-point scale)[40] and the 2003 entering class. Stated mathematically, $\triangle$ LSAT <=> Median2003 – Median1992. Since the inception of its full law school rankings in 1992, *U.S. News* has consistently used median LSAT scores to calculate its law school rankings. Unfortunately, beginning in 1998, it began publishing only 25th and 75th percentile LSAT and UGPA scores.[41] The median LSAT for the 2003 entering class was obtained as part of a survey conducted during the summer of 2004 by the admissions office of the Indiana University School of Law—Bloomington.[42]

Table 1. Aggregate Statistics, by Law School

Variable	Mean	Std. dev.	*N*
Change in median LSAT, 1993–2004	-0.34	2.27	168
Percent change in full-time 1L enrollment (FTE), 1992–2004	7.4%	26.9%	172
Percent change in part-time. 1L enrollment (PTE), 1992–2004	14.3%	136.4%	190
Percent change in full-time 1L composition of law school, 1992–2004	–0.5%	6.8%	173
Number of Am Law 200 firms interviewing on campus, 2004	22.5	36.1	190
Average student loan debt	$63,495	$17,011	179

C. School-Specific Independent Variables

Our data set includes variables from a wide variety of sources. In addition to every published input variable from *U.S. News* since 1992, when the first ranking of all ABA-approved law schools was published, we collected school-specific data based on a number of factors we believed might influence the market for high-LSAT students. For example, during the last several years the authors have heard numerous anecdotal accounts of law schools altering the composition of their entering classes, shifting slots between full-time and part-time programs, or admitting smaller first-year classes and making up the revenue shortfall by actively recruiting transfer students from less prestigious law schools.[43] Because the LSAT and UGPA scores of part-time and transfer students do not count in the calculation of median numbers reported to *U.S. News*, these strategies may be an effective means to "game" these important *U.S. News* input variables. We therefore measured the change in the size of the full-time entering class as well as the change in composition between full-time and part-time students.

Drawing upon Charles Longley's findings that application volume is sensitive to starting salaries,[44] we also hypothesized that a law school's ability to successfully place students in full-time legal employment upon graduation (preferably high paying and high prestige) plays an important role in prospective students' choice of law schools. To measure this relationship, we gathered data on Am Law 200 firms that interviewed at various law schools using data from the 2005–06 directory of the National Association of Law Placement (NALP).[45] Because some multi-office firms complete a separate NALP form for each office while others publish a single form that consolidates information for all branch offices, we counted a firm as interviewing at a law school if any of its offices listed the law school as a site for interviews.[46] We concentrated on Am Law 200 firms both to limit the size of the data collection process to a manageable size and because we believe pre-law students are likely to focus on large-firm recruiting presence at schools as a means of comparing schools since these firms generally pay the highest starting salaries.

Finally, in collecting data for this study, we also assumed that, all else equal (e.g., future employment prospects and earnings), the total cost of a legal education will be a relevant factor on where to apply and enroll. We theorized that students will generally favor law schools that offer them lower tuition and saddle them with fewer student loans.

D. Location-Specific Independent Variables

Although prospective law students are undoubtedly interested in attributes that are unique to each law school, it is likely that some students are willing to trade off attributes such as relative prestige and cost in order to attend a school in a specific geographic location (or type of location). Schools within the same metropolitan area share important locational attributes, such as weather, access to cultural and urban amenities, and geographic proximity to local legal markets. Indeed, it is plausible that some students utilize *U.S. News* rankings, but only to select among schools *within* certain metropolitan areas. Therefore, we collected U.S. Census data on Metropolitan Statistical Areas (MSAs) to generate a series of variables related to change in population and change in the workforce with a Bachelor's degree or higher. We included these variables because certain metropolitan areas have been growing much faster than the nation as a whole;[47] therefore, insofar as regional population of potential law school applicants expands or contracts, there may be a measurable effect on entering LSAT scores.

In addition to broad demographic patterns that reflect the growth (or stagnation) of the regional economy as a whole, there may be important variations in the *legal* job market. Therefore, we also included variables measuring the change in number of lawyers, offices, and firms among Am Law 200 law firms.[48] We theorized that law students would gravitate toward law schools that provided an entree into employment markets where the number of Am Law 200 jobs, which generally offer the highest associate starting salaries, was both large and expanding.[49] Moreover, in contrast to the number of Am Law 200 firms visiting a law school for on-campus interviews, the number and growth of Am Law 200 firms and lawyers within an MSA is arguably a good proxy for the overall health and vitality of the market for corporate legal work in that area. To provide a concrete example, between 1993 and 2003, the San Diego MSA added fourteen Am Law 200 offices and 613 Am Law 200 lawyers. In contrast, the Detroit MSA, which is larger in total population, added two offices (both in the suburbs) and 95 Am Law 200 lawyers. We posit that the legal market for mid-sized corporate law firms is therefore better in San Diego than it is in Detroit.

Table 2 presents descriptive statistics on the 90 MSAs containing at least one ABA-approved law school.[50]

Table 2. Descriptive Statistics, by MSA

Variable	Mean	Std. dev.	*N*
Change in number of Am Law 200 lawyers, 1993–2003	398	1241	90
Change in number of Am Law 200 offices, 1993–2003	4.4	10.7	90
Change in MSA population, 1990–2000	274,306	406,836	89
Change in number of workers over 25 with B.A. or higher, 1990-2000	101,286	152,901	89
Number of law schools in MSA	1.93	2.13	90

NOTE: *N* in this table represents the number of discrete MSAs in the sample, *not* the number of law schools. Some MSAs contain several law schools (e.g., Chicago, New York, Los Angeles) and others contain only one (e.g., Austin, Champaign-Urbana, Phoenix).

Sources: EDWARD L. GLAESER & JESSE M. SHAPIRO, CITY GROWTH AND THE 2000 CENSUS: WHICH PLACES GREW, AND WHY (Brookings Institution Survey Series 2001); NLJ 250, NAT'L L.J., Nov. 15, 2004, at S15; *The Am Law 100 2004: A Special Report*, THE AM. LAW., July 2004, at 91; *The Am Law 200 2004: A Special Report*, THE AM. LAW., Aug. 2004, at 83; Martindale-Hubbell Law Directory, http://www.martindale.com (last visited Nov. 12, 2005).

E. Methodology

This study utilizes multivariate linear regression to model change in median LSAT scores between 1993 and 2004. Obviously, there are multiple categories of influences on a law school's median LSAT. To delineate these influences, we grouped our variables into five analytical categories: (1) initial starting position of the law school, (2) school-specific attributes, (3) locational differences, (4) gaming strategies employed by law school administrators, and (5) changes in reputation.

1. Initial Starting Position

Long-term trends in each of the areas we examine obviously influenced law schools' positions at the beginning of the period of study. To predict the median LSAT in any given year, it would thus be critical to include a relevant measure of the school's initial position to ensure that we measured change in position from the start to the end of the study period (e.g., median LSAT in 1993 to predict LSAT scores in 2004). To isolate the impact of changes in the past decade, we opted to examine the change in median LSAT rather than the level. Although using change variables eliminates the variation due to initial level in each variable, we were still concerned that there would be effects of initial position common to schools. The importance of starting position is evident from the remarkable stability in the very top of the *U.S. News* hierarchy;[51] there is no school ranked in the top 16 in 2004 that was not also ranked in the top 16 in the first *U.S. News* ranking in 1987.[52] (See Appendix 1). Moreover, as seen in table 3, which summarizes several key variables by 1992 "quartile" status (the first year that *U.S. News* ranked all ABA-approved law schools), relative gains in LSAT scores are closely associated with a school's relative starting position.[53]

Based on these observations, we theorized that the market is segmented by relative prestige into "national" and "regional" markets that roughly corresponds to *U.S. News* "Tier 1" status.[54] Therefore, after specifying each regression model, we routinely split our sample into two subsets (1992 Quartiles 2–4, and 1992 Quartile 1) for analysis.

Table 3. Aggregate Statistics by Initial Starting Position

Variable	1992 *U.S. News* Rank	Mean	SE of Mean	Median	Std. dev.	Valid *n*
US. News median LSAT 1993	Top 16	166.50	0.57	166.50	2.28	16
	Rest of first quartile	162.00	0.32	162.00	1.70	28
	Second quartile	158.05	0.33	158.50	2.17	44
	Third quartile	156.59	0.32	156.00	2.15	44
	Fourth quartile	153.13	0.48	154.00	3.02	40
Change in median LSAT 1993–2004	Top 16	1.69	0.42	2.00	1.66	16
	Rest of first quartile	0.46	0.31	0.50	1.62	28
	Second quartile	0.45	0.31	0.00	2.04	42
	Third quartile	-1.56	0.32	-2.00	2.12	43
	Fourth quartile	-1.34	0.35	-1.00	2.15	38
2004 median LSAT	Top 16	168.19	0.48	168.50	1.91	16
	Rest of first quartile	162.46	0.36	162.00	1.90	28
	Second quartile	158.50	0.41	159.00	2.67	42
	Third quartile	155.09	0.45	154.00	2.93	43
	Fourth quartile	151.85	0.49	152.00	3.07	39

Sources: EDWARD L. GLAESER & JESSE M. SHAPIRO, CITY GROWTH AND THE 2000 CENSUS: WHICH PLACES GREW, AND WHY (Brookings Institution Survey Series 2001); *NLJ* 250, NAT'L L.J., Nov. 15, 2004, at S15; *The Am Law 100 2004: A Special Report*, THE AM. LAW., July 2004, at 91; *The Am Law 200 2004: A Special Report*, THE AM. LAW., Aug. 2004, at 83; Martindale-Hubbell Law Directory, http://www.martindale.com (last visited Nov. 12, 2005).

2. School-Specific Attributes

Some law schools may be limited in their ability to respond to market changes due to certain inflexible attributes. For example, public law schools are more resource-constrained than private law schools (but they also have the benefit of state subsidies, which are generally on the wane).[55] Similarly, religiously affiliated schools have a potentially different market for students, since students with the school's religious orientation will be more likely to prefer the religious school to a secular competitor than will students with a different religious orientation. Annual giving and student indebtedness are also indicators of how dependent a law school is on tuition revenues. We tested for the impact of these factors both through dummy variables for status (e.g., public and religious) and with continuous variables that measured the impact of this dependence (e.g., average student loan debt as a measure of cost).

3. Locational Differences

Our model attempts to capture the impact of regional economic growth generally and legal employment market growth in particular. Between the early 1990s and 2004, different regions experienced different rates of overall economic and population growth. We theorized that greater economic growth boosts law schools' relative positions by attracting people to the area. Independently of general economic growth, regions experienced differences in the growth of law firm jobs. For example, both northern California and the Seattle area experienced significant high-tech economic growth in the 1990s,[56] but northern California's law market grew more rapidly than did Seattle's. Between 1993 and 2003, the San Francisco-Oakland-San Jose Consolidated Metropolitan Statistical Area (CMSA) added 786,051 new residents, which is roughly comparable to 644,627 added in the Seattle-Tacoma-Bremerton CMSA, but the San Francisco region added 2937 Am Law 200 lawyers while the Seattle region added only 432. Overall, the increase in the number of Am Law 200 lawyers was strongly (but far from perfectly) correlated with change in total MSA population (.634, $p < .000$) and change in number of workers with a Bachelor's degree or higher (.647, $p < .000$).[57]

4. Gaming

As the influence of the *U.S. News* rankings has climbed, schools have clearly adopted strategies unrelated to educational quality in order to improve (or, more accurately, manipulate) their rankings.[58] Building upon our earlier theory on market segmentation, we hypothesized that the effectiveness of a particular gaming strategy may vary depending upon a school's relative position within the *U.S. News* hierarchy.

For Quartiles 2–4, we attempted to capture a well-known strategy by which schools increase the admission standards for their full-time programs while diluting their standards for part-time candidates. In theory, this shunting strategy (a) bumps up LSAT and UGPA scores reported to *U.S. News* (since the rankings are calculated using the credentials of full-time entering students), and (b) is revenue-neutral.[59] We theorized, therefore, that a decline in the proportion of full-time to part-time students would be associated with a rise in a school's reported median LSAT score.

The shunting strategy is unlikely to be a significant factor within Quartile 1 because only three of these schools (out of forty-four) operated part-time programs between 1993 and 2004. Therefore, for regression models run on this relatively elite cohort, we substituted an alternative gaming strategy we believed would have a similar effect. Based on several anecdotes we had heard over the years, we suspected that some top law schools were shrinking their entering classes, and thus getting a credentials bump from greater selectivity and higher entering credentials, while simultaneously making up the loss in revenues by admitting more transfer or LL.M. students. We used the change in entering 1L enrollment between 1992 and 2004 to model this strategy.[60]

5. Academic and Lawyer/Judge Reputation

If the *U.S. News* rankings have ushered in a new era of law school competition over the academic quality of law school programs, as some commentators have claimed, we should see a positive relationship between *U.S. News* measures of academic and lawyer/judge reputations and entering class statistics, including median LSAT scores. The optimistic assessment is that more productive faculty members and substantial curricular improvements are duly noted by *U.S. News* respondents (law professors, deans, judges, and practitioners) and ultimately filter down to prospective law students through the improved position gained by a school whose reputation scores increase. An alternative, more pessimistic interpretation, which enjoys empirical support from Professor Stake's innovative study, is that changes in academic and lawyer/judge reputation are primarily a function of the previous year's *U.S. News* rankings.[61] Because the reputational scores were reported on different metrics in 1992 and 2004, we standardized all reputation scores to make the mean zero and the standard deviation one for both years. We then generated our change variables by subtracting the 1992 standardized score from the 2004 standardized score.

III. Results

Our results are summarized in Regression Models 1 through 3. We have six specific findings on change in median LSAT scores that merit discussion. These findings fall into the following categories: (1) market segmentation, (2) effect of initial position, (3) cost as measured public affiliation and average student indebtedness, (4) the impact of regional labor markets, (5) the effectiveness of gaming, and (6) the influence of academic and lawyer/judge reputation.

A. *Result 1: There Is a Clear Difference in the Market for Students between "Tier 1" and the Rest of the Law School World*

The results of this study strongly support our initial hypothesis that the market is segmented into a national market, which roughly corresponds to the current "Tier 1" designation, and a regional market, which encompasses the rest of the law school hierarchy. In every regression model we specified, the measures of goodness-of-fit (e.g., adjusted r^2) for predicting changes in median LSAT scores significantly increased when we divided the sample into two groups based on their 1992 *U.S. News* quartile rankings.[62] We examined a number of other possible breakpoints in the data, but the Quartile 1/Non-Quartile 1 distinction was the only one that was both theoretically sound and empirically supported. The theoretical rationale for distinguishing between Quartile 1 and the others is that it reflects a distinction based on *U.S. News*'s practice of ranking schools by placing them into quartile (and tiers beginning in 1994).[63] It also comports with market evidence that law firms rely upon the *U.S. News* rankings to direct their recruiting efforts.[64] We used 1992 Quartile 1 (as opposed to 2004 Tier 1) as the breakpoint in order to avoid a "winner's bias" in our results.[65] [See Tables 4–6.]

The presence of a segmented market is readily illustrated by examining the relationship between average student loan debt and the change in median LSAT scores. Average student loan debt was the only independent variable that was unequivocally important for both the top (Quartile 1) and bottom (Quartiles 2–4) of the law school hierarchy. However, within these two markets, the relationship between debt and LSAT scores was completely different. For schools in Quartiles 2–4, lower student loan indebtedness was associated with gains in median LSAT. This relationship makes intuitive sense: all else being equal, students with marginally higher LSAT scores will prefer law schools that will saddle them with lower total debt. This gives schools with lower costs an advantage in recruiting these students. In contrast, in Quartile 1, higher student loan debt was associated with increases in median LSAT scores. This change probably reflects an underlying relationship between tolerance for debt and job prospects following graduation.[66] Because a degree from a law school at the top of the *U.S. News* hierarchy is almost a guarantee of the opportunity for a job in a major corporate law firm, the demand for these slots appears to be relatively price inelastic. As a result, elite law schools have the luxury of regularly raising their tuition without the worry that the increase will adversely affect their median LSAT scores (and hence their ranking). Indeed, students with marginally lower LSAT scores can be used to cross-subsidize students with marginally higher LSATs, who are more likely to be awarded "discounts" in the form of merit aid.[67]

B. Result 2: Within Each Segment of the Market, a Higher Initial Starting Position Was Associated with Increases in Median LSAT Scores

Efficient markets require the availability of product information at a relatively low cost. For the purposes of our study, 1992 is an important year because it represents the first time that prospective law school candidates and legal employers had access to a *U.S. News* rankings that published data on all ABA-approved law schools. Moreover, this information was formatted for the purpose of facilitating comparisons among similarly ranked schools. Therefore, beginning in 1992, we would expect students to prefer to enroll in the highest-ranked school to which they were admitted. Thus, schools that started in Quartile 2 would generally benefit (i.e., attract students with marginally higher LSAT scores) at the expense of schools that started in Quartiles 3 or 4. Similarly, schools that started in the top 16 would generally benefit at the expense of other Quartile 1 schools. Further, insofar as legal employers began utilizing this information to make hiring decisions among candidates from less prestigious law schools (e.g., Quartiles 2–4), a student's decision to favor a higher-ranked school is certainly rational. Absent any other relevant factors affecting admission decisions (and there are several, which we model), we would expect this initial starting position dynamic to produce an LSAT distribution that at least roughly mirrors the initial starting position hierarchy.

Table 4. Regression Model 1

Panel A. Quartile 1

Influence	Metric	β	Std. error	Std. beta	ρ
	(Constant)	1.003	0.461		0.36
Starting position	Top 16	1.059	0.537	0.299	.056
Cost	Public law school	−0.717	0.531	−0.210	.185
Location	Chg. in Am Law 200 lawyers (1000) in MSA, 1993-2003	0.017	0.095	0.028	.861
Gaming	% Chg. in 1L FTE, 1992–2004	−3.778	2.153	−0.248	.087
	N	44			
	Adj. r^2	.162			

Panel B. Quartiles 2–4

Influence	Metric	β	Std. error	Std. beta	ρ
	(Constant)	−2.151	0.289		.000
Starting position	*U.S. News* Quartile 2 1992	1.518**	0.394	0.318**	.000
Cost	Public law school	1.173**	0.381	0.258**	.003
Location	Chg. in Am Law 200 lawyers (1000) in MSA, 1993-2003	0.163*	0.067	0.201*	.017
Gaming	% Chg. in proportion of 1L FT to 1L FT & PT, 1992- 2004	−6.045**	2.280	−0.210**	.009
	N	123			
	Adj. r^2	.245			

NOTE: * denotes significant at 5% level; ** denotes significant at 1% level.
Sources: *The Top 25*, U.S. NEWS & WORLD REP., Mar. 23, 1992, at 78–80; *The Am Law 100 2003: A Special Report*, THE AM. LAW., July 2003, at 91; *The Am Law 200 2003: A Special Report*, THE AM. LAW., Aug. 2003, at 75; *The Am Law 100 1993*, THE AM. LAW., July/Aug. 1993, SPECIAL SECTION at 1.

The relative gains and declines in median LSAT scores over time strongly support our initial starting position hypothesis. As shown above in table 3, the median LSAT scores for schools in the top 16 schools have increased an average of 1.69 points on the 180 point scale. Similarly, schools that began this "competition" in Quartile 2 experienced a 0.45 increase in their median LSAT scores, whereas schools in Quartiles 3 and 4 experienced declines (-1.56 and -1.34, respectively).[68] The initial starting position hypothesis is also

Table 5. Regression Model 2

Panel A. Quartile 1

Influence	Metric	β	Std. error	Std. beta	ρ
	(Constant)	−1.296	0.943		.177
Starting position	Top 16	0.845	0.537	0.239	.124
Cost	Avg. loan debt ($000)	0.031*	0.015	0.336*	.043
Location	Chg. in Am Law 200 lawyers (1000) in MSA, 1993-2003	−0.014	0.094	−0.024	.883
Gaming	% Chg. in 1L FTE, 1992–2004	−3.697	2.086	−0.242	.084
	N	44			
	Adj. r^2	.211			

Panel B. Quartiles 2–4

Influence	Metric	β	Std. error	Std. beta	ρ
	(Constant)	0.396	0.730		.588
Starting position	*U.S. News* Quartile 2 1992	1.704**	0.380	0.361**	.000
Cost	Avg. loan debt ($000)	−0.034**	0.011	−0.251**	.003
Location	Chg. in Am Law 200 lawyers (1000) in MSA, 1993–2003	0.167*	0.065	0.210*	.012
Gaming	% Chg. in proportion of 1L FT to 1L FT & PT, 1992– 2004	−5.405**	2.219	−0.191**	.016
	N	120			
	Adj. r^2	.269			

Note: * denotes significant at 5% level; ** denotes significant at 1% level.

Sources: The Top 25, *U.S. NEWS & WORLD REP.*, Mar. 23, 1992, at 78–80; *The Am Law 100 2003: A Special Report*, THE AM. LAW., July 2003, at 91; *The Am Law 200 2003: A Special Report*, THE AM. LAW., Aug. 2003, at 75; *The Am Law 100 1993*, THE AM. LAW., July/Aug. 1993, SPECIAL SECTION at 1.

supported by the regression results. In all regression models specified for Quartiles 2–4, a Quartile 2 starting position was a highly significant variable associated with increases in median LSAT scores ($p < .000$). Within Quartile 1, a top 16 starting position was associated with similar gains in median LSAT scores. Although only one of the models results in a p value for top 16 starting position that was less than the standard 0.05 significance level, the p values for Quartile 1 need to be interpreted in light of the small

Table 6. Regression Model 3

Panel A. Quartile 1

Influence	Metric	β	Std. error	Std. beta	ρ
	(Constant)	−2.567	1.092		.024
Starting position	Top 16	2.500*	1.099	0.706*	.029
Cost	Avg. loan debt ($000)	0.046*	0.016	0.494**	.006
Gaming	% Chg. in 1L FTE, 1992–2004	−3.521	2.013	−0.231	.088
Reputation	Chg. academic 1992–2004	2.848	1.409	0.819	.050
	Chg. lawyer/judge 1992–2004	−0.931	0.909	−0.264	.312
	N	44			
	Adj. r^2	.270			

Panel B. Quartiles 2–4

Influence	Metric	β	Std. error	Std. beta	ρ
	(Constant)	0.582	0.797		.467
Starting position	*U.S. News* Quartile 2 1992	1.766**	0.425	0.374**	.000
Cost	Avg. loan debt ($000)	−0.037**	0.012	−0.274**	.003
Location	Chg. in Am Law 200 lawyers (1000) in MSA, 1993–2003	0.160*	0.067	0.200*	.019
Gaming	% Chg. in proportion of 1L FT to 1L FT & PT, 1992– 2004	−5.637**	2.271	−0.199**	.015
Reputation	Chg. academic 1992–2004	−0.246	0.574	−0.040	.669
	Chg. lawyer/judge 1992–2004	0.192	0.356	0.048	.592
	N	120			
	Adj. r^2	.259			

NOTE: * denotes significant at 5% level; ** denotes significant at 1% level.

Sources: *The Top 25*, *U.S. NEWS & WORLD REP.*, Mar. 23, 1992, at 78–80; *The Am Law 100 2003: A Special Report*, THE AM. LAW., July 2003, at 91; *The Am Law 200 2003: A Special Report*, THE AM. LAW., Aug. 2003, at 75; *The Am Law 100 1993*, THE AM. LAW., July/Aug. 1993, SPECIAL SECTION at 1.

sample size (N = 44). Given the small sample size, the p values for the top 16 starting position are relatively low for all three models specified, if not within conventional significance levels.

C. Result 3: In Quartiles 2–4, Lower Cost Law Schools Appear to Have a Better Yield of High-LSAT Students, but in Quartile 1 Prestige Is More Important than Price

As shown in regression model 1, status as a public law school in Quartiles 2–4 was associated with a 1.17-point gain in median LSAT scores (p = .003). To assess whether this relationship was driven by lower tuition offered to in-state students, we specified other models that utilized more precise measures of student cost, such as in-state tuition, out-of-state tuition, and average student debt upon graduation. All of these models corroborated our hypothesis that the change in a school's median LSAT is partially a function of price.[69] Model 2 substitutes average student debt for public law school status. We focused on student debt because it serves as a composite of several relevant factors, including the size of a state subsidy, scholarship aid, and the fiscal management of a law school. After controlling for starting position, gaming, and locational effects, a $10,000 increase in student loan debt is associated with a 0.34 decline in a school's median LSAT score (p = .003).[70]

As mentioned earlier in the narrative for Result 1, within Quartile 1 there is a positive relationship between price and change in median LSAT scores. One possible explanation for this finding is the "Chivas Effect" observed by Longley; that is a law school is perceived as better because it costs more.[71] However, this unusual linkage between price and LSAT scores makes more sense when we consider the interaction between relative prestige, tuition rates, and students' job prospects upon graduation. Specifically, within Quartile 1, *U.S. News* rankings are strongly correlated with tuition.[72] For a risk-averse student, admission to a higher-ranked (and typically higher-priced) law school can be viewed as an insurance policy. In most cases, the significant post-graduation risk of attending a lower-ranked school is not worth the savings in tuition. As a result, schools at the top of the law school hierarchy, by virtue of their favored status among large law firms, are well-situated to extract an economic rent from their students in the form of higher tuition. We will elaborate on this point in Part IV. The nexus between post-graduation job prospects and the market for high-LSAT students is further corroborated by Result 4, which deals with locational effects.

D. Result 4: In Quartiles 2–4, Law Schools Located in Major Am Law 200 Markets Have a Significant Advantage in Attracting High-LSAT Students

As Longley first observed, future employment and earnings is a key factor in determining where students apply to law school. We theorized that students would be attracted to law schools that feed into strong regional economies. Although we specified several models that included various measures of regional prosperity, such as population growth and the increase in the number of college graduates, the only variables that produced significant results (and they were remarkably stable and consistent) were the change in the number of Am Law 200 lawyers and the change in the number of Am Law 200 offices. These results were somewhat surprising in light of the strong collinearity between the Am Law variables and the data on national demographic patterns.[73]

An illustration based on regression model 2 makes these results more concrete. For law schools in Quartiles 2–4, the addition of 1000 Am Law 200 jobs in a metropolitan area was associated with a 0.167 point gain in median LSAT scores. Obviously, this translates into a large competitive advantage for law schools located in large and growing legal markets. For example, between 1993 and 2003, the three metropolitan areas with the largest Am Law 200 growth (measured by number of lawyers) were New York City (9920), Washington, D.C. (4916) and San Francisco (2937). After controlling for initial starting position, cost, and gaming strategies, a regional law school located in these markets would be expected to respectively gain 1.65, 0.82, and 0.49 LSAT points compared to a school in an MSA without any growth in Am Law 200 jobs.

The robustness of the Am Law 200 variables caused us to speculate further on the relationship between high-LSAT students, who will generally have the most admissions offers, and the employment market for new associates. Beginning with the premise that students who attend more prestigious law schools are in higher demand at Am Law 200 law firms, we theorized that the number of Am Law 200 on-campus interviews is a function of (a) a law school's *U.S. News* ranking, (b) a law school's size (which affects competition from other firms), and (c) a law school's geographic proximity to markets with large numbers of Am Law 200 firms. In other words, on-campus interview (OCI) activity is driven by benefits relative to cost.

To test this theory, we specified a regression model in which the number of Am Law 200 firms who participated in the OCI process was the dependent variable, and the independent variables included: (1) status as a top 16 law school, (2) status as a 2004 Tier 1 law school, (3) 2004 median LSAT, (4) the size of the law school, and (5) number of Am Law 200 offices located in same MSA as the law school.[74] The model, which is summarized in Table 7, is a remarkably strong predictor of OCI activity. It also corroborates our earlier findings on the importance of the regional labor market.

Although *U.S. News* rankings, LSAT scores, and law school size are important determinates of OCI activity by Am Law 200 law firms, location in a large corporate market also plays a significant role. This effect can be seen quite clearly when comparing the OCI activity of highly ranked law schools in small market locations to lower-ranked schools in large corporate markets. Consider the following:

- 34th-ranked Fordham Law School in New York City has ninety-one Am Law 200 OCI visits versus ninety-three for 12th-ranked Cornell.
- 56th-ranked American University in Washington, D.C., has forty-five Am Law 200 OCI visits versus thirty-one for 23rd-ranked Iowa.
- 94th-ranked Santa Clara, which is located near Silicon Valley in the San Francisco MSA, has thirty-three Am Law 200 OCI visits versus eighteen for 34th-ranked Brigham Young University.
- Tier 3 New York Law School and DePaul (Chicago) both attracted fourteen Am Law 200 law OCI visits versus four for 40th-ranked University of Alabama and three for 50th-ranked University of Kentucky.

Table 7. Model for Predicting the Number of Am Law 200 Firms Participating in OCI

Metric	β	Std. error	Std. beta	ρ
(Constant)	−252.120	55.188		.000
Top 16 law school	68.851**	5.014	0.537**	.000
2004 median LSAT	15.923**	3.840	0.197**	.000
U.S. News Tier 1, 2004	1.609**	0.355	0.242**	.000
Total enrollment	0.032**	0.010	0.111**	.001
Metric	β	**Std. error**	**Std. beta**	ρ
Am Law 200 offices in MSA, 2003	0.089**	0.021	0.146**	.000
N	174			
Adj. r^2	.840			

NOTE: ** denotes significant at 1% level.
Sources: *America's Best Graduate Schools: Schools of Law*, U.S. NEWS & WORLD REP. (SPECIAL ISSUE) 28 (2004); *The Am Law 100 2003: A Special Report*, THE AM. LAW., July 2003, at 91; *The Am Law 200 2003: A Special Report*, THE AM. LAW., Aug. 2003, at 75.

Obviously, if the objective is to obtain employment with a large, sophisticated law firm in a major market, a high-LSAT student who was not admitted to a national law school—and "national" may be a fairly narrow group[75]—should favor law schools in large and healthy legal markets.[76] Remarkably, our data provides strong empirical support that many students are indeed following this strategy.

E. Result 5: Gaming Works in Both Quartile 1 and Quartiles 2–4

The *U.S. News* rankings are calculated using UGPA and LSAT statistics for each year's entering full-time 1L class. The statistics for transfer students or entering part-time students (even if they eventually switch into the full-time program) are irrelevant.[77] As discussed in Part II.E, this methodology decision by *U.S. News* opens the door for various gaming strategies.

An obvious (and revenue-neutral) way to improve the reported median LSAT score is to shrink the school's full-time program and expand the part-time program, thus permitting a law school to become more selective in its full-time admissions. We tested this strategy for Quartiles 2–4 using a variable that measured the percentage change, between 1992 and 2004, in the ratio of full-time 1L enrollment to total 1L enrollment. As shown in regression models 1–3, this strategy appears to work. For example, in regression model 2, which controls for initial starting position and locational effects, a 10% shift of a 1L entering class from the full-time to part-time program was associated with a 0.54 gain in a school's median

LSAT score. Only three of the forty-four Quartile 1 law schools have part-time programs. As a result, we tested an alternative gaming strategy that focused on change in total 1L full-time enrollment. We assumed that elite law schools were well-positioned to admit fewer entering 1L students, receive a credential bump, and make up any loss in revenues by admitting more transfer students who were anxious to improve the pedigree of their graduating institution. Despite the small sample size (N = 44), the predicted relationship emerges with p values below the .10 significance level. For example, after controlling for initial starting position, cost, and the number of Am Law 200 lawyers in the MSA, a 10% decline in the 1L class was associated with a 0.37 gain in the law school's reported median LSAT score.

F. Result 6: In Quartiles 2–4, Changes in Lawyer/Judge and Academic Reputations Are Unrelated to Change in Median LSAT Scores; In Quartile 1, an Increase in Academic Reputation Is Associated with Higher LSAT Scores

In Model 3, we tested whether change in the lawyer/judge or academic reputation variables was associated with changes in median LSAT scores. In theory, these two reputation variables reflect two plausible strategies for recruiting higher quality students: a law school can (1) improve its stature among judges and lawyers by developing curriculum that specializes in a substantive area of law or emphasizes skills-based training (e.g., law clinics, courses in negotiations, or trial advocacy);[78] or (2) improve its stature among law professors by producing more and better legal scholarship. In Quartiles 2–4, neither of these strategies appeared to be effective. It is worth noting that within this range of the law school hierarchy, change in lawyer/judge and academic reputations were only minimally correlated with each other (r = .121, n = 129, p = .086). Thus, we are confident that our insignificant results are not the product of multicollinearity.[79]

When we ran regression model 3 for Quartile 1, we deleted the variable for change in Am Law 200 lawyers because our earlier results suggested that the local market for new associates was not a significant factor for students choosing among Quartile 1 (i.e., top 44) law schools. Surprisingly, despite the smaller sample size, improvement in *U.S. News* academic reputation was associated with gains in median LSAT scores, even after controlling for initial starting position, top 16 status, gaming, and lawyer/judge reputation. In contrast to Quartiles 2–4, we were concerned about multicollinearity because of the high correlation between changes in lawyer/judge and academic reputation in Quartile 1 (r = .826, n = 44, p = .000). Yet, despite this close linear relationship, changes in academic reputation emerged as a significant variable.[80]

Of course, these results leave open the causal question of whether improvements in *U.S. News* academic reputation are attracting students with higher LSAT scores or vice versa. An alternative theory, modeled by Professor Stake, is that academic reputation is driven by changes in *U.S. News* rankings.[81] Law professors are likely to be more obsessed with *U.S. News* rankings than judges or practicing lawyers; thus, they are more likely to notice minute changes. After all, the prestige of their respective law school, or the law school that might make them a lateral job offer, represents non-monetary compensation. Further, there is at least strong anecdotal evidence that rankings influence placement opportunities for faculty scholarship.[82] Therefore, as schools with higher LSAT scores climb up the *U.S. News* rankings, so does their academic reputation. Professor Brian Leiter, a leading expert on the academic reputation of law schools, who assiduously tracks movement among law school faculty on his weblog, has referred to this dynamic as the "echo chamber" effect.[83]

IV. Discussion

Beginning with the first full rankings of ABA-approved law schools in 1992, *U.S. News* set in motion a competitive cycle that has, over time, produced relative winners and losers. Part of this competition, obviously, is attracting high-LSAT students. The results of this study identify several factors that affect the direction of this market. In this final Part, our discussion is divided into two topics. In Section A, we briefly explore some of the features of the equilibrium that has begun to emerge. The endpoint of this competitive landscape is not particularly attractive. In Section B, we draw upon our results to identify several strategies that could be adopted by law school administrators depending upon their school's current market position. We also make one recommendation to the editors of *U.S. News*, which addresses the gaming loophole.

A. Equilibrium in the Market for High-LSAT Students

In the *U.S. News* rankings era, one fact is unavoidably clear: the rich have gotten richer. In terms of attracting high-LSAT students, law schools in the top half of the law school hierarchy have generally benefited at the expense of those schools at the bottom.[84] Schools in the elite top 16 have done particularly well, their median LSAT scores having increased by an average of 1.69 points.[85] Russell Korobkin has argued persuasively that the primary purpose of the *U.S. News* is to provide a market-clearing device for legal employers and law students.[86] Thus, students with good entering credentials, such as a strong undergraduate record and a high LSAT score, can signal these attributes to the market by accepting admission at a highly ranked law school. Law firms also adjust their expectations for new associates depending upon their relative standing in the market.[87] Our study provides limited empirical support for Korobkin's theory: students obviously make enrollment decisions with an eye toward their future employment prospects, but in many cases this will require them to discount law school rank in favor of (a) law school location or (b) law school cost.[88]

So what is the equilibrium endpoint of this process—can the rich get any richer? The answer appears to be yes. Schools near the top of the *U.S. News* hierarchy continue to have one enormous competitive advantage: they provide an unfettered entree to the Am Law 200 marketplace. Even if an elite law degree is sought for the purpose of securing a coveted job in government, academia, or a public interest organization, it also offers the "safety net" of a high-paying job with a corporate law firm. And, at least anecdotally, a degree from a prestigious law school can play a major role in securing government, academic, and public interest jobs. Not surprisingly, our results clearly show that students are willing pay a premium (i.e., incur more debt) to obtain this attractive bundle of employment options.

Table 8. Tuition, Tuition Increases, and Student Debt by 1992 *U.S. News* Quartile

1992 Rank	Non-resident tuition, 2003		Chg. in non-resident tuition, 1993–2003		Average student indebtedness, 2003	
	Mean	Std. dev.	Mean	Std. dev.	Mean	Std. dev.
Top 16	$31,670	$3,387	$15,616	$1,431	$76,143	$17,876
Rest of first quartile	$25,805	$5,119	$13,320	$2,898	$61,283	$16,882
Second quartile	$23,561	$4,921	$11,999	$2,408	$59,672	$16,225
Third quartile	$22,778	$4,313	$11,545	$1,982	$63,606	$15,842
Fourth quartile	$20,486	$4,659	$10,089	$2,531	$65,067	$17,434

As the market for new law firm associates has matured with the aid of *U.S. News* rankings, elite law schools have arguably emerged as oligopolists who enjoy a fair degree of market power. Conventional economic theory predicts that market power will be used to increase price above marginal cost.[89] The breakdown presented in table 8 suggests that elite law schools have, in fact, levied larger tuition increases than the rest of the law school marketplace. The average nonresident tuition at a top 16 law school increased by $15,616, which is approximately $2300 more than the remainder of Quartile 1, $3600 more than Quartile 2, $4000 more than Quartile 3, and $5500 more than Quartile 4. Of course, law schools do not always charge students the full published tuition. Elite law schools have the advantage of offering merit scholarships (i.e., tuition discounts) to students who help the school's LSAT and UGPA statistics; in turn, any revenue shortfall can be made up by charging full tuition to students with lesser credentials.[90] Further, high-ranking law schools are also perennially successful in raising funds from outside donors, which further reduces any potential financial pressure.[91]

However, as shown in table 8, even students at top 16 law schools rely heavily on student loans, which they intend to repay through the hefty salaries they will later earn at their large firm jobs. Although students of elite law schools have the highest average student debt, their expected post-graduation salaries remain significantly higher than that of graduates of lower-ranked law schools.[92] The result is an effective transfer from the large firms (and so from their clients) to elite and semi-elite law schools. Indeed, the ability to "sell" its graduates at a high price to large corporate law firms enables a highly ranked law school to engage in bidding wars for productive scholars in order to further burnish its prestige. It also finances lighter teaching loads to facilitate more faculty research.[93] The rich are in fact getting richer.

Because deans and faculty at non-elite law schools believe they must emulate the elite law school model of high salaries and light teaching loads in order to improve (or maintain) their current *U.S. News* ranking,[94] there will continue to be enormous upward pressure on tuition costs. It is far from clear how law students benefit from these "competitive" forces. Moreover, it is not obvious that the upward spiral of tuition is sustainable in the long run. This study shows that approximately three-quarters of all law schools are already subject to a tradeoff between higher tuition costs and attracting higher LSAT scores.[95] As tuition continues to outpace inflation (or if interest rates on government-subsidized loans eventually go up), public law schools further up the law school hierarchy will probably be able to skim off more students with marginally higher entering credentials. In the coming decade, the highly uneven growth in the major Am Law 200 law firms, favoring a handful of major and mid-sized markets,[96] is likely to become more pronounced.[97] Lower-ranked law schools in high-growth locations will likely have an easier time recruiting candidates with marginally higher LSAT scores; and these gains will come at the expense of their rivals in low growth locations. Law schools without these endowments will find themselves tilting into ever greater headwinds in the market for better numerically qualified students.[98]

With no tangible institutional benefit for subsidizing faculty research,[99] we predict that the day is coming when cost pressures on low-ranked law schools will cause them to either close their doors or experiment with new models of legal education, such as distance learning or the aggressive use of law firm externships. Steep tuition discounts, made possible only through radical reconfiguration of the current law school model, will be the only way to level the playing field.[100] The specter of economic extinction may cause some low-ranked institutions to challenge the ABA accreditation standards, which mandate a number of items—such as number of full-time faculty, teaching loads, and library volumes—that drive up a law school's fixed overhead.[101] As Dean Matasar recently observed, "we may be reaching the end of a golden era for law schools, beginning a period of decline, and putting many schools' survival at risk."[102]

B. Strategies and Recommendations

When the general manager of the Oakland Athletics, Billy Beane, committed himself to a process of detailed statistical analysis to measure how each player contributed to baseball's ultimate endgame—scoring more runs than your opponent—he identified inefficiencies in the market for talent.[103] Armed with this data, he bucked the conventional wisdom of baseball scouts and fielded a championship caliber team with one-third the budget of his large-market rivals. Similar to baseball, legal academia has an insider's culture that perpetuates certain folklore on how the rankings game ought to be played. But, like the scouts, most law professors are likely to generalize from their own experience, are unduly influenced by recent performances, and are overconfident in their own powers of observation.[104] In contrast, we actually have data.

Based on the results of our study, we offer three recommendations to law deans and faculties who are trying to respond ethically but realistically to the *U.S. News* rankings game. By extension, this encompasses the market for high-LSAT students. The fourth recommendation is directed at the editors of *U.S. News*.

1. Recommendation 1: In a Price-Sensitive Environment, Non-Elite Law Schools Will Fare Better by Emphasizing Scholarships over Scholarship

A law degree is a substantial financial investment that imposes a significant opportunity cost on students. The results of our study suggest that students tend to rationally approach this important career decision. Elite law schools enjoy inelastic demand for their services because the high tuition they charge is typically outweighed by the better employment options that their graduates enjoy upon graduation. However, this tradeoff changes dramatically as a student's best admissions offers come from law schools further down the *U.S. News* hierarchy. In some cases, it makes more economic sense to forgo admission to a Tier 1 school in favor of a Tier 2 school that feeds into a vibrant legal market. Similarly, other students admitted to the same Tier 2 law school may forgo that option in favor of a Tier 3 public law school that offers in-state tuition and a scholarship. In the eyes of that student, the prestige payoff of a Tier 2 school is just too speculative to justify additional student loans.

As the cost of legal education continues to rise relative to a student's expected starting salary, it is certainly foreseeable that these tradeoffs will become more pronounced. The quandary faced by law schools is whether additional tuition or annual-giving dollars should be applied to (a) student scholarships to attract or maintain target LSAT and UGPA scores, or (b) reputation-building activities—such as recruiting renowned scholars, sponsoring a speakers series, or reducing teaching loads to facilitate greater scholarly productivity, with the hope that a future rankings gain will change the price point of the students they are trying to recruit. From the perspective of law faculty, who govern most U.S. law schools, the latter strategy is preferred because it focuses on something about which faculties care a great deal—the relative position of their faculty vis-a-vis other law schools' faculties.[105] The result is what economists refer to as a "positional externality" because each law school has an incentive to allocate excessive resources on a contest that most of them, by definition, are destined to lose.[106]

Professor Russell Korobkin has argued that law school rankings "can serve a valuable social purpose by promoting the production of legal scholarship," which is a public good that would otherwise be "underproduced relative to its social optimum."[107] Although Korobkin may be right that the faculties of the pre-rankings era were less productive than faculties are today, we see the potential for inflation of the price of legal education with no clear social payoff as at least an equally likely outcome since there is now evidence that legal scholarship is worth considerably less than Korobkin assumes. For example, Professor Thomas Smith has commenced a massive citation study to model the network structure of American case law.[108] Smith reports that 43% of all legal commentary never garners a single citation by a court or another law journal article, based on preliminary results of a companion study focusing on legal scholarship.[109]

Perhaps faculty will feel impoverished when deans begin to scuttle the lecture series and conference travel to put more money into student scholarships. (And for law schools at the top of the *U.S. News* hierarchy, the day of reckoning may be a long way off.) If academic reputations are truly a function of a *U.S. News* echo chamber effect, however, there will be no fallout from shifting from faculty scholarship to student scholarships.[110] Faculty can at least console themselves that there is empirical evidence that median LSAT scores are now more likely to go up. Finally, students will be saddled with less debt, which should count for a great deal.[111]

2. Recommendation 2: Provide Legal Employers with Strong Empirical Evidence That the Quality of Education Actually Matters

Legal employers play a key role in this market. When law firms rely upon the *U.S. News* rankings to set their hiring practices, they are basically concluding that the quality of educational inputs (entering credentials) is functionally the same as educational outputs (law school graduates).[112] This is remarkable, for they appear to believe that little that law schools do (or fail to do) during three years of instruction affects students' relative desirability in the job market.[113] In short, employers appear to operate on a model of "good quality in, good quality out." Although some law school administrators lament that legal employers are unimpressed by innovative teaching and curricular reforms—or at least not impressed enough to alter their hiring habits[114]—it is at least fair to ask whether law schools have made a strong enough case that legal employers should do so or whether law schools have innovated enough in their curricula to merit legal employers' attention to such details.[115]

For example, if a law school (a) developed a new curriculum that emphasized team work, presentation skills, and practical knowledge of business; and (b) tracked the career paths of program graduates over time and showed that they outperformed a control group of similarly credentialed students, legal employers might take notice.[116] It is worth noting that several prestigious law firms now pay a substantial signing bonus for new associates with JD/MBA degrees.[117] Are these firms merely paying for a paper credential to burnish their self-image, or are they paying for a valuable skill set that traditional law students lack? This is an empirical question worth exploring.[118] Law schools that provide better or more secure employment opportunities upon graduation than peer law schools will be rewarded with a better yield of highly qualified students and rise in the rankings. Such a strategy, however, requires a multiyear commitment by the school—to develop, implement, and verify the impact of the new curriculum—something a short-term focus on next year's *U.S. News* numbers does not allow. Our data clearly shows that something as simple as geography can confer a significant competitive advantage. We hold out the hope that providing a focused, relevant education ought to pay comparable dividends for law schools.

3. Recommendation 3: Regional Law Schools Should Come to Grips with Long-Term Trends in the Employment Markets for Their Graduates and Consider New (Even Radical) Ways to Overcome a Poor Location

Access to the most coveted legal jobs varies with geography. Students at non-Tier 1 law schools in fast-growing Am Law 200 locations often enjoy better access to corporate law opportunities than their peers at higher-ranked schools in small or dying markets. Not surprisingly, our data shows that students will trade down in reputation in order to get the superior employment options that accompany a large and growing metropolitan area. In order to maintain their current *U.S. News* rankings, geographically disadvantaged regional law schools need to minimize the relevance of location. Although many legal employers are reluctant to incur the time and expense to interview students at inconveniently located regional law schools, this situation can be countered by instituting placement programs that make it easy for prospective employers to conduct initial screening interviews. If the employers will not come to the students, bring the students to the employers. A half dozen thirty-minute interviews with coveted employers would, in many cases, justify a student's travel and lodging costs. Thereafter, regional law schools can expand their beachheads in these major markets and relentlessly promote their national networks to prospective students and alumni.

Regional law schools should also consider more radical options, such as relocation. The industrial economy that once fueled the legal market in the nation's heartland continues to dwindle. Over the last decade, the number of Am Law 200 lawyers has remained essentially flat in several formerly large legal markets.[119] To pick on just one state, none of Ohio's nine law schools in Ada, Akron, Cleveland, Cincinnati, Columbus, Dayton, and Toledo are in fast-growing legal job markets, and those markets are unlikely to turn around in the short (or possibly long) term. This severely hampers these schools in competition for highly qualified students. If even one of the four private law schools relocated to Phoenix, its graduates would enjoy significantly better job prospects (and the remaining law schools in Ohio would be better off).[120]

Merger is another possibility that struggling regional law schools should consider. Some synergies are obvious. An established law school with substantial resources is located in a declining market. As a result, the school's reputation with national law firms is poised to decline. An underfinanced regional law school in a major market lacks the cachet to effectively compete with several cross-town rivals. A merger delivers a brand name, necessary resources, and a market space that solves both schools' most pressing problems.

4. Recommendation 4: The Editors of *U.S. News* Should Revisit Their Methodology and Eliminate the Incentives for the Legal Academy to Engage in Academically Unjustified Behavior

Since the advent of the rankings in 1992, the legal academy has consistently demonstrated that it cannot be trusted to provide consumers with honest, reliable data. Periodically, *U.S. News* has published the names of law schools that have submitted false or manipulated data.[121] Of course, all the scofflaws are not caught—indeed, there is a perception that undetection is rampant—which in turn increases the incentive of remaining law schools to innovate new ways of working the numbers. This pattern has caused the editors of *U.S. News* to rely on publicly available LSAT and UGPA scores submitted to the ABA rather than continuing to rely upon law school self-reporting.[122]

We are going to resist the temptation to heap righteous indignation on law school administrators. As Dean Alex Johnson of the University of Minnesota lucidly explained during his remarks at the Ranking Symposium, his highly principled views of the law school world were exposed as hopelessly simplistic once he was inside the dean's suite.[123] Everyone—students, faculty, alumni, and potential donors—wants higher rankings and there is hell to pay if a law school slips even one notch. Law school deans may despise the effects of the *U.S. News* rankings on legal education, but they simultaneously feel a duty to their constituents (and are under pressure from those constituents) to use every measure reasonably available to protect and improve their *U.S. News* rankings. And over time, the definition of "reasonable" gets stretched to the breaking point. We are indeed caught in a "positional arms race."[124]

This dynamic explains why many law schools are restricting admission to their full-time 1L class while simultaneously expanding their part-time program and/or admitting more transfer students.[125] These maneuvers have little obvious educational merit.[126] But the results of our study provide strong empirical evidence that they work to drive up the median LSAT scores. The deans cannot fix this problem, but *U.S. News* can by eliminating the part-time "loophole" and calculating LSAT and UGPA inputs based on scores for the entire first-year class. Also, they should work to obtain data on the number of transfer students who enter and leave each law school. Insofar as a law school admits more 2L and 3L visiting students than it loses through attrition in the IL class, *U.S. News* should penalize schools in the rankings for engaging in such behavior by including a measure of net transfers in the rankings formula.

Conclusion

In this study we have explained a significant portion of the change in median LSAT scores during the *U.S. News* rankings era. We have six specific findings: (1) the market for high LSAT scores is divided into two segments that operate under different rules; (2) initial starting position is a strong predictor of the future gain or loss in LSAT scores; (3) the allure of the high-end corporate law firms causes a significant portion of students to discount the importance of rankings in favor of locational advantages related to the regional job market; (4) students will pay a tuition premium to attend elite law schools, but are likely to trade a higher ranking for lower tuition when deciding among non-elite schools; (5) neither change in academic reputation nor lawyer/judge assessment correlate significantly to change in LSAT scores; and (6) two well-known gaming strategies for driving up median LSAT scores appear to work. Although median LSAT score is only one of the components of the *U.S. News* ranking system, it is a highly visible one that is often seen by faculties as an important barometer of the efficacy of admissions offices. This use is misplaced as our investigation suggests that many of the factors that influence the change in median LSAT scores are beyond the control of the admissions office. If a law school is going to improve its position in the rankings, its faculty is going to have to stop blaming the admissions office and start taking ownership of the problem.

The practical implication of our study, and other recent empirical work on rankings, is to echo the lessons of Moneyball,[127] which Paul Caron alluded to during his opening remarks to this Symposium. In Moneyball, Michael Lewis recounts how the market for baseball statistics grew first outside baseball management—a puzzle, since there should have been demand for it inside baseball management.

> Everywhere one turned in competitive markets, technology was offering the people who understood it an edge. What was happening to capitalism should have happened to baseball: the technical man with his analytical magic should have risen to prominence in baseball management, just as he was rising to prominence on, say, Wall Street.[128]

Not until Billy Beane, manager of the Oakland A's, grasped the potential of statistical analysis for baseball teams did anyone inside baseball systematically incorporate statistics into management. Just as in baseball in the 1980s, law school management (that is, faculties and deans) have not yet grasped the importance of looking at the right statistics. Old-style baseball scouts based their decisions on whether a player looked right; Billy Beane taught baseball that it was the statistical assessment of a player's performance and potential to contribute to winning games that mattered.

Law school prestige has always mattered to students, faculties, and employers. But the advent of *U.S. News* rankings has heightened the competition among schools by giving prospective students and employers a means of comparing law schools. Therefore, it should not be long before law schools begin to refine their admissions practices (and their strategic plans generally) through the aid of statistical techniques such as multivariate regression of a variety of performance measures.[129] And we predict that those who scoff at this suggestion will eventually pay a price in the *U.S. News* rankings. Although this process might, in the aggregate, damage the collective enterprise of legal education, deans and law faculty who stand on "principle" will do so at the expense of their constituents. Bringing the force of data to bear on legal education will be as difficult as it was to change baseball's attitude toward data—legal education, like baseball, is only quasi-competitive. (Baseball has its league offices; legal education has the AALS and ABA.) But, like it or not, change is on the way.

Appendix. U.S. News Top 20 Law Schools, 1987 and 2004

School	1987 Position	2004 Position
Yale University	1	1
Harvard University	1	2
University of Michigan	3	7
Stanford University	4	3
Columbia University	4	4
University of Chicago	6	6
University of California, Berkeley	7	13
University of Virginia	8	9
New York University	9	5
University of Pennsylvania	10	7
University of Texas, Austin	11	15
Duke University	12	10
Georgetown University	13	14
University of California, Los Angeles	14	16
Cornell University	15	12
Northwestern University	16	10
University of Southern California	17	18
University of Illinois	17	27
University of Minnesota	19	19
University of Wisconsin	20	31
Vanderbilt University	—	17
George Washington University	—	20
Notre Dame University	—	20
Washington University	—	20

Sources: Brains for the Bar, U.S. NEWS & WORLD REP., Nov. 2, 1987, at 72; *America's Best Graduate Schools: Schools of Law,* U.S. NEWS & WORLD REP. (SPECIAL ISSUE) 28 (2004).

Notes

* The authors would like to thank our respective admission directors, Dennis Long (Indiana University) and Barbara Andelman (Case Western Reserve University), for their thoughtful observations on law school admissions. We would also like to thank Jonathan Adler, Olufunmilayo Arewa, Stephen Bainbridge, Jonathan Entin, Peter Gerhart, Michael Heise, Sharona Hoffman, Gerald Korngold, Leandra Lederman, Dale Nance, Jeff Stake, Robert Strassfeld, and participants at the Indiana University rankings symposium for their comments on this paper. Finally, we want to acknowledge the excellent research assistance from Rachael Clarke, David Lundeen, David Maijala, and Elizabeth Wysong.

1. *E.g.*, Mitchell Berger, *Why the* U.S. News and World Report *Law School Rankings Are Both Useful and Important*, 51 J. LEGAL EDUC. 487, 496–98 (2001) (arguing that *U.S. News* rankings serve a useful function because they supply students with relevant information, such as law school reputation, bar passage rates, and faculty-student ratios, in a form that facilitates comparisons and further noting that such information can "promote accountability and positive change" among law schools); Russell Korobkin, *In Praise of Law School Rankings: Solutions to Coordination and Collective Action Problems*, 77 TEX. L. REV. 403, 404, 407–14 (1998) (positing that the primary purpose of the *U.S. News* rankings is to provide a signal to students and legal employers that coordinates the market for entry-level lawyers and defending the rankings as an efficient solution to a collective action problem).

2. E.g., Paul D. Carrington, *On Ranking: A Response to Mitchell Berger*, 53 J. LEGAL EDUC. 301, 301 (2003) (conceding Mitchell Berger's point that the *U.S. News* rankings supply "useful" information to prospective students but arguing that "even that information has an unfortunate tendency to gain unwarranted importance when it is put in quantified form"); Nancy B. Rapoport, *Ratings, Not Rankings: Why* U.S. News & World Report *Shouldn't Want to be Compared to Time and Newsweek—or The New Yorker*, 60 OHIO ST. L.J. 1097, 1099 (1999) (lamenting that "objective" input factors used by the *U.S. News* rankings, such as grade point average (GPA) and LSAT scores, are not "good indicators of quality" because "these numbers don't reflect how well the law school teaches, how cutting-edge its research is, or whether the law school community is cutthroat or supportive") (emphasis in original); David A. Thomas, *The Law School Rankings Are Harmful Deceptions: A Response to Those Who Praise the Rankings and Suggestions for a Better Approach to Evaluating Law Schools*, 40 HOUS. L. REV. 419, 422 (2003) (arguing that the prominence and influence of the *U.S. News* rankings is misplaced because "the magazine does not publish all the relevant data, does not describe all the measures it takes to ensure the accuracy of the data, and does not describe its methodology in enough detail to enable anyone to actually check the results or to isolate and identify the influence of individual factors on the rankings"); LAW SCHOOL DEANS SPEAK OUT ABOUT RANKINGS (Law School Admission Council 2005), *available* at http://www.lsac.org/pdfs/2005-2006/RANKING2005-newer.pdf [hereinafter DEANS SPEAK OUT] (letter endorsed by over 100 law school deans that condemns the *U.S. News* rankings as "inherently flawed").

3. To the extent that the LSAT measures "quality" among the entering class, or at least characteristics that have a positive impact on other characteristics such as bar exam passage, increasing median LSAT may also have an indirect impact through effects on other components of the *U.S. News* formula. See, e.g., Richard Sander, *A Systemic Analysis of Affirmative Action in American Law Schools*, 57 STAN. L. REV. 367, 443–45 tbl. 6.1 (2005) (using logit regression to model factors associated with bar passage and finding that LSAT scores are moderately predictive of bar passage, even after controlling for law school grades).

4. STEPHEN P. KLEIN & LAURA HAMILTON, THE VALIDITY OF THE *U.S. NEWS AND WORLD* REPORT RANKING OF ABA LAW SCHOOLS (1998), http://www.aals.org.proxy.lib.pdx.edu/validity.html.

5. *See*, e.g., Jay Conison, *Financial Management of the Law School: Costs, Resources, and Competition*, 34 U. TOL. L. REV. 37, 37–38 (2002) (quoting dean at Valparaiso who stated that "many more schools are investing far more money—through scholarships and other means—to recruit students with high LSATs"); Howard O. Hunter, *Thoughts on Being a Dean*, 31 U. TOL. L. REV. 641, 643 (2000) (quoting dean at Emory who noted that LSATs "tie in closely with scholarships"). Scholarship money is perhaps the only strategy that law school administrators will discuss in polite company. For example, one purportedly widespread strategy is to spread out scholarship money for prospective candidates with LSAT scores at or slightly above the school's target LSAT median. Thus, instead of one $15,000 scholarship for a student with a 170 LSAT score, the school will offer $3,000 scholarships to five

students with 160 LSAT scores. If a law school's target LSAT is 159, the five candidates with 160 LSAT scores will have a far greater impact than the one candidate with a 170 LSAT score. Another strategy, which we explore in this study, is to decrease the number of full-time students while simultaneously expanding the school's part-time program. Since part-time LSAT scores are excluded from the *U.S. News & World Report* ranking methodology, a law school can theoretically raise its median LSAT score, and hence its ranking, without significantly reducing its revenue from tuition.

6. Abiel Wong, Note, *"Boalt-ing" Opportunity?: Deconstructing Elite Norms in Law School Admissions*, 6 GEO. J. ON POVERTY L. & POL'Y 199, 239–40, 248 (1999); see also Deirdre Shesgreen, *Making the Grade: Schools Look at the 'Whole Person,'* LEGAL TIMES, Jan. 13, 1997, at 2 (reporting a "consensus" among conference participants that the *U.S. News* rankings had caused laws schools to "put too much weight on the LSAT in their admissions decisions").

7. *See Brains for the Bar*, U.S. NEWS & WORLD REP., NOV. 2, 1987, at 72 (listing the top twenty law schools based on a survey of 183 law school deans that asked them to rank the nation's ten best law schools and reporting Yale and Harvard as tied for number one). A terminological note is necessary at this point. *U.S. News* rankings (beginning in 1990) appear in a spring issue of the magazine. The rankings are based on statistics drawn from several law school classes. For example, the 2004 rankings issue used data on the entering classes from fall 2003 and the graduating class of spring 2003, who would have primarily been students who entered law school in fall 2000. The spring 2004 issue of *U.S. News* would, of course, be primarily used by students anticipating entering law school in fall 2004. To be consistent we will refer to particular years of rankings based on the year the data appeared in *U.S. News* rather than by the law school class from which data was derived.

8. Ted Gest, *America's Best Graduate and Professional Schools*, U.S. NEWS & WORLD REP., Mar. 19, 1990, at 59 (ranking twenty-five best law schools and summarizing numerical scores in table form); Robert J. Morse & Elizabeth A. Wagner, *Best Graduate Schools*, U.S. NEWS & WORLD REP., Apr. 29, 1991, at 74 (same).

9. The most recent methodological change occurred this year when *U.S. News* switched from using median undergraduate GPA and LSAT scores to using averages of the 25th and 75th percentile scores. The magazine refers to this number as the "calculated median." See *Law Methodology*, in AMERICA'S BEST GRADUATE SCHOOLS 2006 (2005), http://www.usnews.com.proxy.lib.pdx.edu/usnews/edu/grad/rankings/about/06law_meth_brief.php (defining a median LSAT score as "[t]he calculated median of the scores on the Law School Admission Test of the 2004 entering class of the full-time J.D. program. The calculated median is the midpoint of the 25th and 75th percentile scores.").

10. Although *U.S. News* publishes its methodology each year, something for which it is to be commended, absent the relevant input data the publication of the *U.S. News* methodology has limited value for analysis of the rankings.

11. In its 1990 and 1991 ranking issues, *U.S. News* used average LSAT scores. However, since the publication of its first full ranking issue of all ABA-approved law schools in 1992, *U.S. News* has calculated its rankings using median LSAT scores. *See, e.g., Law Schools*, U.S. NEWS & WORLD REP., Mar. 23, 1992, at 78. Unfortunately, over the last several years, both *U.S. News* and the *ABA-LSAC Official Guide to Law Schools* have only published law school LSAT and undergraduate GPA statistics in 25th and 75th percentile intervals. See e.g., LAW SCHOOL ADMISSION COUNCIL & AMERICAN BAR ASSOCIATION, ABA-LSAC OFFICIAL GUIDE TO ABA-APPROVED LAW SCHOOLS (Wendy Margolis et al. eds., 2005 ed. 2004); *Schools of Law*, U.S. NEWS & WORLD REP., Mar. 29, 1999, at 94. This lack of transparency exacerbates the sense of gamesmanship that already surrounds the rankings process.

12. Leigh Jones, *Law Schools Play the Ranking Game*, NAT'L L.J., Apr. 18, 2005, at 10 (quoting Indiana University law professor Jeffrey Stake).

13. Changes in undergraduate GPA, a factor with almost as large an impact on the rankings, seem to draw less attention from faculties, although we are unsure why this is so.

14. We wish to make clear that the *ranking process* uses LSAT scores as a measure of quality; it is not a normative statement on our part. We believe that skilled admissions officers routinely make correct choices on student quality when they reject some candidates with high LSAT scores in favor of other candidates who present more impressive, but less tangible, indices of quality (e.g., volunteer, leadership, business, or military experience). Unfortunately, the need to set target LSAT scores to nail down an acceptable median for ranking purposes limits their ability to make these tradeoffs.

15. *See generally* Berger, *supra* note 1; Carrington, *supra* note 2; Korobkin, *supra* note 1; Rapoport, *supra* note 2; Thomas, *supra* note 2; DEANS SPEAK OUT, *supra* note 2; see also R. Lawrence Dessem,

U.S. News U.: Or, the Fighting Volunteer Hurricanes, 52 J. LEGAL EDUC. 468 (2002); David C. Yamada, Review Essay, *Same Old, Same Old: Law School Rankings and the Affirmation of Hierarchy*, 31 SUFFOLK U. L. REV. 249 (1997).

16. Two recent studies, which pursue different research questions than those examined here, do an excellent job of filling this gap. See Michael Sauder & Ryon Lancaster, *Do Rankings Matter? The Effects of U.S. News & World Report Rankings on the Admissions Process of Law Schools*, 40 LAW & SOC'Y REV. (forthcoming 2006) (manuscript at 30–31, on file with the Indiana Law Journal) (using regression analysis to show that changes in rankings are closely associated with the volume of applications to law schools, especially among high-LSAT candidates, thus affecting school selectivity—another rankings input—and ultimately influencing the size and direction of any subsequent changes in the *U.S. News* rankings); Jeffrey Evans Stake, *The Interplay Between Law School Rankings, Reputation, and Resource Allocation: Ways Rankings Mislead*, 81 IND. L.J. 229, 250–51 (2006) (using regression analysis to demonstrate how changes in overall rankings subsequently are associated with statistically significant increases in reputation scores the following years, thus suggesting that rankings themselves may ultimately drive the direction of important input variables).

17. See CHARLES LONGLEY, LAW SCHOOL ADMISSIONS, 1985 TO 1995: ASSESSING THE EFFECT OF APPLICATION VOLUME (1998).

18. See CHARLES LONGLEY, WHO GETS THE APP? EXPLAINING LAW SCHOOL APPLICATION VOLUME, 1993 TO 1996 (1998).

19. LONGLEY, *supra* note 17, at 1–2 tbl. 1 (noting that "our analysis focuses on two distinct periods: a cycle of application increase from 1985 to 1992, and cycle of decline from 1992 to 1995").

20. *Id.* at 9–10 tbls.14 & 15 (reporting that relative change in application volume was negatively correlated with acceptance rate at -.4854, $p < .01$ during the 1985 to 1992 period of increase and negatively correlated at -.5627, $p < .01$ during the 1992 to 1995 period of decline; further disaggregating correlation coefficients for public and private law schools).

21. *Id.* at 10 tbls. 14 & 15 (discussing and comparing correlation coefficients for UGPA and LSAT scores and noting that the relationship between application volume and UGPA was only statistically significant for private law schools, whereas the relationship between application volume and LSAT scores was highly significant for both public and private law schools). Longley's findings corroborated a similar study conducted a decade earlier. *See* David H. Vernon & Bruce I. Zimmer, *The Size and Quality of the Law School Applicant Pool: 1982–1986 and Beyond*, 1987 DUKE L.J. 204, 217–19 (observing declines in the average LSAT/UGPA admission index as application volume dropped between 1982 and 1985 and noting that the drop-off appeared to be the least significant at law schools with generally higher entering credentials).

22. LONGLEY, *supra* note 17, at 9.

23. *Id.* at 11.

24. *Id.* at 7 tb1. 10 ("In Table 10 we note that not all law schools enjoyed a rise in the GPA between 1985 and 1992; indeed, about a fifth (36) of the programs saw their entering class median GPA drop.").

25. Id. at 8 tbl. 12.

26. LONGLEY, *supra* note 18, at 1–2.

27. It is worth noting that law school reputation may translate into goods that go beyond starting salary, such as access to more prestigious law firms or government employment. *Cf.* Korobkin, *supra* note 1, at 412–14 fig. 3 (examining the high correlation between law school rank and number of on-campus interviews conducted by legal employers, especially among *American Lawyer* magazine's list of top 100 law firms ("Am Law 100") and arguing that it is rational for students to closely watch rankings if "the primary concern" is to "maximize their chances of securing prestigious employment opportunities").

28. LONGLEY, *supra* note 18, at 5 ("The role of tuition in explaining volume at private schools is particularly noteworthy.... Unlike the pattern at public schools, an increase in fees results in an *increase* in application volume. For every $100 more in charges, between 11 and 21 more applications were filed.") (emphasis in original). Something not controlled for in Longley's study was the correlation between schools in popular locales also being in high cost-of-living locales, which itself suggests a reason for a positive correlation between tuition and application volume.

29. *Id.* at 6 n.18.

30. See *infra* Part IV.A & tbl. 8.

31. Indeed, following the trend at the undergraduate level, tuition at many private law schools has essentially become an individually negotiated item between the law school and the applicant, with highly desirable candidates having the most bargaining leverage. *Cf.* Kim Clark, *Decision Time*, U.S. NEWS & WORLD REP., Apr. 19, 2004, at 53 (reporting the dynamics of appealing financial aid packages and observing that "[p]ublic schools have little discretionary money. And the top schools don't need to bid [to attract top students]. But small private second-and third-tier schools are likely to up an award from [sic] a student whose GPA and test scores are significantly higher than those of the average student at the college.").

32. Of course, a full scholarship costs less to award at a school with lower tuition, so public schools have a compensating advantage in that respect.

33. LONGLEY, *supra* note 18, at 2 n.2 (noting that "the data for the class entering fall 1993 are taken from the March 1992 issue, for the fall 1994 the data are from the March 1993 issue, and so forth. This assignment was made in appreciation of the timing that associates with the application cycle."). We are particularly skeptical of the averaging approach.

34. *Id.* at 3 & tbls. 1 & 2.

35. *See id.* at 6–8. Longley notes that he dropped faculty-student ratio from the objective measure of law school reputation because it "tends to decrease the impact of [reputation] rank on application volume." *Id.* at 7 n.23. The seemingly indiscriminate dropping of purportedly objective measures of quality in order to achieve marginally higher correlation coefficients casts some doubt on whether Longley's objective index of reputation is theoretically superior to the *U.S. News* reputation scores.

36. Sauder & Lancaster, *supra* note 16 (manuscript at 31–32) (examining how rankings affect applications by students and selectivity by schools, which in turn affects future rankings movements); Stake, *supra* note 16 (examining "echo effect" of *U.S. News* rankings).

37. One indicator that this is true is that all three schools report that virtually all of their students are Puerto Ricans. In 2004, 100% of the J.D. student body at Inter American University and Pontifical Catholic University were reported to be Puerto Ricans. At University of Puerto Rico, 673 of the 679 J.D. students were Puerto Ricans, with five of the remaining six students listed as "Hispanic." LAW SCHOOL ADMISSION COUNCIL & AMERICAN BAR ASSOCIATION, *supra* note 11, at 358, 562, 566. All three schools also require the *Prueba de Admision para Estudios Graduados* test as well as the LSAT for admission. *Id.* at 360, 564, 568. This effectively rules out non-Spanish speaking applicants.

38. For a breakdown of these schools in California, see State Bar of California, Law Schools, http://www.calbar.ca.gov/state/calbar/calbar_generic.jsp?cid=10115&id=5128 (last visited June 27, 2005).

39. *See, e.g.*, State Bar of California, Summary of Educational Requirements to Take the California Bar Examination, http://www.calbar.ca.gov/state/calbar/calbar_home.jsp (enter "educational requirements bar exam" into Search Calbar Site; follow "Educational Requirements to Take Bar Exam" hyperlink) (last visited Sept. 15, 2005) (summarizing various ways to satisfy the educational requirements for taking the California Bar Examination, including less stringent standards for law schools accredited by either the ABA or the State Bar of California); State Bar of California, Rules Regulating Accreditation of Law Schools in California, http://calbar.ca.gov/state/calbar/calbar_home.jsp (follow "Attorney Resources" hyperlink; then follow "Bar Exam" hyperlink; then follow "Law Schools in California" hyperlink; then follow "Rules Regulating Accreditation of Law Schools in California" hyperlink) (last visited Sept. 15, 2005) (summarizing standards of law school accreditation for California law schools); Alabama State Bar, Rules Governing Admission to the Alabama State Bar, http://www.alabar.org/public/admissions/RulesAdmissions2003.pdf, 13–14 (Apr. 2004) (summarizing educational requirements for admission by examination, including either graduation from an ABA-approved law school or "satisfactory completion as a resident student [a program of legal studies] at Birmingham School of Law, Jones School of Law of Faulkner University or Miles College of Law").

40. Although we would have preferred to use the earliest median LSAT scores available to calculate our dependent variable, the median scores listed in the 1992 *U.S. News* rankings (published in spring 1992) were based on a forty-eight-point scale. Since the variations in median LSAT over time are typically very small, we decided to use the 1993 LSAT data (published in spring 1993) in order to calculate our LSAT-change variable based on a consistent 180-point scale. We are also assuming that schools reported median LSAT across years in a way that does not introduce bias into the analysis. For example, in the early years, many schools calculated median LSAT by using the highest score for students who took the LSAT multiple times; the reporting rules now require using an average LSAT score for multiple test takers.

41. See *supra* note 11.

42. We would like to thank Dennis Long, Patricia Clark, and Mark Hilycord for supplying us with the 2004 median LSAT scores as well as other interesting and important data.

43. *See, e.g.,* Dale Whitman, *Doing the Right Thing*, AALS Newsletter (Apr. 2002), *available at* http://www.aals.org.proxy.lib.pdx.edu/pmapr02.html (President of the American Association of Law Schools reporting a known example of recruitment of transfer students so that an elite law school "can maintain the overall student body size that fits the building and budgetary needs, while admitting a smaller and more selective first-year class").

44. See *supra* notes 26–27 and accompanying text.

45. The forms are available on NALP's website, www.nalp.org. We gathered the data from the forms in May and June 2005. Thus, there are likely some minor differences between our data and which firms interviewed on particular campuses during the years under study because we did not have access to the pre-2005 forms.

46. In future work we plan to explore additional issues about placement using this data.

47. *See, e.g.,* EDWARD L. GLAESER & JESSE M. SHAPIRO, CITY GROWTH AND THE 2000 CENSUS: WHICH PLACES GREW, AND WHY (Brookings Institution Survey Series 2001) (presenting and analyzing large disparities in regional growth that emerged from 2000 U.S. Census).

48. The Am Law 200 firms used in this analysis were listed in the July and August 2004 editions of *The American Lawyer*. The locational data for most firms was derived from the 2004 and 1994 lists of the nation's largest law firms, published annually by the *National Law Journal*. When a firm was a product of one or more mergers, the locational data from 1994 for each firm was imputed to the current Am Law 200 law firm. To fill in gaps in the dataset, the number of attorneys for each firm location was obtained from the 1994 edition of the Martindale-Hubbell Directory of Lawyers.

49. As we explain in more detail below, the highest-ranked law schools provide access to a national job market in Am Law 200 firms; lower-ranked schools provide more limited access, primarily to Am Law 200 firms located near their campuses. See *infra* Part III.A.

50. Twelve law schools in our sample are not located in an MSA: Cornell (NY), Campbell (NC), Franklin Pierce (NH), Ohio Northern, Southern Illinois, University of Idaho College of Law, University of Mississippi School of Law, University of South Dakota, University of Wyoming, Vermont Law School, Washington & Lee (VA), and West Virginia.

51. This hierarchy began to take shape in 1987 when *U.S. News* published its first law school rankings. However, it was initially limited to the top 25 law schools. Beginning in 1992, *U.S. News* began ranking all ABA-approved law schools. The top 25 law schools were given an ordinal rank with the remaining 150+ law schools divided into first, second, third, and fourth quartiles. The first quartile consisted of the top 25 law schools plus 19 law schools with no ordinal ranking.

52. During this period there has been temporary and brief movement in and out of the top 16. For example, University of Texas was ranked 15th in 1993, 21st in 1994, 18th in 1996 and 1997, 29th in 1998 and back to 15th in 1999, where it has remained for the last several years; from 1996 to 1998, University of Southern California was ranked fifteenth. *The Top 25*, U.S. NEWS & WORLD REP., Mar. 22, 1993, at 62; *The Top 25 Law Schools*, U.S. NEWS & WORLD REP., Mar. 21, 1994, at 72; *The Top 25 Law Schools*, U.S. NEWS & WORLD REP., Mar. 18, 1996, at 82; Ted Gest, *Top Schools: No. 1: Yale University*, U.S. NEWS & WORLD REP., Mar. 10, 1997, at 76; *Schools of Law*, U.S. NEWS & WORLD REP., Mar. 2, 1998, at 78; *Schools of Law*, U.S. NEWS & WORLD REP., Mar. 29, 1999.

53. These figures are entirely consistent with the reflectivity theories advanced by Jeffrey Evans Stake, Michael Sauder, and Ryon Lancaster. See *supra* note 16 (citing sources by these authors).

54. The "tier" terminology is now widely used within the law school environment. However, in order to accurately capture initial starting position, we subdivided our sample using the 1992 "quartile" format. As noted earlier, the quartile format was a precursor to the present-day tier format. Of the 44 schools in the top quartile in 1992, only two law schools (Case Western Reserve University and Tulane) were not categorized as "Tier 1" in 2004, and both returned to "Tier 1" status in 2005. *See America's Best Graduate Schools: Schools of Law*, U.S. NEWS & WORLD REP. (SPECIAL ISSUE) 28 (2004); *The Top 25*, U.S. NEWS & WORLD REP., Mar. 23, 1992, at 78–80. Note that the concept of a national versus a regional or local law school is an old one. *See, e.g.,* Harry W. Jones, *Local Law Schools vs. National Law Schools: A Comparison of Concepts, Functions and Opportunities*, 10 J. LEGAL EDUC. 281, 285–86 (1958) (delineating four criteria to distinguish a national from a local law school,

including selectivity of admissions and likelihood that a graduate will obtain employment as a corporate lawyer in a metropolitan center).

55. A public subsidy is not an unambiguous good. In recent years, elite public law schools have obtained greater financial autonomy from the state by successfully raising funds from private donors. *See, e.g.*, Warren Lutz, *Boalt Hall Looks to Private Funds*, NAT'L L. J., Jan. 24, 2005, at 4 (discussing plan by dean at UC Berkeley School of Law to raise substantial private funds to compensate for declining state support, noting that public law schools at the Universities of Michigan and Virginia "have relied heavily on private money for more than a decade," and reporting that the de minimis 4% subsidy at Michigan permits the law school "to set its own financial agenda").

56. *See* ROBERT D. ATKINSON & PAUL D. GOTTLIEB, THE METROPOLITAN NEW ECONOMY INDEX 7 (2001) (ranking the San Francisco and Seattle CMSAs as the number one and three metropolitan areas in the nation, out of fifty, in terms of economic growth in new economy industries).

57. The following are the MSAs that experienced the largest growth in the absolute number of Am Law 200 jobs: New York-Northern New Jersey-Long Island CMSA (9920), Washington, D.C.-Baltimore-Northern Va. CMSA (4616), San Francisco-Oakland-San Jose CMSA (2937), Los Angeles-Riverside-Orange County, CMSA (2256), Chicago-Gary-Kenosha CMSA (1986), Boston-Worcester-Lawrence CMSA (1808), Atlanta, Ga. MSA (1487), Dallas-Fort Worth, Tex. CMSA (1072), Houston-Galveston-Brazoria CMSA (1046), and Philadelphia-Wilmington-Atlantic City CMSA (996). In contrast, some of the MSAs with the largest population growth are missing from this list. For example, the metropolitan areas of Orlando, Denver, Seattle, Miami, Las Vegas, and Phoenix all added more new residents from 1990 to 2000 than the Boston CMSA, yet the Boston region gained over 1200 more Am Law 200 lawyers than any of these higher growth cities. Similarly, the Philadelphia CMSA, which lost over 30,000 residents between 1990 and 2000, significantly out-gained these same cities by at least 400 Am Law 200 lawyers.

58. *See, e.g.*, Whitman, *supra* note 43, at 1–4 (president of AALS detailing six strategies utilized by actual law schools to boost *U.S. News* rankings, including two specifically designed to increase median LSAT and UGPA scores).

59. Permissive policies for switching to the full-time program after the first year also reduce the burden on the faculty to actually teach evening classes.

60. The ideal way to test this gaming strategy is to have longitudinal data for both entering class size and full-time J.D. enrollment. Unfortunately, we were unable to locate a reliable source for full-time J.D. enrollment. Nevertheless, change in 1L class size is still a theoretically valid, but less precise, measure of this strategy. The credential bump comes from the greater admissions selectivity applied to the 1L class; more liberal admissions of transfer and LLM students are used to make up losses in revenues.

61. *See* Stake, *supra* note 16, at 250.

62. Goodness-of-fit refers to the predictive power of the model specified after adjusting for sample size. In regression models 1–3, the goodness-of-fit measure is the adjusted r^2 value, which reflects the amount of variance in the dependent variable (change in median LSAT score from 1993 to 2004) explained by the independent variables specified. In general, dividing a sample in the two groups will lower the adjusted r^2 except, as here, when the two groups are affected by the independent variables in different ways.

63. As noted in Part I.A, before 1994 *U.S. News* reported ranked results for either the top 25(1990–1992) or the top 20 (1987–1989) and after 2003 it reported ranked results for the top 100.

64. For example, one of the leading attorney recruiting firms, BCG Attorney Search, has created a detailed guide for evaluating law school transcripts, academic honors, and law review membership at the nation's "Top 50 Law Schools." The "Top 50" is based on 2004 *U.S. News* rankings. *See* BCG ATTORNEY SEARCH GUIDE (2004), *available at* http://www.bcgsearch.com/bcgguide.pdf.

65. The breakpoint should reflect the starting point rather than the ending point. Obviously, higher-ranked schools in 2004 are much more likely to have increased their median LSAT scores over time.

66. For a breakdown of starting law firm salaries and student debt based on law schools' *U.S. News* rankings, *see* RONIT DINOVITZER, BRYANT GARTH, RICHARD SANDER, JOYCE STERLING, & GITA WILDER, AFTER THE JD: FIRST RESULTS OF A NATIONAL STUDY OF LEGAL CAREERS 75 fig. 10.3 & tbl.10.3 (2004) [hereinafter AFTER THE J.D.]. These figures show that graduates of top ten law schools have the highest median salaries ($135,000) and the highest median debt loads ($80,000).

67. *See, e.g.*, Conison, *supra* note 5, at 37–38 (stating, as dean at Valparaiso, that "many more schools are investing far more money—through scholarships and other means—to recruit students with high LSATs"); Hunter, *supra* note 5, at 643 (quoting dean at Emory, noting that LSATs "tie in closely with scholarships").

68. The slightly larger decline in Quartile 3 versus Quartile 4 may reflect a perception among students and employers that there is a negligible difference in prestige among schools in this range of the hierarchy. Hence, for students with lower LSAT scores, considerations of cost and geography, which we also modeled, may be predominant in the decisions of where to enroll.

69. For the sake of brevity, we have omitted summaries of these other models. However, to provide the reader with a concrete sense of the price-LSAT relationship, a $5,000 increase in in-state tuition was associated with a 0.28 decline in a school's median LSAT score ($p = .021$).

70. A better model would have controlled for changes in student debt over time. Unfortunately, we were unable to locate a source for this data. The importance of controlling for change is diminished somewhat because of the persistence of a large state subsidy for students at public law schools. For 2004, students at public law schools in Quartiles 2–4 had an average student debt of $48,150 versus $74,455 for students graduating from private law schools in the same cohort.

71. See *supra* note 28–29 and accompanying text. Since Longley served as a pre-law advisor for many years, we are cautious not to dismiss this theory too quickly. It is worth noting that the average socio-economic background of students moves in virtual lockstep with a law school's relative prestige. *Compare* AFTER THE J.D., *supra* note 66, at 20 (reviewing results of large national data set on recent law school graduates and noting that "the more selective the law school, the more likely it is to educate the children of relative privilege, and the less selective law schools are notably more accessible to the less privileged"), *with* SEYMOUR WARKOV, LAWYERS IN THE MAKING 53–56 (1965) (large-scale national study finding that students from more affluent families are much more likely to attend more elite law schools as measured by median LSAT scores).

72. For example, for Quartile 1 schools, the correlation coefficient for 2004 *U.S. News* ranking and in-state tuition is -.576 ($N = 44$, $p < .000$). The coefficient for out-of-state tuition is even higher: -.618 ($N = 44$, $p < .000$).

73. See *supra* note 57 and accompanying text.

74. Inclusion of actual *U.S. News* rankings as an independent variable would have reduced our sample size because only Tiers 1 and 2 (100 law schools) are numerically ranked. Median LSAT, however, is a fairly accurate proxy for *U.S. News* rank. See KLEIN & HAMILTON, *supra* note 4, at 12.

75. The number of Am Law 200 firms interviewing at top 16 law schools ranged from 161 (14th-ranked Georgetown) to seventy-eight (15th-ranked Texas). A total of nineteen schools attract at least seventy-eight Am Law 200 OCI visits. One school in this group is Howard, which is a historically black law school located in Washington, D.C. Although it is ranked in Tier 3, 114 Am Law 200 law firms participate in its OCI process—more than Yale (100) and Stanford (105)! In general, our data suggests that the historically black law schools do very well in attracting Am Law 200 law firms. Tier 4 North Carolina Central has five Am Law 200 OCI visits versus four for 40th-ranked University of Alabama, and Tier 4 Southern Texas (Thurgood Marshall) had nine, which is the same number for 48th-ranked University of Utah.

76. The locational data used in this study provides a remarkable window on how the shift from an industrial to a high-tech information economy has affected the dispersion of Am Law 200 lawyers. For example, MSAs such as Cleveland, Milwaukee, and Detroit, which all had a relatively large base of Am Law 200 lawyers in 1993, added fewer than 100 lawyers each by 2003. In contrast, MSAs such as Austin, San Diego, Phoenix, and Denver, which started with a much smaller base, each added 300 or more lawyers. For a detailed account of these changes, see William D. Henderson, *An Empirical Study of Single-Tier Versus Two-Tier Partnership in the Am Law 200*, 84 N.C. L. REV. (forthcoming 2006).

77. This may be about to change. See Alex Wellen, *The $8.78 Million Maneuver*, N.Y. TIMES, July 31, 2005, §4A, at 18 (noting that in response to our suggestion, *U.S. News* is considering such a change).

78. More and better skills-based courses was one of the key recommendations that emerged from an exhaustive report issued by the American Bar Association in 1992. *See* SECTION OF LEGAL EDUCATION AND ADMISSIONS TO THE BAR, A.B.A., REPORT OF THE TASK FORCE ON LAW SCHOOLS AND THE LEGAL PROFESSION, LEGAL EDUCATION AND PROFESSIONAL DEVELOPMENT—AN EDUCATIONAL CONTINUUM 233–36 (1992). In legal circles, this document is commonly referred to as the MacCrate Report.

79. Multicollinearity refers to the estimation problems that occur in multivariate regression when two or more independent variables are highly correlated with each other. *See* PETER A. KENNEDY, A GUIDE TO ECONOMETRICS 205–06 (5th ed. 2003).

80. The most common estimating error associated with multicollinearity is that the regression coefficients for the two collinear variables will not be statistically significant even though at least one of the variables has important predictive power. See KENNEDY, *supra* note 79 at 208–09. That situation, however, was not present here.

81. See Stake, *supra* note 16, at 250.

82. We are now engaged, together with Professors Olufunmilayo Arewa and Kenneth Dau-Schmidt, in an empirical analysis of legal scholarship that will provide evidence to evaluate this effect. In the meantime we can attest to numerous anecdotes that support such a claim, ranging from a phone call to a colleague from an articles editor apologizing for summarily rejecting a submission because the author's school had been misclassified as a lower tier school to several professors' informal experiments of sending out manuscripts with cover letters on different law schools' stationary and getting markedly better results with the higher-ranked school's stationery.

83. See Brian Leiter, More on the *U.S. News* Echo Chamber, Leiter Updates (weblog) (April 1, 2005), http://leiterreports.typepad.com/blog/2005/04/more_on_the_us_.html (reviewing the 2005 *U.S. News* rankings and observing, "What I'm particularly struck by is the "echo chamber" effect ... namely, that the academic reputation rank of at least the top schools is basically gravitating towards the typical overall *U.S. News* rank of the school—a rank that is, itself, based in large part on that reputation!").

84. See *supra* tbl.3.

85. *Id.*

86. Korobkin, *supra* note 1, at 407–14.

87. For example, an elite firm may concentrate their efforts at top 10 law schools, while a regional mid-sized firm will not waste its time trying to lure students from Harvard.

88. *See supra* Part III.C-D. Regarding the dominant effect of rankings on student enrollment decisions, Professor Leiter has disputed the claim of *U.S. News* editors that law students actually pay attention to individual input variables, observing through his own discussions with prospective students that "students appear to be obsessed with overall rank and only that." Brian Leiter, *Measuring the Academic Distinction of Law Faculty*, 29 J. LEGAL STUD. 451, 452 n.2 (2000). That may be true for the relatively elite cohort in the running for admission to the University of Texas Law School, where Leiter teaches. But it is probably not true for students with less impressive numerical credentials who nonetheless want to maximize their future career options—and that group comprises the majority of the law school population.

89. *See, e.g.*, JEAN TIROLE, THE THEORY OF INDUSTRIAL ORGANIZATION 65 (1988).

90. Note that most students attending elite law schools come from relatively affluent families. *See* AFTER THE J.D., *supra* note 66, at 20.

91. Richard Matasar, who has served as dean at three different law schools, recently observed:

> [Law schools] with the most resources get the most resources.... They can attract new gifts from loyal graduates whose generosity is made more likely by the greater opportunities they received as students at a school whose reputation ensured those opportunities. In short, this market [for fundraising] tracks others—prestige is rewarded.... It reinforces the strength of the strong in the market and underscores the precariousness of the position of lower-ranked institutions.

Richard A. Matasar, *The Rise and Fall of American Legal Education*, 49 N.Y. L. SCH. L. REV. 465, 488 (2004). Data obtained for the study corroborated this assessment. The average annual giving for alumni at top 16 law schools in 2003 was $6.6 million versus $847,000 for the rest of the law school hierarchy. The average for schools in Quartile 4 was $458,000.

92. A law firm associate from a top 10 law school who passed the bar in 2000 has a median salary of $135,000 and a median student debt of $80,000; in contrast, an associate from a top 21-100 law school has a median salary of $73,500 and a median student debt of $65,000. (Note that in determining median student debt only those who had any debt at all were figured into the calculation, those with zero debt equaled 19% within the top 10, and 14% within the top 21-100.) AFTER THE J.D., *supra* note 66, at 75 fig.10.3.

93. There is surely some irony in corporate America paying for the lifestyles of elite law school faculties, whose views are generally thought to be highly liberal and anti-corporate. The clear

segmentation of the law school hierarchy, and the symbiotic relationship that exists between Tier One and the Am Law 200 law firms, is reminiscent of the famous "two hemisphere" theory of lawyers articulated by Heinz and Laumann. *See generally* JOHN P. HEINZ & EDWARD O. LAUMANN, CHICAGO LAWYERS: THE SOCIAL STRUCTURE OF THE BAR 46–52 (revised ed., Northwestern Univ. Press 1994) (1982). Based on a large empirical study of the Chicago bar, Heinz and Laumann observed that lawyers operated in one of two distinct hemispheres defined by the identify of their clients: those that serve organizational clients, like corporations, and those that provided personal legal services, such as personal injury and family law. Heinz and Laumann noted that these two hemispheres seldom overlapped. In essence, the present law school hierarchy corresponds to these two hemispheres in terms of the proportion of their graduates that end up in each sphere.

94. *See* Matasar, *supra* note 91, at 482–83 (noting that faculty are "rankings driven," which causes law schools to "reduc[e] teaching loads to free time for scholars to write (and thereby requiring larger faculties or more adjunct hiring); hir[e] faculty who have interests that may be provocative, press-worthy, or attractive to university press and law review editors (and paying them premium salaries or giving them reduced teaching loads); encourag[e] faculty to travel (and supporting it generously); and promot[e] faculty to appear on television, write editorials, participate in national law reform or other social movements (with appropriate support and staff assistance)"); Harry First, *Competition in the Legal Education Industry*, 53 N.Y.U. L. REV. 311, 324 (1978) (theorizing that law faculty seek to maximize "elitist preferences," which include freedom from commercial pressures, such as the need to practice law, reduced teaching loads to pursue non-classroom activities, and attracting the "best" students, who "provide greater intellectual challenge, and ... may be easier to teach").

95. *See supra* Part III.C.

96. *See* Henderson, *supra* note 76.

97. At some point, this uneven growth may be mitigated by the arbitrage opportunities of major firms in large markets. *See, e.g.*, Bob Sherwood, *The Rise of the All-in-One Law Firm*, FIN. TIMES (London), July 28, 2005, at 9 (reporting that Orrick, Herrington & Sutcliffe, a large west-coast based law firm, has relocated "its entire global back office' functions ... [to] an operations centre in Wheeling, West Virginia" and that the firm is "considering moving much of its fundamental legal research there" as well). Of course, the emergence of a commodity market for corporate legal services is not necessarily good news for law schools or law students.

98. There is a high correlation between entering credentials, law school grades, and bar passage. *See supra* note 75. Because of this, most law schools are unwilling to make ability-to-pay the primary admissions criteria.

99. *Cf.* Marin Roger Scordato, *The Dualist Model of Legal Teaching and Scholarship*, 40 AM. U. L. REV. 367, 369–70 (1990) (questioning whether production of scholarship necessarily produces better classroom instruction).

100. *See* Matasar, *supra* note 91, at 475 (quoting law school dean noting that "financial pressures may soon challenge the capacity of law schools to continue to raise their prices" and thus "undermine the current model for American legal education in non-prestigious, private, expensive law schools").

101. See AMERICAN BAR ASSOCIATION, STANDARDS FOR APPROVAL OF LAW SCHOOLS AND INTERPRETATIONS 2004–05 (2005), http://www.abanet.org.proxy.lib.pdx.edu/legaled/standards/standards.html. *See also* George B. Shepherd, *No African-American Lawyers Allowed: The Inefficient Racism of the ABA's Accreditation of Law Schools*, 53 J. LEGAL EDUC. 103, 133 (2003) (estimating the cost per student of complying with the library standard alone at more than $4000 based on spending by recently accredited schools).

102. Matasar, *supra* note 91, at 475.

103. See Paul L. Caron & Rafael Gely, *What Law Schools Can Learn from Billy Beane and the Oakland Athletics*, 82 TEX. L. REV. 1483, 1491–99 (2004) (summarizing how Billy Beane developed his statistics-driven management philosophy).

104. *Id.* at 1495.

105. *See, e.g.*, Matasar, *supra* note 91, at 483 (noting that resources designed to enhance a law school's academic reputation provide only a "tangential relationship to the core education of law students" but have nonetheless become "essential in the arms battle for reputation").

106. *See* ROBERT H. FRANK, MICROECONOMICS AND BEHAVIOR 629–33 (1991) (discussing concepts of positional goods and positional externalities).

107. Korobkin, *supra* note 1, at 405.

108. Thomas A.C. Smith, *The Web of Law* (San Diego Legal Studies Research Paper No. 06-11, 2005) *available at* http://www.ssrn.com.proxy.lib.pdx.edu/abstract=642863.

109. Thomas A.C. Smith, *A Voice, Crying in the Wilderness, and Then Just Crying*, The Right Coast (weblog), July 13, 2005, http://therightcoast.blogspot.com.proxy.lib.pdx.edu/2005/07/voice-crying-in-wilderness-and-then.html.

110. *See supra* Part III.F.

111. *See* Shepherd, *supra* note 101, at 134 (noting that high cost of legal education "has closed the legal profession to most people with lower incomes.")

112. Korobkin, *supra* note 1, at 408–10 (arguing that the rankings do not measure educational quality, but instead provide a coordinating function that permits the best students, as vetted by the most selective law school admissions, to match up with the most desirable legal employers); Leiter, *supra* note 88, at 454 (contemplating that Korobkin may, in fact, be right); Matasar, *supra* note 91, at 485 (concluding based on his experience as law school dean that legal employers gravitate to highly ranked schools because "they have the highest LSAT scores and the highest undergraduate grades. In short hand: they are the smartest.'"); David B. Wilkins & G. Mitu Gulati, *What Law Students Think they Know About Elite Law Firms: Preliminary Results of a Survey of Third Year Law Students*, 69 U. CIN. L. REV. 1213, 1220 (2001) (observing that "[elite] firms focus primarily on signals (such as law school status and grades) as opposed to substantive skills" as evidenced by the lack of substantive questioning during the interview process).

113. *Cf.* Wilkins & Gulati, *supra* note 112, at 1226 (reviewing results of student survey and finding that "beyond Grades and Eliteness, students do not believe that much happens in law school—neither the courses they take nor the impressions that they make on particular faculty members—is relevant to whether they are hired by elite firms").

114. *See* Matasar, *supra* note 91, at 485–86 (discussing incident where partners from major law firms praised the innovation of Chicago-Kent's legal writing program but explained their reluctance to hire more Chicago-Kent graduates, "We can always train smart people to get better, but we cannot train intelligence").

115. Baylor University is arguably the one law school that has fared well in the rankings by explicitly adopting a model that emphasizes teaching over scholarship. See Baylor Law Faculty & Curriculum, http://law.baylor.edu/faculty_curriculum/faculty_curriculum.htm (last visited Aug. 30, 2005) (stating that Baylor is "one of the only law schools in the nation in which the granting of tenure is primarily based on a professor's teaching effectiveness"). In 2004, when Baylor was ranked 50th by *U.S. News*, it had the largest differential between its lawyer/judges reputation versus academic reputation of any Tier 1 law school. Despite its relatively weak academic reputation, Baylor has an impressive placement rate with law firms.

116. UCLA, Vanderbilt and University of Tennessee have all recently developed formal business tracks for their law students. Based on anecdotal evidence from business law professors at two of these law schools, legal employers have shown a willingness to dig a little bit deeper into the class to hire a student who bonded himself by completing the program. These law schools would provide excellent case studies to measure whether these business tracks alter employer behavior.

117. *See* Mark Horvick & Corey Zarse, Indiana University's JD/MBA Program: Unlocking the Potential (Apr. 11, 2005) (PowerPoint presentation on file with authors) (reporting that Kirkland & Ellis, Latham & Watkins, and Milbank Tweed provide bonuses for new associates with JD/MBA degrees).

118. David Schizer, who was recently appointed dean at Columbia Law School, wants to place a big bet on curricular innovation: "Schizer envisions ... creating special teaching chairs that faculty could apply for, allowing them to spend a year trying out new and, it is to be hoped, innovative, courses to teach. It would allow members of the faculty to spend a semester developing something that doesn't exist in the legal academy.'" Lindsay Fortado, *David Schizer*, 36, NAT'L L. J., May 2, 2005, at S15.

119. *See supra* note 76.

120. University of Nevada's new law school (UNLV), which was founded in 1998, offers a remarkable example of how price and geography can affect a law school's fortunes. As a public law school in one

of the fastest growing MSAs in the country, UNLV has catapulted itself into a secure Tier 2 status. Similarly, twenty-five years after its founding in 1980, George Mason University School of Law, which is a public law school on the border of Washington, D.C., now occupies a relatively secure position in Tier 1. GMU's success is, of course, due to more than its location, but we suggest that its success would not be as great if it had been located in Toledo or Wichita rather than Washington, D.C.

121. *See, e.g., LSAT Scores: Disturbing Discrepancies*, U.S. NEWS & WORLD REP., Mar. 20, 1995, at 82 (pointing out discrepancies between LSAT scores supplied to the ABA and those supplied to *U.S. News*, the great majority of which benefited the reporting schools); *LSAT Scores: Disturbing Discrepancies*, U.S. NEWS & WORLD REP., Mar. 18, 1996, at 81 (same); *Fine Tuning Law Ranking*, U.S. NEWS & WORLD REP., Mar. 10, 1997, at 75 (noting decline in the discrepancy of LSAT scores).

122. *See* Wellen, *supra* note 77 (reporting change in methodology to a calculated median based on the 25th and 75th percentiles and quoting *U.S. News* editor Bob Morse that "we heard that some schools weren't computing their median accurately" and that "we wanted to go with verifiable data").

123. See Alex M. Johnson, Jr., *Destruction of the Holistic Approach to Admissions: The Pernicious Effect of Ranking*, 81 IND. L.J. 309, 348–50 (2006).

124. *See* FRANK, *supra* note 106, at 630.

125. *See* Wellen, *supra* note 77 (discussing actual examples of both strategies).

126. One can justify part-time programs for weaker entering students as giving those students the opportunity to focus their efforts on fewer courses, and thus easing the transition to law school. It is, however, difficult to disentangle the academic motive from the rankings motive when a school dramatically expands such a program.

127. MICHAEL LEWIS, MONEYBALL: THE ART OF WINNING AN UNFAIR GAME (2003).

128. *Id.* at 88.

129. For example, admissions offices can model whether candidates fitting a particular profile are likely to enroll, thus improving selectivity and other *U.S. News* inputs. Paul Caron and Rafael Gely have already constructed a simple model, identifying indices of future scholarly productivity, that debunks conventional theories relied on by appointment committees. See Caron & Gely, *supra* note 103, at 1539–44.

Rankings and Reactivity: How Public Measures Recreate Social Worlds

Wendy Nelson Espeland & Michael Sauder[1]

Introduction

In the past two decades demands for accountability, transparency, and efficiency have prompted a flood of social measures designed to evaluate the performances of individuals and organizations. Measures like the cost-benefit ratios imposed on regulators, standardized tests used to evaluate students and schools, performance measures in firms, assessments of universities, and rankings of schools, firms, and hospitals have become so pervasive, scholars now characterize them as an "audit explosion" (Power 1994), "a tsunami of accountability and transparency" (Caron and Gely 2004:1553), and evidence of an emerging global "audit culture" (Strathern 2000:2).

Such evaluative measures are consequential and controversial. In Great Britain assessment exercises initiated during the 1980s have reorganized higher education, dictating budgets and hiring, reinventing schools as "financial bodies," and generating a "whole host of new institutions and practices" (Strathern 1997:309; Shore and Wright 2000:61). The growing use of quantitative indicators has transformed the meaning of accountability (Hoskins 1996). Where accountability once included many different practices, making institutions accountable now usually means making them "auditable," which often involves devising indicators to measure performance (Power 1997; Strathern 1996, 2000).

Proponents see these measures as making important information more accessible to consumers and clients, motivating organizations to improve, providing crucial feedback about policies, and extending market discipline to other institutions. Critics point to harmful, unintended consequences that occur when professionals lose discretion and actors "play to the test," focusing on indicators rather than on the qualities that the measures are designed to evaluate. Since New York began publicly ranking doctors' performance with criteria including mortality rates, for example, 79% of cardiologists surveyed report that their decision to perform angioplasty or to intervene in critically ill patients was influenced by potential effects on their scorecards (Narins et al. 2005).

Because people are reflexive beings who continually monitor and interpret the world and adjust our actions accordingly, measures are *reactive*. Measures elicit responses from people who intervene in the objects they measure. Understanding the character and consequences of this reflexivity is important. The proliferation of quantitative measures of performance is a significant social trend that is fundamental to accountability and governance; it can initiate sweeping changes in status systems, work relations, and the reproduction of inequality. Given their proliferation, their capacity to foster broad changes, both intended and unintended, in the activities that they monitor, social measures deserve closer scholarly attention.

In sociology, reactivity is usually depicted as a methodological problem. Campbell's (1957: 298) classic statement defines a reactive measure as one that "modifies the phenomenon under study, which changes the very thing that one is trying to measure." Reactivity blurs the distinction between the act of measuring and its object which "contaminates" results. Ethnographers express a similar concern when they advise researchers to minimize the effects of their presence on subjects' behavior so as to "avoid 'distorting' the worlds that they study" (Katz 1983). Other ethnographic approaches (cf. Burawoy 1998) regard reactivity as an inevitable part of research and urge scholars to theorize reflexivity and reactivity rather than try to eliminate it.

We agree that reactivity is an inevitable result of human reflexivity, and that social scientists should investigate reactivity more systematically. To expand our knowledge of reactivity, we propose a framework for investigating the reactivity of social measures. The core issues guiding our framework are (1) which mechanisms shape the reactivity of public measures, and (2) how to characterize the effects of the reactivity of public measures. We develop our framework for analyzing reactivity and illustrate its value through an investigation of one powerful measure, the *U.S. News and World Report* (hereafter, *USN)* rankings of law schools. Our case study of law school rankings demonstrates the distinctive characteristics of particular measures in specific locations—media rankings of law schools—but it also provides a set of concepts and questions that are important for investigating similarities and variation in the reactivity of other measures.

We first sketch the rise of social statistics and their use to describe states and evaluate performances. We next explain why reactivity remains a valuable concept for analyzing the reflexive interactions between people and measures. After briefly describing the history of rankings and how *USN* calculates law school rankings, we explain how two powerful mechanisms, self-fulfilling prophecy and commensuration, generate reactivity. We then identify three important effects of reactivity: the redistribution of resources, redefinition of work, and proliferation of gaming strategies. We conclude by summarizing our framework, suggest its usefulness for analyzing the reactivity of other measures, and highlight the moral implications of quantitative accountability.

Accountability and the Proliferation of Social Measures

Awash in numbers, we now take social statistics for granted so much so that we forget how hard it is to make them and how revolutionary their effects can be. Important historical work has illuminated how numbers have transformed the people they describe (cf. Kula 1986; Hacking 1990; Porter 1995; Carson in press). Social numbers, of course, are nothing new. Rulers and church leaders have long tried to calculate how many men are eligible for conscription or the volume of crops or acreage subject to taxation or tithe. But such numbers were often treated as state or church secrets, the privileged information of elites that, if in the wrong hands, were dangerous (Porter 1986:18–39, 25; Alonso and

Starr 1987:11–13; Hacking 1990:20). What is relatively new is the public nature of social statistics.

Use of statistics is closely linked to advances in probability and the development of nation states and disciplines (Alonso and Starr 1987:3; Porter 1986:156–57). In the nineteenth century, states were expanding, centralizing, and responding to new demands for public services. States needed better information about their empires. The result was an "avalanche" of numbers (Hacking 1990:1–10) that "profoundly transformed what we choose to do, who we try to be, and what we think of ourselves." The spread of numeracy, technical advances, and the increasing legitimacy of quantification all contributed to this trend, but sometimes societies had to change dramatically before states could use these advances. Porter (1995: 35–36, 45–46) describes how, initially, the weak French state was unable to conduct a proper census. Only after the state became more centralized, its administrators more numerous and better trained, and its citizens disciplined enough to permit enumeration, could it do so. Eventually, what it meant to be a state was linked to producing public statistics describing its characteristics and people (Ventresca 1995). Prewitt (1987:261–274) argues that official statistics are closely connected to democratic governance.

For Weber (1978:975), "the peculiarity of modern culture," especially its technical prowess, derives largely from its "calculability."[2] Quantification, with its capacity to enhance predictability, coordination, and impersonality, is the hallmark of bureaucratic authority and helps explain why bureaucracies outperform other institutions. A shift in emphasis from quantification employed to describe relations and make predictions, to quantification used to judge and control these relations, is a small but fateful one (Foucault 1977:183–4). Discipline that constructs compliant, self-policing subjects hinges on "normalization" that defines normal, marks deviance, and creates the experts who maintain the boundaries.

Accountability directed toward controlling human performance through quantification and written assessments first emerged in education around the beginning of the seventeenth century. Not until the nineteenth century were these practices incorporated into the workplace (Hoskins 1996). Quantitative authority and its link to accountability and evaluation are now so secure, so bound up with being modern, that we have trouble imagining other forms of coordination and discipline or other means of creating transparency and accountability.

The long use of social statistics should not detract from the importance of contemporary efforts to extend and transform accountability. Rankings are just one manifestation of a vast proliferation of quantitative performance measures since the late 1970s (Power 1994; Strathern 2000; Hoffer 2000; Shore and Wright 2000). The calculative techniques used in business and finance are being exported to many different institutional domains. This contemporary "accountability movement" has produced diverse and important effects, and its origins are complex. According to Porter (1995), the spread of quantification in decision-making is linked to efforts to mitigate conflict, overcome distrust, and coordinate across both social and physical distance. Others tie accountability and auditing to advances in neo-liberal goals of shrinking government and supplanting social welfare policies with market-based policies, especially in the United States and the United Kingdom.[3] Efforts to integrate economies or governments have also promulgated auditing as a way to enact transparency and accountability, as have international organizations like the United Nations, World Bank, and International Monetary Fund (Halliday and Carruthers 2005).

Rankings are one instance of widespread efforts to control public institutions and make them more accessible to outsiders. *USN*'s goal in creating rankings was not to transform law schools or "hold them accountable." Rather, they wished to provide accessible information to educational consumers (Morse 2005), as well as raise revenue and visibility for the magazine. Editors were surprised by the furor their rankings generated. But, as we will show, we need to scrutinize the response to rankings carefully to understand the important institutional changes that performance measures set in motion.

Reactivity

The concept of reactivity began as a methodological concern about the contaminating influence of measurements on their target object, especially if that object is a person (Campbell 1957; Reiss 1971; Webb et al.1981; Katz 1983). Understood as challenging the validity of findings, reactivity has generated sustained discussions among experimentalists (Orne 1962; Campbell and Stanley 1963; Tedeschi 1981), pollsters, and survey researchers (Converse and Schuman 1974; Suchman and Jordan 1990), as well as qualitative researchers (Reiss 1971; Kazdin 1982; McCall 1984). Although definitions of reactivity vary across approaches, the basic idea is the same: individuals alter their behavior in reaction to being evaluated, observed, or measured.

Some scholars investigate reactivity in substantive rather than methodological terms. Heimer (1985), for example, analyzes reactivity as a generalized problem within the insurance industry, where price is the relevant measure. Insurance changes people's incentives to be prudent, which changes risk. "Reactive risks" are harder to manage than fixed risks, so insurers devise distinctive strategies to control it. Reactivity, for Heimer, is a continuous variable, meaning that people's responses to changing insurance incentives encompass a range of possibilities and that identifying the conditions that produce variability (e.g. institutional development, the number and type of constituencies, use over time) is key for robust explanations. Following Heimer's lead, we broaden the scope and refine the concept of reactivity by identifying patterns of reactivity and the idiosyncratic consequences attending public measures.

Reactivity is a form of reflexivity. Since reflexivity is fundamental to social life, sociology possesses a rich conceptual vocabulary for analyzing the mutuality of our responses. For example, Callon (1998) uses the idea of "performativity" to describe how economic theory shapes the economy, highlighting, as we do, the significance of self-fulfilling prophecy effects (see also Latour 1987; MacKenzie and Millo 2003; Ferraro, Pfeffer, and Sutton 2005; MacKenzie 2006). We restrict our analysis to the effects of social measures and adopt the concept of reactivity for several reasons. Most importantly, its connection to methodological validity makes the legitimacy of knowledge a central issue in analyzing the effects of measurement. Scholarship on knowledge production and evaluation share a fundamental concern with how particular kinds of knowing and judging are made authoritative. The best work analyzes how the authority of different forms of knowledge interact (cf. Porter 1995; Breslau 1997; Heimer and Staffen 1998; Silbey and Ewick 2003; Guetzkow, Lamont, and Mallard 2004; Carson, in press).

Casting reactivity as a threat to the validity of measures draws attention to the dynamic nature of quantitative authority and its capacity to intervene, sometimes dramatically, with other forms of authority. Instead of seeing this relationship as one that can be ameliorated with good technique, we emphasize the tension that adheres to the concept of reactivity as it mediates two understandings of measures: as valid, neutral depictions of the social world, and as vehicles for enacting accountability and inducing changes in performance. In the first view, the independence of measures and the social world they target is threatened by reactivity; in the second view, the job of measures is to harness reactivity, to create a form of reactivity that causes people to change their behavior in desired ways. This tension in seeing reactivity as either a threat or a promise is a contradiction central to the use and effects of public measures and is one that warrants analysis.

Another advantage of the concept of reactivity in capturing the reflexivity of measures is its focus on agency. The concept emphasizes how people *react* to efforts to study them, how being cast as subjects of investigation changes the behaviors of both subjects and investigators. This emphasis makes reflexivity central to the concept of reactivity, highlighting the importance of sense-making as a negotiated process. People interpret measurement in diverse and evolving ways, which can change the location and expression of agency. Emphasizing *reactivity* encourages scholars to make more explicit how actors make discourse meaningful in ways that shape their behavior.

Finally, we find reactivity a useful bridging concept, one that is flexible enough to extend to interdisciplinary scholarly work on measurement, standardization, and evaluation. Reactivity has a history and a literature that resonates across fields. The value of reframing work on the impact of new measurement technologies in terms of reactivity is that it offers a familiar language and a common focus that will encourage scholars to ask similar questions and make connections across a broader range of scholarship. Doing so is crucial for understanding changes in contemporary institutions.

Data and Methods

This article aims to develop a framework for analyzing the reactivity of public measures by identifying and explaining mechanisms that produce reactivity, and patterns in the effects of reactivity. A case study approach is well suited for this goal of theory elaboration because it generates detailed knowledge and sustained analysis of one type of public measure (cf. Steinmetz 2004). *USN* law school rankings were selected because, first, *USN* is the dominant ranker of law schools, virtually monopolizing legal education.[4] Second, unlike most fields in which only the top 25 or 50 schools are ranked, *USN* ranks every accredited law school so the effect of rankings permeate the entire field of legal education. This density of effects enhances our efforts to map the consequences of rankings. Furthermore, pressures for accountability are increasing. All trends suggest that organizational rankings will spread and become more encompassing, so legal education is unlikely to remain exceptional. Finally, legal educators have resisted rankings more vigorously than others. Their resistance makes more explicit the assumptions behind rankings and their effects, which deepens the analysis.

The primary data for this case study is 136 open-ended interviews averaging about 45 minutes with law school administrators, faculty, and staff.[5] These interviews permitted a broad range of respondents to describe the effects and mechanisms of reactivity instead of our presupposing them, as more structured interventions would require. Since respondents were not asked identical questions, interviews were coded for general themes rather than for precisely defined variables; consequently, the frequency of particular responses is only an approximate indication of their importance.

Two waves of interviews were conducted: one designed to capture the breadth, the other the depth, of ranking effects. The first wave ($N = 66$) examined whether and how rankings affected legal education and if these effects varied across different types of schools. These interviews were conducted primarily by telephone. Our sample emphasized variations in rank, ranking trajectory, mission, location, and size. The second wave of interviews ($N = 70$) investigated how rankings permeate these institutions. We visited seven focus schools, interviewing key personnel in different organizational locations, analyzing how ranking effects interact among departments and how they are distributed within schools. Our cumulative sample includes representatives from 70 (52 current and 18 former) of the approximately 190 accredited U.S. law schools, with roughly equal numbers from schools in each of the four tiers.[6] All but five interviews were tape recorded and transcribed. We used Qualrus, a qualitative data analysis program, to organize and code our interview data. Interviews from the first wave were coded using general categories such as types or location of effects (i.e. effects on admissions, effects of quantification, changes in rank, and positive effects). We refined our coding categories based on the first wave and after the second wave recoded all interviews using these modifications.

Other data were collected or re-analyzed to corroborate and help interpret interview data. We compiled a data set from public sources on applications and yields of law schools to determine if changes in school rank affected applications and matriculation (Sauder and Lancaster 2006). We observed an admissions fair for prospective law students attended by admissions personnel from most law schools. At this event, in addition to observing interactions between administrators and students, we conducted 17 interviews, averaging about 10 minutes, with law school admissions staff, as well as 92 short non-random interviews, averaging about 5 minutes, with prospective students. We analyzed organizational material produced by law schools and public information concerning these schools (e.g websites, marketing materials, press releases, and news stories) to learn how rankings affect marketing. We monitored bulletin boards and chat rooms dedicated to prospective law students for an academic year. We conducted 30 in-depth interviews with business school administrators to determine how rankings effects vary across educational fields.[7] Triangulating sources deepens our understanding and helps mitigate the limitations of particular sources.

Law Schools Rankings: History and Methodology

Universities have been ranked for at least a century but until the late 1980s these evaluations were almost exclusively prepared for and used by academics and administrators (Webster 1992). Beginning with *USN*'s rankings of colleges in 1983, graduate and professional schools in 1987, and *Business Week*'s ranking of business schools in 1988, popular media began producing rankings of colleges and graduate programs created for *consumers* rather than insiders. These rankings quickly became lucrative enterprises, providing new information to prospective students and others who wanted measures of "organizational success" (Caron and Gely 2004:1509).[8]

USN first ranked law schools in 1987 and ranked them annually beginning in 1990. Law schools were first divided into four tiers: the top tier listed the fifty highest-rated programs in rank order, with the remaining schools separated into the second, third, and fourth tiers and listed alphabetically within tiers. Beginning in 2004, *USN* reported the top 100 law schools by rank and divided the remaining schools into the third and fourth tiers in an alphabetical list.

The *USN* ranking is comprised of four general categories: reputation, selectivity, placement, and faculty resources. Small changes have been made in rankings but their basic structure has remained the same. Reputation decides 40% of a school's overall score followed by selectivity (25%), placement (20%), and faculty resources (15%). To compile the ranking, each school's score is standardized. These scores are then weighted, totaled, and rescaled so that the top school receives a score of 100 and other schools receive a percentage of the top score (*USN* 2005:50).

Mechanisms of Reactivity

One feature of our framework for analyzing the reactivity of measures is to specify mechanisms of reactivity. Instead of simply identifying relationships between variables, conditions, or events, a mechanism describes causal patterns that generate and sustain these relationships. A mechanism is like a causal switch that, if turned on, directs action in one way rather than another.[9] Analyses of mechanisms produce deeper causal knowledge of social relationships and their dynamism (cf Merton 1967, 1968; Elster 1989; Hedstrom and Swedberg 1998; Stinchcombe 2005). Explaining *how* rankings are reactive, *how* they produce the changes that they produce, helps us better understand why these measures create such powerful effects.

Most generally, rankings are reactive because they change how people make sense of situations; rankings offer a generalized account for interpreting behavior and justifying decisions within law schools, and help organize the "stock of knowledge" that participants routinely use (Schutz 1970:137–145). Administrators consider rankings when they define goals, assess progress, evaluate peers, admit students, recruit faculty, distribute scholarships, conduct placement surveys, adopt new programs, and create budgets. One dean expressed a common sentiment: "[Rankings] are always in the back of everybody's head. With every issue that comes up, we have to ask, 'How is this impacting our ranking?' "

We conceptualize mechanisms of reactivity as patterns that shape how people make sense of things. Patterns emerge in the forms of feedback that rankings elicit, how attention is distributed, and the interpretive scripts people adopt. These patterns influence how people interact with rankings, each other, and other institutions. Two of the most important patterns in sense-making that emerged from our analysis are self-fulfilling prophecy and commensuration. The mechanisms of self-fulfilling prophecy and commensuration produce varied forms of reactivity and, as we will demonstrate, produce some of the most significant consequences of rankings.

Self-Fulfilling Prophecies

For Merton (1968:182–183, 477 original emphasis), a self-fulfilling prophecy is a "dynamic social mechanism" and an "unintended consequence"; it is a "confident error [that] generates its own spurious confirmation," "a *false* definition of the situation evoking a new behavior which makes the originally false definition of the situation come *true*." Merton does not use the term "reactivity" but describes its significance. He suggests that self-fulfilling prophecies create unique methodological problems for social science because subjects change their behavior in response to prediction; prediction, then, becomes a "*new and dynamic* factor" that changes the conditions under which it comes true labeling theory, which harkens back to W. I. Thomas' famous dictum, "If men define situations as real, they are real in their consequences" (Thomas and Thomas 1928: 572).

We do not restrict self-fulfilling prophecies to false beliefs, requiring only that an expectation, once defined as real, amplify or confirm its effect. We define self-fulfilling prophecies as processes by which reactions to social measures confirm the expectations or predictions that are embedded in measures or which increase the validity of the measure by encouraging behavior that conforms to it.[10] Rankings create expectations about law schools, and people change their behavior accordingly. We demonstrate four ways that self-fulfilling prophecies shape the reactivity of rankings: external audiences' reaction to rankings, the influence of prior rankings on surveys that determine future rank, the use of rankings to make funding decisions within universities, and how activities within schools conform to rankings criteria.[11]

The Effects of Rankings on External Audiences

One type of self-fulfilling prophecy created by rankings involves the precise distinctions rankings create. Although the raw scores used to construct *USN* rankings are tightly bunched, listing schools by rank magnifies these statistically insignificant differences in ways that produce real consequences for schools, since their position affects the perceptions and actions of outside audiences. The distinctions produced by rankings are increasingly important and taken for granted, along with the advantages and disadvantages associated with them. As a faculty member at a top law school put it: "[Rankings] create inequality among schools that are rather hard to distinguish. They create artificial lines that then have the danger of becoming real."

Even small differences in rank affect the number and quality of applications a school receives, and its yield—the proportion of accepted students who attend that school (Sauder and Lancaster 2006). Shifts in applications and yield change the selectivity score used by *USN* to compute its ranking and in this way reinforce the original differences which were often largely a product of measurement noise.[12] These results confirm the claims of administrators who carefully analyze cross-application data that describes where students matriculate when they have been accepted by multiple schools. Nearly every admissions director interviewed reported that students' decisions correlate with rankings: if a school's rank declines, they lose students to schools to which they had not lost them in the past and vice versa. Such differences can harden over time.

The experience of two elite schools illustrates this point. Before rankings, school A lost about two-thirds of cross-admitted students to school B. School A, however, has consistently ranked slightly higher than school B, and, over time, students admitted to both schools changed their preferences; now the vast majority (reportedly between 80–90%) of cross-admitted students choose to attend school A. The durability of this difference no doubt increased, changing both schools' student recruitment policies. This form of self-fulfilling prophecy most harms lower-tier schools. For one dean: "If you are in the third tier, it's going to be held against you.... It's harder to solicit your alumni to get more revenue, to have more scholarships or to have more resources to bump up the rankings. It's a self-fulfilling nightmare." Schools must respond not only to the reactions of prospective students, but to other constituents such as trustees, boards of visitors, and alumni, all of whom provide financial and administrative support to the schools. These reactions are most pronounced when a school's rank drops, whether this reflects changes in school quality as measured by *USN* criteria, the improved ranking of a close competitor, or fluctuations in how rankings are calculated. This process was summarized by a dean of a third tier school:

> Law school faculties and the smart administrators all go, "This is a bunch of hooey. We don't care about this." Until they drop and the board of trustees says, "Hey you're dropping; why should we give you more money?" and the board of visitors from the law school say, "Man, your school's really going to pot. You haven't changed a thing.... big changes need to be made here." And your monetary support from alumni say, "Well, I'm not sure I want to support a school that's going in the wrong direction," and your money starts to dry up. And you think, "We have got to have the money; we can't afford to lose funding or else it *will* spiral downhill and we will be a worse law school." So keeping the numbers up is key.

The Influences of Prior Rankings on Survey Responses

A second type of self-fulfilling prophecy occurs when prior rankings shape current evaluations of law schools. *USN* uses two surveys to measure the reputation of the approximately 190 accredited law schools, one sent to academics and one to practitioners. Most deans, even those with long tenures and those active in the accrediting arm of the ABA, admit that they know little about most law schools they are asked to evaluate. Practitioners, whose ties to legal education are often remote, will know even less than deans and faculty. For many deans, one feature they are likely to know about other schools is their *USN* ranking. Consequently, past judgments about a school's reputation, embodied in rank, may influence current evaluations, which reproduce and strengthen these judgments.[13] As two administrators put it:

> Well, hell, I get the rankings and I get 184 schools to rank. I know about [this school], something about [that school], I know about [my school] obviously, and I've got some buddies here and there so I feel like I know something more about some of those schools. But beyond that, guess what, I'm basing these decisions on the rankings; it's a self-fulfilling prophecy. If partners [at a law firm] do anything to prepare them for this [reputational survey], they probably go out and get a copy of past *USN* reports and fill it out from that.

These perceptions are supported by ongoing research on the effects of school rankings on the reputation scores derived from surveys over the fifteen years of rankings. Stake (2006) finds that reputation scores slowly become aligned with overall rank, concluding that past rankings are the strongest predictor of current reputation score.[14]

Distributing Resources by Ranking

A third type of self-fulfilling prophecy occurs within universities if budgets become linked to rankings. Schools affiliated with larger universities must often compete for funds with other programs. Lacking other benchmarks, some administrators use rankings as a heuristic to help allocate resources. A university president informed members of the university planning committee, which included the law professor we interviewed, that "new money" would be allocated partly based on the quality of the program as defined by its *USN* rank. An important criterion was whether or not proposed plans would move a program into a top ten *USN* rank. If budgets are allocated by current rank or potential for moving up in rank, rankings reproduce and intensify the stratification they are designed to measure. How often budgets are directly linked to rankings is unclear; however, many deans worry about how rankings form impressions and how this might influence budgets indirectly.[15]

Realizing Embedded Assumptions

A final example of self-fulfilling prophecy as a mechanism of reactivity is how law schools respond to the conception of legal education that is embedded in rankings factors. Rankings create self-fulfilling prophecies by encouraging schools to become more like what rankings measure, which reinforces the validity of the measure. Rankings impose a standardized, universal definition of law schools which creates incentives for law schools to conform to that definition. LSAT scores, for example, are increasingly used to define merit, and test scores now matter more than other attributes in admissions decisions. Schools may also feel pressure to abandon distinctive missions that are not measured in rankings. One dean reported that his university has always been "an access university," one that "gives students opportunities that they would not have had elsewhere."

> A student can have a very high GPA but a very low LSAT score. That student is not going to help us in the rankings. But let's assume for the moment that that student is a minority—that's the kind of student we like to admit and to give an opportunity to even though that's going to adversely impact our rankings, and even though that student is not going to pass the bar exam the first time around. And that is our mission. We are going to have to change our mission and change our thinking if we are going to take that student's place and give it to a student with a higher LSAT score, if we are going to be driven by the rankings. Our problem, and our challenge and our opportunity, is that we are poised at the top of a tier. So it is almost impossible to resist the temptation to move into that [higher] tier [and] then that becomes a self-perpetuating situation.

When asked if his school would still admit students with the lower LSAT scores along with the higher scoring students, he replied, "It could be that for a couple of years we don't give that student the opportunity. Or we say to that student that we used to have a place for them in the day program but now we have a place for you in the night program, which is part-time and which doesn't count as much toward the rankings."

An even more self-conscious form of this self-fulfilling prophecy occurs when administrators adopt improved rankings as an explicit goal (see Stabile 2000). In framing aspirations using *USN* criteria, organizational members work to produce an organization that conforms to and makes tangible the terms of the measures, a process that renders them increasingly valid. Another version of realizing the assumptions of measurements is when members use rankings to define or market their school to external audiences. When law schools (or central administrations) tout their rankings on their web sites, brochures, or press releases, they are complicit in producing and disseminating identities that align with rankings, which in turn, shape internal processes of identification.[16] The imposed organizational identity that is embedded in rankings and members' sense of identity can interact in complex ways that sometimes reinforce the meaning and legitimacy of rankings.[17]

Commensuration

Commensuration is a second important mechanism that produces reactive responses to rankings. Where self-fulfilling prophecies operate primarily by changing behavior in relation to altered expectations, commensuration works mainly by transforming cognition; it changes the locus and form of attention, both creating and obscuring relations among entities. Commensuration is characterized by the transformation of qualities into quantities that share a metric, a process that is fundamental to measurement. Prices, cost-benefit ratios, survey responses, and standardized tests, like rankings, are forms of commensuration. Commensuration shapes what we pay attention to, which things are connected to other things, and how we express sameness and difference.[18] Three core features of commensuration change sense-making: its capacity to reduce, simplify, and integrate information; the new, precise and all-encompassing relationships it creates among different law schools and among departments within law schools; and its capacity to elicit reflection on the validity of quantitative evaluation. The first two features are inherent in commensuration, while the last one varies.

Simplifying Information

All social forms shape attention by creating patterns of exclusion and inclusion (Simmel 1971: 23–35) and by erecting or transgressing symbolic boundaries (Lamont and Molnar 2002). Commensuration as a mechanism of sense-making is notable for how rigorously it simplifies information and for how thoroughly it decontextualizes knowledge. Commensuration is a means for organizing, integrating and eliminating information.[19] It simplifies in two ways: by making irrelevant vast amounts of information, and by imposing on what remains the same form—a shared metric. Rankings reduce the disparate and variable characteristics that might influence the quality of a law school to a single number. A ranking is the culmination of many commensurative practices that create many important numbers (e.g. LSAT scores, GPAs, survey results, yields, budgets). Rankings are meant to simplify complicated information; they embody decisions that make vast amounts of other information, often qualitative knowledge that is hard to assimilate to this form, irrelevant. Respondents often criticized rankings for oversimplifying law school quality, excluding important factors like student or faculty diversity, teaching, scholarship, cost, social climate, and location. For example, a letter signed by 173 deans last year was sent to all students taking the LSAT cautioning the students: "Several commercial enterprises promote 'ranking' systems that purport to reduce a wide array of information about law schools to one simple number that compares all 192 ABA-approved law schools with each other. These ranking systems are inherently flawed because none of them can take your special needs and circumstances into account when comparing law schools ... The factors [listed by students as] most important ... are excluded entirely or severely undervalued by all of the numerical ranking systems."[20] As attention to rankings increases, it is diverted from information that is not directly linked to rankings.

In addition to making it easier to access and process information, simplification often makes information seem more authoritative. March and Simon (1958) show how processes of simplification obscure the discretion, assumptions, and arbitrariness that infuse information, as well as absorb uncertainty and contingency. Consequently, information appears more robust and definitive than it would if presented in more complicated forms.

The constraints that commensuration imposes stem from how the common metrical relationship is constructed, as well as from the relations of relevancy and irrelevancy, visibility and invisibility, that are conferred. Difference between entities is expressed as an interval on a shared metric. Commensuration makes other categories for expressing difference irrelevant as they are subsumed into this metric. Difference expressed this way is a matter of more or less, rather than kind. The difference, for example, between Yale Law School, ranked 1st, and the University of New Mexico Law School, ranked 99th is 98. Distinctive characteristics not captured in the rankings are less apparent and therefore less salient. Rankings do not reveal that Yale publishes nine student-edited law journals or that the University of New Mexico trains more Native American lawyers than any other law school. These characteristics may indirectly affect a school's reputation but their relevance is highly mediated. The more we attend to schools' ranks, the less we notice these other characteristics. As Simmel (1978:443–445) observed, the more naturalized a social form becomes, the less visible and more 'unreal' the things that are hard to express in that form become. In this way, rankings deflect attention from many important differences among law schools, including whether a law school is public and private, whether graduates typically become solo practitioners or work in large law firms, serve poor communities or large corporations. One dean described responses to *USN* this way: "It kind of dumbs us down. I think it dumbs down students in making selections because they just look at those numbers that reflect so little, and they give them more weight than they deserve."

The radical simplification of commensuration produces decontextualized, depersonalized numbers that are highly portable and easily made public. Numbers circulate more easily and are more easily remembered than more complicated forms of information. Three pages summarize American legal education. The capacity of numbers to circulate widely is enhanced by their abstractness, which appears to eliminate the need for particularistic knowledge in interpreting them. We assume that the meaning of numbers is universal and stable. The erasure of context and the people who make numbers is crucial for their authority. We trust that the methods that accomplished this erasure were rigorous enough to constrain the discretion, politics, and biases of those who create them.

Because we think that numbers transcend local knowledge, we suppose they do not require the same sorts of interpretation and translation as other modes of communicating. This is partly why they are so useful to us. Numbers are easy to dislodge from local contexts and reinsert in more remote contexts. Because numbers decontextualize so thoroughly, they *invite* re-contextualization. Since numbers seem to retain so little of their former context, it is easy to put them to new uses in new places. Believing in the universality of numbers discourages us from noticing how generative they are: that, as numbers circulate, we recreate their meaning by building them into new contexts and reinterpreting their meaning. We can use numbers to do new things without having to acknowledge that they now mean something different. So, for example, many law firms use *USN* rankings to determine the threshold for interviews. Firms interview students with lower class rankings at highly ranked schools and, conversely, require students at lower-ranked schools to have higher class rankings. This use presumes that that student quality is correlated with law school quality, independent of other measures of student quality. Used as recruiting heuristics, the meaning of rankings shifts from the use intended by *USN* (as a guide to prospective law students). This change makes rankings more important and reinforces patterns of self-fulfilling prophecy.

Commensuration Unites and Distinguishes Relations

In addition to making it easier to ignore difference that is not expressed metrically, commensuration shapes attention in other important ways. It simultaneously unifies and distinguishes the objects that it encompasses or evaluates. Commensuration *unites* objects because all entities measured bear a common relationship to each other derived from their shared metric. Instead of simply being lumped together under the general category of "law school," commensuration constructs a specific relationship between each one. With law schools, we already take their unity or coherence for granted because there has already been much cultural work that naturalizes the category, "law schools." This work includes the professional and state struggles to regulate legal education and the accreditation processes of the ABA, which impose standardized practices on law schools and law students, helping to make law schools seem alike.[21] But however alike law schools already seem to us, commensuration unifies them further by constructing a precise hierarchical relationship among them and by making the forms of heterogeneity that exist among them less visible and therefore harder to sustain, as our example of the "access school" on the cusp of tiers illustrates.[22]

The metrical relationships that rankings construct have implications for law schools as an organizational field. Formerly the field of legal education was quite internally fragmented, with a small group of elite schools on top, most of which could make claims to being the best or among the best, and a wide variety of regional or mission-centered schools filling out the field. Rankings challenge this fragmentation by reducing distinctiveness to magnitude. It becomes much harder to make status claims not supported by rankings or to sustain identities that are not linked to rankings. Only Yale can now credibly claim to be "the best" law school.

At the same time that commensuration helps establish law schools as the same, it also *distinguishes* law schools by creating a precise hierarchical relationship among every school. Each law school is assigned a specific number or tier position, a location comprised of a unique configuration of other numbers. Rank establishes for each school a distinct set of relations with every other school, with the interval between schools defining it as "better" or "worse" than every other law school. Over time, commensuration establishes a specific relationship between "this year's law school" and past versions of itself. A school's history can be revised from a narrative form to a series of comparisons of static objects, like photos in a chronological series, permitting schools to track "progress" or "lapses" meticulously. Assigning precise numbers to each school creates and highlights small distinctions. Differences in rankings, even miniscule ones, are closely scrutinized. One professor described the effects of this as " ... horrendous. Students rely on an ordinal ranking system as if it had meaning." Many schools tell painful stories of how tiny, insignificant movement in some factor, a change that reflects "nothing real or important" in their view, caused dramatic downward mobility. One dean described how his school dropped a tier one year because one class performed slightly worse on the bar exam: "It had an enormous impact because everything's at the margins. So many schools are tied in these rankings that you make a marginal switch here or a marginal switch there, you can certainly fall one tier and on occasion you can fall two tiers in these rankings. So it's a devastating kind of problem for people." Especially for schools on the cusp of tiers, small changes matter enormously and are scrutinized meticulously. Administrators complain that the tiny differences that separate many schools take on enormous weight and that such precision is false or misleading. For one law professor, "It would be as if I graded student papers to four digits."

Small differences are closely scrutinized because commensuration makes such comparisons impossible to avoid. In translating difference into magnitude, all one notices is whether one school is higher or lower, better or worse, improving or slipping, no matter how trivial the differences. Rankings are a powerful engine for producing and reproducing hierarchy since they encourage the meticulous tracking of small differences among schools, which can become larger differences over time.

Commensuration Invites Reflection on What Numbers Represent

A final way that commensuration shapes how people make sense of situations is by encouraging people to ponder the relationship between the numbers they make and use and what these numbers are supposed to reflect. This form of reactivity addresses the purchase that numbers have on the "reality" of what they measure. *USN* requires administrators to prepare numbers which it turns into new numbers called rankings. Because these new numbers are important and dissected by many parties, the relationship or "gap" between what the numbers are supposed to represent about their target and what members believe is real about their law schools elicits explanation. In other words, rankings encourage people to think about the ontological status of numbers in relation to the ontological status of the things they measure. Some people begin to question the authority of numbers as well as the production of that authority, and it is fruitful to consider how this ontological scrutiny is distributed among groups.

Desrosieres (2001) describes "four possible attitudes" about the "reality" of statistics: metrological realism, derived from scientific metrology, in which the social relationship that is measured is as real as a physical object; pragmatic accounting or "accounting realism," derived from business accounting, in which the meaning of numbers is inseparable from the trust they inspire, trust that is predicated on the "fair" standardized practices that produce the numbers (cf. Porter 1995); "proof in use" realism, in which statistics are judged real to the extent that their use produces consistent, plausible results; and constructionism which, in contrast to the other forms of realism, understands the reality of what is measured as shaped by measurement conventions. These distinctions are useful to separate analytically, even if in practice they intermingle.

Desrosieres' emphasis is statistics, but his distinctions apply to rankings. We cannot provide a detailed analysis here so we simply note some patterns. The producers of rankings at *USN* understand them as measuring real relations, rather than constructed ones, reflecting both pragmatic and metrological attitudes. Prospective law students, who know little about how rankings are made, more often adopt a metrological realist stance. Most are uninterested in ranking methodology and simply assume that rankings measure something real about the schools. A prospective law student, for example, admitted that she took rankings "quite literally" as "objective measures of quality," ignoring their methodology.

Many administrators think rankings misrepresent their schools in harmful ways. Their deeper knowledge of their school and the effects of rankings, and their experience in helping generate the numbers they often see as arbitrary and only superficially connected to practices at their school, makes clear to them the limitations of straightforward connections between rankings as evaluations of their school and the "reality" of their school. One administrator explained,

> The rankings don't particularly capture what a lot of schools offer. Things like commitments to diversity and missions are not taken into account. These are qualitative factors, and if someone looks at the rankings they are just going to knock out your school without even a cursory review, which is a shame. That's what irritates me. It pressures you to play the numbers game ... It's shameful the things that we have been forced to do because of this. We're a Catholic school and we're all about honesty. Before our placement statistics were really low because we weren't reporting people who were employed in non-legal jobs, but other people were reporting them. We were forced to do the same thing because we couldn't afford for our numbers to be that low.

Detailed knowledge like this encourages constructivist understandings of rankings. But this understanding may change over time, or may be rejected by administrators who invest in rankings as strategies for gauging their performance. The views of a dean at an elite law school, someone who sees rankings as useful measures of quality, can best be classified as "proof in use realism." For him:

> Rankings have always been there. What has changed is the way in which *USN* has tried to make them more precise and to publish then more broadly. When I was looking at law school, everyone in my cohort knew which was the best school. If got you got into Yale, you went there; if you didn't get into Yale, and you got into Harvard, you went to Harvard, and so on down the list. Some schools have moved around on the list but everyone knew then what the list was. So *USN* just put onto paper what everyone was already doing anyway; they have a formula for measuring what everybody cared about ... [*USN* rankings] are simply more complex, with more variables in their formula.

The scrutiny that rankings invite, especially in relation to the construction and meaning of numbers, is an attitude that may extend to other numbers. For example, a former director of career services told us that rankings have "made me much more skeptical about how numbers are used. I don't take them at face value anymore now that I know how loaded they can be."

Commensuration is a powerful, prevalent, and distinctive mechanism of reactivity because it alters the distribution of attention and relevance in legal education. It changes the terms under which people assess change and make decisions; it simplifies and reduces information, standardizes sameness and difference, and inspires members to scrutinize the meaning of numbers. Commensuration and self-fulfilling prophecy represent two distinctive mechanisms of reactivity that help us better understand how rankings transform law schools. Each prompts people to change their behavior: the latter by changing expectations, the former by changing cognition. Because commensuration changes the form of information, its impact can be immediate. Self-fulfilling processes often produce more gradual change, since it takes time for people to alter their expectations and modify their behavior accordingly. Both mechanisms of reactivity will produce varied changes over time; initial responses will be different from those coming later, after rankings have diffused more broadly or become naturalized.

Law schools' initial reactions to rankings illustrate the importance of making over-time comparisons of mechanisms of reactivity. When rankings were introduced most administrators dismissed them, associating them with guidebooks that had little impact on law schools. Administrators had to learn of rankings' increasing influence. Several deans claimed to understand their significance immediately but most ignored rankings. As one administrator said:

> Now the first two or three times around, no one took it seriously. I remember one of my senior colleagues coming in and saying "I tossed [*USN* rankings], in the garbage because it's so stupid." And I said, "So did I." But we didn't know. It seemed absurd to sit here guessing at reputations.

Because deans underestimated their influence, some schools first refused to provide *USN* with the information they requested. *USN* responded by "estimating" the missing data (almost always, schools report, in ways that produced worse scores than schools would have otherwise had). Once angry students and alumni vented their displeasure about their schools' rankings, administrators quickly appreciated their influence.[23] Describing reaction to a disappointing ranking, a dean recalled:

> The effects were immediate hysteria. I had alumni writing me left and right. I had my board of directors asking me what had suddenly happened that [we] had suddenly [dropped in the rankings] ... it was an irrational response because the people writing mostly actually knew about the school. I had my student body protesting, and they're here and they know in the course of one year that nothing had happened. But they all essentially were saying, "What did you do?"

Soon schools submitted information voluntarily and began to analyze their data carefully; eventually schools became more expert in *USN* methodology, contacting *USN* to criticize criteria, clarify definitions, or lobby for changes. A long-time ex-dean explained, "Eventually I realized that eyeballing wasn't enough because you had to look for the little things that create differentiations and then try to game that a little bit. And we did think about that more and more." At several schools, mathematically sophisticated faculty have gone so far as to "reverse engineer" the rankings formulas to learn how their school might improve their scores. One dean said: "We've done a lot of careful studying of the *USN* methodology to figure out what counts the most and what is perhaps the most manipulable, because those are not necessarily the same things." Reactions of students, alumni, media, and peers gradually "taught" law school administrators that rankings mattered. As this lesson spread, more people began treating improved rankings as a strategic project, and their influence widened. So, despite the deep skepticism most administrators still feel toward rankings, they have become crucial professional and organizational facts that generate enormous attention and effort.

Law schools' evolving reaction to rankings suggests several lessons for studying mechanisms of reactivity. In addition to appreciating how the institutionalization of rankings changes their effects, it is important to understand how mechanisms interact. As radical simplifications, rankings circulated more broadly and quickly, and were easier to use than other evaluations of law schools. This made their impact more immediate and pronounced, since they acquired external constituencies quickly, circumventing the professional expertise of the educators who dismissed them. Over time, law schools learned that rankings were fateful, that people made important decisions using rankings, and schools began to invest heavily in improving rankings. This reinforced rankings' impact and legitimacy and set in motion the self fulfilling prophecies described above. Commensuration exacerbated patterns of self-fulfilling prophecies.

Patterns in the Effects of Reactivity

Having described two mechanisms of reactivity, we now turn to the second feature of our framework for analyzing the reactivity of public measures: identifying distinctive effects of reactivity. We describe three ways that law schools react to rankings: maximization involves changing how resources are allocated; redefinition means altering organizational scripts and procedures, including job requirements and admission policies, in conformance with ranking criteria; and manipulation entails the development of gaming strategies.

Maximizing Rankings by Reallocating Resources

One way that law schools react to rankings is by redistributing resources in order to optimize their rank. This reallocation produces tangible and durable changes in law schools since money and time spent for one purpose are unavailable for other uses. The most obvious redistribution of resources occurs when schools funnel large amounts of money into activities that received little funding before rankings and which could influence ranking criteria. Two widespread examples are sharp increases in spending on merit scholarships and marketing one's law school to other law schools.

USN rankings have prompted law schools to place far greater emphasis on LSAT scores than in the past. While LSAT scores have always mattered in admissions, admissions officers and deans agree that schools now do all they can to maximize this measure. Schools use several strategies to boost their LSAT scores, but the most common is to offer merit scholarships to students with high test scores.[24] This has prompted big changes in budgets. A faculty member at a first-tier school recalled how his school tried to raise their average LSAT score: "We were scrapping faculty salaries, not filling lines, raising money out of graduate students through our LLM program, and all of that money was going into funding three or four hundred thousand dollars in scholarships for purely number-driven reasons. And we got the LSAT up a point or two points, and we got a dean of admissions who was, in fact, paid in part based on the numbers he brought in." This redistribution is not limited to highly ranked law schools. An admissions director described the same pattern at a fourth-tier school: "We didn't have merit scholarship awards when I left in 1996. When I came back in 2000, not only were there merit scholarships to attract students with better LSATs, but the budget for [merit scholarships] exceeded the entire financial aid budget ... for the three years that I was there before. And that was just for one year ... It was phenomenally more, it was more than double." Because budgets are complex, it is often hard to know how cuts are distributed; many administrators suggest, however, that this "merit money" reduces need-based scholarships. One dean, for example, said, "I have had to shift dollars away from need-based to the merit-based. The purpose of that is to pump the numbers up to get LSAT scores up. Again, this is not nuclear physics to understand."

A second prominent example of this type of reactivity is increased spending on marketing. A school's reputation is the most influential rankings factor, worth 40% of the total score. Although it is difficult to influence opinions, many law schools now invest heavily in expensive brochures touting their accomplishments, which they send to their peers and practitioners.[25] As one dean put it, "The biggest effect of rankings has been the enrichment of printers." Law schools receive a steady stream of these brochures all year, but they literally clog faculty mailboxes in October just before *USN* surveys are filled out.

These brochures are expensive to produce and distribute because they must be sent to large numbers of potential raters in order to have a chance of influencing the reputational surveys. Many administrators say their schools spend over $100,000 per year on this type of marketing, and estimates of annual spending ranged from the tens of thousands to over a million dollars: "Oh yeah, we've all gone into the spending of, literally, hundreds of thousands of dollars on the glossies that we paper the world with. We sent these to every law professor, every dean, every associate dean, every librarian. We send them to the people who vote for *USN*." Despite huge investments in this strategy, there is no evidence that it works. Nearly every dean we interviewed admitted that they were so inundated with these materials that they barely looked at them: "The mail that I get now from all the schools on these slick glossy things—and I just literally throw them away. My secretary doesn't even give them to me. I can't imagine how bored I'd have to be to read one of those things. But we send them out because we're afraid if we don't ... we need to get our name out there."[26]

Rankings have clearly changed how legal educators make decisions about how resources are allocated. Many deans described feeling conflicted between improving their ranking and improving the quality of legal education they provide. One dean described the pressure this way: "I could hire a faculty member for the amount of money I spend on [marketing]; I could support 20 students for this price; I could buy a substantial number of books for our library; all of which strikes me as what this enterprise ought to be about ... I could almost support an entire legal writing program. I could fund a clinic. I could do any of those things. Instead I'm putting out a magazine which goes to people who aren't interested." For many deans, trying to improve ranking indicators means not investing in other worthy projects. Although administrators may experience these pressures as contradictions, boosting rankings is still broadly understood as doing "what's best for the school" since rankings have important effects on schools. Nevertheless, deans resent the loss of discretion this implies.

Redefining Work and Policies

A second way schools react to *USN* rankings is by redefining work in ways to optimize their rank. This occurs most frequently and dramatically in administrative jobs: career services, admissions, and the dean's office. This type of reactivity can effect enduring changes, especially if new employees are hired with different skills and backgrounds. To illustrate this form of reactivity, we highlight changes in career services work at law schools.

Career Services

Rankings encourage schools to pay more attention to placement statistics. While this sounds like a positive effect, participants do not see it that way. *USN* includes two indicators of placement: percent employed at graduation and percent employed nine months after graduation. To improve these factors, career services personnel now expend much greater effort on learning their graduates' employment status.[27] All 16 respondents working in career services described this effect. One Director of Career Services told us that she and her staff of four spent almost six weeks each year trying to track down graduates who had not replied to their multiple requests for employment information. She admitted to "exploring the possibility of hiring private detectives to locate missing students," but rejected the idea as too costly.

While students clearly benefit from career services departments that are extremely motivated to help them find jobs, there are drawbacks to this emphasis on statistics. Personnel complain that time spent on tracking students' job status decreases time spent counseling students, networking with law firms, and conducting employment seminars. One director estimated that she spent one day every week on employment statistics. As the only career counselor for more than 600 students, she said "That's time when students can't come to me." Another director reported: "The time I spend tracking down those 33 students who don't respond, I should be spending on strengthening employer contacts, developing new programs to help students be successful in their searches. [Searching for missing graduates] is the most aggravating part of my job—but the dean wants those numbers." This emphasis on ranking criteria has changed how career services work is experienced by employees. Most career services personnel we interviewed reported that they had entered this profession because they enjoyed advising students and helping them find satisfying jobs. This part of their job has been compromised, as pressure to maximize placement statistics has increased:

> The best piece of this job typically is when you are helping people, and that's why most people go into it. When you are helping people figure out what they want to do or helping them get a job, that is the piece of it that ... makes up for everything else. [It's] becoming much more statistically oriented; we're a big school to begin with so our resources here are stretched a little bit. The more resources that we spend on *USN* and on the statistics, the less time we have for the students.[28]

This stress on placement statistics creates a pressure like that experienced by many deans; career services personnel report feeling torn between boosting numbers and helping students find the best job for them. For one:

> What do you do when you have a student that has a job offer that is not perhaps what you would want for them and they come to you for some guidance? Do you tell them to hold out a little bit longer ... Or do you tell them to take the job and worry about it later? And I think a lot of folks at this point would tell the students just to take the job and move on to the next one. And you're not helping the students any when you do that.

And if career services personnel do not re-orient their work to boost their placement statistics, they may be fired: "We have focused more closely on placement numbers, we're very concerned about placement numbers, and our placement director is in the process of being forced to resign right now and that is clearly related to the numbers." By all reports, turnover rates are high. Some compare themselves to athletic coaches who must produce results quickly or lose their jobs. If people are fired for their placement statistics, their replacements will likely be hired for their ability to improve these numbers, which further institutionalizes these changes in career services work.[29]

This pattern is repeated in admissions, where the LSAT scores of entering classes are emphasized. Many in admissions believe rankings have, in the words of one director, "completely changed the application and admissions process." Decisions are increasingly based on ranking considerations rather than professional judgments about which students would best fit the school. One dean of admissions said: "We are now torn between decisions that will bring a better class and a class that does better according to *USN* ... There was this student with a 162 LSAT score [a high score for this school] and a low GPA. I thought this guy was probably immature, a slacker ... but I couldn't pass on that score, so I admitted him." This loss of decision-making authority is disturbing to admissions personnel.

And, as with career services positions, admissions jobs appear to be more volatile. As admissions has become more numbers oriented, experienced admissions personnel are sometimes replaced with those who embrace this goal or have better quantitative skills. Some schools are hiring staff with MBAs instead of the conventional JD. These redefinitions of career services and admissions jobs indicate how rankings have changed the conduct of work within law schools. Boosting rankings criteria now threatens to overshadow other goals, a pattern that is echoed in the dean's office.[30]

Gaming Rankings

Perhaps the most direct form of reactivity is trying to "game" the numbers to maximize one's rank. We define gaming as manipulating rules and numbers in ways that are unconnected to, or even undermine, the motivation behind them. Gaming is about managing appearances and involves efforts to improve ranking factors without improving the characteristics the factors are designed to measure. No sharp lines distinguish gaming from other strategic behavior but it is useful to distinguish gaming analytically from other strategic behavior because it produces unique consequences.

Gaming strategies are fateful partly because both actual gaming practices and rampant anxiety about these practices produce similar changes. Because many consider gaming an illegitimate response to rankings, it is subject to gossip and secrets; this secrecy threatens the scientific legitimacy of rankings since it makes it harder to assess whether measures capture what they were intended to. Gaming also changes relations with colleagues at other institutions since it breeds distrust. Distrust speeds the diffusion of gaming strategies because it increases people's anxiety about what colleagues *might* be doing, especially among closely ranked schools. Since tiny differences separate many schools, gaming encourages a "race to the bottom." Many administrators worry that gaming threatens professional values such as honesty, responsibility, and, paradoxically, transparency. Numerous articles have chastised administrators for resorting to gaming, including one written by the president of the Association of American Law Schools (Whitman 2002; see also Wellen 2005).[31]

Respondents described a wide range of gaming strategies deployed by law schools. An early, blatant example entailed schools reporting different numbers to *USN* than to their accrediting body, the ABA. The 1995 rankings issue of *USN* lists 29 (of 177) schools that reported higher median LSAT scores to the magazine than to the ABA. Detroit Mercy and the University of Alabama, for example, had four-point differentials between their *USN* and ABA medians (*USN*, March 20, 1995). This public admonishment was effective. The following year only 13 schools were chastised for discrepant scores (*USN*, March 18, 1996).

Although less nakedly executed than inconsistent reporting, many gaming strategies involve misrepresentation. Law schools now count as employed graduates with any job, including non-legal jobs. One director of career services recounts: "What we did not have to deal with before [rankings] was intense administrative pressure to get the numbers up ... not to help people develop career plans or help people understand how they might be able to use their gifts.... Now it's like 'Can you get a job in the beauty salon painting nails until these numbers are in?' So it's something that has happened on a national level with career services people and it really has a devastating effect."

Another strategy involves re-classifying a portion of admitted students as "part-time" or "probationary" to exclude their scores from the calculation of median LSAT scores.[32]

These uncounted students have lower LSAT scores or GPAs but other desirable characteristics, such as interesting backgrounds, a strong record of public service, or economic, regional or racial diversity. An associate dean at a third-tier school reported:

> I know for a fact that [School X] and [School Y] have created these artificial probation programs where students with low scores come in and they don't have to count them as part of their LSAT. That's complete nonsense.... They have huge numbers of people on probation and it's only in the first year, and it all disappears in the second year. And they do it by taking one fewer course in the first year and then they take a makeup course in the summer. That's the rankings. We suffer because they do that and we don't.

A related strategy is to reduce the size of incoming classes by admitting fewer students into the full-time (day) program and more students into the part-time (night) program. This tactic improves both the median LSAT scores and the student-faculty ratio. A faculty member who chaired admissions at a top-tier school explained: "It's in the nature of any well-structured game that it's subject to strategic choice and strategic influence. So, one thing that we did was to shift students from our full-time into our part-time program, and I'm aware of other schools doing that." This school moved thirty students from its full-time to part-time program, and is considering further cuts in class size to improve rankings, a practice which disproportionately affects lower income, older, and minority students. Other, mostly highly-ranked, schools cut class sizes to improve scores but instead of expanding or creating part-time programs, they solicit transfer students from lower ranked local schools, a strategy that schools losing some of their best students resent. With the exception of one elite school, all of our focus schools reported that this had happened at least once to their best students.

Another gaming strategy employed by some law schools involves pressuring faculty to take spring leaves. Following ABA guidelines, *USN* counts full-time faculty teaching in the fall term for its student-faculty ratio; a faculty member on leave in the fall harms a school's ratio. Several administrators admitted this practice and many claimed it is common (see also Whitman 2002). Given that the student-faculty ratio accounts for just 3% of a school's overall *USN* rank, this suggests how meticulously schools monitor their scores.

Some schools hire their unemployed graduates temporarily to improve their employment numbers, while others (rarely) solicit more applicants, including obviously unqualified applicants, to boost their selectivity numbers. Gaming, according to many administrators, encourages them to be more distrustful of their peers, especially in their reporting of statistics like graduate placement that are difficult to verify.

The redistribution of resources, the redefinition of work, and the adoption of gaming strategies are three prominent types of reactivity that help explain how rankings affect law schools. In each case, organizational actors alter their behavior to try to influence their rank. Our account depicts the reactivity of rankings as producing serious and mostly harmful effects. The few deans who support rankings praise them for making more information available to consumers and for creating accountability. The demand for rankings proves that many find them useful for evaluating the relative performance and stature of law schools and for simplifying decisions. Rankings have also prompted law schools and their professional associations to release more information. But, as many respondents noted, rankings are deeply flawed measures, simplification can result in poorer decisions, and the unintended consequences of rankings can be deleterious. Carefully disentangling the reactivity of measures demonstrates the range and pervasiveness of these effects, whether manifest or latent.

Because rankings shape the stratification of legal education (Sauder 2006) they affect all schools but they do not affect all schools in the same way or to the same degree. Five key sources of variation in rankings effects include: whether schools are on the cusp of tiers, their relative position in the rankings, a dean's commitment to improving rankings, geographical location, and mission. Schools on the cusp of tiers often experience enormous pressure to improve rankings. Because rankings are relative, a school's rank can shift even if nothing changes at that school. Many schools feel they must "swim furiously to stay in place," especially if failing to do so means dropping a tier. A school's position in the rankings also influences ranking effects. While members of lower ranked schools often feel demoralized by their ranking, elite schools are not immune from rankings pressure as some assume. Elite schools may not be stigmatized, but a decline in rank can produce anxiety and vigorous efforts to improve rank.

Leadership produces variation in ranking effects, too. Deans vary in their emphasis on and strategic response to rankings. Deans hired to "improve rankings" or those who adopt higher rankings as an explicit goal, either voluntary or coercively, amplify the reactivity of rankings. Ranking effects may be diminished if a law school dean resists rankings or is not pressured by key constituents to improve them. Geographical location also shapes reactivity. Members of regional law schools may feel less rankings pressure if there are few in-state law schools and if most students wish to practice law locally. For schools aspiring to be a "national" school, rankings matter more, especially if they occupy the same niche in the same region as competitor schools. Finally, the reactivity of rankings is mediated by a school's mission. Schools with distinctive missions, whether this entails commitments to religious traditions, public service, or providing "access," can sometimes resist rankings pressures despite being penalized by the rankings' universalistic and elite-based criteria.

Conclusion

The expansion of public measures and their capacity to change the institutions and the people they describe suggests why it is important to explain their significance. Our framework is designed to help identify the core mechanisms and effects of reactivity. Using the example of law school rankings, we show how rankings evoke self-fulfilling prophecies that gradually transform law schools into entities that conform more closely to the criteria used to construct rankings, and we describe how commensuration changes the form and circulation of information and how people attend to it. We analyze three broad patterns in the effects of reactivity, showing how rankings prompt the redistribution of resources, the redefinition of work, and gaming.

Our framework should be treated as an orienting heuristic, an animating set of concepts and questions to help scholars identify similarities and differences in actors' response to measures; our goal is to facilitate conversations across fields rather than to develop a general theory of reactivity. For Strathern (2000:2), assessment procedures are a "distinct cultural artifact" and appreciating their distinctiveness requires precise comparisons. Our analysis is designed to demonstrate the usefulness of this framework and we conclude by suggesting strategies for using and developing it.

First, the distinction between mechanisms and effects is helpful for framing investigations analytically. Since the same mechanism can produce different effects and different mechanisms can produce similar effects, this distinction helps identify one source of important variation in reactivity.[33] Our framework can help scholars determine if patterns associated with rankings apply to other measures. Recent research on high-stakes testing in public schools, for instance, exhibits self-fulfilling prophecies as teachers, under pressure to raise standardized test scores, "teach to the test" (McNeil and Valenzuela 2001; Meier 2002). Comparing public rankings with private performance measures also reveals interesting variation. Executives' autonomy permits them to impose and change performance measures relatively easily, which affects their institutionalization and mitigates some of the effects described in this analysis. In contrast to media imposed rankings, if corporate performance measures produce counter-productive gaming strategies, firms can simply revise their measures (Meyer 1994, 2002). Analyzing conditions that produce variation in the mechanisms and effects of reactivity will advance our understanding of public measures.

Investigations of measurement can be also be advanced by further specifying the mechanisms and effects of reactivity described here. Commensuration is a broad mechanism of reactivity and its specific forms may generate particular effects. For example, commodification is one form of commensuration that produces effects both comparable and disparate to the effects of commensuration described above. Like other forms of commensuration, price summarizes vast information and directs attention in particular ways. But commodification also elicits distinctive social relations, such as the fetishization of commodities.

Our framework can stimulate scholars to identify new mechanisms and effects of reactivity. Recent research suggests that measures that are adopted voluntarily have different effects than those that are imposed (Zuckerman and Sgourev 2006), so it may be fruitful to consider coercion as a separate mechanism of reactivity. Not only are rankings imposed from the outside, they also create a prisoner's dilemma for schools since they are strictly relative and punish schools who fail to conform. The fate of schools expressed in rankings is not simply intertwined, but is zero-sum: one school's success may come at the expense of many others. Investigating coercion as a mechanism of reactivity may reveal why some forms of resistance failed (e.g. boycotts), why gaming techniques spread so quickly, and why rankings generate such vigilance.

Explaining variation is one crucial way to advance our understanding of the reactivity of measures but it is also important to refine questions and concepts, and to compare explanations across fields. The distinctive approaches of different fields can advance our understanding of the reactivity of measures when they inform one another. Science studies scholars have powerful strategies for analyzing how knowledge becomes authoritative. Organizational theorists explain how fields emerge and change. Psychologists and anthropologists, in different ways, analyze cognition and classification. Scholars of professions emphasize how expertise is expanded and defended. These fields offer unique and complementary insights for understanding the reactivity of measures.

One strategy for developing theory and improving our theoretical explanations of reactivity is to consider the contradictions that measurements generate in their different uses. For example, public measures create a chronic tension between validity and accountability, between taming reactivity and producing it. How to think about this tension is an important question for scholars. Some measures are designed as incentives; their purpose is to change people's behavior. But others are supposed to be neutral descriptions of the world. The contradictions that we, as producers and consumers of public measures, invest in our measures are tricky to reconcile. As scientific depictions, measures should be objective, accurate, and non-reactive. But as incentives or techniques of accountability, measures must offer crucial feedback about people's performance and shape their aspirations. We want to harness the reactivity of measures, but here timing is everything.

We want a sharp temporal break between the act of measurement and the reactivity that responds to it. We want the world to stand still for measurement and, only after, change in relation to it. Measures as a series of snapshots to which people respond are acceptable, but measures as video cameras that encourage our mugging are not. Reactivity that blurs the line between object and measurement threatens the validity of our measures. As Strathern says (1996:4), "When a measure becomes a target, it ceases to be a good measure."

Reflexivity makes the sharp distinction between the act and object of measurement hard to sustain. Because we continually interpret our social worlds, objects are unstable; they emerge and are reconstructed through measurement, just as standardized tests create gifted and under-achieving students, the census produces "Hispanics," and the LSAT defines "merit." Latour (1993) characterizes this tension broadly as pressure to erect sturdy boundaries around the social and the natural. Our perpetual, elusive and misguided efforts to protect the purity of these categories define us as "modern." Reactivity is one form of interaction that reveals how difficult it is to maintain sharp distinctions between measures and objects of measurement, description and inscription, science and society, the social and the natural. It suggests why scientific authority that is grounded in these sorts of dualisms remains a perpetual and perennially incomplete project. The independence of the social and natural worlds is threatened by our reflexivity.

In his investigations of corporate performance measures, Meyer (1994, 2002) suggests that reactivity limits the shelf-life of measures. The challenge of managing reactivity in business is less to protect the purity of the measure than to protect their usefulness as incentives. Since corporations are complex organizations, assessment indicators can never capture all important aspects of performance. Over time, people learn to manipulate measures and their narrowness and simplification can be organizationally self-defeating. As the value of measures declines, it becomes necessary to change them in order to capture other aspects of performance. To remain useful, measures must be a moving target. But these changes may be resisted by those who benefit from particular measures and who have invested in learning to manipulate them. The challenge for *USN* is that, as a journalistic enterprise, they are unqualified to create incentive systems to change law schools. The authority of their rankings rests, precariously, on their status as valid scientific measures and *USN*'s reputation as unbiased journalists reporting "the news" rather than creating it.

Another important set of questions for understanding reactivity involves their moral implications. We do not typically associate ethics with measurement. We have shown that public measures affect the distribution of resources, redefine statuses which can become reified and enduring, produce and reinforce inequality, and transform the language in which power presents and defends itself. Once accountability is understood quantitatively and is equated with good governance, the meanings of many core values—efficiency, improvement, accessibility, transparency, responsibility, responsiveness, and even democracy—are redefined and re-inscribed in our institutions as technical rather than political accomplishments. Accountability is routinely and uncritically invoked as an obvious public good so it is especially important that scholars conduct empirically rigorous analyses.

Assessment measures permit the easy conflation of what *is* with what *ought to be*, of what normal is in the statistical and moral sense. As Foucault (1977), Starr (1987:54), Hacking (1990:163) and others have argued, this conflation is insidious and rhetorically potent. Characterized as decision technologies, benchmarks, guidelines, or even "best practices," performance measures move easily from one location to another, accumulating new uses and constituents. Measures, because they standardize, simplify, and provoke comparison, become sturdy vehicles for transporting practices and values from one site to another: from one country to another, from business to education, from the academy to the military, and so on. The power attending public measures is not the obvious, self-interested power of elites, nor is it monolithic; it enters, inscribes itself, and operates differently than noisy, interested power. Reactivity is nuanced and dispersed.

The blandness of audits and assessments (cf. Porter 1995:51; Strathern 1996) is rhetorically useful, since it defects attention from their capacity to change the places and people that use them. While we suspect that research on the reactivity of measures has been hampered by its rather dreary associations with bureaucrats and statistics, the aim of the present analysis is to stimulate interest in what we think is one of the important and challenging trends of our time—the proliferation of public measures of performance.

Notes

1. Acknowledgements included in original article.

2. Urla (1993:818) contends, "There are probably few features more characteristic of modernity than the notion that we can know ourselves through numbers."

3. Assessment tactics were common in command economies, too. Production quotas monitored productivity in the USSR and were often manipulated (Berliner 1956).

4. Other law school rankings include Brian Leiter's "Educational Quality Rankings of U.S. Law Schools," *The Gourman Report*, *Barron's Guide to Law Schools*, Brennan's Law School Rankings, My-LawSchoolRankings, and lawschool 100. No alternative ranking has the impact of *USN*. Business schools, in contrast, attend to at least five high-profile rankings which powerfully mediates the effects of rankings (Sauder and Espeland 2006).

5. Interviews include 39 deans or ex-deans, 49 other administrators (e.g deans, directors of admissions and career services, personnel in academic affairs, external relations, and development), 33 faculty members, nine other administrators (e.g., marketing, librarians, and secretaries), and six leaders of national legal education associations.

6. Interviews included 21 respondents from fourth tier schools, 26 from third tier schools, 22 from second tier schools and 18 from first tier schools. Of the 1st tier schools, 12 schools from the top 25 and five schools from the top ten were represented.

7. Data from two other projects was re-analyzed. One project included field work and in-depth interviews with 77 law and business students (Schleef 2005). The other involved 18 months of field work in an undergraduate admissions office at a liberal arts college (Stevens forthcoming). We conducted interviews with 12 current and prospective law students and two pre-law advisors. We also interviewed a former editor and current staff member of *USN*.

8. For more on *USN* rankings methodology, see Sauder and Espeland (2006). Mel Elfin, the *USN* editor who helped launch the rankings, said, "It became, essentially, our franchise" (Parloff 1998). In addition to the two regular issues featuring rankings, *USN* publishes two annual guidebooks that summarize rankings for colleges and graduate programs.

9. We thank an anonymous reviewer for this metaphor.

10. Rosenthal and Jacobsen's (1968) famous study of the effects of teachers' expectations exemplifies how measures confirm expectations. Similarly, the creation of often arbitrary categories of people (e.g. "Hispanics") illustrates how the validity of measures increases over time (Porter 1995:41–42). As a category acquires constituencies who use it, those encompassed by the category develop shared interests and identities that make the category more meaningful and "real."

11. Ferraro, et al. (2005:9) describe how theories become self-fulfilling, "regardless of their ability to predict and explain behavior." Focusing on how economic theory has informed management, they describe three mechanisms that produce self-fulfilling effects: redesigning institutions and organizations (including measurement practices), creating norms that presume a theory, and using language that shapes people's interpretations. Our analysis reflects each of these mechanisms, although we label

them somewhat differently and highlight other aspects of self-fulfilling prophecies (see also Callon 1998; Mackenzie 2006).

12. Monks and Ehrenberg (1999) found similar patterns for undergraduate rankings.

13. Most informants believe that these effects are subtle or even subconscious. No one admitted to consulting the rankings as they filled out the survey. They did suggest that prior rankings contributed to their impressions of other schools, especially schools about which they knew little.

14. Some deans dispute this effect since they do not see immediate changes in their school's reputation following changes in rank, which is consistent with Schmalbeck's (2001) analysis. Focusing on *USN* top 50 law schools, he finds that reputations are relatively durable since rankings seem to have little effect on the perceptions of survey respondents: a drop in rank during one year does not harm a school's reputation score in the following year's survey. The effects of prior rankings may be more indirect than is captured in this study. As Stake (2006) suggests, changes often take time to develop and may be most powerful for lower ranked schools since they are less well-known nationally and rankings may substitute for other information.

15. Many university administrators report that they use potential improvement in rank to justify claims on resources, which is confirmed by a quick survey of "strategic plans" and "annual reports."

16. Given law schools' public denouncements of rankings, many commentators note the hypocrisy of this practice. Other organizations publicize their rankings, too. *USN* also ranks hospitals and high-ranking hospitals routinely advertise their standing.

17. Elsbach and Kramer (1996) found that even for elite business schools rankings threaten members' sense of their institution's organizational identity.

18. Espeland (1998) and Espeland and Stevens (1998) provide more detailed discussions of commensuration.

19. Thévenot (1984) describes this sacrificing of information with an eye toward future uses (e.g. coding to produce standardized variables) as an "investment in form."

20. http://www.lsac.org/LSAC.asp?url=lsac/deans-speak-out-rankings.asp.

21. Commensuration is most jarring, it seems less like measurement and more like artifice, when it encompasses things that do not already seem alike. When disparate entities are included in a cost-benefit analysis, for example, we are more mindful that the relations are being *created* among these things, and the unity that commensuration imposes seems more tenuous (Espeland 1998, Espeland and Stevens 1998).

22. Within law schools, rankings factors link the fates of different departments numerically, which makes it easy to notice progress or assign blame.

23. Media reaction to rankings amplified their importance. The annual release of rankings became "news." Local newspapers carried stories about how nearby law schools fared, especially if their rank changed.

24. Twenty-seven administrators reported increases in merit scholarships as an impact of rankings. Opinions varied but most did not see this as the best use of revenue.

25. Thirty-four administrators discussed this effect of rankings. Twenty-five respondents raised this effect without prompting.

26. We asked a law professor to save this promotional material for us. The pile approached three feet in less than a year. Since he was not an administrator, he likely received far fewer brochures than the average dean.

27. The University of Texas School of Law demonstrates the stakes of failing to track employment carefully. In 1998, the school dropped from 18 to 29 in *USN* rankings because 61 recent graduates failed to return their employment surveys, and *USN* assumed that 75% of non-respondents were unemployed (Brooks 1998).

28. Fifteen out of sixteen career service personnel we interviewed discussed this topic. Thirteen reported increased pressure from deans, faculty, or students to improve employment numbers.

29. Deans experience similar pressures. The dean of the University of Houston's law school was recently forced to resign because the school's ranking dropped. One reporter concluded that, "The popularity of the annual rankings, used by prospective students, employers and job-searching scholars

to gauge an institution's credibility, has meant that schools are funneling more resources to boost their placement. It also means that deans can expect the ranking scorecard increasingly to serve as a measure of their individual job performance" (Jones 2006:6).

30. Other personnel also feel rankings pressure. Some schools recruit faculty with an eye toward boosting rankings, change course offerings to boost bar passage rates, or expand marketing staff. Even administrative assistants report spending more time compiling rankings data.

31. 33 respondents described gaming as a problem. Many others described particular strategies used. Only one respondent believed reports of gaming were exaggerated and relatively unimportant. Since gaming tactics are ethically questionable, interviewees were reluctant to admit to gaming at their current schools, describing instead the practices of former employers and competitors. Some tactics are rare and some stories may be apocryphal so we report only strategies that are corroborated with public sources or reflect the direct experience of our informants.

32. Fifteen respondents reported this strategy and most believe its use is increasing. Other reports on the proliferation of part time programs provide corroboration.

33. This parallels Simmel's (1971) discussion of form and content, in which the same form can include different contents and the same content can be organized as different forms.

References

Alonso, William, and Paul Starr. 1987. *The Politics of Numbers.* New York: The Russell Sage Foundation.

Berliner, Joseph. 1956. "A Problem in Soviet Business Administration." *Administrative Science Quarterly* 1:86–101.

Breslau, Daniel. 1997. "Contract Shop Epistemology: Credibility and Problem Construction in Applied Social Science." *Social Studies of Science* 27:363–94.

Brooks, A. Phillips. 1998. "UT Law School Falls from Top 25; Officials Will Appeal *U.S. News.*" *Austin American-Statesman*, Feb. 20, A1.

Burawoy, Michael. 1998. "The Extended Case Method." *Sociological Theory* 16: 4–33.

Callon, Michel, ed. 1998. *The Laws of the Markets.* Oxford: Blackwell.

Campbell, Donald T. 1957. "Factors Relevant to the Validity of Experiments in Social Settings." *Psychological Bulletin* 54: 297–312.

Campbell, Donald T., and Julian C. Stanley. 1963. *Experimental and Quasi-Experimental Designs for Research.* Boston: Houghton Mifflin Company.

Caron, Paul L., and Rafael Gely. 2004. "What Law Schools Can Learn from Billy Beane and the Oakland Athletics." *Texas Law Review* 82:1483–1554.

Carson, John. In press. *The Measure of Merit: Talents, Intelligence, and Inequality in the French and American Republics, 1750–1940.* Princeton, NJ: Princeton University Press.

Coverse, Jean M., and Howard Schumann. 1974. *Conversations at Random.* Ann Arbor, MI: Wiley.

Desrosières, Alain. 2001. "How 'Real' Are Statistics? Four Possible Attitudes." *Social Research* 68: 339–355.

Elsbach, Kimberly D., and Roderick M. Kramer. 1996. "Members' Responses to Organizational Identity Threats: Encountering and Countering the *Business Week* Rankings." *Administrative Science Quarterly* 41: 442–476.

Elster, Jon. 1989. *Nuts and Bolts for the Social Sciences.* Cambridge: Cambridge University Press.

Espeland, Wendy Nelson. 1998. *The Struggle for Water: Politics, Rationality and Identity in the American Southwest.* Chicago: University of Chicago Press.

Espeland, Wendy Nelson, and Mitchell Stevens. 1998. "Commensuration as a Social Process." *Annual Review of Sociology* 24: 312–43.

Ferraro, Fabrizio, Jeffrey Pfeffer, and Robert Sutton. 2005. "Economics Language and Assumptions: How Theories Can Become Self-Fulfilling." *Academy of Management Review* 30: 8–24.

Foucault, Michel. 1977. *Discipline and Punish: The Birth of the Prison.* London: Allen Lane.

Guetzkow, Joseph, Michele Lamont, and Gregoire Mallard. 2004. "What is Originality in the Humanities and the Social Sciences?" *American Sociological Review* 69: 190–212.

Hacking, Ian. 1990. *The Taming of Chance.* Cambridge: Cambridge University Press.

Hacking, Ian. 1992. "The Self-Vindication of the Laboratory Sciences." In *Science as Practice and Culture*, edited by A. Pickering. Chicago: University of Chicago Press.

Halliday, Terance, and Bruce Carruthers. 2005. "The Recursivity of Law: Global Norm-Making and National Law-making in the Globalization of Corporate Insolvency Regimes." American Bar Foundation Working Paper.

Hedstrom, Peter, and Richard Swedberg. 1998. "Social Mechanism, an Introductory Essay." Pp. 1–31 in *Social Mechanisms: An Analytic Approach to Social Theory*, edited by Peter Hedstrom and Richard Swedberg. Cambridge: Cambridge University Press.

Heimer, Carol. 1985. *Reactive Risk and Rational Action: Managing Moral Hazard in Insurance Contracts.* Berkeley, CA: University of California Press.

Heimer, Carol, and Lisa Staffen. 1998. *For the Sake of the Children.* Chicago: University of Chicago Press.

Hoffer, Thomas. 2000. "Accountability in Education." Pp. 529–544 in *Handbook of the Sociology of Education*, edited by Maureen T. Hallinan. New York: Springer.

Hoskins, Keith. 1996. "The 'Awful Idea of Accountability': Inscribing People into the Measurement of Objects." In *Accountability, Power, Ethos and the Technologies of Managing*, edited by R. Munor and J. Mouritsen. London: International Thomson Business Press.

Jones, Leigh. 2006. "Law School Deans Feel Heat from Rankings." *National Law Journal* 27: 6.

Katz, Jack. 1983. "A Theory of Qualitative Methodology: The Social System of Analytical Fieldwork." Pp. 127–48 in *Contemporary Field Research*, edited by Robert Emerson. Prospect Heights, IL: Waveland Press.

Kazdin, A.E. 1982. "Observer Effects: Reactivity of Direct Observation." Pp. 5–19 in *Using Observers to Study Behavior*, edited by D.P. Hartmann. San Francisco: Jossey-Bass.

Kula, Witold. 1986. *Measures and Men.* Princeton, NJ: Princeton University Press.

Lamont, Michele, and Virag Molnar. 2002. "The Study of Boundaries across the Social Sciences." *Annual Review of Sociology* 28: 167–195.

Latour, Bruno. 1987. *Science in Action.* Cambridge, MA: Harvard University Press.

Latour, Bruno. 1993. *We have Never Been Modern.* Cambridge, MA: Harvard University Press.

McCall, George J. 1984. "Systematic Field Observation." *Annual Review of Sociology* 10: 263–282.

Mackenzie, Donald. 2006. *An Engine, Not a Camera: How Financial Models Shape Markets.* Cambridge, MA: MIT Press.

MacKenzie, Donald and Yuval Millo. 2003. "Constructing a Market, Performing Theory: The Historical Sociology of a Financial Derivatives Exchange." *American Journal of Sociology* 109: 107–145.

March, James G., and Herbert A. Simon. 1958. *Organizations.* New York: Wiley.

McNeil, Linda, and Angela Valenzuela. 2001. "The Harmful Impact of the TAAS System of Testing in Texas: Beneath the Accountability Rhetoric." Pp. 127–150 in *Raising Standards or Raising Barriers? Inequality and High-Stakes Testing in Public Education,* edited by Gary Orfield and Mindy L. Kornhaber. New York: Century Foundation Press.

Meier, Deborah. 2002. *In Schools We Trust: Creating Communities of Learning in an Era of Testing and Standardization.* Boston: Beacon Press.

Merton, Robert K. 1967. "On Sociological Theories of the Middle Range." Pp. 39–72 in *On Theoretical Sociology.* New York: Free Press.

Merton, Robert K. 1968 [1948]. "The Self-Fulfilling Prophecy." Pp. 475–490 in *Social Theory and Social Structure.* New York: The Free Press.

Meyer, Marshall. 1994. "Measuring Performance in Economic Organizations." Pp. 556–578 in *Handbook of Economic Sociology,* edited by Neil J. Smelser and Richard Swedberg. New York: Russell Sage Foundation.

Meyer, Marshall. 2002. *Rethinking Performance Measurement: Beyond the Balanced Scorecard.* Cambridge, MA: Cambridge University Press.

Monks, James and Ronald G. Ehrenberg. 1999. "*U.S. News & World Report*'s College Rankings: Why They Do Matter." *Change*: 42–51.

Morse, Robert J. 2005. "*U.S. News and World Report*'s Law School Rankings: How and Why *U.S. News* Does Them." Paper presented at the Law School Admissions Council Annual Meeting and Education Conference, Indian Wells, CA., June 4.

Narins Craig R., Ann M. Dozier, Frederick S. Ling, and Wojciech Zareba. 2005. "The Influence of Public Reporting of Outcome Data on Medical Decision Making by Physicians." *Archives of Internal Medicine* 165: 83–87.

Orne, M. 1962. "On the Social Psychology of the Psychology Experiment." *American Psychologist* 17: 776–783.

Parloff, Roger. 1998. "Who's Number One? And Who's Number 52, 91, And 137?" *American Lawyer*, April 1998: 5.

Porter, Theodore M. 1986. *The Rise of Statistical Thinking, 1820–1900.* Princeton, NJ: Princeton University Press

Porter, Theodore M. 1995. *Trust in Numbers: The Pursuit of Objectivity in Science and Public Life.* Princeton, NJ: Princeton University Press.

Power, Michael. 1994. *The Audit Explosion.* London: Demos.

Power, Michael. 1997. *The Audit Society: Rituals of Verification.* Oxford: Oxford University Press.

Prewitt, Kenneth. 1987. "Public Statistics and Democratic Politics." Pp. 261–274 in *The Politics of Numbers*, edited by William Alonso and Paul Starr. New York: Russell Sage Foundation.

Reiss, A.J. Jr. 1971. "Systematic Observation of Natural Science Phenomena." Pp. 3–33 in *Sociological Methodology 1971*, edited by H. Costner. San Francisco: Jossey-Bass.

Rosenthal, Robert, and Lenore Jacobson. 1968. *Pygmalion in the Classroom: Teacher Expectation and Pupils' Intellectual Development*. New York: Holt, Rinehart & Winston.

Sauder, Michael. 2006. "Third Parties and Status Systems: How the Structures of Status Systems Matter." *Theory & Society* 35: 299–321.

Sauder, Michael and Wendy Espeland, 2006. "Strength in Numbers? The Advantages of Multiple Rankings." *Indiana Law Journal* 81: 205–227.

Sauder, Michael and Ryon Lancaster. "Do Rankings Matter? The Effects of *U.S. News and World Report* Rankings on the Admission Process of Law Schools." *Law and Society Review* 40: 105–34.

Schleef, Debra. 2005. *Managing Elites: Professional Socialization in Law and Business Schools*. Lanham, MD.: Rowan & Littlefield.

Schmalbeck, Richard. 2001. "The Durability of Law School Reputation." *Journal of Legal Education* 48: 568–590.

Schutz, Alfred. 1970. *On Phenomenology and Social Relations*, edited by Helmut R. Wagner. Chicago: University of Chicago Press.

Shore, Chris, and Susan Wright. 2000. "Coercive Accountability." Pp. 57–89 in *Audit Cultures*, edited by Marilyn Strathern. London: Routledge.

Shumar, Wesley. 1997. *College for Sale: A Critique of the Commodification of Higher Education*. London: Falmer Press.

Silbey, Susan, and Patricia Ewick, 2003. "The Architecture of Authority: The Place of Law and the Space of Science." Pp. 75–109 in *The Place of Law*, edited by Austin Sarat, Lawrence Douglas, and Martha Umphrey. Ann Arbor: University of Michigan Press.

Simmel, Georg. 1971. *On Individuality and Social Forms*. Ed. Donald N. Levine. Chicago: University of Chicago Press.

Simmel, Georg. 1978. *The Philosophy of Money*. Trans. T. Bottomore, D. Frisby. Boston: Routledge & Kegan Paul.

Stabile, Tom. 2000. "How to Beat *U.S. News*. A Law School Tries to Manufacture a Better Ranking." *National Jurist* 10(2):19.

Stake, Jeffrey Evans. 2006. "The Interplay between Law School Rankings, Reputations, and Resource Allocations: Ways Rankings Mislead." *Indiana Law Journal* 82: 229–270.

Steinmetz, George. 2004. "Odious Comparisons: Incommensurability, the Case Study, and 'Small N's in Sociology.'" *Sociological Theory* 22: 371–400.

Stevens, Mitchell L. Forthcoming. *Creating a Class: College Admissions and the Education of Elites*, Cambridge: Harvard University Press.

Stinchcombe, Arthur L. 2005. *The Logic of Social Science Research*. Chicago: University of Chicago Press.

Strathern, Marilyn. 1996. "From Improvement to Enhancement: An Anthropological Comment on the Audit Culture." *Cambridge Anthropology* 19: 1–21.

Strathern, Marilyn. 1997. "'Improving Ratings': Audit in the British University System." *European Review* 5: 305–321.

Strathern, Marilyn. 2000. *Audit Cultures: Anthropological Studies in Accountability, Ethics and the Academy*. London and New York: Routledge.

Suchman, Lucy, and Brigitte Jordan. 1991. "Interactional Troubles in Face-to-Face Survey Interviews." *Journal of the American Statistical Association* 85: 232–241.

Tedeschi, J. T. (ed.) 1981. *Impression Management Theory and Social Psychological Research.* New York: Academic Press.

Thévenot, Laurent. 1984. "Rules and Implements: Investment in Forms." *Social Science Information* 22(1): 1–45.

Thomas, W.I., and Dorothy Swaine Thomas. 1928. *The Children in America: Behavior Problems and Programs.* New York: Knopf.

Urla, Jacqueline. 1993. "Cultural Politics in an Age of Statistics: Numbers, Nations and the Making of Basque Identity." *American Ethnologist* 20: 818–843.

U.S. News & World Report, America's Best Graduate Schools, 1990–2005.

Ventresca, Marc. 1995. *When States Count: Institutional and Political Dynamics in Modern Census Establishment,* 1800–1993. PhD thesis, Department of Sociology, Stanford University.

Webb, E. J., Campbell, D. T., Schwartz, R. D. D., Sechrest, L., & Grove, J. B. 1981. *Nonreactive Measures in the Social Sciences* (2nd ed.). Boston, MA: Houghton Mifflin.

Weber, Max. 1978. *Economy and Society.* Eds. G. Roth and C. Wittich. Berkeley: University of California Press.

Webster, David S. 1992. "Rankings of Undergraduate Education in *U.S. News and World Report* and *Money.*" *Change,* March/April: 19–31.

Wellen, Alex. 2005. "The $8.75 Million Maneuver: How Water Bills, Temp Jobs and Backdoor Admissions Help Law Schools Scale the Rankings at *U.S. News.*" *New York Times,* Education Life, July 31, pp. 18–19.

Whitman, Dale. 2002. "Doing the Right Thing." *The Newsletter* (April), pp. 1–4.

Zuckerman, Ezra, and Stoyan Sgourev. 2006. "Peer Capitalism: Social Structure, Motivation, and Learning in the Market Economy." *American Journal of Sociology* 111: 1327–1366.

The Interplay between Law School Rankings, Reputations, and Resource Allocation: Ways Rankings Mislead

*Jeffrey Evans Stake**

Introduction

This article discusses problems created by the annual rankings of law schools published by *U.S. News & World Report* ("*U.S. News*"). Of course all unidimensional rankings of law schools, no matter who produces them, ignore the fact that law schools have different jobs to do for different students, from preparing those who will serve under-represented communities to preparing those who will advise major corporations and the government. Moreover, the consumer orientation of the rankings fails to recognize that law schools have other roles to perform in society, from devising improved laws to augmenting the stock of knowledge about law. In addition, there are serious, particular problems associated with law school rankings—they mislead law schools and prospective applicants. Law schools are misled in the sense that the rankings lead them down a path of operation that reduces the quality of schooling they offer to students. Applicants are misled in the sense that they choose a school that will improve their lives less than would some other law school. There are a number of reasons that rankings can mislead applicants, but one source of invalidity worth highlighting at the outset is that some of the criteria used, such as reputation survey results, are not reliable measures of quality because they are themselves reflexively influenced by the *U.S. News* rankings.

There are three approaches to improving the rankings. One approach is to use rankings to create beneficial incentives instead of harmful ones. In this vein, Russell Korobkin argues that rankings should be constructed to create incentives for the production of public goods.[1] The issue of which public goods should be extracted from law schools deserves further study. Another approach is to attempt to increase the validity of the rankings. There are experts who have spent their lives studying how to evaluate educational programs and curricula and one of the first steps in creating valid rankings ought to be serious consultation with a number of those experts. A third approach is simply to generate more rankings, ones that emphasize criteria different from those included in the current rankings.

However, the primary point of this article is not to prescribe how to create better rankings, but rather to set forth some reasons not to be complacent, including the potential harms and omissions of the current rankings, in the hope that competing rankings published in the future will avoid some of these unintended consequences. It could be argued that this cataloguing of problems is pointless because the market will eventually correct the harms, if indeed any flow from the publication of rankings.[2] The penultimate part of this article discusses the question of why the free market might not solve the problems created by rankings.

Before discussing the harms of rankings, it is critical to distinguish between the data used to make rankings and the rankings made from the data. This article does not argue that any of the information being incorporated into rankings would be better left unpublished. In the present case, it is plain that much of the data used in law school rankings may be useful to those considering where to go to school. For example, it could be extremely helpful for a student to know the Law School Admission Test (LSAT) scores and grades of other students at the schools being considered. A student might want to go where the other students are better, worse, or similar in their ability to take standardized tests. A student might want to go where other students are better, worse, or similar in their ability to get good grades in undergraduate courses. A student might do well in an environment where the students are similar in these abilities, or where they strongly differ. For many such considerations, there is a wealth of information about law schools easily available on the Web, and *U.S. News* publications offer easy access to a few important criteria.

But law school rankings are not presentations of data or other facts. Law school rankings are opinions. It is the opinion of the editors at *U.S. News* that Yale is the best law school. The editors are forthright—unusually and surprisingly forthright—in their presentation of the mechanical calculations that lead them to their opinion. They have also been willing to improve the formula by which they determine their opinions. But none of that elevates the rankings to anything more than opinions.

One other initial caveat is in order. This article does not attempt to tally the benefits of rankings. Rankings do provide information, even if it is essentially opinion. However, the benefits of rankings ought not to be conflated with the benefits of presenting data in manageable forms. Some might argue that the *U.S. News* rankings allow a reader to find a range of schools with a given range of LSAT scores. But omnibus rankings are not necessary or even helpful for performing that function. That function is performed by any list of schools ordered by the LSAT scores of the students. For years, the Ranking Game Web site has allowed users to order law schools from top to bottom on many criteria: LSAT score, reputation, tuition, bar-passage rate, etc.[3] The *U.S. News* Web site now also offers viewers the same functionality, allowing them to rank schools according to some of the criteria it uses in the rankings. These examples show that law schools can be ranked on individual criteria without those criteria being hammered into a thin, unidimensional, omnibus ranking.

Notwithstanding that the information embedded in the rankings can be presented in many other ways, there are still some benefits of omnibus rankings of the sort published by *U.S. News.* Decision makers who lack the ability or time to consider the importance of a number of factors may make better choices in a world with rankings than in a world without them. It is likely that some prospective students would, in the absence of rankings, make errors in weighing the various criteria available to them. Some salient criteria would take on too much importance if these decision makers were presented with no more than the underlying data in an easily digested form. These purchasers of legal education, these lawyers to be, these persons of limited ability to balance multiple criteria in making an important decision, are saved from their own mental infirmities when they are presented with a unidimensional, summary calculation based on weights provided by the ranker.

I. Rankings Can Mislead Suppliers of Legal Education

Many of the stakeholders in legal education, including administrators, students, alumni, and faculty members, care about the rank of their school in the various published rankings. If important ranking systems include a given factor, schools will shift resources to improving that factor and away from factors that count for less in the rankings. This raises the issue of whether those changes in resource allocation improve legal education. If there was no systematic bias against an included factor before the rankings shifted incentives, the rankings push spending on that factor beyond the optimum. The rankings cause schools to devote too many resources to some goals and too little to others. According to Dean Kramer of Stanford Law School, "You distort your policies to preserve your ranking, that's the problem."[4] Here follows a partial list of incentives created by rankings, especially those published by *U.S. News*.

A. Focus More on Grades and Less on Undergraduate Institutions When Admitting Students

Rankings push law schools to give too much weight to some factors in their admissions decisions. Perhaps the best example is the weight given to a student's undergraduate grade point average (UGPA). This factor accounts for 10% of the *U.S. News* rankings. Schools wanting to move up in the rankings will turn down the student with a 3.4 UGPA in engineering from Rose-Hulman in favor of the applicant with a 3.8 UGPA in shuffleboard from Central Ivy State University. The data from the past seven years confirm the effect of this incentive.[5] Both the 75th and 25th percentiles have increased by at least 0.02 UGPA points per school per year, which is significant at the .001 level (regression 1, see Appendix).

There is no reason to believe that admissions committees systematically gave grades too little weight before *U.S. News*'s rankings changed the law schools' strategies. The likely consequence is that the *U.S. News* incentives have led schools away from the proper balancing of the many factors that go into determining which applicants will improve their law schools and will make the best lawyers. Factors such as honesty and empathy lose weight when grades get more attention. The only factor that has probably not lost weight in the admissions process is the LSAT, because *U.S. News* gives it even more weight than grades.

The focus on grades has secondary effects that are equally worrisome. A well-advised student hoping to get into a law school that cares about its ranking will choose an undergraduate school and courses that have inflated grades over ones with tough grading. As the importance of the UGPA increases, law aspirants will try to optimize that credential, to the detriment of their education. Do we want the seats at competitive law schools to go to those who are good at picking an easy curriculum instead of those who signed up for a challenging education?

B. Focus on the LSAT

There are two reasons for using the LSAT in law school admissions: it is the best single predictor of first-year performance, and it can be used to compare English speaking students from any point on the globe.[6] As with grades, the *U.S. News* rankings cause schools to place too much emphasis on the LSAT. Ironically, the Association of American Law Schools (AALS) may have inadvertently played a role in increasing the weight given to the LSAT. The AALS commissioned a 1998 report which concluded that virtually all of the differences in overall ranks could be explained by academic reputation and student selectivity, the latter marked primarily by the median LSAT score.[7] It found the other ten factors to be "superfluous."[8] Law schools learned from this, if they had not figured it out before, that they should place great weight on that single admissions factor. To make matters worse, the ABA stopped collecting median LSAT data from schools. It was a predictable consequence of this decision that *U.S. News* would eventually discontinue use of the median because they no longer had a way to check the accuracy of the medians submitted by the schools.[9] And in fact that was the reason given by *U.S. News* when it made that change from the median to a combination of the 25th and 75th percentiles for the 2005 ranking.[10]

U.S. News's publication of the 25th percentile and, more important, its use of that figure in its ranking formula means that a school wanting to maximize its rank should maximize its 25th percentile LSAT. Another way of saying this is that competitive schools will maximize the LSAT for 75% of their incoming "one-L" class. Some law schools have already succumbed to this temptation and today place great weight on the LSAT, considerably more weight than before rankings were regularly published. The result of this attention has been a yearly increase of 0.220 in the 75th percentile LSAT ($p < .005$), a number which is relatively difficult for schools to increase,[11] and a larger 0.467 yearly increase in the 25th percentile ($p < .001$) during the seven years after the ABA stopped collecting the LSAT medians (regression 1[12]).[13] In the world of law school admissions, staying in place has meant falling behind.

Because the LSAT and UGPA are far from perfectly correlated, maximizing one does not maximize the other. If a school wishes to maximize its medians on both the LSAT and UGPA, it will have to admit nearly all of its class on the basis of those two numbers. When schools put that much weight on the LSAT and UGPA, something has to give. This increased attention to those two criteria necessarily comes at the expense of other criteria that do not count in the *U.S. News* rankings. Those unranked criteria include honesty, integrity, gumption, creativity, and other aspects of fitness to practice as a lawyer.

Professors Marjorie Shultz and Sheldon Zedeck have made a systematic study of the activities of good lawyers. By interviewing lawyers, faculty, students, judges, and clients, they identified twenty-six factors that are important for effective lawyering. Their list includes practical judgment, creativity and innovation, passion and engagement, ability to see the world through the eyes of others, networking and business development, diligence, integrity and honesty.[14] Neither the LSAT nor the UGPA tells the extent to which a person has these qualities. For every applicant admitted on the basis of his LSAT or UGPA, the law school must admit one fewer applicant on the basis of such other indicators of merit.

Each law school admissions committee should be free to attach what weight it considers to be appropriate to all of an applicant's indices of promise for future contributions as law students and practitioners, without any special concern for how the admission of that student would influence its school's rank in *U.S. News*. But committees are constrained. The effect of *U.S. News* rankings on the law school market is similar to that of a command and control economy, with the resulting loss in experimentation and other benefits of decentralized decision making. Rather than 180 different schools deciding independently how much weight to give these two numbers in their attempts to attract and cater to different segments of the market, *U.S. News* commands all schools that care about their rank to use LSAT score and UGPA as the key, essentially exclusive, indicia of student quality.

Law school admissions are decisions with large societal implications. If we were to ask the American public, do you want lawyers in the future to have more cleverness or more integrity, which would they choose? If they would choose integrity, schools are sacrificing the traits the public wants in the quest for higher *U.S. News* rankings. What characteristics should a defendant want in his lawyer when his life is on the line in a capital case? What qualities should citizens want in an official making policy for the government? These are not the attributes being selected for when schools reserve most of their seats for those who are tops in bubble ability, the skill at taking multiple-choice standardized exams. The public interest is not well served when lawyers are those who are good at taking such tests rather than those who are good at written and oral expression. The nation is not strengthened when law schools deemphasize quality of undergraduate school, rigor of courses taken, business and military experience, social intelligence, and interpersonal skills. The effect of *U.S. News* rankings is to give the admissions edge to the applicant with a 163 LSAT who partied hard throughout college over the applicant with a 161 who spent a few years as a soldier and then started a successful business before taking the LSAT. As the influence of *U.S. News* reaches deeper into the admissions process, service to the country through the Marines or Peace Corps, ability to communicate orally with actual human beings, empathy, and a sense of justice will all be forsaken in the pursuit of higher numbers.

The costs of misguided admissions processes are not limited to the world of professional lawyers. Many graduates use their legal educations in non-legal occupations. Law school has become a sort of general education, widely recognized as useful in many positions of leadership within both the public and private sectors. If law schools are admitting the wrong students, the effects may be broadly felt.

There are many indicators of quality in the files of applicants, but *U.S. News* creates an incentive to ignore them all in favor of the LSAT and UGPA. However, this is not inevitable. Rankings could continue to employ LSAT and UGPA data without causing schools to focus entirely on those criteria. *U.S. News* could use each school's 75th percentiles on the LSAT and UGPA as its measures of student quality rather than including the medians or 25th percentiles in the ranking formula.[15] This change would reduce the effects of rankings on admissions practices because maximizing a class's 75th percentile on any criterion can be done with one-half as many students as it takes to maximize the median and only one-third as many students as it takes to maximize the 25th percentile. For a school to maximize its 75th percentiles on both the LSAT and UGPA, it would need to admit no more than one-half of the class by the LSAT and UGPA. Thus, the proposed change would cut in half the portion of the class admitted solely on those numbers, leaving much more discretion with the admissions personnel at each school to admit the students they think will make the greatest contributions as law students and lawyers.[16] Each school would have more freedom than is currently allowed to make its own determination of which students it wishes to admit without worrying about how those decisions will affect its rank in *U.S. News*.[17]

Were this proposal adopted, there would still be a fight over students, and it would be a fight over a smaller pool of students, but each school would need fewer students to make its goal. Because the fight would be over a smaller pool, many students would get large tuition breaks; indeed, many would be offered a full ride. In some ways, this would make the 75th percentile LSAT an even better indicator of school quality. Tuition differences would be wiped out and students would choose among full-ride offers based on other factors. Students' choices would be better measures of their perceptions of quality than when they are influenced by cost considerations. This could have another benefit: more students would get complete scholarships than under the current system. Prospective students would have to be in a school's top 25% to qualify, but many students would be in the top quarter at some school. Since more students would be able to attend for free, more students from the lower economic strata would have an opportunity to attend law school.

Some might argue that a single statistic, the 75th percentile, does not give an accurate picture of student quality. At one time in the past, that might have been true because schools were not so focused on the UGPA and LSAT. But now they are, and what was once a description is now a prescription for success in the rankings. Many schools have striven to increase both percentiles. What will happen if *U.S. News* switches to using just the 75th percentile on the LSAT and UGPA? The switch will make almost no difference to the ranks of schools. In the short run, there is little difference between who will win the competition by the 75th percentile LSAT or a combination of the 75th and 25th because the two figures tell the same story. Using *U.S. News*'s 2004 data, the correlation between the 75th percentile LSAT and the average of the 75th and 25th for all schools is .991. So, although the switch would not affect the ranks of the schools, it would allow schools more freedom to admit students with low numbers. In the long run, some schools would probably make use of this new freedom, and their 25th percentile numbers would decrease. Of course, the 25th percentiles for the schools would continue to be published, so the question is not whether the public would lose information. Rather, the question is whether it is somehow illegitimate for *U.S. News* to ignore that decrease and leave the schools where they are in the rankings. Since the schools are taking students that they think will improve the school or make better lawyers than the applicants with higher numbers that they rejected, it is legitimate to consider the student body to be just as strong as it would have been if the committee had competed with other schools solely on the basis of the numbers.

The point of this proposal is not to eliminate the LSAT from the admissions process, nor even to dethrone it from its seat as the primary factor for many files. The point is to let schools use the LSAT as they see fit. With only a minuscule effect on its ranks, the change by *U.S. News* to using only the 75th percentiles on LSAT and UGPA could dramatically reduce the harmful long-term effects of rankings on law school admissions.[18]

Another alternative that would decrease the impact of the rankings on admissions would be for *U.S. News* to change the ranking criteria from the LSAT and UGPA medians to the median of an index that combines the two. However, because *U.S. News* needs a verifiable number for its rankings, this can only occur if the Law School Admission Council constructs a single index score for each student. As an administrative matter, this would be a trivial task. Of course, the ABA would also have to require that each school report its median index score.

Currently under consideration is another proposal aimed at preventing *U.S. News* rankings from causing schools to overweight the LSAT in admissions. The idea is to replace the current LSAT scores with scores that are scaled separately for each school. There are at least two problems with such a maneuver. First, placing each school on a different scale would make it much more difficult for students to gauge their chances of admission to any school. Second, unless the same were done for grades, *U.S. News* might simply put all of the weight on the UGPA, exacerbating the undesirable incentives and educational consequences noted above.

C. Tweak Other Aspects of the Admissions Process to Increase Numbers

There are a number of other admissions changes a school can make to increase its rank according to *U.S. News*. Below are some of them. None has been shown to improve law education; more likely, they would degrade it.

1. Admit Fewer "One-L" Students and Allow More Transfer Students

The importance of LSATs and UGPAs to a school's rank has created an incentive for schools to reduce the size of the first-year class. With a smaller class it is easier to achieve a high median. To maintain revenues, however, a school reducing the size of the one-L class will need to increase the number of transfer students. This possibility is troubling. There is almost no conceivable benefit to the students who have to start at one school and then move from that school to a preferred school. There is clearly no benefit to the schools losing their more successful students. Aside from increasing ranks, there is also negligible benefit to the schools to which the transfer students are moving. Although schools may argue that transfer students have proved themselves worthy, which they have, if there were a substantial net benefit to the importing schools from skimming large numbers of second-year students from other schools, law schools would have had extensive transfer programs in the past.

Not only is there little benefit to the receiving school, there is a pedagogical cost. Although the lists of first-year courses are similar from campus to campus, any law school worth a high rating will be striving for an integrity of program across the years. Students who have not taken a school's first-year curriculum may learn less in subsequent years and may contribute less to the learning of other students in their classes. A responsible teacher cannot assume that transfer students have been exposed to the basic conceptual building blocks taught in the one-L curriculum. The teacher has to either cover that material again, to the detriment of the students who have been through it, or push on in spite of the fact that some of the students are not prepared, to the detriment of the transfer students.

If this incentive takes hold, average class size will change. The first-year class will become smaller, compared to graduation class size or school size, at those schools to which students want to transfer. A lagged, opposite reaction might appear in the schools from which they move to make up for the students lost through the transfer process. The net effect will not be positive for the students in either group of schools.

2. Reject Some Students with High LSAT Scores

Of the students a school accepts, it is hardest to matriculate those with the highest LSAT scores. Admitting a student with a high LSAT score means admitting a student likely to reject the offer of admission. If "yield" or "acceptance ratio" is a factor in the rankings, as it has been in the *U.S. News* rankings, a school might improve its ranking by rejecting these students. This practice would clearly not be in the interest of the rejected student, and most faculty members would think it does not further the educational mission of a school to reject those applicants with high scores simply because of those high scores. Of course, the LSAT is also a factor in the rankings, so schools will not take this practice so far that they accept just the lowest LSAT candidates. A school maximizing its ranking will reject only those students that are unlikely to accept, the ones with the highest LSAT scores. One way for schools to do this is to interview those students with the highest LSAT scores and accept only those who declare they will matriculate. This process will waste time and could result in students being inappropriately denied admission.

3. Reject Students with Limited Prospects for Employment

If one of the ranking criteria is employment rates, as it has been for *U.S. News*, a school can improve its ranking by accepting only those applicants who appear to be employable. One way to do this is to inquire as to whether the applicant has contacts in the business or law world, so that she will be likely to get a job regardless of performance in law school. Of course, favoring applicants with "old-boy" connections operates to the disadvantage of those from underprivileged backgrounds. Such favoritism also operates to the disadvantage of the educational program of the school when those that are displaced would have made more useful additions to the class.

4. Focus Scholarship Money on Applicants with LSAT Scores Just Above the Median

A scholarship dollar given to one student is a dollar not available to others. In the past, most schools have offered substantial aid to some top students. Since, at most schools, a student with an LSAT score of 177 is half as useful in improving the school's median LSAT as two students with LSAT scores of 168, it would be better to offer two half-sized scholarships to two students with LSAT scores of 168 instead of one full-sized scholarship to a student with a 177 LSAT score. The effect of this could be to draw into the profession fewer of the students with the very highest LSAT scores, by reducing the number of full rides that are available. Notice that the schools that once offered a full ride to the students with an LSAT score of 168 might also switch to offering half a scholarship to two students with LSAT scores of 163. There are countervailing effects here, and the situation is complex, but it is not clear that any of those effects on the supply of talented lawyers are being considered in the struggle to increase ranks.

D. Start a Part-Time Program

Since only full-time students are included in the LSAT or UGPA figures, it behooves a school to start a part-time program and fill it with the matriculants having the lowest admissions numbers. Once again, there is little benefit for the student and not much in it for the school aside from the boost to its rank.

E. Focus the Curriculum on What Is Needed for Bar Passage

Setting aside, for the moment, whether bar passage is a valid measure of school quality, there is no doubt that many schools are paying more attention to it than they did in the past. And bar passage rates may be rising. That is not necessarily a good sign. If there were reason to believe that schools gave too little attention to lessons oriented toward bar passage, improved bar passage could signal an improvement in the curriculum. But there is no reason for such an assumption. Indeed, increasing the relative amount of attention schools pay to bar passage will redound to the detriment of students.

Will teachers teach better if they are told by their seniors and the administration that it is critically important that no one fail the bar on their subject? Teachers that care to please their seniors and the dean will dumb down the essentials so they can be comprehended and retained by the weakest students. They need not worry about the upper portion of the class (from the upper third to the upper 90%, depending on the school) because those students will pass the bar anyway. Teachers concerned primarily with bar passage will teach to the bottom of the class to assure that no student is left behind. Perhaps this would work an improvement. But if so, why have teachers not adopted this strategy already? Would an informed student prefer to attend the school where the teachers are trying hardest to make sure no one fails the bar exam? It is not clear that leaving no law student behind is the best pedagogical policy. This is not to say that schools should not devote resources to helping all students leap the bar. But it is clear that rankings put pressure on schools to change their curriculum in ways that will not produce a net gain. Moreover, if dumbing down the lessons is successful, bar examiners might respond by raising the cut score for passage and, if they do, schools will be under pressure to devote even more time to bar passage and less to teaching important knowledge and skills. The result could well be a detrimental change in the curriculum, without any increase in overall bar passage.

Focusing on bar passage creates another problematic incentive. An admissions committee can help the school on this criterion by rejecting students that are less likely to pass the bar. For example, some students hail from states with difficult bars, such as New Hampshire, California, West Virginia, Alabama, Maine, Maryland, Virginia, and New Jersey. If they are likely to return to their home states to practice, all else equal, a school will be better off rejecting them in favor of students from states with an easy bar. More generally, as noted above, there are many characteristics that are important to building a good lawyer. When bar passage is a factor in the rankings, schools have an incentive to ignore those characteristics in favor of ones that increase the chances the student will pass his or her first bar exam. Should a school deny admission to Mother Teresa if it predicts that she might not pass a bar exam until her second try?

F. Spend Money on Glossy, Colorful Advertising

Since the single largest factor in the *U.S. News* rankings is the reputation among legal academics, schools seeking to raise their reputations have started spending substantial sums on glossy promotional publications and mailing them to legal academics and practicing lawyers. According to one law dean, "Tons of money—not just here, but at other law schools around the country—is being spent on public relations now that was never spent before."[19] A few years ago, one school hoping to make a splash sent a large and colorful poster with a marine motif to all law professors at Indiana University-Bloomington, and presumably many other law schools. Setting aside whether such tactics sacrifice long-run interests for gains that will show up during a dean's tenure, it is doubtful that attempts to increase the "visibility" of schools will advance the legal well-being of society.

G. Raise Tuition for All, but Increase Scholarships for Those with Numbers

Since having more resources matters to *U.S. News*, it is in the interest of a school to raise tuition and give much of it back to the students in the form of scholarships. Thus, by an accounting change, a school can raise its rank without changing the economics of the relationships between the school and its students. But schools might not stop there. Once tuition has been raised, schools could decide that the scholarships need not be granted equally to all students. They could be used to help those who lack financial resources, but if that were the goal it would have been done already. Instead, the school will recognize that the new revenues could be used to attract those with high LSAT and UGPA numbers. One unwelcome side effect would be a reduction in access to legal education for persons of limited financial means.

H. Pay Your Own Utilities

Other accounting practices can make a similar difference to a school's rank in *U.S. News*. At some schools, the university provides the electricity to the law school and deducts the cost from the tuition paid by the law students.[20] The school never sees the money, and it is not part of its resources. Such schools could increase the resources reported to *U.S. News* by collecting the tuition directly from the students and paying the university for the electricity and other services provided by the university.

I. Encourage Everyone and Her Sister to Apply

Since it may be important to have a high rejection ratio, it is important to get every possible applicant to apply for admission. This includes students that have no chance of being accepted. It may be necessary to waive the application fee, but that financial cost could be worth the gains in rank, especially since some of those applicants would not have applied if they had been required to pay a fee. Once applications are up, it becomes even more important to sift them out using the numbers because it is expensive to have committee members study stacks of applications looking for the gems.

J. Hire Your Own

When nine months after graduation rolls around, a school should check to see whether there are any unemployed graduates and hire them so that its employment numbers, which count for a lot in the *U.S. News* rankings, look good.

K. Make It Difficult for Faculty Members to Leave in the Fall

To increase the faculty/student ratio, all possible faculty members must be counted. According to the reporting rules, they are counted in the fall semester. So, schools maximizing their rank could make it difficult for faculty members to leave in the fall. Sabbaticals and other extended leaves will be taken primarily in the spring. This may have the effect of leaving students with too few spring options for learning experiences. If there were no such seasonal incentive created by *U.S. News*, faculty leaves could be divided more or less evenly across the fall and spring semesters, giving students a more useful distribution of courses.

It appears that this tactic might not work in the future. Since the ABA has now decided to collect spring faculty counts in addition to the fall counts and *U.S. News* will use both in an annualized approach, there will be no advantage to allowing faculty members to take leaves only in the spring. The fact that some schools had more faculty members teaching in the fall than in the spring suggests that schools were paying close attention to the incentives created by *U.S. News*. If the balance shifts toward the spring in future years, that will be some evidence that schools were heeding the incentive to have an unbalanced faculty.

L. Increase the Number of "Books" in the "Library"

Libraries are expensive. But not all books are. A school wanting to move up in rank could buy a truckload of cheap books and put them in an "off-site" library annex. If the reporting authorities wise up and require them to be "on-site," schools may stick the books in the basement or attic. Will this increase the net social welfare? Storage space may be cheap, but it is not free and this would be a waste of that resource, as well as an attempt to mislead the public about the quality of the school.

M. Decrease Funding for the Library and Other Units with an Abnormally High Proportion of Positive Externalities

U.S. News creates incentives for schools not to spend too much on library resources. For example, given that the Indiana University School of Law-Bloomington's ("IU-B") law library is ranked above the IU-B Law School, IU-B may be spending too much on its library. This conclusion is not based on a fair appraisal of the value of a great library to the students or faculty, or to the people of the state of Indiana for that matter. Instead, this conclusion reflects the fact that the money spent on the library could give IU-B a better bump in rank if spent on other factors, such as tutorials for students who might not pass the bar. This would clearly be the wrong way to decide how much to spend on a law library. But this is what *U.S. News*, in effect, tells IU-B to do to maintain or improve its position. On the other hand, because library volumes are a factor, *U.S. News* also creates an incentive not to spend too little on the library.

II. General Effects

A. U.S. News *Rankings Could Homogenize Legal Education*

This point about library resources, that a school needs to get the library budget just right, neither spending too much nor too little, applies to other criteria as well. One effect of the hegemony of the *U.S. News* rankings is to create an incentive for schools to calculate and aim for an optimal mix of expenditures. What this means is that *U.S. News* may unwittingly be homogenizing legal education. With time, schools will learn which spending mix yields the greatest rankings bang and the optimum mix will tend to be the same for most schools. *U.S. News* will make it increasingly hard to experiment with different ways of producing an extraordinary product.

A corollary of this homogenization effect is that schools will find it unrewarding to seek a market niche. The *U.S. News* formula discourages diversity and specialization in curricula. For example, a six-hour quantitative methods course of the type once required of first-year students at George Mason could discourage applicants. This could narrow the appeal of the school, which would in turn decrease its LSAT index. It is discouraging to imagine that future instructional innovations might not be implemented because of concerns about the effect on a school's rank in *U.S. News*. Creatively tailored programs could certainly improve some law schools' offerings to students and society, yet it will be a rare school in the upper half that will take the risk of radical innovation or narrow specialization. Law schools are in danger of losing the freedom to create first-class products for the needs of varying consumers and stakeholders.

It could be argued that rankings of law schools will not homogenize legal education any more than the ranking of cars by *Consumer Reports* homogenizes automobile production. But the markets are not the same because car buyers are more able to think and evaluate for themselves. First, car buyers can take a meaningful test drive. A day in the classroom does not give prospective students much of an idea of what it will be like to buy an education from a school. Second, automobile consumers can easily see that factors like handling, acceleration, size, or gas mileage might be more important to them than to *Consumer Reports* testers; law prospects are less able to re-evaluate the weights *U.S. News* attaches to its criteria.[21] Third, consumers in the auto market are repeat players and can learn from previous experiences, while no one buys two J.D.s. Fourth, *Consumer Reports* does not have nearly as much influence on the ultimate value of the product being purchased as *U.S. News* has on the market value of a law degree. Although car buyers might wish to resell the car in the future, those sales are a relatively small factor in selection. Law students buy a product that they will resell at many points in the future, and that resale value is a much larger portion of what they are paying for. Because law students do not expect to drive their degrees into the ground, they cannot afford to ignore the predictions of future market value. For these reasons, rankings of law programs have more power than other rankings to homogenize their products.

If *U.S. News* changed the weights in accordance with the advice of a different panel each year, the rankings would be less likely to homogenize law schools. This would also reduce the sense that the rankings actually reflect a true order of quality, which might encourage consumers to place their own weights on the various factors instead of unquestioningly following *U.S. News*. This might be good for *U.S. News* too, as there would be some reason to buy the new issue instead of relying on the ranking from the previous year.

U.S. News has created a prisoner's dilemma. Each school will rank higher if it defers to *U.S. News*. But all schools will be worse off for that deference. All schools are trying to matriculate the students with high LSAT scores, but the pool of students is not improved. Many schools will end up with smaller first year classes, but more students will have to switch schools part way through their education. All schools will teach to the bar exam, and curricular integrity will diminish. Schools will have an "optimal" library, with fewer expensive books and more donated ones. And for all this, most schools will stay put in the rankings. There can be no net gain for schools as a whole since for every rank step ascended another school must drop a rank. Eventually, law schools may follow the strategems of football coaches, but no one will be better served—neither students nor the society that awaits their services.

B. U.S. News *Is Stratifying Law Schools by LSAT*

Many schools have tried to increase their 75th and 25th percentiles on the LSAT. At the same time, students have been influenced by *U.S. News* in choosing schools. If schools want the highest LSAT scores they can get, they will deny admission to those with scores below the 25th percentile, or the median if that is the critical number. If students choose the highest-ranked schools among those that accept them, they will tend to apply to and attend the school with the highest LSAT numbers, since that correlates highly with the overall ranks. Given these tendencies, over time, the range of student LSAT scores to be found at any school should narrow and there will be an increasing stratification of schools by LSAT score.[22] Indeed, this appears to have occurred. When the difference between LSAT 75th percentile and LSAT 25th percentile was regressed on the year, the year was a significant predictor ($p < .001$). Over the past seven years, the gap has shrunk by one-fourth of an LSAT point per year (regression 1).

Whether this is good or bad is open to debate. It reduces the diversity of LSAT scores in the classroom, making it less likely that students will learn how to negotiate with and make arguments to lawyers who differ in whatever abilities it is that the LSAT measures. If the LSAT does not measure much of importance, this reduction of LSAT ability is not important. But if the LSAT does measure an important difference, classroom uniformity might be detrimental to student learning. This stratification will also exacerbate the LSAT differences between the majority and the students admitted to achieve other sorts of diversity. In the past, the diversity students' LSAT scores blended into the wide range of LSAT scores in the class. As the variation on the LSAT within a school decreases, the LSATs of diversity students will be more noticeably different. On the other hand, some might argue that teaching is more efficient when all students have similar LSAT scores, although there is no formal study supporting this view. Setting aside the issue of whether the stratification is good or bad, it could be argued that by pushing schools to matriculate a narrower band of students, the *U.S. News* rankings have encroached upon one of the "four essential freedoms' of a university—to determine for itself ... who may be admitted to study."[23]

III. Rankings Mislead Buyers of Legal Education

A. The Criteria Used in Rankings Have Not Been Validated

Judging by the sales of *U.S. News*'s rankings, many people want to know about the nation's law schools. The readers want advice, and the rankings provide evaluations done on the cheap. Like many rankings, those published by *U.S. News* are based on a number of factors, most of which make use of readily available data. Many of these criteria are of no inherent interest to the readers of the rankings. A prospective law student wanting to work as a lawyer has no particular interest in the amount of money a school spends, the number of volumes in the library, the grades of the other students in the class, or even the reputation of the school among academics because such reputations are built primarily on faculty publications and not teaching quality.[24] Criteria for rankings are surrogates for experienced quality. The substitutions are poorly declared.

These criteria that are not directly useful are pressed together into a ranking on the unstated theory that they are proxies for what applicants should care about. Readers, and perhaps even the editors at *U.S. News*, assume that there is an integrity of the law school whole that allows the reader to conclude that if the school is good on those measurables, it will also be good on the immeasurables about which the reader truly wants to know. But this assumption is unjustified. First, the data from which the rankings extrapolate are not necessarily correlated to the criteria readers would like to know about, such as whether the school can provide a quality education, or more generally, whether a student's professional or personal life will turn out better for having gone to one school over another. No one has done the careful study needed to validate the criteria by determining whether the available numbers are indeed indicators of the many dimensions of true quality.

Second, even if the criteria used by *U.S. News* were once good indicators, there is little reason to believe that they continue to be good indicators now that they have been announced to the contestants in this ranking game. In other words, the data going into the *U.S. News* rankings are subject to manipulation. Setting aside outright fraud, by employing the strategies discussed above schools can improve themselves on the criteria while doing nothing to improve the whole program, indeed while diminishing the value of the law school experience to their students. For these reasons, the rankings are disconnected from what many readers want to know.

Even if the criteria used by the rankings were shown to be good indicators of what readers want to know, or should want to know, the method used by *U.S. News* to combine the factors into a unidimensional ranking has not been shown to be a valid method for doing so. In other words, the ranks, like the underlying criteria, have not been validated as useful measures of what is important to those choosing a law school.

B. Rankings Devalue Important Criteria

In addition to the serious problem that the rankings have not been validated, the rankings may make matters worse for readers by interfering with the processing of information by the readers who have the ability to balance multiple factors. Numerical indices carry a false air of precision which may lead some readers to give them too much weight.[25] Rankings can cause a prospective student to think a school is better or worse for her than it actually is.

Even when the applicant is not directly rerouted by the rankings, he may be indirectly misguided. By placing all schools on the same scale, rankings give readers the impression that law schools are all trying to win the same competition, that they all have the same goals, that they all serve the same interests and needs. The truth is otherwise. The functions of law schools are many, from providing research and scholarship about the law to preparing students for legal practice. Even within the mission of preparing students, the range is wide, from research and teaching in the academy, to governmental and nongovernmental policy making, to advancing the goals of corporate clients in the national and international markets, to serving the needs of average Americans in matters from the mundane to those of life and death. Unidimensional rankings obscure the multiplicity of roles law schools play in the training of lawyers. The mere inclusion of numerous factors in the rankings does not acknowledge the complexity of purposes in legal education.

Rankings can also indirectly influence students by drawing them away from criteria they think important. Factors left out of the rankings seem less important because of it. Some criteria, like quality of teaching, are hard to define and quantify, and so do not get included directly in the current rankings. Other criteria, like the personal feeling of whether a school would be a comfortable fit, are especially subjective, and cannot be included in published rankings. Still other criteria, like the distance from the school to loved ones and scholarships offered, are quantifiable, but are idiosyncratic to the student, and again cannot be included in rankings published in the mass media. An open letter from many law school deans to prospective students cites many factors that students identify as important, many of which are not considered in the *U.S. News* rankings.[26] The point here is that these omissions not only undermine the value of the rankings but also may have the effect of unjustifiably devaluing criteria that are important to the reader. By their reassuring appearance of objectivity, the rankings lead readers away from criteria they care about to criteria less central to their goals. An applicant might choose Pepperdine University School of Law over Indiana University School of Law-Indianapolis based on Pepperdine's move into the top 100 and IU-Indianapolis's small drop within the second 50, when in fact she would have a much worse experience at consciously religious Pepperdine because she is an atheist. Thus, a person who could weigh the factors on her own might be led to place undue weight on the rankings or their underlying criteria, with the result that she makes a poor decision.

C. Presentations of Data as Ranks Are Inherently Misleading

All rankings present data in a misleading way. They appear accurate and validated, but they actually throw away information. Take, for example, the magnitude of differences. Rankings, unlike measurements or even the summary scores built from measurements, make schools appear less different or more different in overall quality than they actually are. The true differences between closely ranked schools are sometimes small, sometimes large, but are always portrayed as having the same magnitude.

Assume for an imaginary moment that the *U.S. News* criteria are the best indicators of legal education quality and that the *U.S. News* weighting is optimal for the applicant; in other words, assume that the final scores given by *U.S. News* are suitable, at least with regard to the criteria included. Judging by the output of the 2005 *U.S. News* formula, any two schools ranked between 39th and 102nd are less different in quality than the schools ranked 1st and 6th. A difference of sixty places near the middle of the rankings represents about the same difference as six places near the top of the rankings. If a person could sensibly see Chicago (#6) as superior to Yale (#1), then a person could also sensibly see Kansas (#100) as superior to Ohio State (#39). According to *U.S. News*, the difference in quality between Stanford (#3) and Michigan (#8) is greater than the difference between school number 49 and school number 95. The difference between school number 77 and school number 99 is the same as the difference between school number 5 and school number 6. The difference in quality between school number 58 and school number 83 is less than the difference between school 1 and school 2. Thus, according to *U.S. News*, an applicant would make a smaller educational "sacrifice" by choosing Seton Hall (#83) over Loyola (CA) (#58) than choosing by Harvard (#2) over Yale (#1). Of course some students read the rankings correctly, recognizing the microscopic size of middle-range differences in overall quality, and recognizing that mere noise in measured factors can cause large changes in rank. But others appear to attach more importance to the differences in ranks than those differences deserve, judging by the conversations that take place on the Web when new rankings come out.

In the lower half of the ranks, *U.S. News* ignores minute differences by grouping schools into two tiers. This also creates problems. While the difference between the top school in Tier Three and the bottom school in Tier Four might be meaningful, there are other pairs of schools more closely straddling the border between tier three and tier four. For those schools, the division into tiers grossly exaggerates the insignificant differences in overall quality between them.

Figure 1 shows the difference between presenting the scores and presenting the ranks of *U.S. News*'s top 102 schools. The curved line shows that after an initial drop, projected quality diminishes very gradually, at least for the schools included. The lower line graphically represents the fact that ranks continue to drop by the same amount whether the quality differences are large or small. The line is stepped at the bottom because *U.S. News* does not present the ranks of the bottom 77 schools but merely breaks them into groups. This lower line shows the problem with presenting schools in clusters. Such groupings will probably exaggerate the difference between schools across borders of the clusters whose scores are not that different. Finally, note the divergence of the two lines. The difference between the two is a graphic representation of one form of distortion inherent in the *U.S. News* rankings.

Figure 1.

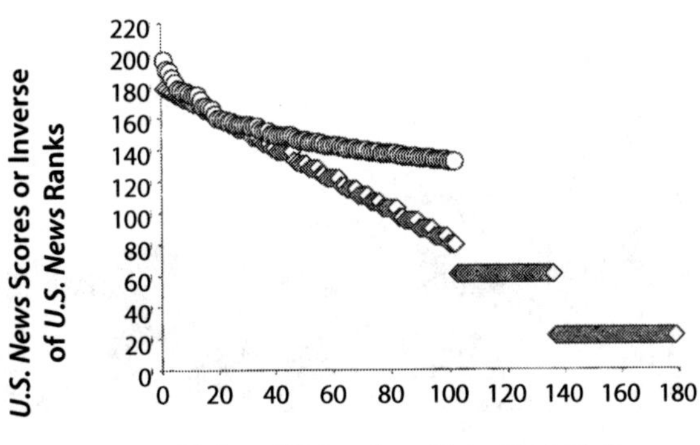

Graphical Presentation of the Difference Between Ranks and Scores, using *U.S. News* Ranks and *U.S. News* Scores for *U.S. News*'s top 102 schools and *U.S. News* ranks for all 179 schools. *Squares* = inverse of *U.S. News* ranks; *circles* = *U.S. News* scores (linearly transformed). The actual *U.S. News* ranks are subtracted from 180. In order to put them on a similar scale, the actual *U.S. News* scores are transformed linearly by adding 97 (making the tangent at school 20). While the shapes of the curves are not arbitrary (one is linear with steps and the other is curved), how they intersect is arbitrary and depends on the choices for the constant used in the transformation of scores. Regardless of which constant is chosen, however, the basic point remains: presenting the differences as ranks distorts those differences in some way. *Data Source: America's Best Graduate Schools: Schools of Law*, U.S. NEWS & WORLD REP., Apr. 11, 2005, at 72–73.

One way of reducing the likelihood that students will exaggerate the differences between schools is to present the differences graphically. One example would be a scatter plot of scores plotted against full-time resident tuition for *U.S. News*'s top 102 schools, as shown in Figure 2.

Figure 2.

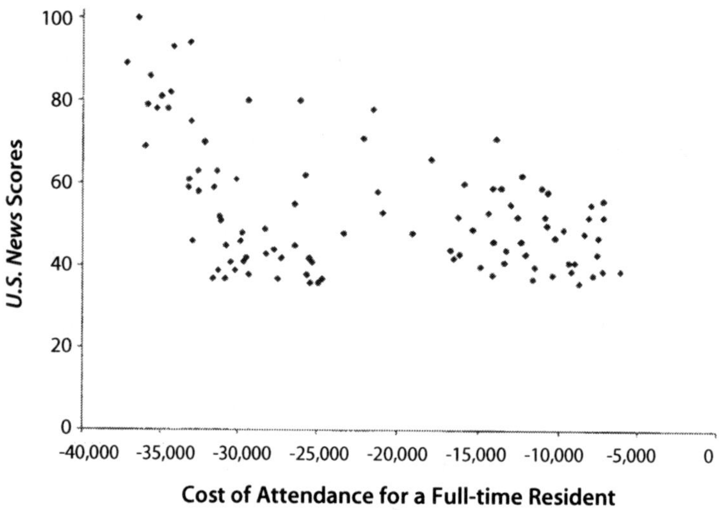

Scatter plot of the *U.S. News* score for the top 102 schools plotted against the cost for a full-time resident to attend. *Data Sources: America's Best Graduate Schools: Schools of Law*, U.S. NEWS & WORLD REP., Apr. 11, 2005, at 72–73.

Another way to present these differences is to graph the scores rather than list them by rank, as in Figure 3.

Figure 3.

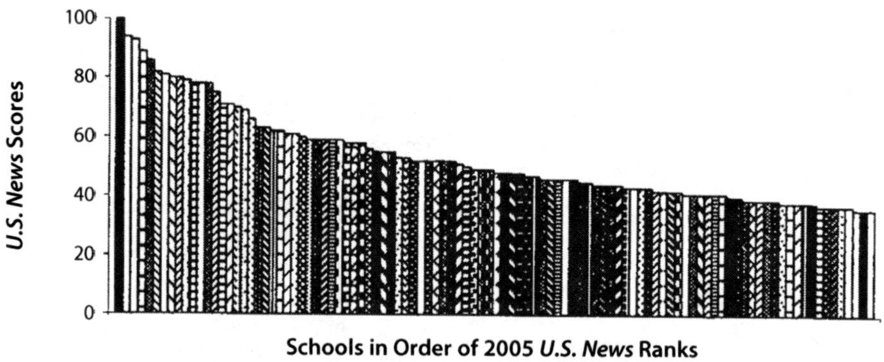

Figure 3. Bar graph showing the top 102 schools by score. *Data Source: America's Best Graduate Schools: Schools of Law*, U.S. NEWS & WORLD REP., Apr. 11, 2005, at 72–73.

Although presentation of differences via rankings is misleading enough, combining rankings to create other rankings is even more dangerous. Suppose that two criteria, *A* and *B*, are to be combined into one summary score. On criterion *A*, three schools score

10, 2, and 0. On criterion *B*, they score 4, 5, and 6. Their ranks are 1st, 2nd, and 3rd, respectively on criterion *A*, and 3rd, 2nd, and 1st on criterion *B*. Combining these ranks will give the three schools the same final score, all tying for first place. Turning cardinal numbers into ordinal ranks has thrown away information. If each point of achievement on the two criteria is equally important to the evaluator, the underlying scores should be added, yielding 14, 7, and 6, which shows that one school is substantially better than the other two, which are close but not the same. If the two criteria, rather than the points achievable on the two criteria, are of equal importance to the evaluator, then the scores should be standardized, yielding combined *z*-scores of 0.16, -0.46, and 0.30, showing the third school to be the best, by a small margin over the first and a large margin over the second.[27] In either case, using the underlying scores instead of the ranks preserves the information as to relative differences. Using rankings in numerical processes is a bad idea; garbage in, garbage out.

D. The Very Act of Publishing Rankings Distorts U.S. News's Reputation Measures

1. *U.S. News* Itself Has Changed How Law Professors View Law Schools

a. Two Hypotheses

The annual rankings of law schools by *U.S. News* do not go unnoticed by members of law faculties. In addition, law professors have very little information about the quality of programs at many competing schools. Given this concern about the rankings and the lack of information from other sources, it would not be a shock to find that *U.S. News* has influenced how law schools were ranked by the law professors that it surveyed. One would expect *U.S. News* to have pulled the reputation of a school among law teachers toward that school's previous ranking by *U.S. News*. For example, if the faculty reputation score of School *X* in a given year was 10th best and *U.S. News* ranked School *X* at 20th that same year, the faculty reputation score would probably move down toward 20th in the following year.

If this is true, the early *U.S. News* rankings may have become self-fulfilling prophecies of the value of schools' degrees. The schools ranked highly by *U.S. News* moved up in faculty reputation score and tended to stay there, and the schools that got low initial rankings moved down. In other words, the rankings were reflexive; there was an echo effect.[28] In the spring, *U.S. News* pronounced Yale to be number one. In the fall *U.S. News* listened carefully for new opinions. But what it really heard coming back was the echo of its own previous publication.

This echo effect would be expected to diminish over time. Suppose the reputation of School *X*, in the hypothetical example above, moves to 15th in year two. Because that reputation is a part of the *U.S. News* rank in year two, but is dragging *X* down less than in year one, *X*'s overall *U.S. News* rank should move up, say to 9th, in year two. In year three, the same thing occurs, with *X*'s reputation moving to perhaps 11th and its overall *U.S. News* rank moving to 8th. In year four, the reputation moves to 8th, the same as the overall rank. Eventually, the system reaches equilibrium and when it does the *U.S. News* ranks will have no more ability to pull the reputations. Of course, if the other factors change, the system never stabilizes completely, but the amount of room for the *U.S. News* ranks to pull the reputations will not be large. Thus, over time, the echo effect should diminish.

From these thoughts, two hypotheses emerge:

1. The *U.S. News* rankings changed law school reputations among the law professors they surveyed.
2. The yearly influence of *U.S. News* on reputations diminished over time.

b. Numerical Evidence

Richard Schmalbeck found in an earlier examination of specific law schools that overall rankings had little or no effect on reputations.[29] So, a more comprehensive examination is in order.

To test the two hypotheses, academic reputation ranks in year $T + 1$ were regressed on academic reputation ranks in year T and *U.S. News* overall scores in year T. The regression was:

$$academicrank_{T+1} = [beta]_0 + [beta]_1{}^* \ academicrank_T + [beta]_2 + usnews_T$$

where $[beta]_1$ and $[beta]_2$ are statistical weights for the two predictors and $[beta]_0$ is a constant. Each year's data, except for the first (1990) and last (2004), was used twice, once as year T and then again as year $T + 1$. Of course the previous year's academic rank was a very strong predictor of the new academic rank; one would not expect much variation in academic reputation from year to year. But the *U.S. News* score was also a predictor of the new academic ranks and was significant at the .05 level (regression 2). A second regression added twenty-six interaction terms, thirteen dummies for years times each of the two variables. In this regression, the *U.S. News* rank in year T increased in significance to the .001 level (regression 3).

For another regression, academic reputation scores were converted into ranks. These academic reputation ranks were compared to *U.S. News* ranks. A difference between the academic reputation rank and the *U.S. News* rank should lead to a change in the same direction in the academic reputation rank in the following year. New variables were constructed from the differences. One new variable was academic rank in year T minus *U.S. News* rank in year T. Another new constructed variable was academic rank in year T minus academic rank in year $T + 1$. If the first hypothesis is correct, the latter new variable should be a function of the former new variable. So, the regression equation was:

$$academicrank_T - academicrank_{T+1} = [beta]_0 + [beta]_1(academicrank_T - usnewsrank_T).$$

Aside from the conversion of scores to ranks,[30] this regression equation is mathematically similar to the previous one, but is more restricted in that the coefficients for $academicrank_T$ and $usnewsrank_T$ are linked together. The result was that the difference between *U.S. News* rank and academic rank was a predictor of the subsequent change in the academic rank, significant at the .001 level (regression 4).[31] This effect was stronger for the schools that were in *U.S. News*'s top 17 in 1990. For the top 17, the coefficient is .200, and for the schools not in the top 17 the coefficient is .045 (regressions 11–12). This difference is significant ($p < 0.05$) (regression 14). It appears that professors of law are following *U.S. News*, and following more closely for the schools initially ranked in the top 17.

The second hypothesis was that this correlation would diminish with time. To test this, the years were divided into halves, T before 1997 and after 1996, and separate regressions were performed on the two subsets. For the earlier years, the difference between

U.S. News and the academic rank was a significant (at the .001 level) predictor of the coming change in academic rank and had a coefficient of .102. For the later years, the difference was not a significant predictor and had a coefficient of .028 (regression 4). A dummy variable for the early years was interacted with the independent variable. When the resulting interaction term was added to the regression for all years, its coefficient was significant at the .01 level (regression 13), showing that the effect was significantly stronger for the early years.

In the past, prospective students might have been well-advised to pay attention to the academic reputations reported by *U.S. News* even though the reputation surveys could have been done better. Now, however, because *U.S. News* rankings have influenced the reputations the surveys were designed to measure, the reputation scores have lost value as independent indicators of quality.

c. Anecdotal Support

There is anecdotal evidence that those entering law teaching are reading and heeding *U.S. News*. One faculty member from a school that rose in the rankings has stated that moving up in *U.S. News* had the effect of improving the pool of hires from which to choose new faculty. Interestingly, the rise in *U.S. News* improved the school's pool of applicants for faculty positions more quickly than it improved the pool of applicants for student positions. Perhaps, since it is their own status as professional educators that is at stake, it is not surprising that legal education insiders follow *U.S. News* more closely than potential applicants. But whatever the reasons, the evidence confirms that law professors parrot back to *U.S. News* what it publishes, and *U.S. News* reports that parrotage as if it were an independent source.

2. *U.S. News* Is Changing Law School Reputations among Lawyers

U.S. News has had a similar effect on the reputation of schools as seen by lawyers. To test for this, the third regression was repeated using lawyer reputations instead of academic reputations. The difference between *U.S. News* rank and lawyer rank was a significant (.001 level) predictor of the subsequent change in lawyer ranks of the schools (regression 5).

However, there are some differences from the results in the academic reputation regressions. *U.S. News* seems to have had a smaller effect on lawyer reputation scores in early years but a larger effect more recently (regression 5). This difference is significant at the .001 level (regression 15). One way to explain this is to assume that during the first few years lawyers did not care much about the *U.S. News* rankings. As the students that had chosen schools based in part on *U.S. News* became lawyers, however, they changed the mix of lawyers surveyed into a group that was paying attention. In addition, it simply may have taken lawyers more time to pay attention to *U.S. News*.

3. *U.S. News* Has Changed Law School Reputations among Matriculants

U.S. News has had a similar effect on the reputation of schools among law school matriculants. If the LSAT scores of entering students are an indicator of the reputation of schools among prospective students, the LSAT and UGPA numbers can be examined with the same lens applied above to the academic and lawyer indicators of reputation. The disparity between the LSAT rank and *U.S. News* rank in year *T* should predict some of the change in LSAT rank from year *T* to year *T* + 1. And it does. As a predictor, the disparity was significant at the .001 level for the 75th and 50th percentile LSAT and at the .005 level for the 25th percentile LSAT (regressions 6–8). The results for the change in UGPA were similar. The difference between UGPA rank and *U.S. News* rank was a significant predictor of the subsequent change in UGPA rank, significant at the .001 level for the 75th and 25th UGPA percentiles (regressions 9–10). Therefore, *U.S. News* may be affecting the behavior of applicants to law schools in the same way that it has affected the reputations among lawyers and academics.[32]

The assumption just made was that the LSAT and UGPA numbers are indicators of the reputations of law schools among prospective students. But are they? At any law school, these numbers are a function of both the attractiveness of the schools to the applicants and the attractiveness of the applicants to the schools. Changes in the median or any other percentile LSAT or UGPA of a school could be due to changes in the admissions process at the school or changes in the attitudes of students toward the school.

It seems unlikely that recent changes in the LSAT numbers at most schools are due to changes in the behavior of admissions committees. Since the late 1990s at the latest, law school admissions offices have been aware that the LSAT statistics are an important component of the *U.S. News* rankings. Many, if not most, law schools, in their attempts to increase their ranks, have increased the weight given LSAT scores to the point that they deny very few applications that would increase their LSAT numbers. When all law schools admit all of the students that will help their *U.S. News* numbers, law school admissions behavior drops out as a confounding factor, leaving the choices of students as the key determinant of the LSAT statistics for each school. Thus, the assumption that changes in LSAT and UGPA percentiles reflect changes in the reputations of schools among applicants is justifiable. The ability of a school to increase its LSAT numbers relative to other schools' depends on the choices of applicants. Their behavior in turn depends on whether the school is attractive to applicants, which depends in part on the reputations of the schools among applicants.

The assumption that UGPA numbers of a school are mostly up to the students is not as safe. Schools have not yet caved in on that criterion and still reject some applicants who would help their UGPA statistics. As a result, changes in law school behavior could account for some of the changes in relative ranks. Nonetheless, if many schools have stable admissions policies, it should still be true that schools will increase their UGPA numbers as students find the schools to be more attractive.

Therefore, the findings that changes in the LSAT and UGPA statistics can be expressed as a function of differences between LSAT and UGPA ranks and *U.S. News* rank supports the conclusion that *U.S. News* has influenced the reputations of schools among prospective students. It is not a surprise that *U.S. News* influences the attitudes of applicants; presumably, that is why applicants buy the rankings issue in numbers large enough to keep *U.S. News* publishing it year after year in the face of heaps of criticism for doing so. Nevertheless, *U.S. News* rankings seem to have been self-fulfilling prophecies: the rankings led students with higher LSATs and UGPAs to more highly ranked schools, and the matriculations of those students cemented the higher rankings, whether or not the rankings were deserved (whatever that means) in the first instance. If a school had an aberrantly good year, *U.S. News* helped to cast that result in concrete, reducing the chances the school would return to its previous rank.

4. Unreliable Reputations Make Up a Large Part of the *U.S. News* Rankings

The bottom line is that a number of the current *U.S. News* factors are polluted by the *U.S. News* rankings and thus should not be considered to be based on independent sources of information. Reputations among faculty members, reputations among lawyers, LSATs, and UGPAs are all influenced by *U.S. News*. Those factors make up 62.5% of the *U.S. News* score. Eventually, if the remaining 37.5% factors are stable, the effect of that 62.5% will diminish nearly to zero. If the other 37.5% are not stable, the effect of the reputation factors will be to slow the movement of the rankings, although those reputation factors will continue to trend toward the ranks that would result from the 37.5% factors alone. The reputation factors will be essentially wiped out of the rankings, except as an occasional stabilizer, and the rankings will settle in to what they would be if constructed entirely from the factors that make up the other 37.5%. Thus those remaining factors must bear all of the weight of the *U.S. News* rankings, making it all the more important that the remaining factors be legitimate indicators of quality. As the next subpart explains, that is a responsibility they cannot bear.

E. A Number of the Remaining Criteria Are Also Problematic

If the goal is to compare the quality of legal education programs offered at the nation's law schools, a number of the criteria included in the rankings are problematic because they do not directly measure anything prospective students care about. It is, of course, possible that these criteria are good indicators even though they are not direct measures of quality of instruction or experience. Careful research might show that they do provide useful insight into the differences between schools. But that sort of research has not been done. It is also possible that there is such a strong logical connection between the factors and what students would want to know that the factors can serve as indicators until it is proved that they do not correlate with quality. The purpose of much of the following discussion is to show that the logical connection between the factors and quality is not so strong that they can stand as indicators without empirical validation.

1. Bar Passage Rate

One of the factors used by *U.S. News* is bar passage. The number used by *U.S. News* for comparing schools is a ratio of the school's bar pass rate in the jurisdiction where the plurality of a school's students take the bar to the overall pass rate in that jurisdiction. This ratio is a poor indicator of school quality because it is statistically easier for a school to exceed the target bar pass rate by a large percentage in states where the overall rate is low—such as in California where the overall pass rate for first time takers is 61%—and harder to have a strong positive result where the overall pass rate is high, such as in Minnesota where it is 92%.

To see why this is so, consider the following hypothetical example. Suppose that there are two states, *X* and *Y*, that have applicants with the same ability taking the same bar exam. State *X* sets the cut score at 125 and has a 60% pass rate and State *Y* sets the cut score at 110 and has a 90% pass rate. Two schools in those states matriculate students with the same aptitude for the bar exam. Without any instruction, 30% of the test takers in either state would score above 110 and 10% would score above 125. But the two schools provide different quality instruction. School *A*, in State *X*, teaches 85% of its students to score above 110, and 70% to score above 125. School *B*, in State *Y*, teaches 100% of its students to score above 110, and 95% to score above 125. *U.S. News* would give School *A* a score of 70/60 or 1.17, and School *B* a score of 95/90 or 1.06. Hypothetical School *B* has done far more to increase the chances a student will score well on the bar exam, yet it receives a lower score on the *U.S. News* bar passage criterion. The ratio used by *U.S. News* is not a valid indicator of quality when the average rates vary as much as they do across states.[33]

Other problems are equally troubling. The bar pass rate is a poor indicator of school quality because students vary greatly in their ability to pass the bar before they matriculate. One cannot tell from the passage rate whether the school has improved or reduced its students' chances of passing. Suppose School *C* doubles the chances its students will pass from 45% to 90% and School *D* increases its students' chances of passing the bar somewhat from 80% to 92%. A valid measure of bar-related teaching quality would rate *C* higher than *D*, but *U.S. News* does just the opposite. The pass rate of 92% from a school with top students might reflect poorer teaching than a 90% pass rate in the same state from a school with less-gifted students. The *U.S. News* method fails to account for differences in student aptitude and effort.

Another problem with the approach employed by *U.S. News* is that the students taking the bar in the home states are often not a representative sample of the whole graduating class. Comparing Indiana University School of Law-Bloomington and the University of Illinois, a greater portion of IU-B's best students do not take the local bar exam. As a result, IU-B will be at a disadvantage compared to Illinois even if the schools do an equal job of preparing students for the bar exam.

The discussion above has assumed that bar passage is a relevant consideration. There are reasons, however, to refrain from considering it at all. For starters, the bar passage rate is not a great measure of school quality. As noted above, preparing students to be good lawyers, for cases from the most routine to the most difficult, is not at all the same as preparing them to pass a single test of legal knowledge.

More important, bar passage might correlate negatively with preparing students for life in the law. The time faculty members have to spend with students is limited, as is the time students have to study. Teaching students what they need to know to pass the bar will reduce the time teachers and students can spend on other lessons. Most teachers expend considerable effort figuring out what their students need to know to be successful and to be good citizens of the legal world. Spending more time on bar passage imposes costs in terms of other educational goals. No one has made a convincing case that law school faculty members have undervalued bar passage in their teaching.

2. Starting Salaries

Another factor that is sometimes thought of as a measure of law school quality is the average starting salary of its graduates. One major problem with this as an indicator is that it, like bar passage, does not account for differences in the income potential of the students before they started school. To account for differences in matriculants, one might construct a value-added model by regressing salaries on LSAT and UGPA, and perhaps other pre-law school indicia of income potential. One advantage of incorporating the results of such a model into popular rankings is that it would reduce the incentive to overweight or lie in order to increase the LSAT, because doing so would reduce the value added. Such a regression ought also to include the geographic region of the employers because there are large regional differences in starting salaries.[34] Without such a factor, schools that produce lawyers for markets that have lower wages and costs of living would look worse than they actually are. One problem with doing such a regression is that it would require data not now available. Another problem is that the numbers do not include gumption and other factors that may be known to the admissions committees. For that reason, assessing the value added by schools might best be done by comparing the success of students that were accepted by a school but attended a lower ranked school to the success of students that were accepted and did attend, as has been done for undergraduate programs.[35] Even constructed to account for those confounding variables, a simple starting-salary factor is problematic because an average or median does not give any indication of the spread of salaries, and a risk-averse student might care as much about that as about the starting level. He might prefer a low starting salary in order to avoid a small risk of an even lower starting salary. Finally, there is reason to believe that some of the jobs with the highest salaries are not the jobs in which lawyers are happiest.[36] If the students that receive the best preparation might vie for jobs that pay less, higher salaries are not a mark of better preparation.

3. Employment at Graduation and at Nine Months Out

It would seem that whether students get jobs at all after law school would be a good measure of the quality of their education. After all, employers want employees who will be good lawyers, not just those who can pass two days' worth of exams. Employment is a proxy for employability which may be a proxy for quality of legal training. Even without considering the complex of issues surrounding the questions of what kind of work will increase a student's happiness as a worker and whether improving the employability of graduates makes them better contributors to society, there are at least two reasons to worry when employment is used as an indicator of school quality. The first is that this factor can be manipulated. Law schools can lie about their employment. More likely, law schools can hire their graduates into temporary positions so that they will be employed at the point in time when the measurement is taken. Clearly, if the rate a month later is only 80%, a 100% employment rate is more misleading than revealing.

The second problem with employment rates is that they may get too much weight in light of the small differences that exist. Because *U.S. News* currently standardizes the scores on each of its criteria and then adds the standardized scores, it does not matter whether the actual differences are small or large; they will get 12% of the weight. If the reputation factors are reflexive and therefore unimportant in the long run, employment at nine months becomes one-third of the critical set of factors. The smaller the actual differences in employment rates, the less likely those differences deserve to make up, effectively, one-third of the rankings. There is some evidence that the spread is decreasing, but more data are needed to confirm or rebut a trend.[37]

Even if there has not been substantial convergence already, it seems likely that there will be substantial convergence in the future because schools are expending considerable effort to increase their employment figures. While this is good for students, it reduces the value of the employment statistic as a measure of school quality to the point where the statistic cannot support the weight it is given.

The third problem with *U.S. News*'s use of employment percentages is that the employment rates reported are not limited to employment in law-related jobs. The *U.S.*

News questionnaire references the American Bar Association (ABA) questionnaire, which in turn references the National Association of Law Placement (NALP) questionnaire. NALP has taken the position that for purposes of its questionnaire, "a job is a job." There is no distinction between clerking for a federal judge and flipping burgers. Data that is so weakly related to the purpose of going to law school cannot carry the weight *U.S. News* loads upon it.

4. Scholarship Money

Another ill-considered factor is the extra credit *U.S. News* gives for scholarship money. First, it paints an inaccurate picture when the discount given to residents by state schools is not considered to be financial support. It is hard to see how tuition discounts for in-state students are different from scholarships given for other reasons.

More important, scholarships are of little to no value to the students who do not get them. Assume that the other *U.S. News* criteria are accurate and properly weighted and School *A* ranks higher than School *B*. And assume that when scholarship money is added to the mix, School *B* rises above School *A*. Should a student that gets no money from either school choose School *B*? Of course not. The inclusion of scholarship money has misled her. For those who do get the scholarship money, it should go into the price consideration, not into the quality-of-product part of the analysis. As long as tuition is not a factor, and it should not be, reductions in tuition should not be a factor either.

The inclusion of what is effectively a price factor into the rankings serves as a good example of the problem with forcing a variety of factors onto a unidimensional scale. For wealthy students, a $100,000 difference in price is of little moment; for others it is critical. This is easy to see when it comes to price. But it is also true for the other factors that go into the rankings. For some students, employment rates matter, for others they do not. For some students, reputations matter, for others they do not. *U.S. News*'s weighting of the factors assumes all buyers want the same thing, when it is obvious they do not. An opportunity to place their own weights on the factors would serve them far better than a single arbitrary weighting.

5. Faculty/Student Ratio

All else being equal, the more teachers there are per student, the better the educational experience probably is for the students. But all else is not equal. Schools impose different course loads on their teachers. Suppose School *X* has 400 students taught by forty teachers for a faculty-to-student ratio of 1:10, while School *Y* has 400 students taught by fifty teachers for a faculty-to-student ratio of 1:8. School *Y* gets the higher ranking. Assume, however, that the teaching load at School *X* is four courses and the teaching load at School *Y* is three courses per year. If all students take eight courses, that is 3200 student-courses to be taught at each school. If the students are evenly distributed, at School *X* there will be twenty students in each course and at School *Y* there will be more than twenty-one students in each course. One might argue that this is not an important difference, but that is beside the point. School *Y* has been given credit in the rankings when it deserves discredit. If the differences in course loads were random, it might be acceptable to ignore this complication. But the teaching loads are inversely correlated with faculty-to-student ratios. Schools that have higher faculty-to-student ratios tend to be the richer schools, and those schools tend to require less teaching of their faculty. This inverse relationship undermines the validity of the faculty-to-student ratio as an indicator of the quality of schooling a student can expect.

One other problem with using ratios of students and teachers is that it is not clear which is more informative, a student/faculty ratio or a faculty/student ratio. For mathematical reasons, it matters to the ultimate rankings which ratio is used, but *U.S. News* has offered no reason for its apparently arbitrary choice.[38]

6. Acceptance Ratio

U.S. News uses the acceptance ratio as one indicator of selectivity. The theory is, of course, that a school that accepts a small portion of the students that apply must be highly selective and that is a good marker of quality. But there are a number of problems with using acceptance ratio as a proxy for quality. For one thing, it is quite likely that some schools attract many applications simply by virtue of being in a major population center. Another serious problem is that the number of applications to a school depends on the clarity of signals it sends with regard to admission standards. A top quality school might be attractive to many students, but if it lets it be known that it accepts applicants only if they have an LSAT above 165, it will get few applications and have to accept many of them to fill the class. It is illogical to conclude that schools that are not highly selective are not high quality. On the other hand it is also not true that schools that are highly selective are high in quality. An average school might be able to attract many applications by announcing that it will randomly select ten students for its class each year. More realistically, a school can keep applications up by making the admissions standards vague. The more students there are that might have a chance of acceptance, the more students that might apply. While it is true that some schools have difficulty attracting enough students to fill the class and will have a low acceptance ratio for that reason, for the majority of schools, the acceptance ratio is more an indicator of the predictability of admission than the quality of the school.

7. Wealth of School—For Example, Faculty Resources

Generally, the more money a school has, the better the experience for its students. For that reason, faculty resources is a valid indicator of educational quality. However, some organizations are more efficient than others and that difference in efficiency weakens the connection between a school's resources and expenditures and the quality of its product.

There are two other problems as well. Some faculties put more effort into teaching and others put more into research. Although research benefits the students by training and informing the faculty, by legitimating an aura of inquiry, and by increasing the reputation of the school, it is quite possible that many faculty members spend less time on teaching than would serve the students well. And the schools that tend to spend more on faculty resources for research than what is optimal for students tend to be the schools that have more money. This further weakens the connection between school resources and the quality of the product the student will purchase. Finally, as with starting pay for graduates, there are substantial regional differences in cost-of-living and lifestyle attractions that allow schools in some regions to attract an accomplished faculty using less money than would be necessary in other regions.

Despite those substantial caveats, it is likely that there is still a positive correlation between resources and merit, so it makes some sense to include resources as a factor in rankings. Indeed, if this is an important factor, it may provide good justification for publishing rankings and not data on the various criteria. Schools would often be unwilling to provide accurate data on resources if that information might be made public. They may, however, be willing to provide the data if it is hidden inside a ranking based on other factors. In this way rankings may serve the purpose of getting into the public domain the useful information on resources that cannot be published outright. Rankings provide a way of publishing secret information without revealing too much of the secret.

To reiterate a point made above, most of the criteria on which the *U.S. News* rankings are based are not direct measures of anything particularly valuable to a prospective student or an employer wanting to hire a student. *U.S. News* criteria might be indicators of quality, but they have not been validated by empirical study, and they have not been established to be logically connected with what readers of the rankings might reasonably hope to learn.

IV. Improving the Validity of Evaluation

If anyone were willing to expend substantial resources to learn more about how law schools compare, he or she might consult experts in educational evaluation. The process of talking to such experts would itself help those interested in law school evaluation to think about criteria for evaluation that they would otherwise not even imagine. Some of those experts would probably recommend close human observation of the schools to learn about the schools directly or to validate numerical indicators of quality. Medical schools employed educational evaluators to help them assess their teaching in the 1970s.[39] But it does not appear that any person or group is interested enough to spend the money required for serious study of law schools.

The question then becomes whether evaluation on the cheap can be improved. Many of those buying the law school rankings issues of *U.S. News* are prospective students, and there are some changes that would make the rankings more useful to those readers. Two improvements suggested above would be to publish the data without constructing summary scores, or if summary scores are calculated, to add a graph that shows the magnitude of differences in those scores. Another improvement would be to find factors that are better indicators of school quality. A list of a few possible factors follows.

A. Student Involvement

One criterion that might improve rankings by indicating the level of learning is the degree of student involvement in learning activities. George Kuh at Indiana University is studying this, but the data are not public, so they cannot be used, at this time, in rankings.[40] Nevertheless, this sort of research might be available in the future to students trying to choose a school.

B. Quality of Teaching

The most obvious deficiency in most of the current rankings is that they lack information on the quality of teaching. As this is a central concern for students, it ought to receive more attention. One of the reasons that it does not is that there are many different aspects of teaching quality. Some schools will be better at teaching skills of policy analysis, some better at teaching legal doctrine, and some better at teaching the arts of legal research and writing.

Surveys of students are sometimes conducted, but it is not clear that students have enough information about what they need to know to evaluate their learning experience. Faculty members who read student evaluations know that students often praise or criticize in ways that show their notions of the goals of legal education differ from those of the faculty. For example, students would probably think "Professor *X* made us learn all of the course ourselves," is a criticism, while many teachers would consider it a compliment.

C. Providing Educational Opportunities

In addition to clinical programs and interdisciplinary studies from biology to economics to feminist studies, special learning opportunities outside the classroom form an important part of the academic life at some law schools. Speakers on campus, library facilities, internships, and other enriching and enhancing experiences await students in varying degrees and in varying formats at different schools. Capturing and presenting some of that variety should help applicants to find a school well-tailored to their interests and aspirations.

D. Obtaining a Desired Job

Instead of surveying alumni about law school reputations, researchers could more usefully survey alumni regarding whether they obtained the jobs they wanted to obtain. Such measures of individual success, if taken at enough schools, would help when added to the rankings. Differences in quality of life as a lawyer, and the lawyers' perceptions of their schools' contributions to those differences, would also be useful to students comparing schools. The University of Michigan has been gathering such data for many years, and Ken Dau-Schmidt and this author have been surveying Indiana University School of Law-Bloomington graduates in recent years. Such data would be more helpful, and useful in rankings, if they were gathered by all schools. And, the gathering of such data could be considered an attribute of good governance. If persons ranking law schools would include a simple factor for whether the school systematically surveyed its graduates, that factor might encourage such surveys and thereby generate information useful to prospective students.

E. Achieving Happiness

Why limit surveys to legal success? It is possible that law school makes a difference to happiness in other dimensions. At least one study indicates that being married improves happiness.[41] A prospective student might sensibly consider whether he or she is likely to find a spouse while in law school. Such data would probably not be too costly for schools to collect. It might also be useful to know whether attendance at any schools led to higher rates of divorce or imprisonment. Gathering such data is too much to expect of *U.S. News*. It would cost a lot and probably not sell many more magazines. But it is not too much to expect of academic research. This kind of information would be useful to the world and parallels existing institutional research.

F. More Rankings Would Help

U.S. News is in the business of supplying a product for a consumer demand, and its success indicates that the *U.S. News* is providing what people want to read. Rankings are popular for a number of reasons. For one, they appeal to our interest in contests. That consumers like contests is shown by the popularity of sports and reality TV shows. That consumers like serious matters to be treated as contests is evident in the media coverage of political campaigns, where the strategies and maneuvers of the candidates get more attention than the issues. Rankings turn the suppliers of legal education into competitors in an entertaining game where the goal is higher rank. In addition to being entertaining, rankings are decisive. When people of modest means face the prospect of spending $100,000 on a product they know nearly nothing about, rankings offer security by resolving doubts. It is much more comforting to be presented with a clear basis for decision, a unilateral ranking, than to be presented with a mass of information from which many choices could be justified. Many consumers of educational rankings do not want arguments, they want answers.[42]

Perhaps the best hope for change, then, is that more sources will cater to this consumer demand for simple answers to complex questions. As is indicated by Michael Sauder and Wendy Nelson Espeland,[43] the students, the public, and the law schools would be better served if there were more rankings. And these rankings should not be limited to those made from a supposedly neutral and general perspective. Special interests should publish their rankings. Environmentalists should identify top schools in the production of environmental lawyers or policy. Corporate and political interests should likewise publish their own partisan rankings. If more legal academics would follow Brian Leiter's lead[44] and collectively and individually create their own rankings, and especially if they were to invest additional time and money in generating valid information on new criteria, the diversity and utility of the rankings would increase.

It should not be assumed, however, that the mere addition of new rankings will solve the incentive problems that afflict the legal academy. Despite the fact that there are a number of popular rankings of business schools, some business educators have argued that rankings are having detrimental effects on business education.[45] Indeed, because business schools are more responsive to incentives and their rankings rely far too much on satisfaction of graduates, business programs may have suffered even more destructive effects than those felt so far in law schools.

V. Will the Market Offer Better Rankings in the Future?[46]

Regarding some of the defects in the *U.S. News* rankings, there is some hope that *U.S. News* will improve its product, and perhaps more hope that another supplier will displace *U.S. News* by providing a better product. Measuring the quality of educational experience offered by schools is not easy, but it could be done better, and better rankings should attract readers, perhaps even readers willing to pay for the information. If Brian Leiter's rankings more accurately depict the relative quality of schooling a student can expect, the market might gradually shift to his product. If this occurs, *U.S. News* will have less influence. Other law teachers—and various lawyer organizations—could join in the competition, offering alternative ranking systems, ones that give students better information on which to base their choices. It is likely that there is sufficient demand to support additional suppliers.

It must be remembered, however, that there are two types of problems with the criteria used in current rankings. One problem is that the criteria do not directly assess something of value to the student: they have not been validated as good indicators of the quality of educational experience a student can expect, and they are not closely enough connected by logic to what the student would want to know to justify an assumption that they are valid measures of quality. There is reason for hope that future suppliers of rankings will base their rankings on criteria of greater validity than those used now.

The second problem, discussed in the first section above, is that the criteria used in the current rankings create harmful incentives for law schools, and to some extent for undergraduate students hoping to attend law school. An increase in the number of rankings taken seriously by employers and prospective students would reduce the influence of *U.S. News* on law school behavior, which could free schools to provide better educational experiences for their students. But little autonomy will be reclaimed if the alternative rankings employ the same criteria currently being used by *U.S. News*. For example, Brian Leiter has included the 25th percentile LSAT figures in his omnibus ranking, so his ranking does little to de-emphasize that criterion in the eyes of law school admissions committees. Is there any reason to believe that new rankings will exclude criteria when they learn those criteria create undesirable incentives? From where would such pressure come?

A. Schools as Facilitators of Rankings: Just Say "No"?

Law schools aid and abet *U.S. News* by providing data for use in the rankings. Faculty members, perhaps proud to have been asked, return *U.S. News*'s surveys, sometimes answering in ways that will serve their own interests rather than the interests of the *U.S. News* readers. Faculty members are unlikely to refuse answering surveys by *U.S. News* in order to support a competing ranking that creates better incentives. Even though the rankings do some injury to their schools, it is not in the interest of faculty members to boycott the questionnaires because those faculty members would lose their voice and power in the *U.S. News* process. By participating, faculty members can improve the relative standing of schools they want to help.

Schools participate, by submitting data requested by *U.S. News*, because they will suffer if they do not provide the data. If a school were to boycott *U.S. News*, it would diminish the authority of the *U.S. News* rankings by a small margin, and that small decrease in the power of *U.S. News* would create a corresponding increase in autonomy for law schools. However, that freedom would be spread across many schools, while the costs of rebuffing *U.S. News*, including the possibility of being excluded from the rankings, would be focused mostly on the boycotting school. Fear of exclusion, not confidence in the legitimacy of *U.S. News* as an evaluator, keeps schools sending data.

Moreover, the costs of *U.S. News* do not fall primarily on the schools or teachers. It is the students, more than the academic organizations, that suffer when the curriculum is aimed at lifting all students over the bar exam instead of presenting lessons tailored to the particular needs of the students or when scarce financial resources are spent on advertising to improve reputations among academics. It is clients and citizens who suffer when teachers teach to the test because that distortion of the educational process produces lawyers less capable than they would have been if the school had focused on students' educational needs rather than the bar exam. For these reasons, law schools and faculty members cannot be counted on to withhold data or in any other way boycott ranking providers in order to keep them from employing harmful criteria.

B. Students as Purchasers of Rankings

The very act of paying attention to *U.S. News*'s rankings increases *U.S. News*'s influence on law school behavior. If so, why do prospective law students do it? One possibility, of course, is that students understand the harms but see the benefits of the information as worth its costs. But that is not the only explanation. It is possible that they simply do not appreciate the ways in which their attention to *U.S. News* causes schools to change their curriculum for the worse. It is also possible that the harms from student attention are delayed, and hence fall on later students, while the benefits of the ranking information are immediate. For example, by the time the applicant chooses her school, *U.S. News*'s inclusion of the 25th percentile or median in the calculations has already influenced the makeup of that student's entering class, and ignoring the rankings cannot undo that harm. A third possibility is that the harms fall on other persons outside law school. To see this, suppose there were two rankings, one that included the 25th percentile or median LSAT and UGPA and another new one that did not. Many applicants would choose the slightly more informative older ranking rather than switching to the newer ranking that benefits future clients by allowing schools to deliver a higher quality of legal education. For these reasons, even if prospective students recognize that the net harm caused by some *U.S. News* criterion exceeds its net benefit, it might not be in the interest of any individual to shift his magazine-purchasing dollar to the supplier of the greater social good. *U.S. News* or other suppliers will produce what readers are willing to buy. Prospective students, as direct purchasers, could demand rankings that create better incentives. But there is no guarantee they will do so when the benefits of those incentives accrue to others.

C. Will Employers Demand Better Rankings?

In some ways there is more hope that employers will demand better rankings since they are more closely connected to the clients' interests in good lawyering. However, as with the students and schools, the clients' interests are not the same as society's interest. First, of course, in many situations, there are social interests not represented by any client. Second, if, at the same cost of education, all lawyers are better educated and therefore better able to serve their clients, it is not clear that the lawyers can capture all of that improvement in the form of higher fees. To the extent lawyers cannot do so, employers have an incomplete interest in improving the quality of legal education.

VI. Other Alternatives

A. Ignore U.S. News

Many harms traceable to *U.S. News*'s rankings result from schools' attempts to raise their ranks. Some legal academics, including deans, have stated that schools should simply ignore *U.S. News* and do what they think is right, whether that be in admissions, placement, or curriculum development. They are right, of course, that this would improve legal education. They are wrong, however, to suggest that there is any chance it will happen on a scale large enough to make a difference. All schools might prefer that there be no *U.S. News* rankings, or that certain criteria be excluded, or that all schools ignore the incentives created by *U.S. News*, but no school can opt out of the game. Refusing to play—refusing to allow the LSAT to drive admissions, refusing to allow bar passage to drive pedagogical choices, refusing to spend extra money on career services offices and advertising—means other schools that do play the game will pull ahead in the rankings. If that happens, some prospective students will not apply,[47] a few students will transfer out, a few faculty "prospects" will refuse interview invitations, a faculty member or two might leave, and perhaps alumni and state governments will provide less support. Any of these could lead to a further drop in rank and another cycle of negative consequences for the school. Because of this possibility, refusing to play the game is not a viable option.

Officials have tried in the past to reduce the impact of *U.S. News*. The American Bar Association stopped collecting the median LSAT.[48] The Association of American Law Schools hired statisticians to analyze the *U.S. News* results and investigate their method. The deans of law schools collectively tried to discourage students from relying on the *U.S. News* rankings.[49] But these efforts had little effect, and law schools might be worried that more serious efforts at coordination would violate the antitrust laws.

Individual faculty members are caught in the same dilemma. Their professional lives might improve somewhat without *U.S. News*, but as long as it publishes law rankings, they will pay heed in one way or another. If a law graduate is choosing a school at which to teach, she will likely care about whether her articles will place well. Because some student law review editors consider the author's institution's rank in *U.S. News*, it is in a prospective employee's best interest to pay some attention to the rankings when choosing employers.

U.S. News has set up a game. The players are the schools being ranked and the faculty members at those schools. Most faculty members and administrators seek to increase their school's rank by various strategic moves. These moves are costly, in terms of money and other resources, but do little or nothing to improve legal education for students. Indeed, it is worse than that. Many of the strategies run contrary to the interests of students and society. Unfortunately, the players cannot exit the game for fear of losing support. This ranking game allows no exit and has no time clock.

B. Ranking the Rankings

It is possible for better rankings to be constructed, and it is possible for legal professionals to help them gain credibility. One way, perhaps, to loosen the grip of *U.S. News* on the law school ranking market is to provide information about the harms of the various rankings. Another is to help students and others evaluate which of the rankings provides the best information. There is just as much need for information about whether *U.S. News* is providing useful information as there is need for the information it attempts to provide. Nonetheless, there may always remain a tension between the predictive validity of a ranking system and the negative incentives it creates. UGPA 25th percentiles serve as an example. A good case can be made that including them in the rankings provides a more accurate picture of the schools. On the other hand, including 25th percentiles in the rankings creates incentives that can only lead admissions committees away from offering admission to the best-qualified applicants. Thus, if rankings are rated on their immediate utility to law students choosing a school, students will ignore many of the problematic incentives created by those rankings. If, because of bad incentives created by the criteria, a meta-ranking gives a low rank to a ranking that is good at informing applicants, the meta-ranking will lose credibility. The same problem that exists at the level of students choosing schools occurs at the level of rankers ranking rankings.

Conclusion

Students looking for law schools and employers seeking employees need useful information about the various products offered by legal educators. Publication of relevant information is a service to them. But rankings are not mere information, they add opinions based on that information. *U.S. News*'s addition of opinion is hard to justify since *U.S. News* is no expert in weighting the criteria and since the addition of that opinion in the form of rankings has a number of negative consequences. Given the various costs of rankings, those who publish rankings ought to try to anticipate those consequences and ought also to do what they can to mitigate them. Rankings will not stop, given a market willing to pay so much for them. But perhaps newcomers will publish rankings based on criteria that more accurately reflect the quality of training offered, or create fewer harmful incentives, or both.

Better rankings might improve the lives of those providing legal education. However, the greater concern is about how the rankings affect the lives of others. *U.S. News*'s rankings have changed and will continue to change legal education. Those changes will be felt directly by the students and indirectly by society. Lawyers and law professors have a strong impact on the economy, the political system, and ethics. Whether that impact will be for the better or worse depends on who is admitted to law school and what training they receive while they are there. It also depends on whether law school faculties are engaged in the sorts of research and service activities that can lead to a more just and efficient legal system, activities that are far outside the incentives created by *U.S. News*. There are deep national interests in what happens in law schools. The nation should therefore be concerned about the changes being wrought in the quest for higher ranks. It is time to move beyond trying to devise a single scale for deciding whether one law school is better than another. It is time to imagine improvements in the law, lawyers, and the system that produces new law and lawyers, and with that in mind to ask how rankings of law schools might be used to achieve those improvements.

Appendix. Regressions

Regression	Dependant variable	Independent variable	β	*P*-value	Adjusted r^2	Number of observations
1	Grades, 75th percentile	Year *T*	0.022	.001*	.044	1026
	Grades, 25th percentile		0.029	.001*	.037	1026
	LSAT, 75th percentile		0.220	.004	.006	1200
	LSAT, 25th percentile		0.467	.001*	.025	1200
	LSAT P75–LSAT P25		−0.247	.001*	.084	1200
2	Academic rank in year *T*+l	Academic rank in year *T*	0.979	.001*	.983	656
		U.S. News score in *year T*	−0.027	.029		
3	Academic rank in year T+l	Academic rank in year *T*	0.972	.001*	.984	656
		U.S. News score in *year T*	−0.075	.001		
		26 Interactive variables 13 years x both of above		only 2 significant at .05		
4	Academic rank in year *T* minus academic rank in year *T*+l	Academic rank in year *T* minus *U.S. News* rank in year T	0.052	.001*	.022	656
	Same as above T+l<1998		0.102	.001*	.100	247
	Same as above T+l>1997		0.028	.114	.004	409
5	Lawyer rank in year *T* minus lawyer rank in year T+l	Lawyer rank in year *T* minus *U.S. News* rank in year T	0.267	.001*	.146	656
	Same as above T+l<1998		0.090	.002	.036	247
	Same as above T+l>1997		0.335	.001*	.189	409
6	LSAT75 rank in year *T* minus LSAT75 rank in year *T*+l	LSAT75 rank in year *T* minus *U.S. News* rank in year *T*	0.260	.001*	.122	359
7	LSAT50 rank in year *T* minus LSAT50 rank in year *T*+l	LSAT50 rank in year *T* minus *U.S. News* rank in year *T*	0.281	.001*	.166	247

Appendix. Regressions *continued*

Regression	Dependant variable	Independent variable	β	*P*-value	Adjusted r^2	Number of observations
8	LSAT25rank in year *T* minus LSAT25 rank in year *T*+l	LSAT25 rank in year *T* minus *U.S. News* rank in year *T*	0.106	.005	.019	359
9	UGPA75 rank in year *T* minus UGPA75 rank in year *T*+l	UGPA75 rank in year *T* minus *U.S. News* rank in year *T*	0.245	.001*	.100	308
10	UGPA25 rank in year *T* minus UGPA25 rank in year *T*+l	UGPA25 rank in year *T* minus *U.S. News* rank in year *T*	0.113	.001	.030	308
11	Academic rank in year *T* minus academic rank in year *T*+l (top 17 schools schools only)	Academic rank in year *T* minus *U.S. News* rank in year T (top 17 only)	0.200	.001*	.103	238
12	Academic rank in year *T* minus academic rank in year *T*+l (schools below Top 17)	Academic rank in year *T* minus *U.S. News* rank in year *T* (schools below Top 17)	0.045	.004	.017	418
13	Academic rank in year *T* minus academic rank in year *T*+l	Academic rank in year *T* minus *U.S. News* rank in year *T*	0.026	.105	.031	656
		Variable above interacted with dummy variable for early years	0.075	.007		
14	Academic rank in year *T* minus academic rank in year *T*+l	Academic rank in year *T* minus *U.S. News* rank in year *T*	0.045	.001	.028	656
		Variable above interacted with top 17 in 1990 *U.S. News*	0.145	.021		
15	Lawyer rank in year *T* minus lawyer rank in year *T*+l	Lawyer rank in year *T* minus *U.S. News* rank in year *T*	0.334	.001*	.169	656
		Variable above interacted with dummy variable for early years	−0.241	.001*		

NOTE: * denotes *P*-value rounded up to .001 from a lower value.

Notes

* The author thanks Robert Stake, Michael Alexeev, Tom Ulen, Ethan Stone, Leandra Lederman, Eric Rasmusen, Stephen Peck, Larry Ribstein, Jim Lindgren, Bill Henderson, Anthony Ciolli, Christopher Smith and participants at the Symposium on the Next Generation of Law School Rankings held at Indiana University School of Law-Bloomington.

1. Russell Korobkin, *Keynote Address, Harnessing the Positive Power of Rankings: A Response to Posner and Sunstein*, 81 Ind. L.J. 35, 44–45 (2006).

2. Larry Ribstein has argued that the market will discipline law schools. See "Ideoblog, Dean's Letters" (May 9, 2005), http://busmovie.typepad.com/ideoblog/2005/05/deans_letters.html; "Ideoblog, The Market for Academic Control" (May 6, 2005), http://busmovie.typepad.com/ideoblog/2005/05/the_market_for_.html; "Ideoblog, Symposium on the Next Generation of Law School Rankings" (Mar. 30, 2005), http://busmovie.typepad.com/ideoblog/2005/03/symposium_on_th.html.

3. The Ranking Game gets about 30,000 page views per month. Jeffrey E. Stake, "The Law School Ranking Game," http://monoborg.law.indiana.edu/LawRank/index.html (last visited Sept. 5, 2005).

4. Alex Wellen, *The $8.78 Million Maneuver*, N.Y. Times, July 31, 2005, §4A, at 18 (quoting Stanford Law School Dean Larry Kramer).

5. It is possible that UGPAs have risen because of grade inflation, although it does not seem likely that grades have inflated that quickly in recent years. It is also possible, and would seem to be more likely, that UGPAs have increased because the size of the applicant pool has increased. And perhaps their qualifications have improved even more than would be expected solely on the basis of the increase in numbers.

6. The superior predictive power of the LSAT as compared to the UGPA is well documented. See William D. Henderson, *The LSAT, Law School Exams, and Meritocracy: The Surprising and Undertheorized Role of Test-Taking Speed*, 82 Tex. L. Rev. 975, 1030 (2004) (citing several validity studies). However, Prof. Henderson's study suggests that the higher predictive validity of the LSAT may be partially attributable to the prevalence of time-pressured exams in the law school curriculum, particularly during the first year. Id. at 1030–34 (discussing mechanics of this relationship).

7. STEPHEN P. KLEIN AND LAURA HAMILTON, THE VALIDITY OF THE U.S. NEWS AND WORLD REPORT RANKING OF ABA LAW SCHOOLS (1998), http://www.aals.org/validity.html.

8. *Id.*

9. I begged the ABA not to stop collecting the median data, but was rebuffed with the dubious claim that *U.S. News*'s use of the 25th percentile would have no more impact on admissions than its use of the median.

10. "We wanted to go with verifiable data," Mr. Morse says, "and we heard that some schools weren't computing their median correctly." Wellen, *supra* note 4, at 18 (quoting *U.S. News* Editor Robert Morse). *See also* Carl Bialik, *Small Change by* U.S. News *Leads To New Controversy in Rankings*, WALL ST. J. ONLINE, April 7, 2005, http://online.wsj.com.proxy.lib.pdx.edu/(subscription required) (on file with the Indiana Law Journal).

11. Most law schools would have accepted most applicants with LSAT scores above their 75th percentile even before the *U.S. News* rankings were published. For that reason, there is not much a school can do through admissions decisions alone to increase its 75th percentile on the LSAT.

12. See *infra* Appendix.

13. It is possible that LSATs have increased because of an increase in the pool of qualified applicants to law schools.

14. Marjorie M. Shultz, *Expanding the Definition of Merit*, BOALT HALL TRANSCRIPT, Summer 2005, at 25, *available at* http://www.law.berkeley.edu/alumni/transcript/summer_05/22-27_feat_23_lsat_final.pdf.

15. I have made this request to *U.S. News* both privately and publicly. See Jeffrey E. Stake, *Reducing the Impact of Rankings on Law School Admissions: A Proposal*, JURIST, Feb. 4, 2003, http://jurist.law.pitt.edu/forum/forumnew93.php. The editor, however, does not seem eager to acknowledge that *U.S. News* influences the behavior of law schools.

16. To some extent the example above understates the benefits of changing to the 75th percentiles. Even before *U.S. News* published its rankings, many schools rejected few of the applicants with LSAT scores above the school's 75th percentile. Thus, rankings based on the 75th percentile LSAT would have a negligible effect on who is admitted to a given law school. By contrast, rankings based on the median LSAT (to say nothing of the 25th percentile) create an incentive for schools to admit dozens of students in the middle of the class who would otherwise be rejected in favor of applicants with slightly inferior numbers but with more promise as lawyers. Thus a shift to the 75th percentile on the LSAT and UGPA could cut the number of students admitted primarily on the numbers by well more than half.

17. The result might be similar to the results one would get with the tournament system suggested by Christopher Avery, Mark Glickman, Caroline Hoxby, & Andrew Metrick, *A Revealed Preference Ranking of U.S. Colleges and Universities*, (Nat'l Bureau of Econ. Research, Working Paper No. 10803, 2004), *available at* http://www.nber.org.proxy.lib.pdx.edu/papers/W10803. The idea common to both methods of ranking is that students' matriculation decisions determine a winner of many head-to-head contests. Because students know that law school admissions are driven heavily by LSAT and UGPA numbers, a decision to attend a school is effectively a decision not to attend all schools with lower LSAT and UGPA medians.

18. After this proposal was presented at the Symposium on *The Next Generation of Law School Rankings*, Dean Robel of Indiana University School of Law-Bloomington gathered signatures from sixty law deans on a letter asking the ABA to return to collecting the median data. The ABA has decided to collect the median LSAT and UGPA from each school and, as expected, *U.S. News* has announced that it will revert to its former use of the medians. Given that change, which will take pressure off the 25th percentiles (which will probably decrease as a result), the benefits of the proposed change to the 75th percentiles would be less dramatic, but would still be considerable.

19. Michael Sauder & Wendy Nelson Espeland, *Strength in Numbers? The Advantages of Multiple Rankings*, 81 IND. L.J. 205, 211 (2006).

20. Wellen, *supra* note 4, at 18.

21. It is also possible that readers of *Consumer Reports* agree more with the underlying criteria being used to rank cars than readers, at least faculty readers, of *U.S. News* agree with the criteria being used to rank schools.

22. The same could be true about grades. However, because the Klein & Hamilton study said that LSAT and reputation were the factors that explained most of the variance, see Klein & Hamilton, *supra* note 7, schools may not have worked as hard at increasing UGPA numbers. In addition, schools are probably less comfortable emphasizing UGPA than LSAT scores because of the more obvious problems noted above with admitting students primarily by grades.

23. *Sweezy v. New Hampshire*, 354 U.S. 234, 263 (1957) (Frankfurter, J., concurring).

24. That is not to say that these criteria are not of direct interest to someone, just not the bulk of those reading the rankings. A prospective student hoping to teach should care about the reputation of a school among teachers, who will be hiring him or her. A law school graduate hoping to teach and publish might well care about the grades of the students he or she might be teaching.

25. See THEODORE M. PORTER, TRUST IN NUMBERS (1995); Patricia McDonough, Anthony Lising Antonio, Mary Beth Walpole & Leonor Perez, *College Rankings: Democratized College Knowledge for Whom?*, 39 RES. HIGHER EDUC. 513, 531 (1995) (stating that rankings shift attention of prospective students from what suits the student to the prestige of schools); Nancy B. Rapoport, *Ratings Not Rankings: Why* U.S. News & World Report *Shouldn't Want to be Compared to* Time *and* Newsweek—*or* The New Yorker, 60 OHIO ST. L.J. 1097, 1099 (1999); but see Mitchell Berger, *Why the* U.S. News and World Report *Law School Rankings Are Both Useful and Important*, 51 J. LEGAL EDUC. 487, 489 (2001) (doubting whether anyone encourages students to take the rankings as gospel).

26. LAW SCHOOL DEANS SPEAK OUT ABOUT RANKINGS (Law School Admission Council 2005), *available at* http://www.lsac.org/pdfs/2005-2006/RANKING2005-newer.pdf [hereinafter DEANS SPEAK OUT].

27. The *z*-scores were calculated as follows: ((score – mean score)/standard deviation). The rounded *z*-scores are 1.39, -0.46, and -0.93 for criterion *A*, and -1.22, 0, and 1.22 for criterion *B*. The numbers reflected above are the sums of the two z-scores.

28. I have borrowed half of this expression from Brian Leiter, who called this the "echo chamber." *See* Brian Leiter, Commentary, *How to Rank Law Schools*, 81 IND. L.J. 47, 51 (2006).

29. Richard Schmalbeck, *The Durability of Law School Reputation*, 48 J. LEGAL EDUC. 568, 576–80, 585 n.21, 586 (1998).

30. It was necessary to use ranks instead of scores because the reputation scores were not published by *U.S. News* until 1998.

31. I ran the regressions with a panel data approach and got essentially the same results.

32. While the general effect is clear, the response of students is complicated in a number of ways. For example, after the median LSAT at Indiana University School of Law-Bloomington rose from 162 to 163, the admissions office saw a substantial reduction in the number of applications from students with LSAT scores of 162, presumably because students rightly deduced that their odds of admission were substantially lower than they would have been the previous year. Professors Sauder and Lancaster have found that *U.S. News* rankings have significant effects on the decisions of applicants. Michael Sauder & Ryon Lancaster, *Do Rankings Matter? The Effects of* U.S. News & World Report *Rankings on the Admissions Process of Law Schools*, 40 LAW & SOCIETY Rev. (Mar. 2006). One study of applications to undergraduate schools also found that changes in rank affect number of applications. James Monks & Ronald G. Ehrenberg, *The Impact of* U.S. News & World *Report College Rankings on Admissions Outcomes and Pricing Policies at Selective Private Institutions* (Nat'l Bureau of Econ. Research, Working Paper No. 7227, 1999).

33. At the 2004 Midwest Law and Economics Conference, a participant suggested that an "odds ratio" might be a better way to represent this factor. While it does account for the differences in state bar pass rates, the odds ratio runs into difficulties when the bar pass rate nears 100%, as it does at some schools, because the denominator approaches zero and the ratios climb dramatically for small changes in number of students that pass. For example, in a jurisdiction with a 90% pass rate, a school with a 99% pass rate gets twice the score of a school with a 98% pass rate, which seems far too great a difference for the one extra student that passes.

34. In their very interesting article, Professors Henderson and Morriss suggest that the regional employment market, particularly for high-paying law jobs, affects a student's choice of law school. *See* William D. Henderson & Andrew P. Morriss, *Student Quality as Measured by LSAT Scores: Migration Patterns in the U.S. News Rankings Era*, 81 IND. L.J. 163, 188–190 (2006).

35. *See* Stacy Berg Dale & Alan B. Krueger, *Estimating the Payoff to Attending a More Selective College: An Application of Selection on Observables and Unobservables*, Q.J. ECON., Nov. 2002, at 1491.

36. Professor Kenneth G. Dau-Schmidt and I will discuss this point further in a piece forthcoming in this volume of the Indiana Law Journal detailing the results of a survey we conducted of Indiana University School of Law-Bloomington alumni.

37. The standard deviation of 0.096 in 2000 had shrunk to 0.063 in 2002. However, it had grown to 0.079 in 2004. (The figures for 1994 and 1996 were for employment at six months out of school, rather than nine, and are not comparable.)

38. To see the difference in operation, play The Ranking Game. See *supra* note 3.

39. The use of educational evaluators at medical schools has been personally communicated to me by Robert E. Stake, an educational evaluator at the University of Illinois.

40. LAW SCHOOL SURVEY OF STUDENT ENGAGEMENT, LSSSE 2004 ANNUAL SURVEY RESULTS: STUDENT ENGAGEMENT IN LAW SCHOOLS: A FIRST LOOK (2004), http://www.iub.edu/ nsse/lssse/2004_annual_report/html/index.htm.

41. Richard A. Easterlin, *Explaining Happiness*, 100 PROC. NAT'L ACAD. SCI. 11176, 11178 (2002).

42. Perhaps The Law School Ranking Game Web site, *see supra* note 3, could increase its viewership beyond the current thousand hits per day if it were marketed more as a source of personalized answers and less as a critique of rankings. It is somewhat ironic that those headed to law school want answers instead of arguments.

43. Sauder & Espeland, *supra* note 19; *see also* Leiter, *supra* note 28, at 52.

44. Leiter's Law School Rankings, http://www.leitterrankings.com (ranking law schools on faculty and student quality) (last visited Nov. 24, 2005).

45. Consider the following abstract from SSRN:

> U.S. business schools are locked in a dysfunctional competition for media rankings that diverts resources from long-term knowledge creation, which earned them global pre-eminence, into short-term strategies aimed at improving their rankings. MBA curricula are distorted

> by quick fix, look good packaging changes designed to influence rankings criteria, at the expense of giving students a rigorous, conceptual framework that will serve them well over their entire careers. Research, undergraduate education, and Ph.D. programs suffer as faculty time is diverted to almost continuous MBA curriculum changes, strategic planning exercises, and public relations efforts. Unless they wake up to the dangers of dysfunctional rankings competition, U.S. business schools are destined to lose their dominant global position and become a classic case study of how myopic decision-making begets institutional mediocrity.

Harry DeAngelo, Linda DeAngelo, & Jerold L. Zimmerman, "What's Really Wrong With U.S. Business Schools?" (unpublished paper, 2005), http://ssrn.com/abstract=766404.

46. I thank Larry Ribstein for suggesting this question to me.

47. I intend to study whether applications increase after rankings increase.

48. Ironically, this effort might have resulted in schools placing more emphasis on the LSAT by shifting *U.S. News* from the median LSAT to the 25th percentile. *See supra* Part I.B.

49. DEANS SPEAK OUT, *supra* note 26.

Why Not Rank Law Schools by Student Credentials?: Replacing the "Junk Science" of U.S. News Rankings

David A. Thomas[1]

"The ratings at least give the impression that all law schools are arranged according to a single hierarchy of talent. Is this self-fulfilling?"[2]

I. Introduction

The latest salvo in the continuing barrage of academic literature over law school rankings was fired by Prof. Theodore P. Seto of Loyola Law School, Los Angeles, in his excellent article, "Understanding the *U.S. News* Law School Rankings."[3] This is a fascinating exploration of the arcane weightings and computations underlying the annual law school rankings issued by the news magazine *U.S. News and World Report* (*USNWR* or *U.S. News*). Professor Seto confesses that he finds the *U.S. News* rankings perplexing, not only with respect to the law school at which he teaches and its peer institutions, but also with respect to law schools at the very top of the rankings. Pointing out obvious anomalies in these upper end rankings of well-known law schools, he wonders whether such serious discrepancies might also affect rankings of less well-known law schools.

As an example of anomalies in the upper ranks, he notes that Harvard, relative to Stanford, had students with stronger academic credentials, a larger law library, and shared with Yale the highest reputation ratings from legal academics; yet, Stanford overall was ranked above Harvard. Similarly, he is puzzled that Yale, with lower student academic credentials, a smaller library, a lower New York bar passage rate, and equivalent reputation rankings, was rated over Harvard (by a "huge" 9-point difference). This has led him to try replicating the magazine's computations and to better understand what impact differences in the components of the rankings have on the ultimate rankings. His article reports the fascinating results of his investigation and includes a section called "Managing Your School's Rankings."

Professor Seto concludes his article with a section, "Improving the *U.S. News* Ranking System," which includes recommendations for the improving both the components of the rankings and the way the rankings are computed. In general, then, while his work shows serious flaws in the *U.S. News* law school rankings, it is premised on the assumption that those rankings are here to stay, and on the hope that perhaps with his friendly suggestions the rankings can be made more serviceable.

Other critics of the *U.S. News* rankings have been less tolerant, many suggesting from the outset that the entire concept of a single ranking system for such diverse institutions as American law schools is not feasible or desirable. Even while condemning the particular ranking scheme of *U.S. News*, however, most critics would concede that there is a huge and diverse demand for some meaningful way of evaluating law schools. That the much-maligned law school ratings of a mere popular news magazine continue to be issued—indeed, continue to be very popular[4]—bespeaks the intensity of the demand. Clearly, critics of the current ratings systems should do more than criticize; they should and do seek better ways to meet the needs reflected in the popularity of current rankings.

Despite the popularity of the *U.S. News* law school rankings, it was clear a long time ago that they were no better than "junk science."[5] Prof. Seto's article confirms that condemnation. The eagerness of the rankings-seekers makes them easy prey for the phony sophistication of the *U.S. News* rankings. This article will (1) analyze the nature of that demand, (2) explain how almost all the components of the *U.S. News* rankings lack relevance (in other words, lack probity) and reliability, or both, relative to that demand, and (3) present a simple but effective way to rate and rank law schools.

II. Why Rankings?

Since the *U.S. News & World Report* began publishing its law school rankings in 1990, probably no single subject has more preoccupied legal educators. The rankings have been heavily and deservedly criticized,[6] but they continue to be frequently consulted by various constituencies, including prospective law students, legal employers, judges and even legal educators and scholars themselves. This anomaly, and the proliferation of alternative ranking schemes, strongly suggest a persisting need for the information the rankings purport to provide, and that those who seek the information are willing to accept it even in flawed form.

The quest for the perfect ranking system and for alternatives to existing ranking systems has spawned many creative approaches to retrieving and evaluating information about the quality of law schools. Some of these are meritorious; some are provocative; some are shallow and silly. It now seems worthwhile to try penetrating this proliferation of lists and orderings with a bright ray of common sense. This effort would raise such common sense questions as: What are the ultimate purposes of law school rankings? Is it possible to produce rankings that serve any such ultimate purposes? What types of information are relevant and reliable foundations for such rankings? How can the needed information be retrieved and presented in the most helpful, reliable and useful way? A thoughtful, common sense approach to these questions might make it possible to identify rational approaches to evaluating law schools, perhaps in different ways for different constituencies.

It would be easy to dismiss this question of "Why Rankings?" with the cynical response that those who promulgate rankings do it mostly for financial reward. However, there would be little financial reward if the rankings were not serving some more significant purposes for those who seek out and consult the rankings. These persons fit into a few main categories—prospective law students, legal employers and judges, and legal educators—and their purposes differ somewhat from one another.

Prospective law students. Simplistically, prospective law students could be said to be seeking the best law school they can be admitted to, but there is more to it than that. Some students would choose not to matriculate into a good school in preference for a lesser school in a locality they considered more favorable; others might choose a lesser school for financial reasons, such as lower tuition and living costs or better financial aid. Still others might prefer a law school because of a religious affiliation or a perceived curricular specialty. Prospective law students usually seek a law school where they can both get a good education and whose prestige will help them get started on their professional career.

Law school rankings could be directly related to the first objective of ensuring a good legal education, if the rankings truly portrayed the comparative quality of law schools. Current ranking systems do not accomplish that. Rankings can also relate to the second objective of helping students in securing professional employment upon completion of law school. Indeed, some students expect the rankings to help them choose a law school whose prestige will best enable the students to obtain the most prestigious and lucrative professional positions upon graduation. However, the large majority of prospective law students are not qualified to realize such benefits from the rankings, even if they wanted to. Reliable rankings information could be of some assistance to most prospective law students in choosing a law school to attend, but in many cases would not be dispositive in their decision-making. The rankings would be only a part of their investigation. Other topics a prospective law student should consider include location, tuition and financial aid, library facility and resources, character and competence of the students, character and competence of the faculty, physical plant, curriculum, academic support, and career services.[7]

Legal employers and judges. Legal employers, too, want the best law school graduates they can hire. The employers naturally assume that the best students tend to matriculate into the best law schools, and it becomes a simple matter to identify and target the top graduates from the top schools. Thus, the law school where one was educated is at least one factor in the credentials considered in the hiring process. It is an important enough factor, in fact, that it may open up interviewing and hiring opportunities not tendered to students from less-respected law schools. Ultimately, it is the person and not the institution the employer hires, so a ranking system of law schools is useful to the prospective employer only insofar as it helps focus the employer on a law school that is assumed to produce good people. Any ranking system that evaluates a law school on criteria not directly related to the quality of the graduates is irrelevant to and may actually do a significant disservice to the prospective employer.

Legal educators. Legal educators, including some who routinely criticize the concept of a ranking system, may also find it convenient or desirable to resort to rankings. Rankings, or the law school reputations emanating from or reinforced by rankings, may influence a law professor's decision about where to seek employment or where to publish a law review article, among other issues. Law school faculties may rely on rankings as a factor in evaluating the credentials of prospective faculty members. Law school dean candidates may promote their candidacies by promising to improve the law school's standing in the rankings if hired. As discussed above, these potential benefits are compromised by the untenability of devising a reliable single ranking system for gauging overall law school quality.

In summary, prospective law students seek the best institution to which they can get admitted, that meets their subjective needs, and that will help them get started in their professional careers. Legal educators want the best institution willing to hire them and that meets their subjective needs, or is willing to publish their scholarly articles. They also want to hire the best persons to join their faculties, and, for public relations purposes, they may want their newly hired colleagues to come from the best schools. Legal employers primarily want to hire the best people, and for public relations purposes they may want the people they hire to come from the best institutions.

So, to the extent these constituencies seek institutional evaluations, there *is* a demand for law school rankings, and even though one may have some impressions about the quality of a particular law school, the impulse to test those impressions against seemingly "objective" information of rankings is irresistible. Law schools do not have won-lost records or conference championships, but they sometimes act as aggressively as collegiate or professional sports teams in upgrading faculties, facilities, and even student bodies, as if they were in intense athletic competition. In fact, law schools see themselves in competition with perceived peer institutions, and law school ranking systems both meet and stimulate needs associated with that competitive attitude.

III. Is It Possible to Rank Law Schools?

This author has previously published an essay asserting that the very concept of a single ranking for law schools is a serious deception.[8] One type of ranking is to merely give a listing in numerical order of items of objective or empirical data. Another type of ranking may list in some sort of numerical order the data generated by normative or qualitative judgments, or the data generated by a mixture of objective and normative sources. If the intent of a ranking is merely to display objective data in numerical order, leaving interpretation and assessment to readers, then criticisms of such a ranking would be limited to the accuracy or validity of the data.

If, on the other hand, the intent of the ranking is to list data that may not be objective and may not be probative, and then to tell the reader what the interpretation of such a listing should be, no intelligent reader should be expected to accept such a ranking. This approach, so lacking in common sense, is unfortunately the *U.S. News & World Report* law school rankings approach.

Another common flaw of law school rankings is the attempt to evaluate and list all law schools in a single ranked list. This is inherently impossible. Even though persons familiar with law schools might be able to identify some aspects of law schools they think are essential to being a good law school, no consensus has ever been attempted or achieved as to what qualities or features in a law school make a good, better, or best law school according to a single, comprehensive scale.

Contrary to common sense, the inference a reader would draw from the *U.S. News & World Report* rankings is that the items listed in the rankings are the accepted criteria one should use in determining the quality of a law school. Not only is that deliberately created impression false and misleading, but, as will be shown below, most of the *U.S. News & World Report* criteria cannot possibly be probative of any reasonable or common sense notion of law school quality, either of absolute quality or of comparative quality. This serious flaw is compounded by placing these erroneous criteria in a single ranked list that is touted as identifying the best or top law schools. Again, persons familiar with law schools would categorically deny that a unitary or consensual judgment about law school quality could be made from assessing a canonical list of criteria.[9]

Also contrary to common sense, the *U.S. News & World Report* rankings report and combine both objective data and non-objective data. Whether or not such data are ultimately probative, the objective statistical data included in those rankings are widely available in other publications and may be validated by reference to verifiable facts about each law school. The non-objective data, specifically the reputation data, are unique to *U.S. News & World Report*, represent opinions founded on perceptions or impressions or idle guesses rather than knowledge, and have no known relation to reality except that they are authentic personal perceptions. To combine these two incompatible and mutually exclusive data sets into a coherent, unitary statistical evaluation of academic excellence in a law school is impossible and irrational.

In a further irrationality, the *U.S. News & World Report* rankings combine objective and nonobjective data in arbitrary ways. The inherent impossibility of rationally combining the objective and non-objective data generated for the rankings is exacerbated by forcing and manipulating the combination according to arbitrary notions of their relative importance. The relative weights assigned to the individual data categories in the rankings are arbitrary and subjective. This is starkly revealed in Prof. Seto's study.[10]

Despite absence of a canon of criteria for determining the "best" law schools according to a single ranked order (and thus the absence of such a canon), certain factual features of law schools are relevant to their relative quality; common sense further suggests that each law school is stronger in some ways than in others, and that even the "best" law schools are not necessarily uniformly strong in all relevant categories. All of these somewhat obvious propositions lend credence to the notion that a single ranked list is neither realistic nor helpful. This notion is sustained by the following additional propositions:

- One can identify some criteria relevant to a law school's quality, but perhaps not gain a broad consensus on all criteria.
- One can agree that reliable data in some or all of the categories does not necessarily produce a single, unitary conclusion about the law school's quality.
- One must concede that a law school's uneven strength in whatever criteria are measured would render a single ranked list inherently irrational.

IV. What Criteria Are at Least Relevant to Evaluating a Law School?

This section evaluates the various criteria used for evaluating law schools in a variety of ranking systems. The evaluations are based on whether the criterion is relevant to or probative of the quality of the law school or of the educational experience it provides. Secondarily, the discussion also reviews whether reliable data pertaining to each criterion is obtainable.

1. Law School Admission Test (LSAT) Scores

The highly interactive style of American law teaching means that one's fellow students can make a big difference in the quality of one's law school experience. Law students frequently participate in class, either by responding to professors' questions or by offering their own comments, with fellow students listening in and, hopefully, vicariously participating in the discussion. Outside of class, students are constantly conversing with each other about class discussions, cases, issues, and current legal events, either informally or in organized study groups. Whether that influence is largely positive or negative is a subjective matter, but in general, a law school with more able students can, in this respect, offer a higher quality legal education experience for all of its students.[11] Thus, it is natural for all higher education institutions, including law schools, to seek out and compete for better students, and it is also natural for any system of rating and ranking law schools to take student quality into account.

The two traditional measures of prospective law students' academic and intellectual credentials are the Law School Admission Test (LSAT) score, and the undergraduate grade point average (GPA). These are both the primary criteria in the admissions process of every law school and key features in law school ranking systems. The LSAT attempts to measure a person's mental abilities in ways that are considered essential for success in law school.[12] It is a standardized test in which performance is not dependent on a specialized educational background, although the scores appear to be somewhat manipulable through intensive preparation and multiple testing experiences.

The only way to tell whether a good LSAT score means one will be a good law student is to measure how accurately the LSAT score correlates to academic performance in law school. Such correlation measurements are very imprecise and can be attempted only for individual law schools rather than for all law schools generally.[13] In general, one may conclude that law school applicants with higher LSAT scores (relative to other applicants at a particular law school), if admitted, achieve a relatively higher class ranking at the end of the first year of law school.[14] However, this is nothing more than a correlation and its predictive value is so weak that no law student need feel precluded from high academic achievement by deterministic limits supposedly imposed by LSAT performance. Moreover, this correlation says nothing about cause and effect relationships. Do the same abilities that generate success on the LSAT also help one to achieve academic success in law school, or does even this weak correlation occur for other reasons? No one knows, least of all those who publish law school rankings.

Despite the inability rationally to correlate strong performance on the LSAT with success in law school or in a legal career, observation and common sense indicate that students with strong LSAT scores tend to enter and graduate from law schools perceived to be relatively stronger law schools. Legal educators observe that students who enter law school with strong LSAT scores are generally stronger students, with numerous exceptions, of course. Observation and common sense also indicate that students with very low LSAT scores relative to the rest of their class frequently struggle to succeed in law school.

The virtues of LSAT scores as a measurement of academic qualifications of entering law students are that the scores are achieved in nationwide test groups and that the scores reflect actual performance rather than subjective evaluation. The main weakness of the LSAT score as an evaluative measure is the inability to know whether a single score is a fluke, or to what extent scores vary from one test administration to another.

Frequently students without strong undergraduate grade point averages achieve high LSAT scores; from this, common sense suggests that the LSAT score and the GPA measure different aspects of intellectual ability, both of which are probably relevant to success in law school.

As between LSAT and GPA, LSAT is currently the predominant measure in the *U.S. News & World Report* ranking system, and probably is the primary focus in the academic credentials aspect of law school admission practices. The LSAT scores of a law school's entering students can be measured by the 75th percentile, the 25th percentile, the median and the mean. For a law school to overload its admitted class with high LSATs, in order to achieve rankings advantage with a high median or high 75th percentile, might leave that law school's entering class with a group of exceptionally low LSAT students seriously struggling in the bottom quartile of the class, which may have a negative effect on the entire instruction program.[15] To the extent LSAT score is a valid measure of entering law students' relevant academic qualifications, that validity is strongest when the LSAT scores are consistently and similarly strong in all quartiles of the admitted class. Despite the apparent relevance and ready availability of LSAT data, the *U.S. News* law school rankings unnecessarily and unhelpfully distort that information. Prof. Seto's study showed that when *U.S. News and World Report* computed LSAT scores as part of its overall ranking system, it first "standardized" them by converting them into percentages, which "conversion significantly changed the effect of LSATs on overall scores."[16]

2. Undergraduate Grade Point Average (GPA)

The other icon of academic ability is the undergraduate grade point average. The GPA's well-known shortcoming as a measurement device is extreme variation in academic rigor and grading standards across the institutions of American higher education, not only across disciplines but also within an individual college or university. Despite this, the GPA has a common sense advantage for applicant evaluation that is completely absent from the LSAT: whatever the variation in grading practices and standards, a strong GPA usually means that the student has relatively good work and study habits and has been able to sustain a consistent effort over a long period of time. Not surprisingly, GPA also has some value as a predictor of academic success in law school.[17] Common sense strongly suggests that the same habits and qualities contributing to a strong undergraduate GPA also aid a strong academic performance in law school.

So, which credential is the better predictor of law school success, LSAT or GPA? The evidence from the author's long term study at his law school is that the LSAT score is a slightly better predictor of academic performance in the first year of law school, and GPA is a better predictor of academic performance for the entire three years of law school, which is logical. Therefore, to emphasize LSAT score as a law school quality evaluation credential at the expense of GPA would be irrational.[18]

Absent from this discussion about student quality, and not subject to measurement, are the personal qualities in students that greatly influence their personal success and their impact on their fellow students, which impact is an important factor in the quality of education at that law school. These are such qualities as whether a law school's students are emotionally stable, free of substance abuse or other self-defeating behaviors, honest, kind and compassionate, and balanced in a professional environment that is often intensely driven and beset by materialism. Assuredly the quality of a law school's students are as much affected by these factors as by students' LSAT scores and GPAs. These factors cannot be measured by reported statistics or by rankings, but local inquiries may help.

3. Student/Faculty Ratio

It would seem self-evident that a lower student/faculty ratio—fewer students per teacher—would be an indication of a higher quality law school program. This assumption would be more valid if faculty numbers were counted and faculty were used the same ways in all law school programs, but in fact practices in this area of law school administration vary widely among law schools. For numerical reporting purposes, law schools operate under a uniform set of rules used by the American Bar Association to calculate student/faculty ratios. The differences among law schools arise in how they assign teaching loads and, in general, how faculty resources are used to provide instruction to law students.

All law schools recognize the pedagogical desirability of smaller classes, but priorities in how to achieve that may differ. Typically, the standard first-year courses are taught in larger-than-average sections, either in sections of equal size or divided into large and small sections. In the standard curriculum, which consists almost entirely of elective courses for second- and third-year students, courses perceived as important—and which are therefore heavily subscribed—are also usually taught in large sections. The class size for almost all other elective courses is usually quite small, and a favorable student/faculty ratio can mean either that more of such smaller courses are offered or that larger courses are sectioned to achieve smaller class size.

Law schools may also differ on how much teaching is expected of their faculty members, and whether faculty members who have administrative responsibilities as deans, assistant and associate deans, and university administrators, also carry partial teaching loads. This in turn makes more vague the significance of the student/faculty ratio in evaluating a law school's quality.

For a prospective law student trying to assess a law school, the most important consequences of the student/faculty ratio are class size and typical teaching loads, both of which affect each teacher's ability to give attention to student needs and present high quality class instruction. The bare numerical data of student/faculty ratio unfortunately do not yield this information. Nor do they reveal whether the law school faculty members promote a culture of caring for students in ways that may profoundly enhance the quality of the students' educational experience, in and out of the classroom. Only an applicant's individual inquiries at selected law schools can begin to yield insights on these important matters.

So, data on student/faculty ratio are relevant, but only as a beginning point for more detailed inquiries about faculty impact on the educational experience, not as conclusory information on the comparative quality of a law school. It would be most helpful to prospective applicants if law schools would publish class size information, either in the *Official Guide* or on their institutional websites.

The natural assumption is that, in general, more favorable student/faculty ratios will help ensure a better classroom experience for the students. Ideally, a law professor should have a moderate load of teaching assignments and a moderate number of students (leaving time for scholarly research and writing, which should also enhance teaching quality), and a favorable student/faculty ratio should help a law school attain those ideals. However, law school policies regarding teaching loads can compromise those benefits, even if the law school has a favorable student/faculty ratio. For instance, if a law school has high expectations for scholarly productivity from its faculty, that could mean less faculty time and energy is left for teaching, which in turn may result in larger class sizes or fewer course offerings, despite a relatively favorable student/faculty ratio. Conversely, if higher teaching loads are the norm, professors may have less time for individual student consultation and mentoring, either in or out of class. The delicate balance struck by law schools on these important issues is not revealed by mere reporting of student/faculty ratios. Disturbingly, American law schools have been inconsistent in how they have reported student/faculty ratios.[19]

4. *Faculty Quality*

It also seems self-evident that faculty quality is an important component of a law school's quality, but this proposition is more complex. If a law school's quality is being assessed for the kind of educational experience it can provide for the students, the main aspect of faculty quality that is important is the quality of classroom experience provided by the faculty. This cannot be and never has been assessed in any meaningful way, especially as a comparison between law schools.

In addition to teaching, law school faculty also engage in legal research and writing, often resulting in published works, but also often resulting in other non-published outputs. A common mantra in law schools, and in higher education generally, is that professors who actively engage in research and writing will become more knowledgeable and therefore better teachers. While this may be true for many professors, widespread observation and anecdotal evidence reveals that many professors engage so enthusiastically in research and writing that their teaching quality and quantity suffer. Achieving the right balance is a delicate and highly subjective undertaking. Law school administrators take part in managing that balance by communicating to faculty members formal or customary publication expectations and by administering and evaluating teaching performance assessments, both from students and colleagues.

The only part of this activity reflecting on faculty quality that is revealed to the public generally is in the form of published works by the faculty. Therefore, it is tempting to count law professors' published works and use the quantitative results as a measuring device to assess faculty quality. Such an approach also enables easy comparisons between law schools. The main problem is that it makes no sense whatsoever to do that. If one is evaluating and comparing law schools as educational institutions, the only part of faculty activity that is meaningful for that purpose is law professors' performance in the classroom, which is unmeasurable.[20]

If law school quality is being evaluated and compared relative to other possible functions of the law school—such as influencing legislation, jurisprudence or public affairs generally—then law professors' publications could legitimately be considered a part of that. Those functions are conceivably important to the law school as an educational institution only if the prominence and prestige of the law school enhance the students' educational experience, such as by making available more career choices. If one were to assume that a more productive faculty results in a more prestigious law school, which provides its students with greater advantages in career choices, then it might make sense to try measuring faculty output.

One is left, then, with the attenuated proposition that faculty output in the form of scholarly activity may contribute to the prestige of the law school, which may enhance that school's students' career choices. This proposition is as impossible to measure and compare as faculty classroom performance.

Despite the utter futility of attempting to assess faculty quality as part of a law school's quality, some nevertheless attempt it.[21] A typical beginning approach would be to quantify faculty scholarly output by counting faculty publications. One then confronts the problem of assessing quality when one has only a quantitative measurement. One approach to this problem is to count how many times faculty publications are cited in other faculty publications. One may attempt to refine the focus on quality by narrowing the citation count to only those citations that appear in top law reviews, and top law reviews are identified by how often the law review's articles are cited in other law reviews.

If one pauses for a "common sense check" at this point, several major flaws are evident:

(1) Articles published in law reviews are an important but not the only important element of a law professor's possible scholarly output. Important articles may be published in other professional journals. Treatises and even casebooks may contain important scholarly contributions and influence court decisions. Professors also write or contribute to court briefs and deliver testimony at hearings and make speeches on important occasions. Any of these activities is as likely to enhance a law professor's performance in the classroom or add to the law school's prestige as publishing law review articles. No attempts have ever been made to measure and compare all of these legitimate and respectable forms of scholarly activity.[22]

(2) It is well known that major law reviews are seriously unbalanced in the subjects represented by the articles they choose to publish.[23] A law professor seeking to publish a fine article not in one of the favored fields must usually publish in a less prestigious law review. This may lessen the readership, number of citations and the prestige associated with the published article, even though the quality of the article is superior.

(3) Scholarly productivity, in whatever form, is not evenly spread out over a law school's faculty. Measuring a law school's overall output, or even a faculty per capita output, says nothing about the influence of scholarly activity on the quality of the faculty or faculty teaching as a whole, since some faculty members may not engage in any significant scholarship at all. There is the possibility that the herculean productivity of a few superstars, who may or may not teach well, will be leveraged into a general prestige for the entire law school. Comparing the numbers and outputs of such superstars between law schools does not solve that problem.

(4) None of this article- or citation-counting even begins to address the problem of quality. An excellent article or book may be ignored, because of its obscure topic, less prestigious publisher, or some other reason.[24]

This discussion has touched on four major flaws in citation studies: (1) the studies ignore other important kinds of scholarly productivity; (2) the citations are unevenly spread out over legal topics, so that high quality works may be undercited; (3) citation counts do not account for faculty who do not produce; and (4) citation counts cannot measure quality. These four flaws are exacerbated by the transcending flaw of the entire enterprise, which is the impossibility of assessing the impact of scholarly activity on law students' experience in the classroom or on the overall quality of the law school.

All of this therefore suggests that purporting to measure a law school's quality on the basis of a limited review of how many articles some faculty members get published, and how frequently the articles are cited by other writers is an irrational exercise in futility.

5. Selectivity of a Law School's Admission Practices (How Hard Is It to Get In? And How Eagerly Do Admittees Select the Law School?)

It is easy to assume that if a law school is selective in its admission practices, it must be admitting better students, which in turn makes it a better law school. It is also logical that the best evidence of this is the academic credentials of the incoming students, that is, their LSAT scores and undergraduate GPAs, data which are readily available and were analyzed as measures of selectivity in preceding sections. Nevertheless, two direct measures of admissions selectivity are available—one from the school's perspective and the other from the student's. Neither is especially meaningful as a measure of a law school's quality, and one is actually misleading.

One measure of selectivity from the prospective student's perspective is interesting and easily compared, but does not necessarily give insight into a law school's quality. According to this measurement, a law school reports the number of admissions offers it has extended and how many were accepted to make up its entering class. These numbers are published annually for almost all law schools.[25] A higher number of acceptances as a percentage of offers supposedly indicates how desirable the law school is, at least in the view of the applicants. However, it is hard to know what is really behind the numbers. The author's own law school typically has a very high acceptance rate, probably because of the school's religious affiliation, which is shared by most students in the school's applicant pool. Even if the students do vote with their feet, because of the way they perceive a law school's suitability, that may offer little insight into a law school's intrinsic quality. And it may also affirm that law school quality is a subjective topic, not subject to single-list ranking.

According to recent statistics, Yale Law School had the highest acceptance rate at 85%; the "top ten" law schools ranged from 58% to 85%; and the large majority of law schools were under 40%. It would make no sense to attach significance, about difference in law school quality, to a comparison of one law school with 33% offer acceptance with another law school with 34% offer acceptance.

Another way to measure selectivity is from the perspective of the law school, by comparing between law schools the percentages of students admitted from the applicant pool. A law school that offers admission to a smaller percentage of applicants, and is therefore more selective, supposedly ends up with higher quality students. Unfortunately, this syllogism, too, is afflicted with multiple flaws. Law school applicant pools differ so widely in composition that using the size of the applicant pool as a standard reference point is silly. Law school applicants have many different reasons for undertaking the time and expense to submit an application, only a few of which are based on a perception that the school is the "best" school. Those perceptions may have no basis in fact.

Prospective law students choose to apply or not to apply for a variety of reasons, and the size of the applicant pool may not indicate the same thing about each law school. For instance, a law school may have a very large applicant pool because it is located in a populous area, admits a large entering class, and can fill the class only by going deep into the ranks of the applicant pool. Another law school may have a very large applicant pool because it is highly ranked or enjoys some other form of prestige. Another law school may have a small applicant pool because prospective law students know that, with their credentials, the chances of admission are small, so they select themselves out of the applicant pool.

The probity of this selectivity information is severely limited, because (1) applicants' reasons for applying vary widely, (2) law schools' reasons for extending offers of admission vary widely, and (3) admitted successful applicants' reasons for accepting offers of admission vary widely. In fact, the size of the applicant pool, the number of offers of admission tendered to that pool, and the percentage of those offers actually accepted are not relevant to the quality of a law school's students, except insofar as they yield an entering class of strong students. The measure of the strength of that entering class is already better indicated by noting directly the entering students' LSAT scores and undergraduate GPAs, so applicant pool numbers are superfluous.

All of this makes attempts to measure a law school's selectivity by other than the academic credentials of the entering class an exercise in irrationality. Law school admissions practices are still mostly driven by consideration of applicants' LSAT scores and GPAs.

Even though the academic credentials of LSAT score and undergraduate GPA are incomplete, flawed, and misused as tools for evaluating law school applicants, they are still the best available measurement of student strength, which in turn is an important factor in assessing the quality of a law school.

Any other attempts to measure a law school's quality by assessing how selective it is in admitting students are redundant and mostly meaningless. They are redundant because those other measures of selection are only indirect ways of learning the same information that is directly given by reviewing academic credentials. They are mostly meaningless because applicants can be motivated by a huge variety of reasons in deciding to accept an offer of admission, only one of which is the perceived quality of the law school.

6. Placement

Almost all law school applicants are urgently interested in knowing how their choice of law school will affect their chances of finding suitable professional positions upon graduation and beyond. Law schools attempt to answer that question by revealing how successful their graduates are in finding those positions. This information is shown in the *ABA-LSAC Official Guide to ABA-Approved Law Schools*, among the charts for each school, in the chart titled "Employment." The chart shows the percentage of graduates employed at the time of graduation in various types of positions. The placement data may also show the percentage of employment several months after graduation, which allows graduates time to take a bar exam, obtain the results, and parlay passing the bar into a job.

These numbers are certainly relevant to one's choice of law school, but only in a general way. They do not distinguish between law schools on a variety of related topics that are of equal or higher importance to applicants. An applicant may want to learn how zealous and effective a law school's placement office (or career services office, or office of some similar title and task) is in helping a student understand the range of professional opportunities, how to identify and best present oneself to prospective employers, how to enlist the assistance of law school alumni, along with many other services. The reported placement percentages may include but not distinguish between legal and non-legal jobs, between first-choice and other than first-choice jobs, and between jobs held before and during law school that were continued after graduation and jobs found first after law school graduation. Quality of professional opportunity is an important issue but is not subject to quantifiable evaluation. Again, on all of these points, the prospective applicant is best advised to call or visit the law schools in which he or she is most interested and gather the impressions and information firsthand.

Because these statistics are relevant to one's choice of law school, it is good that they are gathered and may be analyzed. However, there are severe limits on how useful this information is in making statistical comparisons about law school quality. Employment prospects are certainly affected by the law school's geographical location and the primary geographical market the law school serves. A law school that perceives itself as a national or a regional school is not necessarily, because of that, a better law school than a state school, yet the employment market may be significantly different. Also, placement data is self-reported by the law schools and not subject to independent verification.

The placement statistics for the most prestigious schools are significantly better than the placement statistics for the least prestigious schools, which implies that quality of law school may be reflected in placement success. However, whether the often fine distinctions among law schools closely ranked somewhere between those two ends of the spectrum can yield meaningful comparisons or conclusions about law school quality is problematic. The placement percentages differ from year to year and may follow national trends that impact on employment or law-related employment generally. All these factors make placement data a poorly suited criterion for judging or comparing the quality of law schools, either as educational institutions, or simply as ways to get a job.

In general, the rates of placement success mirror the academic credentials of a law school's entering students. Thus, knowing students' academic credentials provides the more measurable, meaningful and reliable data about law school quality than knowing the placement percentages.

7. *Bar Exam Passage Rates*

Again, the prospective law school applicant would find information about bar exam passage rates interesting and pertinent. Some of this information is reported for each law school in the "Bar Passage Rates" section of the *ABA-LSAC Official Guide to ABA-Approved Law Schools*. Unfortunately, finding out this data is not as simple as getting a report from the state bar organizations, and attempts to meaningfully represent and compare bar passage rates between law schools are false and misleading.

All law schools find their graduates taking the bar exam in more than one state. Seldom is the group of students from one law school taking the bar exam in any one state a representative cross-section of that school's graduating class. This is because even in the states where the largest group of graduates from any one law school take the bar exam usually, the top graduates (or the majority of graduates) have gone elsewhere.

In comparison to overall state bar exam passage rates, no adjustment is made in those states that permit graduates of unaccredited law schools to take the bar exam, and whose presence usually lowers the overall passage rates for that state. Also, it is impossible to know the impact of employers who pay for bar exam review courses and otherwise help their newly graduated employees have the best possible preparation and opportunity for succeeding in the bar exam.

Even the law schools themselves have difficulty in obtaining this data. State bar organizations are not required to report back to law schools which of their graduates have or have not succeeded in any particular bar exam, and the law schools also have no sure way of knowing which of their graduates are even sitting for a particular bar exam.

Most law schools do not explicitly attempt to prepare their students for success in bar exams and, after the first year of law school, do not require students to take courses on subjects that will likely be part of bar examinations. Students with higher academic credentials are naturally more likely to succeed in a bar exam, and law schools with higher credentialed students are more likely to produce graduates who pass bar exams at higher rates than law schools that have students with lower academic credentials. Thus, knowing students' academic credentials provides the more measurable, meaningful, and reliable data about law school quality than knowing the bar passage rate.

8. *Reputation*

In what is surely the most controversial and indefensible part of the *U.S. News & World Report* ranking scheme, two groups of respondents are asked to give an assessment of the comparative quality of law schools, and this reputational data is mysteriously combined, weighted, and folded into the magazine's rankings.[26] Astonishingly and illogically, this most questionable and unverifiable of all the portions of the rankings report is accorded a weight of 40% of the overall score in the *U.S. News & World Report* ranking. After almost two decades, this reputational part of the rankings is probably nothing more than a self-fulfilling prophecy.

The most important criticism of this data is that it is purely subjective and imaginary—indeed, delusional—as indicated by the following self-evident propositions:

No one really knows the intrinsic quality of any law school, including one's own.

No one really knows how the quality of one law school compares with the quality of any other law school.

No one agrees with anyone else about the bases or criteria or priorities in making such comparisons.

The temptations to rate one's own institution high and one's competitor or peer institutions low are irresistible.

The tendency to translate one's ignorance about any particular law school into a low (rather than neutral) reputation rating is universal.[27]

And the respondents may have other limitations. In 1996, Thomas E. Brennan, former Chief Justice of the Michigan Supreme Court and the founder of the Thomas M. Cooley Law School, reported the following:

> Some years ago, I conducted a little informal poll, just to see how much lawyers and judges know about law schools. I asked a hundred or so randomly selected members of the bench and bar to rank ten law schools which I named. They included a good sample of the big names. Harvard. Yale. University of Michigan. And some lesser known schools. John Marshall. Thomas Cooley. As I recall, they ranked Penn State's law school right about in the middle of the pack. Maybe fifth among the ten schools listed. Of course Penn State doesn't have a law school.[28]

All the reputational ratings really reveal is that several dozen otherwise intelligent people agreed to report what they think other people think about something that is unknowable. The common sense approach to reputational data as rankings information is to disregard them entirely. This is especially true at the time of this writing, when the many years of reported reputational data must surely infect and distort the views of those asked to give their reputational rankings each year.

9. Expenditures

Labeled "Faculty Resources" in the *U.S. News* ranking, this category of evaluation includes per student expenditures for instruction, library and supporting services including financial aid, student/teacher ratio, and numbers of volumes and titles in the law library. Professor Seto extensively analyzes flaws in the data, both in the reporting and the computation. His study shows that expenditures per student make an enormous difference in the relative ranking of otherwise comparable schools.[29] He raises two fundamental questions: first, whether the reported expenditure figures actually reflect additional dollars spent on the J.D. programs *U.S. News* is ranking, and second, whether any such additional dollars spent actually improve the quality of those programs in a meaningful way.[30] There is something troubling about rankings based on secret numbers apparently inconsistent with those reported to the law schools' accrediting authority. There is a very real potential that the *U.S. News* rankings may come to measure dishonesty—higher rankings indicating, among other things, a greater willingness to fudge the numbers.[31] To the extent these higher expenditures are attributable in part to higher faculty salaries, Seto argues that this does not necessarily mean better teaching:

> Top-ranked schools hire laterally for scholarship, not for teaching. The inference must therefore be that higher "educational" expenditures per student signal faculties with higher scholarly reputations. Again, it is not clear that the signal is valid; ... Even assuming validity, however, the question remains whether prospective students or employers should care. In physics or chemistry, cutting-edge scholarship matters. In law, by contrast, cutting-edge scholarship often has no relevance whatever to actual practice. Indeed, some professors at top-ranked schools have been accused of not teaching at all.[32]

This discussion has considered nine types of information as possibly relevant to evaluating a law school. Here is a summary of the conclusions reached on these nine types of information:

- LSAT scores: Relevant and measurable.
- GPA: Relevant and measurable.
- Student/faculty ratio: possibly relevant, depending on how faculty are used for the instructional program, but that information is not known; self-reported and inconsistent.
- Faculty quality: Undefinable and unmeasurable.
- Admission selectivity: Measurable but of questionable relevance; academic credentials of matriculated students are more directly pertinent.
- Placement. Not directly relevant; self-reported and inconsistent.
- Bar exam passage rates: Not directly relevant; self-reported and incomplete.
- Reputation: Fictional (without substance and objectivity).
- Per student expenditures: Data and computations not reliable; relevance to quality of instructional program cannot be established.

This review reveals that only the basic data on students' academic credentials are truly relevant and measurable. To the extent the other measures are relevant, they seem to be adequately reflected in the LSAT and GPA data. Indeed, one writer concluded, "[T]he median Law School Admission Test (LSAT) score of a law school's students does much of the work of *U.S. News*'s ranking algorithm (especially since the more subjective factors in the algorithm, such as school reputation and students' college GPAs, are correlated with it)."[33]

Partially at odds with that quoted statement, this review has concluded that it would not make sense to consider LSAT scores alone, since the other empirical student credential, GPA, is the only available measure of other important attributes of student quality. These measures are most reliable if there is no great gap between the 75th, 50th and 25th percentiles in the matriculated class of students. This numerical data about student quality is also relatively more reliable than other measures of law school quality, because it can be objectively documented and verified through authenticated test data and transcripts.[34] Despite the preference of *U.S. News* and Leiter rankings for LSAT over GPA scores, this writer has shown in a previous study that there is good reason to weight them equally in judging student quality.[35]

V. Can the Relevant Information Be Presented and Used in a Meaningful Way?

If one knows that the entering students at a particular law school have a 75th percentile LSAT score at a certain level, that information is most meaningful when considered in the context of similar data from all the other law schools in the *U.S. News* report (a total of 189 law schools in this study). Therefore it makes sense to present this information in a chart or list format that enables such comparisons. The chart below shows for all 184[36] law schools in the *U.S. News* 2008 report (published as the 2009 edition, showing data reported at the beginning of the 2007–2008 academic year) following data relating to entering students:

75th percentile GPA
50th (median) percentile GPA
25th percentile GPA
75th percentile LSAT score
50th (median) percentile LSAT score
25th percentile LSAT score[37]

All the data is drawn from the 2009 edition of the annual *ABA-LSAC Official Guide to ABA-Approved Law Schools*, which was issued in the summer of 2008 and contains data reported at the beginning of the 2007–2008 academic year. In summary, then, the list of law schools is taken from the *U.S. News* report; the data is from the *ABA-LSAC Official Guide*.[38]

In addition to the data, the chart also shows, for each data category, the school's ranking relative to all other law schools. Each category is weighted equally, the rankings are then averaged, and the schools are listed in rank order, according to the overall rankings average. This is in the column headed "Rank for Acad Cred" or ranking for student academic credentials. In the final columns are shown the *U.S. News* ranking for that institution that year, and the *U.S. News* overranking of the law school's ranking in this study (+), or the *U.S. News* underranking (–).

In each category, the 75th, 50th, and 25th percentile figures are all weighted equally. This is a more discerning measure than using only medians, because it identifies admission practices that leave the lower end of an entering class relatively weak.

The chart also shows that LSAT scores and GPA figures are weighted equally. The article acknowledges that both measures have validity and weakness in evaluating academic credentials of prospective law students. Both are relevant and essential; neither alone is sufficient. If they were to be weighted differently, there would be no principled basis for assigning their respective weights.

School	75% GPA	75% GPA Rank	Med GPA	Med GPA Rank	25% GPA	25% GPA Rank	75% LSAT	75% LSAT Rank	Med LSAT	Med LSAT Rank	25% LSAT	25% LSAT Rank	Ave. All Ranks	Rank for Acad. Cred.	*U.S. News* Rank	*USN* Over(+) or Under(–) Rank
Yale	3.97	1	3.89	1	3.77	1	177	1	173	1	170	1	1	1	1	0
Harvard	3.95	2	3.88	2	3.75	2	175	2	173	1	170	1	1.667	2	2	0
Stanford	3.95	2	3.86	3	3.74	3	172	6	170	6	167	6	4.333	3	2	+1
NYU	3.86	7	3.71	11	3.54	7	173	4	171	4	169	3	6	4	5	–1

School	75% GPA	75% GPA Rank	Med GPA	Med GPA Rank	25% GPA	25% GPA Rank	75% LSAT	75% LSAT Rank	Med LSAT	Med LSAT Rank	25% LSAT	25% LSAT Rank	Ave. All Ranks	Rank for Acad. Cred.	*U.S. News* Rank	*USN* Over(+) or Under(−) Rank
Virginia	3.87	5	3.74	7	3.51	12	171	8	170	6	167	6	7.333	5	9	−4
Pennsylvania	3.86	7	3.77	5	3.52	11	171	8	170	6	166	11	8	6	7	−1
Columbia	3.81	27	3.7	12	3.56	6	174	3	172	3	169	3	9	7	4	+3
Cal-Berkeley	3.9	4	3.79	4	3.64	4	170	11	167	13	163	19	9.167	8	6	+2
Duke	3.82	21	3.74	7	3.61	5	170	11	169	11	167	6	10.17	9	12	−3
Vanderbilt	3.83	18	3.74	7	3.54	7	168	15	167	13	164	16	12.67	10	15	−5
UCLA	3.85	13	3.72	10	3.54	7	169	14	167	13	163	19	12.67	10	16	−6
Georgetown	3.82	21	3.67	18	3.44	22	171	8	170	6	167	6	13.5	12	14	−2
Geo. Wash.	3.86	7	3.75	6	3.4	30	168	15	167	13	165	14	14.17	13	20	−7
Northwestern	3.8	32	3.7	12	3.4	30	172	6	170	6	166	11	16.17	14	9	+5
Chicago	3.76	52	3.64	27	3.49	16	173	4	171	4	169	3	17.67	15	7	+8
BYU	3.85	13	3.7	12	3.51	12	167	19	165	25	162	25	17.67	15	46	−31
Cornell	3.78	41	3.66	20	3.54	7	168	15	167	13	166	11	17.83	17	12	+5
Michigan	3.79	37	3.64	27	3.49	16	170	11	169	11	167	6	18	18	9	+9
Boston U.	3.81	27	3.68	16	3.51	12	166	27	165	25	164	16	20.5	19	21	−2
Fordham	3.78	41	3.66	20	3.44	22	167	19	166	18	163	19	23.17	20	27	−7
Texas	3.8	32	3.6	37	3.38	34	168	15	166	18	163	19	25.83	21	16	+5
Maryland	3.84	15	3.65	23	3.47	18	166	27	162	41	160	32	26	22	42	−22
Wm & Mary	3.82	21	3.68	16	3.44	22	166	27	164	28	159	42	26	22	30	−8
Georgia	3.86	7	3.67	18	3.42	27	165	34	163	37	159	42	27.5	24	32	−8
Notre Dame	3.76	52	3.63	7	3.4	30	167	19	166	18	164	16	28.67	25	22	+3
Colorado	3.83	18	3.66	20	3.33	46	165	34	164	28	160	32	29.67	26	32	−6
U Washington	3.82	21	3.65	23	3.47	18	165	34	162	41	159	42	29.83	27	30	−3
So California	3.72	72	3.6	37	3.46	20	167	19	166	18	165	14	30	28	18	+10
Alabama	3.84	15	3.63	29	3.31	48	165	34	164	28	160	32	31	29	32	−3
Boston C.	3.78	41	3.6	37	3.44	22	165	34	164	28	162	25	31.17	30	26	+4
Wash & Lee	3.81	27	3.62	32	3.25	64	167	19	166	18	161	30	31.67	31	25	+6
SMU	3.84	15	3.69	15	3.28	56	165	34	164	28	157	61	34.83	32	46	−14
Iowa	3.86	7	3.62	32	3.41	29	163	52	161	51	159	42	35.5	33	27	+6
Washington U	3.77	6	3.6	37	3.3	50	167	19	166	18	163	19	36.5	34	19	+15
Minnesota	3.78	41	3.55	59	3.28	56	167	19	165	25	163	19	36.5	34	22	+12
Illinois	3.8	32	3.6	37	3.18	84	167	19	166	18	160	32	37	36	27	+9
UNC	3.8	32	3.65	23	3.45	21	164	44	161	51	157	61	38.67	37	38	−1
Cincinnati	3.87	5	3.63	29	3.39	33	162	61	161	51	157	61	40	38	52	−14
Ohio State	3.81	27	3.61	35	3.34	44	164	44	162	41	158	52	40.5	39	32	+7
Geo. Mason	3.86	7	3.62	32	3.11	107	166	27	164	28	159	42	40.5	39	38	−1
Cal-Hastings	3.74	62	3.57	53	3.36	38	165	34	163	37	160	32	42.67	41	38	+3
Cal-Davis	3.75	55	3.56	57	3.38	34	165	34	162	41	159	42	43.83	42	44	−2
Florida	3.83	18	3.65	23	3.44	22	162	61	160	65	156	74	43.83	42	46	−4
Cardozo	3.7	76	3.52	66	3.3	50	166	27	164	28	162	25	45.33	44	55	−11
Loyola Chi	3.75	55	3.58	49	3.35	41	163	52	161	51	159	42	48.33	45	82	−37
Houston	3.79	37	3.58	49	3.3	50	163	52	161	51	158	52	48.5	46	55	−11
Tulane	3.75	55	3.59	45	3.37	37	163	52	161	51	158	52	48.67	47	44	+3
Tennessee	3.82	21	3.59	45	3.35	41	162	61	160	65	157	61	49	48	52	−4
Kentucky	3.79	37	3.63	29	3.36	38	162	61	160	65	156	74	50.67	49	59	−10
Baylor	3.78	41	3.59	45	3.38	34	162	61	160	65	157	61	51.17	50	55	−5
Chi-Kent	3.77	48	3.6	37	3.2	78	164	44	162	41	157	61	51.5	51	66	−15
Wisconsin	3.74	62	3.58	49	3.32	47	163	52	161	51	157	61	53.67	52	36	+16
Pepperdine	3.73	68	3.55	59	3.42	27	162	61	160	65	158	52	55.33	53	59	−6
Florida St.	3.77	48	3.55	59	3.3	50	162	61	160	65	158	52	55.83	54	55	−3
Arizona St.	3.81	27	3.57	53	3.3	50	162	61	159	75	156	74	56.67	55	52	+3
Wake Forest	3.69	83	3.5	69	3.17	87	166	27	163	37	159	42	57.5	56	42	+14
Temple	3.65	102	3.49	73	3.28	56	164	44	162	41	160	32	58	57	59	−2
Utah	3.77	48	3.57	53	3.31	48	162	61	160	65	156	74	58.17	58	51	+7

School	75% GPA	75% GPA Rank	Med GPA	Med GPA Rank	25% GPA	25% GPA Rank	75% LSAT	75% LSAT Rank	Med LSAT	Med LSAT Rank	25% LSAT	25% LSAT Rank	Ave. All Ranks	Rank for Acad. Cred.	*U.S. News* Rank	*USN* Over(+) or Under(−) Rank
Emory	3.62	121	3.42	99	3.28	56	166	27	164	28	162	25	59.33	59	22	+37
Arizona	3.73	68	3.5	69	3.23	67	164	44	161	51	157	61	60	60	38	+22
St. John's	3.74	62	3.58	49	3.19	82	162	61	161	51	157	61	61	61	88	−27
Connecticut	3.64	110	3.47	80	3.24	65	164	44	162	41	160	32	62	62	46	+16
Missouri Colum	3.8	32	3.56	57	3.26	63	161	76	159	75	156	74	62.83	63	59	+4
Brooklyn	3.63	115	3.46	82	3.17	87	165	34	163	37	162	25	63.33	64	63	+1
Loyola LA	3.65	102	3.48	75	3.22	71	163	52	161	51	159	42	65.5	65	63	+2
Lew & Clark	3.73	68	3.5	69	3.15	96	163	52	161	51	157	61	66.17	66	73	−9
Rutgers Cam	3.7	76	3.45	86	3.1	112	163	52	162	41	160	32	66.5	67	77	−10
Nebraska	3.82	21	3.55	59	3.5	15	159	97	156	104	153	111	67.83	68	73	−5
Richmond	3.66	96	3.45	86	3.23	67	162	61	160	65	158	52	71.17	69	68	+1
Toledo	3.74	62	3.6	37	3.1	112	161	76	159	75	156	74	72.67	70		
Oklahoma	3.78	41	3.54	63	3.35	41	160	87	156	104	154	101	72.83	71	68	+3
Villanova	3.63	115	3.4	106	3.14	99	164	44	162	41	160	32	72.83	71	68	+3
Seton Hall	3.65	102	3.45	86	3.22	71	162	61	160	65	157	61	74.33	73	66	+7
Akron	3.76	52	3.51	67	3.16	92	160	87	159	75	156	74	74.5	74		
Indiana-Blm	3.67	94	3.4	106	3.03	134	165	34	164	28	158	52	74.67	75	36	+39
DePaul	3.66	96	3.44	93	3.1	112	162	61	161	51	159	42	75.83	76	88	−12
American	3.59	131	3.4	106	3.14	99	163	52	162	41	161	30	76.5	77	46	+31
Indiana-Ind	3.78	41	3.61	35	3.36	38	158	113	156	104	151	132	77.17	78	68	+10
Oregon	3.68	91	3.45	86	3.27	62	160	87	158	85	156	74	80.83	79	82	−3
UNLV	3.66	96	3.46	82	3.2	78	161	76	158	85	156	74	81.83	80	88	−8
St Louis	3.74	62	3.5	69	3.24	65	159	97	156	104	154	101	83	81	95	−14
U Mississippi	3.79	37	3.59	45	3.28	56	157	122	155	116	152	123	83.17	82		
Pittsburgh	3.65	102	3.4	106	3.11	107	161	76	159	75	158	52	86.33	83	73	+10
Michigan St.	3.64	110	3.45	86	3.21	74	161	76	158	85	155	89	86.67	84		
Kansas	3.77	48	3.45	86	3.09	118	160	87	157	94	155	89	87	85	73	+12
Northeastern	3.61	126	3.39	113	3.14	99	162	61	161	51	156	74	87.33	86	88	−2
Georgia St.	3.62	121	3.37	119	3.11	107	162	61	160	65	158	52	87.5	87	77	+10
Marquette	3.65	102	3.48	75	3.2	78	159	97	157	94	155	89	89.17	88	95	−7
Texas Tech	3.75	55	3.57	53	3.34	44	157	122	154	129	151	132	89.17	88		
San Diego	3.53	149	3.28	147	3.1	112	164	44	161	51	160	32	89.17	88	82	+6
Denver	3.66	96	3.44	93	3.15	96	160	87	159	75	155	89	89.33	91	88	+3
Miami	3.63	115	3.46	82	3.21	74	160	87	157	94	155	89	90.17	92	82	+10
Mercer	3.69	83	3.44	93	3.2	78	159	97	156	104	155	89	90.67	93	100	−7
Wayne State	3.69	83	3.54	63	3.29	55	158	113	155	116	152	123	92.17	94		
Hofstra	3.69	83	3.48	75	3.11	107	159	97	157	94	154	101	92.83	95	99	−4
Louisville	3.74	62	3.42	99	3.12	105	159	97	157	94	154	101	93	96	100	−4
Santa Clara	3.59	131	3.36	124	3.16	92	161	76	159	75	157	61	93.17	97	77	+20
So Carolina	3.69	83	3.37	119	3.04	133	161	76	159	75	156	74	93.33	98	95	+3
Seattle	3.62	121	3.41	102	3.17	87	161	76	158	85	155	89	93.33	98	82	+16
Arkansas	3.7	76	3.51	67	3.17	87	159	97	156	104	151	132	93.83	98		
LSU	3.7	76	3.38	116	3.16	92	159	97	157	94	155	89	94	101	88	+13
Case Western	3.6	128	3.4	106	3.17	87	160	87	158	85	156	74	94.5	102	63	+39
Stetson	3.71	72	3.48	75	3.21	74	157	122	155	116	153	111	95	103	100	−3
SUNY-Buff	3.65	102	3.45	86	3.19	82	159	97	156	104	154	101	95.33	104	100	+4
Hamline	3.7	76	3.48	75	3.22	71	158	113	155	116	152	123	95.67	105		
St Thomas (MN)	3.63	115	3.43	96	3.16	92	161	76	157	94	154	101	95.67	105		
Penn State	3.69	83	3.43	96	3.02	139	159	97	158	85	156	74	95.67	105	77	+28
Pacific McGeorge	3.6	128	3.4	106	3.13	103	159	97	158	85	155	89	101.3	108	95	+13
Hawai'i	3.62	121	3.41	102	3.09	118	160	87	157	94	155	89	101.8	109	82	+27
Montana	3.75	55	3.46	82	3.12	105	158	113	154	129	151	132	102.7	110		
Quinnipiac	3.62	121	3.35	127	3.01	143	160	87	158	85	157	61	104	111		
Creighton	3.68	91	3.49	73	3.23	67	156	136	154	129	151	132	104.7	112		

School	75% GPA	75% GPA Rank	Med GPA	Med GPA Rank	25% GPA	25% GPA Rank	75% LSAT	75% LSAT Rank	Med LSAT	Med LSAT Rank	25% LSAT	25% LSAT Rank	Ave. All Ranks	Rank for Acad. Cred.	*U.S. News* Rank	*USN* Over(+) or Under(–) Rank
Maine	3.69	83	3.38	116	3.06	129	159	97	156	104	154	101	105	113		
San Fran	3.56	140	3.35	127	3.02	139	161	76	159	75	156	74	105.2	114		
West Virg	3.75	55	3.54	63	3.18	84	156	136	153	145	150	149	105.3	115		
Catholic	3.57	137	3.34	131	3.08	124	160	87	158	85	156	74	106.3	116	88	+28
New Mexico	3.72	72	3.36	124	3.09	118	159	97	156	104	152	123	106.3	116	68	+48
Rutgers Newark	3.55	143	3.33	135	3.08	124	161	76	159	75	155	89	107	118	77	+41
Drake	3.72	72	3.35	127	3.11	107	158	113	155	116	153	111	107.7			
Chapman	3.61	126	3.37	119	3.1	112	159	97	157	94	154	101	108.2	120		
Cleveland St.	3.65	102	3.37	119	3.14	99	157	122	155	116	153	111	111.5	121		
So Dakota	3.75	55	3.41	102	3.21	74	156	136	152	157	150	149	112.2	122		
Memphis	3.64	110	3.38	116	3.03	134	158	113	156	104	154	101	113	123		
Dusquesne	3.65	102	3.42	99	3.28	56	155	156	153	145	151	132	115	124		
Pace	3.59	131	3.37	119	3.13	103	157	122	155	116	153	111	117	125		
Wm Mitchell	3.63	115	3.39	113	3.15	96	157	122	154	129	151	132	117.8	126		
Samford	3.52	152	3.27	149	3.07	127	159	97	157	94	155	89	118	127		
Idaho	3.64	110	3.36	124	3.03	134	159	97	155	116	151	132	118.8	128		
No Illinois	3.66	96	3.41	102	3.09	118	157	122	154	129	150	149	119.3	129		
Valparaiso	3.67	94	3.47	80	3.23	67	154	165	151	165	150	149	120	130		
Wyoming	3.63	115	3.43	96	3.18	84	156	136	153	145	150	149	120.8	131		
New York LS	3.57	137	3.34	131	3.08	124	157	122	155	116	153	111	123.5	132		
Ohio Northern	3.7	76	3.4	106	3.1	112	156	136	153	145	148	169	124	133		
Southwestern	3.58	135	3.33	135	3.06	129	157	122	155	116	153	111	124.7	134		
Suffolk	3.49	161	3.3	142	3.03	134	158	113	156	104	154	101	125.8	135		
Baltimore	3.57	137	3.34	131	3	144	157	122	155	116	153	111	126.8	136		
Missouri KC	3.64	110	3.33	135	3.03	134	156	136	154	129	152	123	127.8	137		
Gonzaga	3.54	146	3.34	131	3.06	129	157	122	154	129	153	111	128	138		
Washburn	3.69	83	3.35	127	3.06	129	156	136	153	145	150	149	128.2	139		
Florida Intl.	3.58	135	3.29	145	2.97	149	157	122	155	116	153	111	129.7	140		
Arkansas-LR	3.68	91	3.32	138	2.94	156	156	136	154	129	151	132	130.3	141		
No Kentucky	3.56	140	3.31	139	3.07	127	156	136	154	129	153	111	130.3	142		
Syracuse	3.59	131	3.29	145	3.09	118	156	136	154	129	152	123	130.3	142	100	+42
Willamette	3.52	152	3.22	156	2.85	170	158	113	156	104	153	111	134.3	144		
Vermont	3.54	146	3.25	152	2.95	152	158	113	155	116	151	132	135.2	145		
So Illinois	3.6	128	3.3	142	2.9	162	156	136	154	129	151	132	138.2	146		
Regent	3.66	96	3.31	139	2.95	152	156	136	152	157	150	149	138.2	146		
Campbell	3.55	143	3.21	158	2.94	156	157	122	154	129	151	132	140	148		
Loyola NO	3.56	140	3.39	113	3.09	118	155	156	152	157	149	163	141.2	149		
Albany	3.48	162	3.21	158	2.92	160	157	122	154	129	152	123	142.3	150		
No Dakota	3.73	68	3.3	142	3.02	139	154	165	150	172	147	174	143.3	151		
R Williams	3.55	143	3.31	139	2.96	150	155	156	153	145	151	132	144.2	152		
Capital	3.54	146	3.25	152	2.94	156	156	136	153	145	151	132	144.5	153		
Cal Western	3.53	149	3.24	155	3	144	156	136	153	145	150	149	146.3	154		
John Marshall	3.43	168	3.17	163	2.88	164	156	136	154	129	152	123	147.2	155		
Tex Wesleyan	3.4	171	3.17	163	2.89	164	156	136	154	129	152	123	147.7	156		
So Texas	3.52	152	3.28	147	2.99	148	155	156	153	145	150	149	149.5	157		
Tulsa	3.51	57	3.21	158	2.95	152	155	156	153	145	151	132	150	158		
CUNY	3.47	163	3.14	168	2.92	160	156	136	152	157	151	132	152.7	159		
Franklin Prc.	3.51	156	3.22	156	3	144	155	156	152	157	150	149	153	161		
New England	3.52	152	3.27	149	3.02	139	152	177	151	165	150	149	155.2	161		
Widener (DE)	3.46	166	3.14	168	2.88	164	155	156	153	145	151	132	155.2	161		
W New Eng	3.38	174	3.14	168	2.8	175	156	136	154	129	150	149	155.2	161		
Dayton	3.5	157	3.25	152	2.96	150	154	165	152	157	149	163	157.3	164		
Howard	3.5	157	3.2	162	2.9	162	155	156	152	157	149	163	159.5	165		
St Mary's	3.41	170	3.09	173	2.8	175	156	136	153	145	149	163	160.3	166		

School	75% GPA	75% GPA Rank	Med GPA	Med GPA Rank	25% GPA	25% GPA Rank	75% LSAT	75% LSAT Rank	Med LSAT	Med LSAT Rank	25% LSAT	25% LSAT Rank	Ave. All Ranks	Rank for Acad. Cred.	*U.S. News* Rank	*USN* Over(+) or Under(−) Rank
Nova SE	3.53	149	3.26	151	3	144	151	180	150	172	147	174	161.7	167		
Ave Maria	3.47	163	3.14	168	2.93	159	155	156	151	165	147	174	164.2	168		
Golden Gate	3.37	175	3.09	173	2.82	172	154	165	152	157	150	149	165.2	169		
Mississippi Coll.	3.51	57	3.21	158	2.88	164	153	172	150	172	148	169	165.3	170		
Fla Coastal	3.47	163	3.16	165	2.81	173	154	165	151	165	149	163	165.7	171		
Th Jefferson	3.23	183	3.03	179	2.75	177	156	136	151	165	148	169	168.2	172		
Touro	3.32	178	3.07	177	2.81	173	153	172	151	165	150	149	169	173		
Detroit Merry	3.36	176	3.16	165	2.95	152	154	165	149	177	146	180	169.2	174		
Oklahoma City	3.4	171	3.15	167	2.87	169	152	177	149	177	147	174	172.5	175		
Dist. Colum	3.4	171	3	181	2.7	181	153	172	150	172	148	169	174.3	176		
NCCU	3.45	167	3.13	172	2.88	164	151	180	146	183	143	183	174.8	177		
Whittier	3.19	184	2.99	183	2.56	183	153	172	151	165	149	163	175	178		
St Thomas U (FL)	3.43	168	3.08	175	2.75	177	151	180	149	177	147	174	175.2	179		
Appalachian	3.32	178	3.08	175	2.75	177	153	172	149	177	147	174	175.5	179		
Thos. Cooley	3.35	177	3.03	179	2.75	177	154	165	149	177	145	182	176.2	181		
Barry	3.3	180	3	181	2.7	181	152	177	150	172	148	169	176.7	182		
Texas Southn	3.29	181	3.06	178	2.83	171	151	180	148	182	146	180	178.7	182		
Southern	3.26	182	2.95	184	2.52	184	149	184	145	184	143	183	183.5	184		

It is interesting to note that 56 law schools were "overranked" by *U.S. News* and 43 were underranked. Thirty-three of the 56 overranked law schools were significantly overranked by 10 or more positions by the U.S. News method. These law schools and the magnitude of the overranking are:

USC (10 positions)
Washington U. (15 positions)
Minnesota (14 positions)
Illinois (13 positions)
Wisconsin (17 positions)
Wake Forest (14 positions)
Utah (13 positions)
Arizona (17 positions)
Emory (39 positions)
Connecticut (10 positions)
Villanova (10 positions)
Indiana-Bloomington (52 positions)
American (32 positions)
Pittsburg (12 positions)
Kansas (20 positions)
Georgia State (22 positions)
San Diego (27 positions)
Miami (21 positions)
Denver (14 positions)
Seattle (21 positions)
Santa Clara (12 positions)
South Carolina (11 positions)
LSU (26 positions)
Case Western (57 positions)

SUNY Buffalo (19 positions)
Penn State (48 positions)
Pacific-McGeorge (13 positions)
Hawaii (27 positions)
Maine (13 positions)
San Francisco (16 positions)
New Mexico (39 positions)
Catholic (22 positions)
Rutgers-Newark (31 positions)
Gonzaga (38 positions)

Of these 33 law schools significantly overranked by *U.S. News*, four are religiously affiliated law schools. Of these 18 law schools significantly underranked by *U.S. News*, eight are religiously affiliated law schools. Following is the list of law schools that have been significantly underranked 10 or more positions by the *U.S. News* method:

George Washington (15 positions)
BYU (26 positions)
Fordham (10 positions)
Georgia (11 positions)
Colorado (19 positions)
Maryland (21 positions)
SMU (13 positions)
Tennessee (11 positions)
Cincinnati (14 positions)
Baylor (15 positions)
Loyola Chi (42 positions)
Houston (13 positions)
Temple (18 positions)
Chicago-Kent (26 positions)
St. John's (26 positions)
Rutgers-Camden (10 positions)
DePaul (11 positions)
St. Louis (13 positions)

The main chart shows an authoritative ranking of U.S. law schools for a single category of data relevant to the quality of a law school, academic credentials of entering students. It does not purport to make broader judgments about the overall quality of any law school relative to any other law school, nor is it a comprehensive guide to the suitability of a law school for any particular prospective law student. It is also not necessarily a guide to any of the other constituencies that seek rankings information.

However, it may serve as a rankings guide to what is obviously the most important, relevant, and verifiable component of any law school ranking system, which is the academic credentials of entering students. This may indeed be the reference point for any rankings system, so that any departure from this reference point prompted by the introduction of any other criteria or data would need to be strongly justified as to relevance, objectivity, and verifiability.

This article offers no analysis or explanations for the ranking differences between the *U.S. News* list and the ranking list in this article. However, to the extent those differences emanate from data related to topics other than the academic credentials of entering students, Prof. Seto's work shows clearly that such data lack relevance, objectivity or verifiability, or all three. If this produces large differences in rankings under the two systems, then it is clear that the *U.S. News* rankings are seriously misleading. If approximately one-half of the "top" 104 law schools in the nation are significantly underranked or overranked by *U.S. News*, and if 99 of the top 104 law schools are erroneously ranked, then those who use the rankings are being grossly misled. If, on the other hand and as some may suggest, actual, authentic rankings are not nearly so important as rankings with a wide acceptance no matter how inaccurate, i.e., that appearances are more important than substance, then devotees of *U.S. News* rankings are getting precisely what they deserve.

Notes

1. Rex E. Lee Endowed Chair and Professor of Law, J. Reuben Clark Law School, Brigham Young University.

2. "Some Issues Concerning Law School Stratification," Report, ABA Section on Legal Education: Out of the Box Committee (2008).

3. 60 *SMU L. Rev.* 493 (Spring 2007) [this article appeared in the A Current Index to Legal Periodicals issue of March 27, 2009].

4. See, the magazine's self-proclaimed "#1 Bestseller" logo on the cover of the annual issue containing the graduate school rankings.

5. *See* David A. Thomas, "The Law School Rankings are Harmful Deceptions: A Response to Those Who Praise the Rankings and Suggestions for a Better Approach to Evaluating Law Schools," 40 *Hous. L. Rev.* 419 (Summer 2003). As succinctly stated in Wikipedia, "Junk science is a term used in U.S. political and legal disputes that brands an advocate's claims about scientific data, research, or analyses as spurious. The term conveys a pejorative connotation that the advocate is driven by political, ideological, financial, or other unscientific motives." http://en.wikipedia.org/wiki/Junk_science (visited on April 11, 2009).

6. *See* Theodore P. Seto, "Understanding the *U.S. News* Law School Rankings," 60 *SMU L. Rev.* 493, fn. 1 (Spring 2007, published 2009) for the latest list of the cumulating law review literature on this topic (hereinafter cited as "Seto").

7. In the explanatory paragraph preceding its list of "Third Tier" law schools, the *U.S. News* editors include this statement: "Remember that in considering a law school, you should look not only at its ranking or tier but also at other characteristics—its location, price, course offerings, and faculty expertise, to name a few."

8. David A. Thomas, "The Law Schools Rankings Are Harmful Deceptions: A Response to Those Who Praise the Rankings and Suggestions for a Better Approach to Evaluating Law Schools," 40 *Houston L. Rev.* 419 (Summer 2003). As pointed out therein, this criticism has been the first and most fundamental criticism of law school ranking schemes. *Id.* at 443–449.

9. See Nancy B. Rapoport, "Ratings, Not Rankings: *Why U.S. News & World Report* Shouldn't Want to Be Compared to *Time* and *Newsweek* or the *New Yorker*," 60 *Ohio St. L.J.* 1097, 1100 (1999) (arguing that "[r]anking all of the law schools on the same scale, based only on the measurable factors that *U.S. News* collects," makes no sense).

10. Seto at 506–507.

11. *See* Michael Ariens, "Law School Branding and the Future of Legal Education," 34 *St. Mary's L.J.* 301, 327–328 (discussing advantages of a high-quality student body); Richard A. Posner, "Law School Rankings," 81 *Ind. L.J.* 13 (Winter, 2006). Regarding the importance of student academic quality, Posner writes: "A point that supports the validity of using mean LSAT scores to decide which law school to attend is that a student learns from his fellow students as well as from his teachers; a further point is that the smart students are likely to be successful, and it is helpful to a lawyer's career to know successful lawyers.... [T]he weaker the bottom group of students is, the greater the pressure on the faculty to "dumb down" the teaching so as not to lose the bottom of the class." Id. at 16. "Berkeley is notorious for affirmative action, ... and I would predict the result would be a distinct dumbing down of the teaching there." Id. at 21.

12. Law School Admission Council, *2007–2008 LSAT LSDAS Information Book 1* (2007).

13. *See, id.* at 97: "The correlation between LSAT scores and first-year law school grades varies from one law school to another."

14. *Id.* Studies conducted annually by the Law School Admission Council affirm that LSAT score is a relatively better predictor than GPA of first-year law school academic performance. A study completed by the author, using admissions and academic data for twenty-seven graduating classes of the BYU Law School (with all data in electronic form), indicates that GPA is a better predictor than LSAT score for three-year law school performance. David A. Thomas, "Predicting Law School Academic Performance from LSAT Scores and Undergraduate Grade Point Averages: A Comprehensive Study," 35 *Ariz. L.J.* 1007 (Fall 2003).

15. *See* the Posner comment in note 11, *supra.*

16. Seto at 498.

17. *See* note 15, *supra.*

18. *Id.*

19. "The student/teacher ratios reported in the 2007 issue and used in the 2007 rankings ... do not appear to have been computed on a consistent basis from school to school." Seto at 505.

20. It is also impossible to measure how a professor's research and writing specifically impact that professor's classroom performance. Therefore, assessing classroom performance, if it could be done, would be the only meaningful measure of faculty quality in the context of the law school as an educational institution.

21. Probably the most earnest attempt is by Prof. Brian Leiter. *See* leiterrankings.com.

22. It is undoubtedly common for institutions of higher education generally to require reports of all forms of scholarly productivity, and perhaps even to derive an item count for each faculty member. This does not include any kind of quality assessment.

23. "Most applicants to law school expect to practice law, and faculty publication, the basis some of Leiter's ranking, is increasingly removed from the concerns important even to practitioners, let alone to students, though this phenomenon is more pronounced at elite schools. Current faculty scholarship is, for example, disproportionately concentrated in constitutional law, which few practicing lawyers specialize in." Richard A. Posner, "Law School Rankings," 81 *Ind. L.J.* 13 (Winter, 2006).

24. Professor Leiter indeed catalogs the potential flaws of citation counts with what he calls the "industrious drudge" who writes a lot, the treatise writer who is standardly cited, the "academic surfer" who writes in fad areas, the author of the "classic mistake" who is cited as an example of error, skewing of citations toward senior faculty, and the field-sensitivity of citation studies. He concludes, "So for all these reasons, one would expect scholarly impact to be imperfect measure of scholarly quality. But an imperfect measure may still be an adequate measure, and that is almost certainly true of citation rates as a proxy for impact as a proxy for reputation or quality." www.leiterrankings.com/faculty/2005faculty_impact_cites, at "Faculty Quality Based on Scholarly Impact," 2005, pp. 2–3, visited on April 6, 2009.

25. See the annual *ABA-LSAC Official Guide to ABA-Approved Law Schools.* As of this writing, the current *Official Guide* is the 2009 edition, issued in Summer 2008 and based on statistics gathered in fall 2007. In the statistical charts for each law school, this publication has a chart for "GPA and LSAT Scores" which lists "# of apps" [number of applicants], "# of offers" [number of offers of admission], and "# of matrics" [number of admission offerees who actually matriculated at the law school].

26. See Stephen E. Klein and Laura Hamilton, "The Validity of the *U.S. News and World Report* Ranking of ABA Law Schools" (Feb. 18, 1998) (published and distributed to law school deans as Memorandum 98-10), available at http://www.aals.org/services_deansmemos.php#1998) (last visited Apr. 3, 2009).

27. *See* Nancy B. Rapoport, "Ratings, Not Rankings: Why *U.S. News & World Report* Shouldn't Want to Be Compared to *Time* and *Newsweek*—Or the *New Yorker*," 60 *Ohio St. L.J.* 1097, 1098–1099 (1999).

28. Thomas E. Brennan, *Judging the Law Schools* 5 (1996). Since the time of this statement, a law school has become affiliated with Pennsylvania State University.

29. Seto, at 530.

30. *Id.*

31. *Id.* at 530–531.

32. *Id.* at 543.

33. Richard A. Posner, "Law School Rankings," 81 *Ind. L. J.* 13, 14 (Winter, 2006).

34. Prof. Brian Leiter's ranking of top law schools by student quality lists both LSAT and GPA statistics, but ranks only by 75th percentile and 25th percentile LSAT statistics. He points out, "Many academics and admissions officers, to be sure, favor 75th percentile rankings, because they do not penalize schools for "alternative admissions" procedures which may drag down the numerical credentials at the bottom end of the class. Others point out that the number of "top students" is more important than the average.... On the other hand, some believe the "bottom" of the class matters more." See, www.leiterrrankings.com/students/2007student_quality.shtml. (last visited April 6, 2009).

35. The long-term study completed by the author, using admissions and academic data for twenty-seven graduating classes of the BYU Law School (with all data in electronic form), indicates that LSAT is a slightly better predictor than GPA for first-year law school academic performance, and that GPA is a slightly better predictor than LSAT score for three-year law school academic performance. David A. Thomas, "Predicting Law School Academic Performance from LSAT Scores and Undergraduate Grade Point Averages: A Comprehensive Study," 35 *Ariz. L.J. 1007* (Fall 2003).

36. The published *U.S. News* report lists 189 law schools, but five of those schools appear in both the listing of the "Top 100 Schools" (actually top 104," counting ties) and in the third tier listing. These five duplicated entries are for the law schools at Mercer University, Stetson University, Syracuse University, SUNY-Buffalo and Louisville.

37. The GPA and LSAT data used in this article are those figures reported in the *Official Guide* as pertaining to full time students only.

38. Where data used by *U.S. News* differs from the *Official Guide*, the *Official Guide* is preferred.

Part Four

Paying for Law School

"A Great Devourer of Good Men" and Women: A Review of the Employment and Student Debt Status of Current Law School Graduates

Deborah D. Thornton

In the last year, as unemployment has remained high and new hiring lags, considerable attention has been paid throughout academia and government about higher education and what to do about it. More students than ever before are attending college, mostly on student loans. Many are taking six or more years to graduate, if at all. Either way they have huge debts to pay off. Unemployment and debt among recent graduates are at record highs.

The trends are also affecting legal education. Historically when the job market is tight, people return to or remain in school, to "wait it out." Accordingly, law school admissions and career offices are actively recruiting more students. Being an attorney has long been perceived as a fast track to the "American Dream" of a good job, a high salary, positions of community leadership, and family respect. Going to law school is considered a good alternative, with a guaranteed job. The schools and society promote this image.

As a result, more students than ever before are taking the Law School Admissions Test (LSAT) and, applying for law school. Competition for admissions to the top tier schools remains fierce. Recently, a television show titled "Suits" even featured a bright young man who supported himself by taking the LSAT and Bar exams for others and guaranteeing to earn them the score required for admission to Harvard Law School or to pass the Bar, and thereby assuring their perfect future.

Unfortunately, over the past three years, law school graduates have found their job prospects to be almost as bleak as in other fields, despite the fact that the law schools keep reporting ninety-five to one hundred percent job placement. Many recent (unemployed or underemployed) law school graduates have started to complain about these statistics, using their new legal skills to allege fraud and abuse. The blogs of these graduates are lively and aggressive in their allegations. On Sunday, January 9, 2011, the front page of the *New York Times* business section led with the article, "Is Law School a Losing Game?" The subhead read, "Deans Say Graduates Are Working. They Don't Say how Many Are at Home Depot." Recently, students filed lawsuits against two schools alleging that the institutions purposefully misled and lied to applicants about their employment rates and graduates salaries in order to recruit them.

Whether working as attorneys or not, most law school graduates today are ending their careers in higher education with large debt loads—some as high as $250,000. This creates a significant burden to their future and to their choices. This study attempts to review some of these issues.

National College Enrollment, Student Loan Lending, and Defaults

Before students enter law school, they must complete their undergraduate degree. Even in a very difficult economic climate, increasing numbers of high school students choose to attend college. Nationally, 70.1 percent of high school graduates in 2009 enrolled in either two or four year colleges in the fall immediately following graduation.[1] This is a continuing upward trend line from 68.6 percent in 2008. Fall 2010 enrollment numbers are even higher.[2]

These students must, somehow, pay for college—from either parental or personal savings, work, scholarships and grants, or loans. Unfortunately, college graduates are being devoured by debt, even before they enter graduate studies. As of fall 2009, the Project on Student Debt reported that the nationwide average student debt for those who had earned an undergraduate degree in 2008 was $23,200 and increasing at six percent a year. Sixty-seven percent of graduating students had loans to repay. Young people and children are assuming significant financial liabilities in their attempt to be economically competitive, even before entering graduate school. The U.S. Department of Education publishes an annual report on cohort default rates: The "FY 2008 Official Cohort Default Rates by State/Territory." Nationwide, seven percent of borrowers are in default.[3] If college graduates cannot pay their undergraduate debt, how will they be able to afford law school?

Legal Profession Growth and Current Hiring Situation

Unemployment nationwide remained flat at 9.4 percent in December 2010. The rate for those with a bachelor's degree or higher was less, at only 4.8 percent, slightly lower (-0.1 percent) than a year ago. The largest job gains in December were in "Leisure and Hospitality" at 47,000, followed by "Health Care" at 36,000. Unfortunately, "Temporary Help Services," within the professional and business services category, continued its upward trend, adding 16,000 jobs. Since September 2009, the temporary help services category has added almost 500,000 jobs.[4]

According to the U.S. Bureau of Labor Statistics (BLS), jobs in the legal occupations category (Standard Occupational Classification #23-0000) from now until 2018 will remain less than one percent (0.86 percent) of all jobs nationwide. The total number of jobs in this area, including lawyers, judges, arbitrators, magistrates, paralegals, court reporters, law clerks, and title examiners will be less than 1.5 million (1,439,400) by 2018. This represents a projected fifteen percent overall growth, with a net growth of 397,000 jobs.

In the legal profession, (SOC 23-1011) the expected growth is only 12.98 percent, representing 240,000 new jobs. As a percentage of workers in the broad "legal occupations" category, the largest growth area will be paralegals and legal assistants, at twenty-eight percent.[5] Presumably, paralegals and legal assistants will be hired instead of bar-qualified attorneys, at a lower salary rate.

Table 1. Employment by Occupation, 2008 and Projected 2018

2008 National Employment Matrix Title and Code		Employment				Change, 2008–2018		Total Job Openings due to Growth and Replacement Needs
		Number		Percent Distribution		Number	%	
		2008	2018	2008	2018			
Total, all occupations	00-0000	150,931.7	166,205.6	100.00	100.00	15,273.9	10.1	50,928.5
Legal occupations	23-0000	1,251.0	1,439.4	0.82	0.86	188.4	15.1	397.1
Lawyers, judges, and related workers	23-1000	810.4	910.8	0.53	0.54	100.4	12.4	252.5
Lawyers	23-1011	759.2	857.7	0.50	0.51	98.5	13.0	240.4
Judges, magistrates, and other judicial workers	23-1020	51.2	53.1	0.03	0.03	1.8	3.6	12.1
Administrative law judges, adjudicators, and hearing officers	23-1021	14.4	15.5	0.00	0.00	1.2	8.0	3.8
Arbitrators, mediators, and conciliators	23-1022	9.9	11.3	0.00	0.00	1.4	14.0	3.2
Judges, magistrate judges, and magistrates	23-1023	26.9	26.2	0.01	0.01	-0.7	-2.6	5.0
Legal support workers	23-2000	440.6	528.7	0.29	0.31	88.1	20.0	144.6
Paralegals and legal assistants	23-2011	263.8	337.9	0.17	0.20	74.1	28.0	104.0
Miscellaneous legal support workers	23-2090	176.8	190.8	0.11	0.11	14.0	7.9	40.6
Court reporters	23-2091	21.5	25.4	0.01	0.01	3.9	18.3	7.1
Law clerks	23-2092	37.7	42.9	0.02	0.02	5.2	13.9	10.8
Title examiners, abstractors, and searchers	23-2093	69.5	69.0	0.04	0.04	-0.5	-0.7	10.3
Legal support workers, all other	23-2099	48.1	53.4	0.03	0.03	5.3	11.0	12.4

(Numbers in thousands)
Source: Employment Projections Program, Table 1.2, U.S. Department of Labor, U.S. Bureau of Labor Statistics

This data does not reflect the significant downturn in legal hiring since 2008. Given recent hiring reports, the BLS projections are probably too high. For example, the headline of the National Association for Legal Career Professionals (NALP) fall 2009 hiring report reads, "Entry-Level Recruiting Volumes Plunge." As James Leipold, Executive Director of the NALP wrote, there are "fundamental weaknesses" in the 2009 hiring reports. He added that "it is taking students longer to find a job. More law graduates are taking either part-time jobs, a string of part-time jobs, or taking temporary jobs."[6] The numbers reported by the law schools to NALP, which has collected such data for thirty-six years, show an overall employment rate of 88.3 percent for the class of 2009. This is a drop of almost four percent over the last two years, and the lowest employment rate in the last ten years.[7]

Table 2. Employment Rates Since 2000

Year	Rate
2000	91.5%
2001	90.0%
2002	89.0%
2003	88.9%
2004	88.9%
2005	89.6%
2006	90.7%
2007	91.9%
2008	89.1%
2009	88.3%

Source: NALP Salary Report 2010

Unfortunately, many of those holding newly awarded J.D. degrees, who thought they had jobs on the day they graduated, really did not. NALP reported that in 2009, between 3,200 and 3,700 graduates with jobs in private-sector law firms had their start dates pushed back, or deferred, past December 2009, accounting for almost forty percent of those receiving offers.[8] Some class of 2009 start dates have been deferred as far back as 2011, almost two years. Additionally, many jobs were reported as being temporary, with forty-one percent of public-interest jobs and thirty percent of business jobs falling into that category. In order to address hiring weaknesses, and to keep their hiring numbers artificially high for the national ranking organizations, forty-two percent of the law schools provided jobs for their students after graduation. Of those academic jobs, sixty-nine percent were temporary.[9]

The NALP survey contains employment status results from 191 American Bar Association (ABA) accredited law schools nationwide. It reflects information from 40,833 graduates for whom employment information was known, out of 44,000 who received diplomas. The BLS projections indicate a total of 240,000 new jobs for lawyers between 2008 and 2018. Yet, law schools are graduating at least 44,000 per year. Pretty simple math shows that approximately forty-six percent of those new lawyers will not find jobs in the legal profession. Even if significant numbers of older attorneys retire, it will be difficult to reach 440,000 jobs over those ten years. Even rounding up, and considering that the BLS projections do not reflect the continuing economic recession since 2008, one could infer that almost half of today's law school graduates will not find employment working as attorneys.

However, even a cursory review of the *U.S. News and World Report* law schools ranking reveals that virtually all schools are reporting virtually 100 percent employment of their graduates nine months out, in contrast to the NALP report. These rankings, as we shall see, are critical to the application and enrollment process for the top-tier schools.

The following table outlines more details of the NALP hiring report:

Table 3. National Association for Legal Career Professionals Hiring Report 2007–2009

	2007	2008	2009
Overall Employment	N/A	N/A	88.3%
Offers to Summer Associates	92.8%	89.9%	69.3%
Callback for Summer Jobs	60.0%	46.6%	36.4%
Recruiting of 3L Students	42.0%	25.0%	3.0%
Number of Offers Extended	15	10	7
Large (700+) Firm Offers	30	18.5	8
Colleges Reporting Deferred Offers	N/A	N/A	85.0%

Source: NALP Perspectives on Fall 2009 Law Student Recruiting, http://www.nalp.org/uploads/PerspectivesonFallRec09.pdf.

The *Summer Associate Survey 2010,* compiled by *The American Lawyer,* indicated that hiring by the 114 largest firms was down from an average of fifty-five in 2009 to only thirty-one in 2010, a fall of almost forty-four percent.[10] Some large firms showed even greater drops. For example, Skadden, Arps dropped their summer associate hiring by sixty-five percent, from 223 to seventy-nine.[11]

Table 4. Summer Associate Hiring 2009 Versus 2010

	2009	2010	Percent Drop
Nationwide Average	55	31	43.6%
Nationwide Total	7,034	3,805	45.9%
Skadden, Arps	223	79	64.6%
Shearman & Sterling	129	27	79.1%

Source: "Who is Hiring Now," The National Jurist, September 2010

Michigan State University and the Collegiate Employment Research Institute also publish an annual recruiting trends report. For the 2010–2011 hiring cycle, they show that, while the overall "professional services" market shows signs of recovering, the "legal services" area is still showing a seventeen percent decline, with the average number of hires at 4.2. For their report, the legal services category includes not only attorneys, but also other legal professionals such as paralegals.[12]

In addition to the general economic malaise, William Henderson, a law professor from Indiana University, offered the following thoughts on why the job market for attorneys is changing. One, the traditional use of pedigree (i.e. ranking of the law school) and grades as the basis for hiring is not resulting in the best possible hires. Two, because of the economic downturn, clients and firms do not have the financial "fat" to make bad hires and work with them. Three, law schools are not teaching useful workplace skills.[13]

The Michigan State report indicates that many employers generally find that recent graduates are not adequately prepared to articulate their skills and competencies, and to express their career interests and direction. Additionally, they do not have realistic career expectations, or demonstrate a professional maturity or demeanor.[14] James Leipold of NALP recently stated that it will continue to be a difficult time to find a position, and recommends graduates "take a broader approach, both geographically and by practice area," in applying for jobs.[15] These are all areas in which law school graduates would be well advised to better prepare themselves, and good advice to consider.

Attorney Salary Report and Salary Expectations

Not only must law school graduates get jobs, but most will want to acquire situations which will enable them to not only pay their loans, but possibly marry, buy a house, and support a family. They will want jobs, in other words, that provide "financially profitable" salaries. Based upon 2009 data, this possibility is also in question. Professor Henderson described the job market as "bi-modal," with most jobs in the $40,000–$50,000 range, many in the $140,000–$160,000 range, and few in the middle. The NALP data also supports the "bi-modal" salary theory. Their data reveals two "peaks," or clusters, in salaries. The larger one at the lower end, around $40,000–$65,000, represents thirty-five percent of the reported salaries of the class of 2009. The other, tighter and smaller cluster at the high end, is around $160,000, and encompasses twenty-five percent of salaries.[16] It should be noted that almost all of the $140,000+ annual salary jobs are located in cities with very high costs of living, such as New York City and Los Angeles.

To its credit, the ABA has recently issued a memo stating that in order for a law degree to pay off financially, graduates needed to earn at least $65,000 a year. The outgoing Dean of Northwestern Law School, David Van Zandt, generated this figure.[17] In contrast, national figures report that the starting salary of almost half of the 2008 graduates was below $65,000.[18]

The class of 2009 National Summary Report of Jobs and Salaries by NALP shows that definitive information was reported for eighty-four percent, or 35,528 of the 42,330 law school graduates. Almost seventy percent were in private work, while thirty percent served in the public sector. The salary differences between these two sectors are stark, with the private-sector median at $120,000, compared to $50,000 for government employees, a difference of $70,000.

Many students who enter law school state their altruistic purpose of "wanting to help others." Unfortunately, the person who may need their help is themselves, as they attempt to pay off student loans. This is especially true during the current economic recession, as governments attempt to balance their budgets, and non-profits and public-interest groups deal with reduced charitable giving.

Private-sector employees are considered to be those practicing in either private law firms or business positions. Three-fourths of the private-sector employees, or some 18,750, were making enough to service their student loan debts. When comparing these two aspects—and making the assumption that many of those whose employment situation was not known were unemployed—just under forty-four percent of law school graduates, or four of ten, were being "paid enough" in their first job. Given the trends in employment status of law school graduates, it seems reasonable to assume that those not providing information on their employment status did not have good news to report. If this information was available, it might make the overall picture seem even more bleak.

If one looks at the employment subcategories, those graduates accepting jobs in academia, as judicial clerks, in "unknown" capacities, in government, and in public-interest positions were most likely to be in financial trouble. Only those above the 75th salary percentile in those categories were likely to be financially sound, i.e. making $65,000 or more per year. Only in the categories of business or private practice were the median salaries above the $65,000 level. Even in the business category, those below the median, and certainly those at or below the twenty-fifth percentile, were not in a "financially profitable" situation, with a reported salary of only $50,000 or less.

Graduates accepting positions in these fields might think that after getting some experience, their salaries would rise to more substantial levels. Unfortunately, the numbers do not bear out that belief. The NALP report on public-interest attorneys shows that even after five years, the median salaries for those in civil legal services, public defenders, local prosecuting attorneys, and public-interest organizations remained between $49,000 and $60,000—still not sufficient to pay off law school debt. After eleven to fifteen years, they could expect a salary of $62,500 to $81,000, and would probably still be paying off their student loans.[19]

Other data from the NALP shows that even in positions in which a J.D. degree or bar passage was "required," the median salary was only $65,000. Employees in smaller private firms were more likely to be making less than $65,000, with the median at $50,000 for those in firms with two to ten employees, and right at $65,000 for those in eleven to twenty-five lawyer firms. Only those in private firms of more than fifty-one attorneys could be somewhat assured of making more than $65,000, as the twenty-fifth percentile for those was $75,000. The total number of confirmed jobs in these large, private firms was 8,938.

So, of 42,330 total graduates, only a lucky twenty-one percent were somewhat assured of making enough money to pay their loans. Again, remember that those large firms tend to be in larger, more expensive cities where $75,000 does not go that far. Table 5 outlines these issues.

One may have a job, but is it stable and does it provide enough income? Nationally, the most recent unemployment reports from December 2010 indicate that unemployment, based on unemployment claims, is down to 9.4 percent. However, there are another 11.5 million people who are underemployed and working part-time or who have given up looking for work altogether. This puts the total unemployment rate much closer to seventeen percent.[20]

According to other NALP data, those in academia are at particular risk. This would seem to reflect the reports about law schools hiring their own graduates in order to provide some sort of job, as sixty-nine percent of academic jobs are short-term, and fifty-six percent are part-time. Employees in business and public-interest jobs are also at greater risk for having only a short-term or part-time position. While many law school deans and social activists promote the idea of going to law school to help others, those graduates who are interested in these positions appear to be at significant personal financial risk. [See Table 6.]

Table 5. Class of 2009 National Summary Report Selected Data Only

	Number Reported	Percent Reported	Number with Salary	25th Percentile	Median Salary	75th Percentile	Mean Salary
Total Graduates	42,330						
Employment Known	40,833	96.5%					
Employment by Sector, Total	35,528						
Private	25,006	69.4%	13,767	$65,000	$120,000	$160,000	$111,207
Public	10,522	29.2%	5,733	$42,000	$50,000	$58,000	$50,916
Employment Categories, Total	36,046						
Academic	1,262	3.5%	228	$37,000	$46,000	$55,000	$48,159
Business	4,861	13.5%	1,421	$50,000	$65,000	$90,000	$76,053
Judicial Clerk	3,125	8.7%	2,531	$42,172	$50,000	$58,000	$50,477
Unknown	518	1.4%	13	$33,000	$50,000	$60,000	$51,894
Private Practice	20,145	55.9%	12,346	$70,000	$130,000	$160,000	$115,254
Government	4,092	11.4%	2,161	$44,900	$52,000	$60,000	$54,335
Public Interest	2,043	5.7%	813	$39,000	$42,800	$50,000	$43,971
Size of Firm, Total	20,145						
2–10	6,749	33.5%	2,579	$44,000	$50,000	$62,400	$54,736
11–25	1,526	7.6%	906	$54,000	$65,000	$80,000	$69,360
26–50	946	4.7%	634	$62,500	$75,000	$90,000	$79,486
51–100	912	4.5%	747	$75,000	$95,000	$130,000	$101,915
101–250	1,402	7.0%	1,241	$100,000	$120,000	$150,000	$121,602
251–500	1,468	7.3%	1,365	$120,000	$160,000	$160,000	$140,057
501+	5,156	25.6%	4,796	$160,000	$160,000	$160,000	$155,227

Source: Class of 2009 National Summary Report, National Association for Legal Career Professionals

Table 6. NALP Job Characteristics by Employer Type

Employer Type	Percent Short-Term	Percent Part-Time
Academic	68.6%	55.7%
Business	30.2%	19.8%
Judicial Clerk	100.0%	1.3%
Private Practice	8.4%	5.9%
Government	18.1%	7.7%
Public Interest	40.9%	19.8%
Total	24.9%	10.3%

Source: National Association for Legal Career Professionals, June 2010

The Rest of the Story

In contrast to the optimistic picture painted by law school admissions and recruitment offices, many recent graduates who are not finding jobs are not happy about it. There are multiple blogs and websites dedicated to cussing and discussing the current employment situation. Often the language and photographs used are colorful and crude. The bloggers and commentators on these sites are angry and believe that they were "ripped off," "lied to," and "cheated."

Most of the bloggers are anonymous, but some graduates went public in August with their concerns. One blogger called the law school process a "big Ponzi scheme," saying that schools are just taking students for $45,000 a year.[21] He indicated that since graduating he had accepted a low-level temporary job and toiled in "sweatshop" conditions before opening his own practice. Another graduate from the same school indicated that she would be "paying off her $65,000 student loan until she was 60." In contrast to these two examples, their law school's website indicates the school has a ninety-four percent employment rate, with an average starting salary of $145,000 for attorneys in private practice.

In addition, the data behind *The U.S. News and World Report* law school rankings has been called into question following the revelation that rather than report their "at graduation" employment rates, some schools use an estimated rate, which is typically higher than their actual number.[22] According to an editor at the magazine, only twenty-six percent of law schools are reporting their "at-graduation" employment, which is down from sixty-two percent in 2005.[23] In the same article, a professor at the University of Cincinnati called the employment data "junk" in the first place, indicating that counting "flipping burgers" and hiring your own graduates should not be counted as jobs.

One renowned law school reports a 100 percent employment figure, but provides stipends to employers to induce them to hire their graduates. The number of stipends increased from nine graduates in 2008 to fifteen in 2009, or seven percent of its 219 total graduates. Even without other potential reductions based upon eliminating part-time, temporary, or non-attorney positions, that brings the school's employment rate down to ninety-three percent.

Another law school apparently pays employers $3,500 to hire their graduates.[24] Another implemented a program called the "Legal Corps," which places graduates at public-interest and judicial jobs while paying them a stipend of $2,500 a month, or $30,000 a year, yet allows them to be counted as "employed" in the rankings.[25] Additionally, because of the weak job market, in 2009 the same school offered a $5,000 scholarship to newly accepted students who deferred their admission for a year. Yet, a fall 2010 article in *preLaw* magazine quoted the Assistant Dean of Career Development from that school that she is "optimistic that hiring will start looking up."[26]

Two students of Vanderbilt Law School in Nashville, Tennessee have pro-actively addressed the perceived inaccuracies in the published employment rates. They have used their legal training to form a non-profit called Law School Transparency (LST), dedicated to "encouraging and facilitating the transparent flow of law school employment information."[27] Last July, they made written requests to all 200 ABA accredited schools to provide the job and salary list for all graduates. The surveys asked for employer type and name, position filled, credentials required, full- or part-time status, office location, and salary source. Unfortunately, only eleven schools responded, and only one (Ave Maria School of Law in Florida) offered to provide the requested information.[28]

Other information and reports reveal that some law schools are inflating grades, presumably to make their students more competitive. Most public is the discussion about the Loyola Law School retroactive grade increase, which was used in a comedy piece by Stephen Colbert last summer.[29] Loyola just increased all grades going back to 2007 by .33 points. The mean GPA of first-year students at Loyola, located in Los Angeles, was 2.667. The other schools in California were reporting means of 3.0 or higher. The impression was that the lower Loyola GPAs were resulting in fewer job offers. The dean of the school said that the institution had implemented the change because the "information conveyed by the old grading curve did not accurately convey the high quality of our graduates."[30] Other schools reporting elevated grades include top-tier schools such as New York University, University of California-Los Angeles, and Georgetown Law Center.

Law School Applications and Rankings

Most current undergraduate students considering law school either have not yet received the NALP hiring report, or have not understood the potential implications for their futures, as 60,746 people took the Law School Admissions Test (LSAT) in October of 2009, an all-time high.[31] This number was followed by the 87,500 who actually applied to law school in October, 2010.

Table 7. Number of LSATs Administered

Year	Total	Percent Change
2000–2001	109,030	—
2005–2006	137,444	—
2006–2007	140,048	1.9%
2007–2008	142,048	1.6%
2008–2009	151,398	6.4%
2009–2010	171,514	13.3%

Source: LSATs Administered, Law School Admissions Council, http://www.lsac.org/LSACResources/Data/lsats-administered.asp

The test preparation firm Kaplan asked 1,383 students who took the LSAT in October 2010, "What is most important in picking a law school to apply to?" The number one item was the perceived ranking of the school (thirty percent). Affordability was only considered "most important" by twelve percent. The lowest category was job placement, at only eight percent.[32] Based upon current information, students might want to reverse those rankings and closely investigate both how well the school really does at helping graduates to get well-paying jobs and how much they charge for tuition.

Table 8. Most Important Factor in Choosing a Law School Perceptions of 1,383 Potential Students

Rankings	30%
Location	24%
Academics	19%
Affordability	12%
Job Placement	8%

Source: Kaplan Test Prep November 2010

According to the matriculation reports generated by the Law School Admissions Council (LSAC), the "eliteness" factor weighs heavily not only in choosing which schools to apply to, but in final acceptances. Their research shows that if a student were admitted to two schools with even modest differences in rankings (eight places), the higher ranked school would win over eighty percent of the time. This trend has been well documented since the early 1990s.[33]

A recent report, "The Secret of My Success: How Status, Prestige and School Performance Shape Legal Careers," by professors at the UCLA School of Law and Brooklyn Law School, documents that choosing a school on the eliteness factor alone is inadvisable for most students. Their analysis indicates that the individual's grades while in law school are a better indicator of future earnings than the ranking of the law school. In effect, if you go to a top-tier school that you barely get into, such as Harvard, Yale, or Columbia, and while there earn average or poor grades, you will not be as financially rewarded as you would have been achieving very high marks at a lower-ranked school. Statistically, earning higher grades is "decisively" more important than attending a top-tier school. This effect is part of the driver behind grade inflation and retroactive grade changes such as those reported above. Additionally, as a top-academic recruit at a lower-level school, you might be more likely to receive grant or scholarship money, resulting in less debt to be paid back after graduation.

Table 9. Reality of Criteria Affecting Jobs/Salary

Criteria	Ranking
Performance in Law School	#1
Socioeconomic Factors	#2
Eliteness of School	#3

Source: The Secret of My Success: How Status, Prestige and School Performance Shape Legal Careers, July 2010

The "Secret of My Success" analysis indicates many other interesting demographic factors that are important to post-school economic success, including the fact that those who were undergraduate engineering majors and who are actively religious in "high" denominations receive somewhat higher salary offers than others.

Salary and Career Expectations of Incoming Law Students

The Veritas test preparation company recently released their first survey of law school applicants, in which the one Ls reported their thoughts about applying to law school and their future expectations. Though the survey results were only obtained from 100 applicants, the results are interesting—and the students naïve. Over eighty percent of those surveyed said they would still apply to law school, even if they knew that a "significant number" of graduates did not find jobs in their fields. Only four percent said they would not apply. Concern for an "appealing long-term career path" and achieving "healthy work-life balance" was important to seventy-nine percent. Apparently, few of these young people have talked with first-year associates at major law firms and received a true picture of the work-life balance issues. It was somewhat reassuring that seventy-two percent expressed concerns about being able to pay off their debt. Social contributions were also important to this group, as sixty-nine percent wanted to "make a positive impact on their community."[34]

The *National Jurist* magazine reported in a sidebar that 2010 was a good summer for "self confidence," as fifty-two percent of these pre-law students said they were "very confident" that they would be able to find a job in the legal field after graduating from law school. However, they apparently do not think much of their fellow potential students; only sixteen percent of those surveyed expected other students to be able to find a position in law.[35] This perception—that even though everyone else is struggling, you will somehow be protected and successful—is pervasive throughout many of the responses to pre-law and law-student surveys.

Most interesting is the stated salary expectations of these students. A reasonable salary expectation according to forty-four percent of the respondents was $75,000 to $100,000, while another twenty-nine percent expect salaries of $100,000 to $145,000, and eleven percent expect to earn over $145,000 their first year on the job.[36] Summed up, a total of eighty-four percent believe they will make over $75,000 in their first job after graduating. In the current market, very few will reach that level of financial success, even over the long term.

Law School Costs and Debt

We've seen the facts of the job and salary situation for current law school graduates, and examined their motivations and thoughts about attending school—but how much does law school cost? And what about paying for this education? According to the Veritas survey, only fifty-four percent of potential students considered affordability important in their decision process. There seems to be a disconnect between affordability perceptions and concern about paying debt. This is further demonstrated in that only thirty-eight percent expected to finance their education through student loans. Scholarships and grants were the (unrealistic) expectation of twenty-one percent, while fourteen percent were counting on their parents to pay.[37]

Unfortunately, the reality may not match up with the expectation. Law school costs and resultant borrowing have increased almost as fast as federal government debt. According to the ABA, average in-state public-school tuition and fees in 2008 was $15,621, and increasing at nine percent per year. Out-of-state tuition at publics averaged $26,436 and was growing at seven percent per year. Average private-school tuition and fees were $33,985, increasing at six percent per year.[38] The averages, however, do not reflect the wide swing in prices from the elite private schools such as Yale, Columbia, or Cornell, which charge upwards of $48,000 per year, plus fees, books, and living expenses. At the other end are lower-ranked public schools charging in-state tuition of less than $8,000 per year. Even start-up law schools are charging as much as $30,000 per year.[39]

The *U.S. News* rankings for 2010–11 show an average public-school in-state tuition increase of almost $2,000, to $18,750; out-of-state increases of over $4,000, to $30,750; and private-school tuition of $36,900—a $3,000 increase. The high and low in-state tuition numbers ranged from $7,000 to $43,250, with a median of $17,000. Private schools ranged wildly from $19,960 to $49,000 per year. Again, this does not include costs for living expenses, which can range from sleeping in your parents' basement for free to sky-high prices in Manhattan. It also does not address the lost income potential or lost opportunity cost of working instead of attending school for an additional three years.

Table 10. *U.S. News and World Report* Average Law School Tuition Report

School Year	In-State Public	Percent Increase	Out-of-State Public	Percent Increase	Private	Percent Increase
2008–2009	$15,621		$26,436		$32,070	
2009–2010	$16,836	7.78%	$28,280	6.98%	$33,995	6.00%
2010–2011	$18,750	11.37%	$30,750	8.73%	$36,900	8.55%

Source: U.S. News and World Report Law School Rankings, 2008–2011

A longer-term report on law school tuition by the ABA.net includes data back to 2000. When this data is presented in a graph format, it is easy to see the significance of the increases of the past ten years.

Graph 1. Law School National Average Tuition

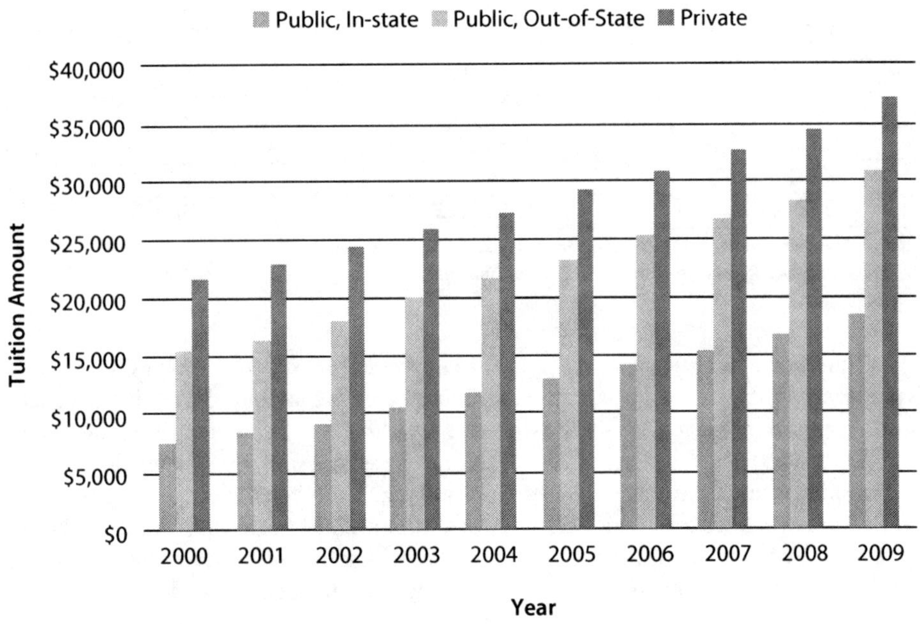

Source: ABAnet, preLaw by National Jurist, Fall 2010

Some administrators reported that these tuition increases enabled their schools to offer more financial aid. In effect, wealthy or highly indebted student "A" pays the full bill, presumably the school keeps a portion for administrative purposes, and some is refunded to student "B" as a scholarship. Interestingly enough, over the last ten years the number of administrative personnel at the law schools, including deans, librarians and other full-time administrators, has more than tripled, from 528 to 1,059, according to an article in the *National Jurist*.[40] The increase in both administrative and teaching staff, and corresponding reduction in teaching loads, accounts for forty-eight percent of the tuition increases.

In contrast to their expectations (only thirty-eight percent of potential law school students expect to finance their education with loans), most do take significant loans. As of 2008, the average public-school debt at the end of law school, according to the ABA, was $59,324, while private-school debt totaled $91,506. Some estimates show average public-school debt as high as $71,436.[41] Note that the amount borrowed does not include private borrowing, only federal loans, and does not include parental borrowing, credit-card debt, and is in addition to any undergraduate loans. This is not the total cost of law school, as the numbers do not include cash expenditures from summer jobs or savings. These amounts are also the average amounts, not median, and do not reflect the upper-end outliers. While some students are able to fund their degree with savings, scholarships, and parental help, a significant number are acquiring six-figure liabilities to attend top-tier schools. The following table outlines the average debt amounts, and the increases in the amounts borrowed for law school in the last few years.

Table 11. Average Amount Borrowed for Law School, 2001–2009

Academic Year	Public	Private
2008–2009	$66,045	$100,003
2007–2008	$71,436	$91,506
2006–2007	$57,170	$87,906
2005–2006	$54,509	$83,181
2004–2005	$51,056	$78,763
2003–2004	$48,910	$76,563
2002–2003	$45,763	$72,893
2001–2002	$43,175	$69,098

Sources: http://www.abanet.org/legaled/statistics/charts/stats%20-%2020.pdf, http://www.ncbex.org/uploads/user_docrepos/790410_Chapman.pdf

One third-year law student at Boston College recently submitted a letter to the dean of his school asking for his tuition back in return for agreeing to drop out of school. The benefit of this arrangement for him was relief from the "crushing weight" of law school loans and the ability to go back to his old life. The benefit for the school was that they would not have to report him as unemployed, and lower their ranking.[42] Another student is using the skills acquired in law school to sue the school in bankruptcy court—alleging that they should have known he would be unable to repay the loans. Yet another posted an online inquiry as to whether he should drop out after one semester with an initial debt burden of $21,000.

While some federal student loans are "subsidized," meaning interest is not charged to the student while they are in school, other loans are "unsubsidized." In the case of unsubsidized loans the interest accrues while the student is in school and capitalizes to the principal. Therefore, the total debt owed at the beginning of repayment is even more. For a public-school student with $66,045 in original loans, this increases the total owed by approximately $6,000, for a total debt of $72,045. For a student in a private school the total can reach almost $112,000.[43]

The regular (ten-year) monthly repayment amount on this debt is $832 and $1,310 respectively. Under the extended repayment plan of twenty-five years it drops to $504 and $807.[44] Keep in mind that a twenty-five year repayment plan means that, even without a one- to two-year hardship deferment, which many students take, a law school graduate would not pay off their loans until they were over fifty years old. The total amount paid by the public-school graduate under this scenario would be over $151,000. For a private-school graduate the total paid is over $242,000. Deferments would increase that total further.

In looking more closely at law school debt burden and outcomes, the chart below illustrates selected examples. The magazine *preLaw* recently issued their "best value" law school rankings. Number one best value nationwide was Georgia State University, with a high first-time bar-pass rate, a high reported employment rate, and low in-state tuition and debt levels. There are three criteria for a best value ranking: first is a bar-pass rate higher than the state average, then an average debt of less than $100,000, and finally—back to the employment factor—an employment rate nine months after graduation of eighty-five percent or more. The magazine then weights the schools, including consideration for in-state tuition.

The chart also shows the results for schools from the Big Ten that are in the best value rankings, compared to the number one best value school—Georgia State. Though all of these schools are public, state taxpayer-subsidized universities, note that debt levels for schools such as Indiana and Minnesota are reaching those of private schools and are almost above the $100,000 level, which would automatically kick them out of best value consideration. The best value rankings did not report data for all Big Ten schools, only the seven which meet their best value criteria. The other four Big Ten universities which offer law degrees—Illinois, Michigan, Penn State, and Northwestern—did not meet the best value ranking criteria. All of these schools are reporting median public service starting salaries in line with national data, all below the $65,000 considered minimally adequate financial remuneration. Additionally, even graduates accepting private-sector jobs that graduated from the University of Nebraska, considered the best value of all Big Ten schools, are not meeting the $65,000 threshold. The low level of average debt at Nebraska, less than $50,000, may compensate somewhat for the poor salary offers.

Table 12. Best Value Ranking of Big Ten University Law Schools

Best Value Rank	Number One Best Value Law School and Big Ten Schools	School's Bar Passage Rate, First-Time Test Takers	Statewide Bar Passage Rate, First-Time Test Takers	Graduates Employed Nine Months After Graduation	Median Private-Sector Starting Salary	Median Public Service Starting Salary	In-State Tuition	Average Debt
1	Georgia State University	94.2%	89.3%	97.3%	$80,000	$51,000	$11,838	$22,129
4	University of Nebraska-Lincoln	92.9%	88.6%	90.5%	$55,000	$44,100	$12,154	$49,946
33	University of Wisconsin	99.3%	91.8%	96.2%	$125,000	$47,500	$16,426	$67,655
38	Indiana University-Bloomington	93.9%	86.7%	92.5%	$97,000	$55,000	$24,891	$91,142
40	Ohio State	90.3%	88.1%	93.5%	$100,000	$46,500	$22,433	$79,855
43	University of Iowa	93.1%	89.7%	94.6%	$92,500	$47,750	$21,432	$81,735
53	Michigan State	84.2%	83.9%	87.1%	NA	NA	$33,054	$65,292
59	University of Minnesota	96.2%	90.8%	96.5%	NA	NA	$28,203	$94,087

Source: "Best Value Law Schools," Fall 2010 Issue of preLaw, *Vol. 14, No. 2, p. 26–27, Bar passage rate, employment, and tuition data derived from the Official Guide to ABA Approved Law Schools 2011 edition*

Alternatives and Conclusion

There are several potential options for avoiding at least some of the law school costs and corresponding debt. First, unless the student is an absolute top-of-the-line brilliant individual, with the highest GPA and LSAT score, and has significant personal cash reserves, they should first consider both the published tuition costs of their preferred school and their potential academic ranking in the matriculated class.

Attending an in-state school, where tuition is more affordable, and where one enters as a potentially higher achieving member of the class, is critical to a future successful career. If it happens to be located in the individual's hometown—hopefully allowing for a lower cost of living by keeping one's old bedroom—so much the better. Additionally, the student should establish and follow a serious, tight budget. Do not borrow a single penny more than is actually required to pay the tuition bill. Be sure your undergraduate loans are well on their way to being paid off, if not completely, before starting law school. Work and save your money for several years before entering law school. Live a frugal lifestyle. Do your homework, ask the hard questions, and do not accept the information presented at face value.

Beyond that, there are other options, including alternative licensing and part-time attendance. If one wants to be in the law field, but is not able to afford law school, or is not willing to assume $100,000 in debt, becoming a paralegal may be an attractive option. Based on job growth projections, that could be a worthwhile field to enter at a relatively low educational cost—and also provide the experience to determine if becoming an attorney is truly the end goal. While working as a paralegal, it may be possible to convince your employer to foot at least part of the tuition bill, or provide a flex-time schedule so that you may attend classes part-time.

Additionally, seven states—California, Maine, New York, Vermont, Virginia, Washington, and Wyoming—offer alternative licensing or law office study programs.[45] Under alternative licensing, a potential attorney finds a mentor to oversee a "reading" program, generally of four years. This is much like the apprentice programs in place from the earliest days of our nation until the 1800s in which someone wishing to become an attorney "read" or studied the law with an established practitioner. The programs require semi-annual study reports and written tests. After one year they take a bar exam, then move on to year two. In California, the first year of study and initial test covers contracts, criminal law, and torts.[46]

Alternatively, at eighty-four schools, or less than half of the ABA accredited law schools, one may attend part-time while working or parenting. These programs generally take four years instead of three to complete. According to *U.S. News and World Report*, about sixteen percent of all law students attend part-time.[47] There is also a ranking of part-time programs. These are based on a peer quality assessment score, LSAT and GPA selectivity, the part-time focus level, and overall school ranking.[48] These schools are presumably pulling most of their students from government or business professionals who believe a law degree will help them advance and who are attempting to pay as they go.

Data reflecting differences in loan debt levels between part-time and full-time students at these schools was not available for my review. A part-time program might, if a student were to budget carefully for a fairly short time period, be a very reasonable option. Additionally, the full-time programs of the top ten part-time schools are generally well respected themselves. One could end up with a perceived "Ivy"-quality degree at significantly less total cost, especially when considering a 25-year loan payoff schedule and accompanying interest.

Law schools may want to seriously consider aggressively implementing and promoting part-time degree programs. This is an area which will be beneficial to current students, who would be interested in part-time programs for other reasons, and might attract students who recognize that they cannot or are not willing to take out the loans and make the financial commitment to a full-time program.

Additionally, administrators and recruitment/admissions personnel would best serve both their potential students and the overall fiscal and economic health of citizens by ensuring that full and accurate data on costs—including total debt, length of time required to pay the debt, and total financial commitment required (including interest paid over 10 vs. 25 years)—are provided to applicants. Law schools must also communicate a realistic picture of potential jobs and income following the awarding of their degree. A student who will be assuming $100,000 or more in long-term unsecured debt needs to understand that only ten of 100 students is in the top ten percent of their graduating class and that only one of those same 100 students is likely to end up with a position paying $160,000 per year.

Potential students need to understand that while public service and helping others has appeal—a $40,000 salary will not go far in paying student loans, buying a home, having children of your own, or saving for retirement. They need to understand that, "Yes, Tommy and Suzie, one day you too will be 50 years old. Do you still want to be paying off your college loans?"

The ABA is beginning to actively recognize and address these issues. President Steve Zack indicated in October 2010 that they are "considering" requiring schools to release full cost and employment statistics to accepted students. A proposal called "Truth in Law School Education" may be considered by the Young Lawyers Division in February 2011. Other subcommittees are reviewing the annual law school questionnaire required by the ABA and Standard 509, which addresses consumer information that law schools must collect and disclose.[49] Currently, only select data is collected and released. Revisions to these requirements could be made as early as the fall of 2011. Zack openly admitted, in front of a "gathering of law school deans and professors," that law schools are "huge profit centers" for colleges. He further said that he thinks some of the "numbers are cooked."[50] These statements were probably considered sacrilegious by some, but he apparently lived to tell the tale. It is to be hoped that law school leaders recognize their responsibility to fully and accurately collect and disclose complete information. Without accurate, factual information, our young people cannot be expected to make good decisions.

Final Suggestions

Though law school may provide the dream career opportunity for some people, those considering applying must seriously review factual information about costs, loans, debt, and jobs. One must weigh the significant long-term debt burden against the current and projected employment market. While personal responsibility and long-term thinking are critical components of all post-secondary education decisions, it is even more important when considering law school. Those counseling undergraduate students who are interested in attending law school must be sure these students are fully briefed on financial issues before making the commitment. These students, who are often only twenty-one or twenty-two years of age, desperately need the cautionary advice and counsel of their parents, their college advisors, and their community leaders.

Notes

1. "College Enrollment and Work Activity of 2009 High School Graduates," U.S. Bureau of Labor Statistics, April 27, 2010, http://www.bls.gov/news.release/hsgec.nr0.htm, accessed on November 19, 2010.

2. Nina Ernest, "Iowa community college enrollment hits all-time high," *The Daily Iowan*, November 19, 2010, http://www.dailyiowan.com/2010/11/19/Metro/20173.html, accessed on November 23, 2010.

3. "FY 2008 Official Cohort Rates by State/Territory," U.S. Department of Education, http://www2.ed.gov/offices/OSFAP/defaultmanagement/2008staterates.pdf, accessed on November 19, 2010.

4. "Employment Situation Summary," U.S. Bureau of Labor Statistics, January 7, 2011, http://www.bls.gov/news.release/empsit.nr0.htm, accessed on January 14, 2011.

5. "Employment Projections: Employment by Occupation," U.S. Bureau of Labor Statistics, November 2009, http://www.bls.gov/emp/ep_table_102.htm, accessed on November 12, 2010.

6. Jack Crittenden and Karen Dybis, "Who is Hiring Now," *The National Jurist*, September 2010, pp. 28.

7. "Market for Law Graduates Changes with Recession: Class of 2009 Faced New Challenges," National Association for Legal Career Professionals, November 2010, pp. 2.

8. "Perspectives on Fall 2009 Law Student Recruiting," National Association for Legal Career Professionals, pp.11, http://www.nalp.org/uploads/PerspectivesonFallRec09.pdf, accessed on November 26, 2010.

9. James Leipold, "Some Perspectives on the Findings for the Class of 2009: Overall Employment Rate Masks Job Market Weakness," Employment for the Class of 2009—Selected Findings, National Association for Legal Career Professionals, November 2010 pp. 1, http://www.nalp.org/uploads/Class_of_2009_Selected_Findings.pdf, accessed on November 26, 2010.

10. Susan Hansen, "Summer Associates Survey 2010: A Chill is in the Air," http://www.law.com/jsp/tal/PubArticleTAL.jsp?id=1202472306807, accessed November 27, 2010.

11. Crittenden and Dybis, pp. 27.

12. "Recruiting Trends 2010–2011," Michigan State University and the Collegiate Employment Research Institute, date published, pp. 17

13. William D. Henderson, "Why the job market is changing," *The National Jurist*, October 26, 2010, http:/www.nationaljurist.com/content/critical-issues/why-job-market-changing, accessed on November 26, 2010.

14. "Recruiting Trends 2010–2011," pp. 30.

15. Jack Crittenden, "Fall recruitment hints at improving job market," Law School News, *preLaw*, October 2010, pp. 8.

16. "Salary Distribution Curve for the Class of 2009 Shows Relatively Few Salaries Were Close to the Mean," National Association for Legal Career Professionals, July 2010, http://www.nalp.org/startingsalarydistributionclassof2009, accessed on November 30, 2010.

17. Debra Cassens Weiss, "Profs Predict Law School Closings as More Grads Earn Less than Break-Even Pay," American Bar Association Journal, October 19, 2010, http://www.abajournal.com/news/article/profs_predict_law_school_closings_as_more_grads_earn_less_than_break-even_p/, accessed November 28, 2010.

18. Leslie Kwoh, "Irate law school grads say they were misled about job prospects," *The Star-Ledger*, August 16, 2010, http://blog.nj.com/business_impact, accessed on December 3, 2010.

19. "New Findings on Salaries for Public Interest Attorneys," National Association for Legal Career Professionals, September 2010, http://www.nalp.org/sept2010pubintsal, accessed on November 26, 2010.

20. "The Employment Situation, December 2010," U.S. Department of Labor, Bureau of Labor Statistics, January 7, 2011, http://www.bls.gov/news.release/empsit.nr0.htm, accessed on January 7, 2011.

21. Kwoh.

22. Robert Morse, "U.S. News Takes Steps to Stop Law Schools From Manipulating the Rankings," Morse Code Inside the College Rankings blog, May 20, 2010, http://www.usnews.com/blogs/college-rankings-blog/2010/05/20/us-news-takes-steps-to-stop-law-schools-from-manipulating-the-rankings.html, accessed on December 10, 2010.

23. Jack Crittenden, "Employment data under fire," *The National Jurist*, September 2010, pp. 5.

24. Ibid.

25. Tim Elfrink, "UM offers firms new law grads for free," *Miami New Times*, November 18, 2010, http://www.miaminewtimes.com/2010-11-18/news/um-offers-firms-new-law-grads-for-free/, accessed on December 4, 2010.

26. Katherine Mangan, "Law Schools Mull Whether They Are Churning Out Too Many Lawyers," The Chronicle of Higher Education, July 9, 2009, http://chronicle.com/article/Law-Schools-Ask-Whether-They/47364, accessed on December 4, 2010.

27. "Law Schools Are on Notice," Law School Transparency, July 12, 2010, http://www.law schooltransparnecy.com/2010/07/law-schools-are-on-notice/, accessed on December 1, 2010.

28. Ibid.

29. Kashmir Hill, "Stephen Colbert Rips Loyola-L.A.'s 'Foolproof' Plan to Get Their Graduates Jobs," Law School Transparency, July 7, 2010, http://abovethelaw.com/2010/07/stephen-colbert-rips-loyola-l-a-s-foolproof-plan-to-get-their-graduates-better-jobs/, accessed on December 3, 2010.

30. Karen Dybis, "Why law schools are inflating grades," *The National Jurist*, September 2010, pp. 18.

31. Rebecca R. Ruiz, "Recession Spurs Interest in Graduate, Law Schools," *The New York Times*, January 9, 2010 http://www.nytimes.com/2010/01/10/education/10grad.html?_r=1, accessed on December 1, 2010.

32. "Kaplan Test Prep Survey: Aspiring Law School Students Place Rankings Above All Else," *BusinessWire*, November 16, 2010, http://www.businesswire.com/news/home/20101116005536/en/Kaplan-Test-Prep-Survey-Aspiring-Law-School, accessed on November 26, 2010.

33. "Law School Admissions Council Matriculation Report," Law School Admissions Council, 2010 http://www.lsac.org/default.asp, accessed on November 10, 2010.

34. "Law School Applicants Willing to Brave Gloomy Job Market," *Veritas Prep*, October 21, 2010, http://www.veritasprep.com/blog/2010/10/law-school-applicants-willing-to-brave/, accessed on December 1, 2010.

35. "Good and Bad," *The National Jurist*, September 2010, pp. 6.

36. "Law School Applicants Willing to Brave Gloomy Job Market."

37. Ibid.

38. "Law School Tuition 1985–2008," American Bar Association, http://www.abanet.org/legaled/statistics/charts/stats%20-%205.pdf, accessed of December 1, 2010.

39. "Best Law Schools, Ranked in 2010," *U.S. News and World Report*, http://grad-schools.usnews.rankingsandreviews.com/best-graduate-schools/top-law-schools/rankings, accessed on November 15, 2010.

40. "Law School Faculties 40% Larger Than 10 Years Ago," *The National Jurist*, March 10, 2010, http://taxprof.typepad.com/taxprof_blog/2010/03/national-jurist.html, accessed on November 29, 2010.

41. "The Value Proposition of Attending Law School," American Bar Association, November 2009, http://www.abanet.org/lsd/legaled/value.pdf, accessed on November 23, 2010.

42. Annie Lowrey, "When law school becomes a bad investment," *The Washington Post*, October 30, 2010, http://www.washingtonpost.com/wp-dyn/content/article/2010/10/30/AR2010103004638_pf.html, accessed on November 26, 2010.

43. Christopher P. Chapman, "The Impact of the Recent Economic Crisis on Law School Borrowers," *The Bar Examiner*, November 2010, pp. 21, http://www.ncbex.org/uploads/user_docrepos/790410_Chapman.pdf, accessed on January 11, 2011.

44. Ibid. p. 22.

45. "Comprehensive Guide to Bar Admission Requirements 2010," National Conference of Bar Examiners and American Bar Association, pp. 10, http://www.ncbex.org/fileadmin/mediafiles/downloads/Comp_Guide/CompGuide_2010.pdf, accessed on January 3, 2011.

46. "First-Year Law Students' Examination Instructions," State Bar of California, http://www.calbarxap.com/applications/CalBar/info/first_year_exam.htm, accessed on January 3, 2011.

47. Robert Morse and Sam Flanigan, "The Part-Time Law School Rankings Methodology," *U.S. News and World Report*, April 15, 2010, http://www.usnews.com/articles/education/best-law-schools/2010/04/15/the-part-time-law-school-rankings-methodology_print.htm, accessed on January 3, 2011.

48. "Best Law Schools Specialty Rankings: Part-time Law," *U.S. News and World Report*, April 15, 2010, http://grad-schools.usnews.rankingsandreviews.com/best-graduate-schools/top-law-schools/part-time-law, accessed on January 3, 2011.

49. Karen Sloan, "ABA May Join Push for Law School Transparency," Law.com, October 19, 2010, http://www.law.com/jsp/article.jsp?id=1202473544557, accessed on January 12, 2011.

50. Ibid.

Part Five

Scholarship on the Law School Experience

Socratic Method and the Irreducible Core of Legal Education

*Donald G. Marshall**

Thanks to all of you for coming today. And a special thanks to the many students—present and former—that are here. This lecture is for them.

Since we are gathered to celebrate the creation of the first endowed position for teaching at the University of Minnesota Law School, I thought it appropriate if I talked about teaching, and in particular, teaching law. I do that with trepidation because I fear that in some respects I will be attempting to describe the indescribable. Although this is my twenty-eighth year of teaching, and I have loved teaching from the moment I entered my first class, I have always regarded the dynamics of the classroom as a fascinating mystery. With teaching, you can intuit that you have had a successful class, and often not know exactly what you and the students did or how you and the students did it.[1] But I will try.

I will give my views of the why, the what, and the how of teaching law. I stress with respect to the how that I will be describing how I think law should be taught; not how I teach it. My description is an aspiration I strive to achieve but sometimes do not. I've titled my talk "Socratic Method and the Irreducible Core of Legal Education." By "irreducible core" I mean the absolutely essential knowledge, thoughtways, values, habits, attitudes, and traditions a student must begin to make her own before undertaking a career in the public profession of the law. My thesis is that that core can be best taught by a variety of different types of dialog adapted to the learning situation of the moment, and which I have called in my title—somewhat misleadingly—Socratic Method.

Popular myth has it that Socratic method is pervasive in American law schools. But nothing could be further from the truth. The fact is that teaching and learning by genuine dialog has all but disappeared from the second and third years of law school, and is fast disappearing from the first. (By genuine dialog I mean a dialog based on respect for the promise of the students' minds and a determination to help them realize that promise by providing intellectual challenge.) Professors are substituting other pedagogical forms: One—the lecture—transmits facts and principles, but not the essentials of legal education, which require teacher-student and student-student interaction. A second—the pro-forma dialog—is a disguised lecture, structured around a series of questions which the teacher asks and then answers himself.[2] A third—the avuncular dialog—is one conducted by a kindly professor who, in his desire to be loved, avoids making any significant demands upon his students. The straightforward lecture is a waste of valuable classroom time and space, and has been ever since the invention of the printing press. The pro-forma dialog is both a waste and a deception. The avuncular dialog an insult to the students, who are entitled to be challenged. Hence, this call for revival of Socratic method.

But I'm ahead of myself. I am already talking about the how of law teaching, when I should be talking about the why and what, because the why and the what lead ineluctably to the how. Furthermore, the why, what, and how follow from the fact that this is, and should be, a professional school.

Why teach law? As far as I am concerned, there is only one correct answer: because you want to help students prepare themselves for entry into the legal profession. Now, a statement of that sort makes some legal academics nervous. They think it is too narrowing. They hear phrases like "preparation for entry into the legal profession" and they immediately think of vocational training in the most parochial of senses. In the sense that the economist, Thorstein Veblen, understood when he said law schools belong in universities about as much as schools of fencing or dancing.[3] Only somebody who has never practiced or has practiced in a mechanical, mundane fashion—without seeing the possibilities for personal redemption through a life in the law—could entertain that view. The fact is that members of the legal profession engage daily in an endeavor which is intellectually based, humanistically motivated,[4] and richly varied.

Intellectually based. That's what Justice Holmes meant when, in an address to the students of Brown University, he said, "The law is the calling of thinkers ... a man may live greatly in the law as well as elsewhere."[5] He should have said that a man or woman can live more greatly in the law than most elsewheres, but he was right about the law being a calling of thinkers. The lawyer must constantly apply the "arts of thought and rationality"[6] as she functions within and contributes to the growth of a variety of legal processes. That requires high-order intellectual capacities including, among others, powers of appropriate generalization, of distinguishing relevant from irrelevant similarities, of discrimination, of particularization, and of reasoned, lucid articulation.[7]

Humanistically motivated. As I understand it, the legal profession is a functional group obliged to master a body of scholarly knowledge, to be applied in light of articulated standards of conduct, for the purpose of providing a public service. Note the three elements of that definition, all worded in the form of obligation: the obligation of professional competence, the obligation of professional responsibility, and the obligation of public service. Humanistic motivation is what underlies the obligation of public service. Lawyers provide public services in many ways. I shall mention only two—provided by every working lawyer and vital to the existence of the Republic. First, every working lawyer fulfills a charge to "maximiz[e] the social interest in tranquility" by providing means for the avoidance or peaceful resolution of dispute.[8] And that charge—that common responsibility of the bar—is no mean thing. After all, it is, in the last analysis, the existence and smooth-functioning of institutional processes for the avoidance and orderly resolution of conflict that permit the release of our people's creative energies and the use of those energies to achieve constructive and socially desirable goals.

Second, every working lawyer provides public service by assuring that all individuals and interests have meaningful access to both the prophylactic and remedial processes of the law. The importance of that service cannot be overemphasized. Law is central to the functioning of American society in a way that is true of few other existing or past societies. De Tocqueville noted that characteristic of this country 160 years ago in his monumental work, *Democracy in America*.[9] Americans go to law. One may deplore that propensity, as increasing numbers of people—in and out of public life—do. But deplore as they may, our use of law is not going to diminish. Too many modern developments reinforce that aspect of our national character: industrialization, urbanization, accelerating mobility, growing cultural heterogeneity, the depersonalizing of markets for the distribution of goods and services, and the unfortunate deterioration of so many nonlegal institutions which used to be agencies of informal control—all centrifugal forces that drive toward a noncommunitarian mindset and lead inevitably to dependence on formal institutions. We as a people have always insisted and will continue to insist on framing urgent social, economic, and political questions in legal terms. In so doing, we will continue to place great problems of social order in the hands of lawyers for definition and in the hands of judges, legislators, and administrators for resolution.[10]

Richly Varied. Lawyers practice in private firms, with the government and in for-profit and not-for-profit corporations. They act as judges, legislators, and governmental administrators. They become private-sector policymakers. And they are influential participants and leaders at every level of community. Such roles, and the tasks within them, are diverse and complex. One consequence of that diversity and complexity is that the image of the lawyer-professional used to guide the content and method of law school teaching is necessarily general. Another is that that image must encompass a broad vision.

There you have it. Intellectually based. Humanistically motivated. Richly varied. To help prepare students for entry into such a profession is not narrowing; it is liberating. Indeed, the law teacher can find derivative redemption in such a life. That's the "why" of law teaching. Now for the what.

I take it as a basic premise that we in the law schools ought not to attempt to teach anything that can be as well or better taught by law firms, broadly defined. We ought to teach only that which we can teach better and which the student absolutely must make her own before entry into the profession. That is an inseparable body of knowledge, thoughtways, habits, and values which are essential to an understanding of the nature of law, and which I call the irreducible core of legal education. All courses at the irreducible core are, or should be, courses where teacher and student, by studying together, develop that constellation of cognitive and moral capacities necessary to understand the nature of law—using "law" here not in the popular and least interesting sense of a body of rules, but in the sense of an "obligatory system that functions through a complex set of decision-making [processes]," each of those processes being in itself law.[11] Rules (what lay persons ordinarily think of as law) are part of those processes, and materials used in those processes, but there are other important materials, such as doctrines, principles, concepts, maxims, conventions, fictions, and, of course, language. Learning how to become a lawyer is very much a matter of learning how to use all of those materials in light of a received tradition of use.

One of those processes—the one I shall concentrate on, for illustrative purposes—is the common law process, by means of which judges in our system create and implement law. A variety of intellectual skills, related cognitive capacities, and professional values are necessary to understand, and operate effectively within, that process. I say not only "understand" but "operate effectively within," because lawyers' participation in judge-created law is a vital aspect of that process; the student must understand the lawyer's role and develop the skills necessary to perform it if she is fully to understand the nature of this form of law.[12]

To start with, the students have to learn how to read and analyze published judicial opinions, for they are the primary visible source of data about the nature of judicially created law. They have to learn how to reduce an opinion to its constituent elements, to analyze each independently and in relation to the others, then through an act of synthesis arrive at a tentative statement of the proposition or propositions for which the opinion stands, and which will be used more or less as a guide to resolution of future disputes.

They have to learn how to analyze a series of related opinions to ascertain how judges in the later cases treat seemingly guiding propositions of earlier cases—and they have to learn how to use this knowledge to determine the effective reach and limits of those earlier propositions.

That involves understanding the concept of stare decisis, the use of precedent, and the creative tension between precedent and the effectuation of public policy. In connection with precedent, the student must master analogical reasoning and the skill of reconciling apparent contradictions.[13]

By analyzing opinions, students have to learn what counts, in light of a received rhetorical tradition, as persuasive justifications for judicial answers to particular legal problems. Concomitantly, they develop a sense of which arguments of counsel are likely to be regarded as convincing, which provocative, and which acceptable. The convincing argument usually appears in the opinion as a justification for decision; the provocative is mentioned and rebutted; the acceptable ignored, but not denigrated.

In addition to developing a feel for what arguments of counsel count, the students must learn how to construct, present, and defend such arguments themselves. To do that, they have to develop, in addition to the intellectual skills I've already mentioned, a series of related cognitive capacities. They must learn how to listen, hear, understand, evaluate, formulate, and articulate; and, to do that, they must hone, to a fine edge, the mental attributes of attention and alertness.

I listed among the essential cognitive capacities the lawyer must have "articulation"—the ability to communicate clearly, concisely and, if possible, with grace. That involves knowledge of and feel and respect for the English language, a mastery of legal language, and the skill of precise expression. The precision of the law student's analyses is disclosed by the precision of her expression. She has to learn to state her process of decision and her ideas in concise, accurate, and lucid language.

In addition, she must commit herself to dialectical reasoning as a valuable means of testing the validity of any proposition—that is, she must recognize the wisdom and instrumental power in the idea expressed by the Poet Richard Eberhart when he wrote:

> Each argument begets its counterpart,
> Only in opposites the truth is human,
> Intelligible....[14]

Finally, the student must learn, and make her own, a series of professional attitudes, values, and habits, including: skepticism toward any generalization when initially perceived, invariant thorough preparation, critical self-awareness, the capacity and temperament for autonomous study, a concern for the welfare of others and the community, and, pre-eminently, a determination to do justice. Only then will she begin to understand the nature of the law we call "common."

There's the what of law teaching. Now, the how. I put it to you that what I have called the irreducible core of legal education can be most successfully taught by use of the dialog method of instruction. All other pedagogical methods, except clinical, are one-dimensional or, at most, two. The dialog, properly conceived and used, is multidimensional.[15] Because the irreducible core of legal education is an inseparable constellation of thoughtways, professional values, personal values, habits, and attitudes, only a multidimensional pedagogical technique will do. Only such a technique allows achievement of multiple teaching-learning goals at the same time. Dialog, artfully employed, does that by facilitating communication at different levels of abstraction, at different times during the class hour, and often at several levels of abstraction simultaneously.

I have used the phrase "Socratic Method" in the title of this lecture as a synonym for dialog. Actually, that use is misleading, because "Socratic Method"—the pedagogical technique used by Socrates in the public market and other meeting places of ancient Athens—is today only one form of dialog. Many others have evolved from Socrates's prototypical technique. Although all forms, skillfully used, are multidimensional, particular forms are best used when a particular learning goal is predominant. The teacher must be ever alert to this fact because it is her or his job to tailor form to goal. I shall briefly describe two of those forms; but before doing so, I want to say something about characteristics common to all dialogs.

A dialog, as I use the term, is simply a conversation between teacher and student—in question and answer form—where the teacher asks the questions, and, in so doing, provides some direction. By selecting the questions, she selects the agenda of conversation. And by varying the nature of the questions, she produces discourse at varying levels of generality with varying degrees of focus. By adjusting the generality and focus of the questions she adjusts the conversation to the learning goal of the moment, allowing her to move from one goal to another or back and forth between goals during a single class hour.

Ideally, the dialog involves two people—teacher and student. That's what President Garfield meant when he was asked for his definition of the ideal university, and responded: "Mark Hopkins at one end of a log and a student at the other."[16] In the law school context, conditions are far from ideal. Class size varies from 20 to 110. One of the consequent challenges for the teacher is to create the illusion that each student is sitting at the other end of the log. In a very real sense each student is, because the theory of the group dialog is that although at any given moment one student is participating in the conversation aloud, every other student is participating silently, ready to jump in at midstream to continue it.

As that description indicates, all group dialogs are multirelational. The relationships are of three sorts. One between the teacher and each student. A second between each student and every other student. And a third between the group and each of its members. Learning opportunities derive from all three relationships. The students not only learn from the teacher, they also learn from each other. And, most interestingly, learning occurs as a result of the relationship between the group and each of its members. The group develops a life of its own—a spirit of inquiry, an ethic of civility and mutual support, a standard of professional behavior. The result of the multirelational nature of the dialog is that products of it are joint creations—all members of the group and the group itself contribute to the learning that occurs. The students tend to believe—at least, when first exposed to the dialog method—that they are only talking, but what they are doing is creating. "They are not simply talking any more than a poem on a printed page is simply a sequence of words."[17]

In addition to being multidimensional and multirelational, the dialog method entails active student participation in the learning process. If I had to pick the single most important virtue of the dialog method, it would be this: dialog is a pedagogy based on the premise that active learning almost always produces understanding of a higher quality than passive learning. It is a recognition of the wisdom conveyed by the old saw: "Tell me, and I will forget. Show me, and I will remember. Involve me, and I will understand." Involvement—at least, informed involvement—in the learning process provides great motivation to learn and produces a qualitatively different form of knowing.

Whatever the form of dialog, when the teacher asks a question, each student has to utilize the six cognitive capacities used by the practicing lawyer daily in the performance of most law jobs. She has to listen, hear, understand, evaluate, formulate a response, and stand ready to articulate and defend it. Moreover, each student has to utilize the same six cognitive capacities with respect to every comment made by a fellow student because she will have to formulate a tentative conclusion about the comment in order to follow the teacher's response or, if called on, to make one herself. In addition, the student hones the mental attributes of attention and alertness because it is only those attributes that allow the use of the other cognitive capacities.

Among the capacities honed by student participation in the dialog is "articulation." In her articulation of a response (to teacher or fellow student) she demonstrates and develops her feel for the English language, the language of the law, and for concise, accurate, lucid expression.

By daily participation in dialogs the student also develops confidence in her ability to speak before a group whose mission it is to evaluate and challenge her ideas or their presentation. And that, after all, is the lawyer's essential milieu. As confidence develops, quality of participation increases, and, eventually, if the process works, the student makes the dialog method and dialectical reasoning her own, using it over a professional lifetime as a means of self-education and self-examination.

Those are some of the features and learning potentials common to all dialogs. Other features and learning potentials are characteristic of particular types of dialog—a fact that allows the teacher to match and mix: match dialog to the dominant learning goal and mix dialogs as the dominant goal changes during a single class hour. There are about four basic dialog types, which by modification and blending can be adjusted to produce almost limitless variety. Time does not permit description of all four. For illustrative purposes, I will briefly describe two used for the first time, as far as we know, in classical Greece, the two which are the prototypical dialogs from which all others derive.

I start with the Socratic dialog, strictly speaking—that is, the dialog as conducted by Socrates in ancient Athens. Socrates did not publish. For an understanding of his distinctive pedagogy we are therefore dependent on descriptions in the writings of others, primarily Plato, Xenephon, and Artistophanes.[18] Of these three, the one who chronicled Socrates's teaching most extensively was Plato, who was Socrates's student. Plato's writings include a number of dialogs which purport to be accurate recollections of exchanges between Socrates and another.

As recounted by Plato, the dialogs of Socrates have a fixed form, structure, and purpose—all related to a distinctive theory of knowledge, a theory which may sound strange to modern ears. As to form, Socrates asked a series of related questions and the student answered them. Each question was responsive to the student answer to the preceding question. Most noteworthy, for present purposes, was Socrates's invariant adherence to questions; he rarely made a declarative statement.

As to structure, the typical Socratic dialog had four stages.[19] In the first, Socrates asked questions until a student answer contained an assertion which Socrates deemed a misconception. In the second, Socrates asked a series of questions designed to lead the student step by step toward realization that his statement was erroneous and why. The third stage was the discovery and acknowledgment by the student that his statement was misconceived. In the fourth, Socrates asked a final series of questions which helped the student discover the relevant valid assertion.

As to purpose, Socrates's dialogs were a form of moral education, the purpose being to discover ethical truth and thereby induce virtuous behavior.[20] (One of Socrates's questionable substantive beliefs was that if men know virtue, they will act virtuously.)

Since Socrates's goal was moral education, his dialogs always dealt with the validity of large propositions.[21]

As to his epistemology, Socrates believed a person's soul contains all ethical knowledge. Teaching ethical truths is, therefore, simply a matter of finding the questions that were keys to unlock the soul and allow the student to discover knowledge he always possessed.[22]

The particular learning potential of the Socratic dialog does not depend on Socrates's theory of soul-possessed knowledge. One can reject that theory and still recognize the wisdom underlying his pedagogy—the wisdom that knowledge has a different quality and a different feel when the teacher-aided student discovers it for himself.

In the law school context, the Socratic dialog, strictly speaking—that is, the dialog where the teacher's only utterances are in the form of questions—should be used, but sparingly. "Sparingly" because such a dialog is time consuming; because many class hours of nothing but questions from the teacher can cause intolerable student frustration; and because the series of questions designed to expose the student misconception can have a destructive effect if not followed by a creative and powerfully restorative series that helps the student discover the valid assertion. Therefore, the Socratic dialog, strictly speaking, should be used only when the truth of large propositions are at stake. For example, discussions of such moral propositions as the nature of justice, or the nature of a particular form of justice, or the demands of justice in a prototypical situation (for example, do and should we have the duty to come to the aid of a stranger in peril) are well suited to the Socratic dialog. Unmodified Socratic technique also works well when examining the validity of large propositions that are not ethical in nature; and the teacher should always be alert to the utility of a mini-Socratic dialog when, during the course of another type of dialog, she discovers a student misconception that can be identified and cured with a limited series of questions. Apart from those three situations, the Socratic dialog should be modified for most law school discussions to make it more directional. That can be accomplished if the teacher intersperses her questions with declarative statements that provide students with less subtle clues to the existence and nature of the misconception and that expedite the timing and impact of the restorative part of the dialog. However, the teacher who modifies Socrates's technique must be ever alert to the danger of significantly diminishing student self-discovery, and to the ultimate sin of making the dialogue avuncular.

A second basic form of dialog is the Protagorean—named after Protagoras, another Athenian, "the leading Sophist and Socrates' rival."[23] Unlike Socrates, Protagoras left some writing. Plato also wrote about Protagoras. In fact, a famous Platonic dialog, the *Protagoras*, recounts an exchange between Protagoras and Socrates.[24] In his teaching Protagoras did not, like Socrates, emphasize the question to the practical exclusion of any other form of statement. Protagoras asked questions, but he made more statements in declaratory than interrogatory form, and the primary form he used was the argument. Protagoras's main goal was to train students in the skills of rhetoric. His typical dialog was a debate with a student in which he illustrated the techniques of effective argumentation.[25]

The Protagorean dialog is obviously useful to the law teacher of today to accomplish a variety of learning goals. Argument and counter-argument (rhetoric) is a useful tool for the law student and the lawyer to test the truth value of almost any proposition. With regard to common law study, in particular, the Protagorean dialog can be used to test the reach and limits of doctrine, to verify a tentatively selected proposition as the, or a, guiding proposition in a judicial opinion, and to apply case-derived guiding propositions to hypothetical situations, to name just a few uses. Used in imaginative combination with other forms of dialog, Protagorean dialog should be a staple of the law school teaching-learning process.

If a law teacher uses a dialog method of instruction—Socratic, Protagorean, Langdellian,[26] in aid of role playing, or a blend or modification of any of those—whatever the form, there are some essential personal characteristics that he or she must demonstrate. Those characteristics follow from the ultimate purpose of the dialog—to maximize learning by encouraging participation in the process of discovery, including, most significantly, discovery of the dialogue as a means of autonomous learning. First, the teacher must have genuine respect for classroom space and time, for the dialog process, and for all potential participants; and she must make that respect evident by her preparation. The neophyte instructor often underestimates preparation time and effort because she thinks that a dialogue, like an ordinary conversation, has its own momentum. Consequently, she enters the classroom with a yellow scratch pad, containing three or four points she wants to cover and starts off with a question to Mr. Jones. Jones gives an answer that she (the teacher) didn't anticipate and therefore doesn't fully understand, or she apprehends its meaning but does not see in the time available to respond how Jones's comment can be used as a step in the collective journey of discovery that is the hallmark of a successful class. She moves to another student, repeating her initial question verbatim, and prays for a response she can immediately understand and use; or, more likely, she lapses into a mini-lecture, checks off the first point on her scratch pad, and moves on to the second. The students perceive that as an effort that failed and may attribute it to lack of professionalism. In addition to all other values lost in the aborted dialog, the teacher has missed the opportunity to model professional behavior.

The instructor could have avoided, or at least minimized, that loss with thorough preparation. That involves mastery of relevant substantive law, but such mastery is only the beginning. The crucial part of preparation—the most demanding and creative part—requires acts of imagination. The teacher has to imagine the class hour before it occurs. She has to conduct a dialog in her head including a variety of responses to her inquiries and a separate branching dialog using each imagined student response as an integral step. Some people call that "scripting," but that term, in this context, is a disservice because it is seriously misleading. It implies a process that is too mechanical and manipulative. The acts of imagination I envision are analogous to the warm ups of an athlete or the finger exercises of a pianist. They are designed to limber the mind of the teacher, so that she doesn't suffer brain cramp during the class hour. But she must not allow herself or her student to become a slave to her imagined dialogs—the purpose of her warm up is to release the creative potential of her intellect so that she can make flexible and productive use of student comment.

A second personal quality or characteristic that the teacher conducting any sort of dialog must possess is compassion. By "compassion" I do not mean sappy sentimentality that leads to the pro-forma dialog or the avuncular dialog. By "compassion" I mean respect for all potential participants in the process and something more—an appreciation that although dialog imaginatively used is the most effective pedagogical vehicle for learning the irreducible core of legal education, it can be, when misused, destructive. Most people have never been required to state their views before an audience whose mission it is to evaluate and criticize those views or their presentation. That is the essential milieu of the lawyer, but not most others. The dialog is potentially threatening to the uninitiated, and the teacher must always be alert to conducting it so as not to wound. She should make it clear by her behavior that she respects the enterprise that is the dialog, and that the dialog is part of, and she should never sharpen her intellect, curry favor, or seek personal satisfaction at student expense. She must not only avoid affirmatively harming students, she must build each and every student's confidence in his ability to perform. She must encourage and foster student willingness to expose themselves by risking mistake and, if the risk materializes, coming back and trying again.

In addition to being thoroughly prepared and manifesting compassion, the teacher must model the constellation of other professional characteristics she wishes the students to make their own. This is the primary way that communication at simultaneous levels occurs. The teacher's participation is like a rich literary metaphor. She teaches excellence by doing excellence—by displaying to the best of her ability professional virtues she wishes her students to make their own.

Lastly, to achieve maximum effectiveness the teacher must do what she can to include everyone in the dialog. Each student must see himself at the other end of the log. The chances of that vision occurring will be maximized if the teacher does a number of things. First, she should call on a mix of volunteers and nonvolunteers. In the ideal dialog, the students would volunteer eagerly to participate. But neither life nor classroom discussion is ideal. In every class, a percentage of the students are reluctant to participate. There are undoubtedly many reasons for that, one being fear of appearing foolish. For some, the prospect of participation is threatening, for a few, overwhelming. But participation is essential if the student is to profit from the process.

I noted previously that the theory of the group dialog is that although one student is participating aloud at any given moment, all others are silently formulating imagined responses to teacher or fellow-student comment. The dialog works, or not, to the extent that silent participation occurs. That form of participation requires enormous self-discipline. In the course of a class hour, it is easy and natural for the student to drift off—thinking of what occurred in his life yesterday, or what will occur tomorrow, or not thinking at all—and in those moments of drift he loses the thread of the conversation. The prospect of being called on for vocal participation reinforces the self-discipline necessary for silent participation. It provides an incentive because the students rapidly learn that if they are called on to participate, the quality of their vocal participation will depend on the extent and quality of the silent participation that preceded it. Insisting on participation by nonvolunteers also provides students with maximum incentive to study assigned materials, because they also rapidly learn—if the teacher has carefully selected the materials—that the quality of their vocal participation will be largely a result of the quality of their preparation, a lesson that every practicing lawyer is reminded of daily.

A sense of group involvement in the dialog is also more likely to occur if the teacher works with more than a few vocal participants during a class hour and if the nonvolunteer participants are randomly selected. Random selection increases the incentive for adequate preparation and silent participation. I say the teacher should randomly select the nonvolunteers. Actually, in a large class—say above fifty—she should randomly select from different physical areas of the class. Selection should be in an order that envelopes the class in the conversation—first a student to the left, then in the rear; a student to the right, then the middle and the front—until, being enveloped, all are on that log.

Finally, maximum involvement depends, in part, on maximum understanding. The teacher can increase the chances of understanding by a judicious mix of question and declarative statement, by providing clues at appropriate stages (in both interrogatory and declarative form), by assuring that she and every vocal student participant can be clearly heard, by welcoming questions (of a sort and at times that do not significantly disrupt the dialog), and by the enthusiasm she brings to the classroom. That last characteristic cannot be overestimated. Enthusiasm is contagious in most areas of life, and certainly in the classroom. Teacher enthusiasm elicits student enthusiasm. And student enthusiasm facilitates learning.

Well, there you have it. Those are my ideas on the why, the what, and the how of teaching part of the irreducible core of legal education. I have ideas about teaching other parts of the irreducible core—other processes which are law, but that's a topic for another day.

I started this lecture by telling you I feared I would be attempting to describe the indescribable. I feared that because, when push comes to shove, teaching is an art form—at least, evocative teaching is; and the quintessential evocative mode, properly used, is the dialog.[27] One can no more convey the essence of a successful dialog than one can convey the overall impact of a painting. Take an O'Keefe or a Hopper, reduce it to its constituent elements—color, line, form, subject matter, medium, application—and what have you said? Not much about its effect on the viewer, because its effect is not reducible to its constituent elements. It is in part a resultant of those elements, but it is much more. It is a creation that ultimately defies analysis. Indeed, analysis may drain it of its life, the way a punch line of a good joke loses its punch when explained. Maybe that's true of evocative teaching also. Maybe, in the end, every serious evocative teacher, through the act of teaching, seeks redemption by expressing his own personal vision in his own personal way. And maybe it is that combination of animating vision and distinctive style that is the crucial, ineffable ingredient of the teaching-learning process.

I end where I began—with thanks. Thanks to about 4,500[28] students with whom I have been privileged to study. They have been the reason for my professional life. If a fair number think I have truly helped them prepare for a life in the law, that's redemption enough for me.

Notes

* This article is a transcript of a lecture I delivered on January 19, 1994, when I was inaugurated as Law Alumni Distinguished Teacher. It has been edited just to delete irrelevances and to add a small number of footnotes. Because the lecture was prepared in December 1993, the sources cited in these footnotes are those I consulted prior to that date.

1. Richard B. Parker, *A Review of* Zen and the Art of Motorcycle Maintenance *with Some Remarks on the Teaching of Law*, 29 RUTGERS L. REV. 318, 326 (1976).

2. *See* THOMAS L. SHAFFER & ROBERT S. REDMOUNT, LAWYERS, LAW STUDENTS, AND PEOPLE 168, 176–77 (1977).

3. THORSTEIN VEBLEN, THE HIGHER LEARNING IN AMERICA: A MEMORANDUM ON THE CONDUCT OF UNIVERSITIES BY BUSINESS MEN 211 (1918).

4. For a discussion of humanistic motivation, see generally Francis A. Allen, *Humanistic Legal Education: The Quiet Crisis, in* ESSAYS ON LEGAL EDUCATION 9 (Neil Gold ed., 1982).

5. Oliver Wendell Holmes, Your Business as Thinkers (February 17, 1886), *in* THE MIND AND FAITH OF JUSTICE HOLMES: HIS SPEECHES, ESSAYS, LETTERS, AND JUDICIAL OPINIONS 31, 31 (Max Lerner ed., 1943).

6. Francis A. Allen, *Mr. Justice Holmes and "The Life of the Mind,"* 52 B.U. L. REV. 229, 233 (1972), reprinted in FRANCIS A. ALLEN, LAW, INTELLECT, AND EDUCATION 2, 6 (1979).

7. *See* Paul T. Wangerin, *Skills Training in "Legal Analysis": A Systematic Approach*, 40 U. MIAMI L. REV. 409 *passim* (1986).

8. Phil C. Neal, *De Tocqueville and the Role of the Lawyer in Society*, 50 MARQ. L. REV. 607, 613 (1967).

9. *See* ALEXIS DE TOCQUEVILLE, DEMOCRACY IN AMERICA 99 (J.P. Mayer ed., George Lawrence trans., Harper & Row 1966) (1835) ("No other nation in the world has organized judicial power in the same way as the Americans.").

10. William J. Brennan, Jr., *The Equality Principle in American Constitutional Jurisprudence*, 48 OHIO ST. L.J. 921, 923 (1987) ("We place great problems of social order in the hands of lawyers for their definition, and in the hands of judges for their ultimate resolution.").

11. Graham Hughes, *Rules, Policy and Decision Making*, 77 YALE L.J. 411, 435 (1968).

12. For a succinct description of the common law as a process and the practicing lawyer's essential role in that process, *see generally* Thomas D. Eisele, *The Activity of Being a Lawyer: The Imaginative Pursuit of Implications and Possibilities*, 54 TENN. L. REV. 345 (1987); Harry W. Jones, *Our Uncommon Common Law*, 42 TENN. L. REV. 443 (1975).

13. *See* Wangerin, *supra* note 7, at 459–64.

14. RICHARD EBERHART, UNDERCLIFF: POEMS 1946–1953, at 59 (1953), *quoted in* Howard Nemerov, *Contemporary Poets*, ATLANTIC MONTHLY, Sept. 1954, at 67.

15. For these and related thoughts I am indebted to JOSEPH AXELROD, THE UNIVERSITY TEACHER AS ARTIST (1973).

16. Mark Hopkins was Garfield's philosophy professor at Williams College. Although some commentators question whether the quote is accurate, *see, e.g.*, Houston Peterson, *Mark Hopkins: 1802–1887*, in GREAT TEACHERS 75 (Houston Peterson ed., 1956), generations of Williams graduates believe with all their hearts that the story is true and that it captures the essence of a Williams education.

17. AXELROD, *supra* note 15, at 8.

18. *See, e.g.*, *Encylopaedia Britannica*, 15th ed., s.v. "Socrates"; Richard K. Neumann, Jr., *A Preliminary Inquiry into the Art of Critique*, 40 HASTINGS L. REV. 725, 729 n.15 (1989).

19. Neumann, *supra* note 18, at 730–31.

20. William C. Heffernan, *Not Socrates, but Protagoras: The Sophistic Basis of Legal Education*, 29 Buff. L. Rev. 339, 407–09 (1980).

21. *Id.*

22. *Id.* at 409.

23. Neumann, *supra* note 18, at 729.

24. PLATO, PROTAGORAS AND MENO (Betty Radice ed., W.K.C. Guthrie trans., Penguin Books 1956).

25. Heffernan, *supra* note 20, at 414–15.

26. Christopher Columbus Langdell was appointed professor at Harvard Law School in 1870 and subsequently became dean. He is generally credited with introducing the case method of study in American law schools. Langdell described his in-class discussions with students about cases as "Socratic," but some, *e.g.*, Heffernan, *supra* note 20, think Langdell's dialogs were more like those of Protagoras than those of Socrates. Indeed, some regard Protagorean and Langdellian dialogs as the same in essential respects. *See, e.g.*, Neumann, *supra* note 18, at 728–29. For a discussion of Langdellian dialogs, see Heffernan, *supra* note 20, at 401–02; Neumann, *supra* note 18, at 739–44.

27. For a detailed description of "evocative" teaching, *see* AXELROD, *supra* note 15, at 7–55.

28. Now, it's about 6,000.

The Relationship between Law School and the Bar Exam: A Look at Assessment and Student Success

*Lorenzo A. Trujillo**

Law schools have a moral and ethical obligation to society—and, to an even greater degree, to their students—to adequately prepare the students to succeed as professionals. Ultimate success for law students is measured by the ability to competently practice in the legal profession, which requires passing the bar exam. A recent downward trend in national bar passage rates highlights the need for law schools to address the factors negatively affecting bar passage rates. Based on research conducted at the University of Colorado School of Law, this article discusses methods to reform new attorney licensure and also highlights strategies to improve bar passage. It suggests ways to minimize the effects of the bar exam's negative factors and recommends ways to better prepare law students.

Introduction

Bar passage rates have been of increasing concern for law schools as the national bar passage rate has declined over the past decade. Undoubtedly, a school's bar passage rate figures prominently into the all-important *U.S. News and World Report* Law School rankings methodology.[1] However, as educational institutions, law schools should be at least equally concerned with falling bar passage rates to the extent that those rates reflect the quality and effectiveness of legal education—or lack thereof. Specifically, law schools should be cognizant of bar passage rates and trends as a function of whether their students are being effectively educated and trained to practice law. [See Figure 1.]

Additionally, a survey of messages from the American Bar Association's Law School Deans' listserv[3] confirms that bar passage rates are of deep concern to deans at law schools throughout the United States.[4] This survey indicates that deans are particularly interested in providing effective, high-quality academic services to aid their students in passing the bar exam.[5] While some schools are simply struggling to improve bar passage rates after their respective states raised the bar passage threshold,[6] others are trying to remedy unexpected and unexplained drops in their institutions' bar passage rates.[7]

Figure 1. National Bar Passage Rates[2]

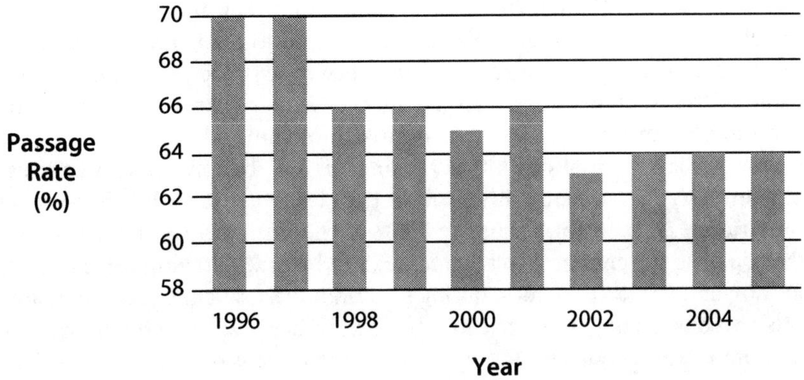

Law schools have a moral and ethical obligation to society—and, to an even greater degree, to their students—to adequately prepare the students to succeed as professionals. Ultimate success for law students is measured by the ability to competently practice the legal profession. This necessarily requires licensure. Therefore, academics should teach and prepare their students for success by ensuring that they are adequately equipped to pass their state's bar examination.

Based on the research provided herein, the author believes that a bar exam is a necessary prerequisite to licensure in the legal profession. However, the time is ripe for the exam to evolve by incorporating multiple testing modalities and a more sophisticated application of technology in exam assessment. This article begins with a discussion of the national concern surrounding the bar exam, followed by an explanation of the methodology of the bar exam and a survey of common criticisms of the exam. Next, suggested alternatives to the current bar exam are evaluated and contrasted with the prevailing arguments supporting adherence to the current examination model. Based on the research, including the author's experience and implementation of strategies at the University of Colorado School of Law ("CU Law School"), the article details and discusses strategies for bar passage. Finally, an analysis of bar passage results at CU Law School is used to illustrate which factors may be negatively affecting bar passage rates. In connection with this analysis, the author also outlines suggestions for minimizing the effects of these factors.[8]

I. Bar Passage: A National Concern

A review of the ABAnet Dean's listserv provided by the American Bar Association reveals that law schools are using a variety of strategies to increase bar passage rates.[9] As noted previously, national bar passage rates have declined significantly over the past ten years.[10]

Correspondingly, the effectiveness of academic support services available for struggling students is a prevalent concern at law schools across the country. Comments on the Dean's listserv indicate that a number of schools are implementing, strengthening, and enhancing academic services in an attempt to combat falling passage rates.[11] Many of these law schools have implemented academic support programs to prepare incoming law students with specific, known weaknesses.[12] Various incarnations of tutorial programs aimed at assisting incoming students during the course of the 1L academic year appear to be the most common ancillary services. Many schools have also begun to offer tutorial sessions and academic services to second- and third-year students whose grades, class rank, or other indicators signify that they may be at risk for failing the bar exam.[13] Not surprisingly, rather than aiming to improve grades or class rank, these tutorials are often specifically designed to assist in bar preparation. Although some schools' bar preparatory courses are voluntary and exclusive to students with the lowest grades, other schools have considered offering preparatory courses for credit pursuant to the limitations established by the ABA.[14] Other options for enhanced academic services include allowing commercial bar preparation companies to teach a course during the traditional academic year. Alternatively, some schools are considering offering scholarships to students who are otherwise unable to pay for bar preparation courses. However, concern that focus on bar passage will label them as "bar review" schools has caused a few schools to express trepidation about offering bar preparation courses as academic classes. This concern stems from a belief that academically rigorous schools do not need such preparation because the quality of legal instruction should be sufficient to ensure bar passage.

Classroom experiences may also have a significant effect on bar passage rates. Two considerations that have been identified as being relevant in this regard are (1) the use of "typical" law school timed-essay exams versus multiple-choice or take-home exams[15] and (2) the use of laptop computers in the classroom.[16] A discussion among colleagues has revealed that one factor contributing to bar passage rates may be whether professors give "traditional" exams or take-home exams.[17] Traditional exams, given under timed-limited conditions, more closely simulate the bar exam experience. As such, there appears to be a disparity in bar passage among students given predominantly take-home exams and those taking more traditional exams, with traditional exam takers passing the bar in greater numbers than those who are given take-home exams.[18]

The use of laptop computers for taking notes in class has also increased dramatically in recent years. However, after observation, professors and students alike have indicated that in some situations computers are simultaneously being used for e-mail, on-line shopping, instant messaging, and note taking.[19] This multi-tasking presents two major concerns. First, students are distracted by their computers and are thus inattentive in class. Obviously, surfing the internet does not support or enhance legal knowledge or skills and does not contribute to classroom interaction or discussion.[20] Second, it has been hypothesized that handwriting notes takes advantage of a different cognitive process than does taking notes on computers. Classroom experience suggests that students who take notes on their computers, accompanied by all of the distractions that inhere in such a machine, are at a disadvantage in terms of actual learning processes and knowledge retention. Interestingly, and perhaps not coincidentally, the introduction of laptops in the classroom coincides with the national decline in bar passage rates. That said, it will be interesting to track how this data changes with the next generation of law students who have grown up with computers and may have adapted to new cognitive modes and learning processes. In 1980, Seymour Papert hypothesized "about how computers may affect the way people think and learn."[21] Papert noted a distinction between the various ways computers might enhance thinking and change patterns of access to knowledge.[22] We are now experiencing the impact of computers on the youth of the 1980s as they enter law schools across the country. Without a doubt, this is an area that requires further study and empirical analysis to provide data to either support or disprove hypotheses about the impact of computers in education.

II. Bar Exam Methodology

Any discussion of the bar exam's effectiveness should begin with the purpose of the bar exam. Licensure generally, and the bar exam specifically, is meant to provide the public with assurances that all practitioners are at least minimally competent.[23] It is important to recognize that the licensure process and the bar exam are not intended to measure all of the skills necessary to competently practice law.[24] If, however, the exam is written in such a way that it measures too narrow a range of skills, the public will not be protected from incompetent lawyers, and the examinees will have fewer opportunities to demonstrate their competence.[25] Specific identified competencies necessary to effective legal practice influence fundamental principles in selecting test content. For example, test questions should measure minimum competence for entry-level lawyers in a wide range of areas.[26] The bar exam tests the abilities to analyze facts and identify issues, in addition to testing knowledge of the law in general.[27] As such, the modern licensure regime used in most states is comprised of the Multistate Professional Responsibility Exam ("MPRE"), the Multistate Bar Exam ("MBE"), the Multistate Essay Exam ("MEE"), and the Multistate Performance Test ("MPT").[28] The MBE measures an examinee's ability to apply broad knowledge, the MEE measures depth of knowledge on a specific topic and the ability to synthesize that knowledge, and the MPT measures practical skills.[29] While not every state uses all of these examination techniques, each remains widely used. For instance, the MBE is required in every jurisdiction except Washington and Louisiana.[30] In addition, over 80% of all bar applicants take the MPT or a similar state exam. Similarly, every jurisdiction except Wisconsin, Maryland, and Washington uses the MPRE.[31] On the other end of the spectrum, the MEE is required in only 18 jurisdictions.[32]

Exam drafters within each individual state have the burden of determining which subjects to test on the state bar exam. *The Code of Recommended Standards for Bar Examiners* suggests that "the emphasis should be upon the basic and fundamental subjects that are regularly taught in law schools."[33] Among the reasons for limiting the subjects tested on the bar exam is the recognition that while the bar exam tests for generalized knowledge, lawyers specialize in particular practice areas. New lawyers may not be well-versed in any subjects while practicing lawyers are expected to conscientiously avoid subjects in which they do not specialize. Therefore, an exam of limited length must be content-limited as well as time-limited.[34]

After determining which areas must be tested, the exam drafters must select specific questions to be asked. Drafters select what issues to test and then write a set of facts drawn to raise the desired issues.[35] In order to assure that questions are tailored to elicit the correct responses, the MBE drafters are divided into six subject matter committees: Constitutional Law, Contracts, Criminal Law and Procedure, Evidence, Real Property, and Torts.[36] A member of each committee writes a draft, the chair of each committee adds draft items, and the committee meets to edit the items.[37] The draft of the test is then sent out for review in each state by the MBE policy committee and at least one impartial outsider.[38]

The MBE is machine-scored. The machine has the ability to flag items that were marked incorrectly by a majority of test takers.[39] Incorrect responses by a majority of test takers are indicative of a substantial statistical variation which indicates a problem with the test item. These questions are then double-keyed, meaning that either the intended correct answer or the incorrect answer marked by a majority of examinees will be accepted as a valid answer.[40] In some instances, questions that were missed by a majority of examinees may be removed from the exam.[41] The MBE raw score, based on the number of questions answered correctly out of two hundred items, is converted into a scaled score so that every test indicates the same relative proficiencies.[42] This standardization performs the essential function of allowing the bar exam to be perceived as both "valid" and "reliable."[43] More particularly, in order to garner support, the exam must actually measure what it purports to measure (validity), and an individual's score must remain the same after multiple assessments (reliability).[44]

Finally, the essay portion of the bar exam must be graded. State bar examiners use one of two methodologies for grading the essay portion of the exams: holistic or analytical.[45] Holistic grading consists of comparing the whole of each essay against a defined performance standard.[46] On the other hand, analytical grading deconstructs the analysis and assigns a point value to each issue and sub-issue.[47] Not all questions lend themselves to analytical grading, and any reliability gained from this process is unlikely to alter the overall reliability of the exam.[48] Bar examiners must also choose whether essays will be graded on an absolute or relative scale.[49] An absolute scale compares the examinee's performance against a predetermined standard while a relative scale compares how each examinee's performance compares to other examinees.[50] Data indicates that a relative grading method better accounts for differences in grading standards and is therefore more reliable.[51]

Clearly, an unreliable exam can never be valid.[52] Therefore, ensuring reliability in both testing and scoring procedure is paramount. Before an exam is drafted, the examiners must agree on the purpose of the exam and the types of skills that ought to be measured prior to licensure.[53] These decisions are reflected in both the examiners' choice of subjects to test and the proficiency required of the examinees to pass. Finally, the examiners must decide what skills and knowledge are best suited to essay questions versus multiple-choice questions.[54] If the examiners choose essay questions, they must decide if more questions with shorter responses or fewer questions with longer responses should be included.[55] That said, asking more questions is generally the preferred method, as it provides a better opportunity for a prepared candidate to demonstrate his or her competence.[56] The use of "optional questions," where the examinee is able to choose one question from a selection of questions, reduces reliability because each examinee is, in essence, taking a different exam.[57] Ultimately, the quality of an essay question and the extent to which it lends itself to consistent grading procedures will affect the reliability of the exam.[58]

III. Criticism of the Bar Exam

Critics of the bar exam rely on three principal arguments. First, critics contend that the bar exam does not verify minimum competence necessary for the practice of law because it does not evaluate proper skills, it relies to a large extent on memorization, it does not test the law itself, and it does not implicate current problems of incompetence.[59] Second, critics assert that the bar exam has a negative effect on law schools because the exam drives curriculum and admission decisions in such a way that actual student education and the educational environment suffer.[60] Third, the bar exam has a disparate impact on minorities and women, which tends to inhibit the goal of having a diverse bar and bench.[61]

Along the same lines, critics believe that the bar exam does not test the skills relevant to the successful practice of law. In 1992, a blue-ribbon commission of judges, professors, and attorneys authored the "MacCrate Report," detailing the ten skills lawyers use most often in their practices.[62] These essential skills include problem solving, legal analysis and reasoning, research, fact investigation, written and oral communication, counseling, negotiation, litigation and ADR procedures, organization, and recognizing and resolving ethical dilemmas.[63] Critics point out that the bar exam tests some of the skills mentioned in the report in cursory fashion while entirely ignoring others. The bar exam in its current form does not emphasize, or even test, such crucial topics as legal research, fact investigation, oral communication, counseling of clients, or negotiation.[64] Because the bar exam ignores nearly half of the skills essential to a career in law, critics assert that the bar exam does not and cannot ensure that applicants who pass the exam are minimally competent to practice law.

Bar exam critics have extended this argument to the debate over whether to raise the cut-score[65] of the bar exam. Nevertheless, because the exam does not test enough of the skills that effectively measure competence, raising the cut-score makes little practical sense.[66] According to critics, raising the cut-score in an effort to ensure competent attorneys cannot protect the public from inept lawyers because the bar exam does not accurately test an applicant's minimal competence to practice law. One critic has stated that raising the cut-score on the bar exam as a method of guaranteeing capable lawyers is "naive, at best, and deceptive, at worst."[67]

Critics also point to the fact that the bar exam does nothing to encourage or test the development of other qualities in applicants that may be beneficial to the profession as a whole. The bar exam does not make an effort to encourage or measure an applicant's empathy for clients, desire to do pro bono or public interest work, or the probability that the applicant will aid poor communities in her career as an attorney.[68]

The second argument made against the effectiveness of the bar exam is that it over-emphasizes memorization of legal doctrine in a profession that does not require—and in fact frowns upon—memorization. A bar examinee memorizes countless legal rules in order to answer the 200 multiple choice questions on the MBE and spot issues on the essay or performance portions of the exam. While the examinee may "know" the law in its black letter form, she may not "understand" the nuances required for practical legal reasoning.[69] Based on this reasoning, the proper test of a future lawyer would be something that does not involve memorization exclusively. A good lawyer does not rely solely on memory. Rather, she relies on legal research and may, in fact, be subject to sanctions or malpractice claims if she attempts to rely solely on faulty memory.[70] Furthermore, if memorization does test the minimal legal knowledge necessary to practice law, then current lawyers and judges should be able to pass the bar exam readily at any point in their careers.[71] Obviously, memorized bar exam information quickly disappears from examinees' minds, and current lawyers and judges likely could not readily pass the bar exam. These facts illustrate why critics argue that the bar exam should not emphasize memorization to such a great degree.

Similarly, critics maintain that the bar exam is inherently flawed given that most law students take an intensive bar review course before taking the exam.[72] Commercial bar preparation courses, which may cost upwards of $3,000, teach the tricks of the bar exam and immerse students in black letter rules.[73] Critics argue that these tricks and concentration on black letter rules demonstrate that the bar exam ignores the nuanced understanding of the law and the synthesizing of rules—skills which are required to be an effective lawyer.[74]

Critics also argue that the bar exam is flawed because it uses artificial testing techniques that have little to do with the practice of law. The MBE multiple-choice portion of the exam is often offered as evidence establishing this point—a practicing lawyer never has to answer a novel multiple-choice question in 1.8 minutes.[75] A competent lawyer presented with a unique question will do the requisite legal research, ask questions, and clarify legal and factual issues before coming to any preliminary determination of a correct answer—if there is one.[76] Also, a practicing lawyer is never given a defined group of answers and forced to choose the "most correct" or "least wrong" answer of a set.[77]

Opponents of the bar exam also point to the time constraints on the exam as a flaw in testing proper legal skills. There are time limits on the multiple choice, essay, and performance portions of the bar exam. In practice, no competent lawyer relies on her first determination of a legal question written in the first draft of a brief. On the contrary, a good lawyer researches, analyzes, writes, and then *rewrites* the answer following a determination made in any given situation.[78] Similarly, the 1.8 minutes allotted to each multiple-choice question or the time constraints of analyzing a file in the performance test places substantial artificial limitations on examinees.[79] In other words, a person who would be a diligent and competent researcher, analyzer, and writer might have all the skills necessary to be a competent lawyer but may have trouble with the onerous time constraints of the bar exam.

Opponents further argue that the bar exam does not test the proper law, even if one assumes the examinees know and understand the nuances of the law they have memorized. They argue that the bar exam tests general and sometimes obscure rules while ignoring specific rules in a segmented profession and local rules of the administering state.[80] While lawyers from different communities may never encounter the same situations, clients, or legal rules, they are all subjected to the same bar examination, the passage of which proclaims their minimum competence to practice law.[81] By ignoring the segmented nature of the legal profession, the bar exam ignores the complex market conditions in which lawyers practice.[82] Lawyers with expertise in one or two subjects are invaluable, while lawyers with a superficial understanding of a plethora of black letter rules cannot be successful advocates for their clients.[83]

The bar exam also fails to test competence because it does not test the local laws of the administering jurisdiction. "In all states, up to one-half of the examination is not based upon the ... state's own laws; in some states the entire exam requires no knowledge of the particular ... state's governing law."[84] Even if one assumes that testing general and obscure rules will lead to a proper evaluation of an examinee's competence, the bar exam still falls short because the MBE multiple choice and the MEE sections test majority/minority general rules, rather than the specific rules of the state.[85] A taker in a particular jurisdiction may memorize, know, and understand a black letter rule that she may never use in actual practice.[86] A state's bar exam cannot possibly measure a lawyer's minimal competence to understand and use legal rules of that state if that state's legal rules are not addressed on the test itself.

Critics also argue the bar exam's failure to test minimal competence can be seen in the fact that the bar exam does nothing to address current problems with incompetence in the legal profession. The leading causes of malpractice claims are problems with the transmission and submission of documents, filing actions in a timely fashion, and properly carrying out investigations.[87] Similarly, communication breakdowns and failures to work with diligence on current cases are the leading issues mentioned in disciplinary proceedings before the bar.[88] Judge William Lucero, Colorado Presiding Disciplinary Judge, reports that the majority of the cases that come before him fall into three areas: (1) neglect and abandonment (usually a communication issue), (2) misappropriation of firm funds and lack of honesty, and (3) misappropriation of client and third party funds, including negligence in handling COLTAF accounts.[89] Opponents assert that the bar exam does not attempt to measure the skills necessary to avoid these problems and thus falls short of its purported goal of protecting the public from incompetent attorneys.[90]

Another major criticism of the bar exam is that it drives curriculum and admissions decisions in law schools throughout the country. Opponents contend that law schools offer, and students choose to concentrate on, the so-called "bar courses" at the expense of clinical, more specialized, and smaller courses.[91] By ignoring clinical courses, students are exposed only to courses driven by black letter rules, and are not exposed to classes "designed to introduce ... the skills required for the actual practice of law."[92] They also complain that in so-called "bar exam courses," law school professors fashion their exams around the bar exam instead of seeking out alternative and possibly better ways to evaluate student performance.[93] Additionally, by ignoring smaller, non-bar courses such as health law, poverty law, environmental law, and law and economics, students "fail to fully engage in a law school experience that will give them ... the jurisprudential perspective that will make them better lawyers."[94]

Moreover, opponents suggest that the bar exam drives admission decisions. Not surprisingly, studies show that students who do well on the LSAT are more likely to do well on the bar exam.[95] If a law school admits "students who know how to take a test almost exactly like the bar exam, and know how to take it successfully, you don't have to do much with those students in law school in order to assure their success on the bar exam."[96] In other words, students who do well on a standardized test such as the LSAT are essentially preprogrammed to do well on the bar exam. As a result, law schools rely heavily on LSAT scores in order to boost their bar passage rate, and in turn, potentially boost their rankings in the oft-cited *U.S. News and World Report*. Unfortunately, law schools often partake in this practice at the expense of admitting students who could be good practicing attorneys, but who do not perform well on standardized tests such as the LSAT and bar exam.

A high ranking in the *U.S. News and World Report* has numerous beneficial effects for a law school. For example, it helps with alumni contributions, gives satisfaction to the faculty, gives students a feeling that they are attending a superior school, and allows the school to attract new students of higher caliber.[97] Therefore, law schools admit students who are likely to pass the bar exam by relying to a significant degree on LSAT scores. This reliance by admissions departments on LSAT scores may lead to the exclusion of students who could have become great lawyers but are not preprogrammed[98] to do well on standardized legal tests. "From the moment they enter law school through graduation, students realize that unless they pass the bar examination, their substantial financial commitment and their years of hard work will be wasted."[99]

The bar exam may also negatively affect how law schools evaluate student performance in law school. Like the bar exam, law school exams are a "one-time make-or-break examination that focuses on only a very few of the many skills that competent lawyers need."[100] If the bar exam tested more skills such as communication, research, and negotiation, law schools would respond in turn, initiating new evaluation techniques that reward mastery of all the skills needed to be a successful attorney rather than simply focusing on skills that can be measured by a paper and pencil test.[101]

Underlying the idea of the bar exam driving curriculum, admissions, and evaluation decisions, is the impression that the bar exam relieves law schools of their responsibilities to prepare competent future lawyers.[102] The bar exam relieves faculty of their responsibility to control the curriculum and evaluate students in the best manner possible at a particular law school, and it relieves the admissions committee of the responsibility to find and admit students who will make a law school the most effective learning environment. The bar exam takes these responsibilities away from law schools and may turn some schools into tuition-collecting institutions that can teach as little or as much as they want, knowing the bar exam will presumably weed out the students who are unfit to practice law.

Critics are also concerned with the disparate effect the bar exam has on minorities and women, thus providing a barrier to a diverse bar and bench. An increase in the number of minorities in the legal profession would lead to an improvement in public perception of the bar and the judicial system, legal services for underrepresented groups would increase, and the bar in general would become a more public-minded body.[103] The lack of diversity in the legal profession can be attributed to the bar exam because of its disparate impact on minorities and women that delay or completely hinder minority and female entrance into the legal profession. A five-year LSAC study found that the first-time bar passage rate was 91.9% for Caucasians, 80.7% for Asian-Americans, 75.8% for Mexican Americans, 74.8% for Hispanics, 66.36% for Native Americans, and 61.4% for African-Americans.[104] Furthermore, a recent study by the National Conference of Bar Examiners concluded:

> Our preliminary analysis showed that men outperform women on the MBE by about 5 points, which is about 1/3 of a standard deviation.... With such a large sample size, a difference of this size is statistically significant; it is also large enough for many people to believe that it is practically significant.[105]

The data provide a substantial argument that the bar exam needs to be carefully studied and revised to level the playing field and to make the assessment fair and equitable for everyone, including minorities and women who have survived the biases imbedded in the education system from kindergarten through twelfth grade, various standardized tests including the SAT, ACT, and LSAT, and undergraduate college level education.[106]

While it is true that applicants may retake the exam and pass, there is significant cost both financially and psychologically for not passing the bar exam on the first try.[107] Failure rates for second- and third-time test takers are often even higher than for first-time examinees.[108]

Figure 2. Passage Rates for First and Repeat Examinees[109]

The data in Figure 2 from the National Conference of Bar Examiners show that repeat examinees pass the bar at less than half the rate of first-time examinees. Therefore, an examinee who fails the exam on his or her first try is more than likely to fail the exam on the second attempt. Clearly, this indicates that the reason for the failure on the first exam was replicated on the second exam. However, if the exam is flawed, then it fails as a fair and equitable assessment of skills and knowledge. The question then becomes whether an assessment that has such a negative impact on admitting minorities and women to the legal profession should be sustained. The answer is no with the bar exam in its current form. Although an assessment is appropriate, the exam must be revised. Validity and reliability must be re-established to create an evaluation system that is fair and equitable.

IV. Proponents of the Bar Exam

Proponents of the bar exam effectively counter each of the contentions leveled against the bar exam. First, they argue that the bar exam measures minimal competence because it tests the proper skills of a lawyer, does not rely on memorization, and properly tests general, rather than specific, areas of the law. Second, proponents assert that there is nothing wrong with the bar exam driving admission decisions, and that critics' curriculum concerns are misplaced. Third, they assert that a disparate impact on minority students exists well before the bar exam is administered. Bar exam proponents also suggest that the answer to the various criticisms of the bar does not lie in changing the exam, instead noting that "[l]earning to think like a lawyer is the key to passing the bar."[110]

Supporters of the bar exam argue that the exam tests the "most basic and essential analytical skills required for the practice of law" and thus, "serves a necessary function."[111] Those in favor of the bar exam agree that it does not test all of the so-called MacCrate skills, but argue that this is a strength of the bar exam rather than a deficiency. Bar examiners have identified the skills that can be accurately tested with a standardized test, and examine only those skills.[112] Thus, the bar exam tests reading comprehension, recognition of legal issues, organization, writing ability, and the ability to follow directions, all of which are "fundamental to the competent practice of law."[113] To do well on an essay question or performance test question, an applicant must effectively read and follow directions, recognize the legal issues involved, and organize and effectively write an answer in the language of the law.[114] Furthermore, greater weight is given to analysis than to "knowing" a particular rule because "credit is given ... for well-reasoned analyses of the issues and legal principles involved even though the final conclusion may be incorrect."[115] Similarly, a multiple-choice question requires an applicant to read a question effectively and recognize a particular legal issue, all under specific time constraints. Bar exam proponents declare that time constraints reflect the realities of the legal profession, where lawyers deal with deadlines on a daily basis, regardless of the area in which they practice.[116]

Supporters also note that the bar exam does not rely on memorization to a fault, because recitation of memorized rules does not play a greater role in preparing or passing the bar exam than it does in any other part of a student's legal education. All law students memorize the elements of causes of action, commit obscure property rules to memory, and learn to extrapolate and remember case law in order to pass law school exams.[117] Even when students take open-book or open-note tests, they must still have basic analytical systems and cognitive paradigms memorized in order to access the information quickly in a timed test situation. In addition, students have been memorizing academic information throughout their careers—from multiplication tables in grade school, to complicated formulas in undergraduate school. The bar exam is essentially no different from these situations. There is a need to memorize a finite number of black letter rules for an applicant to show that she has the ability to work with and understand those rules. Furthermore, a student does not need to memorize every single black letter rule. Generally, a student can pass the bar exam even if she misses eighty questions out of the two-hundred included in the MBE.[118]

Students who fail the bar exam do not fail because they forgot a rule or did not memorize enough rules. Students fail because they cannot identify legal issues, fail to separate relevant from irrelevant information, and lack an ability to properly organize and analyze a legal issue.[119] In other words, students who fail the bar exam may know the black letter law because they took a bar review course and have all the information they need for the exam. However, failure occurs because students do not understand the law. These students do not "recognize a rule when it assumes a different form or appear[s] in language different from what they had memorized."[120] Thus, proponents argue that the bar exam serves its essential purpose of eliminating those applicants who do not possess the requisite skills to practice law effectively.

Proponents further maintain that the bar exam's form is also effective in testing minimal competence. Bar exam critics point out that no lawyer ever encounters multiple-choice questions with four distinct answers. Proponents respond that this has little to do with the administration of the bar exam where a multiple-choice question tests a critical legal skill: the ability to read a set of facts carefully and draw reasonable legal inferences from them.[121] The bar exam is not designed to test legal skills as they are encountered in the real world, rather it is designed as a mechanism to determine whether a particular applicant possesses the skills required to succeed when confronted with real world problems. A multiple-choice question sets up a contained universe to test those skills while providing an efficient and objective way of scoring answers to those questions.

The bar exam also is criticized for requiring students to prepare heavily and take a review course. The answer to this criticism is that the bar exam is no different than any other aspect of a legal education or legal career. Students prepare intensively for law school exams by studying their notes and past exams. Practitioners prepare for trial, motions, and briefs by consulting old work that has been done on similar cases.[122] The bar exam is thus no different from law school or from practicing law. One must prepare intensively to succeed in the legal profession, where good preparation is the hallmark of a good lawyer.

Supporters of the bar exam also effectively counter the criticism that it tests many general areas of the law instead of a few specific areas in an admittedly segmented profession. They answer by stating that the bar exam correctly tests a wide range of legal subjects because most law students end up in a solo or small firm setting.[123] General testing of the law provides students with a broad basis of knowledge from which to draw so that they may pursue a career in whatever specialty they choose. Similarly, law students do not leave law school as experts in any particular field. As critics readily point out, expertise takes a number of years of specialization in a particular area, so testing law students in specific areas is unrealistic for students who are only trained in general fields of law and may not be ready to select an area of specialty.

Those in favor of the bar exam also counter the criticism that it drives curriculum and admission decisions of law schools. They argue that there should be no distinction drawn between "bar courses" and "clinical courses." In regard to admission decisions, they question: What is wrong with admitting people to law school that will do well on the bar exam? A law school's primary responsibility is to prepare students to be successful attorneys, and using indicators, such as the LSAT, to identify students who will do well in law school and on the bar exam is an appropriate method of accomplishing this goal.

Proponents of the bar exam suggest that critics of the exam fundamentally misunderstand the skills required to be successful on the bar exam and, consequently, are misguided in their criticisms of curriculum.[124] Supporters do not disagree that the bar exam may be a determining factor in law school curriculum, but state that designing a curriculum around the subjects tested on the bar exam makes no sense. There is no need to ensure that students take "bar courses" at the expense of clinical courses. In fact, a recent survey indicates that there is "little statistical evidence" that the bar exam factors into curriculum decisions about what upper level courses a school requires.[125] The skills needed to pass the bar exam are the reading, writing, and analytical skills learned in law school, no matter what course a student is taking.[126] For example, a student will acquire the same essential skills needed for the bar exam if she takes a traditional Civil Procedure course or a Clinical Litigation course. In other words, there should be no distinction between "bar courses" and "clinical courses."[127] Therefore, law schools can offer both types of courses without detrimental impact on bar passage rates.

Supporters of the bar exam also contest the idea that the bar exam has a disparate impact on minorities. They argue that research shows that a disparity existed before the bar exam, and, therefore, the exam is not the root of the problem.[128] Research shows the same impact can be found with regard to LSAT scores, law school grade point averages, and bar exam scores.[129] If there are differences in passage rates among different groups they "existed before and during law school."[130] Thus, while something is causing these differences, it is not the bar exam, and the bar exam should not be changed on account of the perceived disparate impact.[131] In fact, research shows that law school GPA is the most determinative factor of bar passage:

> After controlling for law school quality, test reliability, subject matter and test type, time limits, and the ability to take tests, researchers concluded that "the higher the law school grade point average..., the greater the likelihood the applicant will pass. No other measured variable really mattered once there was control for [law school] GPA."[132]

V. Proposed Alternatives to the Bar Exam

The critics of the bar exam have suggested a number of alternatives to the traditional bar exam. First, the Public Service Alternative to the Bar Exam ("PSABE") would consist of a ten to twelve week evaluation in a local court system after law school is completed. Second, the Community Legal Access Bar Alternative ("CLABA") would require a one-year post-graduate apprenticeship with a newly created charitable organization that serves an under-represented community. Third, the Diploma Privilege, which is now only available in the state of Wisconsin, grants a law license to any student who graduates from one of the state's law schools. A fourth proposal is a combination of new testing ideas involving computer-testing and staggered-date testing. Computer testing is capable of evaluating applicants in new ways, while the staggered-date testing would be similar to the method currently used for medical profession board examinations. Finally, some states allow "law readers" to sit for the bar exam after apprenticing with a licensed attorney.[133] Each of these new proposals deals with one or all of the concerns of ensuring minimal competence, completing course curriculum, and making non-bar-specific admissions decisions in law schools, as well as minimizing the disparate impact of the bar exam on minorities and women.

A. Public Service Alternative to the Bar Exam (PSABE)

The PSABE, proposed by Professor Kristin Booth Glen, Dean of the City University School of Law in New York,[134] would involve a ten to twelve week placement in a local court system where a candidate's real world ability to practice law unsupervised could be accurately evaluated.[135] The idea is premised on the assumption "that there is no more valid test of skills than direct observation of ... actual, real-time performance of those skills."[136] The bar applicants would work as lawyers in a local court system and be assigned an assortment of job-related tasks.[137] Applicants would, among other things, write bench memos for judges, assist *pro se* litigants, assist in mediation sessions, or serve as arbitrators in small claims matters.[138] At the same time, court personnel who "are trained and monitored by experienced law school clinical professors" would evaluate the students.[139] If a candidate successfully completed the ten-to twelve-week work process, she would be granted admission to the bar.[140] The only additional requirement of participants in the PSABE would be the completion of 150 hours of pro bono work in the court system of their placement within three years following admission to the state bar.[141]

The principal advantage of the PSABE over the bar exam is that it would ensure competence in the profession by evaluating the essential MacCrate skills that have been identified as necessary components for the competent and successful practice of law.[142] In a real world environment, evaluators would be able to observe such skills as research ability, oral communication, negotiation, counseling, and recognizing ethical dilemmas—abilities which are generally ignored by the bar exam. The PSABE would also address the curriculum and diversity issues that are caused or exaggerated by the traditional bar exam. The PSABE would provide an opportunity for an applicant's entire legal skill set to be observed. Thereafter, law schools would likely offer—and law students would likely take—more clinical courses, where emphasis can be placed on skills relevant to the PSABE but ignored by the standardized bar exam.[143] In addition, the PSABE may avoid the bar exam's disparate impact on women and minorities by eliminating standardized tests that can negatively impact diverse applicants. It would also benefit students with coming out of law school with inadequate financial resources.[144] As discussed in Part IV, *supra*, the bar exam requires even financially-strapped students to invest thousands of dollars into a commercial preparation and review course and to devote many hours to the uninterrupted study and memorization of discrete subjects. The PSABE would eliminate this extra expense and loss of possible gainful working hours by eliminating the need for an expensive bar review course.

The PSABE entirely eliminates the need for a review course, and provides students of limited means the chance of performing PSABE court duties while simultaneously holding a night or weekend job for the ten-week period.[145] Moreover, the PSABE would push future pro bono work by requiring new applicants to perform 150 hours of pro bono work after admission to the bar, thus exposing new lawyers to the urgent need for pro bono work in any local court system.[146]

Professor Glen compares moving from the traditional bar exam to the PSABE to law reviews moving from a "grade-on" system of choosing new members to a "write-on" system.[147] In the past, grades served as a "once-removed proxy" for the skills needed to be a contributing member of a law review.[148] Currently, a writing competition is commonly used to determine new members of a law review because it measures the actual skills that the applicant will use on law review.[149] Similarly, the PSABE would evaluate the actual skills required to be a competent lawyer, whereas the once-removed proxy of the bar exam tests only memorization and knowledge of so-called black letter law.[150] Clearly, the real-time evaluation of the skills essential to be a lawyer is the primary argument for implementing the PSABE as an alternative to the traditional standardized bar exam.[151]

The PSABE is a twelve week practicum in a local court. Although students will work in a real-life courtroom, the practicum is not guaranteed to provide the intensive evaluation of the students' legal abilities in the basic areas that are currently tested by the bar exam. Furthermore, a PSABE student may not have an opportunity to engage in detailed reading comprehension, legal issue organization, or legal analysis and writing. Finally, courtroom exposure presents experiences that are not standardized or guaranteed to be academically rigorous. This author has witnessed a variety of levels of academic rigor when observing externs who are working in courtrooms. The bar exam provides a standard and a common set of skill evaluations. Thus, the PSABE presents a solid real-world test of fundamental skills used in legal practice; however, like other programs urging real-world testing for would-be lawyers, the variety of experiences a student may encounter hinders the ability to measure a standard set of competencies as the bar exam currently provides.

B. Community Legal Access Bar Alternative (CLABA)

The second proposed alternative to the bar exam, CLABA, was initiated by a group of students at the University of Arizona College of Law.[152] The program would provide benefits to both the legal profession and the community in general. As proposed, CLABA would be a one-year, post-J.D. apprenticeship program that "will provide both reduced-fee legal counsel and representation to lower middle-income populations and serve as an alternative method of first-time attorney licensure and bar admission."[153] The one-year apprenticeship program would be implemented by a newly created, freestanding 501(c)(3) nonprofit organization[154] which would serve "individuals, small businesses, and non-profit organizations with incomes of... $15,000 to $60,000."[155] In providing these services, the organization would charge $15 to $35 per hour with limits in place depending on each case.[156] Each apprentice would serve eight weeks in each of six core practice areas: "family law and domestic relations; personal finance and planning; personal and economic injury; business finance and planning; government regulation; and misdemeanor criminal defense."[157] A full-time attorney-mentor would manage each of the core practice areas and "oversee case management, serve as attorney of record, and act as a coach and advisor for apprentices to ensure that all clients receive diligent, competent counsel and representation."[158] Throughout the process, the mentors would carry out both subjective and objective competency-based evaluations of each apprentice.[159] The first week of each core area would be structured as an orientation with the new practice group.[160] The final week of each core area would be spent reviewing files and going through a debriefing conducted by the mentor.[161] After completing work and receiving positive evaluations in each of the six core areas, the apprentice would be granted admission to the bar, subject to passing the standardized Multistate Professional Responsibility Exam ("MPRE")[162] and satisfying any local character screening process.[163] If the apprentice does not complete the program or leaves the program for any reason, she may apply to take the bar exam.[164]

The goal of CLABA would be to provide an evaluation of all essential attorney skills over a long period of time in order to ensure competency. During the year, apprentices would be given multiple objective and subjective evaluations from numerous mentors suggesting improvement in all aspects of their work.[165] Conversely, the bar exam purports to ensure competency with a two-to three-day exam that presents hypothetical situations to which the candidate must respond. CLABA, on the other hand, purports to promote improvement in legal professionalism.[166] The CLABA Institute will hire mentors with the ability to be good role models by promoting good professional ethics and competent legal skills with all of the apprentices.[167] Also, professional conduct will be encouraged because it will be part of the evaluation process.[168] An apprentice who does not return calls to clients, cuts ethical corners, or fails to be civil in her duties will be instructed to improve or she will not be recommended to the bar at the end of the period.[169] Similar to the PSABE, CLABA would likely avoid the disparate impact of the bar exam on minorities and women by eliminating the bar exam. It also supplies a new legal resource for members of the community who may not be able to hire a lawyer otherwise. CLABA proponents believe it evaluates all skills needed to be a lawyer and thus ensures competency among new entrants into the profession.

The CLABA is a one-year apprenticeship program that provides directed experiences in six core practice areas. This program provides higher quality finishing experiences than PSABE. Potential flaws of CLABA will occur if supervising attorney-mentors are not fully engaged in the mentorship of apprentices. Also, different levels of cases worked on by apprentices will result in differing levels of knowledge tested by mentors. The bar exam provides a standard evaluation of legal subjects and skills without regard to the human element of interest or expertise. Again, the skill set a prospective attorney will use in practice are tested—this time for an entire year—however, the problem of evaluation standardization for the entire prospective attorney class yet again provides an argument against the CLABA, just like it did with the PSABE, and also provides a lingering argument in favor of some sort of test like the bar examination.

C. Diploma Privilege

The third proposed alternative to the bar exam is the Diploma Privilege, which provides admission to the bar of a state if a student has graduated from an accredited law school within that state. Although the Diploma Privilege was widespread in the past, only one state, Wisconsin, continues to allow licensure based on graduation from law school.[170] Additionally, in 2006, New Hampshire's Franklin Pierce Law Center initiated an alternative licensure program similar to the diploma privilege whereby participants can gain licensure without taking the full bar exam.[171] The Wisconsin Diploma Privilege operates under the "thirty-credit rule" and the "sixty-credit rule."[172] The thirty-credit rule requires students to take ten specific classes and have a minimum GPA of seventy-seven in those classes.[173] Similarly, the sixty-credit rule "requires students to take at least sixty of their law school credits in thirty subject areas also achieving a seventy-seven average."[174] The thirty-credit and sixty-credit rules ensure that students take certain courses that should prepare them to be competent attorneys.

Proponents of the Diploma Privilege believe it protects the public from incompetent lawyers better than the bar exam. The Diploma Privilege ensures a qualified bar by encouraging substantive work by both law school students and faculty.[175] As a result of the implementation of the Diploma Privilege, law school faculty are encouraged to make exams rigorous and are more likely to fail students who do not fully comprehend the material because the bar exam will not serve as a safety net to weed out deficient students after law school.[176] Likewise, students are aware that faculty will assign failing grades so students work hard to master the material in order to pass the course.[177] The Diploma Privilege also encourages student competence in a wide range of legal subjects instead of limiting knowledge to the six subjects covered on the standard bar exam.[178] As a result, students acquire a mastery of knowledge which includes many legal subjects offered under the thirty- and sixty-credit rules.

Another benefit of the Diploma Privilege is that it mitigates the disparate impact of the bar exam on minorities and women.[179] The Diploma Privilege provides a mechanism whereby the only screener for admission to the state's bar is the law school that the student is attending.

Furthermore, there is no evidence of adverse impact on graduates of Wisconsin law schools when it comes to taking the bar exam of other states. In 1997, ten out of twelve Wisconsin graduates passed the California bar exam, and in the Summer 1996–Winter 1997 and Summer 1997–Winter 1998 academic years, Wisconsin graduates had a 96% and 91% passage rate, respectively, on the Illinois bar exam.[180] Thus, it seems the thirty-credit and sixty-credit rules more than adequately prepare Wisconsin graduates for the traditional bar exam.

One of the biggest concerns about the Diploma Privilege is that it may prevent attorneys from moving throughout the country after practicing locally for a few years. Several state bars do not admit lawyers who have not passed a bar exam, regardless of how long the lawyer has competently and successfully practiced law.[181] This causes concern for students who are readily admitted to the Wisconsin bar, have practiced successfully for many years, and want to leave the state to take a job elsewhere but are confronted with the proposition of taking the traditional bar exam for the first time as a condition of practicing in a new state. As the statistics above show, however, the graduates of Wisconsin law schools are prepared for traditional bar exams in other states by virtue of their thirty-credit and sixty-credit curriculum.

Proponents point to three relevant factors to determine when the Diploma Privilege should be implemented as the mechanism for bar admission in a particular state.[182] First, the state should be small with a correspondingly small practicing bar; second, there should be a close relationship among the state's bar, judiciary, legislature, and law schools; and third, both the public and the bar should hold the state's law schools in high esteem.[183] The size of the state is relevant because only in small states can a close relationship among the bar, the courts, the legislature, and the law schools be established and maintained.[184] This close relationship is vital to the success of the Diploma Privilege because it is the foundation of the ideals and requirements necessary to gain admission to the bar.[185] The dialogue between the bar, courts, legislature, and law schools about current and future expectations of law school graduates is essential to the success of the Diploma Privilege program. It would be significantly more difficult for these relationships to exist in a large state where lawyers generally deal at arms-length and there are few relationships among interested groups.[186] The foregoing factors support a Diploma Privilege system that requires students to take essential courses, promotes hard work and a rigorous curriculum in law school, and mitigates the disparate impact of the bar exam on minorities and women.

The Diploma Privilege would allow graduates of accredited law schools within the state to gain admission to the bar by taking and passing a specified curriculum. However, receipt of a diploma from a law school is not viewed in the profession as a quality assurance of competency because other states do not recognize reciprocity without bar exam passage. Passage of the bar exam provides students with freedom to move to other jurisdictions where reciprocity is granted. The Diploma Privilege licensure does not allow the attorney to move if other opportunities arise or an interest or desire to live in another jurisdiction occurs.

Therefore, unlike the PSABE and the CLABA which seek to provide new attorneys with real-world skill sets, the Diploma Privilege provides an academically competent new attorney. While the Diploma Privilege provides some standardization via the standards set for students in the classroom, it still fails to provide state-wide standardization because no two professors will teach a subject the same nor will any two law schools within the same state offer the same curricula. Thus far, only the bar exam offers that kind of standardization—albeit at the cost of disparate impact. Further, a new attorney under the Diploma Privilege wanting or needing to move to another jurisdiction would still have to take the bar exam for that state. It seems there may be no escaping the bar exam.

D. Computer/Staggered Testing

The fourth suggested alternative to the bar exam proposes a change in how and when the bar exam is administered. This proposal can essentially be broken into two testing methods: computer-based testing ("CBT") and staggered testing. CBT would change the form in which the bar exam is given, moving away from the paper and pencil model to incorporate new technologies that test a wider range of skills in a more effective manner. Staggered testing, on the other hand, uses the medical board examinations as a model in terms of both form and timing of the bar exam, suggesting a system where applicants are required to pass multiple tests at different points in a student's law school education.

Proponents believe that CBT would allow the bar examiners to abandon the paper and pencil approach associated with the typical bar exam and replace it with a more modern testing regime. CBT has the ability to test a broader range of skills in a manner that is more closely aligned with how those skills are actually used in practice.[187] The CBT method is already successfully employed to test future architects on the Architect Registration Examination as well as future doctors on all three parts of the United States Medical Licensing Examination.[188] Advocates of CBT believe it can be used in countless ways to improve the bar exam also.

CBT has the benefit of being able to test skills that the bar exam ignores, such as research, negotiation, mediation, and counseling. CBT can create virtual clients or trials in order to force an examinee to analyze real world situations and determine an appropriate course of action.[189] An examinee could also be presented with the task of interviewing a virtual client by requiring her to watch a client interview and then to write down questions that should be asked in a follow-up interview as well as to address necessary factual inquiries.[190] The CBT interview could also be used to test mediation, counseling, and negotiation skills.

Additionally, some of the memorization aspects of the bar exam could be eliminated by testing actual legal research skills through the Internet or a research-based CD-ROM.[191] Using these tools, an applicant could be given access to the research database and use the information contained therein to respond to a series of questions based on the laws of a particular state.[192] Questions presented could deal with issues as specific as a statute of limitations or as broad as requiring the application of a number of laws to a given fact situation.[193]

The black letter knowledge that is tested on the current bar exam could also be tested in a more practical way using CBT. For example, knowledge of evidence and trial practice could be tested by showing part of a trial and requiring the applicant to offer objections and detail the justifications behind those objections.[194] Proponents of CBT believe new technology can and should be used to improve how the bar exam is administered.[195]

Similarly, proponents of staggered testing believe that method would change not only how but also when the bar exam is administered. One example of a staggered testing model was proposed by Jayne W. Barnard, Professor of Law at the College of William and Mary, and Mark Greenspan, Associate Professor of Surgery at the Eastern Virginia

Medical School and practicing attorney.[196] Their proposal is modeled after the scheme used for licensure in the medical profession.[197] In medical school, students take a series of four tests that become progressively more difficult during the course of their schooling residency.[198] The first test reviews basic foundational material, the second evaluates clinical and communication skills, the third assesses ability to make diagnoses and simple treatments, and the fourth gauges ability in complicated and specialized areas of treatment.[199] Failure to pass any of these tests makes a student ineligible to continue.[200] If a student passes all four tests and proceeds to pass all of the comprehensive examinations in her specialty, the student will become board certified and will be able to practice anywhere in the United States.[201] Staggered testing provides six benefits that the current bar exam does not. First, the process identifies students who will probably not obtain final licensure early. Second, it assesses student work over a longitudinal period of time, instead of during a one-shot exam. Third, it tests clinical skills, not just skills tested by traditional exams. Fourth, it tests the improvement of technique and judgment with increasingly difficult tests. Fifth, it identifies students who may be "book smart" but are not well-suited to be doctors because of a lack of interpersonal skills. Finally, its results are accepted throughout the United States.[202]

The staggered testing model does not attempt to transform the law licensing process into the medical testing process; rather, it tries to apply some of the advantages of the medical testing scheme to the legal licensing process. The staggered testing proposal for law schools consists of five steps: (1) an early test of legal fundamentals, (2) a test of professional and interpersonal skills, (3) a new comprehensive bar exam, (4) post graduate education, and (5) a final bar exam.[203] The early test of legal fundamentals would require law students to take the MPRE and MBE portions of the current bar exam at the end of the second year of law school.[204] Passing the MPRE and MBE would be a prerequisite for continuing into the third year of law school,[205] thus purging students who are not likely to obtain final licensure.[206]

The second part of the staggered testing proposal would be administered during the fifth semester of law school and would test "interpersonal skills, organization skills, and basic writing skills."[207] These skills could be tested by interviewing clients, researching a legal topic, organizing a file, negotiating a contract, drafting a complaint, or making a short oral argument.[208] Computer-based testing could be used to test many of the student's professional and interpersonal skills.

The third part of the test, the comprehensive bar exam, would be taken after graduation and would be structured like the essay and performance portions of the current bar exam.[209] However, the questions would "focus on integrating various bodies of law rather than zeroing in on the minutiae of specific areas of law."[210] The test would require issue spotting and analysis rather than "requiring a regurgitation of specific bodies of law" that require huge amounts of memorization.[211] If an applicant successfully completes the first three steps, she would be granted a provisional license to practice law in the state or states of her choice.[212]

Fourth, an applicant's new provisional license would be renewed every year for up to three years by attending regular Continuing Legal Education (CLE) courses and special CLE courses for new attorneys and "receiving meaningful supervision of, and regular feedback on, her work as a lawyer."[213] This regular supervision would ensure that each new lawyer received good feedback and, thus, obtained the necessary skills it takes to practice law unsupervised. This step would not, in fact, require a new lawyer to practice in a firm or government agency. Solo practitioners would simply have the burden of seeking feedback from attorneys or judges within their community.[214]

The fifth and final step of the staggered testing process would be a second and final bar exam to obtain permanent licensure as a lawyer.[215] This test would look much like the comprehensive exam, with essay and performance portions. However, the candidate would take a test that concentrates on one to three specialties in which the attorney has gained knowledge and is specific to the state where the lawyer has provisionally practiced.[216] This meaningful assessment of a lawyer's skills will rely on the attorney's real world experience in a specific area of law.[217] If the attorney passes the final test, she would be granted permanent admission to the bar of the state and could practice in all areas—not just the one tested—but she would have to disclose to clients the areas in which she has been tested.[218]

The staggered testing proposal captures all of the advantages possessed by the medical profession. Step one provides an early mechanism to identify candidates who do not understand the law and will not obtain a license.[219] Step two provides a way to test practical advocacy skills. At step three, the student would take a new comprehensive exam that would involve one or more essay questions as well as several questions that would require performance-testing. The questions would be like the current essay and performance type inquiries of the bar examinations but would focus on integrating various bodies of law rather than on minutiae of specific areas of law. They would replicate the kinds of questions most lawyers encounter with a new client.[220] Step four helps identify candidates who need help with legal skills that cannot be tested in the form of a standardized test. Step five is the only step geared to a particular state, while a student can go through steps one through four in any state of their choosing. The foregoing illustrates that staggered testing allows comprehensive testing of skills over a longer period of time, while also allowing students the freedom to practice in the state of their choice.

Computer/Staggered Testing is a viable alternative to the current bar exam. However, future attorneys might object to the multiple tiered-testing systems versus a one-time bar exam. This author believes that the Computer/Staggered testing method provides excellent elements to be considered in revising the current exam. This testing system contains all the elements of the current exam but provides students with more time and greater opportunities to demonstrate more skills, including those skills that are identified in the MacCrate Report.[221]

E. Law Readers

Finally, an unconventional approach to legal education may provide bar critics with another alternative. California, Vermont, Virginia, and Washington allow "law readers"—people who have apprenticed for practicing attorneys rather than attending law school—to sit for the bar exam.[222] Law readers participate in what may be characterized as entirely "clinical" preparation but are nonetheless able to sit for and pass the bar exam.[223] This is a highly unusual way to prepare for the bar exam. However, as noted, it is currently only an option in the four states mentioned above.

An entirely clinical preparation for the practice of law in today's competitive and technological society is fraught with inherent potential problems. The potential weaknesses are far too many to enumerate in a paragraph. Briefly stated, while a law reader may have developed the practical skills valued in the MacCrate report, he missed both the formal training and feedback imparted by the fine minds that make up legal academia as well as the broad classroom learning that provides a broad knowledge foundation upon which lawyers who have attended law school and sat the bar use to practice the MacCrate skills when they reach the real world. However, this system is acceptable in four jurisdictions, and the consumer of legal services may be subject to an incompetent attorney as a result.

Not surprisingly, proponents of the bar exam are concerned with the alternatives that critics of the exam have proposed. Their arguments are grounded in the assertion that any bar alternative will eliminate the valuable uniformity that the current system of admission provides. Undoubtedly, there is inherent value in having a uniform test throughout the country because a uniform bar exam compensates for differences in widely varying law schools and law school faculty.[224] Any alternative that does not apply to all law school students, such as the PSABE or CLABA, would be detrimental to the bar exam's uniform structure and would not control for differences among law schools. The disappearance of uniformity from the bar examination process would also create a legal hierarchy based on how a particular individual gained entrance into the profession.[225] Any differences in attaining admission to the bar could "lead to a schism in the profession and create a legal caste system, one caste including those who sat for the bar exam, the other consisting of those who chose" an alternative means of admission.[226]

Another criticism of alternatives to the bar exam is that the skills the alternatives purport to test—oral advocacy, writing memos, drafting pleadings, and other MacCrate skills—are better evaluated *in* law school. Presumably, if a law school is doing its job, a student will not graduate without having been meaningfully evaluated in these areas.[227] Thus, the argument goes, a law student should not earn his J.D. without learning practical MacCrate skills through legal writing, taking practical credits hours like trial advocacy or a clinic, and fulfilling other basic curricula requirements. To the proponents of the bar exam, earning a J.D. is confirmation from the law school that a prospective attorney passes minimum requirements to be an attorney subject to passing the bar exam.

VI. Experiences at the University of Colorado

Although the University of Colorado Law School's bar passage rate was an impressive 97% in 1998, in 2003 it fell nearly ten points to 88%. In response to this drop, this author began to analyze the statistical significance of various factors that may have contributed to the decline. Through research, surveys, and compilation of the resulting data, it became apparent that the single most important predictor of bar passage rate was a student's relative law school class rank. As such, CU Law implemented several academic counseling programs, including a peer tutoring program aimed at providing supplemental academic help to those ranked in the bottom of their respective classes. Based in part on these academic counseling programs, CU Law's bar passage rate rose to 91% in 2005 and remained at that level in 2006.

A. Bar Passage and the Bottom 10%

In 1998, the University of Colorado Law School's Bar Passage rate was 97%. By 2003, however, the University of Colorado's bar passage rate had declined to 88%. In 2004, the tutoring and faculty advising programs were enhanced as a response to the school's lower bar passage rate. Accordingly, in the past two years, the passage rate has increased significantly. Specifically, in 2005, the bar passage rate increased to 91%. Most recently, the 2006 bar passage rate remained steady at 91%.[228]

Figure 3. University of Colorado Bar Passage Rate[229]

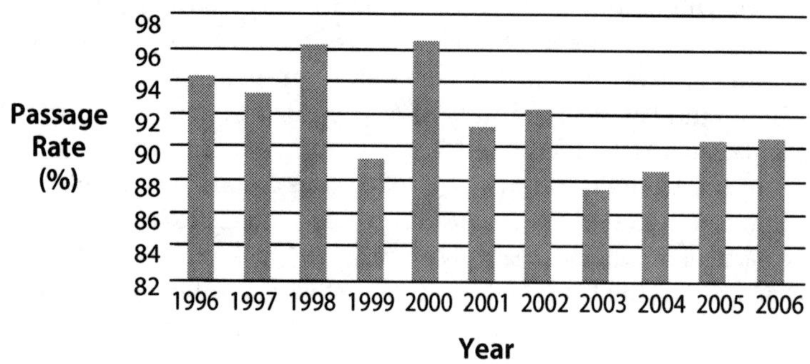

To understand these trends, the CU Law School initiated a survey to correlate students' bar results with their LSAT scores, undergraduate GPA, ethnicity, and their self-reported study habits. Official bar passage rates are calculated by the state. Data from the Colorado Board of Bar Examiners reported herein are for first time examinees only.

In 2004, 117 of 148 graduating students sat for the July 2004 Colorado bar exam and 99 passed. Of the 111 students in the top 75% of the Class of 2004, 84 sat for the exam and 80 passed. Of the 37 students in the bottom 25% of the class, 29 sat for the exam and 15 passed. Of the 14 students in the bottom 10% of the class, 10 sat for the exam and only 1 passed.

The same survey was conducted on the July 2005 Colorado bar exam. In July 2005, 123 CU students took the bar exam for their first time. Of the 129 students in the top 75% of the class, 93 sat for the exam and 92 passed. Of the 43 students in the bottom 25% of the class, 30 sat for the exam and 22 passed. Of the 17 students in the bottom 10% of the class, 8 sat for the exam and only 2 passed.

The same survey was conducted in July 2006, yielding similar results. Of the 119 students in the top 75% of the class, 96 sat for the exam and 92 passed. Of the 39 students in the bottom 25% of the class, 29 sat for the exam and 23 passed. Of the 16 students in the bottom 10% of the class, 9 sat for the exam and only 5 passed. These data indicate a high probability of failure for those students in the bottom 10% of their class.[230]

Figure 4. Bar Passage by Class Rank

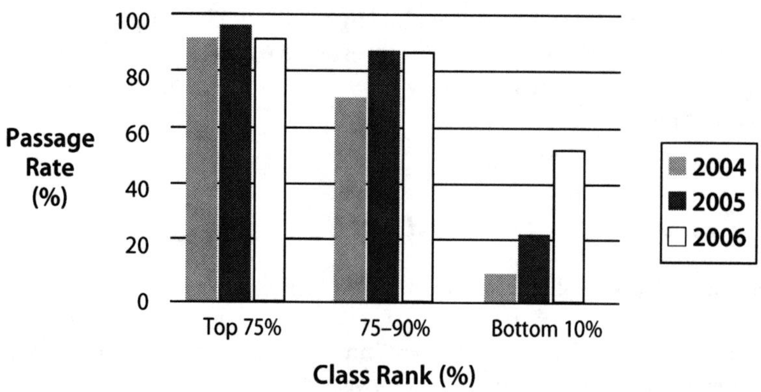

These statistics reinforce the view that those in the bottom 10% are the most vulnerable to failing the bar exam and, therefore, should be provided with the additional academic support necessary to prepare adequately for the exam or, perhaps, should not be allowed to graduate. The critical issue here is that these individuals should not have to wait until the bar exam to understand that they are deficient in their legal knowledge and skills. Confronting a student with his or her deficiencies is more appropriately the role of teaching and evaluation.

These data gain more significance when average undergraduate GPA, LSAT score, and division by class rank are analyzed together.

Figure 5. Average LSAT by Class Rank

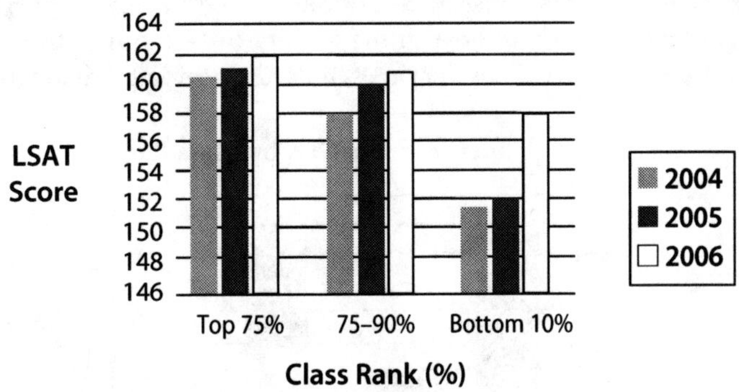

As figure five illustrates, there is a marked difference in the average LSAT scores of the bottom 10% of the class compared to the rest of the class. Importantly, though, the data also reveals that the class of 2006 had a marked increase in LSAT scores amongst all students but an especially higher score amongst those in the bottom 10%. This may explain the marked increase in the passage rate of students in the bottom 10% of the class of 2006. Research shows that LSAT is a predictor of success in law school. However, if LSAT is the single factor relied upon to predict success in law school, then intervention through teaching may be of no consequence for the bottom 10% as shown above.[231]

Figure 6. LSAT Score and Bar Passage Rate

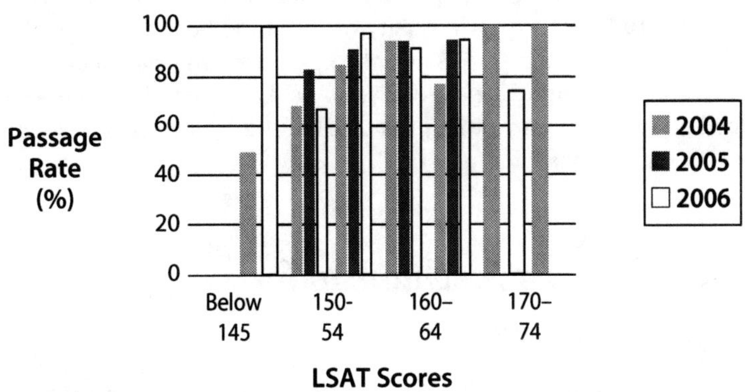

Figure six demonstrates that there is a correlation between LSAT and bar passage. Comparing figure six to figure four, it is apparent that class rank is the strongest predictor of performance on the bar exam. Furthermore, only class rank gives academic support services professionals a meaningful tool for deciding who needs academic support. In discussing class rank, one obvious criticism is often raised: in any ranking, there is always a bottom percentile. While this is necessarily true, it relates to a point discussed in the Conclusion, *infra*. Schools must recognize that there is a minimum standard at which students must be performing. Students who fail to perform at this level are falling below the threshold of necessary competence. Law schools must ensure that students who are not meeting this minimum threshold are both placed on notice, and, if necessary, advised about their potential failure of the bar exam.

Both LSAT and undergraduate GPA data were compiled for the class of 2005. These data show that undergraduate GPA is not an effective or meaningful predictor of bar passage. Figure seven shows that those in the bottom 10% of the class of 2005 had a higher average undergraduate GPA then those in the seventy-fifth to ninetieth percent range. This may be accounted for by widely varying standards at undergraduate institutions.

Figure 7. Undergraduate GPA by Class Rank

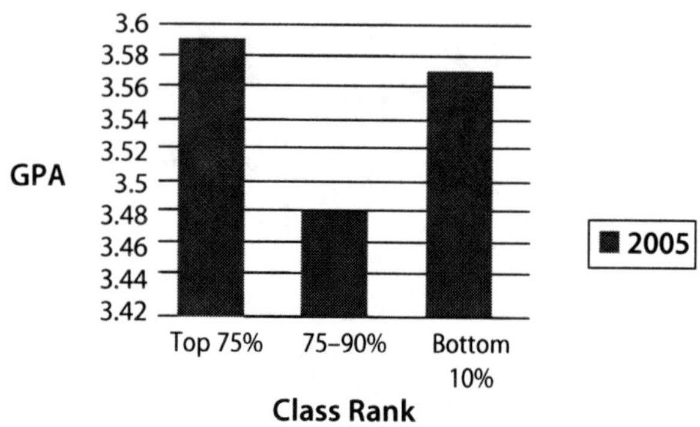

This research indicates that neither the LSAT nor undergraduate GPA are as meaningful indicators of success on the bar exam as class rank, which remains the best predictor for success on the bar exam. It is important that students who fall into the at-risk category in terms of class rank not become self-defeating. Rather, they should recognize that a problem exists in their legal skills, and do everything possible to correct the problem. Some suggestions for overcoming the problems associated with class rank are provided in this article. The students at the University of Colorado School of Law all enter with superior credentials that predict success on the bar exam, and past data show that it is possible for the bar passage rate to exceed 95% at CU Law. Therefore, the recognition of need for remediation and improvement may well be the appropriate response to a low class rank so that bar passage will be assured.

B. Peer Tutoring as a Mechanism for Raising Bar Passage

To aid first-year law students in their studies, the University of Colorado Law School developed the Rothgerber Tutoring program, wherein second and third-year students receive a stipend in exchange for tutoring first-year students. Each first-year section of Torts, Contracts, Property, Civil Procedure, Constitutional Law, and Criminal Law is assigned one tutor who is selected by the professor of the section in which the tutor is assisting. The tutors meet with their respective professors and offer tutoring sessions to first-year students on a biweekly basis. These sessions focus on outlining techniques, explanation of legal concepts and analysis, developing issue-spotting skills, and essay exam writing practice.

While tutoring sessions are open to all students in the appropriate section, ideally, the program works to ensure that tutors focus on issues relevant to those students who are struggling or who feel they need more clarification or explanation of the lectures. The students, however, set the pace of the sessions. The competitive nature of law school has demanded that academic services be open to all students.[232] This challenges the tutors to be all things to all students.

The law school depends on having upper division students tutor first-year students. "At most schools, programs are run and taught by non-tenure track [faculty]."[233] In many schools, academic support program staff is often concerned about infringing upon the "doctrinal" faculty role, function, and realm of authority.[234] Although there have been marked increases in academic support services at many schools, this presence has had "little impact on the day-to-day teaching by the doctrinal faculty."[235]

However, at CU Law School, there has been an impact among some doctrinal faculty.[236] Faculty who teach first-year courses may disseminate information about exam preparation, give advice on second-and third-year course selection, direct students to the school's other academic support services, and provide informal advising about the law school experience. This system was initiated with the incoming class of 2005 on a trial basis. Strategies, such as those identified herein, focus on enhancing faculty involvement in welcoming students and promoting student learning and success.

C. Recommendations for Raising Bar Passage Rate

Based on experiences at CU Law, the author believes that enhancing academic procedures and counseling methods at law schools will better provide students with the requisite skills to pass the bar exam.

Law schools should emphasize the importance of the bar exam from the first day of orientation. They should begin to focus on mastering the law as the essential tool in passing the bar exam from the opening meeting at new student orientation to the final meetings in the third year.[237] Similarly, professors should stress the importance of the bar exam and be willing to answer questions about it.[238] From time to time, professors should review the most recent state bar exam, to answer questions about the exam more effectively and accurately address the knowledge and skills required to pass.[239]

In addition, law schools and professors need to become more cognizant that not all students learn the law easily, and people learn in different ways from one another.[240] Most law school deans and professors graduated at the top of their class from some of the best law schools in the country. For them, learning the law was almost second nature. However, these faculty members need to recognize that law may not come as easily to some students and should be patient in dealing with those who do not possess certain skills or when explaining especially complicated legal problems.[241] Correspondingly, law schools should recognize that students learn in different ways by encouraging students to discover how they learn, and by exploring methods of class presentation that address divergent learning styles. For example, kinesthetic learners make a connection with information in a tactile way through writing it down. Typing the information on a laptop in class may be counterproductive for these students, making it difficult for them to retain the information.[242] Significant research has been done regarding various learning styles and multiple intelligences.[243] Clearly, these bodies of knowledge about how students learn and process information could have a profound effect on how pedagogy is provided in law schools to result in more effective quality instruction and assessment. However, legal pedagogy is not the subject at hand and will require its own article for appropriate analysis and development.[244]

Law schools should encourage students to take and master bar courses for a grade. It should be stressed that mastery of these courses is vital to passing the bar exam.[245] In fact, students who do poorly in these courses should be advised to lighten their course load in order to master the basics of the bar courses.[246] "It is better that a student spend an extra semester or summer to master the bar material than graduate in six semesters and flunk the bar."[247] In order to ensure mastery in these essential courses, law professors should rely on essay examinations and not multiple-choice tests.[248] Faculty should concentrate on crafting effective essay exams that will evaluate the analytical skills needed to be a successful lawyer. If a student possesses these skills, she will likely do well on the bar exam. That said, faculty should not end the teaching relationship with a student after the exam. Professors need to provide feedback to students by deconstructing exams.[249] A professor can help a student immensely by reviewing an exam on which the student has done poorly. The professor can show the student where she went wrong, what issues were missed, and how an answer can be improved. During this process, the student can hone her issue spotting, analytical, and writing skills, all of which are essential to pass the bar exam. A fundamental principle of learning theory is that assessment drives instruction, which leads to quality learning.[250] Law students will gain knowledge and experience from the opportunity to understand their misconceptions, mistakes, and analytical errors.

In a similar vein, law schools need to give better feedback to students by instituting more rigorous grading and retention policies.[251] Many students who failed the bar exam received low B's or high C's in law school, and they did not know they were at risk of failing the bar exam.[252] Professor Christine Jones cogently stated, "[g]rading is like parenting," where sometimes you have to give your children the harsh realities about their lack of achievement so they can develop into mature, competent adults.[253] Similarly, law schools need to give lower ranking students honest assessments of their skills and academic abilities in order to open their eyes to the risk that they may fail the bar exam. These students should also be told that students in their position often do not pass the bar exam, so they have ample opportunity to change their study habits before it is too late.[254] Also, law schools need to institute more disciplined retention policies. "It is kinder to dismiss students from law school after one semester or one year than to re-admit students who have no chance of passing the bar."[255] Law schools should compile statistics that identify the grade point average below which students seldom pass the bar exam. Professor Christian Day proposes that professors should honestly evaluate students rather than collect another few thousand tuition dollars and then hand students a degree that cannot be used to its full capacity.[256]

Law schools should strengthen their academic support offices to advise current students and graduates who fail the bar exam.[257] Effective academic support staff can identify and counsel at-risk students who will probably do poorly on the bar exam without intervention.[258] Support office staff can advise students on what classes to take, how to improve study habits, and how to take exams effectively so they can overcome their at-risk status and improve their chances of passing the bar exam. Likewise, support office staff can continue to advise graduates who fail the bar exam the first time around.[259] The staff can propose alternative study methods to a failing applicant, providing that student with improved methods for writing, preparation, and answering bar questions in order to ensure passage on the second attempt.[260]

Law schools should actively advise students on how to properly prepare for the bar exam. They should inform students about bar review courses and perhaps offer one at the school.[261] This information will help students make educated decisions as to which courses should be taken prior to the bar exam. Equally, law schools should inform students that preparing for the bar is a full-time job, and their personal and financial affairs need to be in order to allow focused study time.[262] It must be stressed that students should not work during the bar prep time because the review is intensive and extremely important to success on the exam. Obviously, studying for the bar will come at a cost to the student who is paying for the review course and cannot earn a wage. However, the cost is small compared to failing the bar exam, and making a six figure investment in a legal education inoperable for a period of at least six months.[263] Most importantly, when reviewing bar exam practice questions, students must learn to fully analyze an issue when responding. Answering hundreds of questions, without an in-depth understanding of the proper response analysis, is a meaningless activity that will not give positive results.[264]

Conclusions and Recommendations

When students enter law school they should be given learning style tests to determine which learning style and note-taking method is most appropriate for them. Law school faculties can greatly enhance the quality of education they provide by engaging in best practices that focus on assessment-driven instruction and quality feedback for students. If students do not effectively use laptop computers to take notes, they should be discouraged from using them. Academic services should be available to all students, but an emphasis should be put on students in the bottom ten to twenty-five percent of their class. These academic services should include involvement of doctrinal faculty, as well as academic support services faculty, and potentially qualified members of the upper classes. Academic services extending beyond the first year should continue to place emphasis on students in the bottom ten to twenty-five percent of their class. Students who are not performing at minimum standards should be notified, and if improvement is not made, should be counseled out of law school. While this is certainly a difficult decision, it should be more difficult to cash tuition checks while knowing that a student is unlikely to pass the bar exam.

In preparing for the bar exam, students should take a bar review course. Students should be discouraged from working during bar preparation and should be reminded that after more than twenty years of investment in education, two additional months and an additional loan may be necessary to ensure bar passage. Students must become keenly aware that failure occurs because of an inability to identify legal issues, failure to separate relevant from irrelevant information, and a lack of ability to properly organize and analyze legal issues.

Finally, although a subject of some controversy, the bar exam has its place in the preparation of future lawyers. However, the time is ripe for the National Conference of Bar Examiners to consider an evolution of the bar exam to incorporate advancing technologies in assessment and understandings of the contemporary practice of law. As a profession, we have an opportunity to engage in research to better address the needs of students, the legal profession, and society to level the playing field for fairness and equity for all students.

Notes

* The author wishes to thank and acknowledge the work of his research assistants, Joseph G. Martinez, William Kozeleski, and Siddhartha H. Rathod, for their assistance in the preparation of this article. The author also thanks Dean David Getches, Marianne Wesson, Clare Huntington, Javier Trujillo, Karen Trojanowski, and Shannon L. Rathod for their review of this article. Special gratitude is given to Jennifer R. Jacobsen for her patient, detailed, and professional editing.

1. William D. Henderson & Andrew P. Morris, *Student Quality as Measured by LSAT Scores: Migration Patterns in the* U.S. News *Rankings Era*, 81 IND. L.J. 163, 165 (2006).

2. National Conference of Bar Examiners, Bar Passage Statistics, http://www.ncbex.org/stats.htm (last visited Dec 18, 2005).

3. The Dean's listserv is an electronic system of e-mail communication among the Deans of United States and Canada law schools. Each dean may subscribe to the system.

4. *See, e.g.*, posting of Joseph Harbaugh, harbaugh@nova.edu, to deans@mail.abanet.org (Oct. 10, 2005); *see also* posting of Jeffrey Brand, brandj@usfca.edu, to deans@mail.abanet.org (Oct. 9, 2005) (copies on file with author).

5. *See* posting of Joseph Harbaugh, supra note 4; *see also* posting of Jeffrey Brand, supra note 4.

6. *See* posting of Jack Guttenberg, jguttenberg@law.capital.edu, to deans@mail.abanet.org (Oct. 10, 2005) (copy on file with author).

7. *See* posting of Jeffrey Brand, *supra* note 4.

8. Factors include LSAT scores, undergraduate GPA, class rank, bar review courses, and whether the student worked during bar preparation.

9. A cross-section of these approaches is analyzed in this article. See discussion *infra* Part V.

10. National Conference of Bar Examiners, *supra* note 2.

11. *See, e.g.*, posting of Jeffrey Brand, *supra* note 4.

12. For example, students with undergraduate grade point averages or LSAT scores that rank significantly below their peers' scores may be targeted for academic support in order to combat potentially low law schools grades—and correspondingly low bar exam scores.

13. The University of San Francisco, University of Baltimore, and Capital University are examples of schools now offering second- and third-year students such academic and tutorial services. *See* posting of Jeffrey Brand, *supra* note 4; *see also* posting of Joseph Harbaugh, *supra* note 4.

14. American Bar Association, Interpretation 302–7 (2005–2006), http://www.abanet.org/legaled/standards/2005-2006standardsbook.pdf.

15. Christian C. Day, *Law Schools Can Solve the "Bar Pass Problem"—Do the Work*, 40 CAL. W. L. Rev. 321, 343 (2004).

16. *See infra* notes 19–20.

17. E-mail from Lucy Marsh, Professor of Law, University of Denver, to Lorenzo Trujillo, Assistant Dean for Students and Professional Programs, University of Colorado (June 22, 2005, 16:53:58 EDT) (copy on file with author).

18. *DU Panel Probes Low Bar Pass Rate...*, LAW WEEK COLO., Jan. 3, 2006, at 1 (identifying too many take-home examinations as one of the reasons for the University of Denver's Law School's "disturbingly low bar passage rates." Id.)

19. E-mail from Lucy Marsh, *supra* note 17. This supposition is also supported by informal conversations with law faculty and colleagues who attended the National Conference of Bar Examiners (Sept. 26–28, 2005) (notes on file with the author).

20. See Kathy Matheson, *More Professors Ban Laptops in Class* (May 3, 2006), http://www.wjla.com/news/stories/0506/324463.html.

21. SEYMOUR PAPERT, MINDSTORMS: CHILDREN, COMPUTERS, AND POWERFUL IDEAS, 3 (1980).

22. *Id.*

23. Mike Kane, Address at the Academic Support Conference—Sponsored by the National Conference of Bar Examiners (Sept. 27, 2005).

24. *Id.*

25. *Id.*

26. Diane Bosse, Address at the Academic Support Conference—Sponsored by the National Conference of Bar Examiners (Sept. 27, 2005).

27. *Id.*

28. Judy Gundersen, Susan Case, and John Kidwell, Address at the Academic Support Conference—Sponsored by the National Conference of Bar Examiners (Sept. 27, 2005).

29. *Id.*

30. *Id.*

31. *Id.*

32. AMERICAN BAR ASSOCIATION, NATIONAL CONFERENCE OF BAR EXAMINERS, COMPREHENSIVE GUIDE TO BAR ADMISSION REQUIREMENTS 21 (Margaret Fuller Corneille & Erica Moeser eds., 2005), *available at* http://www.abanet.org/legaled/publications/compguide 2005/chart6.pdf.

33. Bosse, *supra* note 26.

34. *Id.*

35. *Id.*

36. Gundersen et al., *supra* note 28.

37. *Id.*

38. *Id.*

39. *Id.*

40. *Id.*

41. *Id.*

42. *Id.*

43. Susan Case, Mike Kane, and Doug Ripkey, Address at the Academic Support Conference—Sponsored by the National Conference of Bar Examiners (Sept. 27, 2005).

44. *Id.*

45. Bosse, *supra* note 26.

46. *Id.*

47. *Id.*

48. Stephen Klein, *Option for Assigning Essay Scores*, B. EXAMINER, Feb. 1996, at 24, 25.

49. *Id.*

50. *Id.*

51. *Id.* at 26.

52. Julia Lenel, *The Essay Examination Part II: Construction of the Essay Examination*, B. EXAMINER, May 1990, at 40.

53. *Id.* at 41.

54. *Id.*

55. *Id.*

56. *Id.* at 42.

57. *Id.*

58. *Id* at 43.

59. *Society of American Law Teachers Statement on the Bar Exam*, 52 J. LEGAL EDUC. 446, 446 (2002) [hereinafter "SALT Statement"].

60. *Id.*

61. *Id.*

62. ABA SECTION OF LEGAL EDUC. & ADMISSIONS TO THE BAR, LEGAL EDUCATION AND PROFESSIONAL DEVELOPMENT—AN EDUCATION CONTINUUM, REPORT OF THE TASK FORCE ON LAW SCHOOLS AND THE PROFESSION: NARROWING THE GAP (1992).

63. Kristen Booth Glen, *When and Where We Enter: Rethinking Admission to the Legal Profession*, 102 COLUM. L. REV. 1696, 1699 n.2 (2002).

64. *See* SALT Statement, *supra* note 59, at 447.

65. The "cut-score" is the threshold score which determines whether a candidate passes the bar exam.

66. Andrea A. Curcio, *A Better Bar: Why and How the Existing Bar Exam Should Change*, 81 NEB. L. REV. 363, 369–72 (2002).

67. *Id.* at 372. Currently, New York is in the process of raising the cut-score.

68. SALT Statement, *supra* note 59, at 447. Some readers may question the relevance of promoting pro bono or public interest legal services to the poor. However, in Colorado, for instance, there is a clear value statement in the Colorado Rules of Professional Conduct Rule 6.1 that encourages members of the bar to provide pro bono or public service legal services to the poor. This rule is patterned after the American Bar Association Model Rules of Professional Conduct Rule 6.1. See MODEL RULES OF PROF'L CONDUCT R. 6.1 (2003), *available at* http://www.abanet.org/cpr/mrpc/rule 6 1.html.

69. SALT Statement, *supra* note 59, at 447.

70. *Id.*

71. Curcio, *supra* note 66, at 374.

72. SALT Statement, *supra* note 59, at 448.

73. *Id.*

74. *Id.*

75. *Id.*

76. Curcio, *supra* note 66, at 376.

77. *Id.*

78. *Id.* at 377.

79. *Id.* at 376, 378.

80. Kristin Booth Glen, *Thinking Out of the Bar Exam Box: A Proposal to "MacCrate" Entry to the Profession*, 23 Pace L. Rev. 343, 363 (2003).

81. *See id.* at 363–65.

82. SALT Statement, *supra* note 59, at 448.

83. *Id.*

84. *Id.*

85. *Id.*

86. *Id.*

87. Curcio, *supra* note 66, at 383–84.

88. *Id.* at 384.

89. Interview with Judge William Lucero, Presiding Discipline Judge, Colo. Supreme Court, in Denver, Colo. (Dec. 19 2005). In Colorado, a lawyer may either keep client funds in his possession in an interest-bearing account for the client's benefit or in a COLTAF account. *See* COLTAF About Us, http://www.coltaf.org/about us.htm (last visited Dec. 5, 2006). COLTAF is the Colorado Lawyer Trust Account Foundation, and COLTAF receives the interest from pooled client accounts where the funds are short-term or nominal. *Id.* The interest COLTAF receives is then used to further COLTAF's purposes, including improving the knowledge and awareness of law in the community, providing legal services to the disadvantaged, and improving legal services. *Id.*

90. SALT Statement, *supra* note 59, at 447.

91. *Id.* at 449.

92. *Id.*

93. This statement does not necessarily suggest take home exams or papers. Further, it does not argue against traditional law school exams. Rather, it proposes possible better ways to evaluate student performance which may include traditional exams that use a variety of modalities of language use, essay question types, or hypothetical simulations within the traditional timed exam experience.

94. SALT Statement, *supra* note 59, at 449.

95. Glen, *supra* note 80, at 357 n.43 (citing LINDA F. WIGHTMAN, LSAC NATIONAL LONGITUDINAL BAR PASSAGE STUDY (1998)).

96. *Id.* at 357.

97. SALT Statement, *supra* note 59, at 449.

98. See Elizabeth Rindskopf Parker & Sarah E. Redfield, *The Educational Pipeline From Preschool to Professional School: Working to Increase Diversity in the Profession*, B. EXAMINER, May 2006, at 7, for a discussion of how the education pipeline has a history of preprogrammed academic failure of minorities.

99. SALT Statement, *supra* note 59, at 449.

100. *Id.*

101. *Id.*

102. *See* Glen, *supra* note 80, at 355–56.

103. SALT Statement, *supra* note 59, at 450.

104. Linda F. Wightman, LSAC NATIONAL LONGITUDINAL BAR PASSAGE STUDY 27 (1998).

105. Susan M. Case, *The Testing Column, Men and Women: Differences in Performance on the MBE*, B. EXAMINER, May 2006, at 44. For a more complete understanding of the implications of these data, read the complete article.

106. *See* Parker & Redfield, *supra* note 98, for a discussion of the pipeline.

107. SALT Statement, *supra* note 59, at 450.

108. *See* 2005 Statistics, B. Examiner, May 2006, at 23, 27, *available at* http://www.ncbex.org/bar-admissions/stats/.

109. National Conference of Bar Examiners, Bar Passage Statistics, *available at* http://www.ncbex.org/stats.htm (last visited Dec 18, 2005). The apparent discrepancy between Figure 1 and Figure 2 can be attributed to the fact that Figure 1 includes all examinees while Figure 2 separates first-time from repeat exam takers.

110. Suzanne Darrow-Kleinhaus, *A Response to the Society of American Teachers Statement on the Bar Exam*, 54 J. LEGAL EDUC. 442, 452 (2004).

111. *Id.* at 442.

112. *Id.*

113. *Id.* at 442–43.

114. *Id.* at 444.

115. *Id.* at 445 (quoting New York Board of Law Examiners, The Bar Examination, http://www.nybarexam.org/barexam.htm (last visited June 9, 2004)).

116. *Id.* at 444.

117. *Id.* at 447.

118. *Id.* at 449.

119. *Id.* at 447.

120. *Id.*

121. *Id.* at 449.

122. *Id.* at 451.

123. *Id.*

124. *Id.* at 452.

125. Catherine L. Carpenter, *Recent Developments in Law School Curricula: What Bar Examiners May Want to Know*, B. EXAMINER, Nov. 2005, at 39, 43.

126. Darrow-Kleinhaus, *supra* note 110, at 452.

127. *Id.*

128. *Id.* at 457–58.

129. *Id.*

130. *Id.* at 458.

131. *Id.*

132. *Id.* at 453 (emphasis added) (quoting Stephen P. Klein, *Disparities in Bar Exam Passing Rates Among Racial/Ethnic Groups: Their Size, Source, and Implications*, 16 J. MARSHALL L. REV. 517, 523–24 (1991)).

133. *See infra* Part VI.E.

134. *See* Glen, *supra* note 63.

135. *Id.* at 1702.

136. *Id.* at 1720.

137. *Id.* at 1721.

138. *Id.* at 1725–26.

139. *Id.* at 1721.

140. *Id.*

141. *Id.* at 1723.

142. *Id.* at 1735.

143. *Id.*

144. *Id.* at 1736–37.

145. *Id.* at 1737.

146. *Id.* at 1737–38.

147. *Id.* at 1722.

148. *Id.*

149. *Id.*

150. *Id.*

151. In this system, law schools would be responsible for assuring students' mastery of the basic subjects of law while students are taking law classes. Students would have to fulfill certain prerequisites in law school before they could elect the PSABE as an alternative to the bar exam.

152. Sally Simpson & Toni M. Massaro, *Students with 'CLAS': An Alternative to Traditional Bar Examinations*, 20 GA. ST. U. L. REV. 813, 827 (2004).

153. *Id.* at 817.

154. *Id.*

155. *Id.* at 818.

156. *Id.*

157. *Id.* at 817 n.4.

158. *Id.* at 818.

159. *Id.*

160. *Id.* at 830.

161. *Id.*

162. The MPRE is a short standardized test designed to ensure that all new entrants to the state bar have a threshold understanding of legal ethics and professional responsibility. While not technically a part of the bar exam, passage of the MPRE is a prerequisite to admission to most state bars. National Conference of Bar Examiners Multistate Professional Responsibility Examination (MPRE), http://www.ncbex.org/multistate-tests/mpre (last visited Dec. 4, 2006).

163. Simpson & Massaro, *supra* note 152, at 818.

164. *Id.* at 818–19.

165. *Id.* at 835–36.

166. *Id.* at 837.

167. *Id.*

168. *Id.* at 838.

169. *Id.*

170. See Beverly Moran, *The Wisconsin Diploma Privilege: Try It, You'll Like It*, 2000 WIS. L. REV. 645, 645 (2000).

171. The Franklin Pierce program was initiated with the admission of "an inaugural class of 15 students" in April of 2006. Leigh Jones, *Dream Come True: No Bar Exam—N.H. Honors Program Would Replace Taking the Bar*, NAT'L L.J., May 1, 2006, at 4. The program is described as follows:

> New Hampshire's lone law school has established a first-of-its-kind program that enables graduates to obtain a license to practice law without passing the bar examination.
>
> The program at Franklin Pierce Law Center in Concord, N.H., is designed to give students practical experience during their second and third year of school, which is monitored by faculty, attorneys, and judges. After three years, participants are eligible to practice without enduring the two-day rite of passage....
>
> The Daniel Webster Scholar Honors Program is a collaborative project developed by the New Hampshire Supreme Court, the state's board of bar examiners, the New Hampshire Bar Association and Franklin Pierce Law Center, the only law school in the state.
>
> Students who successfully complete the program can become licensed after passing the multistate professional responsibility examination and satisfying the state's character and fitness requirements....
>
> Participants take regular courses in addition to classes specific to the program. They also work in simulated, clinical and externship programs. They must demonstrate an ability to practice before judges, bar examiners, faculty members and classmates in order to pass....
>
> The American Bar Association (ABA) will be watching the program "with interest,' said John Sebert, consultant on legal education to the ABA. He said he knew of no other programs like Franklin Pierce's. *Id.*

172. Moran, *supra* note 170, at 648.

173. *Id.* at 648 n.35 (quoting Wis. Sup. Ct. R. 40.03(2)(b) (1995)) ("The ten courses are constitutional law, contracts, criminal law and procedure, evidence, jurisdiction of courts, ethics and legal responsibilities of the legal profession, pleading and practice, real property, torts, and wills and estates.").

174. *Id.* at 648 n.36 (quoting Wis. Sup. Ct. R. 40.03(2)(a) (1995)) ("These courses are administrative law, appellate practice and procedure, commercial transactions, conflict of laws,

constitutional law, contracts, corporations, creditors' rights, criminal law and procedure, damages, domestic relations, equity, evidence, future interests, insurance, jurisdiction of courts, legislation, labor law, ethics and legal responsibilities of the profession, partnership, personal property, pleading and practice, public utilities, quasi-contracts, real property, taxation, torts, trade regulation, trusts, and wills and estates.").

175. *Id.* at 649–51.

176. *Id.* at 650–51.

177. *Id.* at 651.

178. *Id.* at 652.

179. *Id.* at 653.

180. *Id.* at 650.

181. *Id.* at 653.

182. *Id.* at 655.

183. *Id.*

184. *Id.*

185. *Id.*

186. *Id.*

187. Curcio, *supra* note 66, at 394.

188. *Id.* at 394–95.

189. *Id.* at 396.

190. *Id.*

191. *Id.* at 396–97.

192. *Id.* at 397.

193. *Id.*

194. *Id.* at 396.

195. Computerized testing may have a negative impact on groups who have not had access to computers and are therefore not comfortable with technology.

196. Jayne W. Barnard & Mark Greenspan, *Incremental Bar Admission: Lessons from the Medical Profession*, 53 J. LEGAL EDUC. 340, 340 (2003).

197. *See id.*

198. *Id.*

199. *Id.*

200. *Id.* at 341.

201. *Id.*

202. *Id.*

203. *Id.* at 359–63.

204. *Id.* at 359.

205. Schools could allow students to continue with the understanding that passage of both tests is required to register for the sixth semester (final semester) of law school.

206. Barnard & Greenspan, *supra* note 196, at 359.

207. *Id.*

208. *Id.* at 359–60.

209. *Id.* at 360.

210. *Id.*

211. *Id.*

212. *Id.* at 361.

213. *Id.*

214. *Id.* at 362.

215. *Id.*

216. *Id.*

217. *Id.*

218. *Id.* at 363. Currently, newly licensed attorneys may practice in any area they decide, even though they may have no experience in that area. In this system, the public would have some degree of assurance of the expertise of new attorneys based on their training and the areas in which they were tested.

219. Many law school faculties rarely fail students. This system is more honest and has integrity because students are not falsely carried through three years of law school debt to only later realize they cannot pass the bar exam.

220. Barnard & Greenspan, *supra* note 196, at 360.

221. *See supra* text accompanying notes 62–64.

222. Rebecca Carroll, *Passing the Bar After Passing on Law School*, ROCKY MTN. NEWS, Sept. 21, 2005, at 46A.

223. *Id.*

224. Darrow-Kleinhaus, *supra* note 110, at 453–54.

225. *Id.* at 454.

226. *Id.* at 455.

227. *Id.* at 454.

228. Colorado Board of Bar Examiners, Pass/Fail Rates by Law School: July 2006 Bar Exam—After Review (Nov. 14, 2006), htp://www.coloradosupremecourt.com/BLE/results/ July2006/Fail%20by%20Law%20School%20Statistics.pdf.

229. Colorado Board of Bar Examiners, Data Compilation (on file with author).

230. A false perception that is sometimes discussed behind closed doors is that diverse/minority students are the group that fall into the bottom 10% and fail. Michael Waggoner, Associate Professor of Law and Assistant Dean of Admissions and Financial Aid, studied this question in detail. He found: "Our students of color pass the bar exam at about the same rate as other takers." Memorandum from Michael J. Waggoner, Assoc. Professor, Univ. of Colo. School of Law, to the Dean's Cabinet of the Univ. of Colo. School of Law (Mar. 1, 2006) (on file with author).

231. However, the data from 1998 inform us that 97% of CU Law students passed the exam. This evidence clearly illustrates that the bottom 10% does not have to fail the bar exam.

232. Ellen Yankiver Suni, *Academic Support at the Crossroads: From Minority Retention to Bar Prep and Beyond— Will Academic Support Change Legal Education or Itself Be Fundamentally Changed?*, 73 UMKC L. Rev. 497, 501–02 (2004).

233. *Id.* at 504.

234. *Id.* at 504–05.

235. *Id.* at 506.

236. The faculty advising programs described above are recent interventions with varied degrees of success as indicated by initial reports back from faculty. Further research on effectiveness and implementation must be done to determine if the interventions work in practice on an on-going basis.

237. Day, *supra* note 15, at 341.

238. *Id.* at 345.

239. *Id.* at 345–46.

240. *Id.* at 341–42.

241. *Id.* at 342.

242. *Id.*

243. *See* HOWARD GARDNER, FRAMERS OF MIND: THE THEORY OF MULTIPLE INTELLIGENCES (1983); DAVID A. KOLB, EXPERIENTIAL LEARNING: EXPERIENCE AS THE SOURCE OF LEARNING AND DEVELOPMENT (1984).

244. As these suggestions are provided, the author fully realizes that not everyone will be able to pass the bar exam. However, important understanding of self through the educational process should eliminate those who are apparently not sufficiently skilled to pass the exam; or, if they continue in the study of law, it should be with the understanding of their deficits. The question is at what point should the notice be given—after a student acquires $100,000 in debt, or before? What is the honest, ethical, and morally correct action?

245. Day, *supra* note 15, at 343.

246. *Id.*

247. *Id.*

248. *Id.*

249. *Id.* at 345.

250. As a general rule, law school professors are not prepared to teach. Their skill set is derived from traditional legal education pedagogy, which does not include methodology of teaching or an understanding of learning processes. It may be valuable for the academy to review the research from the field of education to gain a meaningful understanding of best practices in teaching as a means to enhance legal education in America. For an introduction to best practices that may be transferable to the law school experience, see RICHARD DUFOUR & ROBERT EAKER, PROFESSIONAL LEARNING COMMUNITIES AT WORK: BEST PRACTICES FOR ENHANCING STUDENT ACHIEVEMENT, (1998), and ROBERT EAKER, RICHARD DUFOUR & REBECCA DUFOUR, GETTING STARTED: RECULTURING SCHOOLS TO BECOME PROFESSIONAL LEARNING COMMUNITIES (2002).

251. Day, *supra* note 15, at 347.

252. *Id.* at 345.

253. Interview with Christine Jones, Associate Professor of Law, University of the District of Columbia, Clarke School of Law (Nov. 12, 2005).

254. Day, *supra* note 15, at 345.

255. *Id.* at 347.

256. *Id.*

257. *Id.* at 346–48.

258. *Id.* at 347–48.

259. *Id.* at 346.

260. *Id.*

261. *Id.* at 348.

262. *Id.* at 346.

263. *Id.*

264. *DU Panel Probes Low Pass Rate...*, *supra* note 18 ("A committee of well-known University of Denver law school graduates empanelled to examine 'disturbingly low bar pass rates' has identified nine possible reasons" including too many take-home examinations, inadequate assistance for students scoring lower on the LSAT entry examination and "grade inflation leading to students thinking they are better prepared for the bar exam than they really are." Other reasons identified were failure to require 6–7 courses in law school tested on the bar exam; failure to dismiss students not making satisfactory progress; economic pressure on some to work while studying for the bar; some faculty members' view that "professional licensure" is secondary to developing analytical and expressive abilities; statistics indicating that the bottom twenty percent of the class after first year are unlikely to pass the bar regardless of the course of study; "and a number of repeat takers who were admitted to the College of Law years ago but continue to take the bar drive down the overall passage rate.").

Institutional Denial about the Dark Side of Law School, and Fresh Empirical Guidance for Constructively Breaking the Silence

*Lawrence S. Krieger**

In the day-to-day business of legal education there is remarkably little evidence that we are aware of the unhealthy-unhappy-law-student(lawyer) problem.[1] *The core of this article is a description of recent psychological research on the components of happiness and life satisfaction. This research provides an objective framework for understanding the pervasive problems in legal settings and thus can lead to constructive discussion and intervention. I first review empirical and anecdotal evidence of the dark side of law school, the process of denial among faculty, and failing paradigms at the heart of legal education. I then discuss the helpful recent research, and I conclude by suggesting individual and collective faculty approaches based on this research.*

> Denial prevents us from coming to terms with what is going on before our very eyes. When we will not let ourselves see or know what is happening, we ... perpetuate a dishonest system.[2]

There is a wealth of what should be alarming information about the collective distress and unhappiness of our students and the lawyers they become. We appear to be practicing a sort of organizational denial because, given this information, it is remarkable that we are not openly addressing these problems among ourselves at faculty meetings and in committees, and with our students in the context of courses and extracurricular programs. The negative phenomena we ignore are visible to most of us and are confirmed by an essentially unrebutted body of empirical findings.

The Dark Side of Law School and the Legal Profession

The anecdotal and observational basis for concern is obvious. The tales of law student and lawyer depression, overwork, dissatisfaction, alcohol abuse, and general distress are legion, and many of us see, more clearly than we would like, the undoing of our students' collective energy, enthusiasm, and engagement after only a few months of law school. In another article .... Gerry Hess, director of the Institute for Law Teaching at Gonzaga University, describes his experience:

> In what now seems like another life, I taught second grade. Most of my second graders walked in the first day with new shoes, fresh crayons, and little backpacks. They were excited about school and eager to learn.... My number one goal was for them to leave second grade with those same feelings and expectations.... I was able to achieve my primary goal with most of my students.
>
> I now teach law school. My first-year students enter with new books, the latest computers, and big backpacks. Many of them have the same excitement and expectations as my second graders. When I allow myself to think about this, I conclude that my number one goal in my law school classes ought to be the same as for my second graders. But I don't think about this very often because I have failed so miserably at achieving this goal with law students. The law school experience systematically beats those feelings and expectations out of many of them.[3]

Student observations are similar:

> Harvard Law School continues to represent, for many people both inside and outside the legal community, the pinnacle of legal education, the breeding ground for the nation's leaders. Given this status, one would expect to find HLS full of confident, enthusiastic, optimistic students who are thoroughly comfortable with themselves and fully prepared upon graduation to take on the world.
>
> In fact, one finds quite the opposite. Far from brimming over with personal and intellectual self-confidence, by the second (2L) year, a surprising number of Harvard Law students come to resemble what one professor has called "the walking wounded": demoralized, dispirited, and profoundly disengaged from the law school experience. What's more, by third year, a disturbingly high number of students come to convey a strong sense of impotence and little inclination or enthusiasm for meeting the world's challenges head on.
>
> [A significant number] become subdued, withdrawn, and uncertain of their own self-worth over the course of their legal education. If Harvard Law School routinely generates students who feel insecure, disengaged, and fatalistic about the world and their future in it, one must look to the institution itself for an explanation.[4]

Though we might wish this sad situation were confined to a few law schools, we know it is not. Such observations are discouragingly common throughout legal education,[5] and they are confirmed consistently by empirical studies. In studies by teams of psychologists at the University of Arizona, law students were found to arrive with essentially normal psychological markers but to shift quickly to major psychological distress in the first year. These negative changes persisted throughout law school and into the students' early careers, making it clear that the negative findings in law students do not represent a brief "adjustment" problem at the beginning of law school.[6] The incidence of clinically elevated anxiety, hostility, depression, and other symptoms among these students ranged from eight to fifteen times that of the general population.[7] In their analysis of previous studies on anxiety and depression, Matthew Dammeyer and Narina Nunez observe: "Across studies and measurement instruments, law students almost always reported higher levels of anxiety than comparison groups, including medical students. In some cases they report mean scores on anxiety measures that are comparable to psychiatric populations."[8] Depression measures among law students are no better, with studies showing from twenty to forty percent incidence of clinical depression.[9] A three-semester study that Kennon M. Sheldon (a psychologist) and I have just completed confirms these findings.[10] Our law student sample shifted from strong mental health and life satisfaction measurements during initial orientation to distinctly elevated distress and depression (t values up to 7) later in the first year and into the second year. The data reveal additional changes that are very troubling, including an overall dulling of student motivation and goal-directed striving, and shifts away from initially positive motivation and altruistic values toward external, imposed values and motives. All of these changes predict further decreases in future well-being and life satisfaction.

Research on lawyers is equally negative. In a 1990 Johns Hopkins study, practicing lawyers ranked highest in major depressive disorder among 104 occupational groups.[11] Our graduates rank fifth in the incidence of suicide[12] and show from five to fifteen times the normal incidence of clinical psychological distress as well as very high levels of substance abuse.[13] We might like to believe that future lawyers arrive at law school with these predispositions, but research and our own eyes tell us otherwise.

Individual and Institutional Avoidance

Something distinctly bad is happening to the students in our law schools. Why isn't this a common topic of discussion at our faculty meetings, in our committees, and in our classes? Why are none—or very little—of our resources devoted to trying to understand the sources and then prevent the problems? Certainly many law teachers and deans are aware of the health and distress issues of our students and graduates and are concerned about them. Nonetheless, we maintain the status quo, at times by ignoring the problems outright, and at other times by deflecting concern in ways that avoid any constructive approach to them. Some typical reactions from colleagues, including many who are genuinely concerned about the problems, are the following.

> *It's just as bad in med school.* Actually, research demonstrates that it is not as bad in medical schools.[14] But even if the assertion were true, it would not mean that we should not address the problem. This is a form of denial—rationalizing or justifying the problem (in this case, relying on its purported commonality) in order to avoid confronting it.
>
> *People come to us that way.* Research indicates that this is also not true (see above), and observations of other teachers and students (such as those quoted earlier in this article) confirm that research.
>
> *It's not my job. I'm not trained for this. It needs more study. It isn't that bad. It's always been that way. It's the nature of the business. That's the way the world is now.* None of these responses provides a rational justification for ignoring serious problems. Such statements generate confusion through deflection and minimization,[15] again reflecting a process of denial which allows us to continue our enterprise without grappling with the unpleasant realities.

The current emphasis in law schools on professionalism and civility offers another example of institutional denial. It is wholly unrealistic to expect that depressed or highly distressed lawyers will exemplify professional behavior, no matter how well they are schooled in their obligations.[16] We have our own professional and moral responsibilities to try to prevent or alleviate the distress of our students, and institutional pronouncements about our overriding service mission confirm that point, whether intentionally or not.

Nonetheless, we lecture students on their obligations as good professionals but most often ignore our related obligations.

There are obvious sources of discomfort that encourage our avoidance of these issues. It is inherently unpleasant to reflect on one's darker side; and we may fear that we undermine our own enterprise, or create unwanted anxiety, if we acknowledge openly with our students the significant problems apparently occurring in law schools and awaiting many graduates when they enter practice. Further, we are not clear on the precise causes of the problems, nor do we have ready solutions to offer. It is also true that we are not trained academically for such discussions, and most of us are unaccustomed to dealing with the kind of nonrational, nonanalytical matters such discussions will inevitably entail.[17] We may feel put upon as well. After all, we are basically reproducing the system of legal education which we experienced and for which we had great aptitude as students. And human nature suggests that some of us simply avoid the substantial effort that helpful changes might require—particularly if they come at a cost to our own comfort or convenience. Regardless of individual motives for inertia, the collective result is clear: few faculties address these problems to any greater extent than if the problems did not exist at all.[18]

Failing Paradigms

Beyond the immediate reasons for avoiding the distress problems, the pervasiveness and persistence of the problems and of the institutional denial around them in American law schools suggest that core attitudes and beliefs at the foundation of our educational culture would be threatened by an open look at what is going wrong. The suspect constructs include:

The top-ten-percent tenet—the belief that success in law school is exclusively demonstrated by high grades, appointment to a law review, and similar academic honors. This belief is entirely obvious at most law schools, whether elite or more typical.

The contingent-worth paradigm—the corollary sense that personal worth, the opinions of one's teachers and potential employers, and therefore one's happiness and security in life depend on one's place in the hierarchy of academic success. While there are, of course, comparative evaluations and rankings in other educational settings and in our broader society, in many law schools these considerations virtually dominate the collective thinking and become identified with personal worth.

The American dream—the belief that what is good in work and in life is defined by financial affluence, influence, recognition, and other external indicia of achievement (and that the dream will be secured by academic success in law school).

Thinking "like a lawyer"—defining people (or "parties") primarily according to their legal rights, and trying to understand, prevent, or resolve problems by linear application of legal rules to those rights, usually adopting a zero-sum competitive approach to outcomes. This process requires the closest scrutiny of spoken and written thought to identify any defect that may undermine an adversary's position or create future problems for one's client. Thinking "like a lawyer" is fundamentally negative; it is critical, pessimistic, and depersonalizing. It is a damaging paradigm in law schools because it is usually conveyed, and understood, as a new and superior way of thinking, rather than an important but strictly limited legal tool.

All of these paradigms share a powerfully atomistic worldview and a zero-sum message about life in the law and in law school. For every winner there is a loser, and if anything beyond winning or losing matters, it doesn't matter much. The theme for law students is consistent: you must work very, very hard, and you must excel in the competition for grades and honors, in order to feel good about what you have done, have the respect of your teachers and peers, get a desirable job, and generally be successful. We see these themes dominating the minds of students almost from the instant of their arrival on campus; and as students take on the typically daunting workloads under these competitive pressures, we often see fatigue and anxiety replacing enthusiasm and life satisfaction. All is building toward the day of reckoning, the posting of first-semester grades (and, secondarily, law review selections).[19]

Students obviously may be set up for continuing problems by this overriding emphasis on differentiation, contingent worth, and competitive outcomes. The overall impact is isolating and threatening. In addition, those who succeed in the grades race are likely to experience a performance-based boost in their sense of personal worth, confidence, and security. They feel valued by the institutional culture, and they may be driven to reproduce such victories to maintain these feelings and the sense of relief that accompanies them. Those who falter in the competition by receiving less-than-stellar grades often become thoroughly deflated; their sense of confidence, security, and personal worth plummets. Exacerbating the negative effect of all of the competitive paradigms, the exclusive valuing of thinking "like a lawyer" directly discourages students from being themselves. They learn to inhibit the expression or consideration of ideals, values, and personal beliefs, and they lose sight of the potential satisfaction inherent in cooperation and mutually beneficial outcomes. Enthusiasm and the sense of relevance that would result from engaging more of the student's inborn capacities are simultaneously undermined by this process.

The interplay of these dominant law school constructs ultimately teaches many students to put aside their personal life and health and accept persistent discomfort, angst, isolation, even depression as the cost of becoming a lawyer. This is ominous preparation for professional life, and similar constructs apparently do drive many lawyers, as they vie for status, recognition, and the highest salaries regardless of the toll on their health, happiness, ethics, and professionalism.[20] Three empirical findings related to these law school paradigms are worth noting here. First, among thousands of lawyers surveyed, more than one-third—about fifteen times the incidence in general populations—reported levels of "clinical distress" (indicating the likely need for professional help)[21] in the area of interpersonal sensitivity, a measure of self-esteem and security based on one's need to compare favorably to others.[22] (Given our own acculturation to comparative/competitive law school environments, it may surprise many to learn that the need to compare favorably to others is actually a recognized form of emotional illness!) The Sheldon/ Krieger study of law students provides confirmation: one of the largest maladaptive shifts during the first year of law school that we found was an increasing concern for image and appearance.[23] But research also shows that the general distress and depression among law students is not mitigated by high grades,[24] nor is dissatisfaction among lawyers mitigated by high salaries.[25]

In other words, lawyers are tremendously prone to insecurity and an unhealthy need for status—a likely manifestation of the related law school paradigms around contingent self-esteem and comparative worth—but the top grades and high salaries so much emphasized in law schools and law firms do not improve one's likelihood of a happy and satisfying life. In fact, just the opposite may turn out to be the case, as I explain below.

The suspect paradigms are difficult for us to address critically because academic and analytical superiority, law review experience, and the like obviously reflect the collective experience and special abilities of law teachers. And, as I've said, there are many other reasons we might prefer to simply continue with our current beliefs and educational practices. Nonetheless, the dark side of our enterprise is increasingly documented. This is a particularly appropriate time to put aside avoidance and proceed, because there are also fresh research studies that can provide an objective, empirically supported framework for constructive discussion.

Empirical Insights into the Fundamental Human Needs

Recent research demonstrates that human needs, values, and motivation, and the relationships between them, are all important to understanding well-being and satisfaction. First, as to the human needs, a major cross-cultural study by Ken Sheldon and colleagues provides the latest empirical word on which psychological needs are actually fundamental to a positive life experience. This research is directly relevant to the concerns about life quality among lawyers and law students because needs are defined as those experiences which produce well-being, life satisfaction, and a sense of thriving; conversely, a lack of such experiences produces distress, depressed mood, and loss of vitality.[26]

The researchers concluded that the universal psychological needs include self-esteem, relatedness to others, authenticity,[27] competence, and security (as a foundational need underlying the others).[28] Since a great many lawyers and law students are known to experience high levels of depression and emotional distress, the frustration of their fundamental needs suggests itself as a cause; the common observation that students lose self-confidence and self-esteem after beginning law school, and become insecure and isolated, provides confirmation.[29] Security is particularly important as a threshold issue, because insecurity has undermining effects on all of the other needs.[30] Before discussing the fundamental needs in the law school context, it will be useful to review the related research on motivation, goals, and values, and their impact on these human needs and on well-being.

The Impact of Legal Education on Healthy Motivation, Goals, and Values

Recent empirical studies demonstrate that one's motivational style and the content of one's goals and values predict positive or negative mental health and well-being. Although most of the summarized studies focus on general populations, the implications for lawyers, law students, and law schools are again striking, and the current Sheldon/Krieger study extends these findings directly to law students. For the purposes of these studies, "motivation" implies the reasons why people choose their actions, while "goals" and "values" relate to content—what is sought to be accomplished.

Humanistic Theory as Context

The classic humanistic psychologists, most prominently Abraham Maslow and Carl Rogers, described an individual valuing process underlying behavioral choices. They saw people as naturally striving for their highest level of personal functioning, authenticity, integration, and actualization.[31] Humanistic theory linked the natural striving to be one's best and improve one's society with the experience of satisfaction and well-being; it posited that the source of most psychological distress was the blocking of this movement toward personal and social integration.[32] Actualization or full function would, then, produce highly ethical and prosocial behavior[33]—something particularly relevant for lawyers.

Goals, Motives, and Well-Being: The American Dream as a Failed Paradigm for Life Satisfaction

Many recent studies have found the links between goals, motivation, and well-being that the humanists predicted. With their landmark studies of human goals and well-being, "A Dark Side of the American Dream"[34] and "Further Examining the American Dream,"[35] Tim Kasser and Richard Ryan demonstrated that goals such as money, power, and image, which typify the American dream, do not produce life satisfaction. Their studies, the more recent Sheldon study on human needs, and many others[36] indicate instead that pursuit of the "extrinsic" goals which are common in Western culture, and which are embedded particularly deep in the culture of most law schools and law firms, does not produce a good life and in fact can very well undermine it. These studies consistently demonstrate that, to the extent such goals are primary in a person's life, she will experience decreased life satisfaction compared to people with other primary goals. The Sheldon study is perhaps the most illuminating to date because of its comparison of a wide range of possible experiences. Subjects who identified money, image, or influence as important for life satisfaction consistently experienced the *lowest* well-being in the study.[37] By contrast, persons whose primary goal content was "intrinsic"—toward personal growth, intimacy, and community integration—experienced significantly greater well-being.[38]

As one would expect from the foregoing findings on goal content, research has also found that extrinsic *motivations*—acting for reasons outside of oneself, such as to relieve guilt or anxiety, please others, or gain rewards—predict decreased well-being, sense of meaning, and personal integration. By contrast, intrinsic motivations—working and behaving in ways that are either inherently satisfying or that reflect strongly one's deepest convictions and beliefs—are correlated with enhanced well-being, increased meaning, and increased personal and social integration.[39]

The Interplay of Goals, Motives, and Needs

In addition to affecting life satisfaction directly, one's choice of personal goals and motives also affects the satisfaction of the basic needs. Intrinsic motivation and goals maximize one's opportunity to experience fulfillment of the human needs. For example, doing work one believes is truly important (an intrinsic motivation) will provide experiences of self-esteem and authenticity; working to help others or improve society (an intrinsic value) is likely to support experiences of self-esteem and relatedness to others.[40] Doing work one inherently enjoys (another intrinsic motive) directly provides well-being, enthusiasm, and a sense of thriving, and it also enhances the experience of authenticity and self-esteem. By contrast, extrinsic motivation and goal pursuits tend to replace, or distract one from, the pursuit of more satisfying goals and the fulfillment of the fundamental needs. Extrinsic goals and motives are therefore associated with insecurity and directly produce negative life experiences such as dissatisfaction, stress, and irritation.[41]

All of these findings raise clear implications for law schools and the law practice culture. Assuming that the legal "success" paradigm is, indeed, largely defined by grades, external recognition, and money or position, these inherently competitive goals, values, and motives will promote tension and insecurity and will minimize satisfaction and well-being in the lives of many law students and lawyers. At the same time, this cycle of inherently unfulfilling activity supplants the intrinsic drive for growth, actualization, intimacy, and community, thereby exacerbating the negative effects on well-being. Anxiety or depression is likely to manifest because, regardless of one's level of success within this paradigm, one will not experience internal satisfaction. Sheldon and Kasser summarize many of the relevant research findings as follows:

> [W]hen people are focused on goals with intrinsic content (self-acceptance, affiliation, and community feeling) they are more likely to satisfy their higher psychological needs and thus have many of the characteristics of "fully functioning" individuals, including psychological health and strong interpersonal relationships. In contrast, a focus on extrinsic goals (financial success, popularity, appearance) signals a disjunction from one's true self and a focus on security needs, likely due to non-optimal childhood models and environments. As a result, extrinsically oriented people tend to become "stuck in a vicious cycle" in which they continually experience psychological distress and conflictual interpersonal relationships, not knowing how to escape the cycle.[42]

Beyond "non-optimal childhood models and environments," an educational environment that promotes extrinsic goals and motivation will have a similar effect. This is particularly likely in legal education, which demands of its students a new way of thinking and which typically encourages—either tacitly or explicitly—the rejection of previously held values, preferences for cooperation or mutuality, and other socializing factors.

The Sheldon/Krieger Study

The longitudinal study of law students that Ken Sheldon and I have completed confirms these conclusions in all respects. We measured values, motivation, and well-being in students just after they entered law school, again toward the end of the first year, and during the following fall semester. The arriving students showed healthy well-being, values, and motives—stronger, in fact, than a large undergraduate sample. Within six months, however, the law students experienced marked decreases in well-being and life satisfaction and marked increases in depression, negative affect, and physical symptoms. Perhaps more revealing, their overall motivation and valuing patterns shifted in undesirable (external/extrinsic) directions, with particular increases in the valuing of image and appearance and decreases in altruism and community orientation.[43] These changes predict continuing decreases in life satisfaction and happiness, and they are fully consistent with the reports of distress, dissatisfaction, and loss of ethics and values among practicing lawyers.

In addition to showing negative effects on the values and motivation of new law students, many of our findings directly refute the idea that the problems of law students and lawyers are the inevitable result of self-selection and personal attributes. The entering students were healthier, happier, and more optimally motivated than the comparison undergraduates. Our conclusion, that the problems arising in law students are largely attributable to the process of legal education, has also been reached by psychologists studying another law school. In their studies, normal markers of mental health in incoming students were followed by rapid development of psychiatric distress that persisted throughout law school.[44]

A consideration of the students who performed best according to the usual law school paradigms—those who earned the highest grades—is of further interest. As I said earlier, these students suffered losses in well-being and life satisfaction to the same extent as the rest of their class. An additional finding is revealing: they immediately and significantly shifted away from service-oriented career preferences and toward lucrative, high-status career choices. When matriculating, this group of students had healthier, more intrinsic goals and values than the other law students (who were already quite intrinsically oriented); nonetheless, the more academically successful group shifted toward the most extrinsic career orientations. It may be that these students, who are typically confronted first with choice campus interviews and job opportunities, began first to compromise their personal values to conform to law school norms for "successful" career tracks.[45] This phenomenon of abandoning career preferences that reflect positive (service/community) values for career choices that provide money and status has been reported at other law schools[46] and may foreshadow the common perception of lawyers as valueless and unhappy hired guns. As we have seen, such a compromise is likely to undermine future life satisfaction by decreasing the experience of authenticity, autonomy, self-esteem, and intrinsic motivation, and by displacing intrinsic goal pursuits that would have the capacity to produce well-being.

The Fate of Law Student Needs

A major thrust of this article is to encourage law teachers to individually and collectively undertake a review of our attitudes and educational practices, in order to identify those most likely to have a deleterious effect on the basic needs of law students. To begin that consideration, I will raise here a few such attitudes and practices that are common to many law schools.

First, we might investigate our predilection to work students exceptionally hard.[47] Persistently long hours of high-demand work obviously drain personal resources, encourage students to ignore biological needs that are basic to health and life satisfaction, and at the same time displace normal activities needed to fulfill basic psychological needs.[48] As an experienced litigator, I reject the idea that intensely stressing students in this way is useful professional preparation. Rather, it teaches students to accept constant stress and to associate it with a law career. Once habituated to that experience, students are, likely to make choices that will perpetuate stress as the reality of their future lives and careers.

In addition, the contingent-worth and top-ten-percent paradigms create continuing tension for many students by generating insecurity about future employment, the constant need to outperform peers and friends, the sense that a student is only as worthwhile as his grades and résumé, and the impression that, regardless of any amount of rhetoric about professionalism and the like, in fact personal character, values, ideals, and intentions are largely irrelevant to the new agenda students have undertaken.[49] One could hardly design purposely a more effective belief system for eroding the self-esteem, relatedness,[50] authenticity, and security of an affected population. And schools that have a mandatory or "strongly suggested" grading curve (particularly those requiring very low grades)—a stranger to virtually all other graduate schools—strengthen this effect by promoting the perception among students that their institutions intentionally pit them against each other in order to facilitate numerical differentiation of their contingent worth.[51] Beyond the undermining of basic needs, all of the foregoing pressures contribute to the intense stress experienced by law students—a matter of additional concern because stress is the primary predictor of clinical depression[52] and is thus likely to promote suicidal thinking.

Our traditional teaching methods and our overreliance on objective analysis also promote the undermining of basic needs. The usual classroom atmosphere is one in which students are isolated from each other and the teacher, and encouraged to abandon their preferences, values, and instincts as they are trained to wholeheartedly embrace thinking "like a lawyer." In their description of an innovative approach to teaching designed to avoid this damaging depersonalization, John Mixon and Robert P. Schuwerk observe:

> We intended our approach to be the very antithesis of the traditional law school pseudo-Socratic method of instruction, with its emphasis on "hard" cases and supposedly rigorous and rational cognitive processes at the expense of students' emotions, feelings, and values. These traditional techniques desensitize students to the critical role of interpersonal skills in all aspects of a professionally proper attorney-client relationship and, for that matter, in all aspects of an ethical law practice. They also set students' moral compasses adrift on a sea of relativism, in which all positions are viewed as "defensible" or "arguable" and none as "right" or 'just," and they train students who recognize and regret these developments in themselves to put those feelings aside as nothing more than counter-productive relics from their pre-law lives.[53]

Many law teachers share this evaluation of the effects of traditional teaching methods and the beliefs that underlie them.[54] Again, as with the contingent-worth constructs, one can hardly imagine a better system for undermining the sense of self-worth, security, authenticity, and competence among students. Law students get the message, early and often, that what they believe, or believed, at their core, is unimportant—in fact "irrelevant" and inappropriate in the context of legal discourse—and that their traditional ways of thinking and feeling are wholly unequal to the task before them. It would be quite possible (as I will explain) to teach rigorous legal analysis in a manner that supplements rather than supplants a student's developed values, beliefs, and sense of self—a fact that often leads me to wonder whether we law teachers persist in exclusively valuing thinking "like a lawyer" because of our own adeptness at it or comfort with it.

It is almost too obvious to state that if our operant paradigms, teaching methods, or other practices exert pressures that undermine the physical health, internal values, intrinsic motivation, and/or experience of security, self-worth, authenticity, competence, and relatedness of our students, we should expect the negative results that studies of law students (and lawyers) consistently demonstrate: major deficits in well-being, life satisfaction, and enthusiasm, and flourishing depression, anxiety, and cynicism.

Moving Forward

As we think through the individual and social implications of declining happiness, psychological health, and social consciousness in our students and the profession, we must become willing to dedicate time and resources to preventing or alleviating those problems. The research described in this article guides us forward with the following questions.

- What might we do to promote the regular experience of authenticity, relatedness, competence, self-esteem, and security in our students?
- How can we support intrinsic motivation in law students—inherently enjoyable or personally meaningful work—while we teach the fundamentals of legal analysis and professional technique?
- How can we promote optimal human values in students (toward personal growth, intimacy, community enhancement, altruism), rather than the desire for money, power, status, and image?

As part of this inquiry, we need to specifically identify our individual and institutional practices that tend to undermine the basic needs and optimal values listed, and try to amend those practices.

Colleagues express discouragement about the possibility of changing our systems or the assumptions that underlie them. This is natural; most institutions are endowed with significant inertia, and new directions can seem intimidating. One direct approach to breaking our collective silence around these issues is to provide clear information, perhaps beginning with the published empirical evidence of law student and lawyer distress. Most teachers and students are practically dumbfounded when they see this information. People rarely dispute the findings, and seeing objective quantification of what most already know, or at least suspect, has a powerful focusing effect. After clarifying the need for attention with this negative, problem-oriented research, it is useful to provide the overview of possible solutions contained in the research on needs and motivation.[55] This research also commands attention, provided that its relevance to the likelihood of future happiness and life satisfaction is made clear. In particular, people need to realize that the American dream and the extrinsic goals for money, power, and status that so strongly pervade legal settings are failed approaches to happiness, whereas old-fashioned wisdom about being true to oneself, helping others, maintaining close relationships, and creating community is, according to current research, true and effective for structuring a positive life experience.

As a practical foundation for working with students, it is helpful for teachers to first reflect on our own experiences of the fundamental needs (for self-esteem, relatedness to others, authenticity, and competence); our own internal motivations (for activities that we find enjoyable in themselves, or that support an important personal belief or goal); and our intrinsic goal pursuits (relating to improving oneself, experiencing genuinely close relationships, helping others, or building community). Given the research summarized in this paper, such experiences should be providing us with most of our life satisfaction, and this personal perspective will give us confidence for raising these topics with students. As we then communicate the research findings to students, they become able to make more informed choices about priorities, career directions, and distribution of time during law school and eventual practice. Without deciding the direction any particular student should choose, we have an obligation as the creators of the legal profession to avoid hypocrisy around our institutional service missions and to broaden our message to include at least the scientific research that relates to the health, happiness, and life satisfaction of our students.[56] In addition, we need to remind students regularly that thinking-like-a-lawyer, although a crucial analytical tool, entails a fundamentally negative and dehumanizing worldview. It will have undermining effects if applied generally in life, or in one's career beyond the specific contexts for which it is appropriate.

I will offer some other preliminary observations and suggestions for working with students. Curricular integration is important. Although extracurricular programs, orientation meetings, and such are useful, and may be more easily adaptable for this purpose at first, we should be wary of relying on such venues. Otherwise we perpetuate the institutional message that creating health and well-being in the profession, and in the lives of law students, is not important enough to merit inclusion in the curriculum.

Other teachers and I have experimented with relevant, constructive teaching methods; student feedback and my own observations tell me that results are quite positive.[57] In my classes I inform my students of the research on well-being, values, and motivation; I encourage optimal values; and I promote the regular experience of the fundamental human needs. None of these tasks has been difficult. Once past the initial discomfort of extending the discourse to "personal" career and life issues, the great majority of students welcome such messages, and the students are definitely more engaged in learning when teaching methods calculated to provide for basic human needs are employed.

A teacher may approach these matters in a variety of ways in the context of almost any course, using only a few minutes of class or clinic time each week.[58] For example, if your coverage includes practical or ethical aspects of the profession, you may directly raise and discuss the topics of health and career satisfaction, perhaps overviewing the research on lawyers and giving brief reading and writing assignments.[59] You may also integrate into virtually any course, including those purely doctrinal, questions or assignments that require students to relate their personal values, beliefs, instincts, and conscience to the cases or principles being studied. Such exercises broaden the unnecessarily narrow legal education agenda by promoting personal valuing, and they provide experiences of competence, authenticity, and self-worth in students. In addition, the fact that a teacher encourages discussion of the personal qualities, values, or subjective experiences of lawyers and law students is crucial validation for their continued consideration. We effectively communicate to our students that who they are and what they believe matters, regardless of their overt markers of achievement; and by thus expanding the universe of law school discourse, we begin to undercut the self-fulfilling assumption that law study and practice are per se harmful to one's health and well-being.[60] Collaborative exercises are also useful in diminishing the sense of isolation among students, enhancing their relatedness, and reliably increasing their engagement in the course work. I reemphasize that much thought and collaboration will be required of faculty to develop these and other teaching methods. I offer only first thoughts and a brief overview here.

Beyond working with our students, we need to begin focused, honest dialog among ourselves. Consideration by committees and the general faculty is obviously crucial. It should promote acceptance of the need to address these problems and the appropriateness of doing so, and lead to discussion of directions to be undertaken. Faculty workshops could be instrumental in helping teachers think through methodology while increasing the general level of awareness about these issues. Teachers and administrators interested in the thoughts and experience of involved faculty at other law schools can take part in a dedicated listserv and attend the conferences that its participants organize.[61]

It is not necessary to have answers before we raise the questions and encourage faculty to think about them collectively. Perhaps the initial response will be positive, perhaps not. We should avoid the pessimism of all-or-nothing thinking; institutions by nature change more slowly than individuals.

There are many ways to maintain institutional inertia: waiting for others to conduct more research, focusing on points of disagreement, raising fears of sweeping reforms and unmanageable expenses. But open discussion of important information does not require great cost and, while it will always be useful to conduct more research, all the research to date provides a consistent picture of law student and lawyer distress.[62] Acting within your own sphere of control, by openly raising these issues with colleagues and developing your own teaching style with a view to your students' well-being, you will gain personal satisfaction and make a real contribution to your students, while elevating the overall institutional culture to a more honest and informed dynamic about the health of the profession.

Notes

* Acknowledgements: I thank our dean and administration for their support of this work, and particularly for the opportunities to conduct the empirical research discussed in this article. I am also very grateful for the thoughts and suggestions of Sally Gertz, Calvin Pang, Mary Crossley, and Paul LeBel.

1. See Patrick J. Schiltz, On Being a Happy, Healthy, and Ethical Member of an Unhappy, Unhealthy, and Unethical Profession, 52 Vand. L. Rev. 871 (1999).

2. Anne W. Schaef & Diane Fassel, The Addictive Organization 62 (San Francisco, 1990).

3. Gerald F. Hess, Heads and Hearts: The Teaching and Learning Environment in Law School, 52 J. Legal Educ. 75, 75 (2002).

4. Note, Making Docile Lawyers: An Essay on the Pacification of Law Students, 111 Harv. L. Rev. 2027, 2027 (1998) [hereinafter Making Docile Lawyers].

5. I base this conclusion on numerous discussions with law teachers and administrators. When I assign the Harvard student essay to my students, more than 90 percent confirm that their law school experience has been very similar. See also Hess, *supra* note 3, at 78 (summarizing structured interviews of law students at seven law schools); B. A. Glesner, Fear and Loathing in the Law Schools, 23 Conn. L. Rev. 627 (1991).

6. Matthew Dammeyer and Narina Nunez note that anxiety and depression in third-year students have consistently been found to be as high as, or higher than, in first-year students. Anxiety and Depression Among Law Students: Current Knowledge and Future Directions, 23 Law & Hum. Behav. 55, 61 (1999).

7. See G. Andrew Benjamin et al., The Role of Legal Education in Producing Psychological Distress Among Law Students and Lawyers, Am. B. Found. Res. J. 225 (1986), confirming and extending a previous study, Stephen Shanfield & G. Andrew H. Benjamin, Psychiatric Distress in Law Students, 35 J. Legal Educ. 65 (1985).

8. Dammeyer & Nunez, *supra* note 6, at 63. The article presents a rigorous critique of the methodology of previous studies and suggests additional, expanded research. One is struck by the consistency of the results of the numerous studies summarized here. For a more comprehensive review of research on lawyer and law student distress, see Susan Daicoff, Lawyer Know Thyself: A Review of Empirical Research on Attorney Attributes Bearing on Professionalism, 46 Am. U. L. Rev. 1337 (1997).

9. Dammeyer & Nunez, *supra* note 6, at 65; Benjamin et al., *supra* note 7, at 236.

10. Does Legal Education Have Negative Effects on Law Students? Evaluating Changes in Motivation, Values, and Well-Being (submitted for publication) (manuscript on file with the authors).

11. See William Eaton et al., Occupations and the Prevalence of Major Depressive Disorder, 32 J. Occupational Med. 1079, 1085 tbl.3 (1990).

12. Interview with Carol A. Burnett, National Institute for Occupational Safety and Health, in Cincinnati, Ohio (Aug. 11, 1998).

13. *See* Connie J. A. Beck et al., Lawyer Distress: Alcohol-Related Problems and Other Psychological Concerns Among a Sample of Practicing Lawyers, 10 J. L. & Health 1, 49–50 (1995). *See also* Rick B. Allan, Alcoholism, Drug Abuse and Lawyers: Are We Ready to Address the Denial? 31 Creighton L. Rev. 265 (1997); G. Andrew H. Benjamin et al., The Prevalence of Depression, Alcohol Abuse, and Cocaine Abuse Among United States Lawyers, 13 Int'l J. L. & Psychiatry 233 (1990); Eric Drogin, Alcoholism in the Legal Profession: Psychological and Legal Perspectives and Interventions, 15 Law & Psychol. Rev. 117 (1991).

14. Dammeyer and Nunez, *supra* note 6, summarize the major published studies comparing medical and law student distress. *See also* Robert Kellner et al., Distress in Medical and Law Students, 27 Comp. Psychiatry 220 (1986).

15. *See* Schaef & Fassel, *supra* note 2, at 62; Anne W. Schaef, When Society Becomes an Addict 67 (San Francisco, 1988).

16. For a discussion of the connections between health and professionalism, see generally Daicoff, *supra* note 8; Lawrence S. Krieger, What We're Not Telling Law Students—and Lawyers—That They Really Need to Know: Some Thoughts-in-Action Toward Revitalizing the Profession from Its Roots, 13 J. L. & Health 1, 35 nn. 140–46 (1998).

17. In his recommendations to broaden the law school agenda, Roger C. Cramton describes in more detail some of these inhibitions. Beyond the Ordinary Religion, 37 J. Legal Educ. 509, 512–13 (1987).

18. I posted repeated inquiries to a listserv with more than 200 law teacher subscribers, specifically asking for any experiences of open discussion of these problems in a committee or full faculty meeting. I received a few responses about specific services offered (counseling, orientation meetings, and the like); only one person reported an open faculty discussion of these problems. A look at promotional literature conveys a consistently rosy picture of the law school experience. My teaching assistant reviewed the admissions publications of 20 law schools, half public and half private. Of the hundreds of law students pictured, none showed anything other than happiness and focused attention. The brochures of two schools briefly mentioned the availability of counseling services; one of them also mentioned time/stress management workshops. The others were devoid of any hint of the phenomenon of distress in law school.

19. See Making Docile Lawyers, *supra* note 4, at 2034, describing the excessive anticipation of initial grades at Harvard Law School, and the grades' equally intense impact on students. It is no different at my school or others I am aware of.

20. See Schiltz, supra note 1; Krieger, supra note 16, at 9; Peter A. Joy, What We Talk About When We Talk About Professionalism: A Review of *Lawyers' Ideals/Lawyers' Practices*, 7 Geo. J. Legal Ethics 987, 1007–08 (1994) (book review).

21. *See* Beck et al., *supra* note 13, at 18.

22. Id. at 14; *see* also Krieger, *supra* note 16, at 13 nn. 50–51.

23. Sheldon & Krieger, *supra* note 10.

24. Benjamin et al., *supra* note 7, at 246; Sheldon & Krieger, *supra* note 10.

25. Neither research nor commentary offers any suggestion that lawyers who make more money are more happy; in fact, discussion of distress and dissatisfaction typically centers on the personal toll of the high-paying large-firm practices. Schiltz, supra note 1, details this problem and thoroughly reviews the research on lawyer dissatisfaction; *see also* Sol M. Linowitz, Tile Betrayed Profession (New York, 1994). A recent poll of Florida bar members is confirming: four categories of public service/public agency practice had the highest career-satisfaction ratings. The fifth-ranked category, law firm partners/shareholders, reported average earnings almost triple that of the state lawyers who led them in career satisfaction; and several other categories (including managing partners, lawyers with associates, and corporate counsel) with earnings at least double that of the public service lawyers trailed even further in their career-satisfaction ratings. Mark D. Killian, Lawyers Report Increased Income, Job Satisfaction, Fla. B. News July 1, 2001, at 1.

26. *See* Kennon M. Sheldon et al., What Is Satisfying About Satisfying Events? Testing 10 Candidate Psychological Needs, 80 J. Pers. & Soc. Psychol. 325, 325–27 (2001). Anxiety and depression tend to

occur as fundamental needs are ignored. *See*, e.g., Tim Kasser & Richard M. Ryan, A Dark Side of the American Dream: Correlates of Financial Success as a Central Life Aspiration, 65 J. Pers. & Soc. Psychol. 410 (1993).

27. Sheldon et al., *supra* note 26, at 326. The researchers termed this need autonomy. I use instead the term authenticity, based on the study design and on conversations with the lead author. Two of the three measurement questions went beyond the normal understanding of "autonomy" to include issues of genuineness. Specifically, subjects were asked whether their choices "expressed my true self" and "were based on my true interests and values." Specificity is important because this area of needs is particularly significant in our context. Law students run the substantial risk of losing contact with aspects of their authentic selves, such as their conscience and underlying values, as they are trained to emphasize thinking "like a lawyer" and acting as agents for others.

28. The needs identified in this recent study overlap considerably with Abraham Maslow's hierarchy of human needs, and the definition of *need* is also very similar. *See* Motivation and Personality, 2d. ed., 39–46 (New York, 1970).

29. This conclusion is confirmed by conversations with numerous law teachers and is often raised in commentaries on law school distress (such as those cited in this article). Ken Sheldon and I are currently conducting research to quantify the impact of law school on the basic needs.

30. *See* Sheldon et al., *supra* note 26, at 336–37.

31. Maslow, *supra* note 28; Carl Rogers, On Becoming a Person: A Therapist's View of Psychotherapy (Boston, 1995).

32. Maslow, *supra* note 28, at 57.

33. *Id.* at 168.

34. Kasser & Ryan, *supra* note 26.

35. Further Examining the American Dream: Differential Correlates of Intrinsic and Extrinsic Goals, 22 Personality & Soc. Psychol. Bull. 281 (1996).

36. Approximately 40 relevant studies are reviewed and summarized in Kennon M. Sheldon & Tim Kasser, Goals, Congruence, and Positive Well-Being: New Empirical Support for Humanistic Theories, J. Hum. Psychol., Winter 2001, at 30.

37. Sheldon et al., *supra* note 26, at 337.

38. This research is comprehensively summarized in Sheldon & Kasser, *supra* note 36, at 42–46. For the sake of convenience and brevity, the succeeding footnotes direct the reader to their summary, which of course cites the original studies.

39. *Id.* at 35–47.

40. *See id.* at 42–44.

41. *Id.* at 42–43.

42. *Id.* at 46.

43. Sheldon & Krieger, *supra* note 10.

44. Benjamin et al., *supra* note 7, at 246; Shanfield & Benjamin, *supra* note 7, at 66, 68.

45. One potentially confounding factor is the high debt load of most law students. Our study explicitly sought to eliminate or minimize this factor by instructing students to assume that their debts would be taken care of by any career choice. The reported shift toward higher-paying positions was nonetheless significant. Firsthand observation of the eroding effects of the law-for-money orientation is described in detail in Schiltz, *supra* note 1. Every law student should read this article. I assign it (and related others) in my courses and programs.

46. Robert Granfield, Making Elite Lawyers: Visions of Law at Harvard and Beyond (New York, 1992); Robert V. Stover & Howard S. Erlanger, Making It and Breaking It: The Fate of Public Interest Commitment During Law School 17 (Urbana, 1989). Legal education apparently has changed little in this regard in the last several decades. In 1967 Ervin N. Griswold observed:

> For some years now I have been concerned about the effect of our legal education on the idealism of our students. I have great faith in our students. They are surely as good, as earnest, as sincere, as their predecessors who have come through the years. They bring to

> this school a large measure of idealism. Do they leave with less? And if they do, is that something we can view with indifference? If they do, what is the cause? What do we do to them that makes them turn another way?

Intellect and Spirit, 81 Harv. L. Rev. 292, 300 (1967).

47. For a thorough discussion of the appropriateness of stress in the law school environment, *see* Glesner, *supra* note 5, at 627–41.

48. Maslow's classic motivation theory noted the obvious need to fulfill biological needs (food, rest, shelter) before addressing the psychological needs. Maslow, *supra* note 28, at 38.

49. For a critique of this damaging effect of the narrow law school agenda, *see* Cramton, *supra* note 17, at 512–13.

50. Isolation is a recognized problem among law students. *See* Cathaleen A. Roach, A River Runs Through It: Tapping into the Informational Stream to Move Students from Isolation to Autonomy, 36 Ariz. L. Rev. 667 (1994); Phyllis W. Beck & David Burns, Anxiety and Depression in Law Students: Cognitive Intervention, 30 J. Legal Educ. 270, 274 (1979).

51. Students often share this perception with me; I find it difficult to refute. Our grading systems may reflect numbers-based admissions processes or law firm recruiting preferences, but does that justify the potential depersonalization and distress of law students? All such questions should be open for considered discussion.

52. Eaton et al., *supra* note 11, at 1086.

53. The Personal Dimension of Professional Responsibility, Law & Contemp. Probs., Summer/Autumn 1995, at 87, 102.

54. This conclusion is based on many discussions with law teachers and feedback at educational conferences.

55. I have examples of graphics to convey this information.

56. Griswold deplored the narrowing emphasis of legal education and its stultifying effect on the student spirit:

> [T]he thrust of my point is not anti-intellectual. I am trying to say that we should be more truly intellectual, and take into account all relevant factors, including the inadequacy of many of our premises, and the fact that we are often thinking about the wrong things when we are carrying out our intellectual processes.
>
> If we do, we will get more people who deeply care about society and its problems in our student bodies and on our faculties, people who are willing to do something about these problems as well as debate them.

Griswold, *supra* note 46, at 302.

57. Elsewhere I have described earlier approaches that proved effective in my courses and programs. See Krieger, *supra* note 16, at 17–36. That article relies on humanistic theory, which has largely been confirmed by the research on needs and motivation described in this article.

58. For an overview of teaching approaches appropriate for a variety of settings, *see* Laurie A. Morin, Reflections on Teaching Law as Right Livelihood: Cultivating Ethics, Professionalism, and Commitment to Public Service from the Inside Out, 35 Tulsa L.J. 227 (2000); Ruth Ann McKinney, Depression and Anxiety in Law Students: Are We Part of the Problem and Can We Be Part of the Solution? 8 Legal Writing 229 (2002); Hess, *supra* note 3; Krieger, *supra* note 16.

59. A related listserv provides an ongoing discussion of teaching approaches; *see* note 62, *infra*.

60. In a previous article I discuss the stress of law practice and study. Rather than seeking to "manage" stress, an approach that acknowledges the inevitability of high stress in the profession, I describe ways to substantially decrease stress by changing the attitudes that produce it. *See* Krieger, *supra* note 16, at 8–30. I have since included a control exercise in my classes, to which students constantly refer as a major stress reducer.

61. The Humanizing Legal Education listserv is well subscribed. To subscribe to the listserv, or for conference or other information, send me an e-mail (lkrieger@law.fsu.edu).

62. For a discussion of the many consistent studies, and of recommended directions for future research, see Sheldon & Krieger, *supra* note 10.

Opportunity Lost: How Law School Disappoints Law Students, the Public, and the Legal Profession

*Jason M. Dolin**

I. The Questions

This article answers two questions: 1) How can law schools better prepare students to practice law; and 2) Why do law schools not do this already? This article proposes remedies which many thoughtful and concerned observers of legal education say are obvious and long overdue. This article also argues that the bench and bar are in the best position to initiate change in legal education which is necessary for law schools to produce competent new attorneys.

Since 1998, I have taught a practicum to third year students at Capital University Law School on general practice. In that capacity, I have taught many of the "how to's" of law practice: how to implement doctrine into the work product of a practicing lawyer; how to draft a will; how to draft and file a complaint; and how to deal with clients, to name a few.

As someone who has one foot in law practice and the other in law academia, I have had the opportunity to observe students who are months or weeks from graduation and fear they are not adequately prepared to practice law. Sadly, but not surprisingly, the steep learning curve they will face after graduation will likely be overwhelming to them. Although my students are eager, intelligent, and willing to learn, they know almost nothing about the actual practice of law because they have been taught almost nothing about law as a profession. Most law students have not been exposed to many of the basic skills needed to succeed in practice, such as, how to draft simple transactional documents, how to interview and handle clients, how to deal professionally with colleagues, and how to bill their time. By and large, to the extent that my students know anything about being a practicing lawyer, they have learned it on their own, "on the street."

II. The Problem

The current system of legal education is consistent with the way most practicing lawyers were taught and the way that law students have been taught for generations. So then what is the problem with the current system?[1]

There are two interconnected problems that emanate from failings in the world of legal education. The first problem is that law schools continue to produce large numbers of lawyers, flooding an already drowning market.[2] The second problem is that law schools have refused to teach new lawyers how to practice law.[3] Individually, the effects of either problem would be bad enough. Together, however, the effects of these two shortcomings have had a tremendously damaging effect on law students, the legal profession, and most importantly, the public.

A. *Langdell's Method Ineffectively Prepares Students to Practice*

It is old news that law schools currently do not adequately prepare students to practice law, even at the most minimally competent level. But while law school has not changed, law practice has dramatically changed, and at an ever-quickening pace.

Today, the legal education that many found adequate in the past is inefficient, inadequate, and costly. Law schools still use teaching methods and casebooks modeled on those developed by Christopher Columbus Langdell[4] at Harvard Law School in his contracts course in 1870.[5]

Current law school pedagogy is stuck in Langdell's 19th century. Except for word processing and the greater speed of electronic research, law school has not changed much since those days.[6] The teaching methods and casebooks we use today seek to replicate those taught by Langdell. Despite the passage of over 130 years, Langdell's methods remain the dominant teaching modality,[7] largely unquestioned by those who populate legal academia even though there is no sound pedagogical reason for its pervasive use.[8] By and large, law teaching has stagnated.[9]

Langdell, at least, had an excuse. He did not have access to the substantial scientific studies of how students learn, as well as the advances in educational psychology, social psychology, and neuroscience.[10] Researchers now have a greater understanding of how the brain works and of the critical interplay between emotion and cognition in learning.[11] Researchers now know how students learn and process information,[12] as well as the most effective methods for teaching students of all kinds, including law students.[13] Those advances happened years after Langdell implemented his methods. Further, Langdell did not have the benefit of 130 years of experience in the legal profession. Although Langdell made pioneering advancements in legal education based on the information available to him at the time, today's legal educators have not been nearly as proactive as Langdell. For reasons discussed below, legal educators have refused to acknowledge the 130 years of learning about learning.[14] While other graduate and professional schools have long since adopted more modern teaching methods, including mandatory clinical or field training, law school has made little, if any, progress since Langdell's day.

The Socratic-Casebook method through which law students are taught is not only pedagogically ineffective, but is downright damaging to their mental and emotional health.[15] Substantial evidence, gathered through a number of studies, indicates this damage carries over into the student's future law practice.[16] The results of these studies have been widely known for years. Challenging the pedagogy of the status quo, they have also been widely disregarded in legal academia.[17] Yet, while law school remains mired in the past, law practice today is more complex, more competitive, and more stressful than ever before.[18] In a consumer oriented world, consumers of legal services are demanding greater services at lower price points than ever before.[19] A premium has been placed on speed and efficiency in the delivery of legal services.[20] It is a world and a practice alien to the one that Langdell knew.

B. The Glut of Lawyers in the Legal Market

Driving a lot of the change in the world of law practice has been the glut of lawyers in the legal market—a glut fostered and even encouraged by the American Bar Association (ABA) and by law schools. According to the American Bar Foundation, in 1951 there was one lawyer for every 695 Americans.[21] In 2000, there was one lawyer for every 264 Americans.[22] At this rate, by 2050 there will be one lawyer for every 100 Americans. It is safe to say that the supply of lawyers long ago outstripped the demand for their services.[23] There are simply too many lawyers and too many law schools in the United States. Given the oversupply of lawyers, if law schools were at all sensitive to market forces, they would be shutting their doors, or at least reducing their student headcount.[24] Instead, new law schools continue to open each year. Since 1970, fifty-one new law schools have been approved by the ABA.[25] In 2006 alone, the ABA granted full approval to three law schools and provisional approval to two others.[26]

The overabundance of lawyers is not without consequence. It has hurt the practice and, more importantly, it has hurt the public. This glut of lawyers has made competition for clients greater than it has ever been.[27] While the overabundance of lawyers may have the short term consumer benefit of depressing legal fees,[28] there is more to competent lawyering than cost. The low cost provider is not always the competent provider.[29] The oversupply of lawyers has caused vicious and underhanded competition for clients. When there are too many lawyers and not enough clients, there is a greater temptation for attorneys to over promise and, once the client has been landed, to overbill.[30] Stories of bill padding are common.[31] Lack of business can encourage lawyers on the margin to file frivolous lawsuits, built on little evidence, in the hope of a fast settlement. Further, in a too-competitive market, lawyers are tempted to handle cases that are beyond their competence or outside their area of expertise. The results can be disastrous and the clients pay the price.[32]

The overheated competition for clients has often fostered a win-at-any-cost mentality for fear of losing the client. We hear, too often, of scorched earth litigation and Rambo-like tactics.[33] There has been a loss of civility, independence, and professionalism in practice.[34] A 2004 survey conducted for the State Bar of California found that two-thirds of the attorneys surveyed believed that lawyers "compromise their professionalism as a result of economic pressures."[35] Is it just coincidence that the increased loss of civility and professionalism coincides with the explosive growth of law schools? While one cannot blame the loss of professionalism entirely on the glut of lawyers, it is certainly a large contributing factor.[36] The glut has turned lawyering almost entirely into a business, with an attendant loss of professional values that once made lawyering a great and justifiably proud profession.

The result of all this is that law practice today is faster, more competitive, and more pressurized than ever before. Lawyers today face pressures and challenges unknown by those who practiced as recently as twenty or thirty years ago. Lawyers, many new, but some old, struggle to survive in such a marketplace. The temptation to cut ethical corners increases as it becomes more difficult to make a living. According to former Chief Justice

William H. Rehnquist, "the greater the pressure of maximization of income, the more likely some sort of ethical difficulties will be encountered."[37]

C. Law Schools Make Money

Why then, given the glut of lawyers, do new law schools continue to open and existing law schools continue to graduate new lawyers? The answer, of course, is that by and large law schools make money. Law schools and their affiliated universities have benefited handsomely from the increased number of those who desire law degrees, and they continue to mint graduates in large numbers.[38] Whereas many, if not most, graduate programs are money losers for their universities, law schools are moneymakers and profit centers.[39] Law school tuition is high. There is relatively little tuition discounting, and relatively little outright scholarship assistance. From 1985 to 2005, public law schools' annual tuition and fees have increased from a median of $1792 to a median of $13,107, while private law schools' annual tuition and fees have increased from a median of $7385 to a median of $30,670.[40] According to the ABA:

> Since the early 1970's, there has been a steep and persistent rise in the costs of legal education and in the tuition law schools charge students. From 1992 to 2002, the cost of living in the United States has risen 28%, while the cost of tuition for public law schools has risen 134% for residents and 100% for non-residents, while private law school tuition has increased 76%.[41]

Simply stated, law schools are university cash cows, contributing dollars to the university's bottom line.[42] Langdell's method endures because, although his pedagogy no longer makes sense, his system makes money. As David Franklin, a legal commentator and former clerk to Supreme Court Justice Ruth Bader Ginsberg, wrote:

> Langdell's genius, it turns out, lay in devising a system in which one professor could keep a hundred or more students awake and paying attention for an entire hour without the aid of teaching assistants. Law schools ... are profit centers.... Overhead costs are low, financial aid is the exception rather than the rule.... The Socratic method allows law schools to maintain a high student-to-teacher (tuition-to-salary) ratio.[43]

Cash starved universities are only too happy to take the funds generated by law schools and use them for their general purposes.[44] Indeed, the universities have every incentive to keep the law school classes large and the funds from these larger classes flowing. Law schools, in turn, while sometimes complaining about forking over the money,[45] nonetheless enjoy the prestige and power in their respective university communities that comes from the profit they generate and the funds they supply to the larger university, or main campus.

Regrettably, there is little evidence that the escalating cost of law school education will diminish. The continued increase in tuition has had a damaging financial effect on law students. According to the 2003 Final Report of the ABA Commission on Loan Repayment and Forgiveness, "[t]he typical law student today graduates with debts of around $80,000."[46] The continued increase in tuition has a damaging financial effect on law students. Not only does this debt have negative consequences for students, but society suffers as well. The ABA found that "law school debt prevented 66% of student respondents from considering a public interest or government job."[47] Thus, the crushing burden of law school debt drives graduates away from lower paying public service jobs into higher paying, but less altruistic jobs. While law schools charge high tuitions and spin off excess profits to their universities, law students sink further into debt, and the poorest segments of society suffer from the lack of attorneys able to address a range of social ills.

Having flooded the market with lawyers, many of whom are burdened with high five figure law school debts, one would think, or one would hope, that law schools would do everything they could to prepare these students to make a living. Unfortunately, law schools have done little to prepare students for the dramatic changes they will face in practice when the tuition bill comes due. Of course, law schools would have to revamp their curriculum to successfully prepare students for the challenges of practice, by instituting changes like mandatory supervised internships or meaningful clinical training. Nonetheless, professor-supervised internships and clinical training require lower student-to-professor ratios[48] and are less profitable than the Langdellian economic model of mass production in large lecture halls.[49]

Lawyers in our society are given considerable power and special privileges to handle the sensitive and important matters of a sometimes vulnerable public. That is why the state demands that lawyers be licensed as well as regulated. However, the same cannot be said for academics. The legal profession and the law schools that produce lawyers exist to serve the needs of the public, not to serve as profit centers for affiliated universities, or make the *U.S. News*' top ten.[50] Profitability and accolades are all asides and if they occur along the way to our mission, so much the better. But it is not why the legal profession and law schools exist. Law schools exist to train men and women to become practicing lawyers who serve the legal needs of the law consuming public.[51]

One can understand why universities are happy to accept the spin-off dollars that result from mass production legal education. What is less understandable, however, is the complicity of law schools with this bottom-line system at the expense of their students, the public, and the profession. This may all be the result of a game of internal university politics in the fight for resources, but if it is, it is clear that the law schools, and the profession and public they are supposed to represent, are losing that battle.[52]

Law schools have always called themselves the gatekeepers to the legal profession.[53] They should act as gatekeepers, not toll collectors.

D. Ineffective Pedagogy

Worse still, is that the gatekeepers—law schools—are flooding the market with lawyers who are incompetent to practice. If law schools are flooding the market, let them at least flood it with new lawyers who know what they are doing. Unfortunately, that is not the case.

Practitioners and judges know what it takes to build a good lawyer. Although the skills necessary to be a competent attorney have been known for generations, fourteen years ago the ABA's blue ribbon MacCrate Commission (MacCrate) made the requirements as clear as black and white.[54] Students leave law school virtually in the dark about how to practice law. The ABA, which accredits law schools, does not require that law students take a clinic or practicum, participate in an internship, or have any hands-on client experience in order to graduate.[55] It should come as no surprise that the ABA committees that set law school standards are dominated by those who have succeeded and are comfortable in the current system: law school deans and professors.[56] Further, there is a very real question as to whether the accreditation process effectively monitors the quality or type of teaching in law school.[57]

Legal education is an outlier in the world of professional education. It is virtually alone among professional education in its durable refusal to require practical training prior to licensure. One can hardly think of a profession today that does not require some form of clinical or supervised training prior to licensure.[58] In California, New York, and Ohio the following professions require their practitioners to have either clinical training or apprenticeship practice prior to being admitted to licensure: social workers,[59] medical doctors,[60] accountants,[61] marriage and family therapists,[62] and licensed embalmers.[63] It may provide cold comfort to the deceased, literally, that their embalmer is required to have more practical training prior to licensure than the attorney that drafted their estate plan.

Why are we given this special, virtually exclusive, privilege among the professions to obtain a license to practice without being required to know a thing about practice? Are we that much smarter, that much more intuitive, that much better than every other profession? Have we been blessed with attributes that are not to be found in those who practice other professions? One can excuse a cynic for believing that if lawyers did not control the court system and historically dominate the legislature that the current state of affairs would never be allowed to exist. As this article will discuss later, this system continues to exist because those in legal academia have effectively blocked change.

It is bad enough that law schools do not train their students to practice. What is worse is that the education that law schools do provide—the traditional Socratic-Casebook method—is inefficient, ineffective, and pedagogically unsound. We know, through numerous studies, that the traditional and widely used Socratic teaching method is not only ineffective, but also damaging to the emotional well-being of law students.[64] Studies going back to at least 1986 have consistently shown that the emotional damage caused by law school education does not end with graduation, but carries over into practice.[65] This, of course, has very negative ramifications for the delivery of client services.

Legal practice is a very unhappy and emotionally unhealthy profession. There are many studies and much anecdotal evidence exposing lawyer unhappiness in the practice and the psychological, emotional, and substance abuse problems faced by attorneys.[66] Lawyers experience depression and other emotional maladies at rates between five and fifteen times higher than the general population.[67] The rate of attorney substance abuse and suicide is exceptionally high as well.[68] The difference between lawyer mental health and that of the public starts in law school.[69] Most law professors are unaware of these findings.[70] Those who are aware of them tend to discount them as inaccurate or stemming from other causes.[71]

If the manner in which law school educates its students has not contributed to the high rates of depression and substance abuse, then at a minimum, law school has profoundly failed to address these persistent problems. Yet, although these findings are widely accepted, and have never seriously been refuted, they are also widely ignored within the legal academy.[72] Over the generations, law schools have consistently neglected the best science on learning and educational psychology, choosing instead to stick with the traditional, yet outdated, Langdell methodology.[73] Would this neglect of the best science and practices be allowed to persist in medicine, engineering, architecture, or any other learned profession? If we knew that public school education was causing emotional damage to students, would we let that situation persist? Why then, does it persist in legal education?

The dogged refusal to update curricula and make law school more relevant to the profession of law lies at the doorstep of law faculty, who are quite happy with the way things are and who are reluctant to change. In discussing roadblocks to change in the law school curriculum, Roger Cramton, a pre-eminent legal scholar and former Dean of Cornell Law School discussed the attitude of law faculty to changes in curriculum as follows:

> [W]e are jealous of our prerogatives, comfortable with the way things are, and intensely conservative about matters as central to our selfhood as what and how we teach. Moreover, our special strengths and weaknesses are perpetuated by the hiring process, which tends to filter out people who do not have the same accomplishments and interests, have not attended the same schools and shared the same experiences. We are threatened by discussions of values, by messy human emotions, by personal involvement with students or clients, and we place these matters out of bounds for classroom discussion. We are tied to familiar teaching materials and methods.[74]

One law professor, questioned about the lack of change in the world of legal education, had the following to say: "The present structure of law school is very congenial to us [the faculty].... We're not indifferent to the fact that our students are bored, but that to one side, law school works pretty well for us."[75] Professor Robert Schuwerk of the University of Houston Law Center perhaps said it most succinctly: "Law schools are run primarily for the benefit of law professors—not for the benefit of law students, not for the benefit of the legal community, and most certainly not for the benefit of the public at large."[76]

But while the professoriate may be quite happy with the academic slant in law school, students are not.[77] Students come to law school to be trained as lawyers, not as academics.[78] On a personal level, I frequently hear from my students about the irrelevance of what they learn, especially in the third year. Many express a deep desire for more practical skills such as how to handle clients, how to draft basic transactional documents, and how to operate a law office. A number of them have expressed to me the sentiment that they have spent $90,000 for nothing.

Why then, is the professoriate reluctant to change and incorporate greater skills training in the curriculum? There are a number of reasons. First, in general, any kind of significant change is frequently perceived as uncomfortable and like many of us, law professors resist it. Secondly, and more specifically, law professors are primarily academics, not practitioners. This is the residue of the Langdellian system. By and large, they have spent very little and sometimes no time practicing law prior to teaching. Many of them do not like practice, or are unfamiliar or uncomfortable with it.[79] A 1991 study showed that more than 20% of law professors had no practice experience at all prior to teaching. Overall, the length of practice prior to teaching averaged 4.3 years.[80] A full 37% of the law professors at the seven highest ranked schools had no practice experience prior to teaching.[81] If anything, the anecdotal evidence indicates that recent hires have less practical experience than those hired years ago. Thus, the average length of practice today is even less than the 4.3 years indicated in that 1991 survey. Many law professors continue to go from elite schools to judicial clerkships, and then directly to teaching, or from elite schools to elite firms as low level associates, to teaching.[82]

Practicing attorneys and judges know that the practice of law, even at the small firm level, involves a nuanced and complex set of skills that take many years to acquire and refine. Those who have practiced less than five years are just beginning to develop their lawyering capabilities and have much to learn. Of those first five years of practice, much of it is spent performing legal research, far from the flesh and blood issues faced by practicing lawyers.[83] With all due respect to our law professors, their limited practice experience means that when they exhort their students to "think like a lawyer," very few of them have practiced long enough to know first hand how practicing lawyers think.[84] As such, it is very difficult for academic lawyers to impart through first hand knowledge the mores and practices of the profession about which they teach.[85] Law schools pursue the very laudable goal of having a diverse student body on the theory that diversity brings a variety of perspectives that enhance learning. Unfortunately, most law schools do not pursue a faculty that is *diverse in practical experience*, preferring instead to consistently hire those with little experience in practice. Just as a non-diverse student body diminishes the educational experience in law school, so too does a faculty that is not diverse in practice experience.

Third, law schools are primarily academic institutions.[86] Decisions on promotion and tenure are primarily dictated by academic output, usually meaning the production of law review articles.[87] Law schools recruit and reward faculty members for research, not teaching. There is little, if anything, to be gained by a faculty member who seeks pedagogical reform.[88] Indeed, a non-tenured faculty member seeking to rock the pedagogical boat may be putting his or her academic career at risk. Given the rewards of research and the career risks of promoting teaching reform from within the academy, it is not surprising that most law faculty spend most of their time and energy on research instead of training the next generation of the profession.

Finally, law professors have good reason to be happy with the status quo. Teaching at a law school is a coveted job. Once tenured, law professors have secure jobs, are well compensated,[89] and hold positions of status within both the legal world and society in general. As stated by Nancy Rapoport:

> There's no question that life for a tenured professor at a research university has to be one of the all-time best deals in the world: as long as the university can afford to keep running ... the freedom that the professor has is unparalleled. No boss can dictate to the professor what her field of research should be; most of the time, the professor teaches in areas that complement her research interests; and the service components of the job are often interesting.... Even another of the all-time great jobs ... federal judge ... pales in comparison. The lifetime tenure is the same, but the cases before the judge somewhat dictate the issues that the judge gets to consider.[90]

Why on earth would anyone rock *that* boat? Regrettably, when it comes to examining legal education and what is good for law students and the public, legal educators by and large do not think like lawyers at all. That is, they do not think like people who objectively analyze a problem, break it down into its component parts, and seek a rational and effective solution. Instead, they think like people who are protecting their turf.[91] Despite the obvious shortcomings of the current system, it has its comforts, at least if you are on the professor's side of the podium, and no one in legal academia is penalized for going along with the status quo.[92]

In this environment, it is extremely unlikely that meaningful change will come from within the academy. Since the 1930s, critics including Karl Llewellyn, the father and co-author of the Uniform Commercial Code, and Jerome Frank, Second Circuit court judge, have brought trenchant critiques offering practical solutions to foster better lawyer training in law school.[93] These critiques have gone largely unheeded in legal academia.[94] In recognition of this reality, John Elson, a clinical professor at Northwestern University Law School and a former member of the ABA's Law School Accreditation Committee, has said that:

> [S]ignificant reform in legal education will not come from the voluntary efforts of the leadership of either the law schools or the ABA Section of Legal Education. It will only happen if the leadership of the legal profession ... use their considerable authority to compel law schools to change.[95]

The practicing bar and the judiciary must take the lead to create meaningful change in legal education. The academy cannot be relied upon to fix a system that works all too well for the professoriate, but not very well for anyone else. For too long, the bench and bar have been uninvolved in addressing the shortcomings of legal education. Practitioners have been intimidated by the professoriate, assuming that they know better than practitioners the best way to educate practicing lawyers. However, they do not. In an article published in 2000 entitled *Letter to a Young Law Student*, Professor Corinne Cooper of the University of Missouri Kansas City Law School discusses law school's "ugly little secret." She writes:

> There is one other thing that I hesitate to mention, but it is a fact of law school life. Your professors are not trained to be educators. We got here mostly by being good law students, not because we have any background in higher education theory. This is true of most of graduate school, but it is even worse for law professors, because very few of us go through the traditional doctoral level educational system where one apprentices under a professor who may actually know something about education.[96]

Having a solid grounding in neither educational theory nor in law practice, the professoriate has little experience in either. The average law school professor was trained neither as an educator nor as an experienced practitioner. They were hired to teach primarily because they were outstanding law students.[97] Despite all of their other attributes, in general they know little of practice, receive insufficient feedback as to whether their training is effective, and do not have sufficient personal knowledge in either education or law practice to draw upon in their teaching. It is hard to imagine a less rational system to train new attorneys.

III. Remedies

So the question remains: how to make it better? Recently, there have been signs of hope for an improved and more practice-based brand of legal education. In January 2007, the Carnegie Foundation published its long awaited study on legal education.[98] The Foundation's report echoes the need for the changes that many thoughtful and conscientious observers have been seeking for years. After an extensive survey and review of many law schools, the Foundation concluded that while law school provides its students with important analytical tools, substantial changes are called for, including a curriculum that integrates practical with doctrinal training and a movement towards the medical school training model.[99]

In early 2007, the Clinical Legal Education Association (CLEA) published a multi-year comprehensive study of the existing and best practices in legal education.[100] The study found "the unfortunate reality is that law schools are simply not committed to making their best efforts to prepare all of their students to enter the practice settings that await them"[101] and urged, amongst other things, that legal education would better serve the public if it included a mandatory period of supervised practice before full bar admission.[102]

Further, Harvard Law School recently announced that it is revamping its first year law curriculum to include a greater practical skills component.[103] Included in this new curriculum is a required problem solving course that crosses substantive lines where students, in teams or individually, address fact-intensive problems as they arise in the world and are required to generate solutions.[104]

Finally, in November 2006, Stanford Law School announced changes to the second and third year curricula that combine the study of other disciplines with team-oriented, problem-solving techniques and expanded clinical training. According to Stanford, this change "is being driven by the new demands on modern lawyers, which are fundamentally different from those present when the law school curriculum was formed."[105] Among the other innovations in the Stanford curriculum is a "clinical rotation" where students take only a clinic during a particular quarter—with no competing exams or classes. This approach mirrors the way that medical students have been trained as doctors for the past century."[106]

Harvard's and Stanford's additional focus on legal skills are promising signs, but are only small steps towards a solution. There have been promising signs in the past that have made little headway due to delay-and-stall tactics by the academy.[107] Given the history of delay, avoidance, and denial in the academy, we have little confidence that Harvard's and Stanford's initiatives will advance beyond their nascent stages or even be taken seriously.[108] In particular, pressure is needed from outside the academy, for if the history of legal education has taught us anything, it is that change is almost always resisted.[109] If consistent pressure to change is not sustained on the academy, these initiatives will die a neglected death.

In addition to the changes suggested by Carnegie, the CLEA, Harvard, and Stanford, I offer three suggested starting points.

A. *Medical School Model for Third Year*

The third year of law school is a waste of time and needs to be radically restructured. After two years of pedagogical abuse, third year students have had enough. The evidence, both empirical and anecdotal, is that many of them have mentally checked out and when they do physically attend their classes they are bored and unprepared.[110] The students resent having to suffer one more year of classes and the professors resent the students who, no longer fearful of flunking out, show up unprepared and uninterested.[111]

According to Stanford Law School Dean Larry Kramer:

> Talk to any lawyer or law school graduate and they will tell you they were increasingly disengaged in their second and third years ... because the second and third year curriculum is for the most part repeating what they did in their first year and adds little of intellectual and professional value. They learn more doctrine, which is certainly valuable, but in a way that is inefficient and progressively less useful. The upper years, as presently configured, are a lost opportunity to teach today's lawyers things they need to know. Lawyers need to be educated more broadly—with courses beyond the traditional law school curriculum—if they are to serve their clients and society well.[112]

Law schools do not have resources to waste and should not be wasting students' limited resources. The existing reality is that the third year of law school is, at best, a massive underutilization and, at worst, a frivolous waste of time, energy, and money that could be used for more practical training. The third year should be based on the medical school model of higher clinical and practical concentrations. Thoughtful educators, and now the Carnegie Foundation, have advocated that practical and doctrinal training be integrated throughout the curriculum and that skills training be elevated to a position of greater parity with doctrinal classes.[113] It should be a source of embarrassment to the legal teaching establishment that despite overwhelming evidence showing the need for change, legal educators have not embraced reform.

B. Greater Balance between Scholarship and Clinical Training

In order to create a greater balance between scholarship and practical training, law school resources and faculty incentives should be redirected in part from scholarship to teaching and, in particular, to clinical and practical teaching. Promotion and tenure of law professors is almost entirely dependent upon successful publication in law reviews.[114] It is well known that legal scholarship has become increasingly theoretical and removed from the concerns of practitioners and of little influence with the bench or bar. Roger C. Cramton, former president of the American Association of Law Schools, claims that the scholarly legal writings:

> [A]re not as directly applicable to the problems practitioners face, and because they frequently employ a scholarly jargon and theoretical framework that practitioners do not understand, they are of much less utility to the bench and bar and that [a]s American law schools become more abstract, theoretical, and academic, the role of student-edited reviews diminishes along with close ties to the world of practice.[115]

Once written and used for promotion or tenure, these scholarly articles are almost always ignored.[116] In addition, because these articles are not peer reviewed, the quality of the scholarship is sometimes suspect and has come under increasing scrutiny.[117] Judge Harry Edwards, of the District of Columbia Circuit Court of Appeals has written that "judges, administrators, legislators, and practitioners have little use for much of the scholarship that is now produced by members of the academy."[118] Judge Richard Posner of the Seventh Circuit Court of Appeals has written: "How good is this scholarship? Some of it is good, but much of it is embarrassingly bad, and the overall impression is of enormous variance."[119] And Judge Laurence Silberman, of the District of Columbia Circuit Court of Appeals has characterized the writings contained in law reviews as "dominated by [the] rather exotic offerings of increasingly out-of-touch faculty members."[120]

When was the last time that a legal practitioner, when faced with a thorny legal problem, trotted off to the law library to research an answer in a law review article? That huge investment of time and energy in researching and drafting scholarly articles with little impact can be more effectively utilized for the betterment of a larger audience, law students and the public. Scholarship, of course, has an important place in law school and always should. What I suggest, however, is that a sizable portion of professor-hours now spent on scholarship with little impact, be reallocated to the training of law students in practicums, clinics, and other hands-on programs which have a much larger impact. Such change would need to come incrementally and will require some changes to who law schools hire and how law is taught. It will also necessitate the broadening of the education of many current law professors to include an understanding of the practice of law. The hours put into the production of law review articles with little impact represent a huge underutilized resource of time and energy that can be turned into beneficial practical training.

C. Limit the Reliance on the Overused Socratic-Casebook Method

Move away from the Socratic-Casebook method after the first year. It is a highly inefficient way to learn the law. If there is too much law to learn, as professors always complain, then we need to move to a teaching method that can teach more law in less time. Socratic-Casebook is not that method. After the terror of the first year has abated, students are bored with the Socratic give and take, even if it is well conducted. If our law students have not gotten skills of case analysis after a full year of it, then odds are that two more years of it will not matter. The relatively high failure rate when recent law graduates take the bar exam only highlights the inefficiencies of the current teaching methodologies.[121] Let us get on with the business of teaching students the law in a comprehensive and efficient manner. The Socratic-Casebook method is not it.

IV. Conclusion

The American justice system is premised upon a search for the truth. A good legal education should aim to produce lawyers who seek and have the tools to discover truth. Historically, as a profession, attorneys have not shied away from the truth. Nor have attorneys shied away from the hard corrective work that is sometimes necessitated by advancements in the law and changes in society at large. This quest for truth and progress has been one of the ennobling features of the legal profession.

But it is now time, and long past due, to face the truth about legal education and, more importantly, to do something about it. The current system of legal education is not producing competent lawyers because it is out of date and only held in place by a self-perpetuating, entrenched professoriate. A plethora of studies and educational research shows that legal educators have the knowledge and the means to build a better, more competent lawyer. The entire bench, bar, and academia have the ability to do a much better job. The more important question for the future of legal education and our profession is: does the profession have the will to change?

Notes

* I thank Professors Michael Distelhorst of Capital University Law School, Lawrence Krieger of Florida State University Law School, and Susan Daicoff of Florida Coastal Law School for their review and insights about this article. They are the pathcutters. I thank my wife Lisa, who has heard it all before, but she still keeps listening.

1. This attitude of "If it was good enough for me, it's good enough for you," condemns future generations to the mistakes and inefficiencies of the past and fails to consider changes that have occurred since the time when "it was good enough for me." While the old adage is catchy, it does nothing to advance improvement. Another way of looking at the old adage might be "if it was ineffective enough for me, it's ineffective enough for you."

2. First year law school enrollment at American law schools appears to have been at an all-time high in academic year of 2006–2007, with 48,937 enrolled first year law students. ABA, First Year and Total J.D. Enrollment, http://www.abanet.org/legaled/statistics/charts/stats%20-%206.pdf (last visited Sept. 15, 2007). For the academic year of 2005–2006, American law schools awarded 43,883 J.D. or LL.B degrees. ABA, http://www.abanet.org/legaled/statistics/charts/stats%20-%207.pdf (last visited Sept. 15, 2007). This total is 1211 more than in 2004–2005, 3859 more than in 2003–2004, and 5008 more than in 2002–2003. *Id.*

3. In 2007, the Clinical Legal Education Association (CLEA) concluded that the "unfortunate reality is that law schools are simply not committed to making their best efforts to prepare all of their

students to enter the practice settings that await them. This concern is not a recent development." ROY STUCKEY ET AL., CLINICAL LEGAL EDUC. ASS'N, BEST PRACTICES FOR LEGAL EDUCATION: A VISION AND A ROADMAP 18 (2007). Law school education, unlike other professional schools which emphasize the training of practitioners, evidences its lack of interest in the preparation of legal practitioners by the marginal placement of clinical training in the curriculum.

> With some important exceptions, the underdeveloped area of legal pedagogy is clinical training, which typically is not a required part of the curriculum and is taught by instructors who are themselves not regular members of the faculty. Compared with the centrality of supervised practice, with mentoring and feedback, in the education of physicians and nurses or the importance of supervised practice in the preparation of teachers and social workers, the relative marginality of clinical training in law schools is striking.

WILLIAM M. SULLIVAN ET AL., EDUCATING LAWYERS: PREPARATION FOR THE PROFESSION OF LAW 24 (2007).

4. Christopher Columbus Langdell, once dean of Harvard Law School, "believed that law should be taught, not as a skilled trade, but rather as a science." Jeffrey D. Jackson, *Socrates and Langdell in Legal Writing: Is the Socratic Method a Proper Tool For Legal Writing Courses?*, 43 CAL. W. L. REV. 267, 270 (2007). As a means to this end, Langdell "introduced the case method of law study, in which students learned the law by reading and discussing cases to extract the scientific legal principles." Id. The case method of study, or "Socratic method" involved:

> Having a student analyze each of the cases and then asking a series of questions designed to draw out the legal content of the case. Langdell and the students would then work to synthesize and contrast the cases so that, ultimately, the entire area of the law would be made clear.

Id.

5. Bruce A. Kimball, *Christopher Langdell: The Case of an "Abomination' in Teaching Practice*, THOUGHT & ACTION, Summer 2004, at 23, 24.

6. See SULLIVAN ET AL., *supra* note 3.

7. A survey of law professors in 1994–1995 by Professor Steven I. Friedland sought to find out, amongst other things, the frequency with which the Socratic method was used. Steven I. Friedland, *How We Teach: A Survey of Teaching Techniques in American Law Schools*, 20 SEATTLE U. L. REV. 1, 1–2 (1996) (concluding the data indicates that the Socratic method is entrenched and dominates legal education). The survey found that the Socratic method, Langdell's signature pedagogical device, was utilized by 97% of professors teaching first year classes, 93% of professors teaching upper level classes, 67% of professors teaching seminars, and 54% of professors teaching skills courses. *Id.* at 27. Of the professors using the Socratic method, 30% used it "most of the time" (defined as between 80 and 100% of the time) and 41% used it "often" (defined as 50 to 79% of the time). *Id.* at 28. Of the remainder, 21% used it "sometimes" (defined as 20 to 49% of the time) and only 5% used it "rarely" (defined as 5 to 19% of the time). *Id.* Morrison Torrey, Professor of Law at DePaul University College of Law writes:

> The Socratic Method advocates seem oblivious to, or else attempt to minimize, the negative side of the very attributes they tout.... When the pro-Socratic Method team claims it is an "active" method because a student is responding to a series of questions, they either ignore the fact that the remaining eighty-nine students in the class are passive or they optimistically think all students are ... participating "vicariously." In reality, however, I suspect students are too busy being relieved for not being the immediate victim, desperately hoping they will not be called upon next, to absorb much of the dialogue occurring, much less play along in this "exciting game."

Morrison Torrey, *You Call That Education?*, 19 WIS. WOMEN'S L.J. 93, 103 (2004).

8. *See* sources cited *supra* note 7. *See also infra* notes 13–15.

9. See Michael Hunter Schwartz, *Teaching Law By Design: How Learning Theory and Instructional Design Can Inform and Reform Law Teaching*, 38 SAN DIEGO L. REV. 347, 360 (2001) ("[L]aw school teaching has changed little in the past 130 years."); Russell L. Weaver, *Langdell's Legacy: Living with the Case Method*, 36 VILL. L. REV. 517, 519–20 (1991) (asserting that many of the problems of law school teaching are attributable to the case method).

10. Neuroscience is the study of the nervous system which includes the "brain, the spinal cord, and networks of sensory nerve cells, or neurons, throughout the body." Society for Neuroscience,

What is Neuroscience?, http://www.sfn.org/index.cfm?pagename=whatIsNeuroscience&section=aboutNeuroscience (last visited Sept. 15, 2007).

11. James B. Levy, *As a Last Resort, Ask the Students: What They Say Makes Someone an Effective Law Teacher*, 58 ME. L. REV. 49, 51–52 (2006).

> Because of recent technological advances that allow neuroscientists to peer into the inner workings of the brain, we now have scientific evidence that confirms the essential role socio-emotional considerations play in all cognitive activity, including learning. More specifically, things such as teacher expectations, support, encouragement, and warmth toward students can have a profound effect on their success in school. Law school teachers, however, have been slow to appreciate the power and importance of these considerations.

Id.

12. *Id.* Different students have different learning styles and different methods of processing information. *See, e.g.*, Jayne Elizabeth Zanglein & Katherine Austin Stalcup, *Te(a)chnology: A Web-Based Instruction in Legal Skills Courses*, 49 J. LEGAL EDUC. 480, 482–92 (1999) (discussing the Learning Style Inventory which sets forth various factors that impact a student's ability to learn and characterizes students as "global" learners or "analytic" learners).

13. *See* Rogelio Lasso, *From the Paper Chase to the Digital Chase: Technology and the Challenge of Teaching 21st Century Students*, 43 SANTA CLARA L. REV. 1, 117–18 (2002).

> Studies demonstrate that barriers to learning have more to do with whether the [teaching] methodology is teacher or student oriented.... Teacher-centered pedagogy impedes success in the classroom.... Teacher-centered learning requires all students to adjust their diverse learning styles to fit the professor's teaching style. This does not take into account that different students learn differently.

Id. See also Robin A. Boyle & Rita Dunn, *Teaching Law Students Through Individual Learning Styles*, 62 ALB. L. REV. 213, 215–16 (1998) (discussing the significant improvement upon student performance when students were taught and learned utilizing their respective "learning styles" as opposed to a one-size-fits-all teaching strategy); Daniel J. Givelber et al., *Learning Through Work: An Empirical Study of Legal Internship*, 45 J. LEGAL EDUC. 1, 47 (1995) ("Earlier studies suggest that lawyers attribute much more of their skills education to work experience than to law school in general and more to summer and part-time work than to law school clinical and simulation courses."); Ursula H. Weigold, *The Attorney-Client Privilege as an Obstacle to the Professional and Ethical Development of Law Students*, 33 PEPP. L. REV. 677, 678 (2006) ("In most American law schools, students may graduate having very little practice or experience in many of the skills that lawyers must possess to represent clients competently and ethically.").

14. *See* Pamela Lysaght & Cristina D. Lockwood, *Writing-Across-the-Law-School Curriculum: Theoretical Justifications, Curricular Implications*, 2 J. ASS'N LEGAL WRITING DIRECTORS 73, 76–77 (2004) ("Law schools have seemingly eschewed learning theories in developing their curricula. This is surprising in light of the central mission of the legal academy—to provide students with the necessary knowledge to competently enter the legal profession."). *See also* Lila A. Coleburn & Julia C. Spring, *Socrates Unbound: Developmental Perspectives on the Law School Experience*, 24 LAW & PSYCHOL. REV. 5, 23 (2000); Jay M. Feinman & Marc Feldman, *Achieving Excellence: Mastery Learning in Legal Education*, 35 J. LEGAL EDUC. 528, 529 (1985) ("Law professors have long believed that educational theorists, professors of education or educational psychology, are either charlatans or primitives. That belief is arrogant and anti-intellectual."); Marie Stefanini Newman, *Not the Evil TWEN: How Online Course Management Software Supports Non-Linear Learning in Law Schools*, 5 J. HIGH TECH. L. 183 (2005) (asserting that law professors have been resistant to embrace new teaching strategies); Deborah L. Rhode, *Legal Education: Professional Interests and Public Values*, 34 IND. L. REV. 23 (2000) [hereinafter Rhode, Legal Education].

15. *See* G. Andrew H. Benjamin et al., *The Role of Legal Education in Producing Psychological Distress Among Law Students and Lawyers*, 1986 AM. B. FOUND. RES. J. 225 (1986); Levy, *supra* note 11, at 54 ("Much has been written about how stressful the law school experience is for students and, in particular, how stressful they find the Socratic method."); Kennon M. Sheldon & Lawrence S. Krieger, *Does Legal Education Have Undermining Effects on Law Students? Evaluating Changes in Motivation, Values, and Well-Being*, 22 BEHAV. SCI. & L. 261 (2004).

16. *See* Friedland, *supra* note 7. *See also* Gerald F. Hess, *Heads and Hearts: The Teaching and Learning Environment in Law School*, 52 J. LEGAL EDUC. 75, 79 (2002) ("Unfortunately psychological

distress, dissatisfaction, and substance abuse that begin in law school follow many graduates into practice."); Rhode, *Legal Education*, *supra* note 14, at 36 ("Although the psychological profile of entering law school students matches that of the general public, an estimated twenty to forty percent leave with some psychological dysfunction including depression, substance abuse, and various stress related disorders.").

17. *See* Robert P. Schuwerk, *The Law Professor as Fiduciary: What Duties Do We Owe to Our Students*, 45 S. TEX. L. REV. 753 (2004).

> Most law professors are not familiar with the ever-increasing literature documenting the extreme levels of mental illness and substance abuse that develop among law students while in law school.... Many of those who are familiar with this body of work either do not believe that it is true or else attribute it to causes outside of law school and therefore, beyond our control.

Id. at 764–66. *See also* James J. Alfini & Joseph N. Van Vooren, *Is There a Solution to the Problem of Lawyer Stress?: The Law School Perspective*, 10 J. L. & HEALTH 61, 66 (1995–1996) ("It may seem surprising that the legal academy has given so little attention to such an enormous problem in the legal profession. It becomes less surprising, however, when one considers how little attention law schools give to the current structure and operating realities of the legal profession itself."); Lawrence S. Krieger, *Institutional Denial About the Dark Side of Law School, and Fresh Empirical Guidance for Constructively Breaking the Silence*, 52 J. LEGAL EDUC. 112, 112 (2002) ("In the day-to-day business of legal education there is remarkably little evidence that we are aware of the unhealthy-unhappy-law-student (lawyer) problem.").

18. There appears to be widespread agreement that the practice of law is becoming increasingly stressful. *See, e.g.*, Michael H. Hoeflich, *Legal Ethics and Depression*, 74 J. KAN. B.J. 33, 35 (2005) ("Increasingly, the "law business' has become more competitive and far more stressful. Standards of civility have dropped. Collaborative work among lawyers has become more difficult. Hours worked, particularly among young lawyers, have increased."); William E. Livingston, *De-stressing the Profession*, 81 MICH. B.J. 24, 26 (2002) ("Work overload, competition, dealing with difficult people, and time pressures are stressors found in many professions. Unique to law, however, are the legal role conflicts, an adversarial system of justice, and certain areas of practice with a more pronounced level of conflict.").

19. *See* Austin Sarat, *Enactments of Professionalism: A Study of Judges' and Lawyers' Accounts of Ethics and Civility in Litigation*, 67 FORDHAM L. REV. 809, 829 (1998) ([C]ost-benefit thinking leads to great cost-cutting pressures, to the point that they often feel that the client is unwilling to pay for sufficient preparation."); Patrick J. Schiltz, *On Being a Happy, Healthy, and Ethical Member of an Unhappy, Unhealthy, and Unethical Profession*, 52 VAND. L. REV. 871, 900 (1999) [hereinafter Schiltz, *On Being a Happy*] ("Clients insist on getting good work at low hourly rates. They also insist that lawyers minimize the amount of time that they devote to each file to hold down costs.").

20. One candidate for the Presidency of the Texas State Bar Association summed up the increasing stresses felt by practitioners due to advances in technology as follows:

> Though technological advances have brought much good to our firm, these innovations have in many ways made our individual lives more stressful. Many clients have come to expect 24-hour-a-day access to their lawyers because of cell phones and email. Also, because of instant access they seem to want an instant answer.... Lawyers who cannot strike a good balance between their work life and their personal life tend to burn out.

State Bar of Texas Election: President-elect Candidates Discuss the Issues, 67 TEX. B.J. 268, 271–72 (2004) (quoting President-elect candidate Eduardo Rodriguez).

21. Clara N. Carson & Barbara A. Curran, *Growth and Gender Diversity: A Statistical Profile of the Legal Profession in 2000*, RESEARCHING L., Winter 2005, at 1.

22. *Id.*

23. Some have argued that there is not an oversupply of lawyers but, rather, a misdistribution; that there are substantial unmet legal needs especially amongst the economically disadvantaged. For example, Deborah L. Rhode, a Professor at Stanford Law, has written that the "vast majority of legal needs among low income households are unmet, and many middle income families are priced out of the market for attorney's assistance." Deborah L. Rhode, *Too Much Law, Too Little Justice: Too Much Rhetoric, Too Little Reform*, 11 GEO. J. LEGAL ETHICS 989, 992 (1999) [hereinafter Rhode, *Too Much Law*].

24. However, owing to the peculiar marketplace for legal education, law schools have largely been insulated from the harshness of the marketplace. *See* John Mixon & Gordon Otto, *Continuous Quality Improvement, Law, and Legal Education*, 43 EMORY L. J. 393, 443 (1994) ("Many law schools are

immune from market forces. National law schools' status ensures an abundant supply of applicants who can afford the price of admission. Many regional schools are publicly supported, so tax dollars continue to flow, regardless of whether students, graduates, the profession, or taxpayers are satisfied."); *see also* Richard A. Matasar, *The Rise and Fall of American Legal Education*, 49 N.Y.L. SCH. L. REV. 465 (2004). Matasar states that the law school market is protected by the following factors:

> (1) educational cost is highly leveraged, with students borrowing most of the cost of their education; (2) lenders have been willing to lend to any credit-worthy student; (3) lenders have not been risk averse because substantial portions of students' loans are federally guaranteed; (4) lawyer salaries have been ample to support the debt service that students accumulate in law school; and (5) students have been able to rely on family resources to support them where loans fall short.

Id. at 474–75.

25. ABA, ABA Approved Law Schools, http://www.abanet.org/legaled/approvedlawschools/year.html (last visited May 25, 2007).

26. In 2006, the Council of the Section of Legal Education and Admissions to the Bar ("the Council") granted full approval to Barry University and Florida International University. Provisional approval was granted to Charleston School of Law, Faulkner University, LaVerne College, and Liberty University. *See* ABA, Legal Education and Admissions to the Bar, http://www.abanet.org/legaled/ (last visited May 25, 2007).

27. *See* Keith R. Fisher, *The Higher Calling: Regulation of Lawyers Post-Enron*, 37 U. MICH. J.L. REFORM 1017, 1030 (2004) ("Today, lawyers in private practice, ranging from solo practitioners to partners in large, elite urban law firms, are all endeavoring one way or another to peddle usually fungible services (with rare exceptions) into a saturated, highly competitive market for a shrinking client base."); Schiltz, *On Being a Happy*, *supra* note 19, at 899–900 ("As the number of lawyers has soared, competition for clients has become ferocious."); Matthew S. Winings, *The Power of Law Firm Partnership: Why Dominant Rainmakers Will Impede the Immediate, Widespread Implementation of an Autocratic Management Structure*, 55 DRAKE L. REV. 165, 177 (2006) ("Over the past few decades, the number of lawyers has grown dramatically. Consequently, there is greater competition for clients.").

28. *But see* Deborah L. Rhode, *The Profession and Its Discontents*, 61 OHIO ST. L.J. 1335, 1339 (2000) [hereinafter Rhode, *The Profession*] (stating that the increasing competitive pressures in law practice can produce positive effects, such as reducing prices and promoting efficiency).

29. As with all areas of commerce, there will always be a cheaper purveyor of goods or services. Unfortunately, there is nothing in law or commerce that requires that cheaper equals better. Similarly, there is nothing that mandates that more costly equals better. Given the subtleties of the attorney-client relationship and the high level of skill required for the rendering of many legal services, selecting a lawyer on price alone is often a mistake.

30. William H. Rehnquist, Chief Justice, Dedicatory Address, *The Legal Profession Today*, 62 IND. L.J. 151, 155 (1987).

31. *See* Carl T. Bogus, *The Death of an Honorable Profession*, 71 IND. L.J. 911, 922 (1996) (explaining that "padding time records is a genuine professional plague, one not confined to a few firms or even a few lawyers within most firms. It is a silent epidemic: the realization of what has occurred is so unwelcome that it is largely ignored."); Joseph E. La Rue, *Redeeming the Lawyer's Time: A Proposal for a Shift in How Attorneys Think About—And Utilize—Time*, 20 NOTRE DAME J. L. ETHICS & PUB. POL'Y 473, 478 (2006) ("Lying to clients about their bills [by lawyers] has become so widespread it is now said to have reached epidemic proportions. This has caused even the most ethically-minded associates to feel that they must lie, or else place themselves at a competitive disadvantage when bonuses and raises are determined."); Lisa G. Lerman, *Lying to Clients*, 138 U. PA. L. REV. 659, 665 (1990) (reporting that lawyers use "pervasive deception relating to client billing, some examples involving large amounts of money. These include stories of padding bills, billing two clients for the same time, doing unnecessary work to run the meter, and failing to disclose the basis of the bill.").

32. E.g., Roger C. Cramton, *Furthering Justice by Improving the Adversary System and Making Lawyers More Accountable*, 70 FORDHAM L. REV. 1599, 1602 (2002) ("Numerous studies show that plaintiffs' lawyers in civil cases and underpaid defense counsel in criminal cases often sacrifice their clients' interests in favor of quick settlements or guilty pleas that maximize the lawyer's effort/earnings calculus.").

33. Krista Riddick Rogers, *Comment, Promoting a Paradigm of Collaboration in an Adversarial Legal System: An Integrated Problem Solving Perspective for Shifting Prevailing Attitudes from Competition to*

Cooperation Within the Legal Profession, 6 BARRY L. REV. 137, 137 (asserting that lawyers' adversarial mindset contributes to the legal profession crisis because the "prevailing attitude of 'anything to get ahead' or 'winning at all costs' often manifests itself in intense competition for clients as well as gamesmanship-type tactics and overly aggressive unprofessional behavior often exercised under the guise of 'zealously representing a client.'").

34. Charles I. Nelson & Justin L. Garrett, II, *Beyond Mere Ethics*, 67 ALA. LAW. 180, 180 (2006) (stating that there have been a number of reasons assigned to the decline in professionalism "including the unique stresses of modern society, pressures to increase billable hours, increased competition for clients as lawyer advertising became legal, scorched-earth litigation tactics, and a prevailing attitude that winning is everything."). See David A. Kessler, *Professional Asphyxiation: Why the Legal Profession is Gasping for Breath*, 10 GEO. J. LEGAL ETHICS 455, 483 (1997) ("It is often the case that the lawyer subjugates her own sense of morality for that of the client's, and thereby loses a degree of autonomy enjoyed by previous generations of members of the legal profession."). *See also* Robert W. Gordon, *Money! Power! Ambition Gone Awry!*, LEGAL AFF., Mar.–Apr. 2006, at 26, 32 ("The last thing most lawyers wanted to advertise [in the 1980s] was their superior scruples as monitors of client conduct. They did not wish to present themselves as proponents of legal reforms that their clients might not welcome.").

35. Nancy McCarthy, *Pessimism for the Future: Given a Second Chance, Half of the State's Attorneys Would Not Become Lawyers*, CAL. B. J., Nov. 1994, at 1, available at http://www.calbar.ca.gov/calbar/pdfs/members/1994-Futures-CBJ.pdf (explaining that California attorneys are pessimistic about their profession, and half say that if they had another chance, they would not have become lawyers).

36. *See* Susan Daicoff, *Lawyer, Know Thyself: A Review of Empirical Research on Attorney Attributes Bearing on Professionalism*, 46 AM. U. L. REV. 1337, 1344–45 nn. 16–17 (1997) (explaining that law has become a "business" rather than a profession because of a heightened emphasis on money, and that attorneys and clients both feel less loyalty to law firms).

37. Rehnquist, *supra* note 30, at 155.

38. *See supra* note 3 and accompanying text.

39. *See infra* notes 42–43 and accompanying text.

40. *See* ABA, Law School Tuition, http://www.abanet.org/legaled/statistics/charts/stats%20-%205.pdf (last visited Sept. 15, 2007).

41. ABA COMM'N ON LOAN REPAYMENT & FORGIVENESS, LIFTING THE BURDEN: LAW STUDENT DEBT AS A BARRIER TO PUBLIC SERVICE 10 (2003) [hereinafter COMM'N ON LOAN REPAYMENT & FORGIVENESS], *available at* http://www.abanet.org/legalservices/downloads/lrap/lrapfinalreport.pdf.

42. David Franklin, *Trials of Socrates*, SLATE, July 31, 1997, http://www.slate.com/id/3133/.

43. *Id.*; *see also* ROBERT STEVENS, LEGAL EDUCATION IN AMERICA FROM THE 1850s TO THE 1980s 63 (1983) ("The vast success of Langdell's method enabled the establishment of large-size class. Although numbers fluctuated, Langdell in general managed Harvard with one professor for every seventy-five students; the case method combined with the Socratic method enabled classes to expand to the size of the largest lecture hall."); Benjamin et al., *supra* note 15, at 250 (citing Roger C. Cramton, *The Current State of Law Curriculum*, 32 J. LEGAL EDUC. 321, 333 (1982)); Steven K. Berenson, *Institutional Professionalism for Lawyers: Realizing the Virtues of Civic Professionalism*, 109 W. VA. L. REV. 67, 83 (2006) (reviewing WILLIAM M. SULLIVAN, WORK AND INTEGRITY: THE CRISIS AND PROMISE OF PROFESSIONALISM IN AMERICA (2005)); Andrew Hacker, *The Shame of Professional Schools*, 32 J. LEGAL EDUC. 278, 278 (1982).

44. *See* Philip J. Closius, *The Incredible Shrinking Law School*, 31 U. TOL. L. REV. 581, 584 (2000) ("In many academic settings, universities have utilized the law school as a 'cash cow,' with 'excess' law income being used to fund other programs at the University."); Stephen M. Feldman, *The Transformation of an Academic Discipline: Law Professors in the Past and Future (or Toy Story Too)*, 54 J. LEGAL EDUC. 471, 495 (2004) ("The economic profitability of law schools seems likely to induce universities to maintain them."); Matasar, *supra* note 24, at 482 ("Universities come to appreciate that many law students will pay without regard to price; they urge (and even may require) prices to rise."); Lawrence Ponoroff, *Law School/Central University Relations. Sleeping with the Enemy*, 34 U. TOL. L. REV. 147, 147 (2002) ("There is a pervasive attitude among law faculty that ... the central university is robbing the law school blind."); Richard A. Posner, *Legal Scholarship Today*, 45 STAN. L. REV. 1647, 1655

(1993) ("Relative to most other departments in a university, law schools are awash in tuition income and in gifts from wealthy alums."); Schwartz, *supra* note 9, at 361 ("Law schools traditionally do well economically in large part because, unlike most graduate schools, classes ... range in size from 50 to 120 students."); Randall T. Shepard, *From Students to Lawyers: Joint Ventures in Legal Learning for the Academy, Bench, and Bar*, 31 IND. L. REV. 445, 448–49 (1998) ("Until quite recently, for example, George Washington University siphoned off forty percent of its law school's revenue."); George B. Shepherd & William G. Shepherd, *Scholarly Restraints? ABA Accreditation and Legal Education*, 19 CARDOZO L. REV. 2091, 2106 (1998) ("Viewing the professional school as a cash cow, the university might require that the professional school make payments to the university that far exceed the university's overhead.... Some universities treat their law schools in this manner, using revenue from law school students and alumni to subsidize the university's other programs."); James P. White, *Legal Education in the Era of Change: Law School Autonomy*, 1987 DUKE L. J. 292, 304 n.46 (1987) ("Many still complain that the parent university siphons off too much of the [law school's] excess profits."); William A. Wines, *Lawyer Proliferation and the Social Responsibility Model*, 39 J. LEGAL EDUC. 231, 237 (1989).

45. *See supra* note 44 and accompanying text.

46. COMM'N ON LOAN REPAYMENT & FORGIVENESS, *supra* note 41, at 14.

47. *Id.* at 9.

48. See Margaret Martin Barry, Jon C. Dubin & Peter A. Joy, *Clinical Education for This Millennium: The Third Wave*, 7 CLINICAL L. REV. 1, 21 (2000) (arguing that the higher expense of clinical legal education is associated with lower student to faculty ratios and a "more intensive, and presumably better, learning environments for students."); see also Dionne L. Koller, *Legal Writing and Academic Support: Timing is Everything*, 53 CLEV. ST. L. REV. 51, 60 (2005–2006) (arguing that larger student to faculty ratios in law school further increase the difficulty of teaching effectively and providing meaningful academic support). *See generally America's Best Graduate Programs 2008*, U.S.NEWS, http://gradschools.usnews.rankingsandreviews.com/usnews/edu/grad/rankings/about/indexbrief.php.

49. Franklin, *supra* note 42.

50. Compare Alfred L. Brophy, *The Emerging Importance of Law Review Rankings for Law School Rankings, 2003–2007*, 78 U. COLO. L. REV. 35, 37 (2007) ("There is increasing evidence that law schools have bent their practices of admission, expenditures, hiring, and even their modes of reporting to the ABA in response to the *U.S. News* rankings."), with Lorenzo A. Trujillo, *The Relationship Between Law School and the Bar Exam: A Look at Assessment and Student Success*, 78 U. COLO. L. REV. 69, 82 (2007) ("A high ranking in the *U.S. News and World Report* has numerous beneficial effects for a law school.... It helps with alumni contributions, ... gives students a feeling that they are attending a superior school, and allows the school to attract new students of higher caliber.").

51. Samuel H. Pillsbury, *Learning from Journalism*, 3 OHIO ST. J. CRIM. L. 543, 550 (2006) ("To state the obvious, the basic mission of the American law school is to educate for the practice of law. Law schools exist to form new lawyers.").

52. Robert J. Borthwick & Jordan R. Schau, Note, *Gatekeepers of the Profession: An Empirical Profile of the Nation's Law Professors*, 25 U. MICH. J. L. REFORM 191, 193 (1991) ("Law professors are both the gatekeepers and the molders of the profession."); Bethany Rubin Henderson, *Asking the Lost Question: What is the Purpose of Law School?*, 53 J. LEGAL EDUC. 48, 56 (2003) ("The vast majority of state bar associations require that prospective lawyers earn a law school degree in order to be eligible for state bar admission.... Through the admissions process, law schools select who will ultimately be eligible to sit for the bar examination."). The standards used in approving law schools is "founded primarily on the fact that law schools are the gateway to the legal profession." STANDARDS FOR APPROVAL OF LAW SCHOOLS, Preamble (2007), *available at* http://www.abanet.org/legaled/standards/20072008StandardsWebContent/Preamble.pdf.

53. *See* sources cited *supra* note 52.

54. See Marilyn V. Yarbrough, *Closing Remarks, Legal Education at the Threshold of the New Millennium*, 15 ST. JOHN'S J. LEGAL COMMENT 349, 349 (2001) ("The [ABA's] MacCrate Commission was headed by Robert MacCrate from Sullivan & Cromwell a number of years ago and it was composed of judges, legal educators, practicing attorneys and we were charged with developing a continuum of legal education that was actually pre-law through the end of a legal career.").

55. While, on the one hand, the ABA requires all law schools to *offer* clinical and other hands on training opportunities to its students, on the other, it does not require all students *to enroll* in any of

these practical courses. *See* STANDARDS FOR APPROVAL OF LAW SCHOOLS § 302 at 19–21 (2007), *available at* http://www.abanet.org/legaled/standards/20072008StandardsWebContent/Chapter%203.pdf. Indeed, the Interpretations of Standard 302 make clear that "[a] law school need not accommodate every student requesting enrollment in a particular professional skills program." § 302-4 interpretation at 21. Further, "[t]he offering of live-client or real-life experiences may be accomplished through clinics or field placements. A law school need not offer these experiences to every student nor must a law school accommodate every student requesting enrollment in any particular live-client or other real-life practice experience." § 302-5 interpretation at 21.

56. Roy Stuckey, *Why Johnny Can't Practice Law—And What We Can Do About It*, B. EXAMINER, May 2003, at 32, 41 n.8 ("As long as legal educators control the accreditation process, it will not be an effective tool for ensuring adequate preparation to enter the legal profession.").

57. *See* John S. Elson, *Why and How the Practicing Bar Must Rescue American Legal Education from the Misguided Priorities of American Legal Academia*, 64 TENN. L. REV. 1135, 1142 (1997) [hereinafter Elson, *Why and How*]. Elson, who served on the ABA's Accreditation Committee stated that "after eighteen ABA/AALS site inspection visits and two years on the ABA Accreditation Committee, I can say with some assurance that the ABA/AALS inspections give no more than a pretense of systematically reviewing the effectiveness of teaching that actually goes on in the classroom." *Id.*

58. *See* Borthwick & Schau, *supra* note 52, at 193 ("Law, unlike other professions, requires no formal apprenticeship.").

59. *Compare* CAL. BUS. & PROF. CODE § 4996.2(c) (West 2003) ("Each applicant shall furnish evidence satisfactory to the board that he or she ... (c) [h]as had two years of supervised post-master's degree experience."), *with* N.Y. EDUC. LAW § 7704(2)(c) (McKinney 2001) (stating that to qualify for a license as a "licensed master social worker," an applicant must "have at least three years full-time supervised post-graduate clinical social work experience"), *and* OHIO ADMIN. CODE 4757:19-01(C)(1)(e) (West 2004) ("Not less than four hundred clock hours of supervised practicum and/or field experience, with a primary focus on social intervention coordinated by an individual with an advanced degree in social work.").

60. *Compare* CAL. BUS. & PROF. CODE § 2089.5(d) (West 2003) (stating that of the seventy-two weeks of clinical instruction required for a medical license "54 weeks shall be performed in a hospital"), *with* N.Y. EDUC. LAW § 6528(a)(3) (McKinney 2001) (stating the applicant must have completed "one academic year of supervised clinical training under the direction of such medical school"), *and* OFFICE OF THE PROFESSIONS, N.Y. STATE EDUC. DEPT. § 60.3, (2007) (stating that for issuance of a license to practice medicine, an applicant shall have completed at least one year of postgraduate hospital training), *and* OHIO ADMIN. CODE 4731.291 (West 2004).

61. *Compare* CAL. BUS. & PROF. CODE § 5083(a) (West 2003) (stating that three or four years of experience are required, depending on the applicant's educational qualifications), *with* N.Y. EDUC. LAW § 7404(1)(3) (McKinney 2001) (stating that a certified public accountant applicant must "have experience satisfactory to the board and in accordance with the commissioner's regulations"), *and* OFFICE OF THE PROFESSIONS, N.Y. STATE EDUC. DEPT. (REGULATIONS OF THE COMMISSIONER OF EDUCATION) § 70.2 (2007) (stating that to qualify for a license as a certified public accountant, one or two years of experience are required, depending on the applicant's educational qualifications), *and* Ohio Rev. Code Ann. § 4701.06(D)(2)(a) (West 2004) (stating that in order to sit for the CPA exam, the candidate who otherwise meets the educational degree requirements must have "one year of experience satisfactory to the board in any of the following: (i) a public accounting firm; (ii) Government; (iii) Business; (iv) Academia.").

62. *Compare* CAL. BUS. & PROF. CODE § 4980.40(b) (West 2004) (stating that applicants shall possess a doctor's or master's degree from a program that includes a supervised practicum with "a minimum of 150 hours of face-to-face experience counseling individuals, couples, families, or groups."), *with* N.Y. EDUC. LAW § 4403(3)(c) (McKinney 2001) (stating that to qualify for a license as a "licensed mental health counselor," an applicant shall complete a minimum of three thousand hours of post-master's supervised experience relevant to the practice of mental health counseling"), *and* OHIO REV. CODE ANN. § 4757.30(A)(5) (West 2004) (stating that applicants must have "completed a practicum that includes at least three hundred hours of client contact").

63. *Compare* CAL. BUS. & PROF. CODE § 7643 (West 2003) ("In order to qualify for a license as an embalmer, the applicant shall ... (d) Have completed at least two years of apprenticeship ... and while so apprenticed shall have assisted in embalming not fewer than 100 human remains"), *with* N.Y. PUB. HEALTH LAW § 3423(3) (McKinney 2001) ("The department shall issue an undertaker

or embalmer license to those who, upon payment of a fee of ten dollars, qualify in accordance with the provisions of this section, and who pass (an) examination."), *and* N.Y. PUB. HEALTH LAW §3421(4)(c) (McKinney 2001) (stating that an applicant for a license to practice funeral directing must serve a one year period as a registered resident), *and* OHIO REV. CODE ANN. §4717.05(A)(6) (West 2004) (stating that the applicant must have "completed at least one year of apprenticeship under an embalmer licensed in this state and has assisted that person in embalming at least twenty-five dead human bodies").

64. *See* Benjamin et al., *supra* note 15.

65. *Id.*

66. See Schiltz, *On Being a Happy*, *supra* note 19, at 874–81.

67. *Id.*

68. *Id.*

69. Sheldon & Krieger, *supra* note 15, at 262.

70. *See* Schurwerk, *supra* note 17.

71. Most law professors are unaware of the documented levels of mental illness and substance abuse developing among current law students. *Id.* at 764–65. Studies show that students suffer "from one or more of clinical levels of depression, alcohol abuse, or cocaine abuse rising from 8–9% prior to matriculation to 27% after one semester, 34% after two semesters, and 40% after three years, and persisting after students pass the bar and begin practicing law." *Id.*

72. *See id.* at 764–66.

73. "[T]here's very little innovation at the core of legal education. We're still playing Christopher Columbus Langdell's song—not his song of innovation in legal education, but the monotonous refrain of education in the form of Socratic classes and case law." Nancy B. Rapoport, *Eating Our Cake and Having It, Too: Why Real Change Is So Difficult in Law School*, 81 IND. L. J. 359, 366 (2006).

74. Roger C. Cramton, *The Current State of Law Curriculum*, 32 J. LEGAL EDUC. 321, 333–34 (1982); see also Deborah L. Rhode, *Missing Questions: Feminist Perspectives on Legal Education*, 45 STAN. L. REV. 1547 (1993) [hereinafter Rhode, *Missing Questions*] (arguing that Stanford's faculty has created a structure that maximizes faculty autonomy and "keeps messiness at bay").

> The questions I want to ask are typically missing from the day-to-day curricular decisions at most law schools. Are we as educators effectively equipping students to address the needs of clients as clients perceive them? Are we strengthening commitments to ethical decisionmaking and public service? Are we serving faculty interests at the expense of others in the way we structure the educational experience?

Id. at 1548.

75. Rhode, *Missing Questions*, *supra* note 74, at 1549 (quoting David Margolick, *The Trouble with American Law Schools*, N.Y. TIMES, May 22, 1983, at 21.

76. *See* Schuwerk, *supra* note 17, at 761. *See* Torrey, *supra* note 7, at 105–06, for a discussion of the resistance of the professoriate to change. *See* also Elson, *Why and How*, *supra* note 57, at 1135 ("[S]ignificant reform in legal education will not come from the voluntary efforts of the leadership of either the law schools or the ABA Section of Legal Education."); Henderson, *supra* note 52, at 72 ("Law schools' practices are based on tradition, not on a regular assessment and reassessment of the needs of the public, students, and the legal profession. That these practices persist is largely due to a combination of institutional inertia and financial disincentives for change."). The failure to adequately train students also raises ethical issues because "[l]aw schools have a moral and ethical obligation to society—and, to an even greater degree, to their students—to adequately prepare the students to succeed as professionals. Ultimate success for law students is measured by the ability to competently practice the legal profession." Trujillo, *supra* note 50, at 70.

77. *See* Lasso, *supra* note 13, at 16 (stating that if the measure of law school success is "law student satisfaction, [then] legal education also is surely failing. Law students across the country complain that their legal education leaves much to be desired"). The author adds a footnote that "although mostly anecdotal, there is significant evidence that most law students are not satisfied with the quality of their legal education." *Id.* at 16 n. 62. See also Mitchell Nathanson, *Taking the Road Less Traveled: Why Practical Scholarship Makes Sense for the Legal Writing Professor*, 11 J. LEGAL WRITING INST. 329, 356 (2005) ("Many students are dissatisfied with the skill set they are taking with them

from law school into the legal marketplace and feel that they are not prepared to tackle much of what will be thrown at them by their employers after graduation."). See Posting of Peter Lattman to Law Blog, http://blogs.wsj.com/law/2007/06/08/are-law-students-emotional-wrecks/ (June 8, 2007, 17:30 EST), for a response to a recent WALL STREET JOURNAL article about recently published research by Kennon Sheldon and Lawrence Krieger concerning the negative effects of legal education on law students.

78. See Jay Feinman & Marc Feldman, *Pedagogy and Politics*, 73 GEO. L. J. 875, 876–77 (1985) [hereinafter Feinman & Feldman, *Pedagogy and Politics*].

> The primary function of law schools is to train novice lawyers—yet there is widespread agreement that they do not do this job very well.... [O]nly by constructing a new consciousness of law, lawyering, and learning can law schools perform their most basic task: the training of competent lawyers.

Id.

79. *See* Kevin H. Smith, *How to Become a Law Professor Without Really Trying: A Critical, Heuristic, Deconstructionist, and Hermeneutical Exploration of Avoiding the Drudgery Associated with Actually Working as an Attorney*, 47 U. KAN. L. REV. 139, 140 (1998) ("A recent trend for dissatisfied attorneys, particularly younger attorneys, is to seek employment in legal education.").

80. Borthwick & Schau, *supra* note 52, at 217. The study concluded that "the vast majority of professors teaching law have had very little experience practicing law." *Id.* at 219.

81. *Id. See also* Mary C. Daly, *The Structure of Legal Education and the Legal Profession, Multidisciplinary Practice, Competition, and Globalization*, 52 J. LEGAL EDUC. 480, 489 (stating that law faculty "know very little about the actual practice of law.").

82. Almost one-third of all law professors received their law degree from one of only five schools (Harvard, Yale, Columbia, Chicago, and Michigan). Borthwick & Schau, *supra* note 52, at 226–27. Inasmuch as the faculty at the top schools have a much higher proportion of faculty with no practice prior to teaching (37% vs. 20%), and inasmuch as these top schools produce a disproportionately high number of law professors, "the effects or biases, if any, that flow from professors with little practical experience are presumably passed on at a disproportionate rate." *Id.* at 219–20. According to one commentator, "for many faculty members the road to teaching has been short and narrow: a brilliant record in an Ivy League law school, a clerkship for a distinguished judge or a judge of a distinguished court, and then straight to the classroom." Judith T. Younger, *Legal Education: An Illusion*, 75 MINN. L. REV. 1037, 1041 (1990).

83. Patrick J. Schiltz, *Legal Ethics in Decline: The Elite Law Firm, the Elite Law School, and the Moral Formation of the Novice Attorney*, 82 MINN. L. REV. 705, 758 (1998) [hereinafter Schiltz, *Legal Ethics in Decline*].

> Most lawyers practice in law firms, and the first few years in a law firm rarely give an attorney a realistic impression of the practice of law. A young practitioner's first few years are heavy on legal research and writing, and light on precisely those things that make up the professional life of most lawyers: counseling, negotiation, client contact, trials, firm management.... To gain a real understanding of the practice of law, one must do it for more than a few years.

Id.

84. Nancy L. Schultz, *How Do Lawyers Really Think*, 42 J. LEGAL EDUC. 57, 57 (1992) ("Few [law faculty] seem to recognize that we cannot really teach students how lawyers think without teaching them at the same time what lawyers do. Thinking like a lawyer is a much richer and more intricate process than collecting and manipulating doctrine.").

85. See Harry T. Edwards, *The Growing Disjunction Between Legal Education and the Legal Profession*, 91 MICH. L. REV. 34, 35 (1992).

86. *See* Levy, *supra* note 11, at 61 ("[S]cholarship, rather than teaching, has paramount importance at most [law] schools.").

87. *See* Schuwerk, *supra* note 17, at 762–63; *see also* Ron M. Aizen, Note, *Four Ways to Better 1L Assessments*, 54 DUKE L. J. 765, 770 (2004) ("The "publish-or-perish' mentality that pervades the contemporary legal academy may discourage the use of other, more time-consuming assessment methods."); Schwartz, *supra* note 9, at 360 ("Most law schools hire law teachers based on their record or potential for creating scholarship. Publication is heavily weighted in tenure decisions.").

88. *See* Rhode, *Missing Questions*, *supra* note 74, at 1549 ("Yet even those faculty who are most committed to teaching rarely storm the barricades seeking pedagogical reform. Few academics have anything to gain by underscoring problems that their colleagues find discomfiting to acknowledge, let alone to address."). See also Schiltz, *Legal Ethics in Decline*, *supra* note 83, at 754–56.

89. According to a study conducted by the Ohio Bar Association, median lawyer income for full time lawyers in Ohio in 2003 was $85,000. OHIO STATE BAR ASS'N, 2004 ECONOMICS OF LAW PRACTICE IN OHIO SURVEY 10 (2004), *available at* http://downloads.ohiobar.org/products/2004EconOhioSurvey.pdf. The Bureau of Labor Statistics states that median lawyer income in the United States is $94,930. Bureau of Labor Statistics, Lawyers, http://www.bls.gov/oco/ocos053.htm#earnings (last visited May 26, 2007). Typical salaries for tenured law professors varied. However, of those schools that reported their professor's compensation, typical *median* professor salaries (in the Midwest, for example) from 2005 to 2006 ranged from a low of $110,032 at some schools to a high of $164,774 at others, with the vast majority of the median salaries in the $120,000s and $130,000s. *2005–06 SALT Salary Survey*, SALT EQUALIZER, Mar. 2006, at 2.

90. Rapoport, *supra* note 73, at 363.

> The professor works when he feels like it; and if, on any given afternoon, he decides to go to the ball game, he merely closes his office and walks away.... No one will object, and the odds are a hundred to one that no one will even know he is gone. He is not even required to work on anything that he finds uninteresting or boring or too difficult; and if he encounters some horrible rat's nest of the law ... he is not compelled to stay up struggling with it for four consecutive nights with a wet towel around his head, as is his brother in practice. He can just let it alone, in the serene confidence that [some other professor] will some day work it all out and put it in a book.

William L. Prosser, *Lighthouse No Good*, 1 J. LEGAL EDUC. 257, 260–61 (1948). *See also* R. Michael Cassidy, *Why I Teach (A Prescription for the Post-Tenure Blues)*, 55 J. LEGAL EDUC. 381, 381 (2005) (relating a recently tenured law professor's observation that "with job security in an intellectually challenging, fairly well-paying profession (coupled with relatively high social status and a large amount of autonomy), it is unlikely that many of us [law professors] will ever give up teaching to do something else"); Donald J. Weidner, *The Crises of Legal Education: A Wake-Up Call for Faculty*, 47 J. LEGAL EDUC. 92, 103 (1997) (describing the job of law professor as "surely one of the greatest jobs in the world").

91. Regrettably, this attitude by many of those in legal academia is nothing new. As stated by Robert L. Stevens, then Professor of Law at Yale Law School, in 1973: "Scholars who would seldom be caught with their footnotes down substitute assumptions for evidence when they write about legal education.... Equally disturbing is the "unscientific' participation of many scholars in the debate over legal education." Robert Stevens, *Law Schools and Law Students*, 59 VA. L. REV. 551, 553–54 (1973). *See also* Feinman & Feldman, *Pedagogy and Politics*, *supra* note 78, at 875 ("That most legal educators are anti-intellectual about their primary professional concern is neither surprising nor accidental.... [T]he attitude of unreflectiveness is an important part of the defense of the status quo."); Peter V. Letsou, *The Future of Legal Education: Some Reflections on Law School Specialty Tracks*, 50 CASE W. RES. L. Rev. 457, 460–61 (1999) ("[L]aw school faculties generally take a conservative approach to any significant change in the law school curriculum. This is because curricular reform can often impose substantial and certain costs on a law faculty, while offering only limited and speculative benefits.").

92. James J. Alfini, now Dean of the South Texas College of Law in Houston, and Joseph N. Van Vooren lament the "lack of knowledge and attention" that the legal academy pays to the legal profession. James J. Alfini & Joseph N. Van Vooren, Commentary, *Is There a Solution to the Problem of Lawyer Stress? The Law School Perspective*, 10 J. L. & HEALTH 61, 67 (1996). In talking about changes in law practice, particularly those that relate to the increasing levels of stress in law practice, they state:

> Law professors regularly hear from their law school classmates how much the profession has changed (for the worse), and from recent law school graduates how much they dislike the bottom-line orientation of their law firms. However, we tend to simply shrug our shoulders and go about our business of educating the next crop of law firm associates. The changes in the legal profession merely make us more content in the knowledge that our decision to forego the monetary benefits of legal practice and enter the more comfortable and satisfying world of teaching the law has been confirmed.

Id.

93. Karl N. Llewellyn, *On What Is Wrong with So-Called Legal Education*, 35 COLUM. L. REV. 651 (1935); see also Jerome Frank, *Why Not a Clinical Lawyer-School?*, 81 U. PA. L. REV. 907 (1933); Jerome Frank, *A Plea for Lawyer-Schools*, 56 YALE L.J. 1303 (1947).

94. See Elson, *Why and How*, *supra* note 57, at 1135.

> Anyone who reviews the extensive literature on law schools' duty to prepare students for practice must be struck by how the same critiques and responses have been repeated over the last seventy-five years. It has become something of a ritual attack and counter-attack, where the verbal shots of the attackers always seem to fall on deaf ears.

Id.

95. *Id.*

96. Corinne Cooper, *Letter to a Young Law Student*, 35 TULSA L. J. 275, 278 (2000). *See also* David Lander, *Part Time, But Fully Loaded*, 14 BUS. L. TODAY, July–Aug. 2005, at 45, 47 ("One of the most striking things about law school education is that full-time law school teachers receive virtually no training in how students learn.").

97. *See* Lander, *supra* note 96, at 45, 47.

98. *See generally* SULLIVAN ET AL., *supra* note 3.

99. *Id.* at 58–59. The authors state that:

> [L]earning the law is an ensemble experience, its achievement a holistic effect. From the point of view of student learning, the apprenticeships of cognition, performance, and identity are not freestanding. Each contributes to a whole and takes part of its character from the relationship it has with the others ... we believe legal education requires not simply more additions but a truly integrative approach in order to provide students with a broad-based yet coherent beginning for their legal careers.

Id.

100. *See generally* Stuckey et al., *supra* note 3.

101. *Id.* at 18.

102. *Id.* at 13.

103. *See HLS Faculty Unanimously Approves First-year Curricular Reform*, HARVARD LAW SCHOOL, Oct. 6, 2006, http://www.law.harvard.edu/ news/2006/10/06 curriculum.php (last visited May 26, 2007).

104. *Id.*

105. *See A "3D" JD: Stanford Law School Announces New Model for Legal Education*, STANFORD LAW SCHOOL, Nov. 28, 2006, http://www.law.stanford.edu/ news/pr/47/ (last visited May 26, 2007) [hereinafter *"3D" JD*].

106. *Id.*

107. As some observers have noted, some of these initiatives died "on that immovable rock of opposition—the deans of American law schools." Mitu Gulati et al., *The Happy Charade: An Empirical Examination of the Third Year of Law School*, 51 J. LEGAL EDUC. 235, 236 (1991). The authors, who taught or conducted research at UCLA's law school, conducted a multi-law school survey of 1100 third year law students. The authors indicate that their article, showing the survey results, was intended to, "shed ... some empirical light on long-standing debates about the success of legal education and, in particular, the third-year experience of law students." *Id.*

108. *See generally* ABA, REPORT OF THE TASK FORCE ON LAW SCHOOLS AND THE PROFESSION: NARROWING THE GAP (1992), *available at* http://www.abanet.org/legaled/publications/onlinepubs/maccrate.html.

109. *See* Elson, *Why and How*, *supra* note 57. Indeed, given the peculiar dynamics of the law faculty-law dean relationship, it is extremely unlikely that change will be championed by either law faculties or law deans. *See*, e.g., Howard O. Hunter, *Thoughts on Being a Dean*, 31 U. TOL. L. REV. 641, 642 (2000) ("Faculties naturally tend to resist change in pedagogy and curriculum. Law teachers have substantial investments in their current courses and are accustomed to doing things in certain ways."). Law faculties are resistant to change and unlikely to initiate it on their own, while law deans are unlikely to initiate changes that risk alienating the already change-resistant faculty. ABA regulations regarding law school accreditation insure that the faculty will have substantial input into the dean's appointment or reappointment, further insuring the institutional disincentives for a dean to institute substantial

changes that cut against the desires of the faculty. *See* STANDARDS FOR APPROVAL OF LAW SCHOOLS §206(d) (2007), *available at* http://www.abanet.org/legaled/standards/20072008StandardsWebContent/Chapter%202.pdf.

110. Gulati et al., *supra* note 107, at 244–45. This lack of interest by second and third year law students is nothing new. In 1941, Karl Llewellyn, who was then teaching at Columbia Law School, said, "it is safe to state that the "second-year drop-off' of interest continues, and that the "third-year restlessness' is still with us, both of them on an impressive and disheartening scale." Karl N. Llewellyn, *On the Problem of Teaching "Private" Law*, 54 HARV. L. REV. 775, 778 (1941). To curb this "drop-off," a reconfiguration of the second and third years of law school is recommended.

> Legal education may have a problem of diminishing returns-one that a better integration of cognitive apprenticeship with the practical and professional could help to prevent. On the curricular level, this need for integration points towards a reconfigured third year (and probably some reconfiguration of the second year as well), marked by pedagogies of practice and professionalism that enable students to shift from the role of students to that of apprentice professionals.

SULLIVAN ET AL., *supra* note 3, at 77.

111. *See* Gulati, et al., *supra* note 107, at 244–46.

112. *See "3D" JD*, *supra* note 105.

113. *See* Sullivan et al., *supra* note 3.

114. Arthur Austin, *The Reliability of Citation Counts in Judgments on Promotion, Tenure, and Status*, 35 ARIZ. L. REV. 829, 829 (1993) ("Scholarship is the door to promotion, tenure, and salary increases."); John S. Elson, *The Case Against Legal-Scholarship or, If the Professor Must Publish, Must the Profession Perish?*, 39 J. LEGAL EDUC. 343, 354 (1989) ("The importance of scholarship to the careers of law teachers is difficult to overestimate. Hiring, promotion, pay, collegial recognition, societal prominence, and intellectual satisfaction is mainly a function of the production of scholarship.").

115. Roger C. Cramton, *"The Most Remarkable Institution": The American Law Review*, 36 J. LEGAL EDUC. 1, 10 (1986). See also Judith S. Kaye, *One Judge's View of Academic Law Review Writing*, 39 J. LEGAL EDUC. 313, 319 (1989) ("Prominent law reviews are increasingly dedicated to abstract, theoretical subjects ... and less and less to practice and professional issues, and to the grist of the state court dockets.").

116. *See* MARY ANN GLENDON, A NATION UNDER LAWYERS 205 (1994) ("Anyone who samples the contents of recent law journals, however, might be forgiven for suspecting that many articles will be read by no one at all, other than the writer's promotion and tenure committee.").

117. See Louis Fisher, *Lost Constitutional Moorings: Recovering the War Power*, 81 IND. L.J. 1199, 1234–35 (2006).

> Law reviews are student-run publications. Thousands of manuscripts are submitted to the articles editors but they are not peer-reviewed by scholars and experts. Instead, the articles editors look through submitted articles and choose what to print.... Articles editors, talented and bright as they are, cannot provide a professional, expert read of a manuscript.... Editorial policy is often driven by a desire to publish articles for "their distinctiveness rather than their scholarly soundness."

Id. (citing Robert J. Spitzer, *Lost and Found: Researching the Second Amendment*, 76 CHI.-KENT L. REV. 349, 376 (2000)).

118. Edwards, *supra* note 85, at 35.

119. Posner, *supra* note 44, at 1655.

120. United States v. $639,558, 955 F.2d 712, 722 (D.C. Cir. 1992) (Silberman, J., concurring).

121. Data compiled by the National Council of Bar Examiners shows that for the ten year period from 1997 through 2006, the average bar passage rate for first time bar takers was 76.1%. *See 2006 Statistics*, B. EXAMINER, May, 2007, at 6, 17, *available at* http://www.ncbex.org/uploads/user docrepos/BEMayStatsWeb.pdf. During the same period the average overall passage rate for all bar exam takers (first time and repeaters) was 65.5%. *Id.*

On Being a Happy, Healthy, and Ethical Member of an Unhappy, Unhealthy, and Unethical Profession

*Patrick J. Schiltz**

Dear Law Student:

I have good news and bad news. The bad news is that the profession that you are about to enter is one of the most unhappy and unhealthy on the face of the earth—and, in the view of many, one of the most unethical. The good news is that you can join this profession and still be happy, healthy, and ethical. I am writing to tell you how.

I. The Well-Being of Lawyers

Lawyers play an enormously important role in our society.[1] "It is the lawyers who run our civilization for us—our governments, our business, our private lives."[2] Thus you might expect that a lot of people would be concerned about the physical and mental health of lawyers. You would be wrong.[3] Contrary to the old joke,[4] scientists have not replaced laboratory rats with lawyers, and medical literature has little to say about the well-being of attorneys. At the same time, many law professors—at least those teaching at the fifty or so schools that consider themselves to be in the "Top Twenty"—do not care much about lawyers. Increasingly, faculties of elite schools and aspiring elite schools consist of professors who have not practiced law,[5] who have little interest in teaching students to practice law,[6] and who pay scant attention to the work of practicing lawyers.[7] Even law professors like me—law professors who practiced law for several years, who love teaching, and who are intensely interested in the work of lawyers—often do not have the training or resources to conduct empirical research about the legal profession.[8] As a result, legal scholarship also has little to say about the well-being of attorneys.[9]

If one looks hard enough, though, one can scratch up some information about the health and happiness of attorneys. And this information—although rather sparse and, in some cases, of limited value—strongly suggests that lawyers are in remarkably poor health and quite unhappy.

A. Lawyers' Poor Health

1. Depression

Lawyers seem to be among the most depressed people in America. In 1990, researchers affiliated with Johns Hopkins University studied the prevalence of major depressive disorder ("MDD") across 104 occupations.[10] They discovered that, although only about 3% to 5% of the general population suffers from MDD,[11] the prevalence of MDD exceeds 10% in five occupations: data-entry keyers, computer equipment operators, typists, pre-kindergarten and special education teachers, and lawyers.[12] When the results were adjusted for age, gender, education, and race/ethnic background to determine to what extent those in each occupation were more depressed than others who shared their most important sociodemographic traits,[13] only three occupations were discovered to have statistically significant elevations of MDD: lawyers, pre-kindergarten and special education teachers, and secretaries. Lawyers topped the list, suffering from MDD at a rate 3.6 times higher than non-lawyers who shared their key sociodemographic traits.[14] The researchers did not know whether lawyers were depressed because "persons at high risk for major depressive disorder" are attracted to the legal profession or because practicing law "causes or precipitates depression."[15] They just knew that, whatever the reason, lawyers were depressed.[16]

Other studies have produced similar results. A study of Washington lawyers found that "compared with the 3 to 9 percent of individuals in Western industrialized countries who suffer from depression, 19 percent of ... Washington lawyers suffered from statistically significant elevated levels of depression."[17] A study of law students and practicing lawyers in Arizona discovered that when students enter law school, they suffer from depression at approximately the same rate as the general population.[18] However, by the spring of the first year of law school, 32% of law students suffer from depression, and by the spring of the third year of law school, the figure escalates to an astonishing 40%.[19] Two years after graduation, the rate of depression falls, but only to 17%, or roughly double the level of the general population.[20]

Another study, making use of the data generated by the Washington and Arizona studies, reported that while "the base rate of any affective disorder (which includes depression) is 8.5% for males and 14.1% for females, ... the percentage of male lawyers ... scoring above the clinical cutoff on the measure of depression is nearly 21% and for female lawyers 16%."[21] And finally, a study of North Carolina lawyers found that almost 37% reported being depressed and 42% lonely during the previous few weeks,[22] and that 24% reported suffering symptoms of depression (such as appetite loss, insomnia, suicidal ideation, and extreme lethargy) at least three times per month during the previous year.[23]

2. Anxiety and Other Mental Illness

Depression is not the only emotional impairment that seems to be more prevalent among lawyers than among the general population. The Arizona study also found elevated rates of anxiety, hostility, and paranoia among law students and lawyers.[24] Over 25% of North Carolina lawyers reported that they had experienced physical symptoms of extreme anxiety (including trembling hands, racing hearts, clammy hands, and faintness) at least three times per month during the past year.[25] And the Washington study found indicia of anxiety, social alienation and isolation, obsessive-compulsiveness, paranoid ideation, interpersonal sensitivity, phobic anxiety, and hostility in "alarming" rates among lawyers—rates many times the national norms.[26] For example:

> [T]he base rate [in the general population] for obsessive-compulsiveness is 1.42%, yet nearly 21% of the male lawyers and 15% of the female lawyers in the study score above the clinical cutoff on the measure of obsessive compulsiveness. The same pattern exists in regard to generalized anxiety disorder where the base rate is 4%, while 30% of the male lawyers and nearly 20% of the female lawyers in the study report scores above the clinical cutoff on the measure of anxiety.[27]

Needless to say, these studies "give[] substantial indication of a profession operating at extremely high levels of psychological distress."[28]

3. Alcoholism and Drug Abuse

Lawyers appear to be prodigious drinkers. The North Carolina study reported that almost 17% of lawyers admitted to drinking three to five alcoholic beverages every day.[29] One researcher conservatively estimated that 15% of lawyers are alcoholics.[30] The study of Washington lawyers found that 18% were "problem drinkers," a percentage "almost twice the approximately 10 percent alcohol abuse and/or dependency prevalence rates estimated for adults in the United States."[31] Moreover, the Washington study "reveal[ed] an astounding number of lawyers with a high likelihood of developing alcohol related problems."[32]

Little is known about the frequency with which lawyers use illegal drugs, but the little that is known is not encouraging. The Washington study found that 26% of lawyers had used cocaine at least once, a rate over twice that of the general population.[33] True, the Washington study found that only 1% of lawyers had "abused" cocaine, as compared to 3% of adults generally.[34] But that is hardly cause for celebration. According to the Washington study, *one third* of lawyers in Washington suffer from depression, problem drinking, or cocaine abuse.[35] There is no reason to believe that Washington is anomalous.[36]

4. Divorce

Marriage is good for people. "The research on marriage is striking. For decades, studies have shown that the married live longer and have a lower risk of a variety of physical and psychological illnesses than the unmarried."[37] Also, those who are married report higher levels of career satisfaction than those who are single.[38] The North Carolina study confirmed that what is true for people generally is also true for lawyers specifically: Among lawyers, "changing from single to married status directly increases happiness and satisfaction with life. Marriage also leads to greater job and career satisfaction … and improves health."[39] The North Carolina study identified unmarried lawyers as one of three categories of lawyers least satisfied with their lives.[40]

Likewise, divorce is bad for people, both physically and psychologically (and, for women, economically).[41] Those who divorce die younger than either those who never marry or those who stay married.[42] Indeed, the impact of getting divorced on life expectancy is "only slightly less harmful … than smoking a pack or more of cigarettes per day."[43] Divorced people suffer from cancer, cardiovascular disease, infectious diseases, respiratory illnesses, digestive system illnesses, and other acute conditions more frequently than do single, married, or widowed people.[44] Divorced people are far more likely to abuse alcohol or become alcoholic than those who have never been divorced.[45] Psychologically, divorce is devastating: "Of all the social variables relating to the incidence of psychiatric disorders, or psychopathology, in the population, none appears to be more crucial than marital status."[46] The separated and divorced suffer from psychiatric illness (such as depression and schizophrenia) far more than do the single, married, and widowed.[47] For example, men who are divorced or separated are admitted to hospitals for treatment of psychiatric disorders twenty-one times more frequently than married men.[48] And, not surprising, the suicide rate of those who are divorced is almost triple the rate of those who are married, and significantly higher than the rates of those who have never married or been widowed.[49]

Although empirical research is sparse, there is some indication that the divorce rate among lawyers is higher than the divorce rate among other professionals.[50] Felicia Baker LeClere of Notre Dame's Center for the Study of Contemporary Society compared the incidence of divorce among lawyers to the incidence of divorce among doctors, using data from the 1990 census. LeClere found that the percentage of lawyers who are divorced is higher than the percentage of doctors who are divorced and that the difference is particularly pronounced among women.[51] For example, over 16% of female attorneys between the ages of thirty-five and forty-nine are divorced, as compared to 11% of female doctors in the same age range. Similarly, among ages fifty to sixty-four, over 24% of female lawyers are divorced, as compared to about 15% of female doctors.

LeClere's findings are consistent with an earlier study of divorce rates among female attorneys. That study found that women who have completed six or more years of post-secondary education—a category that obviously includes lawyers—have a substantially higher divorce rate than women generally.[52] The study also found that, among well educated women, the divorce rate for female lawyers was substantially higher than the divorce rates for female physicians and female professors. Specifically, the divorce rate for female lawyers was twice the divorce rate for female doctors and 25% to 40% higher than the divorce rate for women teaching in post-secondary institutions.[53] The study also found that, after their first marriages end, female attorneys are significantly less likely to remarry than female physicians and professors.[54]

5. Suicide

Lawyers reportedly think about committing suicide and commit suicide far more often than do non-lawyers.[55] A review of the death certificates of over 26,000 white male suicide victims by the National Institute for Occupational Safety and Health suggested that the suicide rate for white male lawyers may be over twice that of other white males, although problems with the data made a firm conclusion impossible.[56] The Washington study reported that lawyers are more likely than the general population to experience suicidal ideation and are "at much greater risk of not only acting upon their suicidal ideation but of also being lethal during an attempt."[57] And the North Carolina study found that 11% of lawyers had experienced suicidal ideation at least once a month for the past year.[58]

6. Physical Health

The extremely limited information that is available indicates that the physical health of lawyers may not be much better than their emotional health. As noted, substantial numbers of lawyers report suffering physical symptoms of depression and anxiety, such as appetite loss, trembling hands, racing hearts, and the like.[59] But lawyers also seem not to exercise much[60] and to suffer from ulcers, coronary artery disease, and hypertension in substantial numbers.[61] One troubling study of female attorneys who had graduated from the University of California at Davis School of Law between 1969 and 1985 found that those who worked more than forty-five hours per week while pregnant suffered three times more miscarriages than those who worked less than thirty-five hours per week.[62] As I describe below,[63] working forty-five hour weeks is not only common in the legal profession, but in some sectors—particularly big firms—it is almost considered part-time.[64]

In sum, attorneys seem to be an unhealthy lot. Researchers do not know whether lawyers are unhealthy because unhealthy people are attracted to the legal profession or because something about the practice of law turns healthy people into unhealthy people.[65] But the few researchers who have studied the legal profession are unanimous that lawyers are, as a group, in remarkably poor health.

B. Lawyers' Unhappiness

People who are this unhealthy—people who suffer from depression, anxiety, alcoholism, drug abuse, divorce, and suicide to this extent—are almost by definition unhappy. It should not be surprising, then, that lawyers are indeed unhappy, nor should it be surprising that the source of their unhappiness seems to be the one thing that they have in common: their work as lawyers. "Work satisfaction affects life satisfaction."[66] Almost a century ago, Russian playwright Maxim Gorky wrote: "When work is a pleasure, life is a joy! When work is a duty, life is slavery."[67] If Gorky was right, then life for many lawyers is "slavery," as "job dissatisfaction among lawyers is widespread, profound and growing worse."[68]

A study of California lawyers by the RAND Institute for Civil Justice found that "only half say if they had to do it over, they would become lawyers."[69] On the whole, California lawyers were reported to be "'profoundly pessimistic' about the state of the legal profession and its future."[70] A survey of the North Carolina bar produced similar results. Almost a quarter of North Carolina lawyers said that, if given the choice, they would not become attorneys again; almost half said that they hope to leave the practice of law before the end of their careers; and over 40% said that they would not encourage their children or other qualified persons to enter the legal profession.[71] Along the same lines, a nationwide poll of attorneys conducted by the *National Law Journal* found that less than a third of those surveyed were "very satisfied" with their careers.[72]

For almost thirty years, the University of Michigan Law School has been surveying its former students five years after they graduate.[73] The last survey for which results have been reported was conducted in 1996.[74] Given the stellar reputation of their alma mater, Michigan graduates would presumably have more employment options available than graduates of most other law schools and thus would presumably be among the most satisfied practitioners in America. Yet the annual surveys have discovered surprisingly low levels of career satisfaction in general and a marked decline in career satisfaction over time, at least for lawyers in private practice.

For example, the percentage of graduates working as solo practitioners or in firms of fifty or fewer lawyers who were "quite satisfied" with their careers[75] five years after graduation fell from 45% for members of the classes of 1976 and 1977 (and from a high of 52% for members of the classes of 1980 and 1981) to 37% for members of the classes of 1990 and 1991.[76] The percentage of graduates working in firms of fifty-one or more lawyers who were "quite satisfied" with their careers fell from 53% for members of the classes of 1976 and 1977 (and from a high of 54% for the classes of 1978 and 1979) to 30% for members of the classes of 1990 and 1991.[77] In the rather understated words of the Michigan Law School survey, "this picture is gloomy."[78]

The most comprehensive data on career satisfaction of lawyers were produced by three national surveys conducted under the auspices of the Young Lawyers Division of the American Bar Association ("ABA"). The first survey, conducted in 1984, asked 3000 lawyers of all ages—some of whom were ABA members and some of whom were not—about job satisfaction and many other matters.[79] It was, according to the ABA, "the first in-depth survey of the legal profession in order to accurately study the state of the profession and determine the extent of career dissatisfaction."[80] The second survey, conducted in 1990, resurveyed those who had responded to the 1984 survey, and also questioned just over 1000 lawyers who had been admitted to the bar after the 1984 survey had been concluded.[81] The third survey, conducted in 1995, was more limited. Only "young lawyers" who belonged to the ABA were questioned—"young lawyers" being defined as those who were under the age of thirty-six or who had been admitted to practice for less than three years.[82] Moreover, the focus of the 1995 survey was narrower than the focus of the 1984 and 1990 surveys.[83]

Taken together, the surveys show a substantial decline in the job satisfaction of attorneys. In 1984, 41% of lawyers said that they were "very satisfied" with their jobs; in 1990, only 33% of all lawyers surveyed were "very satisfied,"[84] a decline of one-fifth in just six years. At the same time, the number of lawyers who were "very dissatisfied" with their jobs rose from 3% in 1984 to 5% in 1990.[85] The dissatisfaction was widespread. In the words of the 1990 study:

> In the past six years, the extent of lawyer dissatisfaction has increased throughout the profession. It is now reported in significant numbers by lawyers in all positions—partners as well as junior associates. It is now present in significant numbers in firms of all sizes, not just the largest and the smallest firms.[86]

The decrease in job satisfaction was even more dramatic among those lawyers who were surveyed in both 1984 and 1990. As noted, 40% of them had been "very satisfied" and 3% "very dissatisfied" in 1984. Just six years later, only 29% of these same lawyers (that is, the lawyers who were questioned in both 1984 and 1990) were "very satisfied," and the number who were "very dissatisfied" had risen to 8%.[87] As the study recognized, the sharp rise in job dissatisfaction among the lawyers who were surveyed in both 1984 and 1990 was particularly disturbing, given that these lawyers were "further along in their careers[,] ... better placed, and earning more money in 1990 than they were in 1984."[88]

Because the 1995 survey asked fewer and different questions and surveyed only young members of the ABA, it is difficult to compare its results with the results of the previous two surveys. But the 1995 results were troubling enough on their own. Even though the attorneys surveyed in 1995 had just started their legal careers, over 27% were already "somewhat" or "very" dissatisfied with the practice of law; only about one in five was "very" satisfied.[89] Almost one third of the young lawyers said that they would "strongly" consider leaving their current position in the next two years, and almost another third said that they "might" consider doing so.[90]

I should note two things about these statistics on career satisfaction. First, although most surveys suggest that career satisfaction is relatively[91] low among attorneys and has been declining, there are studies to the contrary.[92] Prominent among them is a recent study of the Chicago bar by John Heinz, Kathleen Hull, and Ava Harter.[93] The Chicago study was not a career satisfaction study as such; rather, attorneys were subject to lengthy personal interviews and, in the course of being interviewed about numerous subjects, were asked a few questions about career satisfaction. Chicago lawyers reported levels of job satisfaction that were similar to those reported by Americans in other lines of work.[94]

Eighty-four percent of Chicago lawyers were "very satisfied" or "satisfied," about 10% were "neutral," 5% were "dissatisfied," and less than 2% were "very dissatisfied."[95]

The authors of the Chicago study acknowledged that their findings were "at variance with much of the common prattle and with some of the academic speculation (insofar as one can distinguish those)."[96] However, the authors did not attempt to explain the variance, other than to speculate that "[l]aw professors may find comfort in believing that practicing lawyers are unhappy" because law professors may "feel better about their perceived (if not real) financial sacrifice," and that "the general public might find it congenial to believe that lawyers are unhappy because it would serve notions of [just] desert."[97] Of course, the problem with this explanation is that it is not law professors and the general public who have been reporting declining career satisfaction among lawyers, but lawyers themselves—in response to surveys conducted by such lawyer-friendly groups as the ABA.[98]

The second thing to note about the data described above is that all of these statistics relate to the overall level of career dissatisfaction among lawyers. It is important to understand, though, that career dissatisfaction is not distributed equally throughout the profession. Lawyers in some practice settings are happier than lawyers in others.[99] And "[l]awyers in large law firms are often among the least happy."[100] This appears to be true for both associates and partners.

A 1997 study of lawyers practicing in the Boston area found that associates in big firms were the least happy of the eight categories of lawyers studied.[101] The Chicago study, which found generally high levels of career satisfaction among attorneys, nevertheless found that "the percentage of 'very satisfied' respondents is ten points lower in the large firm category than in any of the other practice settings."[102] For the last several years, Michigan Law School has found the career satisfaction of its recent graduates who work in big firms to be declining and, on the whole, to be "lower than [that of] any other work-setting group we study."[103] Hildebrandt, one of the largest and most respected consultants to big firms, reported in 1998 that "[e]ven as associates are being paid record-setting salaries, their overall morale has reached new lows."[104] The *Wall Street Journal* recently reported on the efforts of large firms to stem the "exodus of young lawyers" who are so "turned off by the grind of big-time practice" that they are leaving their six-figure salaries behind.[105] The ABA's 1995 survey of young lawyers found that although over 24% of lawyers working in firms of one to two lawyers and almost 14% of lawyers working in firms of seven to twenty five lawyers would "definitely not" consider changing jobs in the next two years, only about 1% of lawyers working in firms of over 150 lawyers were similarly committed to their jobs.[106] And while 26% of lawyers in the seven to twenty-five lawyer firms and about 30% of lawyers in the one to two lawyer firms would "strongly" consider changing jobs in the next two years, over 37% of lawyers in the largest firms were similarly anxious to move.[107] In short, among young associates at big firms, only about 1% were strongly committed to remaining at their firms for at least two more years, while almost 40% had a strong interest in working elsewhere.

It is also telling that lawyers who leave big firms rarely go to other big firms. One study reported that when attorneys who were interested in changing jobs were "asked to indicate the type of firm or other job they were going to look at, only a small percentage of those currently in large firms indicated they were going to look at another large firm."[108] At the same time, "almost no one from a medium or small firm was interested in looking at a large firm."[109] Another study found that only 5% of lawyers who left large Chicago firms went to other large Chicago firms; most went to small firms or in-house.[110]

Many big firm partners are also dissatisfied. Indeed, "[h]appy law partners are a small minority these days."[111] A 1997 survey of partners in the 125 largest American law firms found that one third of those partners—lawyers who, in the eyes of many, have reached the pinnacle of their profession—would choose a different career if they could do it over again.[112] Almost one third of them thought that they would probably or definitely not remain at their firms until retirement,[113] and over 80% said that the nature of private practice in big firms had changed for the worse.[114] Hildebrandt reports that despite the fact that 1997 was "the best year ever" for many firms "due to record demand for legal services in almost all practice areas,"[115] big firm partners are unhappy: "Mo[st] disturbing is the low morale (and almost a disdain for their own profession) we see in partners who wonder whether continuing to practice is worth the effort."[116]

II. Explaining the Poor Health and Unhappiness of Lawyers

A. The Hours

Why are lawyers so unhealthy and unhappy? Why do so many lawyers, in the words of Judge Laurence Silberman, "hate what the practice of law has become"?[117] Lawyers give many reasons. They complain about the commercialization of the legal profession—about the fact that practicing law has become less of a profession and more of a business.[118] They complain about the increased pressure to attract and retain clients[119] in a ferociously competitive marketplace.[120] They complain about having to work in an adversarial environment "in which aggression, selfishness, hostility, suspiciousness, and cynicism are widespread."[121] They complain about not having control over their lives and about being at the mercy of judges and clients.[122] They complain about a lack of civility among lawyers.[123] They complain about a lack of collegiality[124] and loyalty[125] among their partners. And they complain about their poor public image.[126] Mostly, though, they complain about the hours.

In every study of the career satisfaction of lawyers of which I am aware, in every book or article about the woes of the legal profession that I have read, and in every conversation about life as a practicing lawyer that I have heard, lawyers complain about the long hours they have to work.[127] Without question, "the single biggest complaint among attorneys is increasingly long workdays with decreasing time for personal and family life."[128] Lawyers are complaining with increasing vehemence about "living to work, rather than working to live"[129]—about being "'asked not to dedicate, but to sacrifice their lives to the firm.'"[130]

To cite just a few examples: A national survey of lawyers by the *National Law Journal* reported that "most attorneys in the survey believed their careers were putting too much of a burden on their personal lives. When asked what they especially disliked about practicing law, more than half (54 percent) mentioned too many hours/not enough time for a personal life."[131] The 1990 ABA study, after describing increasing job dissatisfaction among attorneys, said that "[t]his increased dissatisfaction is directly caused by a deterioration of the lawyer workplace.... In particular, the amount of time lawyers have for themselves and their families has become an issue of major concern for many lawyers."[132] The North Carolina study identified as "a major factor" in attorney dissatisfaction the "[l]ack of enough time to balance work with time for self, family, the community, pro bono, etc."[133] Respondents to the Michigan Law School survey reported themselves far less satisfied with "[t]he balance of their family and professional lives" than with "[t]heir career as a whole" or any of four other measures of "[l]ife [s]atisfaction."[134] And the report of a national conference convened by the ABA to address "the emerging crisis in the quality of lawyers' health and lives" singled out as a "significant" cause of this crisis the fact that lawyers "do not have enough time for themselves and their families—what many have come to call 'the time famine.'"[135]

Lawyers often suffer from a nostalgic longing for a past that never really existed.[136] But when it comes to their brutal work schedules, lawyers have reason to complain, and they have reason to believe that the problem has grown worse. "Conventional wisdom just a few decades ago was that lawyers could not reasonably expect to charge for more than 1200 to 1500 hours per year."[137] Thirty years ago, most partners billed between 1200 and 1400 hours per year and most associates between 1400 and 1600 hours.[138] As late as the mid-1980s, even associates in large New York firms were often not expected to bill more than 1800 hours annually.[139] Today, many firms would consider these ranges acceptable only for partners or associates who had died midway through the year.

A study conducted by William Ross in 1991 discovered that almost half of the associates in private practice billed at least 2000 hours during both 1989 and 1990, and a fifth billed at least 2400 hours in 1990.[140] Another study conducted by Ross three years later discovered that 51% of associates and 23% of partners billed at least 2000 hours in 1993.[141] Seventy percent of those responding to the Michigan Law School survey worked an average of fifty or more hours per week; over a quarter of the respondents worked more than sixty hours per week.[142] The ABA's 1990 study found that 45% of attorneys in private practice billed at least 1920 hours per year, and 16% billed 2400 or more hours.[143] The same study also found that, although 70% of attorneys are permitted to take more than two weeks of vacation every year, only 48% actually do so.[144] Finally, an extensive survey by Altman Weil Pensa, a prominent legal consulting firm, found that the median number of billable hours for associates in firms of all sizes in 1995 was 1823; 25% of associates billed 1999 hours or more, and 10% billed at least 2166 hours.[145] Not long ago, billable hours at these levels "would have [been] thought unbearable."[146]

Workloads, like the job dissatisfaction to which they so closely relate, are not distributed equally throughout the profession. Generally speaking, lawyers in private practice work longer hours than those who work for corporations or for the government.[147] In the 1990 ABA survey, for example, only 56% of those in private practice agreed that they had enough time to spend with their families, compared to 74% of corporate lawyers and 79% of government lawyers.[148] Similarly, only 46% of private practitioners said that they had enough time for themselves, compared to 53% of corporate lawyers and 66% of government lawyers.[149] In the words of the study, "[t]ime for family and self is a real problem for lawyers in private practice. Far fewer lawyers in corporate counsel and government settings have insufficient time."[150] The findings of the Michigan Law School survey were similar: Only 20% of the respondents working in private practice were "quite satisfied" with "the balance of their family and professional life," as compared to 35% of those working in corporations, 45% of those working for the government, and 50% of those doing public interest work.[151]

Within private practice, the general rule of thumb is the bigger the firm, the longer the hours.[152] For example, a recent study found that over 41% of associates in firms of under 101 lawyers billed fewer than 1800 hours, as compared to about 16% of associates in firms of over 250 lawyers.[153] At the same time, almost 27% of associates in the smaller firms billed over 1900 hours, as compared to approximately 36% of associates in the larger firms.[154] At the biggest firms in the biggest cities, associates commonly bill 2000 to 2500 hours per year.[155] Big firm partners do not have it much better. Junior partners at the nation's 125 largest law firms average 1955.5 billable hours per year,[156] almost 300 hours per year more than partners in small firms.[157] At some big firms, the average number of hours billed by partners and associates alike is 2000.[158]

The long hours that big firm lawyers must work is a particular source of dissatisfaction for them. While roughly half of all attorneys in private practice complain about not having enough time for themselves and their families,[159] in big firms the proportion of similarly disaffected lawyers is about three quarters.[160] The ABA's survey of young lawyers in 1995 found that 62% of those working in firms of at least 150 lawyers were dissatisfied with the amount of time they had to work, while only 28% of those working in firms of fewer than seven lawyers had the same complaint.[161] Among respondents to the Michigan Law School survey, 37% of those working as solo practitioners or in firms of ten or fewer lawyers were quite satisfied with "[t]he balance of family and professional lives," while only 14% of those working in firms of 150 or more lawyers were similarly satisfied.[162] Finally, young attorneys in large firms who are interested in finding a new job are more likely than similarly situated associates in small firms to be motivated by "a desire for more personal time."[163]

The unhappiness of lawyers may puzzle you. At first blush, these billable hour requirements may not seem particularly daunting. You may think, "Geez, to bill 2000 hours, I need to bill only forty hours per week for fifty weeks. If I take an hour for lunch, that's 8:00 a.m. to 5:00 p.m., five days per week. No sweat." Your reaction is common among law students[164]—particularly among law students who are in the process of talking themselves into accepting jobs at big firms. Your reaction is also naive.

There is a big difference—a painfully big difference—between the hours that you will *bill* and the hours that you will *spend at work*. If you're honest, you will be able to bill only the time that you spend working directly on matters for clients. Obviously, you will not be able to bill the time that you spend on vacation, or in bed with the flu, or at home waiting for the plumber.[165] But you will also not be able to bill for much of what you will do at the office or during the workday—going to lunch, chatting with your co-workers about the latest office romance, visiting your favorite websites, going down the hall to get a cup of coffee, reading your mail, going to the bathroom, attending the weekly meeting of your practice group, filling out your time sheet, talking with your spouse on the phone, sending e-mail to friends, preparing a "pitch" for a prospective client, getting your hair cut, attending a funeral, photocopying your tax returns, interviewing a recruit, playing Solitaire on your computer, doing pro bono work, reading advance sheets, taking a summer associate to a baseball game, attending CLE seminars, writing a letter about a mistake in your credit card bill, going to the dentist, dropping off your dry cleaning, daydreaming, and so on.

Because none of this is billable—and because the average lawyer does a lot of this every day—you will end up billing only about two hours for every three hours that you spend at "work."[166] And thus, to bill 2000 hours per year, you will have to spend about sixty hours per week at the office, and take no more than two weeks of vacation/sick time/personal leave. If it takes you, say, forty-five minutes to get to work, and another forty-five minutes to get home, billing 2000 hours per year will mean leaving home at 7:45 a.m., working at the office from 8:30 a.m. until 6:30 p.m., and then arriving home at 7:15 p.m.—and doing this *six days per week*, every week. That makes for long days, and for long weeks. And you will have to work these hours not just for a month or two, but year after year after year. That makes for a long life.

Now do you understand why so many attorneys are unhappy? And why, generally speaking, the more lawyers work, the less happy they are? What makes people happy is the *nature* of the work they do and the quantity and quality of their lives outside of work.[167] Long hours at the office have no relationship to the former and take away from the latter. Every hour that lawyers spend at their desks is an hour that they do not spend doing many of the things that give their lives joy and meaning: being with their spouses, playing with their children, relaxing with their friends, visiting their parents, going to movies, reading books, volunteering at the homeless shelter, playing softball, collecting stamps, traveling the world, getting involved in a political campaign, going to church, working out at a health club. There's no mystery about why lawyers are so unhappy: They work too much.

B. The Money

Why do lawyers work too much? At this point, I'm afraid that we have to leave the realm of fact and enter the realm of opinion. No one knows for certain why so many lawyers work so hard, although many people have opinions. I have one, too—at least about the lawyers who work in big firms (who, as noted, are also the lawyers who work the longest hours[168] and are the least happy with the imbalance between their personal and professional lives[169]). Admittedly, my opinion is just an opinion, but it is based on a lot of experience. I practiced law for eight years in a big firm—six as an associate, two as a partner—and spent much of that time working with and against other big firm lawyers. Most of my law school classmates went on to practice at big firms, as did most of those with whom I clerked. And even today, many of my friends and acquaintances are lawyers who have practiced or are practicing in big firms.

Because my experience is in big firms, and because so many law students want to work in big firms,[170] big firms will be the focus of the remainder of this Article. I recognize, of course, that working for a big firm may not be an option for you. You should nevertheless read the remainder of this article. First, if you are a typical student who does not have the option of working at a big firm, you probably regret that fact and you may even spend a substantial amount of time envying others who can go to big firms. Second, just because you cannot work at a big firm now does not mean that you will not be able to work at a big firm in the future. If you assemble a large stable of clients or if your college roommate is elected governor or if you establish a reputation as a top trial lawyer, the doors of big firms will open to you. Third, even if you never have the chance to work at a big firm, you almost surely will have the chance to work at a firm that acts like a big firm. Small firms, corporate legal departments, government offices, and even public interest firms "have borrowed many features of large-firm practice."[171] Finally, even if working at a big firm—or at a small or medium firm that acts like a big firm—holds absolutely no appeal for you, big firms exercise a disproportionate influence on the profession you are about to enter,[172] and you need to understand the nature of that influence.

In one sense, the answer to the question of why so many lawyers work so much is easy: It's the money, stupid. It begins with law students, who, like most Americans, seem to be more materialistic than they were twenty-five or thirty years ago. In 1970, 39% of students entering college said that "being very well off financially" was either an "essential" or a "very important" life goal; in 1993, the figure had almost doubled to 75%.[173] Of nineteen possible life goals suggested to incoming college students, getting rich was selected most often—even more often than "raising a family."[174] Not surprisingly, then, "the most coveted jobs amongst [law students] are high-paying large law firm jobs."[175] The vast majority of law students—at least the vast majority of those attending the more prestigious schools (or getting good grades at the less prestigious schools)—want to work in big firms.[176] And the reason they want to work in big firms is that big firms pay the most.[177]

Of course, students deny this. Students—many of whom came to law school intending to do public interest work[178]—don't like to admit that they've "sold out," so they come up with "rationalizations, justifications, accounts, and disclaimers" for seeking big firm jobs.[179] They insist that the real reason they want to go to a big firm is the training, or the interesting and challenging work, or the chance to work with exceptionally talented colleagues, or the desire to "keep my doors open." They imply that the huge salaries are just an afterthought—mere icing on the cake. Or they reluctantly admit that, yes, they really are after the money, but they have no choice: Because of student loan debt, they *must* take a job that pays $80,000 per year. $60,000 per year just won't cut it.

Most of this is hogwash. As I will explain below,[180] almost all of the purported non-monetary advantages of big firms either do not exist or are vastly overstated. Moreover, there are few lawyers who could not live comfortably on what most corporations or government agencies pay, whatever their student loan debt.[181] Students are after the money, pure and simple.[182] The hiring partner of any major firm will tell you that if his firm offers first year associates a salary of $69,000, and a competitor down the street offers them $72,000, those who have the choice will flock to the competitor—even if the competitor will require them to bill 200 hours more each year.[183]

I realize that I am not exactly flattering law students. But if this were not true, would big firms get into bidding wars for the services of the best law school graduates? Of course not. But big firms do get into bidding wars—all the time—and, as a result, the salaries of first year associates get pushed to extraordinary levels.[184] In 1997, the median starting salary for first year associates in firms of over 250 lawyers was $71,502.[185] First year associates in some California firms now earn $95,000 per year.[186] And in 1997 some New York firms broke the magic $100,000 barrier and began paying six figure salaries to first year associates—many of whom, of course, had not yet even passed the bar exam.[187]

As the salaries of first year associates go up, the salaries of senior associates must rise to keep pace.[188] After all, no sixth year associate wants to be paid less than a first year associate. And as the salaries of senior associates go up, the salaries of junior partners must rise to keep pace. After all, no junior partner wants to be paid less than a senior associate. And, of course, as the salaries of junior partners go up, so must the salaries of senior partners.

How do firms pay for this ever-spiraling increase in salaries? In theory, they have two options:[189] First, they can raise billing rates. Instead of charging, say, $100 per hour for the time of first year associates, they can charge $115, and instead of charging, say, $225 per hour for the time of junior partners, they can charge $250. Second, they can bill more hours. Instead of demanding 2000 billable hours per year from first year associates, they can demand 2100, and instead of demanding 1900 billable hours per year from junior partners, they can demand 1950.

In reality, though, firms have only one option: They have to bill more hours. The market for lawyers' services has become intensely competitive.[190] As the number of lawyers has soared,[191] competition for clients has become ferocious. Clients insist on getting good work at low hourly rates.[192] They also insist that lawyers minimize the amount of time that they devote to each file to hold down costs. If clients do not get what they want, they will move their business to one of the thousands of other lawyers who are chomping at the bit to get it.[193] Raising billing rates to pay for spiraling salaries is simply not much of an option for most firms. As a result, firms get the extra money to pay for the spiraling salaries in the only way they can: They bill more hours. Everyone has to work harder to pay for the higher salaries. And when salaries go up again, everyone has to work still harder. Associate compensation has increased 1000% in the past thirty years, while billing rates have increased only 400%.[194] Obviously, "law firms have paid for the higher salaries by increasing billable hours rather than charging higher rates."[195]

I am leaving out one wrinkle—an important wrinkle that you should know about if you are contemplating joining a large law firm (or a firm that acts like a large law firm). The partners of a big firm have a third option for making more money. This option involves what big firm partners euphemistically refer to as "leverage."[196] I like to call it "the skim." Richard Abel calls it "exploitation."[197] The person being exploited is you.

It is common for the top partners in the biggest firms to earn upwards of $2 million per year.[198] At some firms, profits per partner approach or exceed $2 million per year,[199] meaning that some partners are paid more than $2 million (because profits are not divided equally among partners). Not one of these highly paid partners could personally generate the billings necessary to produce such an income. Even a partner billing 2000 hours per year at $500 per hour, "both of which figures lie at the outer limits of physical and economic possibility," would generate only $1 million in revenue, "a good proportion of which would be consumed by overhead."[200] So how can big firm partners take home double or triple or quadruple the revenue they generate? They can do so because partner compensation reflects not only the revenue that partners themselves generate, but also "the surplus value law firms extract from associates."[201] Alex Johnson puts the point more dramatically: "[T]he blood and sweat of new associates line[] the pockets of the senior members of the firm."[202]

Basically, what happens is that big firms "buy associates' time 'wholesale and sell it retail.'"[203] Here is how it works:[204] As a new associate in a large firm, you will be paid about one-third of what you bring into the firm.[205] If you bill, say, 2000 hours at $100 per hour, you will generate $200,000 in revenue for your firm. About a third of that—$70,000 or so—will be paid to you. Another third will go toward paying the expenses of the firm. And the final third will go into the pockets of the firm's partners. Firms make money off associates. That is why it's in the interests of big firms to hire lots of associates and to make very few of them partners. The more associates there are, the more profits for the partners to split,[206] and the fewer partners there are, the bigger each partner's share.

After you make partner (*if* you make partner—your chances will likely be about one in ten[207]), you will still be exploited, although somewhat less. You may take home 40% or so of what you bring into the firm as a junior partner. Your take will gradually increase with your seniority. At some point, you will reach equilibrium—that is, you will take home roughly what you bring into the firm, minus your share of the firm's overhead. And, if you stick with it long enough, some day you will reach Big Firm Nirvana: You will take home more than you bring into the firm (minus your share of overhead). You will become the exploiter instead of the exploited.

It should not surprise you that, generally speaking, the bigger the firm, the more the leverage.[208] The median ratio of associates to partners ranges dramatically, from .33 in firms of eight or fewer attorneys in the northeastern United States, to 1.50 in firms of seventy-five or more attorneys in the same region.[209] In general, though, the ratio increases with the size of the firm.[210] Nationally, the median ratio is .51 in firms of eight or fewer attorneys, .66 in firms of nine to twenty attorneys, .64 in firms of twenty-one to forty attorneys, .75 in firms of forty-one to seventy-four attorneys, and .93 in firms of seventy-five or more attorneys.[211] As a result of the disparity in leverage between big and small firms, partners in big firms make dramatically more money than partners in small firms. In 1995, the median income of partners in firms of seventy-five or more attorneys was $190,408—almost 42% higher than the median income of partners in firms of eight or fewer lawyers.[212] (By contrast, the median income of associates in firms of seventy-five or more attorneys was $76,263, just 12% higher than the median income of associates in firms of eight or fewer lawyers.[213]) The stark relationship between firm size and partnership compensation cannot be explained by differences in hourly rates, hours billed, or quality of legal services.[214] Rather, it results from the skim.

This, then, is life in the big firm: It is in the interests of clients that senior partners work inhuman hours, year after year, and constantly be anxious about retaining their business. And it is in the interests of senior partners that junior partners work inhuman hours, year after year, and constantly be anxious about retaining old clients and attracting new clients. And it is in the interests of junior partners that senior associates work inhuman hours, year after year, and constantly be anxious about retaining old clients and attracting new clients and making partner. And most of all, it is in everyone's interests that the newest members of the profession—the junior associates—be willing to work inhuman hours, year after year, and constantly be anxious about *everything*—about retaining old clients and attracting new clients and making partner and keeping up their billable hours.[215] The result? Long hours, large salaries, and one of the unhealthiest and unhappiest professions on earth.

C. The "Game"

But something is wrong here. Something doesn't make sense.

As I have tried to convey, the profession that you are about to enter is absolutely obsessed with money. "[M]oney is not just incidental to the practice, but at its core."[216] Money is at the root of virtually everything that lawyers don't like about their profession: the long hours, the commercialization, the tremendous pressure to attract and retain clients, the fiercely competitive marketplace, the lack of collegiality and loyalty among partners, the poor public image of the profession, and even the lack of civility. Almost every one of these problems would be eliminated or at least substantially reduced if lawyers were simply willing to make less money. The North Carolina Bar Association had it exactly right: "[T]he misguided view of money as the sole goal of practice, sole measure of success and sole measure of self-worth is directly and indirectly responsible for many of the problems in practice today."[217]

The notion that lawyers could get by with less money is not exactly absurd. In 1994, the median income for American men employed full-time during the entire year was $31,612; for women, the comparable figure was $23,265.[218] In 1995, the median income for partners in firms of all sizes was $168,751;[219] one of every four partners made over $230,133.[220] In the largest firms (those of seventy-five or more lawyers), partners' median income was $190,408, and a quarter of big firm partners made over $261,425.[221] Even in the smallest firms (firms of eight or fewer lawyers), the median income for partners was $134,294, and a quarter made over $216,399.[222] These figures are from 1995; although similar figures are not available from later years, we know that the incomes of law firm partners rose dramatically in 1996 and 1997.[223] At those firms qualifying for the "Am Law 100,"[224] the average profits per partner rose to $587,000 in 1997.[225] It's not as if lawyers are just scraping by.

At the same time that lawyers are enjoying these fantastic incomes, many are dissatisfied with their professional lives,[226] and their single biggest complaint is the long hours they have to work.[227] Lawyers could enjoy a lot more life outside of work if they were willing to accept relatively modest reductions in their incomes. Take, for example, a partner who is billing 2000 hours and being paid $200,000. If we assume that a 20% reduction in billable hours will translate into a 20% reduction in pay (an assumption that is unlikely to be exactly true, but that is close enough for our purposes), this lawyer could trade $40,000 in income for 600 more hours of life outside work (assuming that three hours at work translates into two hours billed[228]).

Our hypothetical partner has a choice, then: He can make $200,000 per year and work many nights and most weekends—routinely getting up early, before his children are awake, driving to the office, eating lunch at his desk, leaving the office late, picking up dinner at the Taco Bell drive-through window, and then arriving home to kiss the cheeks of his sleeping children. Or he can make $160,000 per year and work few nights and weekends. He can spend time with his spouse, be a parent to his children, enjoy the company of his friends, pursue a hobby, do volunteer work, exercise regularly, and generally lead a well-balanced life—*while still making $160,000 per year.* If all such lawyers making $160,000 per year sat down and asked themselves, "What will make me a happier and healthier person: another $40,000 in income (which, after taxes, will mean another $25,000 or so in the bank) or 600 hours to do whatever I enjoy most?," it is hard to believe that many of them would take the money.

But many of them do take the money. Thousands of lawyers choose to give up a healthy, happy, well-balanced life for a less healthy, less happy life dominated by work. And they do so merely to be able to make seven or eight times the national median income instead of five or six times the national median income. Why? Are lawyers just greedy?

Well, some are, but it is more complicated than that. For one thing, lawyers don't think in these terms. They don't see their lives as crazy. Lawyers don't see any of this. Lawyers don't sit down and think logically about why they are leading the lives they are leading any more than buffalo sit down and think logically about why they are stampeding. That is the primary reason I am writing this article: I hope that you *will* sit down and think about the life that you want to lead before you get caught up in the stampede.

More importantly, though, the flaw in my analysis is that it assumes that the reason lawyers push themselves to make so much money is the money itself. In other words, my analysis assumes that the reason lawyers want to earn more money is that they want to spend more money and enjoy the things that money will buy. When put in those terms, giving up 600 hours of life for another $40,000 on top of a $160,000 salary makes no sense for most lawyers. What you need to understand, though, is that very few lawyers are working extraordinarily long hours because they need the money. They are doing it for a different reason.

Big firm lawyers are, on the whole, a remarkably insecure and competitive group of people. Many of them have spent almost their entire lives competing to win games that other people have set up for them. First they competed to get into a prestigious college. Then they competed for college grades. Then they competed for LSAT scores. Then they competed to get into a prestigious law school. Then they competed for law school grades. Then they competed to make the law review. Then they competed for clerkships.[229] Then they competed to get hired by a big law firm.[230]

Now that they're in a big law firm, what's going to happen? Are they going to stop competing? Are they going to stop comparing themselves to others? Of course not. They're going to keep competing—competing to bill more hours, to attract more clients, to win more cases, to do more deals. They're playing a game. And money is how the score is kept in that game.

Why do you suppose sixty year old lawyers with millions of dollars in the bank still bill 2200 hours per year? Why do you suppose lawyers whose children have everything money can buy but who need the time and attention of their parents continue to spend most nights and weekends at the office—while continuing to write out checks to the best child psychologists in town? Why do you suppose one big firm partner I know flew into a rage after learning that his year-end bonus would be only—only—$400,000, while the bonus of one of his rivals in the firm would be $425,000? Why do you suppose that another lawyer I know (a lawyer making $1 million a year) came within a whisker of quitting his firm after losing a bitter dispute with one of his partners (a lawyer making over $2 million a year) over a $10,000 payment?

It is not because these lawyers *need* the money. Any of these lawyers could lose every penny of his savings and see his annual income reduced by two-thirds and still live much more comfortably than the vast majority of Americans. What's driving these lawyers is the desire to *win the game.* These lawyers have spent their entire lives competing against others and measuring their worth by how well they do in the competitions. And now that they are working in a law firm, money is the way they keep score. Money is what tells them if they're more successful than the lawyer in the next office—or in the next office building—or in the next town. If a lawyer's life is dominated by the game—and if his success in the game is measured by money—then his *life* is dominated by money. For many, many lawyers, it's that simple.

III. The Ethics of Lawyers

At this point, I should say a few words about ethics. I hesitate to do so. I know that courses on legal ethics (or "professional responsibility") are among the least popular courses in the law school curriculum[231]—even less popular than courses on taxation. I realize that, by raising the topic of ethics, I risk making your eyes glaze over. At the same time, the legal profession is widely perceived—even by lawyers[232]—as being unethical.[233] Only one American in five considers lawyers to be "honest and ethical,"[234] and "the more a person knows about the legal profession and the more he or she is in direct personal contact with lawyers, the lower [his or her] opinion of them."[235] This should concern you.[236]

There are many reasons why ethics courses are so unpopular, but the most important is probably that law students do not think that they will become unethical lawyers. Students think of unethical lawyers as the sleazeballs who chase ambulances (think Danny DeVito in *The Rainmaker*) or run insurance scams (think Bill Murray in *Wild Things*) or destroy evidence (think Al Pacino's crew in *The Devil's Advocate*). Students have a hard time identifying with these lawyers. When students think of life after graduation, they see themselves sitting on the 27th floor of some skyscraper in a freshly pressed dark suit (blue, black, or gray) with a starched blouse or shirt (white or light blue) doing sophisticated legal work for sophisticated clients. Students imagine—wrongly[237]—that such lawyers do not have to worry much about ethics, except, perhaps, when the occasional conflict of interest question arises.

If you think this—if you think that you will not have any trouble practicing law ethically—you are wrong. Dead wrong. In fact, particularly if you go to work for a big firm, you will probably begin to practice law unethically in at least some respects within your first year or two in practice. This happens to most young lawyers in big firms. It happened to me, and it will happen to you, unless you do something about it.

A. Practicing Law Ethically

Let's first be clear on what I mean by practicing law ethically. I mean three things.

First, you generally have to comply with the formal disciplinary rules—either the Model Rules of Professional Conduct,[238] the Model Code of Professional Responsibility,[239] or some state variant of one or the other.[240] As a law student, and then as a young lawyer, you will often be encouraged to distinguish ethical from unethical conduct solely by reference to the formal rules. Most likely, you will devote the majority of the time in your professional responsibility class to studying the rules, and you will, of course, learn the rules cold so that you can pass the Multi-State Professional Responsibility Exam ("MPRE"). In many other ways, subtle and blatant, you will be encouraged to think that conduct that does not violate the rules is "ethical," while conduct that does violate the rules is "unethical."[241]

It is in the interests of your professors, the organized bar, and other lawyers to get you to think about ethics in this way. It is a lot easier for a professor to teach students what rules say than it is to explore with students what it means to behave ethically. (Fortunately, many professors resist the temptation to teach only the rules, but many others do not.[242]) Defining ethics with reference to rules puts tremendous power in the hands of the organized bar that writes those rules.[243] And many lawyers want "the absence of disciplinary measures and adherence to the profession's own Model Rules of Professional Conduct"[244] to be sufficient to qualify a lawyer as "ethical," simply because it is easy to avoid disciplinary measures and to adhere to at least the letter of the formal rules.[245]

I don't have anything against the formal rules. Often, they are all that stands between an unethical lawyer and a vulnerable client. You should learn them and follow them. But you should also understand that the formal rules represent nothing more than "the lowest common denominator of conduct that a highly self-interested group will tolerate."[246] For many lawyers, "[e]thics is a matter of steering, if necessary, just clear of the few unambiguous prohibitions found in rules governing lawyers."[247] But complying with the formal rules will not make you an ethical lawyer, any more than complying with the criminal law will make you an ethical person. Many of the sleaziest lawyers you will encounter will be absolutely scrupulous in their compliance with the formal rules. In fact, they will be only too happy to tell you just that. Complying with the rules is usually a necessary, but never a sufficient, part of being an ethical lawyer.

The second thing you must do to be an ethical lawyer is to act ethically in your work, even when you aren't required to do so by any rule. To a substantial extent, "bar ethical rules have lost touch with ordinary moral intuitions."[248] To practice law ethically you must practice law consistently with those intuitions. For the most part, this is not complicated. Being an ethical lawyer is not much different from being an ethical doctor or mail carrier or gas station attendant. Indeed, long before you applied to law school, your parents had probably taught you all that you need to know to practice law ethically. You should treat others as you want them to treat you. Be honest and fair. Show respect and compassion. Keep your promises. Here is a good rule of thumb: If you would be ashamed if your parents or spouse or children knew what you were doing, then you should not do it.

The third thing you must do to be an ethical lawyer is to live an ethical life. Many big firm lawyers—who can be remarkably "smug[] about the superiority of the ethical standards of large firms"[249]—ignore this point. So do many law professors who, when writing about legal ethics, tend to focus solely on the lawyer at work. But being admitted to the bar does not absolve you of your responsibilities outside of work—to your family, to your friends, to your community, and, if you're a person of faith, to your God. To practice law ethically, you must meet those responsibilities, which means that you must live a balanced life. If you become a workaholic lawyer, you will be unhealthy, probably unhappy, and, I would argue, unethical.

Now I recognize that we live in an age of moral relativism—an age in which "behavior is neither right nor wrong but a matter of personal choice."[250] Your reaction to my claim that an unbalanced life is an unethical life may very well be, "That's just your opinion." It is my opinion, but it is surely not *just* my opinion. I would be surprised if the belief system to which you subscribe—whether it be religiously or secularly based—regards a life dominated by the pursuit of wealth to the exclusion of all else as an ethical life, or an attorney who meets only his responsibilities to his clients and law partners as an ethical person.

B. Big Firm Culture

It is hard to practice law ethically. Complying with the formal rules is the easy part.[251] The rules are not very specific, and they don't demand very much.[252] You may, on rare occasions, confront an extremely difficult conflict of interest problem that will require you to parse the rules carefully. You may even confront a situation in which some ethical or moral imperative compels you to violate the rules. But by and large, you will have no trouble complying with the rules; indeed, you are unlikely to give the rules much thought.

Acting as an ethical lawyer in the broader, non-formalistic sense is far more difficult. I have already given you some idea of why it is hard to practice law in a big firm (or any firm that emulates a big firm) and live a balanced life; I will return to that point in a moment. But even practicing law ethically in the sense of being honest and fair and compassionate is difficult. To understand why, you need to understand what it is that you will do every day as a lawyer.

Most of a lawyer's working life is filled with the mundane. It is unlikely that one of your clients will drop a smoking gun on your desk or ask you to deliver a briefcase full of unmarked bills or invite you to have wild, passionate sex (or even un-wild, un-passionate sex). These things happen to lawyers only in John Grisham novels. Your life as a lawyer will be filled with the kind of things that drove John Grisham to write novels: dictating letters and talking on the phone and drafting memoranda and performing "due diligence" and proofreading contracts and negotiating settlements and filling out time sheets. And because your life as a lawyer will be filled with the mundane, whether you practice law ethically will depend not upon how you resolve the one or two dramatic ethical dilemmas that you will confront during your entire career, but upon the hundreds of little things that you will do, almost unthinkingly, each and every day.

Because practicing law ethically will depend primarily upon the hundreds of little things that you will do almost unthinkingly every day, it will not depend much upon your thinking. You are going to be busy. The days will fly by. When you are on the phone negotiating a deal or when you are at your computer drafting a brief or when you are filling out your time sheet at the end of the day, you are not going to have time to reflect on each of your actions.[253] You are going to have to act almost instinctively.

What this means, then, is that you will not practice law ethically—you *cannot* practice law ethically—unless acting ethically is *habitual* for you. You have to be in the habit of being honest. You have to be in the habit of being fair. You have to be in the habit of being compassionate. These qualities have to be deeply ingrained in you, so that you can't turn them on and off—so that acting honorably is not something you have to *decide* to do—so that when you are at work, making the thousands of phone calls you will make and writing the thousands of letters you will write and dealing with the thousands of people with whom you will deal, you will *automatically* apply the same values in the workplace that you apply outside of work, when you are with family and friends.[254]

Here is the problem, though: After you start practicing law, nothing is likely to influence you more than "the culture or house norms of the agency, department, or firm" in which you work.[255] If you are going into private practice—particularly private practice in a big firm—you are going to be immersed in a culture that is hostile to the values you now have. The system does not *want* you to apply the same values in the workplace that you do outside of work (unless you're rapaciously greedy outside of work); it wants you to replace those values with the system's values. The system is obsessed with money, and it wants you to be, too. The system wants you—it *needs* you—to play the game.

Now, no one is going to say this to you. No one is going to take you aside and say, "Jane, we here at Smith & Jones are obsessed with money. From this point forward the most important thing in your life has to be billing hours and generating business. Family and friends and honesty and fairness are okay in moderation, but don't let them interfere with making money." No one will tell you, as one lawyer told another in a Charles Addams cartoon, "I admire your honesty and integrity, Wilson, but I have no room for them in my firm."[256] Instead, the culture will pressure you in more subtle ways to replace your values with the system's.

Here is an example of what I mean: During your first month working at the big firm, some senior partner will invite you and the other new associates to a barbeque at his home. This "barbeque" will bear absolutely no relationship to what your father used to do on a Weber grill in your driveway. You will drive up to the senior partner's home in your rusted Escort and park at the end of a long line of Mercedeses and BMWs and sports utility vehicles. You will walk up to the front door of the house. The house will be enormous. The lawn will look like a putting green; it will be bordered by perfectly manicured trees and flowers. Somebody wearing a white shirt and black bow tie will answer the door and direct you to the backyard. You will walk through one room after another, each of which will be decorated with expensive carpeting and expensive wallpaper and expensive antiques. Scattered throughout the home will be large professional photographs of beautiful children with tousled, sunbleached hair.

As you enter the partner's immaculately landscaped backyard, someone wearing a white shirt and black bow tie carrying a silver platter will approach you and offer you an appetizer. Don't look for cocktail weenies in barbeque sauce; you will more likely be offered pate or miniature quiches or shrimp. A bar will be set up near the house; the bartender (who will be wearing a white shirt and black bow tie, of course) will pour you a drink of the most expensive brand of whatever liquor you like. In the corner of the yard, a caterer will be grilling swordfish. In another corner will stand the senior partner, sipping a glass of white wine, holding court with a worshipful group of junior partners and senior associates.

The senior partner will be wearing designer sunglasses and designer clothes; the logo on his shirt will signal its exorbitant cost; his shorts will be pressed. He will have a tan—albeit a slightly orange, tanning salon enhanced tan—and the nicest haircut you've ever seen. Eventually, the partner will introduce you to his wife. She will be beautiful, very thin, and a lot younger than her husband. She, too, will have a great tan, and not nearly as orange as her husband's. You and the other lawyers will talk about golf. Or about tennis. After a couple hours, you will walk out the front door, slightly tipsy from the free liquor, and say to yourself, "This is the life."

In this and a thousand other ways, you will absorb big firm culture[257]—a culture of long hours of toil inside the office and short hours of conspicuous consumption outside the office. You will work among lawyers who will talk about money constantly and who will be intensely curious about how much money other lawyers are making. If you want to get some sense of this, leave your tax return on the photocopier glass sometime. (At least one hapless lawyer seems to do this every spring at most firms.) Every lawyer in the firm will know how much money you made last year in about fifteen minutes, and every lawyer who joins the firm during the next quarter century will hear the story of your tax return.

The lawyers in your firm are not unique. Thirty or forty years ago, talking about income and clients and fees "just [wa]sn't done," even among Wall Street lawyers.[258] Today, "the legal profession ... has become extraordinarily self-conscious about making money," and "the new legal journalism [has] hone[d] this self-consciousness to a sharp comparative and competitive edge."[259] Just about every issue of the *National Law Journal* or the *American Lawyer* seems to include at least one article about how much money some lawyer somewhere is making.[260] A couple times a year, these journals publish extensive surveys of lawyers' incomes—focusing in particular on the incomes of associates and partners in big firms.[261] These surveys are pored over by lawyers with the intensity that small children bring to poring over the statistics of their favorite baseball players. Want to know what a first year associate at Irell & Manella in Los Angeles makes? $88,000.[262] How about a sixth year associate at Dewey Ballantine in New York? $166,500, plus a $26,500 bonus.[263] Profits per partner at McDermott, Will & Emery in Chicago? $700,000.[264] Reading about the incomes of your rivals will bring on either intense envy or smug Schadenfreude.

Big firm culture also reflects the many ways in which lawyers who are winning the game broadcast their success. A first year male associate will buy his suits off the rack at a department store; a couple years later, he will be at Brooks Brothers; a few years after that, a salesperson will come to his office, with tape measures and fabric swatches in hand. Similar ostentatious progress will be demonstrated with regard to everything from watches to cell phones to running shoes to child care arrangements to private social clubs. When lawyers speak with envy or admiration about other lawyers, they do not mention a lawyer's devotion to family or public service, or a lawyer's innate sense of fairness, or even a lawyer's skill at trying cases or closing deals, nearly as much as they mention a lawyer's billable hours, or stable of clients, or annual income.

It is very difficult for a young lawyer immersed in this culture day after day to maintain the values she had as a law student.[265] Slowly, almost imperceptibly, young lawyers change. They begin to admire things they did not admire before, be ashamed of things they were not ashamed of before, find it impossible to live without things they lived without before.

Somewhere, somehow, a lawyer changes from a person who gets intense pleasure from being able to buy her first car stereo to a person enraged over a $400,000 bonus.

C. Becoming Unethical

As the values of an attorney change, so, too, does her ability to practice law ethically. The process that I have described will obviously push a lawyer away from practicing law ethically in the broadest sense—that is, in the sense of leading a balanced life and meeting non-work-related responsibilities. When work becomes all-consuming, it consumes all. To succeed in today's big firm, a lawyer must live without a single "compelling, time consuming, and deeply valued interest outside the practice of law."[266] If you are working all the time, you will not—you cannot—meet any other responsibilities that require any appreciable commitment of time or energy.[267] This much is obvious. However, absorbing the values of big firm culture will also push a lawyer away from practicing law ethically in the narrower sense of being honest and fair and compassionate.[268] In the highly competitive, money obsessed world of big firm practice, "[m]ost of the new incentives for lawyers, such as attracting and retaining clients, push toward stretching ethical concerns to the limit."[269]

Unethical lawyers do not start out being unethical; they start out just like you—as perfectly decent young men or women who have every intention of practicing law ethically. They do not become unethical overnight; they become unethical just as you will (if you become unethical)—a little bit at a time. And they do not become unethical by shredding incriminating documents or bribing jurors; they become unethical just as you are likely to—by cutting a corner here, by stretching the truth a bit there.

Let me tell you how you will start acting unethically: It will start with your time sheets. One day, not too long after you start practicing law, you will sit down at the end of a long, tiring day, and you just won't have much to show for your efforts in terms of billable hours. It will be near the end of the month. You will know that all of the partners will be looking at your monthly time report in a few days, so what you'll do is pad your time sheet just a bit. Maybe you will bill a client for ninety minutes for a task that really took you only sixty minutes to perform. However, you will promise yourself that you will repay the client at the first opportunity by doing thirty minutes of work for the client for "free." In this way, you will be "borrowing," not "stealing."

And then what will happen is that it will become easier and easier to take these little loans against future work. And then, after a while, you will stop paying back these little loans. You will convince yourself that, although you billed for ninety minutes and spent only sixty minutes on the project, you did such good work that your client should pay a bit more for it. After all, your billing rate is awfully low, and your client is awfully rich.

And then you will pad more and more—every two minute telephone conversation will go down on the sheet as ten minutes, every three hour research project will go down with an extra quarter hour or so. You will continue to rationalize your dishonesty to yourself in various ways until one day you stop doing even that. And, before long—it won't take you much more than three or four years—you will be stealing from your clients almost every day, and you won't even notice it.

You know what? You will also likely become a liar. A deadline will come up one day, and, for reasons that are entirely your fault, you will not be able to meet it. So you will call your senior partner or your client and make up a white lie for why you missed the deadline. And then you will get busy and a partner will ask whether you proofread a lengthy prospectus and you will say yes, even though you didn't. And then you will be drafting a brief and you will quote language from a Supreme Court opinion even though you will know that, when read in context, the language does not remotely suggest what you are implying it suggests. And then, in preparing a client for a deposition, you will help the client to formulate an answer to a difficult question that will likely be asked—an answer that will be "legally accurate" but that will mislead your opponent. And then you will be reading through a big box of your client's documents—a box that has not been opened in twenty years—and you will find a document that would hurt your client's case, but that no one except you knows exists, and you will simply "forget" to produce it in response to your opponent's discovery requests.

Do you see what will happen? After a couple years of this, you won't even notice that you are lying and cheating and stealing every day that you practice law. None of these things will seem like a big deal in itself—an extra fifteen minutes added to a time sheet here, a little white lie to cover a missed deadline there. But, after a while, your entire frame of reference will change. You will still be making dozens of quick, instinctive decisions every day, but those decisions, instead of reflecting the notions of right and wrong by which you conduct your personal life, will instead reflect the set of values by which you will conduct your professional life—a set of values that embodies not what is right or wrong, but what is profitable, and what you can get away with. The system will have succeeded in replacing your values with the system's values, and the system will be profiting as a result.

Does this happen to every big firm lawyer? Of course not. It's all a matter of degree. The culture in some big firms is better than in others. Every year I steer students who are intent on big firm practice toward some firms and away from others, precisely because some large firms are better places to work than others. I could tell you many stories about big firms going out of their way to show compassion to a partner with a drinking problem or a loyal client who could not pay its bills or a rival attorney who is over the hill and on the verge of embarrassing himself. The big firm at which I practiced was as decent and humane as a big firm can be. Similarly, some big firm lawyers have better values than others. I owe a lot to a partner who sacrificed hundreds of hours of his time and tens of thousands of dollars of income to act as a mentor to me and to many other young lawyers like me.

At the same time, you should not underestimate the likelihood that you will practice law unethically. It is true, for example, that not every lawyer knowingly and blatantly lies on his time sheets. But there is a reason why padding time sheets has been called "a silent epidemic."[270] Lots of lawyers pad time sheets in ways that are less obviously dishonest and more socially accepted.[271] For example, a lawyer who needs to fly from Los Angeles to New York for one client may do the work of another client during the five hour flight, and bill both clients five hours—the first for five hours of travel, the second for five hours of work. Another common practice is for lawyers not to fill out their time sheets until the end of the day—or end of the week—or even end of the month. When a lawyer sits down on July 31 and tries to remember how much time she devoted to a client's work on July 9,[272] it is only natural that she will underestimate the amount of time wasted on coffee breaks and personal phone calls and overestimate the amount of time devoted to the client's work.

Another widely accepted way of padding time sheets is to bill in minimum increments of, say, .25 hours or .30 hours. This permits the enterprising lawyer to engage in four two minute phone calls and bill one hour. I cannot tell you how many times I have seen a lawyer bill a client fifteen minutes for the ninety seconds it took him to leave a voice mail message or to read a one paragraph deposition notice. I recall one occasion on which I sent a letter to an attorney who was representing my client in connection with a lawsuit filed in a distant state. I included in the same envelope copies of two other letters about the lawsuit that I had mailed to other people. I later learned that this lawyer had billed my client .90 hours for reading three letters that I had billed my client .50 hours for writing. How? He billed in .30 minimums and billed separately for each of the three letters he read, while I billed only for the time that I actually devoted to writing the letters. Many lawyers would admire this as clever and creative (if perhaps a bit aggressive) billing.

Likewise, not every big firm lawyer is a workaholic. This, too, is a matter of degree. I know big firm lawyers who make a good living and still eat dinner with their families most nights and spend most weekends away from the office. Unfortunately, though, these lawyers are almost invariably regarded by their partners as "deadwood" or as "semi-retired." If you think I am exaggerating, I challenge you to find *one* big firm partner who lives a balanced life—that is, who does not work regularly on nights or weekends (at home or at the office)—and yet is well respected and considered successful by his peers. And I challenge you to find *one* big firm lawyer who lived anything like a balanced life as an associate and still made partner. I do not know of such a lawyer. Not one. In the last couple years, I have given speeches to various groups of lawyers and judges, and I have challenged my audiences to identify one such big firm lawyer for me. I have yet to be given a name. At best, such partners are rare. They may be nonexistent.

As I say, neither big firms nor big firm lawyers are all alike. But what you need to understand is that they are *becoming* more alike. One of the most consistent findings of the social scientists involved in a recent ABA study of the ethics of big firm litigators[273] was that the cultures of individual firms are weakening, leaving a "void of guidance to junior lawyers."[274] This void, in turn, is being "filled by other powerful systemic or environmental influences," especially influences from outside the firm.[275] In other words, the distinctive cultures of individual big firms are influencing young lawyers less and less, while a generic big firm culture is influencing young lawyers more and more.[276] That is why, no matter which big firm you join, there is a good chance that working at the firm will make you unhealthy, an even better chance that it will make you unhappy, and an almost 100% chance that it will make you unethical—at least if you accept that practicing law ethically includes practicing law in a manner that permits you to meet your responsibilities to someone besides your firm and clients.

IV. On Being a Happy, Healthy, and Ethical Lawyer

I now want to give you some advice—advice about how you can be a happy, healthy, and ethical member of an unhappy, unhealthy, and unethical profession. I want to give you both "big picture" advice and "little picture" advice.

A. *"Big Picture" Advice*

My "big picture" advice is simple: Don't get sucked into the game. Don't let money become the most important thing in your life. Don't fall into the trap of measuring your worth as an attorney—or as a human being—by how much money you make.

If you let your law firm or clients define success for you, they will define it in a way that is in their interest, not yours. It is important for them that your primary motivation be making money and that, no matter how much money you make, your primary motivation continue to be making money. If you end up as an unhappy or unethical attorney, money will most likely be at the root of your problem.

You cannot win the game. If you fall into the trap of measuring your worth by money, you will always feel inadequate. There will always be a firm paying more to its associates than yours. There will always be a firm with higher per-partner profits than yours. There will always be a lawyer at your firm making more money than you. No matter how hard you work, you will never be able to win the game. You will run faster and faster and faster, but there will always be a runner ahead of you, and the finish line will never quite come into view. That is why the game will make your clients and partners so rich and you so unhappy.

Most likely, when you were a child, your parents or grandparents told you that money does not buy happiness. They were right. Even scientists now say they were right.[277] In part, they were right because much of what determines whether you will be happy is outside your control. You cannot control your genetic makeup—upon which happiness seems in part to depend (according to recent studies[278])—nor can you control many of the events in life that, for better or worse, will affect your subjective well-being (for example, you cannot control whether you will be permanently injured in a car accident or whether your spouse will perish at a young age). But the main reason your parents or grandparents were right about money not buying happiness is because—well, because money does not buy happiness.

Research has shown that, with the exception of those living in poverty, people are almost always wrong in thinking that more money will make them happier. "[O]nce people are able to afford life's necessities, increasing levels of affluence matter surprisingly little."[279] When people experience a rise in income, they quickly adjust their desires and expectations accordingly—and conclude, once again, that more money will bring them more happiness.[280] (Psychologists Philip Brickman and Donald Campbell aptly refer to this process as the "hedonic treadmill."[281]) Thus, when, as is true in law firms, more money almost always means more work, money not only fails to buy happiness, but it actually buys *unhappiness*.[282] As one study of lawyers found, "after a certain time commitment (for most people, working more than 225 hours per month), even substantial income cannot negate the reduced quality of life. Because of this ... the net impact of income on career satisfaction is negative."[283] Note that the reference is to *working* 225 hours per month, and not to *billing* 225 hours per month.[284]

Law students and young lawyers—particularly those who have enjoyed academic success at the best schools—have to get their priorities straight. It saddens me that the objects of envy and admiration of many of my students today are not lawyers like Thurgood Marshall or Charles Hamilton Houston—lawyers who sacrificed much personal gain to do much public good—but rather the nameless, faceless attorneys who populate giant law firms, grinding out thousands upon thousands of billable hours, often toward no end other than getting rich and determining whether one huge corporation will have to write out a check to another huge corporation.

Law students and young lawyers have to stop seeing workaholism as "a badge of honor."[285] They have to stop talking with admiration about lawyers who bill 2500 hours per year. Attorneys whose lives are consumed with work—who devote endless hours to making themselves and their clients wealthy, at the expense of just about everything else in their lives—are not heroes. And that is true whether the lawyers are workaholic because they truly enjoy their work or because they crave wealth or because they are terribly insecure. At best, these attorneys are people with questionable priorities. At worst, they are immoral. There are certainly better lawyers after which to pattern your professional life.

Law students and young lawyers must consider the costs, as well as the benefits, of private practice—and particularly of private practice in a large firm. The benefits of big firm life—the high salaries, the plush offices, the conspicuous consumption—are paraded before young lawyers and are easy to understand. Any law student can divide $90,000 by twelve, subtract 40% for federal and state taxes, and fantasize about how she will spend $4,500 a month. By contrast, the *costs* of big firm life are not paraded before young lawyers and are not fully appreciated until a lawyer actually works at a large firm. But the costs are just as real as the benefits.

When you are at that barbeque at the senior partner's house, instead of wistfully telling yourself, "This is the life," ask the senior partner some questions. (I'm speaking figuratively here; you probably don't want to actually ask these questions aloud.) Ask him how often he sees the gigantic house in which he lives. If he's honest, you will find out that he hasn't seen his home during daylight for almost four weeks, and that the only reason he came home at a decent hour tonight is to host the barbeque. Or ask him how often he's actually sat on that antique settee in that expensively decorated living room. You will find out that the room is only used for entertaining guests. Or ask him about his beautiful wife. You will find out that she is the third Mrs. Partner and that the lawyers for the first two Mrs. Partners are driving him crazy. Or ask him about those beautiful children whose photographs are everywhere. You will find out that they live with their mothers, not with him; that he never sees one of them because she hates his guts; and that he sees the other two only on holidays—that is, when he is not working on the holidays, which isn't often. And then ask him when is the last time he read a good book. Or watched television. Or took a walk. Or sat on his porch. Or cooked a meal. Or went fishing. Or did volunteer work. Or went to church. Or did anything that was not in some way related to work.

This is the best advice I can give you: Right now, while you are still in law school, make the commitment—not just in your head, but in your heart—that, although you are willing to work hard and you would like to make a comfortable living, you are not going to let money dominate your life to the exclusion of all else. And don't just structure your life around this negative; embrace a positive. *Believe* in something—*care* about something—so that when the culture of greed presses in on you from all sides, there will be something inside of you pushing back. Make the decision now that *you* will be the one who defines success for you—not your classmates, not big law firms, not clients of big law firms, not the *National Law Journal*. You will be a happier, healthier, and more ethical attorney as a result.[286]

B. "Little Picture" Advice

I have four pieces of "little picture" advice for you.

1. Avoid Working in Large Law Firms—or in Firms That Act Like Large Law Firms

Three years ago, I was a partner in a big firm. Most of my friends and acquaintances were lawyers in big firms, and most of them were unhappy. I had countless conversations with these friends in which we lamented our crushing workloads, the unrelenting pressure to bring in business, the lack of control over our lives, and the tedium of much of our work. When I gave up my partnership in order to teach, dozens of lawyer friends told me how much they envied me, and how much they, too, would like to escape big firm practice.

Then a curious thing happened. I arrived at Notre Dame and found that the substantial majority of my students wanted nothing so much as to join the very same big firms that my lawyer friends wanted so badly to leave. Before I had even taught my first class, students literally lined up outside my door to talk with me about getting big firm jobs. It called to mind the gridlock that often develops outside of open elevator doors: Inside the elevator were my lawyer friends, trying to push their way out, while outside the elevator were my students, trying to push their way in.

You should think very long and very hard before you try to push your way into that elevator—or before you waste a moment of your life regretting that you will not be able to get into that elevator. I fully understand how much pressure law students experience to go to big firms in big cities. At many law schools—particularly the more prestigious schools—going to work at a big firm is considered "the thing to do."[287] Conventional wisdom at the best law schools is that "everyone comes in saying they're interested in public interest and everyone leaves doing large firm corporate work."[288] It is big firms who come to campus to interview, big firms who invite students to fly out for splashy recruiting visits, big firms who get talked about in the student lounge, big firms who get written up in the *American Lawyer*.[289] "The subliminal message of [law school] training is clear to most students: 'Real' lawyers work in large firms representing corporate and affluent clients."[290]

I also understand how easy it is to accept an offer from a big firm. I well remember graduating from law school being burdened by heavy student loan debt and being sick of living in "genteel poverty."[291] I recall how much I looked forward to making real money for the first time in my life—to buying furniture that was not constructed of particle board, to buying bestsellers before they came out in paperback, to buying clothing made of natural fibers. Moreover, like the majority of law school graduates, I had no family commitments, lots of energy, and absolutely no idea of what billing 2000 hours entailed.[292] It was hard not to go to a big firm.

Although I understand the pressures and temptations to join a big firm, I nevertheless encourage you to resist them. If you have already accepted an offer from a big firm, I encourage you not to go to another big firm when you change jobs—which is likely to be sooner rather than later.[293] As you look for a job (or as you look for a second job), weigh carefully the benefits and costs of practicing law in a big firm. I have already discussed the costs at length. Allow me now to say a few words about the benefits. Everyone agrees that the main benefit of big firm practice is the money. But big firms always express the "hope[] that new associates [will] choose to join a [big] firm for reasons other than money."[294] What reasons, exactly? Among those that are routinely given are the following:

a. Training

Many students claim that they will receive better training at big firms than they will at medium or small firms, corporations, or government agencies.[295] Big firms agree.[296] Big firms explain that working for them gives young attorneys the opportunity to learn to do things right. An associate at a small firm or a government agency who is told to draft interrogatories for the first time will likely have to complete the assignment quickly and with minimal supervision; she will learn on the fly. At the big firm, by contrast, an associate can take her time, either because the firm's well-heeled clients will not object to paying the extra cost, or because the well-heeled firm can afford to "write off" some of the associate's time.

There is something to this, but not much. Big firms do indeed get a lot of big cases in which tens or hundreds of millions of dollars are at stake, clients want to pull out all the stops, and associate training costs can easily be tucked away into huge legal bills. But these cases are the exceptions, and as the legal market gets increasingly competitive, these cases are getting increasingly exceptional.[297]

More importantly, the boast of big firms misses a couple of points. First, the breadth of training is as important as its depth. True, it is nice if associates can take the time to learn to draft interrogatories the right way. But it is also nice if associates can get to do something other than draft interrogatories. The life of an associate in a big firm litigation group is dominated by library research, writing briefs, drafting discovery requests, and responding to discovery requests. A typical junior associate will have little client contact, take few depositions, do little negotiating with opposing counsel, argue almost no motions or appeals, and try not a single case.[298] The fact that big firms work on so many big cases in which so much is at stake—the very reason that associates can take the time to do things right—is also the reason associates do not get the chance to do things that matter. AT&T is not going to pay a law firm tens of millions of dollars to fend off a billion dollar antitrust suit, only to see a third year associate show up to take an important deposition or argue a critical summary judgment motion.

Second, the most valuable training that any young lawyer receives comes from observing and being observed by more experienced attorneys. Lawyers can learn only so much from books, in-house training sessions, or continuing legal education seminars. A lawyer learns how to nail down a slippery witness at a deposition or negotiate a deal with an unrealistic lawyer or calm a client who is upset about the size of a bill by watching more experienced lawyers do it, or by doing it and having more experienced lawyers give them feedback. This type of one-on-one mentoring is disappearing in big firms for a number of reasons, including the pressure to bill hours, the pressure to attract and retain clients, the pressure to minimize legal costs, the increasing size of law firms, and the increasing mobility of lawyers.[299] Today "training" by big firms too often means providing brown bag seminars or reimbursing tuition for continuing legal education; the kind of one-on-one training that is most effective is actually less available in big firms than in small firms and other settings. Indeed, one of the most common complaints of big firm associates is the lack of training and feedback they receive.[300]

b. Interesting or Challenging Work

Working in a big firm will unquestionably give you the opportunity to do some interesting work that is not available elsewhere. Large firms work on a lot of big deals and complex cases; AT&T is not going to hire a four lawyer firm in Boise to defend that billion dollar antitrust case. When I was in practice, I worked on the National Football League antitrust case and, very briefly, on the Exxon Valdez oil spill litigation. I litigated several fascinating First Amendment issues for newspapers and religious organizations. I appeared on national television and on radio call-in shows. Working at a big firm made all of this possible. That said, it is nevertheless easy to overstate the degree to which the work that is available at big firms is more interesting or challenging than the work that is available elsewhere.

First, most big firm lawyers—especially big firm associates—spend the bulk of their professional lives working on run-of-the-mill matters.[301] At the same time, many lawyers who do not work in big firms do fascinating work. When Michigan Law School surveyed members of its classes of 1990 and 1991 five years after graduation, it found that only 42% of those in private practice were "quite satisfied" with the intellectual challenge of their work, as compared to 55% of corporate counsel, 68% of government attorneys, and 72% of public interest lawyers.[302] This should not be surprising. After all, who would you rather shadow for a day: a partner at Baker & McKenzie, an Assistant United States Attorney for the Northern District of Illinois, an in-house lawyer at Time-Warner, an attorney for the Sierra Club, or a successful solo practitioner specializing in employment law? The big firm partner would be fifth on my list.

Second, what is "interesting" or "challenging" is in the eye of the beholder. If your idea of challenging work is having the time to research a complicated issue of securities law, then you will find more interesting work in a big firm. But if your idea of challenging work is helping a client get divorced without losing her children or putting a diabolically clever criminal behind bars or helping a client realize her dream of opening a small business, then you are likely to be bored in a big firm. What many lawyers find most gratifying about practicing law is having ordinary people show up at their offices with problems, and then seeing the lives of those people improved in tangible ways as a direct result of their lawyer's efforts. Such lawyers will not find working in big firms to be either very interesting or very challenging.

Finally, whether you are likely to find big firm practice interesting will depend in part upon whether you are the type of person who likes to learn a little about a lot or a lot about a little. Big firm work is highly specialized and becoming more so;[303] "specialization is the name of the game today."[304] As in-house legal departments grow and take on more and more of the "routine" work of corporations, the work assigned to big firms is becoming "more task-specific and ad hoc."[305] Michael Kelly explains "this narrowing of focus, this confining of lawyers to the technicalities of law" as follows:

> As in-house corporate law departments become more professional, that is, more capable and highly respected by management, they do something much more significant than take routine business away from the large corporate law firm. They capture much of the judgment business, the general advising, the work of helping the client to determine the client's real interests, and they limit the role of outside counsel to highly specialized arenas ... in which the in-house group has limited technical expertise.[306]

If you go to a big firm, you will have to find a niche, and the bigger your firm, the smaller your niche is likely to be. If you become an expert in chartering banks, you will charter banks, day in and day out. If you are assigned to defend that billion dollar antitrust action against AT&T, you might spend six or seven years of your life working on that one case—and doing so as the fifth lawyer on a five lawyer team. Some lawyers like to be able to specialize; others do not. It depends on the lawyer. I developed a national reputation for defending religious organizations in clergy sexual misconduct cases. I worked on hundreds of those cases, sending out pretty much the same interrogatories, getting back pretty much the same answers, reading pretty much the same medical records, asking pretty much the same questions at depositions, filing pretty much the same summary judgment motions. I found the work interesting, but the fiftieth case was not as interesting as the first, and the hundredth case was not as interesting as the fiftieth.

In short, some people would undoubtedly find the work done by big firms interesting and challenging. But many other people would find the work far less interesting and far less challenging than work available elsewhere. Big firm work is not inherently superior to other work.

c. Collegiality

Some students want to go to big firms because they want to be surrounded by extremely smart and able lawyers. They see big firms as the place where a young lawyer can be part of an outstanding team, helping and being helped by the best and brightest in the profession. One student told me that he wanted to work at a big firm instead of a small firm for the same reason that any baseball player would rather play for the New York Yankees than the Montreal Expos.

Again, there is something to this. At a big firm you will be surrounded by attorneys who got good grades at good schools. Most of them will even be good lawyers. And it is indeed nice to walk down the hall and talk to the leading tax lawyer in town or to walk farther down the hall and give an assignment to a young associate fresh off a Second Circuit clerkship. I am as critical of big firms as anyone, but I don't think it can be denied that, *on average*, big firm lawyers are more talented and do better work than lawyers in other practice settings. There are, of course, tens of thousands of exceptions—lawyers who do not practice in big firms who are superb, or lawyers who do practice in big firms who are incompetent. But if I had to choose between two law firms to represent me in an important matter, and I knew nothing about the two law firms except that one had 250 lawyers and the other had five, I would hire the big firm in a second. So would most other lawyers.

Again, though, there is another side to this story, one that substantially undercuts this advantage. For one thing, as I just said, outstanding lawyers work in every part of the legal profession. No matter what you do—no matter the setting in which you work—you will meet terrific attorneys. They will help you, and you will help them, and they will refer work to you, and you will refer work to them. Even if you become a solo practitioner, you will, over time, form your own "big firm" of friends and colleagues in the legal profession.

In addition, being part of a law firm with outstanding lawyers does not mean much if those lawyers don't know you or are indifferent to you. Many big firm partners don't even know their partners,[307] much less the dozens of "here today, gone tomorrow" associates. It is even worse if your colleagues are affirmatively seeking to undercut you. Partners at large firms responding to a recent survey reported that just over 58% of their partners were "supportive," while roughly 33% were "competitive" and 10% "undermining."[308] The *National Law Journal*, which conducted the survey, reported that the pressure to attract business was "caus[ing] partners to root for their comrades to stumble."[309] Things aren't much better at the associate level. "The practice of 'leveraging' associates creates competition, stress and a loss of institutional loyalty and sense of belonging. Colleagues are viewed as competitors for partnership."[310] The notion that big firms have an advantage when it comes to "collegiality" is an illusion. Indeed, one researcher taking part in the ABA's recent study of big firm litigators[311] remarked that "[a]ssociates, in particular, conveyed a profound sense of isolation."[312]

d. Keeping Doors Open

Sometimes students, when resisting entreaties to consider alternatives to big firms, say that they are not sure what they want to do, but figure that if they go to a big firm, they will be keeping their doors open, whereas if they go elsewhere, big firms and other elite employers will lose interest in them. I do not know whether this reasoning is sound, but I suspect that it is not.

Without question, lawyers leaving big firms generally have more options available to them—including the possibility of going to other big firms—than lawyers leaving small firms or other employers. But remember that lawyers leaving big firms generally had more options available to them in the first place. Lawyers hired by big firms tend to have better paper credentials than lawyers hired by small firms, so of course they are going to be more mobile when they look for a second job. That doesn't mean that the lawyers are more mobile because they worked in a big firm.

Suppose that two editors of the *Stanford Law Review* graduate the same year and then clerk on the Ninth Circuit. Suppose that, after clerking, one of them joins a big firm in San Francisco, while the other joins a small firm in San José. Suppose further that, three years later, both lawyers decide to look for another job. It is unlikely that the small firm lawyer in San José is going to have much more difficulty finding a job than the big firm lawyer in San Francisco. In fact, depending upon what the lawyers did during their three years in practice, the San José lawyer might actually have an advantage over the San Francisco lawyer.

This raises an important point: Although those leaving big firms always seem to get new jobs, they may have less mobility than is widely assumed. My firm in Minneapolis got hundreds of resumés from attorneys who had spent a few years in big firms in big cities. We rarely interviewed them and almost never hired them. These people generally had not learned anything that would help our firm much. They had often spent several years in the library or reviewing documents or working on one gigantic lawsuit. At the same time, these people generally brought a lot of baggage. They were accustomed to making more money than we could pay. They were accustomed to approaching work in a way that most of our clients would not accept. And they were accustomed to a culture that was inimical to ours. On balance, we almost always preferred hiring lawyers out of law school to hiring associates laterally from other big firms.

When it comes right down to it, then, there is one and only one clear advantage to working at a big firm: money. This was driven home to me recently when I read the final report of the Boston Bar Association's Task Force on Professional Fulfillment.[313] The Task Force was appointed in response to the "growing evidence that a significant crosssection of lawyers are dissatisfied with the quality of their professional lives."[314] The Task Force was asked "to identify the root causes of dissatisfaction in [the legal] profession and to propose ways in which lawyers can reduce or mitigate challenges to their professional fulfillment."[315] The Task Force formed several subcommittees, each of which was charged with studying one discrete part of the profession. Each subcommittee made extensive use of focus groups and individual interviews. The reports of the subcommittees are fascinating, although perhaps in ways not intended by the subcommittees.

For example, the Large Law Firm Partners Subcommittee identified three of the most "fulfilling aspects of the profession for partners [in large law firms]" as "the intellectual stimulation and challenging nature of the work, the opportunities for community involvement and the far greater economic rewards in comparison to the vast majority of society."[316] As I just explained, the first of these is not an advantage of big firm practice; although big firm partners undoubtedly do interesting and challenging work, there is no reason to believe that the work they do is, on balance, more interesting and challenging than the work done by lawyers in other settings. The second of these is ridiculous; if there is one characteristic that defines the lives of big firm partners, it is having to work so many hours that they cannot get involved in the community or anything else outside of work (unless writing the occasional check or attending the occasional benefit is considered "involvement"). Only the third of these has merit; in other words, the only benefit of big firm practice that big firm partners themselves could plausibly identify was money.

Even more interesting was what the big firm *partners* identified as the benefits that big firm *associates* get from big firm practice. The partners first warned that no one should come to a large law firm expecting to make partner,[317] as making partners of most associates would destroy the leverage that makes big firm partners wealthy.[318] However, according to the big firm partners: "Large law firm practice ... can provide new associates with (1) the opportunity to achieve their full potential as lawyers through training and development while associates; (2) candid assessments of their prospects for partnership; and (3) assistance in finding satisfying alternative career paths if partnership is not available."[319]

This is almost laughable. The "training and development" promised by big firms is, as I have explained, largely illusory, which means that the only advantages of big firm practice that big firm partners themselves could plausibly identify were "candid" assessments of whether you are one of the roughly 10% of associates who will make partner,[320] and help in finding a new job if you are not. What's worse, one of these two benefits is as illusory as training and development: The number of big firm associates who receive truly candid assessments of their progress is about as small as the number of big firm associates who live balanced lives.[321]

But don't take my word for it. The Large Law Firm *Associates* Subcommittee of the same Task Force identified as two major complaints of big firm associates the fact that firms do not provide associates with an "honest assessment of one's chances for partnership" and that "firms do not care about associates' professional development."[322] In other words, the things that the associates complained about *not* receiving from big firms were precisely the things that the partners said associates *get* from big firms. (In this and many other ways, big firm associates view big firm practice much differently than big firm partners do.[323]) At the end of the day, about the only thing that the big firm partners and big firm associates could agree upon is that big firms pay a lot of money.

And that is my point: When it comes right down to it, there is one and only one reason to go to a big firm: money.[324] "[T]he old law firm—one characterized by collegiality, intellectual challenge and institutional clients—is dead and gone."[325] What's left? "Money, Money, Money."[326] Mark Byers, the Director of Harvard Law School's Office of Student Life Counseling, put it well: Big firms " 'traditionally held out the ideas of independence, intellectual satisfaction and an affluent lifestyle.... Now not much is left but the affluence.' "[327] "Thus, if seeking wealth is ... the sole driving force in [your] life, and working 60 to 70 hours a week is ... [your] perception of the good life,"[328] then by all means go to work for a big firm. But do not go to work for a big firm because of the "benefits," such as the training, challenging work, collegiality, or increased mobility. Those benefits do not exist.

Also, do not go to a big firm for some of the other reasons given by students. For example, students often say that they must go to a big firm because their student loan debt leaves them no choice.[329] This may be true for some. I have had students with four or five children, an unemployed spouse, and $60,000 or more in debts. For these students, big firm salaries may indeed be necessary. But the number of students whose economic circumstances compel them to take big firm jobs is still substantially smaller than the number of students who *claim* that their economic circumstances compel them to take big firm jobs.[330]

Roughly one in three law students graduates with no student loan debt.[331] Of the remaining two-thirds, the average loan debt upon graduation is $40,000.[332] So let us take a typical student who fears starvation if he does not get a big firm job—say, an unmarried student who graduates with $50,000 in student loan debt. If we assume that this student is being charged 8% interest (compounded annually) and that he must repay his loans within fifteen years (putting aside the fact that he can probably extend payment on his loans for up to thirty years[333]), that student must make about $5,840 in loan payments each year, or about $487 per month.[334] At present, there are thousands of entry-level positions with corporations, as well as with federal, state, and local governments, that pay $40,000 to $60,000 per year.[335] A single lawyer making $50,000 per year would take home (after taxes) roughly $36,000—or about $3,000 per month.[336] After making his loan payment of $487, the lawyer would be left with about $2,500 on which to live for a month. Even if this lawyer goes fifteen years without a raise and never refinances his loan, the amount that he would be able to spend each month after making his loan payment would still almost equal the median gross income for American men and substantially exceed the median gross income for American women.[337] A lawyer who is *spending* more money than most Americans are *earning* will not have to live in poverty.

I have already alluded to a second justification given by students for going to big firms. Many students insist that they really want to practice law in Seattle or Phoenix or Miami—or really want to be a prosecutor or public interest lawyer—but first are going to a big New York or Washington firm to get training or to make enough money to pay off some loans. Then, they say, after three or four years of big firm practice, they will move to the city in which they really want to practice and take the job that they really want to take.[338]

This is self-delusion. First, as I have explained,[339] the vaunted training of big firms does not exist. Second, it is not nearly as easy to walk away from a big firm as these students suppose. Inertia is a powerful force, and lawyers quickly get accustomed to big firm salaries. Young lawyers in big firms are more likely to be pushed out than to walk out. And third, when it is time for big firm associates to leave, it is not nearly as easy to find satisfactory work as students seem to think. True, big firm associates almost always find a new job somewhere, but I doubt that my firm was the only employer that perceived former big firm associates as offering little helpful experience and much unhelpful baggage.

One final thing that students going to big firms sometimes say is that, although they are going to a big firm, they firmly intend to resist big firm culture. In fact, they intend to work to change their big firms from within, and to live balanced lives, no matter what their firms say. All of this is well and good, and if you end up at a large law firm someday, you should indeed advocate reform. But it is a lot harder to resist big firm culture than students think. My own life provides a good illustration.

I could have had my pick of big city, big firm jobs in 1987, as I was completing a Supreme Court clerkship. In fact, many big firms were supplementing their usual astronomical salaries with bonuses for Supreme Court clerks. I decided to turn down the big money and return home to Minnesota, where I joined a large firm with a reputation for treating people well. Within a couple of years, I was married, and our first child was on the way.

I had every intention of leading a balanced life. And, by New York or Washington standards, I suppose I did. By anyone else's standards, I did not. I worked three or four nights and one or two weekend days every week. When I was preparing for a trial or arbitration or appellate argument, I worked almost around the clock. I put hundreds of hours into business development, and, within three years or so, had created a self-sustaining practice. I traveled constantly. What I remember about the times my children first talked or walked or went to the potty was the hotel room in which I was sitting when my wife told me about the event over the phone. I was in Seattle when my grandmother died. I was in Pittsburgh when the worst snowstorm of the century trapped my family in our house for two days. I was in Williamsburg when my wife learned that our third child, with whom she was four months pregnant, had Down Syndrome. I failed miserably in my resolve to lead a balanced life, and neither my family nor I will ever be able to get back what we lost as a result.

You may do better than I did, but don't count on it. No matter how pure your intentions—no matter how firm your resolve—when you go to work at a big firm, the culture will seep in. I grew up in a lower middle class neighborhood. I literally never met anyone who could be characterized as wealthy. I almost never talked about money or thought about money. That all changed when I started practicing law, despite my best intentions. Slowly, imperceptibly, the things that I cared about and the way that I thought about others and the way that I thought about myself changed. I got sucked into playing the game, and even today, three years after leaving the big firm, I still find myself playing the game at times. If you go to a big firm intending to stay for only a couple years, the *job* you choose may be temporary, but the way it *affects* you may not.

2. Seek Alternatives to Private Practice—and Especially to Big Firm Practice

As you look for your first job, do not restrict yourself to private practice. There are tens of thousands of jobs for attorneys in the government, in corporations, and in the not-for-profit sector. A lot of these jobs provide fascinating work, minimal stress, predictable hours, and decent salaries—albeit not the huge salaries paid by big firms. Most importantly, many of these jobs permit you to have a life outside of work. "Time for family and self is a real problem for lawyers in private practice. Far fewer lawyers in corporate counsel and government settings have insufficient time."[340]

Consider the results of the Michigan Law School survey. Members of the classes of 1990 and 1991 were asked about their satisfaction with several aspects of their lives five years after graduation. The classes were divided into four groups—government attorneys, attorneys working for legal services organizations or other public interest employers, private practitioners, and attorneys in corporate legal departments—and the satisfaction levels of each group were reported as follows:[341]

Proportion of Group Who Are "Quite Satisfied" with:	Employment Sector			
	Government	Legal Services	Private Practice	Corporate Counsel
The balance of their family and professional lives	45%	50%	20%	35%
The intellectual challenge of their work	68%	72%	42%	55%
Their current income	21%	11%	55%	31%
The value of their work to society	66%	89%	14%	22%
Their careers overall	67%	78%	32%	48%

The results are telling: Attorneys working in private practice were dead last in career satisfaction, dead last in being satisfied with the intellectual challenge of their work, dead last in being satisfied with the balance of work and family, and dead last in regarding their work as valuable to society. Private practitioners came in first only in being satisfied with their incomes—but, even with respect to income, only slightly more than half of those in private practice were "quite satisfied." Over the past sixteen years, Michigan Law School has found that the career satisfaction of its graduates in private practice has dropped sharply, while the career satisfaction of its graduates working for the government or for public interest organizations has risen sharply.[342]

If you want to practice law in the private sector—as opposed to the government, public interest, or corporate sectors—I recommend that you look at small firms. Not all small firms are alike, of course.[343] Some small firms are structured like big firms; associates are worked to death so partners can profit handsomely.[344] Even small firms that do not act like big firms have their own problems.[345] However, small firms tend to have several advantages over big firms.

First, small firms are small, so you will be closer to your colleagues.[346] You will have a better chance of getting the kind of one-on-one training that is disappearing in big firms. Second, small firms "leverage" associates less,[347] meaning less competition among associates and a greater chance of making partner. Third, small firms are less rigidly structured. They can permit lawyers to work more flexible schedules, or to take longer than seven or eight years to make partner, or to choose not to make partner at all. Fourth, the attrition rate of associates in small firms is smaller than the attrition rate of associates in large firms; young lawyers stick around longer at small firms.[348] Fifth, small firms have more freedom to choose their clients and their cases. If a small firm wishes to do so, it can agree to write a will for a farmer in exchange for a supply of fresh vegetables or to incorporate a gas station in return for free car repairs. Sixth, young lawyers at small firms get more responsibility and get it quicker. Seventh, beginning with the first day of work, small firm lawyers have extensive contact with clients. Eighth, small firms demand fewer billable hours; as a result, lawyers in small firms live more balanced lives.[349] And ninth, and not surprisingly, lawyers at small firms tend to be happier with their careers.[350]

Without question, the attorneys I knew who seemed to be the happiest, who seemed to have the most balanced lives, and who seemed to have the most interesting, satisfying practices were those practicing in small towns (in either small firms or—another option for you—as solo practitioners). But even if you are intent on working in a major city, make an effort to check out small firms. There are many three-to ten-person firms in big cities founded by people who left the rat race—who decided that they were willing to give up some money in order to get some control over their lives. And consider working for the government or for public interest groups. The passion of government and public interest attorneys for their work is unmatched, and the "baptism by fire" that many of these attorneys experience provides better training than brown bag sessions in big firm conference rooms.

Identifying job opportunities with small firms, the government, and public interest groups is difficult, as they do not interview on law school campuses or advertise in major trade journals. Also, unlike big firms, they usually cannot hire a year in advance. It takes a lot of guts to hold out for a small firm, government, or public interest job during the third year of law school, as one of your friends after another signs up with a big firm. But the rewards are worth the effort.

3. If You Go to a Big Firm, Make a Smart Choice

As I have said,[351] big firms are not alike. Some are better than others. If, despite my advice, you decide to go to a big firm, then at least be smart in choosing among big firms. In that way, you will help yourself and you will help the profession.

a. Helping the Profession

As strange as it might sound, you and other future law school graduates have a great deal of influence over the legal profession. Law firms cannot survive without a constant influx of new talent,[352] and they are exquisitely sensitive to the whims and desires of promising young lawyers. The market works. In the recent past, as law students have chosen firms based upon small differences in salaries—and given little heed to substantial differences in workloads—firms have responded by driving both salaries and billable hour expectations through the roof. If law students change what they demand, law firms will change what they offer.

Do not permit yourself to be purchased at auction like a prize hog at the county fair. Do not choose one law firm over another because of a $3,000 difference in starting salaries. Instead, make it clear to prospective employers that salary is only one of many factors that you will consider in choosing a law firm. And then back up your words with your actions. If the past twenty years had seen one law school graduate intent on living a balanced life for every law school graduate intent on chasing the highest salary, big firms would be very different places today.[353]

Any law firm—or any other employer—has the right to expect you to work hard. No matter what kind of law you practice, you will not succeed without putting in long hours at the office (and terrifically long hours when you have a case about to try or a deal about to close). Few legal employers—and even fewer law firms—can guarantee you a nine-to-five, five-day-per-week work schedule. For you to insist on such a schedule would be unreasonable.

That said, you should at least signal to a prospective employer that, while you intend to work hard and be successful, you also intend to do more with your life than rack up billable hours. You can and should let prospective employers know that you do not intend to permit work to consume your life and that you are willing to sacrifice some money in order to have a life outside the office. Sending this message is dangerous; if you are not careful, even a good employer may perceive you as lazy. But if enough students give law firms this message—and back up the message with their actions—it will someday be possible for young lawyers to practice in big firms without giving up their happiness, their health, or their ethics.

b. Helping Yourself

Shortly before the end of each school year, I give a presentation to the third year Legal Ethics classes at Notre Dame. In that presentation, I try to communicate the realities of big firm practice in much the same way as I've tried to do in this article. Invariably, a student will come up to me after class and say, "The big firm at which I'm going to work is not like the ones you describe." When I reply, "How do you know?," the student cites the firm's recruiting materials or her interviews with the firm or her three months experience at the firm as a summer associate.

Understand this: *Firms lie.* They lie in their brochures. They lie during interviews.[354] They lie to their summer associates. To be sure, there are lies and then there are lies. Telling a law student that the firm expects associates to bill 1800 hours per year when, in fact, the firm fires associates who do not bill 2200 hours is a direct, no-doubt-about-it lie. Giving summer associates light workloads, channeling the most interesting projects to them, assigning them to work for the most likeable partners, and smothering them with free meals and social outings is an indirect lie.[355] Either way, though, the firm is holding itself out to be something that it is not.

Law firms have to sell themselves to bright law students, and, like any seller of a product, they work hard to make themselves look good—sometimes at the expense of the truth. Much of what a law firm says "are empty words with no relation to what actually happens at the firm."[356] Yet "law students and associates have often been surprisingly unwilling to look behind the big salaries and empty promises that law firm recruiters ... have thrown at them with increasing vigor."[357] You should shop for a law firm in the same way that you should shop for an apartment or a car or a major appliance. You should first research the product, and then you should ask hard questions of the person trying to sell the product to you.

Before you accept an offer from a firm—indeed, before you even interview at a firm—research the firm thoroughly. Use the *American Lawyer* or the *National Law Journal* to discover the profits per partner at the firm. Roughly speaking, the lower the profits per partner, the better the working conditions. In some ways, the optimal big firm is a firm with high prestige and low profits per partner. At such a firm, big firm benefits will likely be accompanied by a minimum of big firm exploitation. You will find that these optimal big firms tend to be located in cities like Portland and Denver and Milwaukee, rather than New York and Washington and Chicago.

You can look up biographies of a firm's lawyers in the *Martindale-Hubbell Law Directory*,[358] the *West Legal Directory*,[359] *The Best Lawyers in America*,[360] and *The American Bar*.[361] You can look up the firm in such books as *The Insider's Guide to Law Firms*[362] and the *National Directory of Legal Employers*[363] or visit the firm's website.[364] You can use Westlaw or LEXIS to search for references to the firm in judicial opinions, in legal publications such as the *National Law Journal* and the *American Lawyer*, and in general publications such as the *Wall Street Journal* and *New York Times*.[365] You can search the Internet for references to the firm, using search engines such as AltaVista[366] or MetaCrawler.[367] But by far the best information that you will get about the firm will come from lawyers who practice in the same city but do not work at the firm.

If you are interested in a big firm in, say, St. Louis, then you should talk with several lawyers in St. Louis. Talk not only with lawyers working in other big St. Louis firms, but also with lawyers in small firms, in corporations, and in government. Almost every lawyer to whom you will speak will either know someone at the firm or know someone who knows someone at the firm. A particularly good source of information will be lawyers who recently left the firm. These lawyers are easily identified through *Martindale-Hubbell*—or, for that matter, by simply asking around. Obviously, an attorney whom you call out of the blue is less likely to be candid with you than an attorney to whom you have been introduced, so "network." Call an attorney you know, and ask her if she would be willing to introduce you to two other attorneys. Then make the same request of those two attorneys, and of the attorneys to whom they introduce you. Before long, you will have a pretty good picture of the firm.

Of course, you need to be careful to take what you are told about the firm with a grain of salt. What you are told may reflect some envy of the firm, or an attempt to recruit you away from the firm, or resentment at not being hired by or at being forced out of the firm. The more specific you can make people be, the better able you will be to judge their opinions. A lawyer who tells you only that he has heard that "people are unhappy" at the firm has not told you nearly as much as a lawyer who says, "The husband of one of our legal assistants works there. She told me that she has had dinner with her husband only twice in the past month. She said that he billed 2500 hours last year and is on pace to bill 3000 this year."

When you interview with the firm, do not passively accept platitudes. Every big firm claims that it is different. Every big firm denies that it is a sweatshop. Every big firm insists that, although its attorneys work hard, they lead balanced lives.[368] This is almost always false. It *has* to be. There is no free lunch. Someone has to pay for your $80,000 starting salary. And someone has to pay for that office space in the city's most prestigious skyscraper. And someone has to pay for the oak paneling that lines the conference rooms. You cannot get big firm benefits without paying the big firm price. A firm that tells you otherwise is lying.

For a big firm to be truly different, its partners would have to be willing to take less money, and this is something that big firm partners have proven singularly unwilling to do. Marc Galanter and Thomas Palay have described why, in a sense, big firms *cannot* value anything except money: "Money is not all that partners want," Galanter and Palay write.

> But as firms get bigger, securing and monitoring agreement about the priority ordering, the value, and the mix of "goods" they want as their return from practice becomes ever more complex. Since "money" is high (even if not first) on everyone's scale, it is almost always possible to get agreement on more money over any other competing good. As firms get larger, agreement becomes more difficult. This is especially so when firms at the same time become more diverse in terms of gender, ethnicity, class origin, and educational background.[369]

As a result of this phenomenon, "big-firm lawyers insist on taking the gains of firm growth in the form of more money income rather than as sabbaticals, time for child-care, political involvement, greater work satisfaction, or whatever."[370] Presumably, as the culture that most influences a young lawyer shifts from the distinctive culture of her individual law firm (which is created by a couple hundred attorneys) to a generic "big firm" culture (which is created by many thousands of attorneys),[371] the trend toward valuing nothing but material wealth will only accelerate.[372]

Even those within the legal profession who are most concerned about the well-being of lawyers seem incapable of suggesting to their fellow attorneys that maybe, just maybe, a big part of the solution to the profession's problems lies in being satisfied with more modest incomes. Here are a couple examples of what I mean:

In 1991, in response to growing evidence of the unhappiness and unhealthiness of the legal profession, the ABA convened an urgent conference of leading lawyers from across the United States. The conference was dramatically (if long-windedly) titled, *At the Breaking Point: A National Conference on the Emerging Crisis in the Quality of Lawyers' Health and Lives—Its Impact on Law Firms and Client Services.* The lawyers attending the conference were concerned and knowledgeable about the well-being of lawyers, and yet even they could not quite come to grips with the fact that lawyers are unhappy and unhealthy in large part because they have unreasonable expectations about money. To the contrary, much of the conference's report argued (unconvincingly, in my view) that lawyers could use "sound management" and "value billing and value compensation" to make more money without working longer hours.[373] ("Sound management" is to a law firm consultant what getting rid of "waste, fraud, and abuse" is to a politician.)

The more recent Boston Bar Association Task Force on Professional Fulfillment was similarly reluctant to acknowledge reality. The Large Law Firms Partners Subcommittee, after listing three "fulfilling aspects" of big firm practice,[374] identified ten "obstacles to professional fulfillment"[375]—most of which could be eliminated or reduced if big firm partners were willing to make less money. And yet the closest the Task Force came to acknowledging that fact was its hesitant suggestion in the sixth of its six recommendations that the income of big firm partners may have to *grow* more slowly: "The Task Force recommends that … large law firms encourage partners to manage their expectations and to recognize that the annual percentage increases in compensation witnessed in the past few years will inevitably moderate and that monetary rewards alone are not what is meant by professional fulfillment."[376] The other recommendations were mostly vague and hortatory, such as the recommendation that "large law firms ... confront the tension which exists for both firms and partners between increasing revenues and 'having a life'... [by making] the issue of professional fulfillment a key topic at a retreat."[377] And, like the *At the Breaking Point* report, the report of the Boston Bar Association Task Force even hinted that the problem was not that lawyers had come to feel entitled to large annual increases in their already large incomes, but rather that lawyers had not tried hard enough to find ways of making more money without doing more work.[378]

Against this background, you should be skeptical of any claim by any big firm that it is "different." Ask tough questions of the lawyers you meet. When you are at a recruiting dinner with a couple of lawyers from the firm, don't just ask them, "So, do you folks have any kind of life outside of work?" They will chuckle, say "sure," and ask if you want more wine. Instead, ask them how many times last week they had dinner with their families. And then ask them what time dinner was served. And then ask them whether they worked after dinner. Ask them what their favorite television show is or what is the last good movie they saw. If they respond, respectively, *Welcome Back Kotter* and *Saturday Night Fever*, you will know something's wrong. Ask them about their last vacation. Where did they go? How long did they stay? How many faxes did they send or receive while on vacation? Get some sense of what their lives are like.

Similarly, when you are interviewing at the firm, ask tough questions of the lawyers you meet. When a lawyer tells you that she has a lot of client contact, ask her what that means. There is a big difference between sending an occasional letter to the assistant general counsel and flying to client headquarters to engage in all day strategy sessions with the officers. When a lawyer tells you that he gets a lot of interesting assignments, ask for examples. You may be surprised at what passes for "interesting" at the firm. And when a lawyer tells you that associates are happy at the firm, ask for specifics. How many associates were hired five years ago? How many of those associates remain at the firm? Who were the last three associates to leave the firm? What are they doing now? How can you contact them?

Try to get as much information as possible about billable hour requirements. Many firms will tell you that they do not have a target or goal for billable hours. Those firms are probably lying. Almost every firm has a number. In some firms, the number is formal and has "bite"; if you fall below it, you will be fired. In other firms, the number is an unwritten understanding and is used mainly to measure the progress of associates toward partnership; if you fall below it, you won't be fired, but you will draw the concerned attention of partners. Try to discover the firm's number and what the number means. Evasiveness on this score is almost always a bad sign. Also, find out what counts toward the number. Some firms count all the billable hours that a lawyer records, as well as non-billable time that is considered especially valuable, such as time devoted to business development or recruitment or even, in rare firms, pro bono work. Other firms count only hours that can be billed to a paying client. Still other firms count only billable hours that are "realized";[379] if a partner decides to bill a client for only six of the ten hours that you devoted to a project (because you were inefficient or because the client has been grumbling about its bills) you will get credit for only six hours. In short, there can be huge differences among firms with the same nominal goal of 2000 billable hours.

You have to be careful in cross-examining prospective employers in the way I suggest—and the weaker your academic record, the more careful you have to be. You do not want prospective employers to think that you are lazy. Questions about workloads and billable hours and recently departed associates should be mixed in with many other questions about other aspects of firm life. Be polite, not accusatory. Use humor—unless you don't have a good sense of humor, in which case you should go back to being polite, not accusatory. Save the toughest questions for after you get an offer. But ask the questions sometime, in some way, of someone.

By being a smart consumer, you have a chance of distinguishing the good big firms from the bad big firms. Do not expect too much, though. As I have explained at length, big firms just are not set up to give their lawyers a chance to live full lives. The only people who can make big firm money without working big firm hours are the most senior partners who are living off the skim. In the end, big firm life comes down to spending eight years or so being exploited a lot so that you can spend another eight years or so being exploited a little so that you can spend another eight years or so not being exploited so that you can finish your career exploiting others.

4. Develop the Habit of Acting Ethically

As I have explained,[380] whether you practice law ethically will depend primarily upon the hundreds of mundane things that you will do almost unthinkingly every day. To behave ethically, day in and day out, you need to be in the *habit* of doing so. Developing the habit of acting ethically is no different from developing the habit of putting on your seatbelt or cracking your knuckles: You have to do it a lot. If you are going to practice law ethically, you need to decide now, while you are still in law school, what kind of lawyer you want to be, and then act as that kind of lawyer would act. Always. Everywhere. In big things and small. Do not take that first step toward being an unethical lawyer. I'm telling you—I'm *promising* you—that sometime during your first couple years of practice, you will be sitting at your desk late at night with your pen poised over your time sheet, and you will be tempted to pad your hours.[381] Padding time sheets is "the perfect crime";[382] it is profitable for you and it is profitable for the firm and there is virtually no chance that you will get caught.[383] The only thing that will stop you from padding your time sheets is your own integrity.[384]

Do not pad your time sheets—even once. And do not tell lies to partners or clients or opposing counsel. And do not misrepresent legal authority to judges. And do not break your promises. And do not do anything else that is contrary to the values you now hold. And finally, when you screw up—as I did, as every lawyer does—pick yourself up, dust yourself off, and try that much harder to develop the habit of acting ethically.

V. Some Parting Words

To an unfortunate extent, this article has been an exercise in "do what I say, not what I do." As I said, I joined a big law firm after I finished clerking, and, despite the best of intentions, I quickly got sucked into the game. It is very, very hard to avoid the pressures and temptations pushing you toward the big firm, very, very hard to avoid playing the game once you arrive at the big firm, and very, very hard to stop playing the game once you have left the big firm. I failed on the first two counts and continue to fail from time to time on the third. But I want to leave you with the following, by way of illustrating that it is never too late to change—even when you've failed as much as I have.

My firm was lead counsel for the plaintiffs in the Exxon Valdez oil spill litigation. In 1994, while I was still a partner, we won a judgment of over $5 billion.[385] We partners all knew that, if and when we collected that judgment, even the smallest partner's share would be a few hundred thousand dollars. Most of the partners would become millionaires.[386] Because my wife and I would both be partners, we would enjoy two slices of this enormous pie.

At about the time of the Exxon Valdez verdict, my wife and I were beginning to feel that, somewhere along the line, we had lost our way. We were working constantly. We were under constant pressure. We were constantly feeling guilty about the hardships we were imposing on each other and on our children. The life we were leading was not the life we had envisioned. We had strayed from the values with which we were raised.

In early 1995, we decided to leave big firm practice, and to leave the Exxon money behind.[387] We decided to give up a ton of money in return for work that was more enjoyable and less stressful, and for more time with each other and our children.[388] All of this, we decided, was more important than money—even lots and lots of money.

I don't claim that we made an enormous sacrifice. We did give up a lot of money, but we still get paid well, and we have great jobs. Nor do I claim that we have stopped playing the game—that we have no regrets, that we never look back, that we don't care about money any more. None of that would be true. Living a balanced life and defining success for yourself are lifelong struggles, and they do not end once you leave a big law firm. The one thing I can promise you is that, as we rediscover every day, they are struggles well worth undertaking.

Notes

* I am grateful to Paul D. Carrington, Mark Chopko, Roger C. Cramton, John S. Elson, Stephen Gillers, Geoffrey C. Hazard, Jr., Douglas Laycock, Howard Lesnick, Sanford Levinson, Thomas D. Morgan, John Copeland Nagle, Michael Stokes Paulsen, Robert E. Rodes, Jr., Elizabeth R. Schiltz, Thomas L. Shaffer, David A. Skeel, Jr., and Kent D. Syverud for their comments on earlier drafts of this Article, and to William L. Esser, John J. Laxague, Rosemarie K. Nixon, and Scott R. Williams for their research assistance. I am also grateful to the students enrolled in the Spring 1999 session of the "Religious Consciousness and Legal Thought and Practice" seminar at the University of Pennsylvania Law School for vetting this article for me.

1. *See* MARC GALANTER & THOMAS PALAY, TOURNAMENT OF LAWYERS: THE TRANSFORMATION OF THE BIG LAW FIRM 1 (1991); MARY ANN GLENDON, A NATION UNDER LAWYERS: HOW THE CRISIS IN THE LEGAL PROFESSION IS TRANSFORMING AMERICAN SOCIETY 283–84 (1994); GARY A. MUNNEKE, CAREERS IN LAW 5–7 (1997); A. Leon Higginbotham, Jr., *The Life of the Law: Values, Commitment, and Craftsmanship*, 100 HARV. L. REV. 795, 803–04 (1987).

2. FRED RODELL, WOE UNTO YOU, LAWYERS!, at 7 (1957).

3. *See* Amiram Elwork & G. Andrew H. Benjamin, *Lawyers in Distress*, 23 J. PSYCHIATRY & L. 205, 206 (1995) (asserting that the health of lawyers has received "scant attention from scholars in either the legal or the mental health communities").

4. Why are scientists replacing laboratory rats with lawyers? There are more lawyers than rats. Scientists can become emotionally attached to rats. And there are some things that rats will not do.

5. *See* Robert J. Borthwick & Jordan R. Schau, *Gatekeepers of the Profession: An Empirical Profile of the Nation's Law Professors*, 25 U. MICH. J. L. REFORM 191, 220 (1991); Patrick J. Schiltz, *Legal*

Ethics in Decline: The Elite Law Firm, the Elite Law School, and the Moral Formation of the Novice Attorney, 82 MINN. L. REV. 705, 756–62 (1998).

6. *See* Talbot D'Alemberte, *Keynote Address*, *in* THE MACCRATE REPORT: BUILDING THE EDUCATIONAL CONTINUUM 4, 12 (Joan S. Howland & William H. Lindberg eds., 1994); Schiltz, *supra* note 5, at 754–56; Barbara Bennett Woodhouse, *Mad Midwifery: Bringing Theory, Doctrine, and Practice to Life*, 91 MICH. L. REV. 1977, 1993 (1993).

7. *See* MICHAEL J. KELLY, LIVES OF LAWYERS: JOURNEYS IN THE ORGANIZATIONS OF PRACTICE 19 (1994); Harry T. Edwards, *The Growing Disjunction Between Legal Education and the Legal Profession*, 91 MICH. L. REV. 34, 35 (1992); Schiltz, *supra* note 5, at 762–71; Laurence H. Silberman, *Will Lawyering Strangle Democratic Capitalism?: A Retrospective*, 21 HARV. J. L. & PUB. POL'Y 607, 616 (1998).

8. *See* Michael A. Livingston, *Reinventing Tax Scholarship: Lawyers, Economists, and the Role of the Legal Academy*, 83 CORNELL L. REV. 365, 400 (1998); Craig Allen Nard, *Empirical Legal Scholarship: Reestablishing a Dialogue Between the Academy and Profession*, 30 WAKE FOREST L. REV. 347, 368 (1995).

9. *See* James J. Alfini & Joseph N. Van Vooren, *Is There a Solution to the Problem of Lawyer Stress? The Law School Perspective*, 10 J. L. & Health 61, 66 (1995–1996) ("[I]t may seem surprising that the legal academy has given so little attention to such an enormous problem in the legal profession. It becomes less surprising, however, when one considers how little attention law schools give to the current structure and operating realities of the legal profession itself.").

10. *See* William W. Eaton et al., *Occupations and the Prevalence of Major Depressive Disorder*, 32 J. OCCUPATIONAL MED. 1079 (1990).

11. *See id.* at 1081.

12. *See id.*

13. *See id.* at 1081–83.

14. *See id.* at 1083. Pre-kindergarten and special education teachers suffer from MDD at a rate 2.8 times higher than expected, while secretaries suffer from MDD at a rate 1.9 times higher than expected. *See id.* Thus, an attorney who drops off his child at pre-school on the way to work and greets his secretary as he arrives at the office can hit the "Depression Trifecta" before 9:00 a.m.

15. *Id.* at 1085.

16. *See id.*; *see also* AMIRAM ELWORK, STRESS MANAGEMENT FOR LAWYERS 15 (2d ed. 1997); SOL M. LINOWITZ, THE BETRAYED PROFESSION: LAWYERING AT THE END OF THE TWENTIETH CENTURY 242 (1994); BENJAMIN SELLS, THE SOUL OF THE LAW 99 (1994); Elwork & Benjamin, *supra* note 3, at 215.

17. G. Andrew H. Benjamin et al., *The Prevalence of Depression, Alcohol Abuse, and Cocaine Abuse Among United States Lawyers*, 13 INT'L J. L. & PSYCHIATRY 233, 240 (1990) (footnote omitted). By "statistically significant elevated levels of depression," the researchers are referring to elevated scores on a self-report instrument known as the Brief Symptom Inventory ("BSI"). *Id.* at 237. According to the researchers, "[a] significant elevation of the BSI depression symptom (a score that exceeds two standard deviations above the normal population mean) is strongly correlated with clinical impairment, and suggests the need for specific treatment." *Id.*

18. *See id.* at 234 (citing G. Andrew H. Benjamin et al., *The Role of Legal Education in Producing Psychological Distress Among Law Students and Lawyers*, 1986 AM. B. FOUND. RES. J. 225, 246 [hereinafter *Psychological Distress*]).

19. *See id.* The Arizona study measured depression through use of the BSI, as well as three other standardized self-report instruments (the Beck Depression Inventory, Multiple Affect Adjective Checklist, and Hassles Scale). *See Psychological Distress*, *supra* note 18, at 228–31.

20. *See* Benjamin et al., *supra* note 17, at 234.

21. Connie J. A. Beck et al., *Lawyer Distress: Alcohol-Related Problems and Other Psychological Concerns Among a Sample of Practicing Lawyers*, 10 J. L. & HEALTH 1, 50 (1995–1996) (footnote omitted). A subject was considered to be above the "clinical cutoff" if he or she scored more than two standard deviations above the mean of a normal population on the instruments used by those who conducted the Washington and Arizona studies. *See id.* at 3. At this point, the subject is "considered clinically distressed and needing treatment." *Id.* at 3–4. This "is not synonymous with a full-blown psychiatric diagnosis." *Id.* at 49 n.200.

22. *See* ELWORK, *supra* note 16, at 14.

23. *See* NORTH CAROLINA BAR ASS'N, REPORT OF THE QUALITY OF LIFE TASK FORCE AND RECOMMENDATIONS 4 (1991).

24. *See* ELWORK, *supra* note 16, at 14–15.

25. *See* NORTH CAROLINA BAR ASS'N, *supra* note 23, at 4.

26. Beck et al., *supra* note 21, at 23.

27. *Id.* at 50 (footnotes omitted).

28. *Id.* at 49.

29. *See* NORTH CAROLINA BAR ASS'N, *supra* note 23, at 4.

30. *See* Eric Drogin, *Alcoholism in the Legal Profession: Psychological and Legal Perspectives and Interventions*, 15 LAW & PSYCHOL. REV. 117, 127 (1991).

31. Benjamin et al., *supra* note 17, at 241.

32. Beck et al., *supra* note 21, at 50–51.

33. *See* Benjamin et al., *supra* note 17, at 241.

34. *See id.*

35. *See id.* at 242.

36. *See* ELWORK, *supra* note 16, at 15; Benjamin et al., *supra* note 17, at 242.

37. DAVID B. LARSON ET AL., THE COSTLY CONSEQUENCES OF DIVORCE: ASSESSING THE CLINICAL, ECONOMIC, AND PUBLIC HEALTH IMPACT OF MARITAL DISRUPTION IN THE UNITED STATES 1 (1995); *see also id.* at 41–88; Beck et al., *supra* note 21, at 7; Lee A. Lillard & Linda J. Waite, *'Til Death Do Us Part: Marital Disruption and Mortality*, 100 AM. J. SOC. 1131 (1995); David G. Myers & Ed Diener, *Who Is Happy?*, 6 PSYCHOL. SCI. 10, 15 (1995); Hara Estroff Marano, *Debunking the Marriage Myth: It Works for Women, Too*, N.Y. TIMES, Aug. 4, 1998, at F7; Jennifer Steinhauer, *Studies Find Big Benefits in Marriage*, N.Y. TIMES, Apr. 10, 1995, at A10.

38. *See* David L. Chambers, *Accommodation and Satisfaction: Women and Men Lawyers and the Balance of Work and Family*, 14 J. L. & SOC. INQUIRY 251, 255, 274 (1989).

39. NORTH CAROLINA BAR ASS'N, *supra* note 23, at 7.

40. *See id.* at 4. Lawyers working more than 250 hours per month and associates working at law firms were the other two categories. *See id.*

41. *See generally* LARSON ET AL., *supra* note 37, at 41–88; JUDITH S. WALLERSTEIN & SANDRA BLAKESLEE, SECOND CHANCES: MEN, WOMEN, AND CHILDREN A DECADE AFTER DIVORCE (1989); JUDITH S. WALLERSTEIN & JOAN BERLIN KELLY, SURVIVING THE BREAKUP: HOW CHILDREN AND PARENTS COPE WITH DIVORCE (1980).

42. *See* LARSON ET AL., *supra* note 37, at 44–58 (collecting and describing studies).

43. *Id.* at 1.

44. *See id.* at 46–47, 58–61 (collecting and describing studies).

45. *See id.* at 61–62 (collecting and describing studies).

46. *Id.* at 63.

47. *See id.* at 62–70 (collecting and describing studies).

48. *See id.* at 64.

49. *See id.* at 50–57.

50. *See* ELWORK, *supra* note 16, at 16; Micheal [sic] Hall, *Pressure Blamed for Lawyers' Divorce Rate*, L.A. DAILY J., Jan. 20, 1988, at 5; Richard J. King, Jr., How Lawyers Can Cope With Stress, *PA. LAW.*, Oct. 1995, at 8, 8 (book review).

51. LeClere's findings, broken down by age, were as follows:

Male Lawyers/Male Doctors				
Age	*20–34*	*35–49*	*50–64*	*> 64*
Never Married	41.7%/29.1%	9.3%/6.7%	3.0%/2.2%	2.9%/2.1%
Currently Married	54.6%/67.4%	81.1%/86.5%	85.3%/88.7%	38.7%/87.4%
Currently Divorced	2.9%/2.5%	7.7%/5.1%	8.5%/6.6%	3.9%/3.5%
Currently Separated	.8%/.9%	1.8%/1.4%	1.6%/1.3%	.8%/.6%
Currently Widowed	.0%/.1%	.2%/.2%	1.6%/1.2%	8.6%/6.4%

Female Lawyers/Female Doctors				
Age	*20–34*	*35–49*	*50–64*	*> 64*
Never Married	48.6%/35.0%	18.8%/13.0%	8.4%/10.3%	11.7%/11.5%
Currently Married	45.6%/59.9%	61.6%/73.2%	56.8%/65.7%	44.6%/41.2%
Currently Divorced	4.9%/4.0%	16.2%/11.0%	24.3%/15.3%	14.3%/11.3%
Currently Separated	.8%/1.1%	2.2%/1.6%	1.8%/.8%	.4%/.8%
Currently Widowed	.1%/.0%	1.1%/1.1%	8.6%/7.8%	29.0%/35.2%

1990 Decennial Census Public Use Microdata Samples (5% Persons Sample).

52. *See* Teresa M. Cooney & Peter Uhlenberg, *Family-Building Patterns of Professional Women: A Comparison of Lawyers, Physicians, and Postsecondary Teachers*, 51 J. MARRIAGE & FAM. 749, 751 (1989).

53. *See id.*

54. *See id.* at 752.

55. *See* Deborah K. Holmes, *Learning from Corporate America: Addressing Dysfunction in the Large Law Firm*, 31 GONZ. L. REV. 373, 377 (1995–1996); Laura Gatland, *Dangerous Dedication: Studies Suggest Long Hours, Productivity Pressures Can Cause Serious Health Problems and a Higher Suicide Rate for Attorneys*, A.B.A. J., Dec. 1997, at 28, 28; Doretta Zemp, *Turned-Off Lawyers*, STUDENT LAW., Nov. 1981, at 23, 37.

56. *See* Carol A. Burnett et al., Suicide and Occupation: Is There a Relationship?, at 2 (Nov. 19–22, 1992) (unpublished paper, presented at the American Psychological Association—National Institute for Occupational Safety and Health Conference on Workplace Stress in the 90's, on file with author).

57. Benjamin et al., *supra* note 17, at 241.

58. *See* ELWORK, *supra* note 16, at 14.

59. *See supra* notes 23–25 and accompanying text.

60. Half of lawyers do not exercise regularly. *See* NORTH CAROLINA BAR ASS'N, *supra* note 23, at 4; YOUNG LAWYERS DIV., AMERICAN BAR ASS'N, THE STATE OF THE LEGAL PROFESSION 1990, at 51 (1991).

61. *See* NORTH CAROLINA BAR ASS'N, *supra* note 23, at 4.

62. *See* Marc B. Schenker et al., *Self-Reported Stress and Reproductive Health of Female Lawyers*, 39 J. OCCUPATIONAL & ENVTL. MED. 556, 557 (1997).

63. *See infra* Part II.A.

64. *See* Sheila Nielsen, *The Balancing Act: Practical Suggestions for Part-Time Attorneys*, 35 N.Y.L. SCH. L. REV. 369, 370 (1990) ("In many large firms and other prestigious workplaces nine-to-five is considered part-time."); Jennifer A. Kingson, *Women in the Law Say Their Paths are Limited by the "Mommy Track,"* N.Y. TIMES, Aug. 8, 1988, at A1 ("[The] legal profession has its own definition of 'part-time' work. At some of the largest and most competitive firms ... 'part-time' hours are 9 to 5, five days a week.").

65. *See* Benjamin et al., *supra* note 17, at 245; Eaton et al., *supra* note 10, at 1085.

66. Myers & Diener, *supra* note 37, at 15 (citation omitted).

67. MAXIM GORKY, THE LOWER DEPTHS act I, *in* FOUR MODERN PLAYS 289 (Henry Popkin ed., Alexander Bakshy trans., Holt, Rinehart & Winston 1961) (1902).

68. David Margolick, *More Lawyers Are Less Happy at their Work, a Survey Finds*, N.Y. Times, Aug. 17, 1990, at B5; *see also* Carl T. Bogus, *The Death of an Honorable Profession*, 71 Ind. L.J. 911, 940 (1996); Holmes, *supra* note 55, at 375–76.

69. Nancy McCarthy, *Pessimism for the Future: Given a Second Chance, Half of the State's Attorneys Would Not Become Lawyers*, CAL. ST. B. J., Nov. 1994, at 1, 1.

70. *Id.* In an unscientific survey of the California bar (the survey reflected the views of only those who chose to fax in a response to questions published in *California Lawyer* magazine), only 40% of attorneys reported being even "[r]easonably" satisfied with their careers; 36% reported being "[s]o unhappy I'd change careers," 16% "[u]nhappy but inert," and 8% "[i]ndifferent." *See* "It's Become a Miserable Profession," *CAL. LAW.*, Mar. 1992, at 96, 96. Almost three-quarters of the California lawyers responding to the survey agreed that they "enjoyed practicing law less now than they did when they first began," and a similar percentage said that they would not advise their children to become attorneys. *Id.* The respondents were almost certainly not representative of the entire California bar.

71. *See* NORTH CAROLINA BAR ASS'N, *supra* note 23, at 4.

72. Margaret Cronin Fisk, *Lawyers Give Thumbs Up*, NAT'L L. J., May 28, 1990, at S2, S2.

73. *See, e.g.*, The University of Michigan Law School, The University of Michigan Law School: A Report on the Class of 1991 Five Years After Graduation 1 (1996) (unpublished report, on file with author). I am grateful to David L. Chambers for making the Michigan reports available to me.

74. *See id.*

75. Defined as those "[i]ndicating a 1 or 2 on a 7-point scale." *Id.* at 15.

76. *See id.*

77. *See id.*

78. *Id.* at 16. The survey also found that, among the members of the class of 1991, those who were not practicing law five years after graduating were "substantially more satisfied [with their careers] than their classmates practicing in firms." *Id.* at 7.

79. *See* YOUNG LAWYERS DIV., *supra* note 60, at 1.

80. *Id.*

81. *See id.* at 2–3.

82. YOUNG LAWYERS DIV., AMERICAN BAR ASS'N, CAREER SATISFACTION 1995, at n.1 (1995).

83. Those questioned in 1984 "were sent a lengthy survey covering many aspects of their work environment, job history, educational background, health and psychological profile, and basic demographics." YOUNG LAWYERS DIV., *supra* note 60, at 1. Those questioned in 1990 were sent an almost identical survey, with a few questions added "primarily ... to gather detailed empirical data on the issue of gender bias and sexual harassment." *Id.* at 3. The 1995 survey, by contrast, was focused much more narrowly on the career satisfaction of young lawyers. *See* YOUNG LAWYERS DIV., *supra* note 82.

84. *See* YOUNG LAWYERS DIV., *supra* note 60, at 52 tbl.66.

85. *See id.* The number who were "somewhat satisfied" rose from 40% to 43%, "neutral" from 4% to 5%, and "somewhat dissatisfied" from 12% to 14%. *See id.*

86. *Id.* at 81.

87. *Id.* at 53 tbl.68.

88. *Id.* at 53.

89. *See* YOUNG LAWYERS DIV., *supra* note 82, at 13 tbl.13.

90. *See id.* at 9.

91. It is important to bear in mind, when reviewing data regarding the career satisfaction of attorneys, "[t]hat research indicates that most employed persons, in all professions and in all types of positions, are satisfied with their careers." John P. Heinz et al., *Lawyers and Their Discontents: Findings from a Survey of the Chicago Bar*, 74 IND. L. J. 735, 736 (1999); *see also* Chambers, *supra* note 38, at 259, 274. Roughly 85% of American workers are at least " 'moderately' " satisfied with their careers. Heinz et al., *supra*, at 736. Thus, lawyers could be relatively dissatisfied with their work, even if a majority (or even a substantial majority) were satisfied.

92. A 1991 survey of attorneys practicing in Toronto, a 1987 study of graduates of the Minnesota Law School, and a 1994 survey of members of the New York bar found generally high levels of career satisfaction among lawyers. *See generally* JOHN HAGAN & FIONA KAY, GENDER IN PRACTICE: A STUDY OF LAWYERS' LIVES (1995) (Toronto); Paul W. Mattessich & Cheryl W. Heilman, *The Career Paths of Minnesota Law School Graduates: Does Gender Make a Difference?*, 9 LAW &

INEQ. J. 59 (1990) (Minnesota); Edward A. Adams, *Legal Career Exacts Steep Personal Price, 'Law Journal' Poll: Attorneys Accept Long Hours, Absence from Families*, N.Y.L.J., Feb. 7, 1994, at 1, 1 (New York).

93. *See* Heinz et al., *supra* note 91.

94. *See supra* note 91.

95. *See* Heinz et al., *supra* note 91, at 736.

96. *Id.* at 757. Of course, the authors of the Chicago study did not have the opportunity to read this article, whose prattle, I'd like to think, is far from "common."

97. *Id.*

98. Some possible explanations for the differences between the Chicago survey and most (but not all, see *supra* note 92) surveys of lawyer satisfaction include the following:

First, all of the data on career satisfaction are derived through surveys that ask lawyers to characterize their own happiness; survey data are less reliable than that produced by more rigorous (but far more difficult and expensive) behavioral studies. *See* Chambers, *supra* note 38, at 254–55. All surveys run a strong risk of response bias, although, with respect to career satisfaction surveys, it is difficult to know how that bias would cut. Perhaps those who are least satisfied with their careers would be more likely to respond to a survey, as they would feel the need to let off steam. Or perhaps those least likely to respond to such a survey would be "those who feel so beleaguered by their work and other responsibilities that they do not have time to respond." *Id.* at 261 n.47. It is also possible that survey responses "are biased toward the positive side of the scale by the respondents' desire to present themselves as successful persons." Heinz et al., *supra* note 91, at 750. Presumably, this problem, if it exists, would be exaggerated in those studies that involve face-to-face interviews (such as the Chicago study) as opposed to anonymous questionnaires.

Second, the surveys ask different questions. Some ask about satisfaction with "the law," some about "life," some about "careers," some about "current jobs," and some about particular aspects of "the law," "life," "careers," or "current jobs." Some use four-point scales, some five, some seven, and some don't use scales at all. Some ask whether lawyers would become lawyers again (a question that the authors of the Chicago study characterize as "an invitation to dream," *id.*), some ask whether lawyers want their children to become lawyers, and some ask whether lawyers plan to remain lawyers through the end of their careers.

Third, the surveys focus on different populations. Some study the lawyers of a single city or state, some study the graduates of a single law school, and some study lawyers at a single point in their careers.

Fourth, the surveys are billed differently. Some are expressly presented as studies of career satisfaction, while others bury questions about career satisfaction in a long series of questions on other topics. Surveys that are expressly billed as focusing on career satisfaction may, on the one hand, attract a disproportionate share of responses from the dissatisfied, or may, on the other hand, cause respondents to think more carefully about various aspects of their working lives before answering (or may do both).

Fifth, those who conduct these surveys find significance in different things. Some authors focus on the number of lawyers who report being "very satisfied" and "very dissatisfied," while others focus on the number of lawyers who report being either "very satisfied" or "satisfied," on the one hand, or either "dissatisfied" or "very dissatisfied," on the other hand.

Finally, some of these studies are undoubtedly better than others; they are better designed, they attract higher response rates, they analyze the data more carefully. I am grateful to John Heinz for suggesting some of these explanations to me.

99. For example, according to the Michigan Law School survey, only 32% of the members of the classes of 1990 and 1991 who were in private practice were "quite satisfied" with their careers five years after graduation, as compared to 48% of corporate counsel, 67% of government attorneys, and 78% of public interest lawyers. See University of Michigan Law School, *supra* note 73, at 9 tbl.3.

100. Fisk, *supra* note 72, at S2.

101. *See* TASK FORCE ON PROFESSIONAL FULFILLMENT, BOSTON BAR ASS'N, EXPECTATIONS, REALITY AND RECOMMENDATIONS FOR CHANGE 2 (1997); *see also* Gatland, *supra* note 55, at 29. The eight categories were Large Law Firms (Partners), Large Law Firms (Associates), Sole Practitioners and Small Firms, In-House Counsel, Public Service and Academia, Senior Lawyers, Law Students and Recent Graduates, and Women Attorneys and Attorneys of Color.

102. Heinz et al., *supra* note 91, at 745. At the same time, big firm lawyers were less likely to report themselves as "dissatisfied" or "very dissatisfied." *See id.* at 743–45.

103. University of Michigan Law School, *supra* note 73, at 15 tbl.8.

104. HILDEBRANDT, CLIENT ADVISORY 1998, at 7 (1998).

105. Richard B. Schmitt, *From Cash to Travel, New Lures for Burned-Out Lawyers*, WALL ST. J., Feb. 2, 1999, at B1.

106. *See* YOUNG LAWYERS DIV., *supra* note 82, at 9 tbl.9.

107. *See id.*

108. AMERICAN BAR ASS'N, THE REPORT OF AT THE BREAKING POINT: A NATIONAL CONFERENCE ON THE EMERGING CRISIS IN THE QUALITY OF LAWYERS' HEALTH AND LIVES—ITS IMPACT ON LAW FIRMS AND CLIENT SERVICES 11 (1991).

109. *Id.*

110. *See* ROBERT L. NELSON, PARTNERS WITH POWER: THE SOCIAL TRANSFORMATION OF THE LARGE LAW FIRM 142 (1988).

111. *Is It Possible to Put Passion Back into the Practice of Law?*, PARTNER'S REP., Nov. 1994, at 1, 1 [hereinafter *Is It Possible?*].

112. *See* Chris Klein, *Big-Firm Partners: Profession Sinking*, NAT'L L. J., May 26, 1997, at A1, A24. Of course, even among partners who say that they would become lawyers again, "many admit[] that they would [do so] only for financial reasons, or because, as one partner said, 'I don't know what else to do with myself.'" *Is It Possible?*, *supra* note 111, at 2.

113. *See* Klein, *supra* note 112, at A24.

114. *See id.* at A1; *see also* NORTH CAROLINA BAR ASS'N, *supra* note 23, at 5 (finding that attorneys working in rural and suburban areas were more satisfied with their careers than attorneys working in urban areas); Alex M. Johnson, Jr., *Think Like a Lawyer, Work Like a Machine: The Dissonance Between Law School and Law Practice*, 64 S. CAL. L. REV. 1231, 1231 (1991) (reporting that, among the author's former students, the larger the law firm for which the student works, the less satisfied the student seems to be).

115. HILDEBRANDT, *supra* note 104, at 1.

116. *Id.* at 7.

117. Silberman, *supra* note 7, at 615.

118. *See* COMMISSION ON PROFESSIONALISM, AMERICAN BAR ASS'N, "... IN THE SPIRIT OF PUBLIC SERVICE:" A BLUEPRINT FOR THE REKINDLING OF LAWYER PROFESSIONALISM (1986), *reprinted* in 112 F.R.D. 243, 259–61 (1986); ELWORK, *supra* note 16, at 22; NORTH CAROLINA BAR ASS'N, *supra* note 23, at 12; TASK FORCE ON PROFESSIONAL FULFILLMENT, *supra* note 101, at vii; David A. Kessler, *Professional Asphyxiation: Why the Legal Profession is Gasping for Breath*, 10 GEO. J. LEGAL ETHICS 455, 457–64 (1997); Carla Messikomer, *Ambivalence, Contradiction, and Ambiguity: The Everyday Ethics of Defense Litigators*, 67 FORDHAM L. REV. 739, 758–59 (1998); Robert L. Nelson, *The Discovery Process as a Circle of Blame: Institutional, Professional, and Socio-Economic Factors that Contribute to Unreasonable, Inefficient, and Amoral Behavior in Corporate Litigation*, 67 FORDHAM L. REV. 773, 778 (1998); Schiltz, *supra* note 5, at 729–30 & n.76; Fisk, *supra* note 72, at S2; Klein, *supra* note 112, at A1.

119. *See* NORTH CAROLINA BAR ASS'N, *supra* note 23, at 12; Schiltz, *supra* note 5, at 741 & n.110; *Is It Possible?*, *supra* note 111, at 3; Klein, *supra* note 112, at A1, A24–A25.

120. *See* ELWORK, *supra* note 16, at 19; GALANTER & PALAY, *supra* note 1, at 52; Douglas N. Frenkel et al., *Introduction: Bringing Legal Realism to the Study of Ethics and Professionalism*, 67 FORDHAM L. REV. 697, 704 (1998); Schiltz, *supra* note 5, at 741 & n.113; Klein, *supra* note 112, at A24–A25.

121. ELWORK, *supra* note 16, at 20; *see also* Fisk, *supra* note 72, at S11.

122. *See* NORTH CAROLINA BAR ASS'N, *supra* note 23, at 11, 12.

123. *See* ELWORK, *supra* note 16, at 20; NORTH CAROLINA BAR ASS'N, *supra* note 23, at 12; TASK FORCE ON PROFESSIONAL FULFILLMENT, *supra* note 101, at vii; Austin Sarat, *Enactments*

of Professionalism: A Study of Judges' and Lawyers' Accounts of Ethics and Civility in Litigation, 67 FORDHAM L. REV. 809, 834 (1998); Schiltz, *supra* note 5, at 726 n.63; Fisk, *supra* note 72, at S11.

124. *See Is It Possible?*, *supra* note 111, at 3; Klein, *supra* note 112, at A25.

125. *See* NORTH CAROLINA BAR ASS'N, *supra* note 23, at 12; Frenkel et al., *supra* note 120, at 704; Robert W. Gordon, *The Ethical Worlds of Large-Firm Litigators: Preliminary Observations*, 67 FORDHAM L. REV. 709, 717 (1998); Nelson, *supra* note 118, at 786; Schiltz, *supra* note 5, at 744.

126. *See* ELWORK, *supra* note 16, at 20; NORTH CAROLINA BAR ASS'N, *supra* note 23, at 13; TASK FORCE ON PROFESSIONAL FULFILLMENT, *supra* note 101, at vii.

127. *See, e.g.*, AMERICAN BAR ASS'N, *supra* note 108, at 3–4, 9; WALT BACHMAN, LAW v. LIFE: WHAT LAWYERS ARE AFRAID TO SAY ABOUT THE LEGAL PROFESSION 103 (1995); ELWORK, *supra* note 16, at 4, 19; ANTHONY T. KRONMAN, THE LOST LAWYER: FAILING IDEALS OF THE LEGAL PROFESSION 301–03 (1993); LINOWITZ, *supra* note 16, at 107–08; NALP FOUND. FOR RESEARCH & EDUC., KEEPING THE KEEPERS: STRATEGIES FOR ASSOCIATE RETENTION IN TIMES OF ATTRITION 106 (1998); NORTH CAROLINA BAR ASS'N, *supra* note 23, at 4, 10, 11; YOUNG LAWYERS DIV., *supra* note 82, at 15–16; YOUNG LAWYERS DIV., *supra* note 60, at 17, 81; Chambers, *supra* note 38, at 287; Deborah K. Holmes, *Structural Causes of Dissatisfaction Among Large-Firm Attorneys: A Feminist Perspective*, 12 WOMEN'S RTS. L. REP. 9, 13–14 (1990); Kessler, *supra* note 118, at 465; Nelson, *supra* note 118, at 783; Note, *Why Law Firms Cannot Afford to Maintain the Mommy Track*, 109 HARV. L. REV. 1375, 1378 (1996); Fisk, *supra* note 72, at S12; Gatland, *supra* note 55, at 28, 29; Stephanie B. Goldberg, *Bridging the Gap: Can Educators and Practitioners Agree on the Role of Law Schools in Shaping Professionals? Yes and No*, A.B.A. J., Sept. 1990, at 44, 44; Nancy D. Holt, *Are Longer Hours Here to Stay? Quality Time Losing Out*, A.B.A. J., Feb. 1993, at 62, 62; Klein, *supra* note 112, at A1, A24.

128. Alfini & Van Vooren, *supra* note 9, at 63; *see also* ELWORK, *supra* note 16, at 25 ("The single most frequent complaint about the practice of law is the 'hours.'").

129. Kessler, *supra* note 118, at 466.

130. AMERICAN BAR ASS'N, *supra* note 108, at 3 (emphasis added) (quoting an unnamed participant in the conference).

131. Fisk, *supra* note 72, at S12.

132. YOUNG LAWYERS DIV., *supra* note 60, at 81.

133. NORTH CAROLINA BAR ASS'N, *supra* note 23, at 11.

134. University of Michigan Law School, *supra* note 73, at 3 tbl.1. The other four measures were "their legal education at Michigan," "their current family life," "the intellectual challenge of their work," and "their income." *Id.*

135. AMERICAN BAR ASS'N, *supra* note 108, at 3.

136. Several authors have discussed this phenomenon. *See*, e.g., Harry T. Edwards, *A New Vision for the Legal Profession*, 72 N.Y.U. L. REV. 567, 571–72 (1997); Marc Galanter, *Lawyers in the Mist: The Golden Age of Legal Nostalgia*, 100 DICK. L. Rev. 549 (1996); Judith S. Kaye, *Women Lawyers in Big Firms: A Study in Progress Toward Gender Equality*, 57 FORDHAM L. REV. 111, 115 (1988); Deborah L. Rhode, *The Professionalism Problem*, 39 WM. & MARY L. REV. 283, 303–07 (1998).

137. Deborah L. Rhode, *Institutionalizing Ethics*, 44 Case W. Res. L. Rev. 665, 711 (1994).

138. *See* WILLIAM G. ROSS, THE HONEST HOUR: THE ETHICS OF TIME-BASED BILLING BY ATTORNEYS 2–3 (1996); *see also* BACHMAN, *supra* note 127, at 103 (noting that "[t]wenty years ago ... [l]awyers with average billings of 1,500 hours per year often became partners"); Bogus, *supra* note 68, at 924 (stating that "in the 1960's the median number of billable hours was about 1500 per year for partners and associates alike").

139. *See* ROSS, *supra* note 138, at 20.

140. *See id.* at 27.

141. *See id.*

142. *See* University of Michigan Law School, *supra* note 73, at 3 tbl.1.

143. *See* YOUNG LAWYERS DIV., *supra* note 60, at 22 tbl.19.

144. *See id.* at 23. The North Carolina study found that 17.3% of lawyers did not take more than one week of vacation in 1989. *See* NORTH CAROLINA BAR ASS'N, *supra* note 23, at 4.

145. *See* ALTMAN WEIL PENSA, INC., THE 1996 SURVEY OF LAW FIRM ECONOMICS, at III-3 (1996).

146. Silberman, *supra* note 7, at 615.

147. *See* ELWORK, *supra* note 16, at 30.

148. *See* YOUNG LAWYERS DIV., *supra* note 60, at 17.

149. *See id.*

150. *Id.*

151. *See* University of Michigan Law School, *supra* note 73, at 9 tbl.3.

152. *See* ALTMAN WEIL PENSA, *supra* note 145, at III-2, III-6; TASK FORCE ON PROFESSIONAL FULFILLMENT, *supra* note 101, at 9; Holmes, *supra* note 127, at 14; Rhode, *supra* note 136, at 300; David B. Wilkins & G. Mitu Gulati, *Reconceiving the Tournament of Lawyers: Tracking, Seeding, and Information Control in the Internal Labor Markets of Elite Law Firms*, 84 VA. L. REV. 1581, 1602 (1998); Frank J. Roan, *Large Firm vs. Small Firm Practice*, FLA. B. J., Jan. 1994, at 28, 28.

153. *See* NATIONAL ASS'N FOR LAW PLACEMENT, EMPLOYING ASSOCIATES IN 1997: PATTERNS & PRACTICES 11, 15 (1997).

154. *See id.*

155. *See* Holmes, *supra* note 127, at 14; Nielsen, *supra* note 64, at 370; Rhode, *supra* note 137, at 710; Benjamin L. Sells, *Workaholism*, A.B.A. J., Dec. 1993, at 70, 70.

156. *See* Klein, *supra* note 112, at A25.

157. *See* ALTMAN WEIL PENSA, *supra* note 145, at III-6.

158. *See* John E. Morris, *Too Good to Be True?*, AM. LAW., July/Aug. 1998, at 5, 5.

159. *See* NORTH CAROLINA BAR ASS'N, *supra* note 23, at 4; YOUNG LAWYERS DIV., *supra* note 60, at 17.

160. *See* Fisk, *supra* note 72, at S12; Klein, *supra* note 112, at A24.

161. *See* YOUNG LAWYERS DIV., *supra* note 82, at 15.

162. University of Michigan Law School, *supra* note 73, at 12 tbl.7.

163. YOUNG LAWYERS DIV., *supra* note 82, at 10.

164. *See*, e.g., NALP FOUND. FOR RESEARCH & EDUC., *supra* note 127, at 23.

165. Unless, like so many attorneys, you work while you are on vacation, or in bed with the flu, or at home waiting for the plumber. One of my lawyer friends was relieved to find that he could receive faxes and Federal Express deliveries at Disney World, as it helped him to work through his honeymoon. (Perhaps not surprisingly, he got divorced just eight months later.) Another acquaintance was back at the office, billing time, less than 24 hours after giving birth; her newborn child, suffering from low birth weight and other problems, remained hospitalized in the intensive care unit. And one of the lawyers with whom I worked as a summer associate explained to me how, by disciplining himself to think about client matters while showering every morning, he was able to bill an extra hour per week.

166. For similar approximations, *see* BACHMAN, *supra* note 127, at 108; ELWORK, *supra* note 16, at 19; LINOWITZ, *supra* note 16, at 107; ROSS, *supra* note 138, at 27; Bogus, *supra* note 68, at 925; Robert W. McMenamin, *Lawyers at Bay*, 31 LAW OFFICE ECON. & MGMT. 370, 373 (1991); Manuel R. Ramos, *Legal Malpractice: The Profession's Dirty Little Secret*, 47 VAND. L. REV. 1657, 1685 (1994).

167. *See* NORTH CAROLINA BAR ASS'N, *supra* note 23, at 5, 6, 10; Beck et al., *supra* note 21, at 7; Myers & Diener, *supra* note 37, at 15–17; Rhode, *supra* note 136, at 310–11; Robert E. Lane, *Does Money Buy Happiness?*, PUB. INTEREST, Fall 1993, at 56, 56.

168. *See supra* notes 152–58 and accompanying text.

169. *See supra* notes 159–63 and accompanying text.

170. *See infra* notes 175–77 and accompanying text.

171. GALANTER & PALAY, *supra* note 1, at 18.

172. *See* CYNTHIA FUCHS EPSTEIN, WOMEN IN LAW 176 (2d ed. 1993); KRONMAN, *supra* note 127, at 273; NELSON, *supra* note 110, at xi; Bryant G. Garth, *Legal Education and Large Law*

Firms: Delivering Legality or Solving Problems, 64 IND. L. J. 433, 433 (1989); Kaye, supra note 136, at 113; Graham C. Lilly, *Law Schools Without Lawyers? Winds of Change in Legal Education*, 81 VA. L. REV. 1421, 1449 (1995); Mark C. Suchman, *Working Without a Net: The Sociology of Legal Ethics in Corporate Litigation*, 67 FORDHAM L. REV. 837, 837 n.1 (1998).

173. Myers & Diener, *supra* note 37, at 12.

174. *See id.*

175. Roger E. Schechter, *Changing Law Schools to Make Less Nasty Lawyers*, 10 GEO. J. LEGAL ETHICS 367, 386 (1996); see also *Pay for Class of '97 Is $63K, But Money Isn't the Only Issue*, LAW OFFICE MGMT. & ADMIN. REP., Feb. 1998, at 2, 2 [hereinafter *Pay for Class of '97*] (asserting that receiving an offer from a large law firm is "the feather that most [students] want to add to their caps").

176. Eighty-one percent of Michigan Law School's class of 1991 took an initial job in private practice; 46% of the class took an initial job in a firm with more than 50 lawyers. *See* University of Michigan Law School, *supra* note 73, at 6. Harvard's statistics are similar. *See* Schiltz, *supra* note 5, at 760 n.219.

177. This point was drily made by a big firm associate writing under the *nom de plume* "The Rodent" in *Explaining the Inexplicable: The Rodent's Guide to Lawyers*:

> A law degree offers many diverse career options such as teaching, working as in-house counsel for a company, representing a public interest or nonprofit organization, working for the government, forming a small firm with other lawyers, or opening up your own law office. If all else was equal, law students would set their sights on any of these various types of legal service.
>
> All else is not equal because The Firm pays the highest salaries to new lawyers. Thus, instead of considering what type of legal career would be most suitable for them, most law students maneuver for a job with The Firm.

THE RODENT, EXPLAINING THE INEXPLICABLE: THE RODENT'S GUIDE TO LAWYERS 33–34 (1995); *see also* Wilkins & Gulati, *supra* note 152, at 1637 (noting that "many students state that the high salaries paid by corporate firms are the primary reason why they choose jobs in this sector over what they consider to be more rewarding work in government or in public interest practice").

The universal perception that big firms pay better than other legal employers is accurate. In 1997, the median salary offered to first year associates by firms of 251 or more lawyers was $71,502. *See* Margaret Cronin Fisk, *Stratospheric Salary Gap Reflects National Trend*, NAT'L L.J., June 1, 1998, at B8, B11; Mark Hansen, *Big Pay Day for New Associates*, A.B.A. J., Mar. 1998, at 25, 25; *Pay for Class of '97*, *supra* note 175, at 2. At the same time, the median salary offered to first year associates by firms of 10 or fewer lawyers was $40,000, and starting salaries for entry level jobs with corporations, the government, legal services organizations, and public interest organizations generally ranged from $25,000 to $60,000. *See* Fisk, *supra*, at B8, B11–B15.

178. According to the Michigan Law School survey:

> About a quarter of the class started law school without a plan for what to do with their law degree. Of those who did have a plan, about half expected to enter private practice and most of the rest hoped to work in government, politics or legal services.... (Eight years later, five years after graduation, the great majority of those who planned to work in private practice are working there, but so also are the great majority of those who had no plans and a near majority of those who planned to work in government or public interest work.)

University of Michigan Law School, *supra* note 73, at 5.

179. ROBERT GRANFIELD, MAKING ELITE LAWYERS: VISIONS OF LAW AT HARVARD AND BEYOND 149 (1992).

180. *See infra* notes 295–312 and accompanying text.

181. *See infra* notes 329–37 and accompanying text.

182. *See* NALP FOUND. FOR RESEARCH & EDUC., *supra* note 127, at 13; Edward A. Adams & Bruce Balestier, *As Associates' Pay Increases, 'Going Rate' Becomes History*, N.Y.L.J., Aug. 19, 1996, at 1.

183. *See* BACHMAN, *supra* note 127, at 106.

184. *See* GALANTER & PALAY, *supra* note 1, at 56–57 (describing bidding wars among New York firms).

185. *See* Fisk, *supra* note 177, at B8.

186. *See id.* at B11.

187. *See id.*

188. *See* GALANTER & PALAY, *supra* note 1, at 56 (describing how changes in starting salaries for first year associates in New York City resulted in salary increases for more senior lawyers in New York City and for attorneys in firms outside of New York City); NORTH CAROLINA BAR ASS'N, *supra* note 23, at 12 ("Firms strap themselves (and the people being recruited) with high time demands from the overhead stemming from high starting salaries and the spiral effect on other associate salaries."); Rhode, *supra* note 136, at 308–10 (describing how increases in starting salaries for first year associates lead to increases in the salaries and workloads of all lawyers).

189. I am putting aside the option of cutting overhead by, for example, switching to a cheaper brand of stationery or a cheaper supplier of health insurance, as savings produced by such measures are relatively minor. Moreover, I am putting aside the option of implementing "value billing," "alternative billing," or other schemes that promise to help lawyers enjoy increased compensation without having to work harder. Although such schemes are talked about a lot, *see, e.g.*, AMERICAN BAR ASS'N, *supra* note 108, at 15–18; BEYOND THE BILLABLE HOUR: AN ANTHOLOGY OF ALTERNATIVE BILLING METHODS (Richard C. Reed ed., 1989); Barbara Franklin, *Alternative Billing: Flat Fees, "Value" Bills Favored over Hourly Rates*, N.Y.L.J., Aug. 13, 1992, at 5, 5; *Law Firm Billing: Clock's Running on Billable Hours*, NAT'L L.J., Dec. 19, 1994, at C1, C1; they remain largely untried, and their success remains largely unproven, *see* HILDEBRANDT, *supra* note 104, at 7 (noting that "[d]espite all the talk of alternative billing arrangements, 75–80% of all law firm revenues continue to be based on hourly billing"); Franklin, *supra*, at 5 (concluding that "[l]awyers who are experimenting now with alternative fee arrangements say it is either too soon to draw any conclusions or concede their profit margins have shrunk"); Randall Samborn, *Vanguard of a Fee Revolt: Fred Bartlit's New Litigation Boutique Is Betting the House on How It Charges for Its Work*, NAT'L L.J., Apr. 4, 1994, at A1, A1 (finding that "[a]lthough alternative billing practices are in vogue at many firms today, the experiments are, in most cases, loss-leaders for lawyers willing to cut their fees without changing their hourly ways"); Dale H. Seamans, *Is Time Running Out for the Hourly Rate?*, Mass. Law. Wkly., Nov. 11, 1996, at B3, B3 ("Alternative billing ... has been cast about in most law firms and corporate board rooms, but some observers say the concept is slow to become a practice. In spite of a grimly competitive marketplace, the hourly rate is hanging on."). Billing by the hour "remains the bread-and-butter of the legal profession." *Id.; see also* RICHARD C. REED, BILLING INNOVATIONS: NEW WIN-WIN WAYS TO END HOURLY BILLING 99 (1996) (noting that "hourly charges remain the dominant billing system at large U.S. law firms (77% of billings)").

190. *See* Schiltz, *supra* note 5, at 741.

191. According to the American Bar Association, the number of attorneys in the United States grew from 221,605 in 1951 (one for every 695 Americans) to 805,872 in 1991 (one for every 313 Americans), and is expected to grow to 1,005,842 by 2000 (one for every 267 Americans). *See* BARBARA A. CURRAN, AMERICAN BAR ASS'N, WOMEN IN THE LAW: A LOOK AT THE NUMBERS 7 (1995); SECTION OF LEGAL EDUC. & ADMISSIONS TO THE BAR, AMERICAN BAR ASS'N, LEGAL EDUCATION AND PROFESSIONAL DEVELOPMENT—AN EDUCATIONAL CONTINUUM 15 (1992). The Bureau of Labor Statistics reports similar increases in the absolute number of lawyers and in the percentage of lawyers in the general population. *See* Silberman, *supra* note 7, at 610–11.

192. *See* Sarat, *supra* note 123, at 829.

193. *See* GALANTER & PALAY, *supra* note 1, at 50; KRONMAN, *supra* note 127, at 27677; SECTION OF LEGAL EDUC. & ADMISSIONS TO THE BAR, *supra* note 191, at 78–79; Frenkel et al., *supra* note 120, at 704; Gordon, *supra* note 125, at 717; Holmes, *supra* note 55, at 380.

194. *See* ROSS, *supra* note 138, at 2.

195. *Id.*; *see also* NORTH CAROLINA BAR ASS'N, *supra* note 23, at 12.

196. *See* Ronald J. Gilson & Robert H. Mnookin, *Coming of Age in a Corporate Law Firm: The Economics of Associate Career Patterns*, 41 STAN. L. REV. 567, 584 (1989); Peter D. Sherer, *Leveraging Human Assets in Law Firms: Human Capital Structures and Organizational Capabilities*, 48 INDUS. & LAB. REL. REV. 671, 672 (1995).

197. RICHARD L. ABEL, AMERICAN LAWYERS 193 (1989).

198. *See, e.g.*, John E. Morris, *What It Means to Have a Good Year at Skadden, Arps*, AM. LAW., July/Aug. 1997, at 13, 13 (listing 16 partners at Skadden, Arps, Slate, Meagher & Flom who made at least $1.5 million in 1996).

199. *See* Anna Snider, *Survey Shows Wachtell with Highest Profits*, N.Y.L.J., July 1, 1998, at 1, 1 (reporting that profits per partner exceeded $1 million at nine New York firms and $2 million at one New York firm in 1997).

200. ABEL, *supra* note 197, at 191.

201. *Id.* at 192; *see also* D'Alemberte, *supra* note 6, at 10.

202. Johnson, *supra* note 114, at 1250–51.

203. NELSON, *supra* note 110, at 77.

204. *See* ABEL, *supra* note 197, at 192; NELSON, *supra* note 110, at 77.

205. *See* ABEL, *supra* note 197, at 192.

206. *See* Gilson & Mnookin, *supra* note 196, at 585.

207. *See* Wilkins & Gulati, *supra* note 152, at 1603.

208. *See* ABEL, *supra* note 197, at 191.

209. *See* ALTMAN WEIL PENSA, *supra* note 145, at V-3.

210. *See* ABEL, *supra* note 197, at 191.

211. *See* ALTMAN WEIL PENSA, *supra* note 145, at V-3. According to Marc Galanter and Thomas Palay, large firms have become more highly leveraged over time. *See* GALANTER & PALAY, *supra* note 1, at 59.

212. *See* ALTMAN WEIL PENSA, *supra* note 145, at IV-6.

213. *See id.*

214. *See* ABEL, *supra* note 197, at 193–94.

215. *See* Frenkel et al., *supra* note 120, at 704 (describing how, in large firms facing increasingly competitive markets, "firm-wide insecurity trickles down").

216. AMERICAN BAR ASS'N, *supra* note 108, at 12.

217. NORTH CAROLINA BAR ASS'N, *supra* note 23, at 9.

218. *See* BUREAU OF THE CENSUS, U.S. DEP'T OF COMMERCE, STATISTICAL ABSTRACT OF THE UNITED STATES 1996, at 469 tbl.725 (116th ed. 1996).

219. *See* ALTMAN WEIL PENSA, *supra* note 145, at IV-3.

220. *See id.*

221. *See id.* at IV-6.

222. *See id.*

223. *See* Fisk, *supra* note 177, at B8.

224. Every year, in its July/August issue, the *American Lawyer* provides highly detailed financial information on the 100 largest American law firms—the "Am Law 100."

225. *See* Morris, *supra* note 158, at 5.

226. *See supra* Part I.B.

227. *See supra* Part II.A.

228. *See supra* note 166 and accompanying text.

229. *See generally* Note, *Making Docile Lawyers: An Essay on the Pacification of Law Students*, 111 Harv. L. Rev. 2027 (1998).

230. *See* D'Alemberte, *supra* note 6, at 13 ("To students, usually possessed of extremely talented minds and competitive personalities, law schools send a message about values. That message is that the path to success—the way to 'win'—is to get a job with a large law firm.").

231. *See* Roger C. Cramton & Susan P. Koniak, *Rule, Story, and Commitment in the Teaching of Legal Ethics*, 38 WM. & MARY L. REV. 145, 146–47 (1996) ("[L]egal ethics remains an unloved orphan of legal education.... Many law school faculties remain convinced that the subject is unteachable or believe that it is not worth teaching."); David Luban & Michael Millemann, *Good Judgment: Ethics Teaching in Dark Times*, 9 GEO. J. LEGAL ETHICS 31, 3738 (1995) ("[T]he legal ethics course is—not to put too fine a point on it—the dog of the curriculum, despised by students, taught by overworked deans or underpaid adjuncts and generally disregarded by the faculty at large.") (footnote omitted).

232. *See generally* COMMISSION ON PROFESSIONALISM, *supra* note 118; SECTION OF LEGAL EDUC. & ADMISSIONS TO THE BAR, AMERICAN BAR ASS'N, TEACHING AND LEARNING PROFESSIONALISM 2-5 (1996); YOUNG LAWYERS DIV., *supra* note 60, at 33–34; Lawrence J. Fox et al., *Report, Ethics: Beyond the Rules, Historical Preface*, 67 FORDHAM L. REV. 691, 691 (1998); Gordon, *supra* note 125, at 719, 736; McCarthy, *supra* note 69, at 1.

233. *See* Gary A. Hengstler, *Vox Populi: The Public Perception of Lawyers: ABA Poll*, A.B.A. J., Sept. 1993, at 60, 60–65 (ABA poll); Chris Klein, *Poll: Lawyers Not Liked*, NAT'L L. J., Aug. 25, 1997, at A6, A6 (Harris poll); Leslie McAneny & Lydia Saad, *Honesty & Ethics Poll: Pharmacists Strengthen Their Position as the Most Highly Rated Occupation*, GALLUP POLL MONTHLY, Dec. 1997, at 21, 21 (Gallup poll); Randall Samborn, *Anti-Lawyer Attitude Up*, NAT'L L. J., Aug. 9, 1993, at A1, A1 (*National Law Journal*/West Publishing Co. poll).

234. Hengstler, *supra* note 233, at 62.

235. *Id.*

236. Judge Laurence Silberman argues that it is the public's low regard for lawyers that has led law firms to become obsessed with money. He cites the work of anthropologist Robert Ardrey, whose "thesis was that humans, like all mammals, have two drives (other than the basic ones): to acquire property and status. If you depress the opportunity to acquire one, the second becomes much more important." Silberman, supra note 7, at 615. In Judge Silberman's view, "[a]s lawyers' place in society... ha[s] dropped, they have been driven to acquire more property." Id.

237. It was precisely because so many blatant ethical violations were being committed by so many "talented partners at major establishment law firms" that the American Bar Association's Section of Litigation convened a task force of legal scholars and social scientists—known as the *Ethics: Beyond the Rules* task force—to study the ethics of big firm litigators. Fox et al., *supra* note 232, at 691–92; *see also* Sarat, *supra* note 123, at 813–14. The members of the task force used "a series of focus groups, open-ended conversations, and semi-structured interviews" to collect empirical evidence about the attitudes and behavior of partners and associates litigating in the nation's largest law firms. Suchman, *supra* note 172, at 838. Each member of the task force presented his or her tentative conclusions in a paper, and the papers were published by the *Fordham Law Review*. *See generally* Report, *Ethics: Beyond the Rules*, 67 FORDHAM L. REV. 691 (1998).

238. MODEL RULES OF PROFESSIONAL CONDUCT (1983).

239. MODEL CODE OF PROFESSIONAL RESPONSIBILITY (1969).

240. The Model Rules have been adopted in about four-fifths of the states (often with modifications), while the Model Code is still in force in about one-fifth of the states (again, often with modifications). *See* Laws. Man. on Prof. Conduct (ABA/BNA), at 01:101, 01:301 (1997).

241. *See* Frenkel et al., *supra* note 120, at 705–06.

242. If the casebooks and articles that they author are any indication, most of the academy's leading ethicists do not succumb to the pressure to teach only the rules. But at many law schools, professional responsibility courses are not taught by leading ethicists—or, for that matter, even by non-leading ethicists—but rather "by overworked deans or underpaid adjuncts." Luban & Millemann, *supra* note 231, at 37–38.

243. "Unlike governance structures in other nations and professions, regulation of the American bar has remained under almost exclusive control of the group to be regulated.... The Committee that drafted the Code of Professional Responsibility included no lay members; the 13-member Model Rules Commission had only one." Rhode, *supra* note 137, at 687.

244. Hengstler, *supra* note 233, at 62.

245. *See infra* notes 251–52 and accompanying text. I agree with Deborah Rhode that:

> [m]ost attorneys want a process that is sufficiently responsive to clear abuses to protect clients and the profession's public image, as well as forestall more intrusive state regulation. But few lawyers have supported a system that would require major increases in their own bar dues, that would significantly expand oversight of their own conduct, or that would impose substantial risks of serious sanctions.

Rhode, *supra* note 137, at 694.

246. Rhode, *supra* note 137, at 730.

247. Frenkel et al., *supra* note 120, at 703; *see also* Gordon, *supra* note 125, at 710, 732; Messikomer, *supra* note 118, at 743.

248. Rhode, *supra* note 137, at 675.

249. Messikomer, *supra* note 118, at 760.

250. Margaret Steinfels, *The Catholic Intellectual Tradition*, 25 ORIGINS 169, 173 (1995).

251. *See* Gordon, *supra* note 125, at 711.

252. *See* Cramton & Koniak, *supra* note 231, at 172.

253. *See* Frenkel et al., *supra* note 120, at 706 ("[T]he conditions under which lawyers ... make daily judgments are increasingly inhospitable to calm and reasoned analysis."); Gordon, *supra* note 125, at 717 ("Everyone in the [big] firm feels the pressures of overburdened time and the need to make snap decisions on insufficient sleep and reflection: 'There's too much to do and no time to think.'" (citation omitted)); Nelson, *supra* note 118, at 783 ("The lawyers agreed that many litigators were under tremendous time pressures in their practice and, thus, often did not have very much time to reflect on what they were doing.").

254. I have provided a lengthier defense of this proposition in Schiltz, *supra* note 5, at 713–20.

255. KELLY, *supra* note 7, at 18 ("[T]he culture or house norms of the agency, department, or firm play a dominant role in the way a lawyer practices. The organization profoundly affects the lives of lawyers."); *see also* Frenkel et al., *supra* note 120, at 698 (discussing research showing that "the settings in which lawyers work are among the most powerful, contextual factors shaping enactments of professionalism").

256. Actually, someone might tell you this. *See* Gordon, *supra* note 125, at 718:

> An associate who raises an ethical objection, or even just a question, about what a partner or client wants is taking a risk of being perceived as a difficult or obstructive person.... An associate whose ethical fastidiousness poses the risk of displeasing or even losing a client will not last long.

257. *See* Messikomer, *supra* note 118, at 759 (describing how big firm associates absorb "knowledge, techniques, norms, rules, and behavioral patterns" through "a process of 'osmosis'" (citation omitted)).

258. GALANTER & PALAY, *supra* note 1, at 69 (quoting PAUL HOFFMAN, LIONS IN THE STREET: THE INSIDE STORY OF THE GREAT WALL STREET FIRMS 71 (1973)).

259. KELLY, *supra* note 7, at 170.

260. *See, e.g.*, Edward A. Adams, *Have Go-Go '80s Returned?*, NAT'L L. J., Sept. 1, 1997, at A4, A4; Harvey Berkman, *Starr Keeps Going and Going*, NAT'L L. J., Sept. 29, 1997, at A4, A4; Lisa Brennan, *N.Y. Firms Grab Jersey Lawyers*, NAT'L L. J., June 22, 1998, at A6, A6; Cynthia Cotts, *How Firms Keep Their Associates on the Job*, NAT'L L. J., June 8, 1998, at A1, A1; Eric Herman, *The Stealth Firm*, AM. LAW., Sept. 1997, at 59, 59; Morris, *supra* note 198, at 13; Amy Schroeder, *For Top GCs, 1996 Was a Lucrative Year*, AM. LAW., July/Aug. 1997, at 36, 36; Amy Singer, *The Next Face of Cravath?*, AM. LAW., May 1997, at 45, 45; Darryl Van Duch, *Merrill Deal Paves Way for New ADR*, NAT'L L. J., May 18, 1998, at B1, B1; Bob Van Voris, *Secondhand Smoke Deal Draws Fire*, NAT'L L. J., Oct. 27, 1997, at A7, A7; Nicholas Varchaver, *What Have You Done for Me Laterally?*, AM. LAW., June 1996, at 74, 74.

261. *See, e.g.*, Fisk, *supra* note 177, at B11; *The Am Law 100*, AM. LAW., July/Aug. 1998 (insert); *The NLJ 250: 20th Annual Survey*, NAT'L L. J., Nov. 10, 1997, at C5.

262. *See* Fisk, *supra* note 177, at B11.

263. *See id.*

264. *See id.* at B10.

265. Several researchers involved in the *Ethics: Beyond the Rules* project, *see supra* note 237, noted the "lack of connection" between the daily work of big firm litigators and "the lawyer's moral sense." Frenkel et al., *supra* note 120, at 706. In other words, the researchers found that the ordinary "moral sense" that lawyers use to guide their personal lives has little impact on their professional lives, and—consistent with my observation that big firm culture works on young lawyers over time to replace their values with the system's—the researchers also found that "moral sensitivity beyond [complying with] the rules ... is more apparent in associates than partners." *Id.*

266. Nielsen, *supra* note 64, at 371.

267. You should also bear in mind that the pressure to work constantly is strongest on associates, who are generally in their late twenties and early thirties, and on junior partners, who are generally in their middle to late thirties. This is, of course, precisely the time when many people seek to marry and begin a family. It is, in a sense, the "formative years" for the rest of a lawyer's life. It is a particularly bad time to be ignoring personal life.

I should note one other fact: This time period is pretty much the only time that female attorneys can bear children. Although male attorneys can raise children as well as female attorneys, "[c]hildrearing continues to be viewed primarily as 'mother's work' even if 'mother' happens to be a lawyer." Rebecca Korzec, *Working on the "Mommy-Track": Motherhood and Women Lawyers*, 8 HASTINGS WOMEN'S L. J. 117, 117 (1997); *see also* Robert L. Nelson, *The Futures of American Lawyers: A Demographic Profile of a Changing Profession in a Changing Society*, 44 CASE W. RES. L. REV. 345, 380 (1994) ("Numerous studies report that female attorneys who are married and have children bear primary responsibility for childcare."). As a result, big firm life forces upon female lawyers a choice that it does not force upon men: They can keep chugging along on the partnership track or they can raise children, but they can't do both. *See* University of Michigan Law School, *supra* note 73, at 13 (reporting that, five years after graduation, nearly half of the female graduates of the Michigan Law School who had children were employed part-time or not employed at all, whereas "not one man with children ... reported working part-time or not working at a job in order to take care of children"). In this and many other ways, the terrible toll that big firm life exacts from all young attorneys is magnified many times over for female attorneys. *See generally* EPSTEIN, *supra* note 172; MONA HARRINGTON, WOMEN LAWYERS: REWRITING THE RULES (1994); Leslie Bender, *Sex Discrimination or Gender Inequality?*, 57 FORDHAM L. REV. 941 (1989); Cynthia Fuchs Epstein et al., *Glass Ceilings and Open Doors: Women's Advancement in the Legal Profession*, 64 FORDHAM L. REV. 291 (1995); S. Elizabeth Foster, *The Glass Ceiling in the Legal Profession: Why Do Law Firms Still Have So Few Female Partners?*, 42 UCLA L. Rev. 1631 (1995); Kaye, *supra* note 136; Note, *supra* note 127.

268. To the extent that big firm culture contributes to the poor physical and emotional health of lawyers, it also makes it more likely that lawyers will practice unethically in the most narrow sense of all—failing to comply with the formal rules of professional responsibility. The substantial majority of all disciplinary and malpractice actions against attorneys are associated with alcoholism, drug abuse, or mental illness. *See* Michael A. Bloom & Carol Lynn Wallinger, *Lawyers and Alcoholism: Is It Time for a New Approach?*, 61 TEMP. L. REV. 1409, 1413 (1988) (estimating that 50–70% of disciplinary cases against lawyers relate to alcoholism); John Mixon & Robert P. Schuwerk, *The Personal Dimension of Professional Responsibility*, 58 LAW & CONTEMP. PROBS. 87, 96 (1995) (estimating that 60–80% of all disciplinary and malpractice actions against lawyers nationwide are associated with substance abuse or mental illness); Patricia Sue Heil, Comment, *Tending the Bar in Texas: Alcoholism as a Mitigating Factor in Attorney Discipline*, 24 ST. MARY'S L. J. 1263, 1265 & n.6 (1993) (reporting that, according to various state bar studies, a majority of attorney discipline cases arise from alcoholism or chemical dependency).

269. Gordon, *supra* note 125, at 735; *see also* Suchman, *supra* note 172, at 860 (reporting that, in the opinion of big firm litigators, many features of the incentive system within big firms—such as "billing pressures[,] ... competitive compensation, emphasis on rainmaking, and the favorable treatment of aggressiveness in evaluation"—are "designed to reward behavior that is at best unrelated to ethicality, and at worst destructive of it").

270. Bogus, *supra* note 68, at 922.

271. *See* Rhode, *supra* note 137, at 679 (noting that "some qualitative research suggests that lawyers' 'creative billing' practices are often fraudulent or on the fringes of fraud: inflating hours, charging two clients for the same work or the same travel time, failing to describe the basis of bills, and so forth"). For a "funny-because-it's-so-true" account of the "creative" ways in which lawyers inflate their

bills, *see* THE RODENT, *supra* note 177, at 89–115. For less funny, but equally true accounts, *see generally* Symposium, *Unethical Billing Practices,* 50 RUTGERS LAW REV. 2151 (1998).

272. *See* Lisa G. Lerman, *Lying to Clients*, 138 U. PA. L. REV. 659, 706–07, 710, 716–17 (1990).

273. *See supra* note 237.

274. Frenkel et al., *supra* note 120, at 705; *see also* Gordon, *supra* note 125, at 717; Nelson, *supra* note 118, at 792; Sarat, *supra* note 123, at 824–25, 827–28; Suchman, *supra* note 172, at 857, 864.

275. Frenkel et al., *supra* note 120, at 705.

276. *See id.*; Douglas N. Frenkel, Ethics: *Beyond the Rules—Questions and Possible Responses,* 67 FORDHAM L. REV. 875, 880 (1998); Suchman, *supra* note 172, at 868.

277. *See generally*, e.g., JONATHAN L. FREEDMAN, HAPPY PEOPLE: WHAT HAPPINESS IS, WHO HAS IT, AND WHY 133–51 (1978); DAVID G. MYERS, THE PURSUIT OF HAPPINESS (1992); David Lykken & Auke Tellegen, *Happiness is a Stochastic Phenomenon,* 7 PSYCHOL. SCI. 186 (1996); Myers & Diener, *supra* note 37; Rhode, *supra* note 136, at 310–11; Daniel Goleman, *Forget Money; Nothing Can Buy Happiness, Some Researchers Say,* N.Y. TIMES, July 16, 1996, at C1; Lane, *supra* note 167; Dan Seligman, *Why More Money Won't Buy You Happiness,* MED. ECON., Sept. 8, 1997, at 207, 207.

278. *See generally* Lykken & Tellegen, *supra* note 277; Goleman, *supra* note 277; Lane, *supra* note 167, at 58–59; Seligman, *supra* note 277, at 214.

279. Myers & Diener, *supra* note 37, at 13.

280. *See id.*; Rhode, *supra* note 136, at 310–11; Lane, *supra* note 167, at 61; Seligman, *supra* note 277, at 207–08.

281. Philip Brickman & Donald T. Campbell, *Hedonic Relativism and Planning the Good Society, in* ADAPTATION-LEVEL THEORY: A SYMPOSIUM 287, 289 (M.H. Appley ed., 1971).

282. *See* TASK FORCE ON PROFESSIONAL FULFILLMENT, *supra* note 101, at 2–3:

> One of the most interesting and ironic findings of the Task Force was a reiteration of the theme that money does not buy happiness. Of the Task Force's eight subcommittees, associates in large firms expressed the most dissatisfaction.... Ironically, by contrast to the unhappiness of highly compensated large law firm associates, small firm and solo practitioners were among the most professionally fulfilled even though they often face serious financial struggles in the practice of law.

283. NORTH CAROLINA BAR ASS'N, *supra* note 23, at 11.

284. A lawyer working 225 hours per month is likely billing about 150 hours per month, or 1800 hours per year. *See supra* note 166 and accompanying text.

285. Nielsen, *supra* note 64, at 369.

286. *See* Brickman & Campbell, *supra* note 281, at 300 ("[T]here may be no way to permanently increase the total of one's pleasure except by getting off the hedonic treadmill entirely. This is of course the historic teaching of the Stoic and Epicurean philosophers, Buddha, Jesus, Thoreau, and other men of wisdom from all ages.").

287. NALP FOUND. FOR RESEARCH & EDUC., *supra* note 127, at 21–22.

288. GRANFIELD, *supra* note 179, at 147; *see also* RICHARD D. KAHLENBERG, BROKEN CONTRACT: A MEMOIR OF HARVARD LAW SCHOOL 118 (1992) ("Everyone was going to firms, even the most vocal radicals. And if everyone did it, it had to be right. Right?").

289. *See* GRANFIELD, *supra* note 179, at 141–42, 143–67; KAHLENBERG, *supra* note 288, at 93–118; NORTH CAROLINA BAR ASS'N, *supra* note 23, at 23; D'Alemberte, *supra* note 6, at 4, 7, 11, 13; Duncan Kennedy, *Legal Education and the Reproduction of Hierarchy,* 32 J. LEGAL EDUC. 591, 601–02 (1982); Frank J. Macchiarola & Joseph Scanlon, *Lawyers in the Public Service and the Role of Law Schools,* 19 FORDHAM URB. L. J. 695, 701–03 (1992); Schechter, *supra* note 175, at 385–86; James M. Wakefield, Note, *Attitudes, Ideals, and the Practice of Environmental Law,* 10 UCLA J. ENVTL. L. & POL'Y 169, 187–88 (1991); Note, *supra* note 229, at 2032–33, 2034–35.

290. Henry Rose, *Law Schools are Failing to Teach Students to Do Good,* CHI. TRIB., July 11, 1990, at 17.

291. Rhode, *supra* note 136, at 309.

292. *See id.*

293. A study by the National Association for Law Placement of over 10,000 associates who had been hired by over 150 law firms of all sizes between 1988 and 1996 reported that:

> nearly 1 in 11 (9.2%) left their firms within a year of being hired. The attrition rate was nearly double that over each of the next two years, so that 43% of new associates had departed within three years.... About two-thirds of new associates departed within five years, and three-quarters did so within seven years.

NALP FOUND. FOR RESEARCH & EDUC., *supra* note 127, at 53. A study of large law firms in Chicago produced even more dramatic results: 18% of big firm associates were gone within a year, 30% within two years, and over 50% within four years. *See* NELSON, *supra* note 110, at 137. The Michigan Law School survey found that, by 1996, only 38% of the members of the class of 1991 remained in the first job they took after graduation (or after clerking, if they clerked). At the same time, 30% of the class had already held *three or more* jobs in the five years after graduating. *See* University of Michigan Law School, *supra* note 73, at 6. The legal profession as a whole is experiencing increasing lateral movement, *see* GALANTER & PALAY, *supra* note 1, at 54–55; KRONMAN, *supra* note 127, at 277–78; Holmes, *supra* note 127, at 23; Chris Klein, *Associate Job 1: Land Clients*, NAT'L L. J., Mar. 31, 1997, at A1, A25, and the turnover rate of associates—especially associates in big firms—is particularly high, *see* GALANTER & PALAY, *supra* note 1, at 54–55; NELSON, *supra* note 110, at 139; Holmes, *supra* note 127, at 23.

294. Hansen, *supra* note 177, at 25.

295. *See, e.g.*, GRANFIELD, *supra* note 179, at 160–61.

296. *See* Wilkins & Gulati, *supra* note 152, at 1642 ("[I]t is now common for many law firm interviewers to state expressly that young lawyers should join their firm 'for the training' even if they only intend to stay for a few years.").

297. *See* Gordon, *supra* note 125, at 726; Nelson, *supra* note 118, at 802.

298. *See* Messikomer, *supra* note 118, at 765.

299. *See* Schiltz, *supra* note 5, at 739–46; *see also* Frenkel, *supra* note 276, at 878, 881; Messikomer, *supra* note 118, at 752; Nelson, *supra* note 118, at 784; Sarat, *supra* note 123, at 824–25; Suchman, *supra* note 172, at 864.

300. *See* NALP FOUND. FOR RESEARCH & EDUC., *supra* note 127, at 105–06; TASK FORCE ON PROFESSIONAL FULFILLMENT, *supra* note 101, at 9–10; Holmes, *supra* note 127, at 16; Suchman, *supra* note 172, at 862; Ruth Hochberger, *Money Can't Buy Job Satisfaction*, NAT'L L. J., Sept. 1, 1986, at 13, 13.

301. David Wilkins and Mitu Gulati have described how large law firms make two kinds of work available to associates: "training work" (that is, work that is interesting, that develops the skills and judgment of young lawyers, and that helps young lawyers develop strong relationships with their senior colleagues) and "paperwork" (that is, work that is boring, that does little to develop the skills and judgment of young lawyers, and that provides little opportunity for contact with partners). *See* Wilkins & Gulati, *supra* note 152, at 1608–1610. Wilkins and Gulati also describe how, in most big firms, the (abundant) paperwork is shared among the (many) associates who are not destined for partnership, while the (scarce) training work is channeled to the (few) associates who have a chance of making partner. *See id.* at 1610–13.

302. *See* University of Michigan Law School, *supra* note 73, at 9 tbl.3.

303. *See* KRONMAN, *supra* note 127, at 275–76; SECTION OF LEGAL EDUC. & ADMISSIONS TO THE BAR, *supra* note 191, at 40–46; YOUNG LAWYERS DIV., *supra* note 60, at 14; Roger C. Cramton, *Delivery of Legal Services to Ordinary Americans*, 44 CASE W. RES. L. REV. 531, 608 (1994) (noting that "[i]ndividual lawyers know more and more about less and less"); Rhode, *supra* note 137, at 680 (describing "an era of increasing specialization where lawyers know more and more about less and less").

304. HILDEBRANDT, *supra* note 104, at 5.

305. GALANTER & PALAY, *supra* note 1, at 50.

306. KELLY, *supra* note 7, at 175. According to Kelly, this "is part of the reason that in-house counsel jobs have become so much more attractive [as compared to large firm jobs]: because they offer the pleasures of collaboration with a client, rather than episodic fire fighting or technical servicing." *Id.* at 177.

307. *See* Suchman, *supra* note 172, at 868 (reporting that "a recurrent theme" among big firm litigators was reflected in the statement of a big firm partner that he knew "very little about my partners, except what I hear from other firms").

308. KLEIN, *supra* note 112, at A24.

309. *Id.* at A25.

310. NORTH CAROLINA BAR ASS'N, *supra* note 23, at 19.

311. *See supra* note 237.

312. Suchman, *supra* note 172, at 863.

313. *See* TASK FORCE ON PROFESSIONAL FULFILLMENT, *supra* note 101.

314. *Id.* at iii.

315. *Id.*

316. *Id.* at 5.

317. *See id.* at 6.

318. *See* Holmes, *supra* note 127, at 15.

319. TASK FORCE ON PROFESSIONAL FULFILLMENT, *supra* note 101, at 6.

320. *See* Wilkins & Gulati, *supra* note 152, at 1603.

321. *See id.* at 1592 ("[A]ssociate evaluation at [large] firms tends to be both infrequent and, when done, cursory."); *id.* at 1666 ("[M]ost [young] lawyers have relatively little information about their partnership chances.").

322. TASK FORCE ON PROFESSIONAL FULFILLMENT, *supra* note 101, at 8–9.

323. Every one of the researchers involved in the ABA's *Ethics: Beyond the Rules* project remarked on "the widely divergent perceptions of senior and junior lawyers about the climate in their firms and the prescription for addressing problems." Frenkel et al., *supra* note 120, at 705; *see also* Messikomer, *supra* note 118, at 747–48; Nelson, *supra* note 118, at 794; Sarat, *supra* note 123, at 826; Suchman, *supra* note 172, at 844–45.

324. The Michigan Law School survey reported the following:

> For those working in firms, and particularly those in large firms, satisfaction with income has not declined over time. It has in fact remained high while overall satisfaction has declined. (Money, once again, does not buy happiness.) On the other hand, there has over this period been a precipitous decline among the five-year graduates in firms in their satisfaction with the intellectual challenge of their work, with the balance of their family and professional lives, and with their perception of the value of their work to society. There has also been a precipitous decline in the proportion who expect to be working at the same firm in fi[v]e years.

University of Michigan Law School, *supra* note 73, at 16.

325. Klein, *supra* note 112, at A24.

326. *Id.*

327. *Id.*

328. Roan, *supra* note 152, at 30.

329. *See, e.g.*, Granfield, *supra* note 179, at 151–53; David L. Chambers, *The Burdens of Educational Loans: The Impacts of Debt on Job Choice and Standards of Living for Students at Nine American Law Schools*, 42 J. LEGAL EDUC. 187, 193 (1992); Robert Granfield, *Constructing Professional Boundaries in Law School: Reactions of Students and Implications for Teachers*, 4 S. CAL. REV. L. & WOMEN'S STUD. 53, 74 (1994); Lewis A. Kornhauser & Richard L. Revesz, *Legal Education and Entry into the Legal Profession: The Role of Race, Gender, and Educational Debt*, 70 N.Y.U. L. REV. 829, 832 (1995); Giovanni Anzalone, Note, *AIDS and Mandatory Pro Bono: A Step Toward the Equal Administration of Justice*, 8 GEO. J. LEGAL ETHICS 691, 718 (1995).

330. *See* GRANFIELD, *supra* note 179, at 152–53.

331. *See* Cynthia Cotts, *Largest Provider of Loans to Law Students Pushes New Frugality*, NAT'L L. J., Jan. 12, 1998, at A14, A14.

332. *See id.*

333. *See id.*

334. *See* JACK C. ESTES, HANDBOOK OF INTEREST AND ANNUITY TABLES 450 tbl.6 (1976).

335. *See* Fisk, *supra* note 177, at B8, B13–B15.

336. Using 1998 rates, a single lawyer with no dependents grossing $50,000 per year would have $43,050 in taxable income (after taking the personal exemption ($2,700) and the standard deduction ($4,250)) and would be required to pay $8,758.50 in federal income taxes and $3,825 in Social Security taxes. *See* Rev. Proc. 97–57, §§3.01 tbl.3, 3.04(1), 3.08(1), 199752 I.R.B. 20, 21–23; 1998 U.S. Master Tax Guide (CCH) P 49 (1997). State and local income tax rates and income tax thresholds vary widely from state to state, *see* RESEARCH INSTITUTE OF AMERICA, ALL STATES TAX GUIDE 114–20 (1998), but a state and local income tax bill of about $1,800 would be typical, leaving the lawyer with almost $36,000 in disposal income.

337. *See supra* note 218 and accompanying text.

338. *See* Wilkins & Gulati, *supra* note 152, at 1606 ("It is impossible to spend time talking to law students about their career goals without coming to the conclusion that many of the young women and men who join large law firms have no intention of staying long enough to become partners.").

339. *See supra* notes 295–300 and accompanying text.

340. YOUNG LAWYERS DIV., *supra* note 60, at 17; *see also* ELWORK, *supra* note 16, at 20.

341. *See* University of Michigan Law School, *supra* note 73, at 9 tbl.3. A respondent was considered "quite satisfied" if he or she circled one or two on a seven-point scale. *See id.*

342. *See id.* at 15 tbl.8.

343. *See* GALANTER & PALAY, *supra* note 1, at 108–10; KELLY, *supra* note 7, at 17.

344. Generally speaking, the bigger the city in which a small firm is located, the more likely it is that the small firm acts like a big firm.

345. For example, small firms are often less stable than big firms; if half of the business of a six-person firm is generated by one partner, the firm is unlikely to survive if that partner gets hit by a truck. Also, personality conflicts are more of a problem in small firms than in big firms. If you don't get along with a partner at a six-person firm, you're unlikely to last long. If you don't get along with at least one partner at a 600 person firm, something is wrong with you.

346. *See* GALANTER & PALAY, *supra* note 1, at 126.

347. *See* ABEL, *supra* note 197, at 191; ALTMAN WEIL PENSA, *supra* note 145, at V-3.

348. *See* NALP FOUND. FOR RESEARCH & EDUC., *supra* note 127, at 53 & 54 tbl.1.

349. *See* YOUNG LAWYERS DIV., *supra* note 82, at 15–16; University of Michigan Law School, *supra* note 73, at 12 tbl.7.

350. *See* TASK FORCE ON PROFESSIONAL FULFILLMENT, *supra* note 101, at 3; University of Michigan Law School, *supra* note 73, at 12 tbl.7, 15 tbl.8.

351. *See supra* text preceding note 270.

352. *See* D'Alemberte, *supra* note 6, at 10.

353. *See* Rhode, *supra* note 137, at 711 ("If more talented applicants and associates voted with their feet, more firms would likely respond.").

354. *See* THE RODENT, *supra* note 177, at 64 ("[M]ost of those things typically said about The Firm when associates are interviewing for jobs are just big Law Fibs.").

355. Working as a summer associate at a firm is unlikely to give you a good understanding of what it will be like to work as a permanent associate at the same firm. *See* Amy M. Colton, *Eyes to the Future, Yet Remembering the Past: Reconciling Tradition with the Future of Legal Education*, 27 U. MICH. J. L. REFORM 963, 983 (1994); Talbot D'Alemberte, *Teaching About Justice and Social Contributions*, 40 CLEV. ST. L. REV. 363, 372–73 (1992); Johnson, *supra* note 114, at 1254–55 & n.99; Sukhjit Purewal, *Ain't No Time for the Summertime Blues*, AM. LAW., June 1998, at 16, 16.

356. AMERICAN BAR ASS'N, *supra* note 108, at 15; *see also* NALP FOUND. FOR RESEARCH & EDUC., *supra* note 127, at 14.

357. Wilkins & Gulati, *supra* note 152, at 1673.

358. MARTINDALE-HUBBELL LAW DIRECTORY (131st ed. 1999). *Martindale-Hubbell* biographies are also available on LEXIS (MARHUB Library) and on the Internet (<http://www.martindale.com>).

359. *The West Legal Directory* is available on Westlaw (WLD database).

360. STEVEN NAIFEH & GREGORY WHITE SMITH, THE BEST LAWYERS IN AMERICA (1997).

361. THE AMERICAN BAR (Diane R. Irvine ed., 80th ed. 1998).

362. THE INSIDER'S GUIDE TO LAW FIRMS (Francis Walsh & Sheila V. Malkani eds., 4th ed. 1998).

363. NATIONAL ASS'N FOR LAW PLACEMENT, NATIONAL DIRECTORY OF LEGAL EMPLOYERS (1998).

364. Links to law firm websites can be found at <http://www.findlaw.com>.

365. The *National Law Journal* also has an Internet site (<http://www.ljx.com/nlj>). Some local legal journals, such as the *New York Law Journal*, have their own websites (<http://www.nylj.com>).

366. See <http://www.altavista.com>.

367. See <http://www.go2net.com/search.html>.

368. *See* AMERICAN BAR ASS'N, *supra* note 108, at 5; NALP FOUND. FOR RESEARCH & EDUC., *supra* note 127, at 14; Johnson, *supra* note 114, at 1252–53; *Pay for Class of '97*, *supra* note 175, at 3.

369. GALANTER & PALAY, *supra* note 1, at 128.

370. *Id.*; *see also* Sarat, *supra* note 123, at 826 (" 'The only common value among a firm of 300 lawyers is money. There will be no other common values.' " (citation omitted)). For an illustration of Galanter and Palay's observation in action, *compare* Michael Kelly's case study of the money-oriented, quite diverse large firm of "McKinnon, Moreland, and Fox", with his case study of the other-than-money-oriented, less diverse small firm of "Mahoney, Bourne, and Thiemes." *See* KELLY, *supra* note 7, at 25–52 (McKinnon), 53–83 (Mahoney).

371. *See supra* notes 273–76 and accompanying text.

372. I have heard many lawyers speculate that another reason why no big law firm has made a serious and sustained attempt to reward its attorneys with better lives instead of more money is because such a firm would lose clients. According to this theory, clients respect a firm made up of lawyers who work constantly; clients know that such lawyers will put everything aside to do their clients' work, 24 hours a day, 7 days a week. Thus, a firm made up of lawyers who bill 1800 hours per year will lose business to a firm made up of lawyers who bill 2200 hours per year. I am not aware of any evidence suggesting that this theory is actually true.

373. *See* AMERICAN BAR ASS'N, *supra* note 108, at 14–18.

374. *See* TASK FORCE ON PROFESSIONAL FULFILLMENT, *supra* note 101, at 5. As I explained, *see supra* text accompanying note 316, only one of these—the "great[] economic rewards"—was convincing.

375. TASK FORCE ON PROFESSIONAL FULFILLMENT, *supra* note 101, at 5–6.

376. *Id.* at 6–7.

377. *Id.* at 6.

378. For example, first on the list of obstacles to professional fulfillment identified by big firm partners was "the increased pressure on productivity created by the ascendancy of the billable hour as the primary source of a firm's revenue," *id.* at 5, while one of the recommendations of the Task Force was that "large law firms consider accelerating their efforts to shift revenue production away from a dependency on the billable hour," *id.* at 6–7. This tendency to blame the billable hour for the unhappiness of big firm lawyers is a bit odd. The main source of "the increased pressure on productivity" is presumably the expectations of partners to enjoy high and perpetually increasing incomes. Admittedly, the billable hour is a poor vehicle for meeting that expectation, but to blame the vehicle, while ignoring the expectation, seems short-sighted.

379. An hour that is recorded by a lawyer as billable, billed to a client, and paid for by the client is known as "realized." An hour that is recorded by a lawyer as billable, but that is not billed to the client (but instead "written off") or that is billed but not paid for by the client, is known as "unrealized." The "realization rate" of a lawyer reflects the portion of the time recorded by the lawyer as billable

that is eventually paid for by a client. Firm managers use realization rates as a measure of a lawyer's efficiency and profitability to the firm.

380. *See supra* text preceding note 253.

381. "[T]he notion of padding ... crosses the mind of almost anyone who has kept a time sheet.'" Stephanie B. Goldberg, *The Ethics of Billing: A Roundtable*, A.B.A. J., Mar. 1991, at 56, 57 (quoting Geoffrey C. Hazard, Jr.).

382. ROSS, *supra* note 138, at 23.

383. *See* Wilkins & Gulati, *supra* note 152, at 1594.

384. *See* Gordon, *supra* note 125, at 716 (describing how the big firm litigators questioned by the ABA's Special Task Force on *Ethics: Beyond the Rules* consistently reported that "there were few positive incentives, other than self-respect and the good opinion of judges and of lawyers from other firms[,] to practice ethically").

385. *See* DAVID LEBEDOFF, CLEANING UP: THE STORY BEHIND THE BIGGEST LEGAL BONANZA OF OUR TIME 291–93 (1997).

386. *See id.* at 314–15.

387. Our firm had adopted a policy that lawyers who left the firm voluntarily would not share at all in the Exxon Valdez recovery. I should note that, as of this writing (four years after entry of the verdict), the Exxon Valdez case is still on appeal and the $5 billion judgment remains unpaid. *See* David Phelps, *Big Payoff Comes with Even Bigger Wait for the Check*, STAR TRIB. (Minneapolis), Mar. 16, 1999, at D1.

388. My wife received a part-time, tenure-track appointment to the Notre Dame Law School faculty, which has permitted her to spend more time with our children and to become active in advocating for the rights of the disabled.

About the Authors

Jason M. Dolin started his legal career in 1979 as an Assistant District Attorney in the Manhattan District Attorney's Office. Since 1998 he has been an adjunct law professor at Capital University Law School in Columbus, Ohio where he teaches a general practice practicum to third year law students. He has written several articles addressing the need for a more practice-integrated legal education that better prepares law students for the rigors and realities of law practice. He has advocated for greater transparency in the reporting by law schools of the employment outcomes of their graduates.

Wendy Espeland is Professor of Sociology and the Charles Deering McCormack Professor of Teaching Excellence at Northwestern University. She received her B.S. degree from Arizona State University and her Ph.D. from the University of Chicago. Her current research investigates quantification as a complex social process that changes how we understand the world and how, and to whom, we cede authority. She is completing a book with Michael Sauder entitled, *Fear of Falling: How Media Rankings Changed Legal Education in America*, which analyzes the effects of media rankings on higher education. She has recently published articles about quantification in the *European Journal of Sociology*, *American Sociological Review*, *American Journal of Sociology*, and the *Annual Review of Law and Social Science*. She has received fellowships from the Russell Sage Foundation, Radcliffe Institute for Advanced Study and Wissenschaftskolleg zu Berlin.

Ellen Grigsby (Ph.D., Political Science, University of North Carolina-Chapel Hill, 1987) is Lecturer and Pre-Law Advisor at the University of New Mexico. She is the author of *Analyzing Politics* (5h ed., Cengage, 2012) and *Reading Ideologies* (Pearson/Longman, Forthcoming 2016).

Bethany Rubin Henderson is a social entrepreneur. She founded the non-partisan national service corps City Hall Fellows, which is empowering the next generation to go local, and lead their cities. The impact Bethany has had on both cities and Millennials has won her numerous accolades, including a coveted Echoing Green Fellowship. Bethany earned her J.D. from Harvard Law School and a B.A. and M.A. in political science from the University of Pennsylvania. A former big firm litigator, Bethany has spoken and written regularly over the past 10 years on topics ranging from intellectual property law to cities' human capital crises.

William D. Henderson is professor of law at the Indiana University Law School. Before that, he held a visiting appointment at Chicago-Kent College of Law and clerked for U.S. Court of Appeals for the Seventh Circuit. His scholarship focuses on legal profession and legal education, and he has published articles in the *North Carolina Law Review*, the *Indiana Law Journal*, the *Texas Law Review*, the *Michigan Law Review*, and the *Stanford Law Review*. Henderson also serves as a research associate with the Law School Survey of Student Engagement (LSSSE) and as director of the Law Firms Working Group, a joint initiative of the Indiana Law and the American Bar Foundation. He is also a regular contributor to the Empirical Legal Studies Blog (www.elsblog.org).

Richard Ippolito received his Ph.D. in economics from the University of Chicago in 1974. He was the chief economist at the Pension Benefit Guarantee Corporation for many years before joining the faculty at George Mason University Law School, where he penned the article that appears in this volume. He has published many articles and books, mostly about pensions and mutual funds. His "Economics for Lawyers" lectures at the law school were published by Princeton University Press. He is now retired.

Jeffrey S. Kinsler is a professor of law at Elon University School of Law. He has also served as dean of Appalachian School of Law and held teaching positions at the law schools at Valparaiso University, the University of Denver College, the University of Tennessee, Marquette University, the University of Sydney, and Griffith University. He served as a Fulbright Scholar at the University of Queensland. Kinsler practiced law with the Chicago firms of Katten, Muchin & Zavis and Mayer, Brown & Platt. He is member of the Virginia, Tennessee, Illinois and Wisconsin bars. He has published articles in a number of law reviews and co-authored eight books. He graduated first in his class at Valparaiso University School of Law and secured an LL.M. from Yale Law School.

Russell Korobkin is Professor of Law at the UCLA School of Law. Before coming to UCLA, he held faculty appointments or visiting professorships at the University of Illinois College of Law and the University of Illinois Institute of Government and Public Affairs. He has also taught at Harvard Law School, the University of Texas School of Law, the University of Arizona, the University of Houston, the University of Nevada-Las Vegas, Pepperdine University, Vanderbilt University, LaTrobe University, the Heilbronn Business School. Korobkin obtained his undergraduate and law degrees from Stanford University, clerked for the U.S. Court of Appeals for the District of Columbia Circuit, and worked at the law firm of Covington & Burling in Washington, D.C. He has published more than forty articles on subjects as diverse as behavioral law and economics, negotiation and alternative dispute resolution, contract law, the health care law, and stem cell research. In 2007 Yale University Press published his *Stem Cell Century: Law and Policy For A Breakthrough Technology* (Yale University Press), and in 2009 the Aspen Law and Business Press published the second of his *Negotiation Theory and Strategy* textbook.

Lawrence S. Krieger has served as Clinical Professor of Law at the Florida State University College of Law since 1991. Before that he worked as a litigation attorney for 11 years, most recently serving as Chief Trial Counsel for the Florida Divisions of Securities and Finance. His academic research focuses on the wellness and integrity of law students and lawyers. He is founder and moderator of the Humanizing Legal Education listserv and founding Chair of the Section on Balance in Legal Education (Association of American Law Schools). He was selected as one of 26 teachers nationwide as subjects for the forthcoming book, *What the Best Law Teachers Do* (Harvard Press, 2013).

Ryon Lancaster is an assistant professor of sociology at the University of Chicago, where he focuses on organizational sociology, the sociology of law, economic sociology, and historical sociology. His current project examines bureaucratization of the Catholic Church in England in the 12th century. He is also conducting research on the founding of Reformation-era English churches. Lancaster is working on two projects related to law and organizations in the United States. The first considers how the economic behavior and organizational structures of large American law firms changed over time. The second project, affiliated with the American Bar Foundation, and examines how the Equal Employment Opportunity Commission processes employment discrimination cases.

William P. LaPiana is the Rita and Joseph Solomon Professor of Wills, Trusts and Estates at New York Law School and Director of Estate Planning Studies for the Graduate Tax

Program at NYLS. He holds the A.B., summa cum laude (1973), the A.M. in history (1975), the J.D. cum laude (1978), and the Ph.D. in history (1987) from Harvard University. From 1979 to 1983 he was associated with Davis Polk and Wardwell where he worked primarily in the estates group. He began teaching in 1983 at the University of Pittsburgh School of Law and joined the New York Law School faculty in 1987.

David S. Mann is professor emeritus of the College of Charleston. He received his B.A. in Political Science from Cal-State Long Beach, an M.A. from the University of Southern California, and a Ph.D. from Washington State University. He taught at Washington State University as a graduate student. Dr. Mann's teaching interests emphasized public law, criminal justice, constitutional law, civil liberties, judicial process, and jurisprudence. His research interests included state government policies, judicial politics, criminal justice, and political behavior. He is co-editor (with Luther F. Carter) of two books: *Government in the Palmetto State* and *Government in the Palmetto State: Toward the 21st Century*. He has also published articles and reviews in *Women's Law Journal*, the *Journal of Dental Education*, *American Political Science Review*, the *Journal of Politics*, and *Political Science Book Review*. He also contributed chapters to *Court Management in the United States*, *Reapportionment Politics*, and *Public Policy Formation*.

Donald G. Marshall (B.A., Williams College; LL.B., Yale University), now deceased, was honored many times for his teaching and was a respected national expert on torts and evidence. After completing his studies at Yale, he clerked for Justice Haydn Proctor of the New Jersey Supreme Court. From 1961 to 1967, he worked with the firm of Lowenstein and Spicer in Newark. Marshall joined the University of Minnesota law faculty in 1967 and taught there until he retired in 2005. In 1995, he was appointed as the first Law Alumni Distinguished Teacher. Marshall served as a consultant to the New Jersey Corporation Law Revision Commission and drafted much of the New Jersey Business Corporation Act. He also authored the Rules of Procedure and Official Forms for Minnesota Probate-Juvenile Courts.

Andrew P. Morriss is the D. Paul Jones, Jr. and Charlene A. Jones Chairholder in Law and a Professor of Business at the University of Alabama. He also taught at Case Western Reserve University (where he served as Associate Dean) and the University of Illinois. He is the author or coauthor of more than 60 book chapters, scholarly articles, and books.

Amelia A. R. Murphy, Ph.D. (Political Science, 1998) is Co-Director of the Public Deliberation Center of New Mexico. Dr. Murphy is an applied social scientist who specializes in qualitative and quantitative research design, implementation, and analysis in a variety of policy arenas.

Michael Sauder is associate professor of sociology at the University of Iowa and Robert Wood Johnson Fellow in Health Policy at Harvard University. With Wendy Espeland, he is currently examining how the production of educational rankings affects the organizational activities and status systems of higher education. His theoretical work explores how third parties, legitimacy, and ambiguity influence status relationships at both the individual and organizational levels of analysis.

Patrick J. Schiltz graduated *summa cum laude* from the College of St. Scholastica and *magna cum laude* from Harvard Law School, where he was an editor of the *Harvard Law Review*. After serving as a law clerk to U.S. Supreme Court Justice Antonin Scalia, Schiltz practiced for six years as an associate and two years as a partner at Faegre & Benson in Minneapolis. Schiltz left private practice in 1995 to join the faculty of Notre Dame Law School, where he taught Civil Procedure, Evidence, and Sports Law. In 2000 Schiltz became the founding associate dean of the University of St. Thomas School of Law. In

2002 he was named the St. Thomas More Chair in Law, the first endowed chair at the School of Law. Schiltz was nominated to the federal bench by President George W. Bush on December 14, 2005, and his nomination was unanimously confirmed by the United States Senate on April 26, 2006.

Jeffrey Evans Stake holds the Robert A. Lucas chair at Indiana University Maurer School of Law, and often chairs the admissions committee. In addition to examining effects of rankings and steps that might be taken to improve them, he maintains his interactive website, the Law School Ranking Game, monoborg.law.indiana.edu/lawrank/, which allows users to enter their own weights for factors in a ranking. His ranking game was discussed by Malcolm Gladwell in the February 14, 2012, issue of *The New Yorker* (2011). In addition to writing on rankings, he writes on property law, trust law, law and evolution, divorce law, the First Amendment, and law school grading.

David A. Thomas is the Rex E. Lee Endowed Chair and Professor of Law Emeritus at Brigham Young University's J. Reuben Clark Law School, where he taught fulltime from 1974 until his retirement in 2010. He continues teaching parttime. He was educated at Brigham Young University (B.A., 1967; MLS, 1977) and Duke University Law School (J.D., 1972), where his legal education was interrupted for military service in Vietnam. His scholarly work includes over 40 books and several dozen law review articles in the areas of real property, civil procedure, legal history and legal education. He received several teaching awards and served for fifteen years on his law school admission committee. He and his wife Paula have eight children and 19 grandchildren, and reside in Orem, Utah.

Deborah Davis Thornton is a public policy analyst and writer for the Public Interest Institute (PII) in Mount Pleasant, Iowa. She has been published in over 100 Iowa newspapers and has been a guest on a variety of radio shows. She is a member of *the Iowa City Press-Citizen* writers group. She has written recently on the following topics: college costs and student loan debt, law school transparency, K-12 education reform, public pension reform, Tax and Expenditure Limits (TELs), and Tax Increment Financing (TIF). She edits the PII "Iowa Economic Scorecard" and "Facts and Opinions." Deborah has an M.B.A from the University of Maryland, a B.A. in Journalism and Political Science from Indiana University, and has taught at Iowa Wesleyan College.

Dr. Lorenzo A. Trujillo (Ed.D., J.D.) is the Deputy Director for the National Association of Counsel for Children (NACC). Prior to his work with the NACC, he served as the Assistant Dean of Students and Professional Programs and Professor at the University of Colorado Law School. Also, he is the Past General Counsel to the National Hispanic Bar Association. He has practiced law; consulted, taught, lectured, and published concerning matters in juvenile law, education law, estate and non-profit corporate law, immigration law, family law, business law, language equity, the arts, and public policy. Dean Trujillo received awards as the 2007 National Hispanic Bar Association Attorney of the Year and the 2006 Outstanding Hispanic Attorney for the Colorado Hispanic Bar Association.

About the Editors

Tim Alan Garrison (Ph.D., Kentucky; J.D., Georgia) is a professor of history at Portland State University (Portland, Oregon). He has also served as the university's Director of Native American Studies (2005–2009). Garrison is a member of the State Bar of Georgia and practiced law for seven years. He has been advising pre-law students for over fifteen years, served as president and treasurer of the Western Association of Prelaw Advisors, and sat on the Prelaw Advisors National Council.

Garrison has written extensively on the Indian Removal Crisis of the 1830s and federal Indian policy in general. He is the author of *The Legal Ideology of Removal: The Southern Judiciary and the Sovereignty of Native American Nations* (University of Georgia Press, 2001, paperback, 2009). He is the co-editor, with Paul Finkelman, of *The Encyclopedia of United States Indian Policy and Law* (Congressional Quarterly Press, 2008). His recent articles include "The Shades of Loyalty: Elisha W. Chester and the Cherokee Removal," in *New Directions in Southern Legal History* (eds. Sally Hadden and Patricia Minter), "Pan-Nationalism as a Crisis Management Strategy: John Ross and the Tahlequah Conference of 1843," in *Between Settler and Indigenous Governance* (eds. Timothy Rouse and Lisa Ford); "The Foundations of Jackson's Removal Policy: U.S.-Indian Relations, 1775–1815," in *A Companion to Jacksonian America* (ed. Sean Patrick Adams); "On the Trail of Tears: Daniel Butrick's Record of the Roundup, Internment, and Removal of the Cherokees," in *Removing Peoples: Forced Removal in the Modern World* (eds. Richard Bessel and Claudia Hakke); and "United States Indian Policy in Sectional Crisis: Georgia's Exploitation of the Compact of 1802" and "The Devil and Andrew Jackson: Historians and Jackson's Role in the Indian Removal Crisis," both included in *Congress and the Emergence of Sectionalism: From the Missouri Compromise to the Age of Jackson* (eds. Paul Finkelman and Donald R. Kennon.

Frank Guliuzza (Ph.d., Notre Dame) is the Dean of Academic Affairs at Patrick Henry College and was formerly Chair of the Political Science and Philosophy Department at Weber State University. One of the leading pre-law advisors in the United States, he served as President of the Western Association of Pre-Law Advisors (2001–2007) and as Chair of the Pre-Law Advisors' National Council (2007–2009). He is currently President of the American Collegiate Moot Court Association and is on the Executive Committee of the American Mock Trial Association. He founded the mock trial programs at Weber State University and Patrick Henry College, and has coached 20 teams into national competition – including several that have placed in the top ten at AMTA national tournaments. He is also the co-coach of the Patrick Henry moot court teams that captured the 2009, 2010, 2011, and 2012 intercollegiate national championships.

Dr. Guliuzza has authored works in several journals, including the *Drake Law Review, Marquette Law Review, Willamette Law Review*, the *Review of Politics, Academe, American Political Science Review*. He is also author of the book, *Over the Wall: Protecting Religious Expression in the Public Square*. Guliuzza has received a number of honors and awards for his teaching, including: "*Utah Professor of the Year*" by the Carnegie Foundation for the Advancement of Teaching and Council of Advancement and Support of Education (2003) and "*Outstanding Teaching in Political Science*" by the American Political Science Association and Pi Sigma Alpha (2000, 2003, 2004, 2008).

Index

Note: *USN* denotes *U.S. News & World Report*.